AN INTRODUCTION TO PERSONALITY

PRENTICE-HALL PSYCHOLOGY SERIES

Richard S. Lazarus, Editor

SECOND EDITION

AN INTRODUCTION TO PERSONALITY

RESEARCH, THEORY, and APPLICATIONS

DONN BYRNE

Purdue University

Prentice-Hall, Inc., Englewood Cliffs, New Jersey

Library of Congress Cataloging in Publication Data

BYRNE, DONN ERWIN
  An introduction to personality.

  Bibliography: p.
  1.–Personality. 2.–Psychology—Methodology.
  I.–Title. [DNLM: 1.–Personality. 2.–Psychological
  tests. BF698 B995i–1974]
  BF698.B9–1974   155.2   73–17157
  ISBN 0–13–491597–6

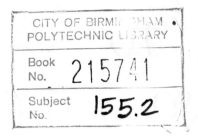
© 1974, 1966 by Prentice-Hall, Inc., Englewood Cliffs, New Jersey

PRINTED IN THE UNITED STATES OF AMERICA
10 9 8 7 6 5 4 3 2

PRENTICE-HALL INTERNATIONAL, INC., *London*
PRENTICE-HALL OF AUSTRALIA, PTY. LTD., *Sydney*
PRENTICE-HALL OF CANADA, LTD., *Toronto*
PRENTICE-HALL OF INDIA PRIVATE LIMITED, *New Delhi*
PRENTICE-HALL OF JAPAN, INC., *Tokyo*

Contents

v

II
Personality Dimensions As Predictors of Behavior
63

III

Situational Determinants of Behavior

307

Preface

Whether a student enrolled in a course in personality eventually becomes a psychologist or decides never to take another course in the area, acquaintance with the workings of a behavioral science constitutes an integral part of his education. Because of the intrinsic interest of the research problems central to personality psychology, this field is in many ways a potentially ideal context in which to introduce undergraduates to the science of behavior.

In the time that has passed since the original version of this book was published in 1966, there have been a great many changes in the field of personality and in our society. Two of these changes are reflected strongly in the present volume and have led to an essentially new book rather than simply to a revised one.

First, I and many of my colleagues have become increasingly critical of personality tests and the individual differences approach. The reasons for this change are spelled out in some detail in Chapter 9. One consequence is that the already ambiguous borderline between personality and social psychology has become even more indistinct. This shift in emphasis in the field has influenced many areas of research and is best reflected here in four completely new chapters dealing with interpersonal attraction, aggression, sexual behavior, and altruism. At the same time, the study of individual differences is not neglected, and the chapters on authoritarianism, need for achievement, manifest anxiety, intelligence, and self-concept provide an overview of both past and current developments in this area.

Second, there is an unprecedented demand both within the field and outside of it for an indication of the relevance of our work to the more general needs of the student and of society. In the present book, an attempt is made to deal with these concerns in several ways. The necessity for basic research is emphasized, and an effort is made to show that at times such work progresses only very slowly toward the solution of real life problems. At the same time, there is a strong interest among personality and social psychologists in problems which are of very real and immediate interest. These parallel lines of development in the field need not be seen an antagonistic and alternative roads to salvation but rather as mutually interdependent ways to reach our goals. With all types of research and theorizing, it is possible to communicate about the conceptual and empirical activity of psychologists without ignoring the important connections between this enterprise and the more obvious and immediate concerns of the student.

In the author's undergraduate course in personality, and hence in this book, there are four primary aims. Even though these aims may not be successfully attained, it may be helpful to make them explicit.

(1) There are a great many bits of factual information being generated daily by those active in research; any informed citizen can benefit from becoming acquainted with at least a part of what is currently known about such important aspects of behavior as intelligence, aggression, sex, and so on. A course and a textbook represent only the first step in what may be a lifetime of keeping informed about a specific set of problems, but that first step is a crucial one. This, by the way, must be a selective procedure, and any description of the activities of a field as broad as personality represents only a sampling of what is being done.

(2) It is essential to provide an idea of the basis on which psychologists can legitimately come to conclusions about behavioral issues. It is important for all of us to learn to distinguish between opinions which do and opinions which do not have a basis in empirical findings. This does not imply that only statements based on research are worthwhile. It does imply that we should know whether we are listening to firmly established facts, well supported theories, tentative ideas, wild speculations, value judgments, or assertions based on faith. If one reads in the newspaper or sees on television that some spokesman has denounced the evil effects of pornography or has stated that threats of retaliation will deter aggression or has advocated marriage counselling based on the idea that opposites attract, how can these declarations be evaluated? If the student learns nothing more than to examine the basis of such statements with a critical eye, his contact with personality psychology can be considered a resounding success.

(3) Increased understanding of how science works is the third goal. Science is an intellectual undertaking, but it is sometimes difficult to make it clear that ideas are the mainspring of science. Personality psychology grew

out of philosophical speculations as to why man behaves as he does. Formal attempts to develop broad theories of personality were begun about the beginning of this century. Such theories are an integral part of the history of personality and in various guises they tend to influence much of our current thinking. The five major theoretical influences on personality psychology are presented in descriptions of the formulations of Freud, Jung, Sullivan, Rogers, and the numerous psychologists identified with a stimulus-response approach to personality. In addition to such broad theoretical contributions, the day-to-day work of science makes more sense if one sees it not just in terms of instrumentation, or statistics, or isolated research findings, but as a way of generating and validating ideas. In this text, the student is shown where ideas originate, how the ideas are translated into research, and the way in which theoretical speculations and research findings are interconnected. Successful scientific activity leads man to think about himself in a new way, and this outcome is probably more characteristic of psychological science than any other.

(4) The application of research findings and theories to our own lives is an important goal but one which can cause much disagreement among psychologists. It is clearly possible to attempt to oversell psychology as a cure-all for worry, sexual hang-ups, war, unpopularity, flat feet, and acne. It is also possible to back completely away from such spurious claims and attempt to present psychology as a pure science dealing only with esoteric laboratory issues. Between these two extremes, we can try to consider the impact of psychological knowledge on our decisions, evaluations, and judgments. Research in personality and social psychology has not yet produced a technological equivalent to moon landings, cures for diseases, or new weapons of destruction. This research does, however, deal in large part with the kind of problems we each must face, for example, in interacting with others, attending school, selecting a mate, raising children, and striving for success. If you saw a magazine cover which had the following teaser headlines, you might decide that the articles inside were of possible value to you: What child-rearing practices result in the development of fascist ideology? What causes an individual to become oriented toward achievement and success? How does anxiety affect school grades? Are blacks intellectually inferior to whites? Does psychotherapy lead to an increase in self-esteem? What causes two people to become friends? Does violence on television make children act aggressively? Do men and women respond differently to pornography? Will most people come to the aid of a stranger in distress? These questions deal not only with our everyday concerns, but they are also the focus of a considerable amount of current psychological research. In this sense, much of the work of personality and social psychologists can be seen to be of rather direct and immediate applied value.

Despite these goals, the student who has finished this text will *not* possess a theory which provides an understanding of all behavior or the key to optimal adjustment or the solution to all of the behavioral problems of mankind. The student *will* have an introduction to the ideas, the procedures, and some of the findings in one of the most exciting and challenging of activities —the scientific study of human behavior.

Among the many individuals whose comments and suggestions contributed to this edition of the book, I would like to give special thanks to Robert Baron, William Griffitt, Walter Mischel, Joseph Rychlak, and Jerry Wiggins whose comments and criticisms were extremely helpful. In addition, I would like to acknowledge the very basic contribution of my wife, Lois, who typed the manuscript, wrote letters seeking permission to use copyrighted material, and spent endless hours in proofreading. Her collaboration is gratefully and lovingly acknowledged.

DONN BYRNE
West Lafayette, Indiana

AN INTRODUCTION TO PERSONALITY

I

Background

I

Science
and the
Study of Personality

To live in the latter half of the twentieth century is to live in an era in which science has become a powerful force in influencing human activities. In the world's most highly developed nations scientists are accorded an honored position in society and scientific education is encouraged and supported. A survey of occupations in the United States has found that scientists are outranked in prestige only by supreme court justices and physicians. Occupations ranked below scientists include those of state governor, cabinet member, banker, factory owner, and artist (Abelson, 1964).

At the same time, ideas about what it is that scientists do or what it means to utilize the scientific method seem to be a bit fuzzy. For most people, "science" evokes images of men in white jackets surrounded by gleaming equipment or memories of biology labs in which the "experiments" never quite worked out the way the lab manual said they should. To some, whatever scientists do seems incomprehensible and somewhat frightening, like the activities of a powerful secret society.

Given this context, students who enroll in an introductory course in psychology are often surprised to learn that psychologists describe their work as a science. Perhaps because of its relative youth and perhaps because of its potentially threatening possibilities, the phrase "science of behavior" most often brings forth either amused ridicule or open hostility. Three journalistic items provide a flavor of this negative reaction:

Nothing raises eyebrows faster than the idea that science can find "laws" of human behavior. Human differences are too vast for generalizations that apply with any exactitude to individuals (*Time* magazine, Feb. 14, 1964, p. 43).

Psychology, which is the study of things people with common sense know already, has discovered that kids are ornery.

The earnest gents and ladies in sensible shoes have been "understanding" the little disgusters for the last generation, with the result that our jails are full, the streets of our cities are unsafe after nightfall. . . .

. . . It may make normal readers retch, but psychologists describe spanking as "some form of primary negative reinforcement."

Negative reinforcement is what bred the sturdy race that spanned this continent, and I'd like to see it return to fashion (Richard Starnes, columnist for the Scripps-Howard newspaper chain, quoted in the *American Psychologist,* 1963, p. 510).

For me, the whole concept of behavioral science and practitioners thereof is hilarious. The expression itself is repellent, if not actually a contradiction of terms. If it was a science, how could it explain human behavior? If it was behavior, how could science help explain it?

Human behavior is far more mysterious than the distant galaxies, and thank God. Ask any cop, any advertising man, any priest, even any city editor.

As students of human behavior I should place behavioral science somewhere below baseball umpires and somewhere above Titans of Finance. The whole hi-falutin' name is at once an extraordinary pretension and an ignoble confession. . . .

Nobody has measured people yet. (Charles McCabe, *San Francisco Chronicle,* October 18, 1966, p. 20)

If these quotations represent widespread public opinion, the beginning pyschology student must feel that he is face-to-face with an enormous credibility gap when his instructor, with a straight face, identifies psychology as a science. In order to accept such an unlikely notion, the typical student must: (1) alter somewhat his conception of science and (2) have some contact with psychological research. That is what the next several hundred pages are all about.

GOALS OF A SCIENCE OF PERSONALITY

Research and Theory as Procedures for Making Sense Out of the World

Man is an animal who is bright enough to recognize that he is confronted by a threatening and confusing environment. He perceives himself the victim of discomfort, disease, natural disasters, and the sometimes unpleasant activity of other human beings. Anything which results in bringing order out of chaos by providing understanding and prediction of external events would obviously be to man's benefit. That is, such activity should be rewarding in that it reduces fear and anxiety. If the activity also leads to some degree of control over the environment, the feeling of satisfaction should be even greater. In addition to the positive emotional component, such activities should be adaptive in an evolutionary sense because the ability to predict and control any portion of the threatening environment increases the odds that the individual will survive at least long enough to have offspring. Concepts which lead, for example, to the accurate prediction of seasonal changes, the securing of food, a way to protect oneself from predators, or some means to prevent disease would help preserve life and provide the opportunity to procreate. Human beings are obviously not dependent solely on genetic selection, and the survival of a group would also be enhanced by passing on knowledge to companions and to one's children. Specific ideas such as the regularity of the phases of the moon, the utility of a club as a weapon, the uses of fire, the advantages of a bow and arrow, the secret of planting seeds to secure a crop, the way to make gunpowder, or the relationship between energy and matter need only occur one time to one individual.

Conceptualized in this way, all of man's intellectual products may be seen as attempts to make sense out of the world, to gain predictive knowledge, and to achieve the means for controlling that world. At first, the concepts must have been relatively simple, such as the relationship between fire and the feeling of warmth. In time, ideas were developed in a more elaborate form as religious beliefs, myths, political ideologies, folk sayings, and science. There are many similarities among these seemingly different conceptual systems. Each involves the creation of abstractions, a narrow focus on crucial elements, and a simplification of that which originally was complex. Strangely enough, this abstraction, narrowness, and simplification eventually lead to greater generality and hence broader understanding in each instance. Russel Lynes (1968, p. 23) makes a similar point in a discussion of cartoonists: "This is not to say that the best cartoons are the most elaborate drawings of place and people. On the contrary it is the simplification of the complex by the deftest shorthand that evokes (as in the drawings of Steinberg) the most comprehensive view of the world."

In Figure 1-1 is a very general depiction of conceptual activity as a means of making sense out of the world. The left and right portions of the figure represent, respectively, the problems and the goals of all conceptual systems. The center portion of the figure could be taken as a description of theology, communism, astrology, or physics. Such activities differ primarily in their procedures and in the kind of evidence which is acceptable. They differ in the way they go about confirming and extending the conceptual system and in the rules of evidence for determining when they are correct. The procedures and criteria of science will be the focus of our attention with respect to the field of personality. There is, incidentally, no reason to compare dif-

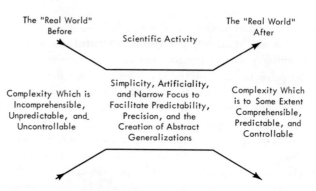

Fig. 1-1 Science and Other Conceptual Activities as Intermediate Processes Between the Complexity of Experience and the Same Complexity Brought at Least Partially under Man's Control. (After Byrne, 1971, p. 17.)

ferent conceptual systems in an attempt to show that one is more sensible than another. There are no logical grounds on which to assert that science is superior, say, to black magic. They are two different intellectual games with different rules. Science can be defended primarily on pragmatic grounds with respect to its own criteria of success. Scientific conceptions have led to repeated instances of accurate prediction and to numerous ways to control some portion of our surroundings. We may not be happy with all of the technological fruits of science, but one cannot argue that science is ineffective. By comparison, the rain dance, human sacrifice, Grandmother's proverbs, astrological charts, the prayer wheel, voodoo, palm reading, and the worship of divinities on Mount Olympus have not done very well in providing predictions or technology.

It might further be noted that the rate of change for both our physical and our conceptual tools in the older sciences is an increasingly rapid one. The time between the first use of fire and the invention of the wheel was considerably longer than the time between the invention of the wheel and the flight of the first airplane. Considering a more recent time span, at the beginning of this century the indoor toilet was just being installed in the homes of those with enough money and enough adventurous spirit to try out new gadgets. Two-thirds of a century later, color television broadcasts from the moon were familiar to all of us. Comparable changes over the next seventy years are likely to be even greater. If behavioral science undergoes an equally astonishing rate of development and change over the coming decades, we can expect literally unimaginable alterations in human life.

On the basis of past success and future hope, science would seem to be one of man's more useful developments. In what way does scientific activity lead us to understanding, prediction, and control?

UNDERSTANDING: WHY? HOW?

Describing and Naming as Understanding. Each of us wants to know why things happen in the world or how it is that they come about. And, when an explanation is available, we seem to feel better; understanding has been achieved. It is sometimes said (for example, Marx, 1951), that understanding is the basic goal of science. In one sense, however, understanding is the easiest thing in the world to attain. Skinner notes:

> When we say that man eats *because* he is hungry, smokes a great deal *because* he has the tobacco habit, fights *because* of the instinct of pugnacity, behaves brilliantly *because* of his intelligence, or plays the piano well *because* of his musical ability, we seem to be referring to causes. But on analysis these phrases prove to be merely redundant descriptions (Skinner, 1953, p. 31).

Simply naming an event or process may somehow be sufficient for providing an aura of understanding. Perhaps children first gain some degree of mastery over the world by learning to name parts of it. A frightening and inexplicable noise becomes "thunder," and an unexpected and blinding light becomes a "flashbulb." To have a word means that adults are familiar with such things and are not afraid of them. The next time that the event occurs, it is no longer a mysterious unknown but something specific with a label. The label provides a feeling of mastery over the situation.

As we grow older, much the same word-magic still is effective in reducing uncertainty and in providing what seems to be understanding. We hear or devise verbal explanations all the time. A murderer was motivated by watching violence on TV programs. A Ph.D. received his intelligence from one of his great-grandfathers who was a "whiz at numbers." The permissive philosophy expounded by various political leaders brought about crime in the streets and topless bathing suits. A housewife explains her headaches by saying that they are psychosomatic. A colleague of the author was once asked by a student in class, "Why did the Eskimos develop the custom of abandoning their old people in the snow to die?" Attempting a joke, the instructor replied, "Because they subsist on a diet of whale blubber." Apparently satisfied with this "explanation," the thirty-five students carefully wrote the material in their notes.

A somewhat elaborate and sophisticated verbal explanation may be developed as part of a more general conceptual scheme. For example, a small boy is drowned, and his parents in their despair wonder *why* this terrible thing happened. What attempts might be made to give them understanding? The suggestion could be made that the event happened because the River God was hungry. It happened as part of God's mysterious plan. It happened because the boy had a strong need for independence which led him to venture away from his home into exciting activities. It happened because the corrupt capitalist system exploited his parents and made it impossible for them to supervise him closely. It happened because his father had spent an immoral youth, and this was divine punishment. It happened because a neighborhood witch put a hex on him. It happened because the boy of his own free will chose to die. It happened because the boy had an unconscious need for self-punishment. Each of these explanations seems to offer understanding, and each could be extended to explain a wide variety of specific events. Is there any way to make distinctions among alternative explanations? Is there any basis on which to select some as more reasonable than others?

After-the-Fact Explanations. One difficulty in comparing and evaluating such alternative explanations is that the event has already taken place. Man is creative enough that almost any notion can be elaborated to provide a convincing after-the-fact explanation of any event. This holds true whether the concepts are provided by psychoanalysis, stimulus-response theory, religion, or the delusional system of a paranoid schizophrenic. Any ideas which depend entirely on their ability to offer what seems to be "understanding" are not likely to be devastated by contradictory data. One is reminded of the patient who complained to a visitor that the psychiatrists were poisoning his soup. The visitor took a sip and said that it tasted all right to him. The patient nodded, "You see how clever they are?"

"Why" questions are essential in building theoretical systems in science, and understanding is clearly an important goal. What is needed is some way to determine when it is that understanding has been achieved.

PREDICTION: WHEN? WHAT?

Predictive Accuracy as the Criterion of Understanding. The criterion of understanding adopted by scientists is prediction. This particular criterion is perhaps the major distinction between science and most other conceptual systems. Thus, we say that any attempts to increase understanding (naming, describing in different terms, or building complex verbal explanations) are of value only if the result is: (1) a more accurate prediction of the original phenomena, or (2) an accurate prediction of additional phenomena. For example, as will be discussed in Chapter 8, the observation of the behavior of clients in psychotherapy led to the proposition that individuals strive to maintain self-consistency. Once the elements of an individual's self-concept are determined, it should be possible to make specific predictions about his behavior in therapy—what topics will be talked about, what material will be distorted, what ideas will arouse defenses, and so forth. Further, predictions can be made about quite different kinds of situations in which self-congruent and self-incongruent elements are involved: situations including learning, perception, physiological responses, and the like. If these various predictions prove accurate, the concept of self-consistency is a useful one. If the predictions are not confirmed, the concept will be altered or discarded.

The term "prediction" is being used here in a very general sense to mean any situation in which we make the statement, "If X is true, then we should be able to observe Y." It may be that Y actually occurred sometime in the past, so we are really "postdicting". For example, predictions in archeology may be tested by observations of the remains of a civilization that disappeared centuries ago. Similarly, various geological explanations of the composition of the moon were confirmed (or disconfirmed) by observations of lunar rocks that were older than mankind. If a psychologist proposes that severe childhood illnesses may lead to attempts to overcompensate and achieve in adulthood, he should be able to show that very successful individuals have different medical histories than unsuccessful ones. Thus, theoretical statements in science are expected to have observable consequences. If someone tells you that the ancient Babylonians had transistor radios or that the moon is made of Kraft cheese or that adult achievement depends on childhood exposure to *The Three Bears*, they should be able to make a predictive statement about what would constitute appropriate evidence. If they cannot, the ideas may be interesting or even exciting, but science cannot deal with them. It can be seen that insistence on prediction provides scientists with a built-in system for correcting and improving their explanations.

Subjective Feeling of Understanding vs. Predictive Accuracy. In our everyday lives, when we say that we really understand something, we often mean that there is a gut-level feeling of sudden illumination. Holt (1962) has pointed out that this empathic, intuitive feeling of knowing a phenomenon from the inside is different from a scientific statement of the determinants of the phenomenon. As an example, he notes that social scientists feel that they have an understanding of juvenile delinquency if they can take variables such as economic status, the social disorganization of a neighborhood, and family structure and use these variables to predict delinquency rate. That kind of formulation is not what most people are likely to think of as understanding. Instead, understanding comes from firsthand contact with a delinquent and his family, from reading a book such as *Studs Lonigan,* or from seeing a powerful movie that portrays a delinquent with artistic power and vividness. Thus, the artist is better able to provide understanding in the usual sense than is the scientist. An artist can make you feel it. A scientist can provide you tools with which to predict it.

The two types of understanding are quite different, and each is important. Trouble sometimes arises when individuals fail to make the distinction and are disappointed to find that a theoretical principle fails to evoke a visceral response or that an emotionally stirring artistic achievement fails to provide predictive accuracy. Science strives for intellectual insight while art strives for emotional insight. Science and art can peacefully coexist so long as one does not attempt to evaluate the other according to its own standards.

Correctness of Explanations. When a prediction or a series of predictions fail, then the conceptualization which led to that prediction must be altered to take account of the inaccuracy. It may seem odd, but accurate prediction is no guarantee of the correctness of one's theoretical formulation.

For example, even when the earth was considered to be the center of the universe, astronomers were able to make relatively accurate predictions of the movements of the moon, sun, and planets. The planets offered the greatest difficulty, but the theories utilized complex loop-the-loops (epicycles) as the planetary pathways "around the earth." The only thing wrong with this formulation was that it turned out to be inconsistent with later data. When the sun was conceptualized as being located at the center of the solar system, the new theory depicted all of the planets as traveling in smooth elliptical orbits around it. The new formulation yielded the same accurate predictions provided by the old theory, and in addition it enabled astronomers to account for previously inconsistent data. All theoretical statements are tentative in that they are accepted to the extent that they are consistent with existing data and are subject to change if new data become available.

Another sort of example is provided by the various ideas concerning the causes of yellow fever. At one point night air was thought to bring on the disease because some protection was afforded when windows were kept closed at night. The reason that this conceptualization led to accurate predictions concerning prevention, of course, was because the closed windows were preventing the entry of mosquitoes. Once the idea of mosquitoes as the causal agent was proposed, a test involved having volunteers expose themselves to mosquito bites. The test showed that yellow fever developed after such exposure; thus, the night air was irrelevant. At still another level, the mosquito is irrelevant, too, unless it is carrying the yellow fever virus.

It is also true that an hypothesis can be falsely rejected because it fails to predict accurately. Ideas in science must be rejected tentatively as well as accepted tentatively. A classical problem in comparative psychology has been whether other animal species could be taught to use human language. The idea of being able to talk to the animals is appealing to others besides Dr. Doolittle. Because chimpanzees are highly intelligent, they have frequently been chosen as subjects in experiments designed to explore this possibility. The hypothesis that chimpanzees could be taught to communicate was tested by various investigators who raised chimps from infancy so that their experience would be like that of a human baby. Hayes and Hayes spent six years in such an effort with a chimpanzee named Viki and yet were only able to teach her to make four sounds that approximated English words. It could be concluded, then, that even a very bright animal given intensive training could not be taught a language system. Somewhat later, Gardner and Gardner (1969) decided to start over again with the same hypothesis and a different method. These experimenters reasoned that chimpanzees are not naturally vocal but that they do use their hands a great deal to gesture and to manipulate objects. A chimp named Washoe was selected for study, and the investigators tried to teach her the sign language of the deaf. With a gestural language rather than speech, Washoe was able to learn thirty signs in the first twenty-two months and was continuing to add to her vocabulary each week. Even more surprising, she learned to combine signs into sentences to tell the experimenter to "give me a tickle," "open the refrigerator for food and drink," and "listen to the dog." Such results suggest that the original hypothesis was correct; it was the method of testing it that was wrong.

The fact that an idea may be accepted at one point and later rejected (or vice versa) may be a bit upsetting, but that kind of uncertainty is part and parcel of the way science proceeds. The "real" world cannot be ascertained independently of the outcome of our predictions about it. Therefore, accurate predictions should be taken to mean that one's present conceptualization is provisionally "correct," but that it may at some point be supplanted by a better one. Inaccurate predictions mean that one's present conceptualization is provisionally "incorrect," but new methodology may later revive it.

Control: What Are the Practical Implications?
Of What Use Is It?

In the laboratory, the ability to control phenomena means that the scientist is able to manipulate certain independent variables and predict accurately the effect on certain dependent variables. Such control also suggests that it may be possible to control some aspect of the world outside of the laboratory. What are some of the issues involved when the application of scientific knowledge is considered as a goal of science?

Seeking Knowledge for Its Own Sake versus Seeking Solutions to Practical Problems. There is an old and honored academic tradition which places a high value on the principle that knowledge should be sought not for practical reasons but for its intrinsic worth. Thus, support is gained for sciences such as archeology which are unlikely to yield applied benefits and for the humanities. This tradition has been described well by Walter Lippmann (1966, p. 19).

If we say that the vocation of the scholar is to seek the truth, it follows, I submit, that he must seek the truth for the simple purpose of knowing the truth. The search for truth proceeds best if it is inspired by wonder and curiosity, if, that is to say, it is disinterested—if the scholar disregards all secondary considerations of how his knowledge may be applied, how it can be sold, whether it is useful, whether it will make men happier or unhappier, whether it is agreeable or disagreeable, whether it is likely to win him a promotion or a prize or a decoration, whether it will get a good vote in the Gallup poll. Genius is most likely to expand the limits of our knowledge, on which all the applied sciences depend, when it works in a condition of total unconcern with the consequences of its findings.

Despite this tradition, a certain amount of conflict tends to exist between those individuals actively engaged in basic research and those who feel that the ultimate outcome of such work should be useful to society. The general culture, as represented in Congressional support for research grants and popular articles describing scientific discoveries, is clearly oriented toward the application of laboratory findings for the benefit of mankind. Basic research seems less important and is sometimes viewed as a waste of time. The single most notable area of agreement between the political left and right is a negative attitude toward basic research. If research isn't relevant, it isn't worthwhile. For some, relevant means "of immediate benefit in improving the quality of life" and to others it means "of practical utility in increasing industrial or military efficiency." As one individual remarked in discussing the scarcity of jobs for Ph.D.s, "The tight market for Ph.D.s is a good thing. There are too many people with a lot of knowledge about unimportant things" (Lofton, 1972, p. 364). Support for basic research can generally be obtained, however, by pointing out that basic research has repeatedly led to findings with practical implications. For example, prior to the early 1940s, the work of nuclear physicists was seemingly far removed from application. Today, the applied aspects of this field are all around us. In addition, the history of science suggests strongly that work on immediate applied problems has not necessarily proven to be the most effective way to solve such problems. One need only think of alchemists attempting to transmute lead into gold. It is also true, of course, that solutions at times come first, and then basic research is conducted afterward to discover how or why something works. For example, aspirin has long been used as a means to reduce pain, but the reasons for its effectiveness are still being sought.

The fact that there is not necessarily a smooth and direct relationship between laboratory research and useful applications is not always made clear. If we can agree that certain problems are of critical concern, why don't scientists concentrate all of their efforts on solving these problems? In a field as highly developed as physics, it frequently is possible to set a goal (the atomic bomb or a manned rocket to the moon) and with enough money and engineering effort, that goal is achieved. In less developed fields such as biomedicine and psychology, the creation of a Manhattan project does not appear to be a useful way to proceed. A crash program to cure arteriosclerosis or prevent crime is probably doomed to fail. It is not because we don't desire to solve such problems, but because relatively young sciences must proceed in a different way. Rather than identify a problem and then seek the solution, it may be necessary to establish reliable knowledge and then seek a problem for which it is applicable.

There are many instances in which experimental methodology or experimental findings are developed in basic research and later are found to be applicable in work on an applied problem. Such research fall-out may be accidental in that the concerns of those conducting the original research may be far removed from the use to which it is eventually put. For example, the discovery of X radiation (itself an accident) was of considerable importance in theoretical physics; at the same time, the utilization of X-rays in medical diagnosis constituted an application in a quite different field. Townes (1968) has documented the basic research which led to the development of the laser beam which then became a tool for solving many applied problems. He then raises a question (p. 702):

> Consider now the problem of a research planner setting out twenty years ago to develop any one of these technological improvements—a more sensitive amplifier, a more accurate clock, new drilling techniques, a new surgical instrument for the eye, more accurate measurement of distance, three-dimensional photography, and so on. Would he have had the wit or courage to initiate for any of these purposes an extensive basic study of the interaction between microwaves and molecules? The answer is clearly No... It was the drive for new information and understanding, and the atmosphere of basic research which seem clearly to have been needed for the real payoff.

Two questions illustrate the different emphases which may be placed on the same finding: Is it relevant to the theoretical formulation? Could it serve a utilitarian purpose? Perhaps an ideal situation is one in which both questions are asked and an ideal finding is one which provides a "yes" to each question. Weinberg (quoted in Greenberg, 1966) suggests that science is like a basketball game in which a team keeps the ball moving; every now and then the opportunity arises to make a good shot. Basic research keeps knowledge moving; every now and then there is an opportunity to exploit it for some practical use.

Control Outside of the Laboratory: Value Judgments. With the application of scientific knowledge, value judgments must be made. Should thousands of men, women, and children be destroyed in order to hasten the end of a war? Is it right to fluoridate a town's water supply over the protests of a frightened minority in order to aid in the prevention of dental cavities? Is it right to pass a compulsory sterilization law in order to decrease the incidence of schizophrenia in the population? Is it right to use subliminal messages flashed on a movie screen in order to increase the sales of a particular product? Is it right to design neighborhoods in such a way that interpersonal contacts are increased and personal isolation is decreased? These decisions are different from those usually required of scientists; there are no generally accepted criteria for moral concepts such as "right."

Part of the problem, undoubtedly, is the fact that control activities which affect human behavior, even in minor ways, can arouse our anxieties. Farber has discussed this phenomenon:

It was stated earlier that, if the determinants of behavior were known, and if enough of them were susceptible to manipulation, then it would be possible to control behavior. It was also noted that this proposition arouses the most intense annoyance and anxiety in many people, including psychologists, who for good reasons, abhor the idea of a totalitarian technocracy (Bergmann, 1956). In its superficial aspects, one can rather readily understand why the concepts of "control" and "despotism" are sometimes equated. If behavior can indeed be controlled by manipulating its determinants, then individuals with the requisite knowledge could and very possibly would exercise this control.

On the one hand, we must recognize that different societies and different individuals have different goals. What is desirable or reinforcing for one may be frustrating and punishing for another. We are only too liable to the delusion that our own goals are the only reasonable ones. Thus, when I try to change a person's behavior or attitudes, I am appealing to his better judgment; when you try to do so, you are using propaganda; and when "they" do so, they are brainwashing. To complicate matters further, this multiplicity of motives and goals extends to the intrapersonal sphere. The behavior that is instrumental to the satisfaction of one motive may frustrate the satisfaction of another.

On the other hand, our respect for the rights of others to their particular goals and the instrumental acts whereby they are achieved should not lead us to the romantic delusion that these are spontaneous products of unfettered choice. No one escapes control by the physical environment short of death; and no one escapes control by his social environment short of complete isolation. Almost the entire period of childhood is given over to the acquisition of new behaviors, goals, and motives, under the guidance of parents, family, and teachers. Be it wise or unwise, deliberate, impulsive, or unconscious, such guidance inevitably has its effects. It is difficult, in fact, to think of any kind of social interaction that has absolutely no effect on behavior. That the effects are unintentional or unwanted does not negate them (Farber, 1964, pp. 12–14).

Validity of the Application. One final question which arises in the application of scientific knowledge is that of validity. Does the procedure actually do what is claimed for it? Does it work? The question here is not one of deliberate falsehood or the activity of con men. Rather, the question deals with honest differences of opinion in evaluating the relevant evidence and with differences among scientists in their willingness to utilize imperfect techniques. It is here that some relatively basic conflicts may arise between those oriented toward prediction and those oriented toward control.

One applied field closely related to personality psychology is that of clinical psychology. Here we find the application of assessment techniques and of procedures designed to bring about changes in personality. For many academic psychologists, clinical practice today is analogous to the medical practice of previous centuries. That is, the patient's distress clearly merits attention and the motivation of the professionally oriented psychologist to provide help is genuine, but the available techniques are perceived as no more effective than the leeches, lancets, and laudanum of a previous medical era. On the other hand, many clinicians criticize academic psychologists as too cautious or even socially irresponsible in focusing on artificial laboratory problems when there are real-life problems to be met. The professional man often feels that like the proverbial drunk: "...the academician spends his time looking under the lamppost, where the light is good, for the ...quarter that was dropped in the gutter half a block away" (Rodgers, 1964, p. 677).

Probably the goals of prediction and control are sufficiently different that they tend to appeal to different individuals. Recognizable distinctions exist between a science and a profession, and psychology may someday follow the example of other disciplines and formally divide into two separate (but equal) groups engaged in these different types of activity.

If personality research is directed toward the goals of understanding, predicting, and controlling human behavior, the question may be raised as to whether this is a reasonable undertaking. Throughout man's history, including the present time, the prevailing opinion has been that there cannot be a science of behavior. What assumptions must one make in order to embark on such an unpopular task?

TWO ASSUMPTIONS UNDERLYING PERSONALITY RESEARCH

ASSUMPTION I—BEHAVIOR IS PREDICTABLE

The lawfulness of behavior is the basic premise in psychology; animal organisms, including human beings, do not behave in a random or otherwise unpredictable manner. There is a lawful regularity in every aspect of behavior, regardless of its simplicity or complexity, regardless of its importance or unimportance in human affairs. This assumption is often designated as determinism.

Free Will. Though a deterministic assumption is obviously necessary for behavioral science, it tends to arouse opposition and arguments against it, even from many behavioral scientists. For the most part, the opposition may be attributable to the fact that our cultural heritage does not include the notion that behavior follows natural laws. In fact, most human societies have assumed that man is a free agent propelled by inner forces that defy prediction (Immergluck, 1964). When Skinner (1971) attempted to convince the general public that this idea of individual freedom of behavior is a delusion, he aroused widespread anger and criticism. To some, he was more than the messenger with unhappy tidings; he was accused of wanting to take our freedom away.

Can psychologists assume that individuals ever choose to perform specific behaviors on the basis of an autonomous, unknowable force such as free will? May one engage in behavior which is independent of the predictable regularities of natural laws? If Assumption I is accepted, the answer obviously is "No." Every behavior is conceptualized as the result of lawful interactions between it and antecedent events. If Assumption I is not accepted, behavioral science disappears in a puff of smoke, for there can be no science of behavior. There is no direct way to settle such controversy; one cannot prove that there is or is not free will. The fruitfulness of the assumption can only be determined through the success or failure of those who are attempting to build a science of behavior.

A philosopher, Peter Caws (1971), has pointed out a basic reason for our very different reactions to the idea of lawfulness in the physical sciences as opposed to the behavioral sciences. We accept laws of gravity which have been tested with ball-bearings and laws of genetics derived from the study of sweet peas and fruitflies. We even acknowledge that such laws will apply to us if we fall from a tower or become parents. Such concepts as mass or genes refer to things we *have* and about which nothing can be done. Behavioral science, on the other hand, deals with things we *do*. Our actions are seen as reflecting what we *are*, our individualism. If our actions are nothing but the end point of a series of determining influences (genetics, past experiences, and current environmental events), where does that leave us? The notion that we have no greater choice about whether to be shy or outgoing than about whether to fall down or up is an extremely threatening one. In a way, psychology represents the last great threat to man's conception of himself. At various times in history, ideas of the earth's place in the solar system or man's position in an evolutionary scheme were equally threatening. It should be noted, however, that we have survived these previous threats and adjusted to them. One more is not likely to do us in. Skinner (1971, p. 215) takes a very positive view of man's future, "He is indeed controlled by his environment, but we must remember that it is an environment largely of his own making. . . It is often said that a scientific view of man leads to wounded vanity, a sense of helplessness, and nostalgia. But. . .man remains what he has always been. . .A scientific view of man offers exciting possibilities. We have not yet seen what man can make of man."

Limitations. Two other, somewhat minor, problems are raised by the assumption of lawfulness and predictability. Confusion sometimes arises to the effect that psychologists are planning to compete with palmists and readers of tea leaves in predicting the future. A more precise statement of the proposition would be that behavior *in a given stimulus situation* is predictable. Therefore, any behavioral law must be specific with respect to the stimuli involved. We may find in an experiment that pain evokes aggression, but that does not necessarily mean that a patient will hit his dentist. We should note that the fact that a lawful relationship is found in a controlled laboratory situation does not necessarily mean that the same relationship will be found in the uncontrolled stimulus situations outside of the laboratory. In physics, the effect of gravitational force on falling bodies is specified *in a vacuum*. When the falling speed of an object in "the real world" is under consideration, the effects of many additional variables (for example, wind speed and direction, resistance offered by the shape and size of the object) must be known. A feather and a rock fall at the same rate in a vacuum but are quite different if you drop them from your roof on a windy day.

The second problem is the fact that organisms change over time; hence the predictions for a given organism with respect to the same stimulus situation on two different occasions might well be different. As an obvious example, the amount of fear aroused in response to an unexpected clap of thunder should differ from the amount of fear aroused when it thunders a second time. Similarly, a joke is not as funny after the first hearing. One's response to the words on a menu at a French restaurant is different before and after having learned the language. In short, organisms are affected by what has occurred previously, and this influences their response to subsequent events. Perhaps, then, we should state Assumption I as follows: *behavior in a given stimulus situation is predictable if the relevant variables affecting the organism are known.*

Assumption II—Scientists Can Investigate Only Operationally Defined Variables

Operationism. The scientific method and the philosophy of science have evolved over the centuries as a set of procedures and concepts for advancing the acquisition of knowledge. One of the more useful concepts is operationism. An operational definition of a term is simply a verbal statement which specifies the observable conditions or procedural rules under which the term is used in defining a concept or variable (Bechtoldt, 1959).

In our usual conversations, when someone indicates that a given person is "anxious," for example, he may convey to each different person who hears it a very special kind of meaning picked up over the years from friends, relatives, books, movies, and other sources in the culture and from his own private, subjective, internal world of experience. Such meanings may be highly individualistic, inconsistent among various individuals, and even inconsistent over a period of time for the same individual. If an experimenter used such terms in this manner and reported that he found male adolescents to be more anxious than female adolescents, he might have in mind most any meaning of anxiety. In turn, the finding might convey fifty different meanings to fifty different readers.

In order to bring such a hodgepodge of vague elements into the realm of scientific inquiry, concepts must be defined in quite a different way, that is, operationally. A person may be defined as being anxious if he is one who says, "I feel nervous," has trembling hands, reports that he worries about the future, complains of numerous vague physical ailments, goes about hurriedly, or obtains a high score on a psychological test measuring anxiety—all of which are observable aspects of behavior. When the variables under investigation are defined in this way, other experimenters are able to use precisely the same variables. An experimenter does not simply employ "an unpleasant stimulus" but rather an electric shock of a specified voltage attached to the right index finger of each subject. Subjects are not simply differentiated into "anxious and nonanxious" individuals, but are selected in terms of the scores they receive on a specific measure of anxiety. "Operationism" involves only the recognition that knowledge can best be gained and communicated through procedures which are observable, specific, and open to repetition by other investigators. Even so, the concept is of central importance in science and, strangely enough, has been a matter of controversy.

Science and the Unobservable. If scientists deal with that which is tangible, what about concepts which cannot be defined in that way? If a concept cannot be tied to observables (hell, for example), it is simply not open to scientific inquiry and is, therefore, not the business of science (Simpson, 1964). Utilizing the scientific method, there is literally no way even to begin answering the question of whether there is a hell. Science cannot and does not deny the existence of nonmaterial, unobservable phenomena. Science and theology are not in disagreement; they simply deal with different problems in different ways.

Pseudo-Problems. One benefit of operationism is that scientists are able to avoid false problems such as the ancient question of whether a tree falling in an uninhabited forest makes a noise. If "noise" is defined as dial readings on a machine that detects sound waves, then one can easily demonstrate that noise does occur even in an uninhabited forest. If, on the other hand, "noise" is defined as a verbal report about auditory stimulation, then noise cannot occur in such a forest. And, either definition of noise is acceptable, providing that it is clear which one you mean.

An equally false problem is the question of whether the operationally defined variable is *really* a measure of the concept. Does the Manifest Anxiety Scale *really* measure anxiety? Does the Stanford-Binet *really* measure intelligence? Does a thermometer *really* measure temperature? Does a self-rating scale *really* measure sex arousal? Such questions assume that some identifiable, pure, formless, nonoperational anxiety or intelligence or temperature or sex arousal exists somewhere. It is meaningless to talk about the amount of correspondence between operational measures and the real variable, because there is no *real* variable. What *is* meaningful, however, is to determine the relationship between one operationally defined variable and other operationally defined variables.

Criticisms of Operationism. Critics say that an operational definition is too narrow and that the rich meaning of a term is lost when it is reduced to something as specific and limited as a test score or an experimental procedure. No one claims to encompass all of the rich cultural meaning of concepts such as anxiety, intelligence, or hunger into a single score or a specific condition. In order to formulate an operational definition which more closely matches the cultural meaning, one probably must employ a large number of discrete operations which together are something like the cultural meaning. Most definitions from the culture are probably too broad and too vague for scientific investigation. Often, scientists find that they are better off with more than one operational definition of a given concept if the different definitions represent unique variables which are at least partially independent of one another. As Zubin (1965) has pointed out, the temperature reading of a mercury thermometer does not encompass all that is meant by an individual when he expresses feelings of being hot or cold. The mercury readings plus the humidity level plus barometric pressure plus wind speed probably do account for most of the perceived temperature differences. Nevertheless, these entities are separate variables, operationalized in quite different ways, and each has its own antecedents and consequents.

Allport (1961, p. 573) repeatedly criticized any approach to personality which failed to recognize man as possessing qualities over and above the operations and constructs of science. "He is more than a bundle of habits, more than a point of intersection of abstract dimensions. He is more than a representative of his species, more than a citizen of the state, more than an incident in the movements of mankind. He transcends them all." Such a statement expresses a commendable view of the value of human beings. As representatives of that group, we can agree enthusiastically with Allport. What all this has to do with the means by which scientists go about studying behavior is, however, a mystery. To determine that a man weighs 190 pounds and is 5' 11" tall says nothing about your philosophical views concerning humanity. It is, nevertheless, useful if you wish to find a suit which fits him. The quantification of observable behavior is no more demeaning or antihumanistic than is stepping on the scales or holding up a tape measure. A second type of negative reaction to operationism is of a somewhat different order. The necessity for defining variables in terms of specific observables in research is sometimes misinterpreted to mean that it is improper even to speculate in nonoperational terms. Some psychologists equate operationism with a narrow and old-fashioned and antagonistic experimental psychology (Shontz, 1965). The term "operationism" has been credited with a great deal of negative meaning. In contrast, Stevens points out that operationism:

> ...is not opposed to hypotheses, theories, or speculation. It seeks merely to discover criteria by which these things may be detected and labeled. It is not opposed to poetry, art, or religion. It wants only to know the difference between these things and science (Stevens, 1939, p. 230).

If any scientist felt compelled to stick so close to operations that he was afraid to engage in vague, ill-defined speculative thinking, his scientific contributions are likely to be quite limited. The most creative aspects of scientific activity may, in fact, be much closer to art than to science.

HOW DOES SCIENTIFIC ACTIVITY PROCEED?

In a book intended to give laymen some understanding of what science is all about, James B. Conant (1947) indicated that he hoped to dodge the problem of defining science, feeling that science could best be understood by reading about how individual scientists have actually proceeded in their work.

Science is not defined by technological apparatus and not by memorization of the facts which have been gathered. The technological apparatus is often forbidding to the uninitiated, but the use of most techniques, from a centrifuge to an electronic computer, can be learned by any normally functioning individual who has recevied the proper instruction. All of the accumulated facts do not have to be memorized by each investigator; having them available in written form is much more efficient. Science, instead, is a dynamic, often exciting, often frustrating process in which a reciprocal interaction takes place between observation and conceptualization. A few examples may make this activity seem less mysterious.

UNCONTROLLED OBSERVATION

A science of behavior has many possible starting points, but most include observations of behavior. The observation may be of oneself, others in one's everyday environment, animals, patients in psychotherapy, or experimental subjects.

When scientists engage in uncontrolled observations, what are the characteristics of this procedure? At the observational stage, there is no reason to be concerned about experimental rigor. One of the most exciting and important aspects of science can be seen in the attempt of an acute observer to make conceptual sense of some aspect of the world. For example, a therapist notes that a patient's paralyzed hand can be moved after the patient expresses hostility toward his father for the first time. A child psychologist hears a small girl attribute blame for an accident to an inanimate object. A professor observes that his students seem to joke and laugh uproariously just before an examination is administered. If an individual observes such events, wonders about them, and tries to make sense of them, he has engaged in the initial activity necessary for a science of behavior. The aim is to arrive at fruitful concepts which will then lead to more refined observations. Rogers makes a similar point:

> It is my opinion that the type of understanding which we call science can begin anywhere, at any level of sophistication. To observe acutely, to think carefully and creatively—these activities, not the accumulation of laboratory instruments, are the beginnings of science. To observe that a given crop grows better on the rocky hill than in the lush bottom land and to think about this observation, is the start of science. To notice that most sailors get scurvy but not those who have stopped at islands to pick up fresh fruit is a similar start. To recognize that, when a person's views of himself change, his behavior changes accordingly, and to puzzle over this, is again the beginning of both theory and science. I voice this conviction in protest against the attitude which seems too common in American psychology, that science starts in the laboratory or at the calculating machine (Rogers, 1959, p. 189).

GENERALIZATION

As soon as the observations are expressed in symbols which go beyond what was observed, generalization to a class of events is taking place. This process constitutes the first step or the most primitive level of theory building. We each accumulate a series of concepts, often unverbalized and often incorrect, which influence our interpretations of behavior. Novelists have long been aware of these guiding speculations which people hold. Quite often a fictional character is made to express a generalization or series of generalizations about behavior.

Not only novelists, but waitresses, kindergarten teachers, bus drivers, and used-car salesmen all observe human behavior and all develop general notions about it. "Fat people are jolly." "Mexican kids can't be trusted." "It's human nature to have wars and revolutions." "Any guy who walks like that must be queer." "Spare the rod and spoil the child." "Everybody's out to make a fast buck." Most people, of course, do not go beyond their original generalizations. The reason is that they do not have adequate means by which to check their ideas in order to discard the incorrect ones and expand

on those that are valid. In order to move from the generalizations of everyday life and the pages of novels, one must specify operations and engage in
empirical research to test the validity of the generalizations.

VERIFICATION

Outside of science, most individuals seem to rely primarily on congruent
validation to "test" their generalizations. That is, any new observations
which are congruent with the generalizations are accepted as evidence that
the ideas are correct. Contrary observations are conveniently ignored. For
example, a belief that long-haired boys are dirty may be confirmed by observing a few such individuals who are in need of a bath. But, as an old
Jewish saying puts it, *"For instance* is not proof." The fact that some short-
haired boys may also be unclean or that many long-haired boys are not dirty
can easily be ignored.

In science, on the other hand, an effort is made to verify the generalizations by seeking new data as objectively as possible. The primary concern is
to carry out the verification procedure in such a way that one is not deceived
into accepting that which is not so or rejecting that which is. Examples of
how this is done in the field of personality will be given throughout the
remainder of this book.

THEORY BUILDING

Theory building is the attempt to formulate increasingly broader generalizations which take the established relationships beyond the particular events
involved in a specific observation. By giving a more comprehensive explanation of the observation, theories are created, hypotheses can be deduced, and
hypothesis testing leads to new observations. Rogers gives an example:

> I like to think of the discovery of radioactivity by the Curies. They had left
> some pitchblende ore, which they were using for some purpose or other, in a
> room where they stored photographic plates. They discovered that the plates
> had been spoiled. In other words, first there was the observation of a dynamic
> event. This event might have been due to a multitude of causes. It might have
> been a flaw in the manufacture of the plates. It might have been the humidity,
> the temperature, or any one of a dozen other things. But acute observation and
> creative thinking fastened on a hunch regarding the pitchblende, and this
> became a tentative hypothesis. Crude experiments began to confirm the hy-
> pothesis. Only slowly was it discovered that it was not the pitchblende, but a
> strange element in the pitchblende which was related to the observed effect.
> Meanwhile a theory had to be constructed to bring this strange phenomenon
> into orderly relationship with other knowledge. And although the theory in its
> most modest form had to do with the effect of radium on photographic plates,
> in its wider and more speculative reaches it was concerned with the nature of
> matter and composition of the universe (Rogers, 1959, p. 190).

Where does psychology, and more specifically the field of personality, stand with respect to theory? As will be described in the following chapter, much that we label as "personality theory" is not theory in the formal sense but rather a mixture of observations, generalizations, pretheoretical speculation, and hypotheses. It is easier to extend the speculations than it is to carry out the data-gathering procedures necessary to support the speculations and thus to extend the network of facts. Considerable agreement exists that our present theories are lacking in many respects and that the construction of better behavioral theories is badly needed.

Most personality theories are broad in scope and attempt to supply an explanatory framework covering essentially every aspect of human behavior. Existing personality theories tend to be far too ambitious in their aims and far too limited in their predictive power. What then, is our solution? Spence pointed out:

> It should be noticed that...comprehensive physical theories...are formulated only after there is available a considerable body of empirical laws relating concepts of a fairly abstract nature, i.e., highly generalized laws. It would hardly seem necessary to have to say that no such comprehensive, highly abstract theories exist today in psychology, for the simple reason that we do not even have a well developed body of very general laws in any area of our field (Spence, 1960, p. 82).

Thus, a potentially fruitful approach to theory building in the science of personality would seem to be the establishment of behavioral laws and the construction of small theories dealing with specific and limited behavioral events rather than the development of a general theory of personality. These small "personality theories" would, initially, be limited in scope but predictively powerful. As such theories are built, the formulation of more general concepts will tie them together into increasingly broad overall theories. This, however, is an end point rather than a starting point. First, we need to devise psychological laws analogous to those of the pendulum, of gases, of the lever, of the effect of gravity on momentum, and so forth. As satisfying and useful as it would be to have a complete theory of behavior immediately available, a more limited goal is the first step.

THE FIELD OF PERSONALITY

From the viewpoint of the physical sciences and the biomedical sciences, the history of man's development is one of constant and ever more amazing progress. In the highly developed industrialized nations at least, an astounding proportion of the general population is living in a manner not available to the most wealthy and powerful citizens as recently as the early 1900s. There is, for example, an astonishing degree of physical comfort with central heat-ing, air conditioning, king-sized beds, automatic washers and dryers, vacuum cleaners, supermarkets with food from around the world, and refrigerator-freezers with automatic ice-makers (regular or crushed). With a few exceptions, most of the major diseases of the past can be prevented or cured; as recently as the 1950s, polio epidemics were a recurring horror to mothers each summer. With automobiles and airplanes, our mobility is miraculous. We can cross the country in the time it took George Washington to travel from Mount Vernon to Washington, D.C. Almost continuous entertainment in the form of movies, television, radio, and recordings is available with the flick of a switch. It could be said that things are getting better and better, and we should all be filled with optimism.

As Pogo once noted however, "We have met the enemy and he is us." When we examine the behavior of mankind during the twentieth century, rapid change and improvement is not the outstanding feature. Just consider a few examples. The technical skills and organizational ability of a cultured and advanced European nation was directed toward the identification, apprehension, transportation, and efficient extermination of over 6 million "undesirable" men, women, and children. The uneven possession of wealth is such that at the same moment in time one woman can pay $1 million for a piece of decorative jewelry while another stays awake in a Ghetto room to keep the rats from attacking her sick baby. A student, and former Boy Scout, rode an elevator to the top of a university tower and shot over forty individuals at random before he himself was shot. A Latin American dictator employed a midget whose fearsome specialty was biting off the genitalia of male prisoners. Powerful cars and an expensive highway system are built in the United States, and one result is the annual death of over fifty thousand individuals with family holidays as the peak fatality period. Policemen become the random targets of snipers and bombers. Russian intellectuals who are critical of their government's policies have been apprehended, placed in mental institutions, and systematically tormented with sophisticated medical techniques to cause pain and suffering. Groups of American students who have protested against official policies have sometimes been physically abused, often been arrested, and on a few tragic occasions been killed. More children in the United States die annually as the result of physical abuse from their parents than from leukemia, cystic fibrosis, and muscular dystrophy. Uncontrolled population growth and uncontrolled exploitation of natural resources have resulted in overcrowded cities in which individuals breathe unspeakably filthy air and drink water contaminated with chemical and organic refuse; the arguments among ecologists tend to be about the number of years left to our species and the precise form our self-destruction will take. Bombs are dropped, bodies are burned, prisoners are tortured, and anyone walking alone on the streets of a big city at night is risking his life. The picture of man's progress is somewhat marred when we focus attention on man himself.

Chad Oliver once wrote a science fiction novel about a planet on which the order of development of behavioral and physical sciences was reversed compared to our own. Their behavioral theories and behavioral technology were infinitely superior to ours, while the development of the physical sciences was still at a primitive level. Considering how things have worked out on our planet, that reversed procedure sounds appealing.

The problems of mankind are perceived by almost everyone, and numerous solutions have been offered. One such solution would be the rapid development of behavioral science. This is not to suggest that behavioral scientists now have the answers for all human problems. Rather, the hope would be that there is time for psychology and other fields to pursue the science of behavior as successfully as physicists have done in making sense out of the physical world.

Not until the latter part of the last century was the notion of studying behavioral variables seriously pursued. Over time, the type of behavior investigated has widened from relatively simple processes, such as perceptual thresholds and reaction time, to include *any* behavior of *any degree of complexity*, ranging from light avoidance in amoebas, to learning in the flatworm, to mental illness in man, to international hostility.

Within the field of psychology, there are many areas of research interest. No psychologist investigates all types of behavior. Thus, some psychologists work only with animal learning, some psychologists investigate only leadership behavior in small groups, and other psychologists deal only with man-machine systems. Where does the field of personality fall within all of this?

Whereas the background of experimental psychology lies in the traditional laboratory approach to science in which independent variables are manipulated and the effect on dependent variables determined, the historical background of personality psychology is much closer to everyday life experiences. For thousands of years before there were any psychologists, there was a general awareness of and interest in individual differences. The language developed in such a way that we tend to describe other individuals in terms of their standing along an indefinite number of *dimensions.* Whether we are characterizing a political candidate or a blind date or a character in a novel or a next-door neighbor, the same sorts of dimensions are utilized in each instance. For example, someone is described in terms of the extent to which he is intelligent–stupid, kind–cruel, dominant–submissive, liberal–conservative, anxious–calm, contented–unhappy, ambitious–lazy, crazy–sane, devious–straightforward, creative–commonplace, social–unsocial, crude–refined, impulsive–cautious, interesting–dull, outgoing–withdrawn, and so on and so on. In fact, if one were to take any such description of a given person and list all of the dimensions utilized plus that person's position on each, the end product is what we mean by that individual's "personality".

In its earliest stages, the field of personality psychology did not go a great deal beyond that point. There was speculation about which dimensions should be included in personality descriptions, speculation about why people differ in various ways, and speculation about the factors responsible for changes in personality. In more recent times, this interest in dimensions of individual differences has grown in sophistication, and attempts are made to measure the dimensions of personality with some precision, to determine the extent to which relationships exist between and among these dimensions, and to provide personality descriptions in a more specific and more quantified fashion.

At the present time, the study of personality encompasses both the experimental approach and an interest in individual differences.

Personality in Relation to Other Fields of Psychology

In this text, the *personality* of an individual will be defined as the combination of all of the relatively enduring dimensions of individual differences on which he can be measured. The *field of personality* is defined as that branch of psychology which deals with dimensions of individual differences and with situational determinants of the behavior of individuals. Thus, behavior is conceptualized as resulting from a combination of personality characteristics and situational factors.

In many respects, personality is the broadest and least specific field of psychology with respect to subject matter. It has been characterized as the last refuge for general psychologists and also as psychology's garbage bin in that any research which doesn't fit other existing categories can be labelled "personality". For this reason, the work described in this text necessarily touches on fields such as social psychology, clinical psychology, learning, developmental psychology, physiological psychology, and others. The one common link to the various areas of work to be described is the goal of understanding, predicting, and controlling human behavior.

In many respects, psychologists whose interests place them in the field of personality (or personality-social psychology) occupy a middle ground within the field of psychology. The identification of broad areas of interest often divides psychologists roughly into experimental and clinical psychologists. The identity of the former rests on the historical base of psychology as a laboratory science, and the label "experimentalist" most often refers to a psychologist who engages in research in the areas of learning, perception, or psychophysiology. Clinical psychology is largely a post-World War II phenomenon, a rapidly growing area of interest within the American Psychological Association (APA). While research methodology has consistently been included as part of the graduate training of clinicians, their identifying characteristic is an interest in the application of diagnostic and therapeutic skills for the purpose of identifying and alleviating the emotional problems of maladjusted individuals.

Psychologists in the personality-social area, on the other hand, are somewhat different from either experimentalists or clinicians. They share a research orientation and methodology with experimentalists, but the content of their research tends to be relatively complex human behavior. Like clinicians, personality psychologists are interested in the variables determining human behavior, but they are much more inclined to focus on normal rather than abnormal functioning and are less likely to be engaged in service work in an applied setting.

Division 8 of the APA (Personality and Social Psychology) has recently been one of the fastest growing areas in the field. Between 1948 and 1960, the membership of Division 8 increased 297 percent; by way of comparison, Division 3 (Experimental Psychology) increased 40 percent, and Division 12 (Clinical and Abnormal Psychology) increased 189 percent (Tryon, 1963). Since about 1960, personality has emerged as a major field of specialization among doctoral candidates (Vance and MacPhail, 1964).

As of 1968, Division 8 was found to have the largest membership of the various APA divisions (4,168 members) representing about 15 percent of all APA members (McGuire, 1968). Division 8 also was found to have a very young membership, indicating that this field has become increasingly popular among graduate students and new Ph.D.s during the past five to ten years. Both in number of individuals and in the publication of research, personality and social psychology are growing faster than psychology as a whole (McGuire, 1968). In Table 1-1 may be seen the employment settings

**Table 1-1. Employment Settings and Principal Work Activities
of Personality and Social Psychologists**

Employment Setting	Percentage	Work Activity	Percentage
College or University	72.7	Teaching	45.8
Federal Government	5.1	Basic Research	23.6
Nonprofit Organization	4.9	Management	9.6
State Government	3.4	Applied Research	7.5
Private Industry	2.4	Management, other than	
Medical School	2.2	research/development	6.3
Military, USPHS	1.8	Clinical Research/Investigation	2.2
Nonprofit Hospital/Clinic	1.8	Clinical Practice	1.0
Junior College	1.2	Report or Technical	
Self-Employed	1.0	Writing/Editing	.9
Secondary School System	.9	Development	.8
Private Hospital/Clinic	.7	Counseling Practice	.4
Other Government	.6	Administration, Psychological	
Research Center	.5	Tests	.2
Other	.6	Consulting	.1
		Design	.1
		Other	1.13

(Data from Cates, 1970)

and principal work activities of personality and social psychologists responding to the 1968 National Register of Scientific and Technical Personnel
(Cates, 1970). As a field, it consists primarily of individuals employed in a
college or university setting and engaged in teaching and/or basic research.

THE PLAN OF THIS BOOK

This text is divided into four sections. The first section contains two introductory chapters. In the present chapter, an attempt has been made to
introduce the notion that personality psychology is an area of scientific research interest, to outline some of the general goals toward which scientific
activity is directed, to consider some of the assumptions underlying personality research, and to give a brief overview of personality psychology and
its relationship to the rest of the field. The following chapter will summarize
three major personality theories which constitute the historical basis of the
field and will attempt to show the way in which theoretical development
influences current personality research.

The second section of the book concentrates on individual differences as
a focus of the study of personality. First, there is a description of the methods
used in investigating individual differences in terms of personality measurement, personality development, personality structure, personality dynamics,
and personality change. Following this introduction are five chapters describing in some detail what is known with respect to a representative sample
of five personality dimensions: authoritarianism, need for achievement,
manifest anxiety, intelligence, and self-concept. These particular five dimensions were selected as examples because (1) there has been a considerable
amount of research dealing with each, and (2) they represent quite varied
kinds of personality dimensions. The five variables provide a sampling of
research on individual differences in ideology, motivation, emotion, ability,
and self-image.

The third section shifts to a consideration of the situational determinants
of behavior. In an introductory chapter, the emphasis on built-in behavioral
tendencies (either through heredity or early experience) will be contrasted
with the emphasis on current influences on behavior. The implication of
these contrasting emphases will be examined in some detail. This introductory material is followed by four chapters describing what is known about
the determinants of interpersonal attraction, aggression, sexual behavior,
and morality.

Thus, the study of personality will be approached in a relatively broad
way to provide a picture of the variety of methods and approaches characteristic of the field and in a relatively narrow way to provide a close-up
in depth of a limited number of personality dimensions and important areas
of human behavior. The emphasis throughout this text will be on an exami-

nation of research aimed at gaining knowledge about behavior rather than on attempts to describe and characterize particular individuals. Nevertheless, the final section will show that it is possible to take the variables which are usually studied one or two at a time and "put them back together again" with respect to a specific individual. The relatively molecular way in which science must proceed does not eliminate the possibility of learning something about the molar functioning of a whole person: rather, it makes such learning possible.

SUMMARY

Though the latter half of the twentieth century is in many respects an age of science, there are many misunderstandings concerning the scientific method. In addition, reactions to the idea of a science of behavior range from amusement to hostility. A major goal of this book is to provide the student with an appreciation of science in general and of the study of personality as a specific part of this endeavor.

One of the many ways in which individuals have attempted to bring order and predictability into their lives is by means of the conceptual and procedural activities which constitute science. The goals of science are often identified as understanding, prediction, and control. Without a clear criterion, understanding is not a satisfactory goal in that it is relatively easy to achieve an illusion of understanding through simple naming, elaborate verbal descriptions, or after-the-fact explanations. Prediction may be defined as the primary goal of science and as the necessary criterion of understanding. Explanation at any level of complexity is useful if it increases predictive accuracy. Accurate prediction is no guarantee of the correctness of a theoretical formulation; all conceptualizations are only provisionally correct and may be supplanted by better ones. When laboratory control of phenomena is attained, it is often possible to control some aspect of the world outside of the laboratory. There is a long standing academic tradition, unpopular on both the political left and right, that knowledge should be sought for its own sake rather than for practical reasons. A useful strategy in any science, and a necessary one for a young science, is to encourage basic research and at the same time to seek problems for which the resulting knowledge is applicable. One difficulty for the scientist in applying his findings is that value judgments must be made which have nothing to do with science. The validity of the application also can be an issue for applied science. For this and other reasons, many fields are divided into those individuals engaged in basic research and those engaged in professional application.

The basic assumption underlying research in the field of personality asserts that behavior is lawful. This idea runs counter to many of the thoughts and values characteristic of Western civilization; the predictability of behavior is incompatible with the doctrine of free will. Those in the humanistic movement tend to reject a deterministic model of behavior as somehow degrading to mankind. A science of behavior must, however, rest on the assumption that behavior in a given stimulus situation is predictable if the relevant antecedent variables affecting the organism are known. A second assumption is that science can investigate only operationally defined variables. In order to achieve uniformity of meaning, to make clear which concepts are amenable to scientific inquiry, and to avoid pseudo-problems, variables must be reducible to observable operations or procedures. The meaning of an operationally defined concept is seldom identical to the cultural definition of the concept. Further, operationism does not imply a criticism of speculation or nonoperational thinking; it simply clarifies the difference between such activities and the formal propositions of science.

Science is a dynamic process in which a reciprocal interaction takes place between observation and conceptualization. Scientific activity begins with observation, often in informal, uncontrolled situations. When the observations are expressed in symbols which go beyond the immediately observed stimulus, there is generalization to a class of events. Generalization constitutes the first step or the most primitive level of theory-building. Though it is a universal practice to observe and generalize about behavior, the process of systematic verification is unique to science. A primary concern of scientists is to carry out the verification procedure in such a way that one is not deceived into accepting that which is not so or rejecting that which is. The next step, theory-building, involves the formulation of ever broader generalizations and more basic principles. On the basis of theories, one may make deductions which lead to new observations and to the unification of previously unrelated empirical events in a comprehensive framework. Seemingly, a fruitful approach to theory-building in the field of personality is the establishment of behavioral laws and the construction of small theories dealing with specific and limited behavioral events rather than the development of a general theory of personality.

The rapidly accelerating progress of the physical and biomedical sciences present a picture of man's development as one of constant and almost unbelievable improvement. A view of man's behavior, however, presents a picture of war, crime, and assorted cruelties for which behavioral science is one possible source of amelioration. The background of experimental psychology lies in the traditional laboratory approach to science in which independent variables are manipulated and their effect on dependent variables determined. The historical background of personality psychology is in the centuries-old way of describing other individuals in terms of their standing along an almost infinite number of dimensions. This description of individuals has led to attempts to measure personality dimensions and to investigate their antecedents and their correlates. The most distinctive feature of the field of personality at the present time is the tendency to combine experimental psychology with an interest in individual differences. An individual's personality is defined as the combination of all the relatively enduring dimensions of individual differences. The field of personality is defined as that branch of psychology which deals with dimensions of individual differences and with situational determinants of the behavior of individuals. The field of personality or personality-social is a rapidly growing one which shares a research orientation with experimental psychology and an interest in complex human behavior with clinical psychology. The Division of Personality and Social Psychology is the largest division of the American Psychological Association, and this field has become increasingly popular among graduate students and new Ph.D.s during the past five to ten years. Most personality-social psychologists are employed in a college or university setting and are engaged in teaching and/or basic research.

This text is divided into four sections. The first section contains two introductory chapters which deal with general issues pertinent to the study of personality and with a summary of three major personality theories. The second section concentrates on individual differences as a focus of the study of personality. Following a description of research methodology, there are five chapters covering the research which has been conducted on the personality dimensions of authoritarianism, need for achievement, manifest anxiety, intelligence, and self-concept. The third section shifts to a consideration of situational determinants of behavior. There is an introductory chapter contrasting the individual differences approach with the emphasis on stimulus events. This is followed by four chapters describing what is known about the determinants of interpersonal attraction, aggression, sexual behavior, and morality. The final section consists of a discussion of the problem of combining personality variables and the knowledge of situational determinants in order to provide a description of an individual.

2

Theories

of

Personality

Originally, the field of personality was primarily identified with personality theories such as those of Sigmund Freud, Carl Jung, and Harry Stack Sullivan. At one time a description of these theories would have served as an accurate reflection of the concerns and interests of those working in personality. Today, an acquaintance with the early theorists provides an important historical perspective to the origins of personality psychology. In the present chapter, three of these theories will be described.

PERSONALITY THEORIES AND OTHER THEORIES IN SCIENCE

In the description of science in the previous chapter, the interaction between conceptualization and empirical research was discussed. Conceptualization involves the creation of abstract explanations which are more general than any specific observation and which are directed toward the identification of basic principles which can account for a wide array of phenomena. The development of atomic theory, bacteriological theory, and genetic theory are examples of powerful formulations which have been of immense importance in stimulating empirical research, in generating applications, and in altering man's conception of himself and his universe. Successful theories can be expected to yield those three effects; research, application, and an alteration in man's self-concept.

THE SPECIAL CHARACTERISTICS OF
PERSONALITY THEORIES

The historical roots of experimental psychology and much of modern personality-social psychology lie in the laboratories of nineteenth-century biology and physics. For that reason, our conception of theory tends to be consistent with that in other sciences. The historical roots of personality psychology lie in the consulting rooms of nineteenth-century medical practitioners. Oddly enough, the result has been that "personality theories" have been closely related to the formulations of philosophers, theologians, and novelists. This is not said to disparage the enormously creative products of personality theorists but simply to emphasize the basic differences between their theoretical products and the kinds of theories developed elsewhere in psychology.

In the preceding chapter, a process was described in which scientific activity moves from observation, to generalization, to verification, to theory-building. In the verification phase, such elements as operational definitions, controlled observational techniques such as experiments, and the quantification of variables differentiate the procedures of scientists from those of the man in the street and from others who have attempted to make sense out of their world. What would happen if very bright, hard-working, dedicated investigators were to use a different kind of verification technique? What if verification consisted of additional uncontrolled observations? Since that was the procedure of early personality theorists, we will be able to see some of the strengths and weaknesses of that approach in the following pages.

When someone with the brilliance and creativity of Sigmund Freud engaged in theory-building of that kind, the result, while less than a set of empirical laws or an acceptable theory, was considerably more than a literary exercise. Many of the conceptualizations have had an influence on research even though the reverse was not true and certainly they have influenced man's self-concept, as evidenced repeatedly in artistic creations. The proof of any scientific pudding is prediction and control, and it has turned out that these various efforts have not yielded impressive predictive powers nor exciting techniques for influencing behavior. The flaws of these theories will be discussed at the end of this chapter. But this is not to suggest that these theoretical efforts were a waste of time or should otherwise be dismissed as irrelevant. Early personality theories constitute interesting attempts to by-pass the empirical procedures of science, they offer amazing insights into human functioning (some correct and some incorrect, undoubtedly), and they have influenced human thought to a wide extent. Therefore, for some time to come, personality theories are likely to remain influential in determining the kinds of variables we investigate and the kinds of explanations we consider reasonable.

THE PSYCHOANALYTIC THEORY
OF SIGMUND FREUD

BACKGROUND

In Freud's (1935) own words, "I was born òn May 6th, 1856, at Freiberg in Moravia, a small town in what is now Czechoslovakia. My parents were Jews, and I have remained a Jew myself." His family moved to Vienna when he was four. He completed medical school at the University of Vienna with the intention of becoming a research scientist. He was not greatly interested in his medical studies and spent much of his time in laboratory research. Shortly after receiving the M.D. degree in 1881, he joined the Institute for Cerebral Anatomy as a researcher. His salary was low, and in addition, advancement in an academic-research setting was hampered by a prevailing anti-Semitism. He eventually made the decision to seek the possible financial rewards of private practice. Even so, he remained more interested in research than in the practice itself. Even after the development of psychoanalysis, his major concerns were not with his practice or with curing individual patients, but with theory-building. He thought of himself not as a physician but as a scientific scholar.

Freud grew interested in a number of somewhat unorthodox approaches to the treatment of emotional problems. These included hypnosis as practiced by Jean Charcot, a French psychiatrist, in treating hysterics and a novel procedure devised by Joseph Breuer, a Viennese physician, which involved directing the patient to talk about symptoms and problems. Freud did not find hypnosis to be particularly useful, but he was quite impressed with the "talking-out" technique. After disagreeing with Breuer concerning the role of sexual conflicts in the development of hysterical symptoms, Freud went his own way in developing both psychoanalytic theory and the therapeutic techniques which constitute psychoanalysis. He himself felt that the great turning point in his thinking came in July, 1895, when he first had the insight as to the nature of dreams. Freud worked at the time when the first psychology laboratories were being established in Germany. While his contemporaries were dealing with conscious processes and simple responses, Freud spent over forty years in trying to understand man's unconscious functioning and his most complex behavior.

Freud's life was spent in the practice of psychoanalysis and in writing and developing his theory of personality in a prolific outpouring of articles and books. His work attracted numerous disciples and eventually led to the establishment of the International Psychoanalytic Association in 1910. In addition to his profound effect on the practice of psychiatry, his work became extremely important in psychology, as well. An acknowledgement of this fact was provided by G. Stanley Hall, an American psychologist, who invited Freud to give an address at meetings commemorating the founding of Clark University. Late in his life, the Nazis overran Austria, and Freud managed to escape to England. He died in London in 1939.

In examining Freud's theoretical system, it is helpful to keep in mind the nature of his theory-building procedures. In therapy, his observations consisted primarily of the verbalizations of his patients. Because the technique was new and unusual, Freud was in the unique position of hearing, in voluminous detail, the innermost thoughts, early memories, sexual secrets, dreams, wishes, and other details about the lives of numerous individuals. To an even greater extent than is true for a priest in a confessional, Freud was exposed to aspects of human behavior not ordinarily on public display. Because this talking seemed to lead to an improvement of symptoms and to a greater feeling of well-being, Freud could easily have been content only to develop and practice an important new therapeutic technique. He did much more than that! He continually tried to make sense out of his observations, to devise constructs to account for the behavioral panorama to which he was exposed, and to build his generalizations into a theoretical superstructure which could potentially explain all of human behavior. A number of writers have compared his methods to those of Sherlock Holmes. Why should conversation about a long-forgotten childhood incident lead to a dramatic improvement in a physical symptom? Why should a man report dreams in which he had intercourse with his mother? Why should an individual block and be unable to think of what to say next when his associations dealt with certain topics? Freud was a thoroughgoing and devoted exponent of the assumption that behavior is lawful and that it is possible to determine the antecedents of any behavior—whether they be dreams, slips of the tongue, forgetting, or neurotic symptoms. As his theory grew, he was constantly modifying it on the basis of his observations of additional patients and on the basis of deductions and logical difficulties he encountered with his existing formulations. Thus, Freud's work is an excellent example of scientific functioning and the development of a theory of behavior. Only his choice of verification procedures ultimately proved to be a fatal error for this particular theory and for this general approach to theory-building. At the end of the nineteenth century, however, that was not at all obvious. To deal with one's theory in the form, "If X is true, then Y should follow," means that you are necessarily attuned to prediction and at some point in the chain of reasoning, to observables. Rychlak (1968) points out that Freud's medical research activity involved techniques such as dissection almost exclusively rather than experimentation. His three attempts at experimental research were unsuccessful, and he never published an experimental article.

Freud went on to build his personality theory without the feedback, discipline, and corrective power of the procedures of experimentation, and without concern for operational definitions of his constructs. It is an interesting paradox in that his range of interests would have been severely restricted if he had bound himself to the methods and procedures of the experimental psychologists of his day. By going his own way, he was able to deal with problems and to generate ideas that were far beyond those considered by behavioral scientists. It is clear now that the final outcome of Freud's endeavor was to be closer to literature than to science. Nevertheless, what an impressive achievement it was!

THE STRUCTURE OF PERSONALITY

Mehrabian (1968, p. 54) gives an interesting overall picture of the kind of thinking characteristic of Freud's theory:

> The metaphor which Freud employed during the early stages of his theorizing can be easily summarized. The relevant psychological structures of an individual are represented as two adjacent compartments, which are separated from each other by a permeable membrane. Elements stored in the lower compartment try to find their way into the upper compartment but are prevented in varying degrees by the permeable membrane. The greater the number of elements in the lower compartment, the greater is the tension in the membrane. The elements which succeed in finding their way into the upper compartment are considerably modified in the process of passage through the membrane. In psychological terms, the upper compartment is the location of the conscious psychological functions, and the lower compartment is the location of the unconscious, unacceptable impulses or wishes. Also, the membrane represents the defenses, and the tension in the membrane is the anxiety associated with defensive functioning.

States of Consciousness. Freud categorized mental functioning into three levels or states: conscious, preconscious, and unconscious. That of which we are fully aware is the *conscious.* Psychologists later translated this to mean that which is verbalized. If an individual has a particular visceral reaction and says to himself "I am hungry," that is a conscious experience. Included here are our perceptions of internal and external events and our wishes and plans which are represented in our thoughts and our discussions.

The *preconscious* includes those memories from the past which are more or less available to consciousness when needed. If I ask you your telephone number or your mother's maiden name or the capital of Illinois, you will probably be able to bring the material into consciousness, sometimes with a mental effort or struggle. The relationship between conscious and preconscious material is seen in the tip of the tongue phenomenon in which the name of a song or a movie actress or whatever is almost but not quite recalled. Sometimes, it is hours or days later when the forgotten material is suddenly and clearly remembered. It has been suggested that the preconscious is like a darkened room in which consciousness is represented by a small speck of light which flits from point to point in the room.

Freud described the *unconscious* as a repository of past events and of current impulses and desires of which one is not aware. Here, we have a much larger and much darker room into which the speck of light cannot penetrate. The thought processes here can run free without constraint by rules of grammar or logic, by realistic considerations, or by moral issues. When the restrictive forces are relaxed, unconscious material can burst to the surface in either direct or disguised form; examples include dreaming, the thoughts and actions of someone under the influence of alcohol or other drugs, and the delusions and hallucinations of psychotics. The disguised material can often be deciphered or interpreted by someone trained in the ways of the unconscious (in Sherlock Holmes style). Undisguised material is often disowned by the individual himself: "How could I dream such non-sense, I've never thought of things like that!" "Did I really say those things at the party?"

The Three Systems of Personality. In observing the things that his patients felt and wanted, things they did and failed to do, things that they felt were right and wrong, Freud organized these behaviors in a conceptual scheme by suggesting that the personality is composed of three interacting systems: the id, ego, and superego. That is, he proposed that behavior is the result of whatever compromises we work out among our primitive desires, the constraints of reality, and our acquired moral code.

In the beginning, there is only the *id*. As babies we know only desire—hunger, thirst, pain-reduction, for example. We want our desires fulfilled right now. This demand for immediate satisfaction of our bodily needs was labeled the pleasure principle. If satisfaction were always supplied instantly, our thought processes would never develop beyond the simplest representations of needs. Hunger would lead to food, thirst to drink, and lust to sexual gratification, without delay, without complication, without consequences. Failure to achieve gratification is temporarily solved by providing ourselves with mental images of the goal in the form of wish-fulfilling fantasies and hallucinations. Instant gratification is seldom possible outside of the womb, and day dreams fail to satisfy tissue needs. Pure id functioning, then, is seen only in the behavior of infants.

We do not remain as infants, so it is apparent that some other kind of functioning (*ego*) must develop. Freud proposed that, to survive, the individual must begin to come to terms with the objective world beyond himself. One must learn the difference between milk and the idea of milk, between the memory of mother's voice and her presence in the room, between what one wants and what is actually obtained. From this ability to differentiate reality from fantasy there gradually develop behaviors which allow some manipulation of factors in the real world. Included here is the tendency to plan ahead and then to test the usefulness of the plan by trying it out. In contrast to the pleasure principle of the id, the workings of the ego are described as the reality principle. In the previous chapter, the development of science and other conceptual systems was described as a means of attaining prediction and control of the environment. Freud would describe those activities as ego functioning in the service of the reality principle.

The aim of the id is to obtain pleasure and to avoid pain. The ego functions to obtain the same ends, but it is tempered by the demands of reality. Development may halt at this point, but there is a third system which can develop. When parents are able to teach the child the traditional values of his society and when this moral code becomes internalized so that the child truly believes and genuinely feels the rightness of the values, the *superego* is said to have developed. The aim here is not pleasure but to do the right thing, to be good, to achieve perfection according to a particular moral code. A more familiar term is "conscience," which refers to a kind of built-in reinforcement process which makes a person self-satisfied when he does right and guilty when he does wrong. At times the pleasure-oriented aims of the id are in direct conflict with the morality-directed aims of the superego. Most often, personality is seen as functioning relatively well with the ego coordinating and compromising the demands of the id, the superego, and the objective world.

PERSONALITY DYNAMICS
AND PERSONALITY DEVELOPMENT

Energy and Instincts. Freud viewed man as a machine which consumes food, water, and oxygen and converts these into energy which is expended in both physical and mental work. Freud was strongly influenced by the thinking of physicists, and he assumed that the conservation of energy was as true in biology as in physics. Thus, energy could be stored, transformed from one state to another, or expended, but it could not be destroyed or lost to the system. Freud proposed that the source of psychic energy for personality functioning was in the id-instincts. He defined an instinct as an innate psychological representation of a physiological excitation. Thus, physiological needs become represented psychologically as wishes. The total amount of energy available to the personality is the sum of the instincts.

The resulting motivational theory built by Freud is a familiar one in psychology. Bodily needs lead to wishes and to the behavior necessary to satisfy the need. When the need is satisfied, the organism comes to rest until another need arises. There are individual differences in the means adopted to satisfy the need and in the specific object chosen as a goal. Freud classified the instincts as those involving life (for example, hunger and sex) and those involving death. Libido was the name he gave to the energy underlying the life instincts, but he had no comparable name for the energy of the death instincts. The life instincts serve to insure the survival of the individual and of the species, and Freud concentrated primarily on the sex instinct. The death instinct is directed toward returning the organism to the inorganic matter from which it originated. The death wish frequently is frustrated by the life instincts and hence other goals must be substituted for self-destruction. The problem is solved by turning the death-wish on others in the form of the aggressive drive. The notion of a death instinct was prompted by observations of widespread savagery unleashed in World War I. Had Freud lived beyond 1939, he could have observed additional examples of human behavior impelled by the death instinct.

Stages of Development. During the first five years of life, according to Freud, each individual passes through a series of developmental stages. Freud was convinced that the first few years of life were crucial in forming later personality.

The first source of contact with the external world is through the mouth. The oral stage centers around the pleasures received from eating, sucking, and (later) biting. Freud reasoned, by analogy, that fixation at the early oral stage would lead to an oral incorporative personality with the desire to acquire things. Dependency needs are also described as tied to the early oral stage in which an individual passively receives help from others. Fixation at the later oral stage would lead to an oral aggressive personality with the need for abusing others verbally. Such phrases as "He nearly bit my head off" or "She has a biting wit" come to mind. Adult behaviors as diverse as licking an ice cream cone, biting on a pipe stem, asking others for help, and enjoying hostile debates could be interpreted as reflecting the outcome of the individual's early oral experiences.

The next interaction between the child and the external world is through his bowel functions, and thus the anal stage follows the oral. Pleasure is experienced with defecation and, when toilet training begins, the child is forced to control and regulate this behavior in accordance with an external set of relatively arbitrary demands. Once again, later character is determined by the events occurring during this stage. Control of one's bowel activity is a way of conforming to society's demands, of pleasing mother, and of being able to produce a product at the right time and in the right place. Anal retentiveness was thus seen as related to later conformity, stinginess, and an excessive concern with things being neat and orderly but also to socialization and achievement. Anal expulsiveness was seen as related to messiness, cruelty, and explosive displays of temper. Power with respect to the adult world can be attained either through conformity or through rebellion.

The next arena of interaction between the individual and the external world is with respect to the genital organs. In the phallic stage, masturbatory activities are discovered to be pleasurable, and there are enjoyable sexual fantasies associated with self-manipulation. A dramatic outcome of this early sexual activity is the feeling of desire for the parent of the opposite sex and hostility toward the same sex parent: the Oedipus complex. Much of one's later interpersonal behavior (friendship, courtship, reactions to authority figures) is presumably dependent on what occurs during the phallic stage. At this time, the male is afraid that his jealous father will cut off his genitals (resulting, not unreasonably, in castration anxiety). Defenses arise here in that both the sexual desire for the mother and the hostility toward the father are repressed. The ideal resolution occurs when the feelings toward the mother are transformed from lust to affection ("I'd walk a million miles for one of your smiles.") while those toward the father are transformed from hate to a desire to be like him and thus to identify with his strength and power ("My old man can beat up your old man.") Both aspects of the resolution are expressed in the line, "I want a girl just like the girl who married dear old Dad." For females, the analogous process (sometimes labeled the Electra complex) is more complicated in that she also first loves the mother because of her tender care during infancy. The young girl then discovers that boys have a penis while she does not. This revelation leads her to reject the mother who is also built defectively and to love her father who is properly equipped with a penis. Mixed with her love for her father (and other males later) is penis envy because males have something which she lacks. For girls, the resolution of the Oedipus complex is not as clear, and there is less massive repression of her love for the father or of her hostility toward the mother.

Assuming that the individual successfully gets through the oral, anal, and phallic stages, there is a later and final step in development: love of others in addition to one's self and one's parents. In the genital stage (during adolescence), there is the development of genuine friendships, love, and other nonselfish social attachments. Many individuals never successfully resolve the Oedipal conflict and hence never reach the genital stage. The end result of these various stages is the adult personality which is in part determined by the events of each stage.

With this brief overview of several of Freud's major concepts, his work on anxiety will be examined in more detail.

FREUD'S CONCEPTUALIZATION OF ANXIETY AND DEFENSES AGAINST ANXIETY.

Among the earliest detailed observations and speculations concerning anxiety were those reported by Freud (1926) in his monograph, *Inhibitions, Symptoms, and Anxiety*. Freud's writings on most topics tend to be organized without differentiation of observations, generalizations, and speculations. A somewhat different order from the original presentation will be followed here, in an attempt to examine the basic points of his monograph.

1. *Descriptive Definitions of Anxiety.* Freud defined anxiety in terms of subjective feeling:

> Anxiety, then, is in the first place something that is felt. We call it an affective state, although we are also ignorant of what an affect is. As a feeling anxiety has a very marked character of unpleasure (Freud, 1926, p. 132).

In addition to "unpleasure," further qualifications were added in that this particular emotion was described as one which involved expectation, the lack of a specific focus, and a generalized feeling of helplessness. Still other characteristics were the physical sensations accompanying the emotional experience, especially those involving breathing and the heart.

Though Freud himself was content to leave the concept at this relatively abstract level, one could rather easily translate his observations into operational terms.

2. *Speculations Concerning the Antecedents of Anxiety.* Freud saw clearly that there were marked individual differences with respect to anxiety level, but he confessed his inability to specify how these differences came to be. In more general terms, he suggested that the psychical and physiological components of anxiety have their origin in the responses evoked by the process of birth:

> In man and the higher animals it would seem that the act of birth, as the individual's first experience of anxiety, has given the affect of anxiety certain characteristic forms of expression.
> ...We are therefore inclined to regard anxiety-states as a reproduction of the trauma of birth (Freud, 1926, pp. 93, 133).

Specifically, Freud believed that the crucial element in the birth trauma with which later stimulus conditions were associated was a particular type of danger. At birth, one suffers a great and frightening loss and is helpless to do anything about it. Later situations involving loss reawaken the same feelings of helplessness.

The difficulty with such formulations is that this colorful comparison of adult subjective feelings with those of the newborn infant is not really testable. The hypothesis in its literal form concerns the unobservable elements of subjective experiences. While we might be able to utilize the subjective reports of adults as a convenient substitute, there is no conceivable way to translate the internal perceptions of the infant as he emerges from the birth canal into terms amenable to scientific inquiry.

In addition, everyone is born and everyone experiences anxiety, so differential prediction from the theory is not possible. Freud recognized much of this and indicated that Otto Rank had a more useful notion in suggesting that variations in the initial amount of anxiety (for example, quick vs. protracted birth, births which lead to interference with breathing) produce variations in adult anxiety and hence neurosis. Rank's formulation accounts for individual differences and is open to empirical verification, but Freud (1926, p. 152) rejected it because it was too simple and because "...it floats in the air instead of being based upon ascertained observations."

3. *Speculations Concerning Stimuli which Evoke Anxiety.* In earlier writings, Freud (1895) had proposed that anxiety was evoked whenever "excitation" (sexual energy) accumulated because of some interference with its discharge. An anxiety attack was seen as something of a misfired act of intercourse with heavy breathing, perspiration, and so forth. By 1926, he had quite different ideas about the process.

Freud hypothesized the occurrence of certain traumatic situations which lay bare the helplessness of the ego and thereby elicit automatic anxiety. Depending on the developmental stage which the individual has reached, these situations are birth, loss of mother, loss of penis, loss of another person's love and loss of the love of one's own superego. The response of anxiety does not solve the problem, but the organism is simply built that way.

Other stimuli which arouse anxiety are those which indicate a threat that a traumatic situation will occur. Here, anxiety acts as a signal which is useful to the organism in that the organism is alerted to prevent situations of danger from occurring. In Freud's (1926, p. 134) words: "...anxiety arose originally as a reaction to a state of *danger* and it is reproduced whenever a state of that kind recurs."

4. *Speculations Concerning the Consequents of Anxiety.* Though Freud himself did not rely on the concept in this way, perhaps his greatest influence on subsequent research and theorizing about anxiety was with respect to its motivating properties. Anxiety is sufficiently unpleasant that it acts as an instigation to other behavior, the goal of which is anxiety reduction. Because of the specific type of behavior with which his work brought him in contact, he was primarily concerned with neurotic forms of anxiety reduction:

> Anxiety is a reaction to a situation of danger. It is obviated by the ego's doing something to avoid that situation or to withdraw from it. It might be said that symptoms are created so as to avoid the generating of anxiety. But this does not go deep enough. It would be truer to say that symptoms are created so as to avoid a *danger-situation* whose presence has been signalled by the generation of anxiety (Freud, 1926, pp. 128–29).

Given operations for measuring anxiety, one can see that these general ideas lead to a number of possible empirical tests. That is, specific cues are hypothesized to evoke anxiety, which, in turn, is hypothesized to evoke a wide variety of possible behaviors which should serve to bring about anxiety-reduction. Further, interference with the performance of those behaviors should re-evoke anxiety.

5. *Speculations Concerning Techniques to Reduce Anxiety.* As in much of Freud's description of therapeutic activity, a major goal was to render unconscious material conscious. Neurotic symptoms are retained because the individual is unaware of the stimulus which evoked the anxiety which led to the symptoms. The ability to verbalize accurately concerning the danger cues was seen as the only way in which the individual could regain control of the situation:

> Real danger is a danger that is known, and realistic anxiety is anxiety about a known danger of this sort. Neurotic anxiety is anxiety about an unknown danger. Neurotic danger is thus a danger that has still to be discovered. Analysis has shown that it is an instinctual danger. By bringing this danger which is not known to the ego into consciousness, the analyst makes neurotic anxiety no different from realistic anxiety, so that it can be dealt with in the same way (Freud, 1926, p. 165).

Defense Mechanisms. Extreme anxiety could be relieved by defensive behavior, and the principal defense mechanisms are repression, projection, reaction formation, fixation, and regression. They operate unconsciously, and they involve some distortion of reality. It's as if the ego fools itself. Repression involves unconscious forgetting or denial or misperception. If sexual attraction toward one's sister is threatening and anxiety-evoking, the anxiety can be reduced if one is literally not aware of his sexual desires. Projection involves assigning the cause of the anxiety to an external source which is easier to deal with than one's own impulses. Unacceptable sexual desires can be denied as relevant to oneself; instead, they are attributed to someone else. Thus, one can be worried about the blacks who are notoriously eager to rape nubile young white women. With reaction-formation, there is a reversal of impulse so that the original anxiety-evoking impulse is denied by the presence of its opposite. He could not be sexually attracted to his sister if he disliked her. If a given source of anxiety arises during a later developmental stage, one way of solving the problem is to remain at an earlier stage (fixation) or to return to that earlier stage (regression). If he can remain a child in his thoughts and wishes and behavior, there can be no sexual threat.

We will now examine the work of two other theorists more briefly. As a second example of the early personality theories, let us look at the formulations of one of Freud's first and most illustrious co-workers.

THE ANALYTICAL THEORY
OF CARL JUNG

BACKGROUND

Carl Jung was born in Switzerland in 1875, the son of a pastor. Though originally planning to go into philosophy or archeology, he was influenced toward the natural sciences and medicine by a dream. Jung became an M.D., obtaining his degree from the University of Basel. His interest was psychiatry, and he worked in a mental hospital in Zurich. Like Freud, he studied for a time in Paris. He later taught at the University of Zurich, but eventually quit in order to spend all of his time in private practice and in developing his theoretical system.

A momentous event in Jung's life was his reading of Freud's (1900) first book, *Interpretation of Dreams*. He was immensely impressed by it and began gathering data which seemed to confirm Freud's ideas. Though Jung carried out several research studies, he later expressed strong doubts about the value of laboratory experimentation and the collection of empirical data. The two physicians began corresponding in 1906, and when the International Psychoanalytic Association was founded, Jung was elected its first president. Freud and Jung were closely attached, both professionally and personally. Jung was seen as Freud's heir-apparent in psychoanalysis, but their association came to an abrupt end in 1914, in part because of Freud's emphasis on the importance of sexuality. At this point, Jung withdrew from the International Psychoanalytic Association and began working exclusively on his own theoretical system and his technique of psychotherapy, *analytical psychology*.

Over the succeeding years as a practitioner and theorist, Jung educated a great many therapists who travelled to Switzerland to undergo analytic training. He died in 1961 at the age of 85.

Analytical psychology never achieved the popularity of psychoanalysis, and Jung has had less influence on the field of personality than is true for Freud. His two major contributions to current research have been quite specific and often completely divorced from Jungian theory: the concept of introversion-extraversion and the word association technique. His theoretical system had a more direct effect on the early research and theorizing of Timothy Leary prior to his involvement with LSD research and the counter-culture. Leary's discussion of the drug experience and reincarnation (for example, in a 1966 interview in *Playboy* magazine) is also quite compatible with Jung's theoretical formulations. In any event, Jung's work is an interesting illustration of the way in which the kind of approach to theory-building used by Freud and Jung can lead to extraordinarily different end products even when two theorists begin at the same point and employ the same general techniques. Jung, incidentally, did not think of his work as a theory so much as a set of extended observations which revealed the way that man functioned.

Jung himself (1961, p. 337) has supplied a general overall description of his mode of theorizing: "I see in all that happens the play of opposites." Jung (1963, p. 235) traced his thinking to the influence of Goethe:

> In my youth (around 1890) I was unconsciously caught up by this spirit of the age, and had no methods at hand for extricating myself from it. *Faust* struck a chord in me and pierced me through in a way that I could not but regard as personal. Most of all, it awakened in me the problem of opposites, of good and evil, of mind and matter, of light and darkness. Faust, the inept, purblind philosopher, encounters the dark side of his being, his sinister shadow, Mephistopheles, who in spite of his negating disposition represents the true spirit of life as against the arid scholar who hovers on the brink of suicide.

An unusual aspect of Jungian theory is its emphasis on the religious experience and his continuing interest in primitive people, psychotics, alchemy, and mythology. Bischof (1970, p. 122) summarizes Jung's position:

> In many ways Carl Gustav Jung was the "grand old man" of personality theorists. He lived through the earliest era of personality theory, wrote voluminously, gathered many honors, and continued until his death to write, treat a few patients, and excite the psychological world with his work. Jung's influence has been unique. His theories are not popular in the sense that many papers at the psychological meetings are oriented toward them. Most psychologists are bothered by Jung. They cannot ignore him. The usual reaction is an attack on his theory; then, with a feeling that all has been put in its proper place, the psychologist continues with his main thesis. But to ignore Jung does not seem to satisfy psychologists. Jung irritated them because he was different, mystical, circuitous in writing style, provocative. He led one to accept vigorously or totally reject his theories on personality. There seems to be little room for halfhearted responses. Although Jung was quite aware of the world of psychologists, his position in it left him unimpressed, as he continued to feel that truth is truth whether it happens to be popular or not.

The Structure of Personality

It is quite difficult and probably somewhat misleading to attempt to describe Jungian theory in a few pages. It is analogous to presenting *War and Peace* by noting the names and one or two foibles of Tolstoy's leading characters. In any event, the following material is at best a brief introduction to the kind of theorizing in which Jung engaged.

Jung retained Freud's concept of ego in his theory, but his description of unconscious functioning led him far away from the explanations provided by psychoanalytic theory.

The Personal Unconscious. Any experiences which have been unnoticed, forgotten, or repressed are contained in the personal unconscious. This "region" was seen as the repository of complexes. A complex consists of an organized collection of associated concepts and images. Jung was interested in the word association test as a research tool, and his observation of responses to this test undoubtedly contributed to the idea of there being clusters of associated concepts to which an individual responded in a particular fashion. For example, if someone were to respond to a number of different stimulus words with references to control, subjugation, winning, manipulating, and so forth, he could be described as having a power complex. Other groups of associated responses could lead to the diagnosis of a mother complex, homosexual complex, or inferiority complex. Such complexes can be at various levels of consciousness and sometimes pass from the personal unconscious to the ego and vice versa.

The Collective Unconscious. Here, we find a formulation quite removed from traditional psychological or even psychoanalytic thought. In the collective unconscious are the inherited influences from one's own ancestors, from the entire human race, and even from man's animal progenitors. Jung (1939, pp. 24ff) describes the general idea:

> This psychic life is the mind of our ancient ancestors, the way in which they thought and felt, the way in which they conceived of life and the world, of gods and human beings. The existence of these historical layers is presumably the source of the belief in reincarnation and in memories of past lives. As the body is a sort of museum of its phylogenetic history, so is the mind. There is no reason for believing that the psyche, with its peculiar structure, is the only thing in the world that has no history beyond its individual manifestation. Even the conscious mind cannot be denied a history extending over at least five thousand years. It is only individual ego-consciousness that has forever a new beginning and an early end. But the unconscious psyche is not only immensely old, it is also able to grow increasingly into an equally remote future. It forms, and is part of, the human species just as much as the body, which is also individually ephemeral, yet collectively of immeasurable duration.

The evolutionary sequence of our anatomy is recapitulated from conception to birth as we develop from a one-celled organism to a complex human being. We resemble other species along the way, and even develop such specialized features as gill slits for a time during the gestation period, but we eventually end as a distinctly human organism. In a similar way, the evolutionary sequence of experience is recapitulated and retained as unconscious memory in the collective unconscious. Because we all have a common evolutionary history, we all share the same collective unconscious. These memories are not directly available in conscious thought, but they reveal themselves by predisposing us to respond to particular stimuli in a given way. Thus, there are a number of characteristics which are shared across widely diverse cultures such as the tendency to believe in a Supreme Being, to fear snakes, and to exhibit mother love. Jung's explanation of these commonalities was that we share common primitive ancestors who repeatedly had certain experiences. If one never saw a snake, for example, that particular primitive fear would never be aroused. We are predisposed to such a reaction, however, and our first contact with a snake should automatically involve the arousal of fear.

One of Jung's beliefs was that man can benefit from becoming aware of the wisdom stored in his collective unconscious. Many of man's difficulties arise when he ignores or behaves in opposition to the urgings of his collective unconscious. Thus, much of Jung's therapeutic effort was directed at facilitating this awareness.

Archetypes. The archetypes in the collective unconscious were created by the accumulated experiences of numerous generations of our ancestors. For example, there is a mother archetype, and this blends with our own experiences with our actual mother who is frequently glorified into a kind of ideal figure because of archetypal influences. Not only is this archetype crucial in determining attitudes about one's mother, but it is reflected repeatedly in art, literature, religion, and mythology from the Virgin Mary, to the Earth Mother, to Mary Worth, to Whistler's Mother, to the Fairy Godmother, and in customs such as the celebration of Mother's Day. In addition, thousands of primitive experiences with angry and even cruel mothers lead to variations in the mother archetype which are reflected in such figures as the Wicked Witch of the West, the she-devil, the whore, and Cinderella's step-mother. Other archetypes include rebirth or resurrection, the young hero who can solve all of our problems, God, and the old wise man. The recurring and unending popularity of such figures in our legends, novels, and religions can thus be explained by Jung.

One way in which archetypes are discovered is through observation of repeated themes in myths or in art. Why is there story after story of a divine being who comes to earth and mingles with its citizens? Why is there a circle or circular arrangement in primitive drawings, in early architecture, in sculpture, in Renaissance art, and in the scribblings of young children? Jung's answer was that they are based on shared racial memories. Another approach is to ask why a certain theme in literature, or drama, or any form of art, has a universal appeal that goes beyond the artistic merit of the material itself. Why are people caught up by the primitive symbols of Moby Dick, Oedipus the King, and Prince Charming? Again, the power of these symbols is seen as evidence that they are evoking inherited memories from the collective unconscious.

The Persona. Role theorists have described much of our behavior in terms of social roles in which we play a given part in particular social situations. In Jungian theory, this idea is carried even further in that the persona represents the mask which each of us adopts. It reflects the part we are assigned to play in our interactions with others. If one is not aware of the discrepancy between this public version of himself and his true inner self, he becomes shallow and is cut off from his own feelings and emotions. The search for inner truth in the form of encounter groups, mystical experience, or drugs would be seen as a way of trying to get behind one's mask to discover who is really there.

The Anima and the Animus. Here, Jung observes that elements of both sexes are present in each of us. In spite of the fact that an individual is a man, he carries within his collective unconscious the racial memories of interactions with women, an archetype of femininity or the anima. Analogously, each woman has an archetype of masculinity, the animus. A failure to recognize these archetypes leads to emotional difficulties, as when a male fails to perceive his own gentleness and tenderness or a female ignores her own ambition and drive. The unisex look and the Women's Liberation Movement would be seen as attempts to express recognition of the anima and animus.

The Shadow. The unconscious antithesis of overt behavioral trends is the shadow. It is of great importance for an individual to become aware of these unconscious trends even though they are the opposite of his conscious functioning. Whatever is emphasized by the person consciously, the opposite is emphasized unconsciously. The shadow is the dark reflection of the selves of which we are aware.

The Self. Jung felt that there is a desire for unity or oneness in man's strivings. This desire was represented as the self. It is an archetype which is expressed in a variety of ways from the mandala, or magic circle, to the desire men have to form groups or join organizations. Our personal goal is to achieve unity, or selfhood, or wholeness, and is sometimes seen in religious experiences. Attempts to realize such a feeling have been made in the form of self-starvation to attain a mystical state, Yoga, and the use of numerous drugs. When the self is attained, it is usually after man reaches middle age and begins seeking a more unified inner picture by moving from the persona toward his shadow and the collective unconscious.

Extraversion and Introversion. Jung defined one of the basic attitudinal divisions into which man could be categorized as the direction taken by the libido in relation to the outside world. These inborn temperamental differences led either to subjective (introverted) functioning in which the self is uppermost or to objective (extraverted) functioning in which the outside world is uppermost in importance. Jung (1928, p. 41) describes these attitudes as follows:

> The first, if normal, is revealed by a hesitating, reflective, reticent disposition, that does not easily give itself away, that shrinks from objects, always assuming the defensive, and preferring to make its cautious observations as from a hiding place. The second type, if normal, is characterized by an accomodating, and apparently open and ready disposition, at ease in any given situation. This type forms attachments quickly, and ventures, unconcerned and confident, into unknown situations, rejecting thoughts of possible contingencies.

This dichotomy was adopted by many theorists and has led to a considerable amount of research. We should note that several of Jung's assumptions about introversion-extraversion are often neglected by those who have adopted the terms: the genetic basis of the types, the unconscious development of the type opposite from the overt one, and the danger of neurosis or psychosis resulting from overdevelopment of either attitude type.

Thinking, Feeling, Sensing, and Intuiting. Jung classified psychological functions into four categories. Of the two modes of judgment, there is the creation of ideas (thinking) and the evaluation of internal and external events (feeling). The two modes of apprehension are the realistic perception of objective events (sensing) and the subjective perception of events (intuiting). Differential development of these four functions commonly occurs, and the stronger of each mode pair is emphasized while the weaker is repressed. It is important to strive for equal functioning. Jung (1933, p. 107) explains how these four functions work together to provide complete understanding:

> ...a certain completeness is attained by these four. Sensation establishes what is actually given, thinking enables us to recognize its meaning, feeling tells us its value, and finally intuition points to the possibilities of the whence and whither that lie within the immediate facts. In this way we can orientate ourselves with respect to the immediate world as completely as when we locate a place geographically by latitude and longitude.

The four functions are also relevant to a discussion of the meaning of symbols to mankind. Jung differentiated signs (sheriff's badge, state flag on the capital building, H_2O) from symbols. The latter refers to those words, ideas, or images which constitute "the best possible formulation of a relatively unknown thing which cannot conceivably, therefore, be more clearly or characteristically represented." (Jung, 1923, p. 601). In part, the thinking and sensing functions are involved in responding to symbols but much more important are intuition and feeling. A true symbol evokes feelings, fears, and wishes which are deeper than logical, rational thought processes. Examples are the cross for early Christians, the swastika for the Nazi party, the number 13, and the sacred word "Om" intoned by Allen Ginsberg.

THE DYNAMICS OF PERSONALITY

Psychic Energy. Jung described that which powers the personality as psychic energy or libido. He defined libido as the life energy underlying natural phenomena. The value of anything is the amount of psychic energy invested in it. The conscious value system of an individual can be determined by asking him for his relative preferences or by observing the way in which he spends his time. His unconscious values are more difficult to establish. It is necessary to find out how many groups of items are associated with the nuclear element of a complex. This can be done through careful observation and deduction (for example, interpretation of the true meaning of a given behavior), the noting of complex indicators (for example, slips of the tongue, blocking in giving a word association), and the intensity of expressed emotions (for example, physiological responses as revealed by a lie detector). In primitive groups and in the young, most psychic energy is expended in staying alive and in sexual activity. When there is surplus psychic energy it can be expended in creative activities. If one has wealth or lives in a well-developed society, less energy is needed for staying alive. As one grows older less energy is employed in sexual pursuits. In such instances creativity should flourish.

Equivalence. Jung proposed a version of the first law of thermodynamics in suggesting that energy expended in one part of the system will subsequently appear elsewhere in the system. In other words, energy cannot be lost. Energy extracted from work will be expended on a hobby. If sexual fantasies are repressed, the energy will reappear in artistic creation or dreams. Such dreams frequently point toward the resolution of conflicts.

Entropy. This principle is related to the second law of thermodynamics and describes forces moving toward equilibrium. Thus, the personality moves toward (but never reaches) a state of equilibrium in which psychic energy is evenly distributed throughout the system. There is tension associated with disequilibrium, and this tension motivates a variety of possible responses. For example, a man who denies the influence of his anima is under considerable tension and strain because forces toward entropy would tend to redistribute energy. If the man fights this redistribution of energy he will have to use defense mechanisms and pay the price in terms of fatigue, discontent, and maladjustment. With complete entropy, perfect balance is achieved and there is no motivation for any activity. Complete entropy would thus be fatal to the organism.

STAGES OF DEVELOPMENT

Much like Freud, Jung described the investment of psychic energy in different activities as the individual develops from birth through various age levels. He did not, however, describe these as related exclusively to sexual pleasure and bodily processes. It seemed to him unnecessary and misleading to label all bodily satisfactions as sexual in origin.

The infant faces the problems of nutrition and growth primarily through his first four years. Jung saw this as a presexual period during which the individual is learning to speak and to think, gradually becoming interested in the world beyond himself and his parents. Sexual functioning can begin when the individual reaches puberty, but true sexual maturity does not necessarily follow then—or ever. The parents are seen first as protectors and suppliers of nutrition and later as the objects of sexual longing. Jung thus accepted the incestuous desires of the Oedipus and Electra complexes.

On the subject of development Jung's greatest deviation from Freud was his concentration on the changes of the middle years and old age. In middle age, interests move away from the body and into artistic, philosophical, and intellectual concerns. Religion becomes important as one tries to define his relationship to the external world. If an individual fails to develop these interests and remains locked in the earlier stage of physical pleasure or work, he is seriously harming himself in that his development is stopped.

Jung also described development in more general terms, the development of mankind itself. Thus, there is progress from generation to generation toward greater self-realization. He saw no reason to suppose that evolutionary progress in man's personality was not as striking as in biological structures and functions. Jung's description of man's past development and his future potential represents a hopeful and optimistic characterization of behavior.

THE INTERPERSONAL THEORY OF
HARRY STACK SULLIVAN

BACKGROUND

Harry Stack Sullivan, the third personality theorist to be considered here, was an American psychiatrist. His approach to theory building was much like that of Freud and Jung, and once again the final product was quite different from that of either of his predecessors. Freudian theory is concerned with the personal unconscious and its control by the ego, the superego, and the demands of reality. Jung's theory may be seen as focussing on the collective unconscious, man's racial wisdom, and his evolutionary potential.

Sullivan's theory is one in which the focus is turned outward on man's inter-personal relationships. Sullivan's position is somewhat compatible with the work of current psychologists in that he stressed the observable interactions between and among people rather than the hypothesized inner workings of the psyche. In fact, he identified psychiatry with social psychology and recognized that personality is an abstract construct derived from observed social interactions (Sullivan, 1950).

Sullivan was born on a farm in New York State in 1892. He, too, became a physician, receiving his M.D. degree from the Chicago College of Medicine and Surgery in 1917. After serving in World War I, he held medical posts with two governmental agencies before he entered the field which was to be his life work. During one year at Saint Elizabeth's Hospital in Washington, D.C., he began his association with William Alanson White, a neuro-psychiatrist. From the early 1920s until the early 1930s he worked at Saint Elizabeth's Hospital, at the University of Maryland Medical School, and at the Enoch Pratt Hospital, concentrating largely on the problem of schizo-phrenia. His next step was private practice in New York City. From an initial somewhat Freudian orientation, he moved toward the development of his own theoretical position. During the late 1930s he became director of the Washington School of Psychiatry which was funded by the William Alanson White Foundation. He also edited the journal, *Psychiatry,* published by the foundation. He died suddenly in 1949 in Paris, while on his way home from a world mental health meeting in Amsterdam.

Sullivan, then, may be seen as a man of diverse successful roles—practitioner, teacher, editor, and administrator. Unlike Freud and Jung, he did not produce a series of theoretical books. Only one book (Sullivan, 1947) was published during his lifetime. His other five books were assembled and edited after his death and are based on his lecture notes and recordings of his lectures.

THE STRUCTURE OF PERSONALITY

It is interesting that the notion of personality structure is not compatible with Sullivan's theory. Viewing personality as a verbal abstraction rather than a concrete entity, Sullivan found no reason to build an elaborate theory describing the structural details of "the personality." Rather, individuals interact with other individuals (present or absent, alive or dead, real or fictitious) and it is these interpersonal interactions which characterize human behavior. Our habits, our dreams, our hopes and fears, and everything else which distinguishes us from other animals all are made up of inter-personal concerns. Bischof (1970, p. 588) draws an interesting distinction between Freud and Sullivan:

The analogy of Freud's work was that of a building constructed brick by brick and quite unchangeable after the foundation is constructed. The analogy of the interpersonal theory of Sullivan's is that of a kite, which is held together by the tension between its parts. The entire structure, although retaining a basic shape, may be altered and changed depending upon the tensions within the system.

Sullivan did find it useful to identify a few subconstructs within personality. One of these is the dynamism. Essentially, a dynamism is a habit, a recurring behavior pattern. For Sullivan, the important human dynamisms are those involving other human beings. Many of the personality variables discussed in the following section of this book, such as authoritarianism, anxiety, and achievement need, would be labeled as dynamisms. His particular focus of concern, however, was on the dynamism of self. In formulating a self theory, there are many similarities between Sullivan and Carl Rogers (who will be discussed in Chapter 8).

Sullivan described the development of the self as a protective device in the interactions between the infant and his parents. Being completely dependent upon the parents for his physical well-being, the child becomes sensitive to parental approval and censure. On the basis of positive and negative parent-child interactions, the child learns that certain behavioral acts are approved and these aspects of the self are perceived as good-me. Other acts bring disapproval, and they become conceptualized as bad-me. Sullivan (1947, p. 10) suggested "The self may be said to be made up of reflected appraisals" and (p. 21) "It is built largely of personal symbolic elements learned in contact with other significant people." The self-system functions to protect the individual from anxiety. The emphasis is on maintaining a consistent and positively valued self-picture as good-me. Maintaining this self-image often requires misperceptions, forgetting, and other defensive maneuvers. Sullivan viewed inadequate or defensive self-functioning not as a product of internal malfunctioning, but as the product of an irrational society. If it were not for the unreasonable demands of parents and other representatives of society, one's self-system would not have to develop crippling defenses against anxiety.

Another interpersonal construct discussed by Sullivan was that of personification. By this term, he meant the concept built up about oneself or about any other person. As we shall see in Chapter 10, when interpersonal attraction is discussed, Sullivan's views fit in well with current reinforcement formulations. If another person is associated with positive experiences, his personification is a favorable one. If that person is associated with anxiety and pain, the personification is negative. Once such concepts are formed, there is a tendency to perceive the other person in a consistent way which can, of course, interfere with accurate perception of his or her behavior.

Widely shared personifications take the form of stereotypes and prejudices. If both kinds of interaction have occurred, positive and negative personifications may be established side by side (good-me and bad-me, good-mother and bad-mother).

THE DYNAMICS OF PERSONALITY

Sullivan, like Freud and Jung, proposed an energy system but he felt no need to posit psychic energy as something different from any other energy. Primarily, the organism is motivated to reduce tension, caused both by biological needs (for example, hunger, thirst, and sex) and by anxiety (primarily interpersonal in origin). Most of the behavior which is of interest to psychologists is motivated by anxiety which results when the individual perceives that his security is threatened. This kind of tension-reduction theory of human behavior is common to both personality theories and learning theories. Sullivan (1950, p. 85) suggested:

> Tensions can be regarded as needs for particular energy transformations which will dissipate the tension, often with an accompanying change of "mental" state, a change of awareness, to which we can apply the general term, *satisfaction*.

It should be noted that Sullivan's emphasis was on learned needs and learned modes of tension-reduction rather than on instincts or inherited demands. This emphasis also places him closer to American psychologists in many fields than did the conceptualizations of Freud and Jung.

STAGES OF DEVELOPMENT

The most distinct of Sullivan's concepts was his categorization of the three modes of experience as prototaxic, parataxic, and syntaxic. Prototaxic functioning is the earliest and most primitive form of experience. For example, the infant is bombarded by sensations which he is unable to perceive as coherent or meaningful events. There is no relationship between events, no sense of time, and no distinction between self and the outside world. As we begin to perceive meaning and relationships and to distinguish self from the external world, our thought processes shift to the parataxic mode. The experiences and images may be entirely erroneous or unrealistic, but the meaning is very real to the individual himself.

To get a personal feel of the parataxic mode, the reader who has access to one of his own preschool picture books might try leafing through and noting the very special memories and meanings evoked by the pictures. Similarly, the return to a town, a house, or a vacation spot not visited since early childhood can give one an echo of his own early parataxic perceptions.

As adults, we may occasionally slip back to parataxic thinking and under special circumstances revive childhood beliefs, images, or confusions. False perceptions and other defensive reactions to anxiety are labelled parataxic distortions in that autistic meaning interferes with realistic perceptions. Many of the thought processes of psychotics, such as delusions, hallucinations, and noncommunicable perceptions, represent parataxic functioning.

When one learns to perceive as others do and to share their language, beliefs, and explanations, thinking has entered the syntaxic mode. Functioning here depends on consensual validation and agreement. Interpersonal communication is possible only for those functioning syntaxically. It might be noted that the agreement may be arbitrary (the meaning of words and numbers) or inaccurate (a flat earth or witches), but the fact that these symbols and meanings are shared is all that is necessary. Sullivan suggested that most of us respond both syntaxically and parataxically in our everyday functioning. We communicate as if our language were entirely syntaxic, but in fact we are also responding to parataxic meanings. Such dual functioning necessarily causes confusion and a failure of communication. For example, if someone labels himself "a political radical", the subsequent conversation is going to be colored for each participant, not by a dictionary definition of radical, but by all the meanings and feelings, positive and negative experiences he associates with that word. Or, although you and I may agree that we favor free speech each of us perceives specific instances of outspoken behavior quite differently with respect to whether they fit our personal meanings of "free speech."

Developmental Stages. Sullivan's description of seven developmental stages was tied to interpersonal experiences rather than to internal events or biological processes. Sullivan also recognized that the pattern of development would vary from culture to culture and that his description was based on observations within European and American societies.

He identified the first stage as infancy, the period from birth to the development of speech. Oral activity is predominant in this stage because oral behavior provides the primary interaction between the child and other individuals. The child's first conceptualizations involve the nipple (either on mother's breast or attached to a bottle) which can be associated with pleasure and satisfaction (good nipple) or with anxiety and frustration (bad nipple). During this stage, there is also the progression from prototaxic to parataxic thinking. The second stage is childhood, in which language develops and syntaxic thinking becomes possible. Interpersonal behavior at this stage involves playing with peers and being the object of training efforts by parents. In addition to the expanding world of other individuals, the child's self image becomes increasingly articulated, and the child begins to learn various roles he is to play—boy, girl, clown, mother's helper, bully, or whatever. He also learns that there are others who dislike him and who may even be dangerous. Within his family, a child may easily come to believe that everyone loves him and is interested in his welfare; negative interactions outside of the family can come as a great surprise. The third stage, the juvenile era, coincides in our society with attendance of elementary school. The child begins a life away from his family in an expanded social sphere. The complexities of interpersonal interactions increase, and the child must learn a variety of roles and interpersonal strategies. The individual has a reputation and tends to see himself and the world in the stereotyped terms of his culture. His behavior also begins to be guided by self-criticism and self-approval. For a great many individuals, the juvenile stage is as far as development progresses.

The fourth stage, preadolescence, is characterized by the move from completely egocentric concerns to the establishment of an intimate relationship with a friend of the same sex. This is the individual's first genuine human relationship—complete with affection, shared confidences, and mutual trust. This is the first expression of love, which is the feeling that the satisfactions and the security of another person are as important as one's own satisfactions and security. When circumstances are such that this kind of relationship is not formed, the result is acute unhappiness, loneliness, and an impairment of future interpersonal functioning.

The fifth period is early adolescence, during which time sexual relationships are paramount. There are, of course, the physiological changes which initiate sexual desire (the "lust dynamism"), but for Sullivan the most important aspect of the period involves the interpersonal expressions of that desire. Adolescence is a confusing period in which sexual desire centers on members of the opposite sex yet sexual satisfaction is most likely to be achieved by oneself, and intimate friendships exist only with members of one's own sex. Maturity involves the fusion of desire, satisfaction, and intimacy with someone of the opposite sex. Given the difficulties of working out such interpersonal relationships in the context of societal taboos and induced guilt, it is hardly surprising that sexual behavior is frequently a source of severe conflicts or that the outcome of this period is often unsatisfactory. Sullivan did not view sexuality in children or adolescents as a special problem except for the fact that society responds with anxiety and hence gives added meaning to this particular behavior. When individuals remain psychologically in the juvenile era, their heterosexual activity is limited to what Sullivan labeled "instrumental masturbation." The other person is not part of an intimate human relationship but merely an animate object providing physical pleasure.

The sixth stage, late adolescence, begins with the establishment of one's preferred genital activity and moves toward the acquisition of a mature repertory of interpersonal relations. Hall and Lindzey (1970, p. 149) describe the endpoint of this developmental process, adulthood:

> When the individual has ascended all of these steps and reached the final stage of adulthood, he has been transformed largely by means of his interpersonal relations from an animal organism into a human person. He is not an animal, coated by civilization and humanity, but an animal that has been so drastically altered that he is no longer an animal but a human being—or, if one prefers, a human animal.

AN APPRAISAL OF PERSONALITY THEORIES

PERSONALITY THEORIES AND THE GOALS OF SCIENCE

How may personality theories be evaluated with respect to the scientific goals of understanding, prediction, and control? Our focus here is on the early physician-theorists who founded the field of personality and not on the research oriented theorists such as Henry A. Murray (who will be discussed in Chapter 5) and Carl Rogers (who is discussed in Chapter 8). The three theorists presented in this chapter demonstrate the way in which personality was studied during the first half of this century. What have we learned from these creative efforts?

The theorists themselves sought primarily to understand human behavior. Hitherto baffling or mysterious behavior was brought within man's comprehension when constructs such as the id, ego defenses, collective unconscious, and parataxic distortion were devised. We can now explain dreams and slips of the tongue, suicide and rape, psychosis and war, and all of the other puzzling things that men do. The problem, of course, is "How do we know our explanation is correct?" How do we know that we understand these phenomena? If you say "I'd like you to meet my wife, Mother...I mean Martha," I can explain your mistake on the basis of an unresolved Oedipal conflict and propose that you were attracted to a spouse who serves your unconscious incestuous needs. If you agree, my explanation is confirmed. If you deny my interpretation, I can point out your strong resistance to admitting your repressed wishes into consciousness, thus confirming my interpretation. If you hit me in the mouth, you provide even stronger confirmation of the anxiety and threat raised by my accurate interpretation of your verbal slip—further, you have identified me as a threatening father figure and reacted with primitive rage at this rival for your mother's bed. If you gradually come to accept what I said, you are showing insight and a widening of your consciousness. It should be clear that if we were really to play this kind of game, I could not lose. My explanation is "correct" no matter what. Personality theories which rely on subjective understanding provide no way to separate correct from incorrect assertions. The theoretical system is accepted or rejected on the basis of faith and consensual validation. The same could be said for religion, astrology, and devil worship.

When we turn to prediction, it becomes very difficult to give a fair evaluation of personality theories. This is, the theories were not built with prediction as their goal, and the formulations are not expressed in predictive terms. What does it mean, predictively, to say that man first passes through the oral stage? We know that everyone begins life by sucking milk from a nipple, but nothing is added to our predictive ability by this knowledge. What can one predict from the notion that each man possesses an anima and each woman an animus? Of what use is it to say that the cognitive functioning of young infants is prototaxic when there is no way to verify such a statement and when it leads to no predictions about the infant's behavior? One could take many of the constructs and propositions of existing personality theories and show them to be of no utility in scientific terms. The unfairness of this attack should also be obvious. One is viewing the theoretical product with a very different pair of glasses than was used by the creators of the product. Instead of trying, for example, to confirm Freudian theory, one might do better to either accept it on its own terms or to attempt to build a scientifically based theory, utilizing insights and hypotheses borrowed from Freud.

Control is the third goal. What have these theories accomplished in the way of application? It is possible to say that the obvious application has been psychotherapy, beginning with psychoanalysis. This is not entirely true, however. First, the development of therapeutic techniques may be seen as an enterprise which paralleled the development of personality theory. If anything, the theories tended to grow out of observations made by those engaged in psychotherapy rather than therapy developing as an application of the theories. It may be granted that some of the specifics of therapy were influenced by theoretical considerations. For example, one therapist might stress sexual conflicts, another might stress the patient's creative potential, and a third might stress anxiety aroused in interpersonal interactions. Second, the controversies surrounding the effectiveness of traditional psychotherapy are scarcely comforting to adherents of personality theories if psychotherapy is to be heralded as the culmination of the theoretical endeavor. Third, even if psychotherapy were a direct product of the theories and even if psychotherapy were an unqualified success, theories whose only application consists of a single basic technique would be considered somewhat limited.

It is suggested here that personality theories have not been successful in terms of reaching the goals of science. This conclusion does not in any way detract from the intellectual brilliance of the various achievements. It also does not suggest that it should have been obvious at the outset that the theories inevitably would lead to scientific failure. Only Monday morning quarterbacks are free of errors. It also does not mean that personality theories have nothing to offer. Scientific success is not the be-all and end-all of human existence. For some time to come, novelists, theologians, artists, and personality theorists are likely to have more to offer toward making sense out of human existence than are experimentally oriented psychologists.

The successful future theories of behavior will probably not resemble the often beautiful literary productions of the early personality theorists but rather the mathematical formulae of physicists. Future personality theories will not be as much fun to read as the old ones, but they can be expected to lead to precise behavioral predictions and to applications not yet even envisioned.

PERSONALITY THEORIES
AND CURRENT RESEARCH CONCERNS

In addition to specific theoretical hypotheses and constructs which influence much of our present research in personality, the early theorists also exemplified and contributed to the two primary current orientations to the study of human behavior. The present book represents each of these orientations: personality is conceptualized either as based on relatively enduring dispositions or on situational determinants acting upon easily modifiable habits.

Both Freud and, to a lesser extent, Jung contributed to the conceptualization of human behavior as determined by a combination of genetic factors and the lasting effects of early experience. Freud's emphasis was on childhood events which determined the individual's basic characteristics for the remainder of his life. Jung's emphasis was on inborn determinants and on variations along a few universal dimensions (for example, introversion-extraversion). The following six chapters are in agreement with the Freudian and Jungian orientation that personality is relatively stable, even when the specific research has no direct relationship to the writings of Freud and Jung.

A more recent emphasis in personality research is on the situational determinants of behavior. It may be seen that Sullivan represents this quite different orientation in the field. His refusal to conceptualize personality as an anatomical object to be charted and diagrammed and his emphasis on the interpersonal situation as the major stimulus to which individuals respond place him in the mainstream of the research presented in the five chapters of the third section of this book.

One final word must be added about these contrasting approaches to personality because of their quite different therapeutic and even political implications. A focus on the individual and his internal characteristics leads toward a therapeutic concern with adjustment and with altering the person so that he is better able to adapt to the demands of external reality. The world is as it is, and psychology's task is to find out how to mold individuals into that world. On the other hand, a focus on the situational determinants of behavior tends toward a therapeutic concern with restructuring the situation so that it does not have a harmful effect on human beings. The world has many negative aspects, and it is psychology's task to find out how to alter those negative features in order to benefit mankind. These are quite different philosophical positions, and they lead to quite different kinds of research, theory, and application. These contrasting approaches will be pointed out from time to time throughout this book.

SUMMARY

The field of personality originally was identified with the personality theories created by a series of medical practitioners engaged in psychotherapy. Successful scientific theories stimulate empirical research, generate applications, and alter man's conception of himself. The early personality theories primarily achieved the third of these accomplishments and resembled the productions of philosophers, theologians, and novelists more closely than they resembled scientific theories. A major reason for this is that their verification procedures involved additional uncontrolled observations rather than a concern with operationism, experimental manipulations, and quantification.

Sigmund Freud (1859–1939) engaged in private medical practice in Vienna, developing a therapeutic technique known as psychoanalysis and devising the first comprehensive theory of personality. He was convinced of the lawfulness of behavior, and his work involved the description of the human psyche, using a method of deducing underlying events in a manner reminiscent of Sherlock Holmes. Freud categorized mental functioning as conscious, preconscious, and unconscious. Further, the personality is composed of three interacting systems—the id (concerned with pleasure), the ego (concerned with reality), and the superego (concerned with evaluations of right and wrong). Freud viewed man as a machine which consumes various products, converts these into energy, and then expends the energy in physical and mental work. The life instincts (libidinal energy) serve to insure the survival of the individual and the species while the death instinct strives to return the organism to inorganic matter. Each individual moves through a series of developmental stages and the events occurring in each stage are crucial determinants of later personality characteristics. The stages are oral, anal, phallic (during which the Oedipal complex arises) and, if there is successful resolution of the Oedipal complex, the genital stage. With respect to anxiety, Freud defined it as an unpleasant subjective feeling involving expectation, the lack of a specific focus, and a sense of helplessness. He suggested the origin of anxiety as the emotional state evoked by the process of birth. Anxiety is aroused by various traumatic situations which involve loss and by situations which indicate a threat that a traumatic situation will occur. The presence of anxiety leads to behavior which serves to reduce anxiety, behavior including defense mechanisms and other neurotic responses. Anxiety was said to be amenable to therapeutic reduction if the patient could be enabled to accurately verbalize the danger cues and thus regain control of his own behavior. Defense mechanisms operate unconsciously, and they involve some distortion of reality. The principle defenses are repression, projection, reaction formation, fixation, and regression.

Carl Jung (1875–1961) was a Swiss psychiatrist who was an early colleague of Freud. He eventually parted from Freud both personally and professionally. He developed his own personality theory which is termed analytical psychology. Jung's concept of the personal unconscious was similar to that of Freud, but a unique contribution was the collective unconscious which contains influences inherited from one's own ancestors, from the entire race, and even from man's animal progenitors. These inborn factors are not directly available in consciousness, but they predispose us to respond to particular stimuli in a given way. For example, repeated ancestral experiences have led us to have the tendency to believe in a Supreme Being, to fear snakes, and to exhibit mother love. Within the collective unconscious these images or ideas which lead to universal responses are called archetypes. Archetypes are revealed in myths, art, religion, and literature. The persona is the mask we wear in social interactions. The anima and animus represent the unconscious elements of the opposite sex present in men and women. The shadow is the unconscious antithesis of overt behavioral trends. The self is an archetype representing a desire for unity or oneness. In relation to the outside world, the libido either functions in an introverted or extraverted fashion. In addition, Jung classified the psychological functions into two modes of judgment (thinking versus feeling) and two modes of apprehension (sensing versus intuiting). Symbols are words, ideas, or images which constitute the best possible formulation of a relatively unknown thing. Jung, like Freud, conceived of the personality as a closed energy system. The libido is the life energy underlying all natural phenomena, including the personality. The principle of equivalence states that energy cannot be lost to the system. The principle of entropy states that the personality moves toward (but never reaches) a state of equilibrium. For Jung, the stages of development were not tied to sexual pleasure. The greatest divergence from Freud's developmental schema, however, was in Jung's concentration on the developmental changes of later life when the libido can be invested in artistic, philosophical, and intellectual concerns. He also saw mankind as steadily progressing through evolutionary changes in personality.

Harry Stack Sullivan (1892–1949) was an American psychiatrist who also served as an educator, editor, and administrator. The major portion of his theoretical contribution was published after his death on the basis of tape recordings and notes of his lectures. Sullivan viewed personality as a verbal abstraction. Human behavior is determined by interpersonal interactions. Rather than deep-seated and unchanging characteristics, there are only habits, or dynamisms, which provide some stability of behavior across situations. The dynamism of self (including the good-me and bad-me) is extremely important, and is built up through parent-child interactions. A personification is the concept one acquires about oneself or about any other person. The organism is primarily motivated to reduce tension, both biological needs and interpersonally-aroused anxiety. Sullivan described three modes of experience as prototaxic (primitive, unrelated sensations), parataxic (differentiated but highly personal images and meanings), and syntaxic (sharing the perceptions and language of others). The developmental stages were seen as tied to interpersonal experiences. They are infancy (birth to the development of speech), childhood (syntaxic thinking and interactions with peers), juvenile era (elementary school and the learning of stereotypes about self and others), preadolescence (establishing an intimate relationship with a friend of the same sex), early adolescence (sexual desires for opposite sex, satisfaction in masturbation, and friendship with members of one's own sex), late adolescence (establishment of one's preferred genital activity), and adulthood (mature repertory of interpersonal relations).

Personality theories have primarily provided us with an understanding of human behavior though there is no way to establish the validity of most of the theoretical propositions. Personality theories were not designed to provide predictions of behavior. With respect to application, psychotherapy tended to precede the theoretical developments rather than emerge from the theories. Current research in personality tends to involve either an emphasis on internal characteristics which stems from the tradition of Freud and Jung or an emphasis on situational determinants which is closer to the model advanced by Sullivan. These contrasting theoretical and research approaches also have implications for perceiving the solution to behavioral problems either as the alteration (adjustment) of the malfunctioning individual and his traits or as the alteration of the malfunctioning situation.

II

Personality Dimensions

as

Predictors

of Behavior

3

The Study
of
Individual Differences

When we are asked to describe another person, to say what they are *really* like, we tend to respond with a series of adjectives. We indicate where they fall on various dimensions. In a rough way, we compare those we describe by saying that John is smarter than Bill or that Kathy is more outgoing than Linda. We apparently share the assumption that descriptions and comparisons of this kind provide useful predictive information. That is, you might decide to study for a test with John or spend time at a party with Kathy on the basis of such information.

The field of personality grew out of this general tradition, and much of personality research has been concerned with efforts to identify and operationalize the important dimensions of personality in order to be able to study them within the field of psychology.

A SUGGESTED MODEL FOR DESCRIBING RESEARCH ON INDIVIDUAL DIFFERENCES

The basic question is, "What do we want to know about any given personality dimension?" Stripped of all the trappings of research detail, what we want to know is why people differ on this dimension, how such differences are related to other behaviors, and what causes people to change their standing on this dimension.

It may be helpful to think of this type of research as fitting the five categories shown in Figure 3-1. These categories will be used throughout the present section of the text and will now be briefly defined.

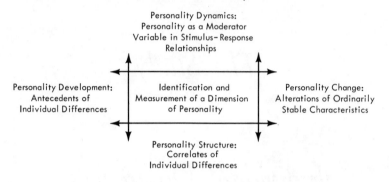

Personality Dynamics:
Personality as a Moderator
Variable in Stimulus- Response
Relationships

Personality Development:
Antecedents of
Individual Differences

Identification and
Measurement of a Dimension
of Personality

Personality Change:
Alterations of Ordinarily
Stable Characteristics

Personality Structure:
Correlates of
Individual Differences

Fig. 3-1 A Schema Depicting Research on Individual Differences Involving Personality Measurement, Development, Structure, Dynamics, and Change.

Personality Measurement

The starting point for such research is the identification of a dimension and an attempt to measure it. For example, one might observe that others differ in the amount of prejudice they express toward various groups of people. You probably are able to compare those you know and can say that your uncle is more prejudiced than your aunt, or whatever. If you pursue the question further, you may find that the concept of prejudice is too broad because people differ as to the targets of their prejudice. Some express negative feelings about blacks, others about Catholics, others about Midwesterners, and still others about those who wear beards. You might decide, then, that to describe others in terms of their degree of prejudice, you need to break the concept into smaller units such as anti-black prejudice, anti-Catholic prejudice, and so forth.

If you were to continue this process of specifying what you mean by prejudice, it would lead you to the problems and procedures of personality measurement. Your observation that other people differ in, say, anti-black prejudice could be verified by constructing a measuring instrument which would provide an objective way to determine the position of each individual on this dimension. Research in the area of personality measurement involves test construction and the evaluation of existing tests.

Personality Development

Once a dimension has been identified and a measuring device constructed, one obvious type of interest is the determination of the reasons for the individual differences. What are the antecedents of differences along the dimension? With respect to anti-black prejudice, for example, we could try to find out the conditions under which prejudice develops and those under which it fails to develop. It might be important to find out whether the prejudice of parents is taught directly to their children, whether actual positive and negative experiences with blacks has anything to do with general feelings about blacks, and whether such broad concerns as economic security contribute to prejudice or its absence. Research on personality development includes studies of environmental influences, and, in many cases, studies of genetic and prenatal influences.

PERSONALITY STRUCTURE

In general, personality structure refers to the way in which the various personality dimensions fit together to form an overall structure. Because many specific genetic, prenatal, and environmental factors influence more than one personality dimension, such dimensions tend to be related to one another.

For example, when a group of individuals is measured on a scale of racial intolerance, it is possible to find out whether these scores are related to differences on a scale measuring political conservatism. If a relationship is found, we can begin seeking the common antecedents which lead to the association. The discovery of such relationships also provides predictive power. Thus, if we know an individual's level of prejudice, we can make better than chance predictions about how he will respond to liberal and conservative political candidates.

When several such dimensions of personality are found to be interrelated, we speak of clusters or factors within the overall structure of personality. There may come a time when personality psychologists can identify all the relevant dimensions and state how they fit together in clusters. At present, there is still much to be done in identifying, measuring, and determining the relationships among the dimensions.

Research on personality structure includes correlational studies of the relationship between dimensions and more elaborate mathematical determinations of the way in which the dimensions are organized. The end point of the study of structure is a way to describe an individual's personality, a cross section of his characteristics at a given point in time.

PERSONALITY DYNAMICS

If the study of personality structure leads to a descriptive cross section of what a person is like, personality dynamics is concerned with the effect of personality variables on the individual's response to an ever-changing stimulus world.

As we will see in the third section of this book, much psychological research is concerned with establishing lawful relationships between stimuli and responses. It is often found, however, that these stimulus-response laws are different for different groups of people. It is here that personality variables can be of great value in providing a way to group individuals so that we can determine how the stimulus-response relationships operate in each group. Used in this way, personality variables are conceptualized as moderator variables. That is, they moderate or influence the effect of external stimuli on behavior.

An example of this type of research is an experiment in which white subjects are asked to read several passages and afterward to recall as much as possible of what had been read. The content of the passages for some subjects is negative to blacks and for others is positive to blacks. Which type of passage will be remembered better? In a random group of subjects, we are likely to find that neither antiblack nor problack statements are recalled any better. If we first divide each group of subjects into those scoring high on a measure of antiblack prejudice and those scoring low on the prejudice measure, we may then find that high-prejudiced subjects remember more of the material in the antiblack condition while low-prejudiced subjects remember more of the material in the problack condition. Thus, a stimulus variable (content of the passages) is moderated by a personality variable (prejudice) in determining the response (recall of the passages).

Research on personality dynamics consists primarily of experimental investigations in which there is a manipulation of stimulus variables and a division of the subjects on the basis of one or more personality variables.

PERSONALITY CHANGE

The fifth area of research on individual differences is concerned with the alteration of personality variables. Even though such characteristics are defined as being relatively stable and enduring, changes are presumably possible at any age level under the right conditions.

Experimental research might be designed, for example, to determine the effect of different types of persuasive appeals for tolerance on anti-black attitudes. Similarly, field studies could be conducted to determine the effect of school integration on prejudice.

A few of the basic details of these five types of research will now be described.

THE MEASUREMENT OF BEHAVIOR

Among the essential requirements of any science is the development of reliable and valid instruments with which to measure the variables being investigated. In examining the history of a field, one of the changes which may be observed as that field advances is the steady improvement in measuring instruments. No advantage is gained in developing precise measuring tools in the absence of theoretical developments, but theoretical advances in the absence of adequate measurement are necessarily limited. Much of the history of science is made up of the reciprocal contribution of theory and methodology.

In investigations of human behavior, the problem of measurement has been a difficult one. We will examine some of the solutions which have been developed to solve those problems. Bear in mind that the measurement problems which face psychology are not in any way conceptually different from the measurement problems which have faced other fields. The major difference is the fact that analogous problems are being solved in different centuries.

MEASUREMENT IN THE PHYSICAL AND BEHAVIORAL SCIENCES

An example of the parallels between the development of physical measures and behavioral measures was given by Zubin (1965) at a symposium on the problems of measuring anxiety. He noted that all measurement begins in an intuitive and subjective way and is initially unreliable and invalid. Even in the physical sciences, the first approach to measuring length, weight, time, and temperature, for example, was intuitive. Zubin speculated on what a prehistoric Ice Age symposium on measuring temperature would have been like. One cave man proposes that warmth depends on the number of bear skins you wrap around your body, so temperature could be measured by counting skins. Another claims that warmth is a function of how long you are exposed to sunlight. A third says that warmth increases when you run, so distance is the best measure of temperature. A medicine man says that he has evidence that body temperature rises without any bear skins, exposure to sunlight, or running. The symposium breaks up without any conclusion, and someone writes a paper pointing out that it is impossible to measure temperature because it is subjective and because no one can agree about its determinants.

In fact, the first breakthrough in measuring this variable took place in Egypt where a subjective rating scale was devised. Temperature was estimated as falling at four points along a scale ranging from "the hottest day in summer" to the "coldest day in winter." Much later, it was discovered that mercury expands when it is heated and that mercury could be placed in a tube marked off by regularly spaced lines. At that point, an objective measuring device had been created. We will see that many of the variables in personality research are still measured by self-rating scales the way temperature was in ancient Egypt while some can be measured by objective devices analogous to the thermometer.

QUANTIFYING MEASURES OF BEHAVIOR

What is there about a rating scale or a device such as a thermometer that makes it a measuring instrument? The primary characteristic of measurement is that of differentiating a variable along a scale. The differentiation may be along a simple *ordinal scale,* which defines an order of events (hottest day in summer to coldest day in winter) or along a more precise scale with *equal intervals* (division marks on a mercury thermometer). Quantification occurs when we assign numbers to the points on these scales; this is a great advantage because we can then handle data mathematically.

Ranking. As an example of behavior measurement, let's say that you are interested in measuring intelligence. One of the simplest approaches is to rank individuals along the dimension. If no other measuring instrument were available, judges could be asked to rank a group of subjects from brightest to dumbest. This kind of ordering of people becomes extremely difficult when the group gets relatively large. You can rank three people in terms of brightness much more easily than you can rank thirty people, and ranking three hundred people is practically impossible. Ranking also gives information only within a given group, and the information often has no meaning across groups. For example, the individual who is ranked number one in brightness in one group may be the least bright in another group.

Rating Scales. Variables can be classified along a two-point scale (hot-cold or smart-dumb), but further differentiation and discrimination can be obtained by extending the two-point scale into a longer ordinal scale. With intelligence, for example, the ratings can be made along a three-point, five-point, or nine-point scale. Instead of simply bright-stupid, a series of terms could be used:

Extremely Bright   _____
Bright   _____
Average   _____
Stupid   _____
Extremely Stupid   _____

Theoretically, such a scale could contain any number of points, but in fact people are not able to make meaningful differentiations beyond approximately seven or nine points.

Two difficulties are common to both ranking and rating techniques. First, close agreement between judges is difficult to obtain, though intensive training and practice will help. A more basic problem is the limited degree of differentiation provided by these measures. There are built-in restrictions on the fineness with which subjects can be ordered and discriminated.

Relying on Physical Dimensions. One familiar method of improving measurement in psychology is through the use of a scale developed for other sciences. For example, behavior can be measured in terms of time, and the objectivity and differentiation is as great as in any other science because the measure is a well-developed one. Time has been used in measuring intelligence by determining how long it takes subjects to solve a complex task. The smaller the amount of time required to master the task, the greater the intelligence.

Frequency Counts. Still another way of dimensionalizing behavior is through the use of a frequency measure. A response can occur over and over. A behavior measure can be the total number of times the response occurred during a given period of time. With intelligence and many other behavioral variables, there are special problems in trying to use a frequency approach. The number of times a subject solves a complex task would be meaningless. Human beings learn very quickly and easily grow bored. Frequency of performing such tasks might be an indication of tolerance for repetitious tasks or of lack of imagination rather than of intelligence.

A more fruitful approach is a variation on the principle of frequency. Instead of determining the number of times a given response follows a given stimulus, frequency counts are made of the number of times a particular kind of response follows a variety of different stimuli which have something in common. Frequency counts, then, are made across different behaviors which are related. The subject is asked to solve a series of complex tasks, and the number of times he can do so is the measure of intelligence.

RELIABILITY OF MEASUREMENT

A variable is measured when one can order it along a dimension. The consistency with which this ordering is done is the reliability of measurement. Obviously, good measurement is consistent, and bad measurement is inconsistent. Inconsistency in measurement is called measurement error. In any field, the more consistent the measuring device, the better the data. A set of numbers obtained from an unreliable instrument is partly garbage because such numbers not only reflect the variable under study but also random measurement errors. The lawful relationships which the scientist is seeking are often obscured by such errors of measurement. Imagine the task of attempting to work with time measures if one's only instrument were a clock in which the minute hand moved around the dial in irregular stops and starts at varying speeds.

Stimulus Consistency. It is never possible to control all of the stimuli present in the testing situation. When a test is administered, the test materials

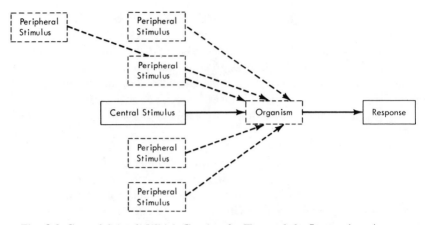

Fig. 3-2 Central Stimuli Which Consist of a Test and the Instructions Accompanying it and Peripheral Stimuli Which Consist of All of the Other Stimulus Variations Which can Influence Test Responses.

themselves are only a part of the stimuli to which the subject may be responding. In Figure 3-2 is depicted the situation in which the test is the "central stimulus" and all other external factors are the "peripheral stimuli." Let us say, for example, that a psychologist is measuring responses to four cards of the Thematic Apperception Test (TAT); subjects are asked to write stories for which each picture might be an illustration. The central stimulus consists of those four pictures and the instructions. Individual differences in responding to such pictures have proved to be a useful indicator of need for achievement as will be seen in Chapter 5. What if the four pictures were changed in some way from subject to subject? Under these circumstances, individual differences in the stories might obviously be a function of differences in the pictures. While no experimenter would deliberately change the stimulus for each subject, the possibility of accidental changes in the peripheral stimuli is always possible. Therefore, every investigator needs to describe the central and peripheral stimuli in painstaking detail so that they may be reproduced as exactly as possible by any other experimenter who wishes to study the same variable. Thus, the stimuli are kept as constant as possible from experiment to experiment. When this is not done, stimulus inconsistency can result in less reliable measurement.

A related problem arises when different stimuli are combined in a test because they are known to be equivalent in some way. For example, when several vocabulary items are administered in an intelligence test, these separate stimulus units are assumed to have something in common even though each word is different. Test items are judged to be equivalent if they elicit correlated responses. This type of reliability may be determined by correlating items or groups of items with one another. The resulting correlation is known as the *coefficient of internal consistency*. When one-half of the test is correlated with the other half, the result is called split-half reliability.

When more than one version of the test has been constructed, it is necessary to know whether the two sets of stimuli are equivalent. The correlation between two test forms is called the *coefficient of equivalence*.

Response Consistency. Objective measurement requires that different individuals who judge each response arrive at approximately the same numerical score. Without very high *interjudge consistency*, reliable measurement is impossible. Careful training of scorers is needed to improve this type of reliability, especially when there is a great deal of subjectivity in the judgments that are made. Interjudge consistency is highest when response measurement is based on simple perceptual judgments such as counting black marks on a true-false answer sheet or reading a number on a dial.

With personality tests, responses are expected to be stable over time. The *coefficient of stability* or test-retest reliability is the correlation between scores on the test given at two different points in time.

VALIDITY OF MEASUREMENT

Validity refers to the "truth" of the measure, the degree to which the test is capable of achieving certain aims. As with reliability, different types of validity have been defined.

Content of the Items. The simplest form of validity is defined by the nature of the items. A measure has *face validity* to the extent that the items are related logically or reasonably to the construct which the test is supposed to be measuring. For example, if someone constructed an intelligence test, the instrument would have face validity if it contained material dealing with vocabulary, arithmetic, reasoning, and memory. An "intelligence" test which required the subject to lift weights, inquired about his sexual habits, or tested his knowledge of Swahili would not be considered by most of us to be a likely measure of intelligence.

A more sophisticated version of face validity is *content validity*. If a test is supposed to constitute a sample of a particular body of material, there should be evidence that it is an adequate sample. For example, an algebra test should consist of an adequate sample of algebra problems. For most measuring instruments in personality, we do not have a specific body of material that the items are supposed to sample. Therefore, there is no way to specify content validity for the usual personality test.

Predicting Criterion Behavior. The type of validity which is most often discussed in introductory texts is suited primarily to applied situations in which there is a specific criterion behavior that the test is designed to predict. In a manufacturing plant, employees are needed on the assembly line who can perform a mechanical task quickly and accurately. The development of an employee-selection device which predicts that behavior can be very useful in saving time and money. The validity of a test used for this purpose would be the correlation between test scores and the number of parts assembled without error. The higher the correlation, the more valid the test, and the better the prediction of job performance. A distinction is sometimes made between *predictive validity* and *concurrent validity*. Predictive validity refers to the correlation between test scores and criterion performance at a later time. Concurrent validity refers to the correlation between test scores and criterion performance at about the same time.

To What Are Scores on the Test Related? Except for tests designed to predict a specific behavior, no single comparison or correlation can be interpreted as indicating the validity of the test. *Construct validity,* however, refers to a consideration of many indicators of what the test measures (French and Michael, 1966). The major point is that there is no single criterion by which most personality tests can be "validated." How could you determine if a test of prejudice is a valid one? Prejudice refers to many different behaviors and attitudes. A test of prejudice would have to be related to many different kinds of responses in different situations.

Construct validity, then, is determined by investigating as many relationships as possible. It is not quite accurate to speak of personality tests as valid or invalid. Rather, it is more realistic to indicate that a given test has been found to be related to such and such variables. The most meaningful validational question in personality is: "To what are scores on the test related?"

CONSTRUCTING RELIABLE MEASURING INSTRUMENTS

Intuitive Approach. In any test construction procedure, the initial step is that of obtaining or devising a series of stimulus items which make logical sense. There are no hard and fast rules to follow, and there is probably a degree of both theory and art in devising any behavior measure.

At first glance, it does not seem likely that simply putting a group of items together would yield a reliable instrument. However, the research literature in personality demonstrates the usefulness of just this approach. The measure of anxiety (described in Chapter 6) and the measure of self-concept (described in Chapter 8) were initially constructed in this way. It is assumed that, should the measure prove to be of value, greater precision can be obtained by subsequent improvements in the test.

Internal Consistency or Bootstrap Approach. Item selection can be evaluated beyond simple intuitive judgments by determining the extent to which each item is related to the others. Those which prove to be unrelated are discarded. In a sense, the test is "lifted up by its own bootstraps."

The usual procedure is to begin with the intuitive approach and then to evaluate each item. The test is administered to a large number of subjects, and their responses are scored according to the intuitively based scoring system. Then, the relationship between the score on each item and the score on the total test is determined. A good item is one which is related to the total score; that is, it is measuring the same thing. A bad item is one which is unrelated to the total score. This type of analysis provides an empirical check or verification of the investigator's skill in building a consistent measuring device. The measure of authoritarianism described in the following chapter was developed by means of the bootstrap approach.

External Criterion Approach: Correlational. Whenever an external criterion exists for the variable being measured, it is desirable to use it as the basis for selecting test items. All potential items are evaluated in terms of their relationship with the criterion.

In the correlational method, groups which differ on the criterion variable are given the test. Those test items which differentiate between groups are assumed to measure some aspect of behavior which is different in the two groups. The measure of intelligence discussed in Chapter 7 was built in this way, using different age groups as the criterion.

External Criterion Approach: Experimental. If it is possible experimentally to manipulate the behavior to be measured, another type of test construction may be considered. Rather than depend on correlations with other behaviors, the investigator is able to bring about the condition he wishes to measure and then determine those items that measure it best. In the test construction phase, an experimental and a control group are used. The central stimulus is kept the same for both groups, and a portion of the peripheral stimuli is varied in a particular way. For example, an experimenter might present two groups with a picture of a steak dinner and ask the subjects to rate the picture on a scale of one to ten (the higher the rating, the more they liked the picture). This would be the central stimulus. The peripheral stimulus to be varied might be hunger. The experimenter would instruct one group—the erperimental group—not to eat for six hours before they came to the experiment. He would give the other group—the control group—no special instructions. The experimental group then represents the hunger condition, and the control group represents the "normal" condition.

In this particular experiment, the results would probably show that the hungry experimental subjects rated the picture of the steak dinner higher than the control subjects. If the experimenter found this to be consistently the case, he would give the test only under neutral conditions to subjects who were not given any special instructions about eating or not eating before the experiment. It could be assumed that those subjects whose responses were like those of the original experimental group behave under ordinary conditions as the experimental group did under special conditions. That is, it could be assumed that they were hungry.

This approach to test construction has not been used as extensively as have the other approaches. In part, this is a function of our inability to manipulate many of the variables we desire to measure. It is not possible, for example, to create experimental conditions to make subjects more intelligent. Motivational states can, however, be manipulated. The development by this method of a TAT measure of need for achievement is described in Chapter 5.

PERSONALITY DEVELOPMENT: DETERMINING THE ANTECEDENTS OF INDIVIDUAL DIFFERENCES

Within an experimental situation it is possible to manipulate independent variables and determine their influence on specific dependent variables. Such research allows us to describe many relationships in cause-effect or antecedent-consequent terms. The typical personality variable, on the other hand, is more complex, general, and stable than the usual dependent variable studied in the laboratory. A personality characteristic is likely to have developed as a function of many antecedents operating over a long period of time. Such characteristics are sufficiently stable that they are usually found to be unaffected by variations in stimulus conditions. If we cannot manipulate antecedent variables, how can we discover the determinants of individual differences in personality?

It might be noted that knowledge of such determinants is potentially one of the most important aspects of personality research. Knowledge of the antecedents of individual differences is of theoretical importance because developmental theories can tie together a great many findings which are otherwise independent. With respect to application, mankind stands to benefit greatly from the discovery of developmental influences. It seems that the most likely way to develop intelligent, achieving, adjusted, creative, independent, adaptive adults would be through knowing how to manipulate the variables involved in heredity, the prenatal period, and child-rearing. One of society's best hopes for eliminating mental illness or of increasing the incidence of genius is through alterations of developmental influences. With these probably distant goals in mind, we will briefly consider the three areas of developmental research.

GENETIC DETERMINANTS OF PERSONALITY

Man has had some notions about the transmission of characteristics across generations for many thousands of years. The idea of breeding dogs, for example, in order to obtain desired physical or behavioral characteristics is at least ten thousand years old. The same concept was generalized to human beings, as when Plato in *The Republic* proposed that the best men in the society should mate with the best women in order to improve the quality of the group.

Knowledge of the mechanisms involved in hereditary transmission was lacking until comparatively modern times, however. It is interesting that Darwin's (1859) theory of evolution was developed in the absence of basic knowledge about the way in which inheritance worked. He was puzzled, for example, as to why a given characteristic is sometimes inherited and some- times not. The work of an Augustinian monk in a monastery in Brunn, Moravia, constituted the first important step toward modern hereditary thought. Gregor Mendel investigated the effects of crossing different varieties of pea plants, and he traced the distribution of various characteristics through many generations. He proposed that certain elements must be responsible for determining attributes such as shortness and tallness. Though Mendel's work was first reported in 1865, not until its rediscovery in 1900 did it begin to influence other investigators. Mendel's elements, now called genes, are accepted as the basis for transmitting characteristics from one generation to the next.

What type of research has been conducted in the study of behavioral genetics?

Family Resemblances. As everyone knows, genetic determinants of various physical characteristics are responsible for the similarities in appearance which occur within a family. Similarities among siblings or between parents and their children are taken for granted with respect to hair and eye color, height and weight, and so forth. The notion that behavioral traits are inherited and lead to family resemblances in personality is a little more difficult to verify, and exceptions are easy to find. There are several techniques, however, that can provide information about whether or not a given behavioral character- istic is influenced by genetic factors.

Early investigators attempted to provide relevant data by studying several generations of a single family to seek behavioral similarities (for example, Goddard, 1912). A major difficulty is built into this family-pedigree approach; environmental and genetic influences are necessarily confounded. Common experiences as well as common genes are shared among family members. What is needed is a means of separating the two types of antecedents.

A most convincing comparison in a family resemblance study is that be- tween siblings born at the same time (fraternal twins) and siblings born at the same time who also share the same genetic properties (identical twins). When identical twins are found to be more similar in a particular charac- teristic than are fraternal twins, there is strong evidence that degree of genetic similarity is responsible for the difference.

Experiments of Nature. It is sometimes possible to utilize a naturally occurring situation as if it were a laboratory experiment. That is, real life variations in stimulus conditions are treated just as though they had been manipulated by an experimenter. This approach lacks the degree of control possible in a laboratory situation, but certain types of information can be obtained in no other way.

If children were separated from their natural parents at birth and placed in a different family, it would be possible to compare the effects of heredity and environment. Behavioral variables which are determined by hereditary factors should be similar for children and their natural parents while resemblances between children and their foster parents would be expected for characteristics which are determined by experience. Though such experiments cannot and should not be undertaken, precisely that same situation is provided through natural causes when infants are adopted or placed in foster homes. Comparisons of foster children as a technique for studying human genetics will be described with respect to studies of intelligence in Chapter 7.

In the relatively rare instances in which identical twins have been separated in infancy and reared separately in different families, a unique opportunity is provided to determine the extent to which behavioral variables are independent of environmental determinants. Any similarities between identical twins reared together can be a joint function of identical genes and nearly identical environments. Similarities between identical twins reared in different families are presumably almost entirely the result of genetic influences.

Selective Breeding. Experimental research on behavior genetics at the human level is not possible for obvious ethical reasons. As an alternative possibility, selective breeding may be studied in other species. One of the outcomes of this research is the generalization of the findings to human behavior.

PRENATAL DETERMINANTS

One of the most persistent and widespread beliefs concerning human development over the past centuries has been the idea that the experiences of a pregnant women determine various characteristics in her offspring. It was suggested, for example, that a frightening experience will leave its mark on an unborn child; a mother who was frightened at the sight of a gorilla in a zoo would be likely to give birth to an especially hairy child. A great many individuals believed at one time that it was possible to influence an unborn child's interests and attitudes through the activities of the pregnant mother; women would attend concerts and read the classics for the sake of the child's later cultural tastes. With increasing sophistication in the last several decades, these colorful beliefs are rapidly disappearing.

Probably in part as a reaction to these earlier propositions, it was taught in medical schools for many years that the fetus is well insulated in the womb and hence is more or less unaffected by events occurring outside of the womb (Montagu, 1959). Even though the mother's exposure to Beethoven may not have a notable effect on the musical tastes of the fetus, it has been equally wrong to assume that the nature of all events which take place during the nine months of pregnancy are irrelevant. The developing child is bathed in a chemical environment and is wholly dependent on the mother for the intake of nourishment and the elimination of wastes. These circumstances lead to the probability that the mother's physiological functioning is of great importance in determining many aspects of the development of the fetus. An example of the effect of the mother's diet on the intelligence of her offspring will be given in Chapter 7.

EXPERIENTIAL DETERMINANTS OF PERSONALITY

By far the greatest amount of research on the antecedents of personality has been concerned with experience. Studies of child-rearing attitudes and practices, of childhood learning, and of cultural influences on development all fit within this general framework.

Parental Behavior and Behavior of Their Offspring. Many studies involve only the parent or only the offspring. For example, it is possible to measure a mother's child-rearing attitudes and to ask her questions about her child's behavior. Similarly, it is possible to measure a child's behavior and ask him questions about his mother's child-rearing practices. It cannot be known for sure whether we are dealing with accurate representations of the other person in the parent-child interactions or with distorted perceptions. For that reason, whenever possible experimenters obtain data on the parent and the child independently rather than depend on what either one says about the other.

Cross-Cultural Comparisons. A popular approach to experiential antecedents of individual differences has been that of cross-cultural comparisons. Within the typical American community, an investigator can obtain parental differences in punishment techniques, for example, and attempt to relate these differences to the behavior of children. In the total range of punishment techniques practiced in other cultures around the world, the American samples offer only a small variety of different practices. In some cultures parents are much more punitive than Americans while in others parents are more indulgent. The gain of a wider range of child-rearing practices is a major benefit of the cross-cultural approach. One problem with this research should be noted. If Society A and Society B differ in child-rearing practices and in some other behavior, the child-rearing practices may well have been the cause of the behavior. Since the societies are also likely to differ in countless ways in addition to the way they raise children, it is not really possible to isolate the variables with certainty. When cross-cultural findings fit in well with findings from other types of investigations, they can be accepted with greater confidence.

Experimental Studies of Children. There are two somewhat different types of experimentation with children. Some experimental child psychologists approach the problem with established concepts and findings from general experimental psychology and then investigate their applicability to children. Other investigators begin with a problem from the field of personality and then devise experimental situations in which such variables may be studied in the laboratory.

Experimental Studies of Animals. Another avenue to the study of personality antecedents is the utilization of nonhuman subjects in experiments. One of the obvious reasons for using animal subjects is that much of the theorizing about the effects of early experience centers around traumatic and disruptive events to which human subjects could not ethically be exposed. If stressful early experience is found to affect the later behavior of mice or monkeys, we are inclined to believe that similar effects hold true for human beings.

PERSONALITY STRUCTURE

Most of the research on personality structure is several steps removed from the problem of the overall organization of personality. Most such investigations involve the establishment of simple relationships between and among a limited number of personality dimensions.

When a psychologist establishes that there is a relationship between two different responses made by an individual, neither of these responses is conceptualized as causing the other. Rather, the fact that there is a link means that there is some other factor responsible, and that factor may be sought in future research.

A correlational situation is shown in Figure 3-3. Whenever a lawful relationship is found between R_1 and R_2, it suggests that an unobserved variable within the organism is common to both. Something has made the responses at least partially equivalent. There may be physiological attributes or traces of past learning experiences which intervene between the stimulus and response in each instance. Such findings are not only of theoretical importance, but in a practical sense it is often useful to be able to predict one response

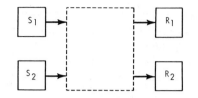

Fig. 3-3 A Representation of the Correlation Between Two Responses.

from another. The use of test responses to predict job performance is one example of how correlational data may be useful.

Whenever ability or skills are involved in two correlated responses, it seems probable that common physiological factors are involved. For example, reaction time for the hand is highly correlated with reaction time for the foot. Each behavior requires approximately the same sensory, neural, and muscular functioning which is different for different individuals. Possibly these differences are genetic in origin and possibly they are partly influenced by experiential differences such as training, exercise, and nutrition.

With other responses, the same kind of guesses could be made but the connections are less obvious. In an intelligence test for children, the vocabulary section asks such questions as, "What is a microscope?" Individual differences in vocabulary clearly reflect experiential factors such as the vocabulary of the parents, the child's contact with reading material, and the quality of the school he attends. Another part of the test involves following a pattern to copy a design using blocks of various colors. Again, there are individual differences in the number of designs a child can complete and how fast he can do it. With the block design task, the effects of parents, reading, and school would not seem to be particularly important. Nevertheless, there is a substantial correlation between how well children do on the vocabulary test and how well they do on the block design test. It seems likely that both genetic and learning variables account for the relationship between the two behaviors.

Still other response-response relationships seem to be entirely attributable to learning experiences. On an attitude scale, college students who express favorable opinions about drinking tend to be favorable toward smoking; those who oppose one tend to oppose the other. One would guess that in the students' families there was either a relatively positive or a relatively negative orientation toward both tobacco and alcohol, and this consistency is reflected in the correlation between the two attitude responses.

PERSONALITY DYNAMICS

The study of personality dynamics is defined as any research which involves the manipulation of a stimulus variable and the division of subjects into subgroups on the basis of a personality variable. In this type of research, the two major emphases in personality research can be seen to merge. The present section of the book describes research on individual differences with its emphasis on establishing response-response relationships. The third section of the book describes research on the situational determinants of behavior with its emphasis on establishing stimulus-response relationships. Personality dynamics brings together these two approaches.

The drawing in Figure 3-4 depicts the general case of a personality dynamics experiment. Though a lawful relationship may be established between

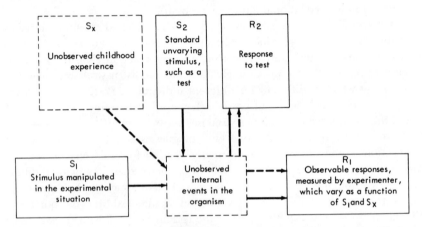

Fig. 3-4 An Experiment in Personality Dynamics in Which a Stimulus Variable and a Personality Variable Jointly Influence a Response Variable. (Adapted from Byrne, 1964, p. 41.)

S_1 and R_1, the fact that there are variations among subjects in R_1 suggests that there are other antecedents to this response in addition to S_1. If the antecedents are unobserved internal processes in the subjects and if these internal processes are caused by unobserved events in the past history of the subject (S_x), no amount of experimental rigor will increase the accuracy with which R_1 can be predicted from S_1.

The solution to this dilemma lies in the use of a personality test. If we can assume that the effects of S_x on the organism influence a variety of responses, we can construct a standard stimulus $(S_2,$ a test) and obtain responses to it $(R_2,$ test performance) which vary as a function of S_x. By means of this approach, we are able to use individual differences in R_2 to increase the accuracy with which we can predict the S_1–R_1 relationship. Since we cannot observe or control S_x or its effects, only through the use of R_2 as a substitute can we increase the accuracy of our predictions. The personality characteristic measured in the S_2–R_2 procedure is conceptualized as a moderator variable in the S_1–R_1 relationship.

PERSONALITY CHANGE

By definition, the major focus of interest in research on individual differences is on the consistent, unchanging aspects of behavior. At the same time, there is considerable theoretical and practical concern with the possibility of bringing about changes in behavior. When we consider issues such as political indoctrination or brain-washing, the rehabilitation of criminals, the effectiveness of advertising, or the effects of racial integration on interpersonal attitudes, it is obvious that the applied implications of work on personality change are enormous.

The personality change research which is described in the next five chapters centers on two types of influence. Change can be brought about deliberately, as in psychotherapy or in a Marine boot camp, and it can occur as a by-product of other events, as with aging or the availability of the birth control pill. Because of the potential value and potential danger of knowledge about how to change behavior, this type of research tends to raise more optimism and more fears than any other in the study of individual differences.

SUMMARY

The field of personality grew out of the general cultural tradition in which we describe one another as falling along various dimensions. One approach to the study of behavior has been the effort to identify and operationalize the basic dimensions of personality in order to study them with respect to personality measurement, personality development, personality structure, personality dynamics, and personality change.

Among the essential requirements of any science is the development of reliable and valid instruments with which to measure the variables under investigation. The reason that the measurement of behavior appears to be a different sort of problem than the measurement of variables in the physical sciences is simply the difference in the ages of the different fields. The primary characteristic of measurement is the ability to differentiate along a scale, and the quantification of these differences gives us the ability to handle our data mathematically. Behavior can be measured by means of ranking a series of individuals or rating them along an ordinal scale. With these techniques, interjudge agreement is difficult to obtain, and the degree of differentiation among subjects is limited. These difficulties can be overcome by the utilization of physical dimensions and by the construction of measures based on response frequency. The consistency with which a variable is ordered along a dimension is the reliability of measurement. Measurement error can be caused by inconsistencies in the stimulus variable. When stimuli are combined to form a test, they must be equivalent in that they elicit correlated responses as determined by a coefficient of internal consistency. When two different stimuli or sets of stimuli are utilized as alternate measures of the same variable, they must yield correlated responses as evaluated by the coefficient of equivalence. Response inconsistencies occur if there is not high interjudge consistency in identifying the response or if there is not a great consistency of responses over time as determined by the coefficient of stability. Validity of measurement is the extent to which a test measures what it purports to measure. Face validity refers to the logical connection between test materials and the variable being measured; content validity refers to how well a specific universe of material has been sampled by the test. When the measure is designed to predict a specific criterion behavior, validity is the correlation between test scores and the criterion; depending on the time sequence of the two behaviors, this is either concurrent or predictive validity. In personality research there is generally no specific criterion by which to evaluate a test. Instead, construct validity is important, and the question is: "To what are scores on the instrument related?" Tests may be constructed by the intuitive approach, the internal consistency or bootstrap approach, and by the use of an external criterion with either a correlational or an experimental methodology.

The study of personality development is of potential importance to both theory and application. Speculations about the heritability of behavioral characteristics are of ancient origin, but detailed knowledge of the laws of heredity began in 1865 with Mendel's work with pea plants. The study of human behavior genetics has included the family resemblances method with early studies on family pedigrees and much better research on the comparison of fraternal and identical twins. By capitalizing on experiments of nature, psychologists have compared the similarity of adopted children and their natural versus their foster parents and have examined the similarity of identical twins reared separately versus those reared together. The laboratory method of selective breeding is used with nonhuman subjects. Developmental research has also been concerned with the prenatal period. The greatest amount of research on personality development has been with the effects of early experience on behavior. Some studies have dealt with the responses of either a parent or a child along with that person's perception of the other. Other experiments involve the direct and independent investigation of parents and their children. Because of the relatively narrow range of child-rearing practices within a single culture, some investigators have turned to cross-cultural research. Experimental studies of children involve the application of the concepts and methodology of general experimental psychology to child subjects and the study of personality in a laboratory setting. In addition, the effects of early experiences are sometimes investigated in laboratory experiments with animals.

Personality structure involves the representation of the interrelationship among personality variables. The establishment of a relationship between responses indicates a link between them, the cause of which may be sought in subsequent research. There may be common genetic factors, common learning experiences, or some combination of the two which results in a relationship between responses.

Personality dynamics refers to research in which behavior is studied with respect to both a stimulus variable and a personality variable. Work on personality dynamics brings together the two major research emphases of situational determinants and individual differences.

Though a major focus in the study of individual differences is on the unchanging aspects of behavior, there is also concern with the possibility of bringing about changes in behavior. Personality change can be brought about by deliberate procedures and as a by-product of other events. This type of research is the source of more optimism and more fears than any other in the study of individual differences.

4

Authoritarianism

An attitude is a predisposition to respond either positively or negatively toward an object or a class of objects. Each of us holds a large number of relatively enduring beliefs, opinions, and values which involve attitudinal elements. Subjectively, our attitudes appear to be relatively independent of one another and seem to be based, at least in one's own case, on an objective evaluation of factual evidence. An individual feels that his judgments about the Catholic Church, liberal political philosophy, communism, radicals, modern novels, labor unions, pornography, nuclear testing, television programming, big business, sports cars, and everything else are those which would be made by any sensible person who knew the facts. The possibility that such attitudes are the inevitable consequents of past experiences or that these judgments tend to group themselves in ideological clusters is not readily acceptable. One of the best examples of personality research directed toward an attitudinal variable is provided by work on authoritarianism. Authoritarianism refers to an attitudinal system which consists of interrelated antidemocratic sentiments including ethnic prejudice, political conservatism, and a moralistic rejection of the unconventional.

HISTORICAL BACKGROUND

The streets of our country are in turmoil. The universities are filled with students rebelling and rioting. Communists are seeking to destroy our country.

Russia is threatening us with her might and the Republic is in danger. Yes, danger from within and from without. We need law and order. Yes, without law and order our nation cannot survive. Elect us and we shall restore law and order. (Adolph Hitler, Hamburg, 1932)

Our psychological interest in authoritarianism owes a debt, of sorts, to Adolf Hitler. When the Nazi party obtained political power in Germany in 1933, the world witnessed the formation of one of the most thorough-going authoritarian regimes to control a major nation in modern times. Authoritarian ideology and its associated behaviors pervaded every aspect of German life. Prompted in large part by the horrors of Hitler's systematic and barbarous anti-Semitism, the American Jewish Committee established a Department of Scientific Research for the purpose of initiating fundamental studies of prejudice and of stimulating such studies by others. This group was interested in learning the characteristics of those who establish authoritarian societies and of those who readily accept this ideology. Specifically, they hoped to be able to identify and describe the *potentially* fascistic individual and to seek the determinants of this pattern of behavior. It was hoped that a scientific understanding of authoritarianism would provide the means to prevent its future reappearance in Germany or in any other nation.

Among the products of the research directed toward such problems was a monumental work entitled *The Authoritarian Personality* by T. W. Adorno of the Institute of Social Research, Else Frenkel-Brunswik of the University of California, Daniel J. Levinson of the Harvard Medical School, and R. Nevitt Sanford of the University of California. The work of this group and their colleagues was carried out throughout the late 1940's and was published in 1950. Their interests ranged over ethnocentrism, anti-Semitism, antidemocratic ideology, and political and religious beliefs. Their methods included a unique and fruitful blend of clinical insight and empirical research. The impact of this project on subsequent psychological theory and research has continued to be strong for over two decades.

THEORETICAL BACKGROUND

The underlying theory of the nature of the authoritarian personality was based on many sources—previous research, psychoanalytic theory, observations of actual behavior, and attempts to make theoretical sense out of the diverse characteristics of the fascists in control of Nazi Germany. Fromm's (1941) description of the sometimes empty values of modern man in a "free" society was another source of ideas. Nine variables were postulated as representing central trends in an authoritarian individual. The plan of the Berkeley investigators was to form a tentative definition of authoritarian characteristics and then to construct test items to measure these characteristics. In general, authoritarians were described as individuals who use repressive defenses to control their sexual and aggressive needs and who develop conforming, submissive, conventional patterns of interpersonal behavior. Their own repressed sexuality is projected onto others, and their repressed hostility is both projected outward and expressed in "justifiable" ways (for example, against the enemies of the nation or against those who violate the laws). In the descriptions of the specific characteristics given below, the definitions are taken from Adorno et al. (1950), but many of the examples are drawn from more recent events.

CONVENTIONALISM

Rigid Adherence to Conventional, Middle-Class Values. The proposal that conventionalism constituted a factor in the authoritarian make-up was based on the observations that (1) facism characteristically develops in conventional middle-class environments and (2) unconventional individuals tend to be free of prejudice. The fact that a great many conventional individuals are democratic, tolerant, and equalitarian in outlook presented some problems. It was, therefore, proposed that when conventional values are based on a well developed superego, such values are not related to antidemocratic trends. When the values are external in origin, however, a different situation exists. An individual whose ideas of right and wrong are simply a function of contemporary, external social pressure would be expected to be receptive to antidemocratic ideology. The difference is seen, for example, in those who truly value the American ideals of democracy, freedom of speech, and equality versus those whose values seem to represent only a shallow, flag-waving patriotism. "America—love it or leave it." While this distinction between two different types of conventional behavior makes sense, it is a difficult distinction to make operationally and one which would be hard to translate into test items. That is, subjects would have to indicate the basis of their conventionalism, not just their beliefs and behavior.

AUTHORITARIAN SUBMISSION

Submissive, Uncritical Attitude toward Idealized Moral Authorities of the Ingroup. Because the Nazi creed stressed submission to authority, desire for a strong leader, and the subservience of the individual to the state, this type of submission was included among the probable characteristics of authoritarians. In writing the items, the guess was made that authoritarian submission would characterize the individual's relationship to all authority figures— parents, older people, supernatural beings, or anyone who could be seen as a leader. "I did not question the orders. I only obeyed them" Complete submissiveness was hypothesized to occur because of a deficiency in superego development. In addition, the threat of having any negative or hostile feelings toward authority could lead to a defensive overemphasis on the reverse, the submission to such authority.

AUTHORITARIAN AGGRESSION

Tendency to Be on the Lookout for, and to Condemn, Reject, and Punish, People Who Violate Conventional Values. It was hypothesized that individuals who are forced to adhere completely to a conventional mold and to submit to authority without complaint would necessarily experience feelings of hostility. The outward expression of this hostility would seem most justifiable (and most safe) if it could be directed toward those who violate whatever is conventional. "I don't hate my father; it's the hippies who make my blood boil." Thus, hostility is displaced from the appropriate targets in the ingroup onto inappropriate targets in the outgroup. The latter, depending on the particular environmental circumstances, could consist of Jews, communists, sexual offenders, members of the Women's Liberation Movement, or any other identifiable group. Not only is the authoritarian able to give vent to his hostility, but he does so for "good" reasons based primarily on a distorted version of religious morality and patriotic concerns.

DESTRUCTION AND CYNICISM

Generalized Hostility; Vilification of the Human. In addition to displacing hostility onto outgroups, another outlet for authoritarians is a generalized hostility which includes the expression of aggression toward mankind, contempt for human nature, and cynicism concerning the motives of others. Among other things, one's own hostility is more acceptable if everybody acts that way or if it is seen as natural. "Everybody's out for a fast buck. People are no damn good."

POWER AND TOUGHNESS

Preoccupation with the Dominance-Submission, Strong-Weak, Leader-Follower Dimension; Identification with Power Figures; Overemphasis upon the Conventionalized Attributes of the Ego; Exaggerated Assertion of Strength and Toughness. Because of internal weaknesses and fears, the authoritarian is hypothesized to react with an overemphasis on strength and power—his own and that of his group. It is especially important to have a leader who provides power and to be identified as a member of a group with such attributes: strongest nation on earth, master race, world-wide communist movement, and so forth. The authoritarians would be expected to submit completely to the orders of such power sources and, in turn, to be ruthless in exercising power when the situation arises. An example would be a Gestapo underling who obeyed his superiors without question and displayed his own tyranny over his subordinates and victims. "Might makes right."

SUPERSTITION AND STEREOTYPY

The Belief in Mystical Determinants of the Individual's Fate; the Disposition to Think in Rigid Categories. Among the mechanisms which may account for the authoritarian's belief in mystical and fantastic forces is the tendency to avoid personal responsibility for various feelings, acts, and consequences by placing the blame on outside forces rather than on oneself. If some unknowable factor is responsible for what happens, the individual is guiltless. "The war must be just with God on our side." "It was written in the stars." By stereotypy, or the disposition to think in rigid categories, is meant the tendency to resort to primitive, oversimplified, black-and-white explanations of human affairs. Successful authoritarian leaders capitalize on these tendencies by providing a simple rationale for past difficulties and future achievements. Such complex events as war, depression, crime, and a utopian society emerge as straightforward problems with straightforward solutions promised by slogans and catch phrases. In addition, these leaders do well when they attach elements of the mysterious to themselves and their regime. An authoritarian ruler is wise to provide himself with supernatural ancestors, as did Roman and Japanese emperors. They appear in public rarely and then only with pomp and ceremony, as with the spectacular Nazi rallies with searchlights, banners, and gigantic stage settings. Their destiny is mystically intertwined with that of the nation, they are free from illness, and they have divine protection from assassins.

ANTI-INTRACEPTION

Opposition to the Subjective, the Imaginative, the Tender-Minded. It was hypothesized that authoritarians tend to respond to concrete, clearly observable, tangible facts and to oppose reliance on feelings, fantasies, speculations, and imagination. "Keep your feet on the ground and your head out of the clouds." The underlying dynamics are suggested as fear of "wrong" thoughts, of feelings and emotions which might get out of hand. The sort of "prying into the mind" that is characteristic of psychological testing and psychotherapy is viewed with great suspicion and concern. Interestingly enough, prying by governmental authorities on external behavior by means of wiretapping or secret agents is seen as acceptable. Totalitarian nations and authoritarian political groups also tend to reject any artistic endeavor which tends to arouse frightening or dangerous thoughts and feelings. Thus, censorship of art, including books, movies, and plays, seems necessary and right to the authoritarian. The greatest dangers come from creative material which is sexually arousing or which contains ideas that are critical of those in power.

PROJECTIVITY

The Disposition to Believe that Wild and Dangerous Things Go on in the World; the Projection Outwards of Unconscious Emotional Impulses. One of the most pervasive characteristics of authoritarians, as postulated by the Berkeley group, is the ability to transfer internal problems to the external world—taboo impulses, weaknesses, fears, responsibilities. Thus, the authoritarian sees the most unacceptable aspects of himself in the world around him. Especially prominant are the projections of sexual and aggressive impulses. He is surrounded by depraved individuals engaging in sexual excesses—outgroup members, foreigners, people in high places, college students, neighbors. Equally rampant in the world around him is hostility—crime waves, subversion, plots in the government, threats from abroad. "At least half the college professors are Commies and most of the rest are pansies." Such projection shades rather easily into paranoid delusions, and the beliefs of authoritarians sometime assume a rather bizarre form. For example, stories were widely circulated in 1963 that the government was secretly training cannibals in Georgia and that millions of Red Chinese troops were massed just over the Mexican border. In 1970, a syndicated columnist reported that all of the student unrest in the United States had been planned years ago by a secret group which met outside of Prague.

SEX

Exaggerated Concern with Sexual "Goings-on." The authors of the authoritarian scale felt that sexual concerns were sufficiently basic to give this characteristic a prominent and separate position in their description. As has been discussed, there is the desire to punish those who violate sexual standards, to censor sexual material, and to project sexual excesses onto others. It is suggested that for authoritarians, sexual impulses must be strongly attached to anxiety cues. The anxiety is reduced by means of projection of the impulses onto others and by an expression of hostility toward those who express such impulses. "I would never even think of engaging in premarital intercourse, but half of the kids down at the high school belong to wild sex clubs." In terms of Freudian theory, unresolved Oedipal complexes would lead to the association of incestuous fears with any unrestrained sexual activity.

CONSTRUCTION OF THE CALIFORNIA F SCALE

BUILDING THE SCALE

Tests were first built to measure such specific characteristics as anti-Semitism, ethnocentrism, and conservatism. Then, the investigators attempted to measure the more general concept of authoritarianism by writing test items which corresponded to their theoretical description. The Fascist Scale (or F Scale) was to become the most valuable of these instruments. An effort was made to write items which were indirect and which were neither too obviously irrational nor too objectively factual. Each item was written in the form of a declaratory statement, and the subject was asked to respond by indicating the appropriate degree of agreement on a scale as follows:

Response	Score
Strong support, agreement	7
Moderate support, agreement	6
Slight support, agreement	5
Slight opposition, disagreement	3
Moderate opposition, disagreement	2
Strong opposition, disagreement	1

(omitted items receive a score of 4)

In the first scale which was assembled, 38 items were written, mixed with other items in a questionnaire, and administered to four large groups of subjects. The split-half reliability of the F Scale was .74. The responses of this group of subjects were used for item-analysis. The discriminatory power technique was employed. The mean item score of the lowest scoring 25 percent was subtracted from the mean item score of the highest scoring 25 percent *for each item.* The larger the difference, the better the item distinguished between those with the highest and lowest scores on the entire test and hence the better the discriminatory power (DP) of the item.[1] A DP of zero would mean that the item was not measuring what the rest of the scale was measuring.

In an effort to improve the measuring instrument, the Berkeley group constructed a second version of the F Scale. They retained the nineteen best items of the first scale, rewrote four of the worst items, and devised eleven new ones. This second form of the F Scale was administered to five large groups of subjects. The item-analysis and subsequent revision were well worth the effort in that the new split-half reliability was found to be .87.

---

[1] The authors also considered each item's discriminatory power with respect to the Anti-Semitism Scale, but for reasons of clarity the present discussion will omit that analysis.

Once again, the DP of each item was obtained in order to provide a basis for an improved third version of the scale.

For the third scale, more items were discarded and a few new ones were added. This final F Scale was administered to over fifteen hundred subjects. The reliability was found to be .90. Thus, the test measured authoritarianism consistently enough to warrant its utilization in research. The items in this final scale and the specific characteristics of authoritarianism which each was designed to measure are shown in Table 4-1 in the order of their DPs. The first item shown in the table is the best measure of authoritarian ideology, the second item the second best, and so forth.

Table 4-1. The California F Scale

Rank	DP	Item
1	4.00	Sex crimes, such as rape and attacks on children, deserve more than mere imprisonment; such criminals ought to be publicly whipped, or worse. (AA, S)
2	3.82	What the youth needs most is strict discipline, rugged determination, and the will to work and fight for family and country. (AA, PT)
3	3.71	There is hardly anything lower than a person who does not feel a great love, gratitude, and respect for his parents. (AA)
4	3.56	Every person should have complete faith in some supernatural power whose decisions he obeys without question. (AS, SS)
5	3.38	Young people sometimes get rebellious ideas, but as they grow up they ought to get over them and settle down. (AS)
6.5	3.31	Obedience and respect for authority are the most important virtues children should learn. (C, AS)
6.5	3.31	Homosexuals are hardly better than criminals and ought to be severely punished. (AA, S)
8.5	3.17	Nowadays when so many different kinds of people move around and mix together so much, a person has to protect himself especially carefully against catching an infection or disease from them. (P)
8.5	3.17	People can be divided into two distinct classes: the weak and the strong. (SS, PT)
10	3.16	No sane, normal, decent person could ever think of hurting a close friend or relative. (AS)
11	3.06	Some day it will probably be shown that astrology can explain a lot of things. (SS)
12	3.00	Nowadays more and more people are prying into matters that should remain personal and private. (AI, P)
13	2.97	If people would talk less and work more, everybody would be better off. (C, AA, AI)
14	2.93	An insult to our honor should always be punished. (AA, PT)
15	2.88	Most of our social problems would be solved if we could somehow get rid of the immoral, crooked, and feeble-minded people. (AA)
16	2.83	When a person has a problem or worry, it is best for him not to think about it, but to keep busy with more cheerful things. (AI)

Table 4-1. (cont.)

Rank	DP	Item
17	2.72	Science has its place, but there are many important things that can never possibly be understood by the human mind. (AS, SS)
18	2.71	The wild sex life of the old Greeks and Romans was tame compared to some of the goings-on in this country, even in places where people might least expect it. (P, S)
19	2.65	Human nature being what it is, there will always be war and conflict. (DS)
20	2.64	The true American way of life is disappearing so fast that force may be necessary to preserve it. (DC)
21	2.60	What this country needs most, more than laws and political programs, is a few courageous, tireless, devoted leaders in whom the people can put their faith. (AS, PT)
22	2.58	No weakness or difficulty can hold us back if we have enough will power. (PT)
23	2.55	Familiarity breeds contempt. (DC)
24	2.51	Some people are born with an urge to jump from high places. (SS)
25	2.26	Most people don't realize how much our lives are controlled by plots hatched in secret places. (PT, P)
26	2.19	A person who has bad manners, habits, and breeding can hardly expect to get along with decent people. (C, AA)
27	2.00	Nobody ever learned anything really important except through suffering. (AS)
28	1.98	Wars and social troubles may someday be ended by an earthquake or flood that will destory the whole world. (SS, P)
29	1.73	The business man and the manufacturer are much more important to society than the artist and the professor. (C, AI)

Key: C = Conventionalism; AS = Authoritarian Submission; AA = Authoritarian Aggression; DC = Destructiveness and Cynicism; PT = Power and "Toughness"; SS = Superstition and Stereotypy; AI = Anti-intraception; P = Projectivity; S = Sex.

ANTECEDENTS OF AUTHORITARIANISM

THEORETICAL CONSIDERATIONS

The most obvious origins of a system of attitudes and beliefs such as authoritarianism would seem to lie in the early experiences between an individual, his parents, and others. Two kinds of influence seem likely. Of greatest importance are those forces which contribute to the development of the underlying characteristics of a fascist orientation: repression, denial of aggressive and sexual impulses, projection, and displacement. In addition, there must be contact with the specific ideas and beliefs that form the content of authoritarian ideology.

In the original Berkeley studies, a number of clinical investigations (utilizing interviews, case histories, and projective tests) were carried out in order to provide information about the highest and lowest scoring subjects. These observations led to many hypotheses which could be confirmed or refuted in future research.

Of course, when subjects talk about their parents or their childhood experiences, these recollections may or may not be accurate representations of what actually happened. The position taken by the Berkeley group, however, was that all such material was of potential importance in understanding differences between those high and low in prejudice, ethnocentrism, and authoritarianism. On the basis of the material that was collected, several conclusions were tentatively drawn concerning differing family experiences of those who gave extremely authoritarian or extremely equalitarian responses. Subjects high in authoritarianism reported that relatively harsh and threatening discipline was used by their parents. The child was expected to be submissive and to suppress unacceptable impulses. The family seemed to be anxious about status and to stress rigid conventional values as a way to succeed socially. Such values were simply imposed by the parents and not really integrated by the offspring. Because parents became morally indignant when their child failed to conform, he later expressed moral indignation toward anyone else who behaved according to different values. Any rules and ideas seemed to represent a set of cliches to be memorized. The relationships in the home were based on prescribed roles with an emphasis on duties and obligations rather than on affection. Any expression of hostility toward the parents was forbidden, and the child tended to overreact by glorifying and idealizing them in a stereotyped fashion. Male authoritarians, expecially, reported having a "stern and distant" father who made them feel weak and helpless. Among other things, the son would later try to be strong like his father by being aggressive and stressing rugged masculinity.

With respect to the equalitarian individuals on the opposite end of the prejudice-ethnocentrism-authoritarianism continuum, family characteristics are described more or less as the reverse of those outlined above. That is, less obedience is expected of the children, and parents are less status-ridden, less anxious about conformity, and less intolerant of socially unacceptable behavior. Equalitarian individuals report more affection within their families, and they seem more emotionally free.

TRADITIONAL FAMILY IDEOLOGY

Among the many hypotheses which emerge from the foregoing material, several basic contrasts in family structure and functioning seemed to differentiate authoritarians and equaliterions. Levinson and Huffman (1955) termed the general beliefs of the autocratic extreme as "Traditional Family Ideology" and predicted that the democratic-autocratic dimension of family structure would be found to be associated with the equalitarian-authoritarian dimension of personality.

Their first step was the construction of a scale to measure attitudes about family organization: the Traditional Family Ideology (TFI) Scale. This instrument was conceptualized as an extension or application of the material from the clinical interviews discussed above. The five major characteristics of autocratic families included in the TFI Scale were conventionalism (emphasis on conformity, cleanliness, practicality, and upward mobility), authoritarian submission (emphasis on obedience), exaggerated masculinity and femininity (emphasis on role differences between the sexes), discipline (emphasis on rules and punishment for violating the rules), and a moralistic rejection of desires (emphasis on inhibition and denial of emotions, especially sex and hostility).

The original TFI Scale consisted of 40 items to which subjects responded on an agree-disagree basis. This test was found to have a split-half reliability of .92. Levinson and Huffman performed an item-analysis, using the Discriminatory Power technique. Five of the items failed to discriminate high and low scorers and were discarded. Of the remaining 35 items, the seven best ones were:

A child should not be allowed to talk back to his parents, or else he will lose respect for them.

The family is a sacred institution, divinely ordained.

Women who want to remove the word obey from the marriage service don't understand what it means to be a wife.

There is a lot of evidence such as the Kinsey Report which shows we have to crack down harder on young people to save our moral standards.

A man can scarcely maintain respect for his fiancee if they have sexual relations before they are married.

Some equality in marriage is a good thing, but by and large the husband ought to have the main say-so in family matters.

It goes against nature to place women in positions of authority over men.

In the initial investigations with this instrument, the TFI and the California F Scale were found to correlate about .70. Authoritarianism appears to be associated with adherence to traditional family ideology. Levinson and Huffman rightly indicated that this correlational finding should be considered an initial step in a series of investigations of the antecedents of authoritarian characteristics. The correlation between the two tests suggests the possibility that authoritarians are raised in autocratic homes, equalitarians in democratic homes. One could guess that the nature of these homes and the interpersonal interactions in them are largely responsible for later differences in authoritarians and equalitarians.

CROSS-CULTURAL STUDIES

Descriptions of the family characteristics of authoritarians very often contain words such as "traditional" and "conventional" which reflect an "old-fashioned" and "old-world" way of organizing families and raising children. Such families are contrasted with the more "modern" and "progressive" American spirit of equality and permissiveness and Dr. Spock. One implication of this contrast is that, as a group, Americans should be lower in authoritarianism than the citizens of various countries, especially of countries in which family traditions change very little over time. In a similar way, the children of newly arrived immigrants to this country should be higher in authoritarianism than the offspring of families who arrived earlier and hence are more thoroughly assimilated.

Turkish-American Comparisons. Kagitcibasi (1970) observed that the typical Turkish family is restrictive with respect to discipline though combining this restrictiveness with emotional warmth. On the average, one would expect to find a much greater proportion of traditional, father-dominated, restrictive families and hence a higher mean level of authoritarianism in Turkey than in the United States.

His subjects consisted of a large group of high school students in Turkey and in the San Francisco area. As expected, the Turkish students were higher in authoritarianism than were the American students. In addition, the Turkish subjects scored higher than the Americans in patriotism, rejection of foreigners, and respect for authority.

Mexican-American Anglo-American Comparisons. Ramirez (1967) has pointed out the similarity between the Mexican family structure and that of authoritarians in that both are characterized by dominating fathers, strict discipline, and a strict separation of sex roles.

> Both the Mexican and high authoritarian families are typically father dominated and employ strict child-rearing methods emphasizing submission and strong obedience to the will and dictates of authority figures. In both groups interrelationships are based on roles of dominance and submission and both believe in strict separation of the sex roles.

Thus, the average Mexican-American should be more authoritarian than the average Anglo-American. To test this hypothesis, Ramirez obtained college students from each group to serve as subjects. They were given the F Scale and a special scale dealing with family values. As expected, the Mexican-American subjects scored significantly higher on the F Scale than did the Anglo-American subjects. Similar differences were found on the items dealing with family values. For example, the Mexican-American subjects were much more likely to agree with items suggesting that the mother should be the dearest person in existence for the child, that it helps a child in the long run if he is made to conform to his parents' ideas, that the word of an adult should never be questioned, and that it does no good to try to change the future because the future is in the hands of God. Ramirez speculated that adherence to these values could be a source of continuing conflict as these individuals are caught between the Mexican and Anglo cultures.

DISCIPLINARY TECHNIQUES

Contained within the description of the autocratic family are a number of specific elements. In his doctoral dissertation at Duke, Hart (1957) focused on one of these: disciplinary techniques.

The way in which parents attempt to control their children's behavior in the socialization situation has been hypothesized as one of the consequents of authoritarianism-equalitarianism and also as one of the antecedents of that personality dimension. Hart utilized the Whiting and Child (1953) conceptualization of punishment techniques: a dimension varying from love-oriented to nonlove-oriented. The former serve to maintain the child's striving for parental affection and include denial of love, threats of denial of reward, and threats of ostracism. Nonlove-oriented techniques, on the other hand, tend to focus on the importance of obeying rules and on punishment when the rules are violated. Included are physical punishment, threats of physical punishment, and ridicule. On the basis of earlier speculations by Adorno, et al. and by Levinson and Huffman, Hart hypothesized that authoritarian parents would select nonlove-oriented techniques in disciplining their children.

A group of mothers was selected for study; each had at least one preschool child. Individual interviews were scheduled, and each mother was asked a series of questions about her most probable response to her child's behavior in a series of situations such as not eating, handling genitals, and destroying property. The mothers were also given the F Scale. Three judges decided which disciplinary category the mothers' responses indicated. Two out of three judges had to agree for the scoring to be made.

To test the hypothesis concerning the relationship between disciplinary techniques and authoritarianism, each mother's F Scale score was correlated with the number of situations in which she indicated that she would respond with a nonlove-oriented technique. The correlation was .63, thus confirming the hypothesis.

PERMISSIVENESS-RESTRICTIVENESS

Block (1955) at the Institute of Personality Assessment and Research at the University of California administered a group of items dealing with "restrictiveness" versus "permissiveness" in child-rearing attitudes to a group of military officers. Restrictive statements included:

When adults are entertaining, a child should "be seen but not heard."
Firm and strict discipline makes for strong character in later life.
Children need some of the natural meanness taken out of them.

Permissive statements included:

A child should be permitted to have secrets from his parents.
Jealousy among brothers and sisters is a very common thing.
Children have a right to make a mess just for the fun of it.

On the basis of responses to the items, the most and least restrictive fathers were selected for additional study. The restrictive group was found to score significantly higher on the F Scale than the permissive group.

On the basis of the various correlational findings that have been reported, we may reasonably speculate that a circular pattern of cause and effect links child-rearing practices and authoritarianism. The relationships are shown schematically in Figure 4-1. The authoritarian or equalitarian characteris-

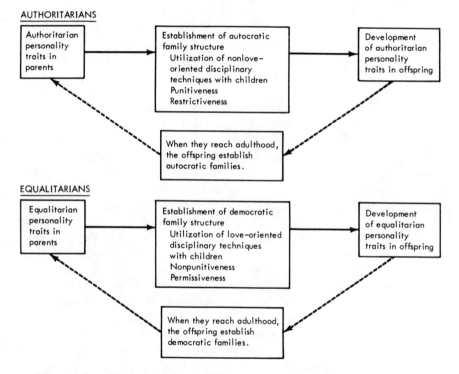

Fig. 4-1 Possible Antecedents and Consequents of Authoritarianism.

tics of parents lead them to structure their families and raise their children in quite different ways. The consequences for the children include the development of personality characteristics like those of the parents. On reaching adulthood, these individuals repeat the pattern, and so it continues from generation to generation.

Authoritarianism and Traditional Family Ideology
Across Generations

In order to confirm the sort of relationships depicted in Figure 4-1, a great deal of additional research must be undertaken. The major flaw in the data thus far presented is the reliance on intra-individual approaches in which scores on the F Scale are found to be related to some other behavior within a group of subjects. Two untested assumptions are built into the generalizations about the child-rearing antecedents of authoritarianism. Husbands and wives are tacitly assumed to be similar to one another in both authoritarianism and in child-rearing practices. Even more strongly, parental authoritarianism and child-rearing techniques are assumed to lead to the development of these same characteristics in their offspring. Without studying husband-wife and parent-child relationships, assessing the probable accuracy of these formulations is not possible.

In an attempt to answer such questions, Byrne (1965) administered the F Scale and TFI Scale to a group of college students plus the mothers and fathers of each. As in the studies reported earlier, the correlation between the two tests was substantial (r = .62 for students, r = .61 for fathers, r = .61 for mothers). Across generations, however, the relationships are considerably smaller. For the male students, their F Scale scores correlated only .33 with the TFI scores of their fathers and .14 (not significant) with the TFI scores of their mothers. For the female students, the corresponding coefficients were .10 and .14, neither of which is statistically significant. The most useful information for predicting authoritarianism in the offspring was found to be the F Scale scores of each parent. If the authoritarianism of both parents is considered, a multiple correlation of .40 for male offspring and .33 for female offsping is found. Though such relationships mean that we can predict the level of authoritarianism of an individual with a moderate degree of accuracy on the basis of knowledge about his parents' scores, it seems that other variables must also be involved.

One possible clue lies in differences between the parents. Similarity between husbands and wives was significantly greater than zero for each scale (r = .30 for the F Scale and r = .26 for the TFI Scale), but the relationships are not very large. When the parents were divided into high, medium, and low thirds on the basis of their authoritarian scores, all possible patterns of husband-wife combinations were found. It was suggested that the influence of parental authoritarianism on the ideology of their offspring could quite possibly be affected by such husband-wife differences. For example, a family with an authoritarian father and equalitarian mother might have a different effect on children than a family with the reverse pattern; similarly, such husband-wife differences could affect sons and daughters differently. Authoritarian offspring were found to be most likely to develop in families in which neither parent is low F and the same-sexed parent is high F. Equalitarian offspring are most likely to be found in families in which at least one parent is low F and the same-sexed parent is not high F.

We may conclude that the rather simple picture that has been drawn in the past to contrast authoritarian and equalitarian home atmospheres and their effects on offspring will need to be replaced by a somewhat more complicated description of family patterns and their effects.

THE PLACE OF AUTHORITARIANISM IN THE STRUCTURE OF PERSONALITY

A great many of the investigations of the California F Scale have consisted of establishing correlational relationships with other personality dimensions and with behavior in various types of situations. A few of these findings will be described.

PREJUDICE

One of the initial reasons for developing the F Scale was the desire by Adorno, et al., to construct a scale that would measure prejudice in a relatively indirect way without mentioning any minority group by name. Authoritarianism was conceptualized as a general trait, while prejudice toward any specific group represented a particular manifestation of the trait. Two of the other scales which the Berkeley group developed dealt with prejudice more directly, and the F Scale was expected to correlate with these measures.

The group's starting point in the study of prejudice was an investigation of anti-Semitism, partly because the world had recently witnessed what happens when the horror of prejudice is carried to an extreme and partly because of the long unhappy history of the Jewish people as the objects of bigotry and persecution. The suggestion was made that organized anti-Semitism presents a major threat to democracy because it serves as a rallying-cry for antidemocratic political movements. As Levinson put it:

> The irrational quality in anti-Semitism stands out even in casual everyday discussions. The fact that people make general statements about "the Jew," when the Jews are actually so heterogenerous—belong to every socioeconomic class and represent every degree of assimilation—is vivid evidence of this irrationality. This striking contrast between the Jews' actual complexity and their supposed homogeneity has suggested the hypothesis that what people say against Jews depends more upon their own psychology than upon the actual characteristics of Jews (Adorno, et al., 1950, p. 57).

The Anti-Semitism (A-S) Scale included the following type of items:

I can hardly imagine myself marrying a Jew.
There may be a few exceptions, but in general Jews are pretty much alike.

The trouble with letting Jews into a nice neighborhood is that they gradually give it a typical Jewish atmosphere.

In some of the original investigations of the A-S and F Scales, the two tests correlated .53. Thus, as was hypothesized, authoritarianism is positively related to espousal of anti-Jewish attitudes.

Still another part of the original series of authoritarian studies dealt with ethnocentrism. Ethnocentrism refers to cultural narrowness, the tendency to accept one's own culture while rejecting anything different from it. The Ethnocentrism (E) Scale which was constructed included items from the A-S Scale along with such additional items as:

The worst danger to real Americanism during the last 50 years has come from foreign ideas and agitators.

Filipinos are all right in their place, but they carry it too far when they dress lavishly and go around with white girls.

It is only natural and right for each person to think that his family is better than any other.

The E Scale was found to correlate .73 with the F Scale. Thus, a strong tendency exists for authoritarianism to be associated with ethnocentrism.

In the United States, perhaps the central object of prejudice is the Negro race. Because of the number of individuals involved and the complex historical and legal elements intermixed, psychological and sociological studies of antiblack prejudice have tended to predominate in investigations of bigotry. Probably in part because other factors (for example, regional differences) serve to confound the relationships, authoritarianism is generally found not to be as highly correlated with attitudes toward blacks as might be expected from the anti-Semitism and ethnocentrism findings. The relationship between the F Scale and measures of antiblack prejudice has been reported to be as low as .17 (Klein, 1963) and as high as .33 (Kelly, Ferson, and Holtzman, 1958). Both coefficients are statistically significant, but of relatively low magnitude.

HOSTILITY

One of the basic characteristics originally ascribed to the high authoritarian individual is that of hostility. This hostility is hypothesized to be a generalized drive but it is directed primarily toward outgroups and toward those who violate cultural norms. Many of the items on the F Scale were designed to reflect this hostile component. In addition to the prejudice studies, other empirical evidence also supports the hostility hypothesis.

In his doctoral dissertation at Case Western Reserve University, Meer (1955) investigated the hostility of authoritarians as revealed in their dreams.

From a group of undergraduates, high-authoritarian and low-authoritarian subjects were selected. Dream reports had been collected during the semester by the students' instructors. High and low authoritarians did not differ in how many dreams they reported having. Each dream was scored by a judge for aggressive and friendly encounters with various characters appearing in the dreams. Characters were divided into members of the ingroup (family members, friends, and acquaintances) and of the outgroup (strangers). The intensity of the aggression was scored on a scale ranging from "feeling hostile but no outward expression" to "intentional killing." Those high in authoritarianism reported significantly more aggression toward outgroup characters than toward ingroup characters; those low in authoritarianism did not show this difference. With respect to friendly acts, authoritarians reported significantly more such acts with ingroup than with outgroup members; again, equalitarians did not make the differentiation. Even in their dreams, authoritarians seem to make a distinction between the ingroup and the outgroup.

Both on the basis of the general background description of authoritarianism and on the basis of the child-rearing data, one might expect to find that authoritarians are convinced that punishment and retaliation are the best way to solve problems. When President Kennedy was assassinated, Sherwood (1966) hypothesized that authoritarians would be most likely to respond with righteous indignation and to be concerned with blame and punishment. He compared this kind of response with what Piaget calls "moral realism" in children. That is, from about three to eight years of age children tend to view both rules and the punishments for violating them as givens which remain unquestioned and unchangeable. Tied in with this view of the world is a conception of justice in which the wrongdoer should suffer with a punishment that fits the crime. It seemed to Sherwood that adult authoritarians would respond in the same as was way observed by Piaget in children. One week after the assassination in Dallas, questionnaires were mailed to a group of past and present officers of various Midwestern organizations which had expressed public concern with "Americanism"; the same questionnaires were also given to liberal arts college students. The organization sample was not only higher in authoritarianism than the students, but their mean score was one of the highest ever reported. In Table 4-2 are shown some of the items which differentiated the two groups.

A follow-up experiment involved a management problem which a group of industrial administration students was asked to study and then to recommend the best course of action. Once again, high authoritarians in the group were much more likely to recommend punishment as a solution than were the equalitarians. Sherwood concluded that the morality of authoritarian adults is much like that observed in small children.

Perhaps the extreme manifestation of hostility is in warfare. Again, it would be expected that authoritarians would differ from equalitarians in

Table 4-2. Comparison of Authoritarians and Equalitarians in Responding to Questions about the Assassination of President Kennedy

	Authoritarians	Equalitarians
The assassination of the President was part of the Communist conspiracy.	4.51	1.95
The most important consideration facing the nation after President Kennedy's death is finding who is guilty and punishing him.	5.32	2.44
Lee Harvey Oswald got what was coming to him when he was shot.	6.03	3.31
The important thing is that the wrongdoer should suffer.	4.81	2.21
Rewards and punishments should be decided by those in charge, even if it means unequal punishments for the same crime.	5.05	2.63
We spend too much time worrying about being just and fair when we know all the time that someone is guilty.	4.87	2.12

(After Sherwood, 1966, pp. 266–67)
On each item, 7 = strongly agree and 1 = strongly disagree.

their attitudes about warfare. The conflict in Vietnam provided an especially relevant attitudinal topic in that opinions about various aspects of the American presence in Vetnam were sharply divided and strongly expressed. Izzett (1971) predicted a relationship between such opinions and authoritarianism in that pro-Vietnam war attitudes correspond to the official government position while anti-Vietnam war attitudes constitute a break with authority. The proposed relationships were studied by going to a direct measure of relevant behavior. On October 15, 1969, a great many individuals participated in a moratorium on the war. Izzett hypothesized that students who observed the moratorium by refusing to attend classes on that day would have significantly lower F Scale scores than the students who did attend classes. In addition, a paper and pencil questionnaire dealing with attitudes about the war was expected to show that authoritarians were more prowar than equalitarians. A large group of students at the State University of New York at Oswego was administered the F Scale and a series of items dealing with the Vietnam war. At the class meeting before the Vietnam moratorium day, it was announced that classes would be held as usual but that students should follow the dictates of their own beliefs with respect to coming to class on that day. It was found that the students who observed moratorium day by staying away from class had significantly lower F Scale scores than those who attended class. On the questionnaire items, authoritarianism was positively related to responses indicating that the United States should invade North Vietnam, resume bombing of North Vietnam, and send more troops and supplies to South Vietnam. Authoritarianism was negatively related to responses indicating that the United States should withdraw its troops immediately and that the United States should press for a coalition government in South Vietnam which included the Viet Cong. Individuals scoring low in authoritarianism have also been found to be more likely to engage in protest actions against the war such as signing petitions, writing letters to political leaders, and attending antiwar rallies (Granberg & Corrigan, 1972). Thus, both in questionnaire responses and in their overt behavioral acts, authoritarians and equalitarians were shown to respond quite differently to U.S. military involvement in Southeast Asia.

Sexual Behavior and Attitudes

Concerns with sexuality and sexual "goings on" were given an important theoretical place in the description of authoritarians. Studies of the relationship between F Scale responses and attitudes about sex have consistently verified this proposition.

In an unpublished study of undergraduates at the University of Texas, John McCoy found that authoritarians were more likely than equalitarians to feel that children should not be given frank explanations about sex until they are old enough to have some self control. These students also indicated that their dates were likely to end up in conversation rather than in necking.

Similarly, authoritarians have been found to be more likely to evaluate stimuli with sexual content as being pornographic than do equalitarians. Eliasberg and Stuart (1961) presented color slides of works of art showing nudes including Modigliani's *Reclining Nude, 1918,* Gauguin's *Woman with Mangoes,* and Chabas's *September Morn* to male and female students. Subjects were asked to judge each as pornographic or not pornographic. The correlation between the number of pictures judged to be pornographic and F Scale scores was .46.

Political and Economic Beliefs

One of the basic dimensions of political ideology is that complex combination of beliefs and values concerning man and his relation to the state and to the existing social order: liberalism versus conservatism. Because such beliefs cover a great many aspects of life, it is not surprising to find that liberalism-conservatism is related to various personality variables. That is, one's political views are based on internal needs and values as much as on external arguments and "facts."

In their original series of investigations, Adorno, et al. (1950) suggested that adherence to right-wing or conservative politics should be related to antidemocratic beliefs because fascism is the most extreme right-wing political and economic structure and ideology. A Politico-Economic Conservatism (PEC) Scale was built in an attempt to measure such trends as support of

American status quo, resistance to social change, and support of conservative values. It includes items of the form:

America may not be perfect, but the American Way has brought us about as close as human beings can get to a perfect society.

In general, full economic security is bad; most men wouldn't work if they didn't need the money for eating and living.

Correlation between the PEC Scale and the F Scale is .52. Other investigators in subsequent studies have confirmed this relationship between authoritarianism and conservatism. Consistent with these findings is Rim's (1970) research with a group of Israeli students. Both high and low scorers on the F Scale ranked a series of values with respect to their importance. Those high in authoritarianism ranked it as more important to be polite and clean than did those low in authoritarianism; the reverse was true with respect to the importance of being ambitious, independent, and broadminded.

Since a number of quite specific issues are involved in liberal-conservative differences, it is not surprising to find the F Scale related to the position which individuals take on many topics. As his doctoral dissertation at Stanford, Mahler (1953) built a Socialized Medicine Attitude Scale; examples of items are:

The quality of medical care under the system of private practice is superior to that under a system of compulsory health insurance. (Disagree)

A compulsory health program would be a realization of one of the true aims of a democracy. (Agree)

Any system of compulsory health insurance would invade the privacy of the individual. (Disagree)

With a group of Stanford students, Mahler found that his scale correlated − .30 with the F Scale. That is, the more positive the attitude toward socialized medicine the less authoritarian the individual tends to be.

Authoritarianism is correlated with and hence predictive of other types of political behavior besides that of marking responses on an attitude scale. In the 1960 presidential campaign, Wrightsman, Radloff, Horton, and Mecherikoff (1961) found a relationship between presidential choices and the F Scale scores of college students. They found that authoritarian scores of those who supported different candidates were consistently related to the assumed liberal-conservative stance of the preferred candidate. The more conservative the candidate the more authoritarian are his supporters.

The importance of the candidate's political ideology in determining his relative appeal to authoritarians and equalitarians was shown by Leventhal, Jacobs, and Kudirka (1964) in two investigations. The first was conducted just before the 1960 presidential election. The hypothesis was made that

Kennedy's advocation of the New Frontier would appeal to those low in authoritarianism, while Nixon's preference for the status quo would appeal to those high on this dimension. In the period one to two weeks before the election, undergraduates at Yale indicated their preference with respect to the two candidates and also took the F Scale. A significant relationship was found between F Scale scores and political choice, with authoritarians preferring Nixon.

In an attempt to extend these findings, Leventhal, et al. (1964) then employed an experimental situation in which a candidate's ideology could be manipulated. At the time of the 1962 congressional elections, pairs of candidates were described to three different samples of students. One group was presented with a conservative Republican versus a liberal Democrat, one with a liberal Republican versus a conservative Democrat, and the third group was given two candidates who had the same ideology. The subjects were undergraduates at Yale. The ideology of the candidates was given in terms of their opinions about federal aid to urban redevelopment, increased social security benefits, increased minimum wages, greater unemployment benefits, federal aid to education, and stricter antitrust legislation. Those with high scores on the F Scale voted for the conservative candidate, and those with low scores voted for the liberal candidate, regardless of party label. When the two candidates had the same ideology, authoritarianism was not related to choice. The authors point out that authoritarianism would be expected to affect choice of candidates only in the relatively small and well-educated segment of the population, only if the candidates are reasonably consistent in espousing liberal or conservative ideology, and only if such ideological positions are more salient than other characteristics of the candidates.

For the 1964 presidential election, Milton and Waite (1964) utilized the TFI Scale rather than the F Scale. In the summer of 1964, the TFI Scale was administered to students at the Universities of Tennessee and Georgia. The students were then asked which of the following three men they preferred as President of the United States: Goldwater, Johnson, Wallace. As hypothesized, the highest TFI Scale scores were attained by those preferring Wallace and the lowest scores by those preferring Johnson. Prior to the 1968 presidential election, Stanford undergraduates were asked by the author to indicate their first choice among the candidates. Those who named Nelson Rockefeller or Richard Nixon had the highest scores in authoritarianism, and those who named Robert F. Kennedy had the lowest mean scores. Supporters of George Romney and Lyndon Johnson fell between these two extremes.

Still other types of politically relevant behavior have been found related to authoritarianism. Beginning in 1949, the University of California at Berkeley was shaken by what became known as the "loyalty oath controversy." The Regents of the University, in the summer of that year, sent out a special noncommunist oath with the academic contracts for 1949–1950. A great many individuals refused to sign this oath on the grounds that: (1) there were no Communists on the faculty, and (2) the oath constituted a violation of tenure. In the suceeding furor, eighteen nonsigning faculty members took their case to court, while a number of nontenure employees (mostly graduate students) lost their positions. Handlon and Squier (1955) located a group of the nonsigners who were fired and selected a random sample of nontenured individuals who did sign the oath. Each subject was interviewed and given the F Scale. Though there were many similarities between these two groups, one of the findings was that those who refused to sign were significantly less authoritarian than those who did sign the oath.

Maladjustment

In the theoretical description of authoritarians, a number of the proposed characteristics suggest less than optimal psychological functioning. Thus, authoritarians were described as rigid, conforming, repressing, denying, projecting, and displacing. Equalitarians, on the other hand, were indicated to be flexible, free, aware of their impulses, and less likely to utilize unconsciously determined defense mechanisms. Masling suggested that the primary reason for these differences in characterization stemmed from a lack of objectivity in the social scientists who were investigating authoritarianism. His general point is a good one: "There seems to be a tendency to use the term 'authoritarian' as a mild profanity which one could use to describe other people (never oneself)" (Masling, 1954, p. 318). Masling also indicated that at that time only four studies had investigated the relationship between authoritarianism and mental health and that not one of them found any relationship. Obviously, considerably more evidence would be needed to be able to conclude with any degree of confidence that authoritarians are or are not more maladjusted than equalitarians.

Despite the general antiauthoritarian bias in much of the literature, Sanford (1956) has pointed out that a low score on the F Scale is not a guarantee of mental health. He describes five distinct types of individuals who are low in potential fascism, and at least two of these categories involve elements of maladjustment. For example, the rigid low authoritarians are as totalitarian as those with high scores. It is just that their compulsivity and paranoia are in support of such ideals as minority rights and against right-wing ideology. It is obviously possible to do the "right" things for the "wrong" reasons.

Criminal behavior represents a particular type of maladjustment. Among the groups who were given the final version of the F Scale by Adorno, et al., San Quentin prisoners obtained the highest score. Aumack (1956), in an investigation of murderers at San Quentin, reported that their mean authoritarian scores were the highest yet reported in any investigation.

Though it is difficult to make any sweeping conclusions about authoritarians and mental health, individuals who score high on this dimension do not appear to be greatly different from those with low scores on most measures of adjustment. It is possible, of course, simply to define authoritarianism as an abnormal adjustment on logical or even on moral grounds. On the basis of the type of evidence we usually use, however, authoritarianism does not seem to be related to psychological adjustment.

INTOLERANCE OF AMBIGUITY

Authoritarians have been described by Else Frenkel-Brunswik (1950) and others as being more intolerant of ambiguous situations than equalitarians. The authoritarian is said to have no place in his cognitive structure for ambivalence or ambiguity; he sticks with simple, firm, preconceived categories. Because of the many different operations that have been used to define tolerance of ambiguity, the data with respect to this hypothesis are not as clear-cut as they might be.

Intolerance of ambiguity has been defined as the tendency to interpret ambiguous situations as sources of threat and tolerance of ambiguity as the tendency to interpret ambiguous situations as desirable (Budner, 1962). Budner developed a 16-item scale to measure tolerance-intolerance of ambiguity. Sample items are:

What we are used to is always preferable to what is unfamiliar. (Agree)
A good teacher is one who makes you wonder about your way of looking at things. (Disagree)

This test and the F Scale were administered to nine groups of subjects. In each instance the correlations were positive. While other investigators have also found that authoritarians are more intolerant of ambiguity than equalitarians (for example, Kelman & Barclay, 1963), some find no relationship between the two variables (for example, Davids & Eriksen, 1957). The most plausible reason for these contradictory findings is that the various measures which have been proposed for intolerance of ambiguity are not measuring the same thing (Kenny & Ginsberg, 1958).

INTELLIGENCE AND EDUCATIONAL ATTAINMENT

In the original California studies, scores on the F Scale were found to be negatively correlated with measures of intellectual ability. Subsequent studies have been consistent in finding that individuals who are high in authoritarianism do less well than low authoritarians on college entrance tests (Jacobson & Rettig, 1959), receive lower grades (Davids, 1956), and complete fewer years of school (Lindgren, 1962).

Why should there be any relationship between intellectual functioning and authoritarianism? One possibility is that only those of relatively low intellectual ability are able to accept the kind of ideology represented by an extreme fascistic orientation. A second line of reasoning points out that intelligence and educational attainment are related to social class as will be discussed in Chapter 7. Perhaps class differences in child-rearing practices lead to differences in authoritarianism and it is this variable which is responsible for any correlations with intellectual-educational measures. Still a third possibility is that those in our society who are low in IQ, low in socioeconomic status, and low in education feel threatened and frustrated and hence turn to authoritarian beliefs as a solution to their problems. Whatever the ultimate explanation of these findings, the negative relationship between authoritarianism and intellectual ability is well established.

RELIGIOUS AFFILIATION AND RELIGIOUS ACTIVITY

Several aspects of religious behavior have been found to be associated with authoritarianism and ethnocentrism. Jones (1958) examined the relationship between scores on the F Scale and responses to a background information form. He used two large samples of Naval Aviation Cadets. The questions and the mean scores of subjects giving each response are shown in Table 4-3.

Table 4-3. Authoritarianism and Religion

Are you affiliated with a religious group?

	No	*Yes, Protestant*	*Yes, Jewish*	*Yes, Roman Catholic*
		Mean Scores		
Sample 1	105.0	114.8	89.1	114.3
Sample 2	108.6	118.6	102.4	122.3

Did you attend church regularly prior to coming into the Navy?

	Yes	*No*
	Mean Scores	
Sample 1	117.5	106.4
Sample 2	119.7	114.9

We see that, compared to equalitarians, those high in authoritarianism: (1) are more likely to be Protestant or Roman Catholic than to be Jewish or unaffiliated with any church, and (2) are more likely to attend church regularly.

Data obtained by David Dustin and Robert K. Young using college undergraduates are consistent with these findings. In terms of religious preference, those students who indicated that they were Baptists, Episcopalians, or Catholics obtained the highest mean scores, while those with no religious affiliation were the least authoritarian. In between were students who were Jewish, Methodist, Presbyterian, or members of miscellaneous Protestant groups. Similarly, those who attended church more regularly (weekly or twice a month) were significantly more authoritarian than those who never or almost never attended church. Even among those with religious affiliations, individuals who attend church regularly are significantly more authoritarian than those who stay away from church. Similarly, a study of Stanford undergraduates by the author reported a correlation of .44 between frequency of church attandance and scores on the F Scale. There was approximately a thirty-point difference in the authoritarian scores of those who never attended church and those who reported weekly attendance.

If the traditional Christian values stress tolerance, brotherhood, and equality, why is it that these values are held more firmly by individuals outside of organized religion than by those with church affiliations? Adorno, et al. (1950) have suggested that the majority of middle-class Americans belong to a religious group as a matter of course and not because they consider the matter carefully or accept its ideology. Thus, church membership and church attendance for many individuals may represent simply socially acceptable responses. It has also been found that authoritarian churches (Mormon, Catholic, Seventh Day Adventist, Southern Baptist) attract the most converts during times of economic hardship while nonauthoritarian churches (Congregational, Northern Baptist, Presbyterian, Episcopal) are most successful when the economic situation is good (Sales, 1972). It may be that in times of threat, authoritarians are highly motivated to turn to organized religion.

DYNAMICS OF AUTHORITARIANISM

REPRESSION, PROJECTION, AND OTHER
RESPONSES TO SEXUAL STIMULI

One of the basic characteristics of authoritarian individuals in the original theoretical description was the tendency to utilize repressive defenses. One of the best designed investigations testing this hypothesis was an experiment by Kogan (1956). If the repression hypothesis were accurate, it was proposed that authoritarians would find it more difficult to recognize threatening aggressive and sexual material than would equalitarains. Kogan selected 42 sentences to be recorded on tape, partially masked by white noise in order to make recognition difficult. Subjects were given 14 neutral, 14 aggressive, and

14 sexual sentences in random order. Samples of the three types of sentences are:

Neutral
  You like to go swimming during the summer season.
  The thought of a good meal increases your appetite.
Aggressive
  Only your death would be a just punishment for you.
  Your mother is to blame for your worst faults.
Sexual
  You have been unable to break your ugly sex habits.
  You would have loved to share your father's sex life.

The subjects were male undergraduates. Each sentence was played, the tape stopped, and the subjects were asked to write down what they had heard; then the next sentence was played. Because of the white noise, accurate perception of the sentences was difficult. Recognition of the threatening material was measured in relation to recognition of neutral material so that any differences in hearing ability were controlled. It was found that as authoritarian scores increased, ability to perceive the threatening material decreased.

A study of authoritarian projection was undertaken by Griffitt (1973). He presented slides depicting explicit sexual themes to a group of unmarried undergraduates at Kansas State University. In addition to self-ratings of their response to the erotic stimuli, the subjects were asked to guess the way in which a member of the opposite sex would respond. Authoritarianism in both sexes was associated with the projection of negative responses to members of the opposite sex. Thus, opposite sex individuals were seen as angry, disgusted, and restrictive about erotica by those high in authoritarianism. In addition, female authoritarians had interesting perceptions of the response of males. They differed from equalitarian females in guessing that undergraduate males would be relatively more aroused by themes of female homosexuality and oral-genital sex and relatively less aroused by conventional heterosexual intercourse. Griffitt (1973) notes that the themes projected as arousing

> . . . involve activities which have traditionally been considered as religiously, morally, and socially unacceptable forms of sexual behavior while (the theme projected as unarousing) represents one of the few generally accepted forms of "normal" sexual expression. Female authoritarians assume that males are sexually aroused by the "unacceptable" but not by the "traditional" behaviors.

When authoritarians are found to repress or to project in response to sexual stimuli, it is reasonable to assume that such stimuli bring about negative emotional responses. That is, authoritarians and equalitarians may not differ in the extent to which erotic stimuli are arousing or sexually stimulating, but they may very well differ in whether such arousal is perceived as pleasant or unpleasant, a source of enjoyment or a source of concern. In an experiment to be described in more detail in Chapter 12, Byrne and Lamberth (1971) presented a series of sexual themes to married students at Purdue University and obtained their reactions on various scales. As expected, authoritarianism was unrelated to sexual arousal, but it was consistenstly related to negative feelings about being aroused. For example, as authoritarianism increased, self ratings of disgust and depression increased. In addition, authoritarianism was associated with the judgment that the sexual stimuli were pornographic and the belief that there should be legal restrictions on the production and sale of such material. It may be seen, then, that the crucial variable in the response of authoritarians to sexual material is in their attitudes and emotional reactions to sexuality. For them, sex arousal is a negative experience and one which should be severely limited and controlled. Legal restrictions on erotic stimuli would serve as a protection against such arousal.

AGGRESSION

Experimental studies have also dealt with the proposed relationship between authoritarianism and aggressive responses. Epstein (1965) pointed out that authoritarians are supposed to be sensitized to power relationships such as strong-weak or superior-inferior and hence should feel that aggression is justifiable against low status rather than high status persons. It is as if weakness and lower status confers a permit or license to aggress. This is one explanation, for example, of why it is that harsh repressive measures are more likely to be directed against minority groups, the victims of poverty, or "hippie types" than against members of the majority group, those who are wealthy, or advocates of the establishment. In an experiment at Wayne State University, Epstein (1965) selected high and low authoritarians on the basis of a pretest. As in many of the experiments to be described in Chapter 11, a version of the Buss (1961) aggression machine was used. The subject is supposedly teaching another subject (the victim) a verbal learning task by administering shocks when incorrect responses are given. Actually, the interest of the experimenter is in the magnitude and duration of the shocks which the subject believes he is administering. In Epstein's experiment, the victim was either low-status (old disheveled clothes, family making under $1500 annually, planning to drop out of school, parents who have a grade school education and are unemployed) or high status (well dressed, planning to obtain a graduate degree in business administration, family making $20,000 annually, parents who have a college education, and father a vice president in an advertising firm). There was an interaction between the authoritarianism of the subject and the status of the victim. That is, authoritarian subjects administered more intense shocks to a low status victim than to a high status victim while the reverse was true for the equalitarian subjects. It was suggested that perhaps high and low scorers both tend to express differential aggression on the basis of status, simply in opposite directions. Epstein (1965, p. 588) suggested the possibility that "... some low scores on the F scale may be indicative of an 'authoritarianism of the left' which is characterized by hostility and rejection of groups that appear economically privileged or powerful."

In quite different experimental situations, the general tendency of authoritarians to respond with punishment has been found repeatedly. For example, Dustin and Davis (1967) placed subjects in a setting supposedly designed to measure their leadership ability. The follower purportedly had to perform a simple task and it was the leader's responsibility to maximize that person's performance. After each trial, the subject could choose one of various sanctions to communicate to the follower: awarding of money, taking money away from him, saying he did well or poorly, or simply telling him to go on to the next trial. The equalitarian subjects used the negative sanctions significantly less often than did the authoritarians. Since the follower's performance was the same for all subjects, the findings suggest that individuals scoring high and low in authoritarianism differ in their beliefs concerning the effectiveness of different kinds of sanctions. That is, authoritarians seem to think that people will work best if they are punished or scolded while equalitarians feel that performance is enhanced by rewards or praise.

These various studies do not seem to indicate that the responses of authoritarians are indiscriminately hostile and aggressive, but that they respond with punishment and negative interpersonal sanctions only when the situation provides a convenient justification for the negative behavior and especially if the recipient "deserves" it. In fact, the studies of the way that authoritarians raise their children, respond to transgressions, teach others, or try to motivate their followers are very consistent in showing a preference for punishment, pain, and various other negative reinforcers. It is as if authoritarians hold quite different views from equalitarians about how human beings function. It is also possible that such situations provide a socially acceptable way to aggress against others. One setting which provides a splendid opportunity for justifiable aggression is the courtroom in which one can do one's duty as a citizen and advocate various kinds and degrees of punishment toward a very acceptable victim—the defendant. In a simulated jury experiment, Mitchell and Byrne (1973) gave identical evidence to authoritarian and equalitarian subjects about a case in which the defendant had supposedly stolen an examination. In addition to the evidence, the testimony included statements mentioning a number of irrelevant attitudes supposedly held by the defendant, and these were made either to agree or to disagree with the attitudes of each subject. Both authoritarians and equalitarians liked the agreeing defendant better than the disagreeing one, but for the authoritarians this liking also influenced their judicial decisions. The authoritarians were less sure of the guilt of a defendant they liked and were more severe in the punishment they recommended for a disliked defendant. Once again, then, authoritarians are found to respond punitively if there is social support for such a response and especially if there is a "good" reason to aggress against the victim.

<small>CONFORMITY, OBEDIENCE, AND OTHER GROUP BEHAVIOR</small>

The characteristics of conventionalism and authoritarian submission within the authoritarian syndrome have led a number of investigators to hypothesize that those scoring high on the F scale should be conformists. In the widely used conformity procedure devised by Asch (1956), subjects are given a task such as judging the length of lines or matching the size of a standard object with an adjustable one. Presumably, the subject is one of a group of subjects carrying out the task. Actually, each subject is mixed in with a group of experimental confederates who are instructed to give unanimously incorrect responses on specified trials. Conformity is defined as the number of trials on which the subject goes along with the group on the incorrect decisions.

In his doctoral dissertation at Case Western Reserve, Nadler (1959) utilized an Asch length-of-line judging task. Subjects were 70 college students. Nadler found a correlation of .48 between F Scale scores and frequency of yielding to incorrect group judgments about the line lengths. Barron (1953) has constructed a test which discriminates between those who are independent and those who conform in the Asch situation. With San Francisco laundromat customers as subjects, Lindgren (1962) found that authoritarianism correlated negatively with independence.

At the Institute of Personality Assessment and Research at the University of California, Crutchfield (1955) studied conformity in groups of five men each. Slides were projected on a wall directly in front of the subjects, and each slide presented a question calling for a judgment by the subject. Some were perceptual judgments such as length of lines; some were matters of opinion. Each subject responded in order by pressing a button to indicate his choice among a series of alternative answers. Whenever the subject was in the fifth position, the "other members of the group" responded incorrectly. Actually, the information about the other members' choices was faked; the experimenter was the source of all of the information. The conformity score was the number of trials on which the subject responded as he believed the group had done. Scores on the F scale were found to correlate .39 with this measure of conformity.

Wells, Weinert, and Rubel (1956) studied conformity by using the drawing shown in Figure 4-2. In the control group, college students were shown the

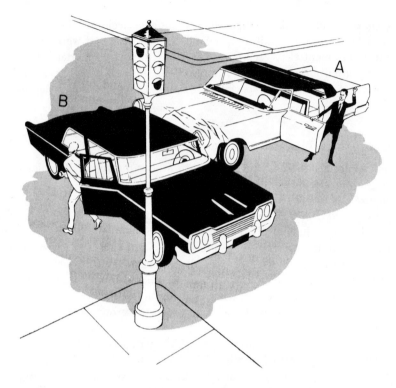

Fig. 4-2 Which Driver was at Fault? (In the original drawing by Nancy Secol, the lower light was colored green and the upper light was colored red.) (Adapted from Wells, Weinert, and Rubel, 1956, p. 134.)

picture and asked which driver was at fault in the accident. Only two blamed Driver B; the remaining sixty blamed Driver A. In the experimental group, other students were shown the picture in a conformity situation. Each subject sat in a circle with four other students who appeared to be fellow subjects. Actually, they were confederates who said that Driver B was at fault; the real subjects responded last. In this situation, twenty-one subjects blamed B and forty-one blamed A. The mean F Scale score of those who yielded to conformity pressure was significantly higher than for those who did not yield.

In spite of the number of investigations reporting a positive relationship between authoritarianism and conformity, we should note that for reasons which are as yet not determined, negative evidence is sometimes reported (for example, Gorfein, 1961; Moore & Krupat, 1971).

Related to conformity, but perhaps of greater importance, is the question of obedience to authority. When someone is ordered by an authority figure to exterminate Jewish prisoners in a gas chamber, to shoot unarmed women and children, or to maintain public silence about matters which it seems the public should know, what does he do? Some individuals obey and gas the prisoners, shoot the women and children, and keep the official secrets while others fail to do so. Clearly, it would be hypothesized that authoritarians would be more likely to obey and equalitarians likely to defy authoritative commands. Milgram (1963, 1965) has conducted a series of experiments in which subjects thought they were administering electric shocks to a fellow volunteer in a "learning experiment." The experimenter tells him to give higher and higher levels of shock. Some subjects obey this directive even when they must force the unwilling victim's hand onto the shock apparatus while others refuse to obey such orders even when they cannot see or hear the victim. Elms and Milgram (1966) hypothesized that these differences in the tendency to obey unreasonable commands were in part a function of differences in authoritarianism. They selected extreme subjects who had defied or obeyed the experimenter's orders. As predicted, those who obeyed were significantly higher in authoritarianism than those who refused to do the experimenter's bidding.

RIGIDITY AND RESISTANCE TO CHANGE

Authoritarians are expected to be more rigid in their behavior and more resistant to change than are equalitarians.

Resistance to changing one's opinion on the basis of new evidence was investigated by Mischel and Schopler (1959) who took advantage of an event that occurred while their research was in progress. Shortly after Russia launched Sputnik I in 1957, students in two psychology classes were asked a number of questions including: "Which of the two countries (U.S. or USSR) do you think is most likely to get to the moon first?" About three-fourths of the students chose the United States; choice was *not* related to authoritarianism. Within a month, Sputnik II carrying a live dog was launched; the United States had not yet had a successful satellite launching. At this point, when the questions were readministered, only about one-fourth of the students still chose the U.S.; the others changed their minds. It was suggested that those who still thought that the U.S. would be first to reach the moon were rigidly holding to their original position in the face of contradictory evidence. In each of the two classes, those who changed their predictions had significantly lower F Scale scores than those who maintained their original position.

A finding by Steiner and Johnson (1963) could be interpreted as further evidence of the resistance of authoritarians to change on the basis of new information. The subjects were students at the University of Illinois. After arriving at the laboratory, each was introduced to two other "subjects" who were actually working for the experimenter. After taking the F Scale, the subjects were informed that the research dealt with impression formation. In response to questions, Accomplice I indicated that he was a premedical student, a junior, and had a grade-point average better than B. Accomplice II reported that he was a physics major, a junior, and also had a grade-point average higher than B. The real subject answered similar questions about himself, and then each subject was asked to rate the other two students on rating scales dealing with personality characteristics, knowledge, and skill. As a source of new information, an oral test of factual material was administered by the experimenter to each individual. Accomplice I gave unusual and incorrect answers to about one-third of the items while Accomplice II gave correct answers to all items. Presumably, this behavior provided negative information concerning the knowledge or ability of Accomplice I. Following this procedure, each subject judged the others on the rating scales a second time. In comparing the two sets of ratings, Steiner and Johnson found that the high F Scale subjects resisted the negative information and rated the two partners equally favorably, just as they had done in the original rating. The low F Scale subjects lowered their evaluation of Accomplice I after seeing him perform less well on the oral test.

CHANGES IN AUTHORITARIANISM

Authoritarian characteristics are generally assumed to be relatively stable and enduring. As with any personality variable, however, authoritarianism is subject to alteration under suitable conditions. A few studies have begun the task of specifying those conditions under which authoritarian tendencies are likely to increase and those under which a change away from authoritarian beliefs occurs.

Increased Authoritarianism

Kahn, Pollack, and Fink (1960) investigated the effects of convulsive therapy on authoritarianism in a group of patients at Hillside Hospital in New York City. The F Scale was administered during the week before treatment began, on the day following the twelfth treatment, and two weeks after treatment was terminated. The patients were divided into an experimental group which received convulsive therapy and a control group which received much weaker electro-stimulation. All patients were treated for at least four weeks. Only in the experimental group did F Scale scores increase significantly during treatment. In addition, it was found that the greater the amount of brain dysfunction induced by the treatment, the greater the increase in authoritarianism. When members of the control group were later placed in treatment, they too revealed a significant increase in F Scale scores. Following treatment, the scores returned to their original level. It was concluded that the effect occurs because convulsive therapy leads to an increase in stereotyped behavior and to difficulty in making fine discriminations. Since these characteristics are associated with authoritarianism, F Scale scores increase.

A brief report is available of what appears to be a situation which might be expected to bring about a more lasting increase in authoritarianism. One would predict that interpersonal rewards in an authoritarian context should lead to ideological shifts in the direction of greater acceptance of authoritarian beliefs. Christie (1952) administered the F Scale to inductees in an Army basic-training center before and after completion of six weeks of infantry training. The group as a whole made no significant shift in authoritarianism. However, sociometric data were available concerning the degree to which each individual was accepted or rejected by other recruits and by the noncommissioned training personnel. The recruits who were more accepted than rejected by *both* peers and superiors became significantly more authoritarian over the six-week period. Their mean score was not significantly different from that of the other recruits on the original administration of the F Scale.

DECREASED AUTHORITARIANISM

An investigation with interesting implications was carried out by Singer (1960) as his doctoral dissertation at the University of Pennsylvania. Singer attempted to alter responses to the F Scale by means of verbal reinforcement of democratic statements made by the subjects. The F Scale and the E Scale were administered and female subjects were selected to serve in either the experimental or the control group. Items of the F Scale were read to each subject who was asked to indicate agreement or disagreement with each. In the experimental group, each prodemocratic response was reinforced by the statement "good" or "right" from the experimenter. In the control group, no reinforcement was given. Singer found that in the experimental group, subjects gave more prodemocratic responses than they had previously. Generalization beyond the experimental situation is another matter, of course. Singer attempted to test this possibility by readministering the E Scale immediately after the reinforcement task. For half of each group, the experimenter remained in the room; for half, the experimenter was out of the room. Generalization of prodemocratic attitudes to the E Scale took place only in the condition where the experimenter remained in the room with the subject. When subjects were left alone, no change in ethnocentrism occurred. The results suggest that the subjects were responding to social influence rather than changing their basic authoritarian beliefs.

In Singer's experiment, there was a direct reinforcement by an experimenter of equalitarian responses to the F Scale. Grossman and Eisenman

(1971) carried out a more elaborate experiment in which group pressure was employed to both increase and decrease authoritarianism. Subjects participated in a panel discussion with three other students who were actually confederates of the experimenter. The experimenter read F Scale statements one at a time, the three confederates give their views on the topic, and the last to respond was the subject. With the authoritarian subjects, the confederates all expressed equalitarian views and with equalitarian subjects, they all expressed authoritarian views. Examples of the kind of interaction are given below in response to the item, "The wild sex life of the old Greeks and Romans was tame compared to some of the goings on in this country, even in places where people might least expect to find them." With an equalitarian subject, a sample interaction was:

Confederate 1: I would say true considering the fact that (pause) that they weren't so wild back then as we consider them. The things that they consider wild are almost commonplace nowadays.

E: They held sex to be something noble and beautiful while we debase it more today?

Confederate 1: More or less.

Confederate 2: I'd say it was true—even if it was a little wild then, it was the whole society in general that acted this way at that time.

E: Today?

Confederate 2: Right today it's different. It's large and more pronounced.

Confederate 3: I think it's true. Back then it was most likely more just common sex whereas now we have perversions (pause) like you take stag movies for instance. They start out back in the early twenties with normal sex and now they're getting more perverted and more perverted. (looking at E) You know what I mean?

E: (nods affirmatively)

S: I guess it's true.[1]

With an authoritarian subject, a sample interaction was:

Confederate 1: I have to say that's definitely false. (pause) You don't see what's going around in Greece or Rome in those days happening now. People running around the streets. (pause, smiles lasciviously at group) It's definitely false. (emphatically)

E: You don't think it's any worse today?

Confederate 1: No! No, we don't have orgies like they had.

Confederate 2: (chuckling at F Scale statement) I'm going to say that it is false also, I—I don't think (pause) I think generally things now are overplayed, sensationalism of newspapers (pause) just to sell a paper they build sex up.

[1] Grossman, J. C. & Eisenman, R., "Experimental manipulation of Authoritarianism and its Effect on Creativity." *Journal of Consulting and Clinical Psychology*, 1971, *36*, 241–42. © 1971 by the American Psychological Association and reprinted by permission.

E: You don't think sex changes across the ages?

Confederate 2: No, no, it's natural order of things.

E: There's only so much you can do.

Confederate 2: Yeah.

Confederate 3: I also agree that's false. Sexual energy or libido is, uh, an innate thing in all people that they're born with and uh, (long pause).

E: And Greece had just as much as we have?

Confederate 3: Right, and sexual behavior must, uh, come out otherwise you'll be messed up.

S: That's false (weakly) (referring to F Scale statement).[2]

In both conditions, the group experience proved to be a powerful determiner of F Scale scores. An interesting observation was that when the subjects were told about the details of the experiment afterward, they expressed great disappointment with themselves that they could have been swayed so easily.

Another investigation of change involves less experimental control than the previous two studies but has a great deal of social significance if it proves to be a consistent finding. Levitt (1955) reported an investigation dealing with the influence of teachers' behavior on authoritarianism in grade-school children. The teachers in three grade-school classes took part in a "causal" training program for a one-year period. The goal of this type of training program is indicated by the following definition:

> Theoretically, a "causal" teacher is one who is pupil-centered rather than class-centered, who recognizes the dynamic complexity of human motivation in dealing with classroom problems, and whose reactions to classroom situations are based to a maximum possible extent on the motivations for pupil behavior rather than on that behavior itself. Concomitant with this general orientation are various attempts to assess pupil motivation, rather than to assign stereo-typed causes to behavior (Levitt, 1955, p. 449).

Shortly after the teachers had finished the training program, the three experimental classes and six control-group classes were administered a children's version of the F Scale. The students in the experimental classes were found to be significantly less authoritarian than the students in the control classes at each grade level.

As might be expected from the discussion of the relationship between education and authoritarianism, it has been suggested that the educational process itself tends to reduce authoritarianism. Simpson (1972) proposed that such findings would occur only when the educational system empha-sizes cognitive learning and only when nonauthoritarian teachers are em-ployed. By contrast, a system emphasizing rote learning in an authoritarian atmosphere should not lead to a reduction in authoritarianism as education

---

[2] *Ibid.*

increased. A comparison of the relationship between authoritarianism and years of schooling is shown in Figure 4-3 for Mexico and the United States. It is clear that years of education is unrelated to authoritarianism in Mexico and strongly related in the United States. It would seem from both Levitt's (1955) study and this one by Simpson (1972) that it is the type of education which is crucial.

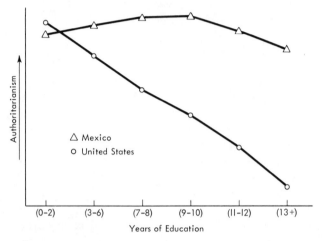

Fig. 4-3 Authroritarianism Decreases as Years of Education Increase in the United States but the Two Variables are Unrelated in Mexico. Presumably, the Type of Educational Procedures and the Atmosphere of the Classroom are Crucial Factors in Determining this Relationship. (Adapted from Simpson, 1972, p. 230.)

CURRENT ISSUES IN RESEARCH ON AUTHORITARIANISM

The preceding description of research dealing with the California F Scale shows clearly that authoritarianism has proven to be a useful concept as a dimension of personality. What issues seem to be important in influencing future research on the variable?

ACQUIESCENT RESPONSE SET

A large amount of methodological criticism has been leveled at the F Scale because of the fact that each item is worded so that agreement with the content of the item indicates authoritarianism. Thus, the scores obtained on this instrument potentially involve a confounding of authoritarian tendencies with another personality variable: acquiescent response set. Acquiescence refers to the tendency of some individuals to indicate agreement with almost any sweeping generalization that is stated as a test item. One difficulty with having the F Scale confounded with acquiescent response set is that correlations between it and other tests may be a function of an actual relationship between authoritarianism and another variable or possibly only an artifact caused by the common element of acquiescence. On the basis of a number of theoretical and empirical considerations, Samuelson and Yates (1967) conclude that there is little evidence of the existence of a serious acquiescence bias. More importantly, they criticize the entire controversy over acquiescence as a blind alley for research which had the unfortunate effect of dampening research interest in authoritarianism. Among others, Rorer (1965) has proposed that the entire issue is a tempest in a teapot.

Jackson and Messick (1958) and Chapman and Campbell (1957) have argued for the desirability of building an F Scale with response set controlled. For example, half of the items could be worded in the opposite way so that disagreement with the item content indicates the trait being measured. Some investigators (e.g., Kerlinger, 1967; Rokeach, 1967) have argued that the democratically worded items are unlikely to discriminate authoritarians and equalitarians because both groups in a democratic society are likely to indicate agreement with such statements. For this reason, it is suggested that there is no need to seek suitable reversed items and that the use of such items would actually detract from the measurement of authoritarianism rather than improve it.

To get around some of these problems, a necessary step in building a successful balanced scale is the identification of reversed items which actually correlate with the original scale. It is not difficult to write a logically reversed item, but that is obviously not a guarantee that authoritarians will disagree with it and equalitarians endorse it. One such attempt by the author contained a large number of reversed items which were given to various samples of undergraduates along with the original F Scale. The eleven reversed items which correlated best with scores on the original test were retained. These cross-validated items are:

1. The findings of science may some day show that many of our most cherished beliefs are wrong.
2. It is highly unlikely that astrology will ever be able to explain anything.
3. People ought to pay more attention to new ideas even if they seem to go against the American way of life.
4. Insults to our honor are not always important enough to bother about.
5. It's all right for people to raise questions about even the most sacred matters.
6. There is no reason to punish any crime with the death penalty.
7. Anyone who would interpret the Bible literally just doesn't know much about geology, biology, or history.
8. When they are little, kids sometimes think about doing harm to one or both of their parents.

9. It is possible that creatures on other planets have founded a better society than ours.

10. The prisoners in our corrective institutions, regardless of the nature of their crimes, should be humanely treated.

11. Some of the greatest atrocities in man's history have been committed in the name of religion and morality.

When these reversed items were combined with eleven of the usual F Scale items, the result was a twenty-two item balanced scale which controls for acquiescence. Results with this test suggest that it correlates with various tests and questionnaires in the same way as does the original F Scale but with slightly lower coefficients (presumably because the original relationships also involve acquiescence). In any event, it has proven possible to construct a balanced F Scale, and the correlation between this test and the original one is .84. Whether or not such a test represents even a minor improvement in the original scale is a question for future research.

DOGMATISM

Almost from its inception, the work on authoritarianism has been criticized as being influenced by the liberal biases of those conducting research. The objectivity of the data is not questioned, but the types of behavior selected for study and the interpretations of research findings are characterized as having an antiauthoritarian bias. To the extent that this state of affairs represents the equalitarian, democratic, liberal values of many behavioral scientists, perhaps it is inevitable. If these values or biases lead investigators to overlook certain problems, greater objectivity would obviously lead to better research.

One possible example of such a tendency is the equating of certain general characteristics, such as rigidity, conventionalism, and intolerance of ambiguity with conservative or right-wing political philosophy. Quite likely, many of these same characteristics hold equally true for those with an extreme left-wing political orientation. A major research effort to investigate this possibility was undertaken by Milton Rokeach. His interest was in the structure rather than the content of beliefs. "A person may adhere to communism, existentialism, Freudianism, or the 'new conservatism' in a relatively open or in a relatively closed manner" (Rokeach, 1960, p. 6).

To measure this more general characteristic of open- and close-mindedness, Rokeach devised the Dogmatism Scale which contains such items as "In a heated discussion I generally become so absorbed in what I am going to say that I forget to listen to what the others are saying," and "A group which tolerates too much difference of opinion among its own members cannot exist for long." Research with the instrument has demonstrated that left-of-center groups (for example, communists) and right-of-center groups (for example, Catholics) both score high on the Dogmatism Scale. Only the right-of-center groups score high on the F Scale. In one study of English political groups, the communist party members scored lowest of all groups on the F Scale and E Scale and highest of all groups on the Dogmatism Scale. Other research has suggested that the measures of authoritarianism and dogmatism are not essentially different (Thompson & Michel, 1972). Much of the dogmatism research has been reviewed by Vacchiano, Strauss, and Hochman (1969).

Though more research data will help to clarify these relationships, it seems likely that many of the characteristics which have been ascribed to right-wing authoritarians are, in fact, characteristic of the dogmatic, closed-minded individual of whatever political persuasion.

SUMMARY

An attitude is a predisposition to respond either positively or negatively toward an object or a class of objects. Some attitudes are grouped into ideological clusters. Authoritarianism refers to an attitudinal system which consists of a number of interrelated, antidemocratic sentiments. Research on authoritarianism was pioneered by Adorno, Frenkel-Brunswik, Levinson, and Sanford just after World War II.

The underlying theory of the nature of authoritarianism had its origin in diverse sources. Authoritarians were described as characterized by conventionalism, authoritarian submission, authoritarian aggression, destruction and cynicism, power and "toughness," superstition and stereotypy, anti-intraception, projectivity, and an exaggerated concern with sex.

Questionnaire items were written by Adorno, et al., in an attempt to tap the various aspects of authoritarianism. A preliminary scale was subjected to an item-analysis, using the Discriminatory Power technique. The best items were retained, some items were rewritten, and some new ones added. This second form of the scale was again item-analyzed. The final scale has a split-half reliability of .90.

Research on the antecedents of this dimension has dealt with child-rearing attitudes and practices. On the basis of early observational data, it was hypothesized that authoritarian-producing families are characterized by expectations of obedience from the children, concern with status, parental anxiety about conformity, and intolerance of socially unacceptable behavior. Subsequent research has found positive relationships between F Scale scores and traditional family ideology among adults and greater authoritarianism in traditional Turkish and Mexican-American cultures than in the Anglo-American culture. Authoritarianism is also related to the use of nonlove-oriented disciplinary techniques among mothers and restrictiveness rather than permissiveness in child-rearing attitudes among males. One investigation utilized families consisting of mother, father, and offspring. Rather than traditional family ideology, the best predictor of offspring authoritarianism was parental authoritarianism.

Research on personality structure has demonstrated correlations between F Scale scores and a number of other behaviors. Authoritarianism is positively related to prejudice as defined by anti-Semitism, ethnocentrism, and antiblack attitudes. Hostility is also characteristic of authoritarians in that, compared with equalitarians, they indicate more aggression toward outgroup characters and more friendly acts with ingroup characters in their dreams, are overly concerned with assigning blame and administering punishment, and were more favorable toward the Vietnam war. The negative response of authoritarians to sex is indicated in their attitudes about sex education and pornography. With respect to political and economic beliefs, authoritarians are found to be conservative, to be against socialized medicine, to prefer conservative rather than liberal political candidates regardless of party label, and to be more apt to sign a controversial loyalty oath. While authoritarians are often described as maladjusted, evidence supporting this idea is lacking. When intolerance of ambiguity is defined by responses to paper and pencil tests of this characteristic, F Scale scores are positively related to ambiguity intolerance though other measures of response to ambiguity show no relationship. A great many findings indicate a negative relationship between authoritarianism and both intelligence and educational attainment. Compared to equalitarians, those high on the F Scale are more likely to be Protestant or Roman Catholic than to be Jewish or unaffiliated and are more likely to attend church regularly.

Research on the dynamics of authoritarianism has been of several types. In a perceptual defense situation, authoritarians have relatively more difficulty perceiving sexual and aggressive auditory stimuli. Members of the opposite sex are perceived by authoritarians as responding negatively to sexual stimuli, and they themselves respond negatively and restrictively to erotic stimuli. In experimental studies, authoritarians are found to respond with greater aggression toward low status victims than toward high status victims, to prefer negative reinforcement as a way to motivate others, and to let their liking for a defendant influence their judicial decisions. In a wide variety of conformity experiments, authoritarians have been found more responsive to group pressure than equalitarians, and they also are more likely to obey unreasonable commands from an authority figure. Authoritarians show greater resistance to changing their opinions on the basis of new evidence.

A few investigations have been concerned with changes in authoritarianism. Increases in F Scale scores have been found during the course of convulsive electro-shock therapy and among recruits accepted by both peers and superiors during infantry training. Decreases in F Scale scores have been found to be a function of reinforcement of prodemocratic responses by an experimenter, group pressure, and of teachers who had received special training. In the United States authoritarianism tends to decrease as education increases; this is not the case in Mexico.

Among the issues which may influence future research in authoritarianism are acquiescent response set and the difference between the structure of beliefs (for example, dogmatism) and the content of beliefs (for example, liberal vs. conservative).

5

Need
for
Achievement

Achievement need is a learned motive to compete and to strive for success. Because almost any activity from gardening to managing an industrial organization can be viewed in terms of competition and success, the need to achieve influences many kinds of behavior. And because it is a *learned* motive, there are wide differences among individuals in their past experiences and hence in their achievement motivation.

Traditionally, motivational concepts have been important in theories of personality, and often they play a crucial role (Hall and Lindzey, 1970). Most accounts of behavior include some sort of moving, driving, or energizing force which propels the organism. Brown (1961, p. 24) notes: "The ubiquity of the concept of motivation, in one guise or another, is nevertheless surprising when we consider that its meaning is often scandalously vague."

As was noted in Chapter 1, motivational propositions such as "man eats *because* he is hungry" are not explanations at all but circular descriptions. If, however, we define hunger in terms of independent conditions, such as hours of food deprivation, the proposition becomes predictively meaningful. That is, "man eats when he has been deprived of food for six hours or more." Since the latter sort of statement refers to observable variables, what purpose is served by throwing in hunger drive as an intermediate concept? Drive is simply a higher-order generalization which permits us to conceptualize a wide variety of different behaviors within a single framework. Thus, eating hamburgers, driving to a grocery store, opening a can of soup, ordering a meal in a restaurant, placing a dime in a candy machine, turning right in a T-maze, and pressing a lever in a Skinner box all have a common conceptual component if we use the motivational term of hunger. What else is involved in the use of motivational concepts? (1) The organism's state under specific conditions may be described in terms of *drive level*. As hours of deprivation increase, hunger drive increases. (2) The fact that the organism responds differently to different motivational conditions (for example, food deprivation, water deprivation, pain) leads to the concept of *drive stimulus*, a hypothetical internal cue which leads the organism to make the appropriate external response. For example, rats can learn to make one response to obtain food and a different response to obtain water; under conditions of food deprivation or water deprivation, the appropriate response is made. (3) There are many different *instrumental responses* which may be learned as ways of obtaining (4) a given *goal* which reduces or satisfies the drive. Not only are there many alternate instrumental responses, but there are many different goals which may satisfy the same drive.

A distinction is usually made between *physiological* or *primary drives*, such as hunger, thirst, and sex, and *learned* or *secondary drives*, such as fear, affiliation, and need for achievement. To complicate matters, it is sometimes suggested that achievement behavior is actually a socially acceptable expression of the more basic drive of aggression. Whatever its origin, achievement motivation is a meaningful concept (1) if we can specify the stimulus conditions under which drive level is increased or decreased, (2) if subjects distinguish between this drive and other motivational conditions in terms of making differential responses, (3) if instrumental responses can be learned as ways of obtaining (4) identifiable goals which satisfy the drive. For example, we might attempt to arouse the achievement motive by telling subjects engaged in a group task that their individual performance on the task is a predictor of future success and that they should try to do better than their fellow group members. These instructions should lead to different behavior than instructions involving other motivations, such as stressing the importance of being liked by the other group members. The subjects who succeed in outperforming their competitors after achievement arousal should be better satisfied than subjects who fail. Specific goal-directed responses such as increased effort and persistence should be observed when the achievement need is aroused.

Since our interest here is in achievement need as a personality variable, the major emphasis will be on the determination of individual differences in the strength of the motive. Presumably, the stimulus conditions which increase the level of this drive do not affect all individuals in the same way because of differences in past learning experiences. Since we cannot deal directly with these past experiences, a test is used to measure such differences.

THEORETICAL BACKGROUND OF THE CONCEPT OF ACHIEVEMENT NEED

MURRAY, *n* ACH, AND THE THEMATIC APPERCEPTION TEST

Historical Background. Henry A. Murray (1893–   ) is a physician, chemist, psychoanalyst, and psychologist who has described his primary motivation as ". . . a stout affection for human beings coupled with a consuming interest in their emotions and evaluations, their imaginations and beliefs, their purposes and plans, their endeavors, failures, and achievements" (Murray, 1959, p. 9). Murray was born in New York City, was graduated from Harvard University in 1915 as a history major, and then entered medical school at Columbia. After receiving the M.D. degree in 1919, he spent two years as an intern in surgery and then five years working in research in the areas of physiology and the chemistry of embryology. This work led to a Ph.D. degree in physiological chemistry at Cambridge University.

His educational background is obviously a nonpsychological one, and the change in Murray's career plans took place as the result of a number of factors. He has indicated that one determinant was his greater interest in the motives and thoughts of human beings than in the physiological aspects of their bodies. In addition, he had come to believe that human personality was the major problem of our time and ". . . not very far from proving itself an evolutionary failure. . ." (Murray, 1959, p. 11), that psychoanalysis was making great progress in the study of mental processes, and that he was personally best suited in terms of temperament to work in an area on the unknown frontiers of science. His early contacts with the academic psychology of the day had left him disappointed, however, and he turned instead to the medical practitioners of psychotherapy as a source of knowledge. A major influence was his first contact with Carl Jung in 1925:

> . . . I had no scales to weigh out Dr. Jung, the first fullblooded, spherical— and Goethian, I should say—intelligence I had ever met, the man whom the judicious Prinzhorn called "The ripest fruit on the tree of psycho-analytical knowledge." We talked for hours, sailing down the lake and smoking before the hearth of his Faustian retreat. "The great floodgates of the wonder-world swung open," and I saw things that my philosophy had never dreamt of. Within a month a score of bi-horned problems were resolved, and I went off decided on depth psychology. I had experienced the unconscious, something not to be drawn out of books (Murray, 1940, p. 153).

Even though he had no formal training in academic psychology, Murray became an Instructor in psychology at Harvard in 1927 and the following year became an Assistant Professor and director of the Psychological Clinic there. His training in psychoanalysis was completed in 1937. At the Harvard Psychological Clinic in the 1930's, he and his students and colleagues from a variety of fields undertook a large scale investigation of human personality. A portion of this work led to the more recent research on achievement need and will be described shortly.

In 1943, Murray joined the Army Medical Corps. He established and directed a project designed to screen and assess candidates for the Office of Strategic Services. His work in this connection brought him the Legion of Merit in 1946. After his return to Harvard in 1947 and until his retirement in 1962, his teaching and research interests continued to encompass the fields of personality and clinical psychology.

Explorations in Personality. The work of Murray's group at Harvard culminated in a book, *Explorations in Personality* (Murray, 1938), which was to have considerable impact on the field of personality. In fact, it was Murray and a Harvard colleague, Gordon Allport, who created and defined the field of personality in American psychology. Murray's unusual background affected the way in which his group approached the study of personality. He has indicated that the practice of medicine taught him to arrive at a valid disagnosis by inquiring about the patient's memories of interior sensations and emotions. He says, "...I have never ceased to elicit direct expressions and reports of interior experiences—somatic, emotional, and intellectual—not only as sources of indications of overt actions to be executed in the future, but as indications of occurrences that are intrinsically important" (Murray, 1959, p. 10). Medical practice also left him with the conviction that a group of trained collaborators using many different assessment techniques on a single subject could arrive at a more accurate appraisal than could a single investigator with a limited range of methods.

In studying "personology," the unit with which the Murray group chose to work was the life history of a single individual (or as much of it as could be sampled). Beginning with existing personality theories, the goal was to test hypotheses, develop new methodologies, discover empirical relationships, and in the process develop a new personality theory. The philosophical basis of Murray's approach to a science of personality is suggested by the following:

> Now, at every stage in the growth of a science there is, it seems, an appropriate balance between broad speculation and detailed measurement. For instance in the infancy of a very complex science—and surely psychology is young and complicated—a few mastering generalizations can be more effective in advancing knowledge than a mass of carefully compiled data. For in the wake of intuition comes investigation directed at crucial problems rather than mere unenlightened fact-collecting. Here we may point to the undeniable enrichment of our understanding and the impetus to further studies which has come from psychoanalytic theory. In its present stage personology seems to call for men who can view things in the broad, that is, who can apperceive occurrences in terms of the interplay of general forces. A man who has been trained in the exact sciences will find himself somewhat at a loss, if not at a disadvantage. He will find it difficult to fall in with the loose flow of psychologic

thought. He will find nothing that is hard and sharp. And so if he continues to hold rigidly to the scientific ideal, to cling to the hope that the results of his researches will approach in accuracy and elegance the formulations of the exact disciplines, he is doomed to failure. He will end his days in the congregation of futile men, of whom the greater number, contractedly withdrawn from critical issues, measure trifles with sanctimonious precision (Murray, 1938, pp. 21–22).

The specific project described in *Explorations in Personality* involved small groups, about 13 subjects at a time, who came to the Clinic three or four hours per week over a period of several months. The subjects were examined individually on as many as two dozen different tests and in experimental situations by as many as 24 experimenters. Subjects wrote autobiographies, filled out questionnaires, took ability tests, were given a hypnotic test and a level of aspiration test, responded to projective devices, were placed in an emotional conditioning situation with measures of galvanic skin response and tremor, and took part in experiments involving such things as cheating, frustration, and memory for success versus failure. The observations and measurements of each subject's behavior in these situations were then put together by a five-man Diagnostic Council, and the end-product was a psychograph or reconstruction of the subject's personality from birth onward.

The personality theory which emerged from this project is in many respects an eclectic one, borrowing terms and concepts from many theorists and combining them with original notions. The most influential portion of Murray's theory has been his approach to needs.

n *Ach.* One influence on Murray's work from his medical and biological days was his conviction that an early step in any discipline should be a classification of the entities and processes with which one is dealing. His taxonomy of human needs is one example of this concern. He distinguished and defined 28 needs, each designated by abbreviations such as n Aff (affiliation need), n Dom (dominance need), n Sex (sexual need), and the one which will be the focus of this chapter, n Ach or achievement need. This motive, n Ach, was defined as "...the desire or tendency to do things as rapidly and/or as well as possible" (Murray, 1938, p. 164).

Thematic Apperception Test. One of the assessment procedures developed in the Harvard Clinic, the TAT, was a projective device which has become a standard instrument in the practice of clinical psychology and which has also become the object of intensive research interest. The idea was to have subjects create a story, and in the process to reveal wishes, fears, and memories of which he was unaware or which he would not ordinarily want to reveal to others. A series of pictures was used to stimulate the story-telling process.

The investigators settled upon a set of pictures which were administered as a test of "creative imagination." Subjects were instructed to make up a plot or story for which each picture could be used as an illustration. In the Harvard project, the TAT was interpreted in terms of many variables, including the expression of needs.

For Murray's group, then, the TAT was only one assessment procedure among many, and achievement need was only one personality variable among many. More specific attempts to use fantasy material to measure n Ach were not made until the late 1940's with the development of a quantified n Ach scoring system for thematic apperception stories.

CONSTRUCTION OF THE n ACH SCORING SYSTEM

THE WESLEYAN PROJECT

Building upon the work of Murray, David C. McClelland (1917–   ) initiated a research project in 1947 at Wesleyan University which resulted in an extremely fruitful approach to the study of the need to achieve. Wesleyan was also the institution at which McClelland did his undergraduate work. He received the A.B. degree in 1938, the year in which *Explorations in Personality* was published. He went to Missouri for an M.A. degree in 1939 and then entered graduate school at Yale. After the Ph.D. degree was awarded him in 1941, McClelland spent a year as an Instructor at the Connecticut College for Women. He then returned to Wesleyan for a very productive fourteen years during which his initial work on n Ach was carried out. In 1956, he moved to Harvard as chairman of the Center for Research in Personality and then as chairman of the Department of Social Relations.

From 1947 to 1952 the achievement motive was the central concern of the Wesleyan group. This work was summarized in book form in 1953 by McClelland, John W. Atkinson, Russell A. Clark, and Edgar L. Lowell. Interestingly enough, though they utilized Murray's concept of n Ach and Murray's TAT as a measurement technique, their approach to the study of personality was in dramatic contrast to Murray's:

> . . .We have discovered that concentration on a limited research problem is not necessarily narrowing; it may lead ultimately into the whole of psychology. In personality theory there is inevitably a certain impatience—a desire to solve every problem at once so as to get the "whole" personality in focus. We have proceeded the other way. By concentrating on one problem, on *one motive,* we have found in the course of our study that we have learned not only a lot about the achievement motive but other areas of personality as well. So we feel that this book can be used as one basis for evaluating the degree to which a "piece-meal" approach to personality is profitable, an approach which proceeds to build up the total picture out of many small experiments by a slow process of going from fact to hypothesis and back to fact again (McClelland, et al., 1953, p. vi).

One impetus for research on n Ach was the belief that experimental work on secondary drives at the human level had been relatively neglected by psychologists. The TAT was chosen as a measuring device because fantasy, which is analogous to Freud's use of dreams, appeared to be a good place to look for the effects of motivation. Experimental work with animals suggested the usefulness of being able to manipulate motives experimentally. Thus, the original plan was to devise a way to experimentally manipulate a secondary drive and to determine the effect of this manipulation on fantasy material produced by the subject. The researchers would then be able to determine the specific aspects of fantasy which were indicators of the aroused motive rather than simply to rely on clinical inferences about the meaning of such material.

As a first step, Atkinson and McClelland (1948) took a primary motive about which a good deal is known (hunger) and tested the effects of food-deprivation on thematic apperception stories. Male Naval personnel at a submarine training school were divided into groups that had been without food for one hour, four hours, or 16 hours. Seven thematic apperception pictures were projected on a screen, and the subjects wrote stories in response to each. Significant relationships were found between hours of deprivation and content categories such as an increase in the number of deprivation themes in the stories and an increase in the number of plots about overcoming food deprivation. There was found to be a decrease in the amount of eating in the stories and in invitations to eating. Given this success in measuring n Food with fantasy material, the experimenters moved on to the construction of an n Ach scoring system.

Need for Achievement

First reported in 1949 by McClelland, Clark, Roby, and Atkinson, the test construction procedure involved having groups under achievement-arousing conditions and groups under nonarousing conditions each write thematic apperception stories, scoring these stories for a number of achievement-related categories, and determining statistically which categories were reliable indicators of aroused n Ach. Only male students were used.[1]

The four pictures employed were:
1. Two men in a shop working at a machine, often seen as inventors.
2. Boy in checked shirt at a desk, an open book in front of him.
3. An older and a younger man, often seen as father and son.
4. Boy with vague operation scene in background.
The subjects were told:

[1] The achievement motive in females apparently has different characteristics than in males, and almost all of the work to be described in this chapter is confined to male subjects. The problem of female n Ach is discussed in a later section.

This is a test of your creative imagination. A number of pictures will be projected on the screen before you. You will have twenty seconds to look at the picture and then about four minutes to make up a story about it. Notice that there is one page for each picture. The same four questions are asked. They will guide your thinking and enable you to cover all the elements of a plot in the time allotted. Plan to spend about a minute on each question. I will keep time and tell you when it is about time to go on to the next question for each story. You will have a little time to finish your story before the next picture is shown.

Obviously there are no right or wrong answers, so you may feel free to make up any kind of a story about the pictures that you choose. Try to make them vivid and dramatic, for this is a test of *creative* imagination. Do not merely describe the picture you see. Tell a story about it. Work as fast as you can in order to finish in time. Make them interesting. Are there any questions? If you need more space for any question, use the reverse side (McClelland, et al., 1953, p. 98).

Several different procedures were used to arouse the achievement motive and both the aroused and nonaroused groups were given the TAT cards immediately afterward. Story content was scored by judges, and then the frequency of each content category occurring in the various experimental conditions was compared. Each scoring category which yielded significant differences across groups was then defined as a fantasy response which indicated the presence of *n* Ach.

Of the twelve categories which were found to vary across experimental conditions, two examples are given below:

1. Achievement Imagery is scored for stories in which an achievement goal is included.

Example: A group of medical students are watching their instructor perform a simple operation on a cadaver. A few of the students are very sure they will be called on to assist Dr. Hugo. In the last few months they have worked and studied. The skillful hands of the surgeon perform their work. The instructor tells his class *they must be able to work with speed and cannot make many mistakes.* When the operation is over, a smile comes over the group. Soon they will be leading men and women in the field.

2. Instrumental Activity is scored if the activity of at least one of the characters in the story indicates that something is being done to attain an achievement goal, whether successfully or unsuccessfully.

Example: James Watt and his assistant are working on the assembly of the first steam engine. They are working out the hole for a slide valve of the first successful steam engine...All previous experiments have failed. Successful use of steam has not been accomplished. If the slide valve works, the first compound steam engine will be harnessed. *James Watt is pulling the pinion in place for the slide valve.* His assistant is watching. The purpose is to make a pinion to hold the yoke in place which will operate the slide valve. If the slide valve works satisfactorily, they will perfect it for use in factories and for use on the railway. *It will work.*

To construct the test, the achievement motive was manipulated in order to identify and to validate those aspects of fantasy material which are affected by motive arousal. In subsequent research the thematic apperception pictures are given and the subjects' stories written under nonarousing conditions. The assumption is made that differences in achievement fantasy in a neutral situation reflect differences in the characteristic level of this motive for each individual. Those who obtain very high *n* Ach scores in a nonarousing condition are assumed to function normally at the level attained by the experimental subjects when the drive has been deliberately aroused. Individual differences in a neutral situation constitute the personality variable of need for achievement.

RELIABILITY

Interjudge Consistency. When relatively complex subjective judgments must be made in order to score a set of responses, considerable care is needed to be able to obtain adequate interjudge consistency. With *n* Ach, categories are defined in some detail, actual examples of scorable and nonscorable instances of each category are provided, and practice protocols are available for those learning the system. With about a week of preparation, one can learn the system well enough to attain an interjudge consistency of over .90 (McClelland, et al., 1953).

Internal Consistency. Attempts to build internally consistent sets of pictures have met with some difficulties. Atkinson (reported in McClelland, et al., 1953) utilized an eight-picture set by combining the four original ones with four others in various orders of presentation. After elimination of the least reliable picture, the split-half reliability of the remaining pictures was found to be .78. On the basis of more extensive data, both published and unpublished, Entwisle (1972) estimates that reliability is much lower than that.

Consistency over Time. Test-retest reliability is not much more impressive than measures of internal consistency. Reported coefficients have ranged from .03 over an eighteen-month period (Birney, 1959) to .64 over a five-week period (Morgan, 1953). Using a three-week time period, Haber and Alpert (1958) found test-retest coefficients of .36 for cards which elicit few *n* Ach stories and .59 for cards which elicit a relatively large number of *n* Ach stories. Murstein (1963) has summarized much of this research. At best, the scores appear to be only moderately stable over a fairly brief period of time.

EFFECTS OF PICTURE CUES ON RESPONSE
TO TAT CARDS

In questionnaire tests, it seems obvious that alterations in the wording of the items can lead to different responses from subjects. When the test materials consist of pictures, it is equally reasonable to suppose that picture changes would lead to response changes. A pictorial stimulus is quite complex, however, and it is by no means easy to determine precisely which aspects of the picture are eliciting which responses. For example, Alper and Greenberger (1967) found that when the figures in the picture are facing one another, more achievement imagery is evoked than when faces are averted.

It was pointed out by Veroff, Feld, and Crockett (1966) that individuals with different social backgrounds may not be measured comparably when they are exposed to the same set of pictorial stimuli. For example, the characters and settings must necessarily represent a given social class; would individuals who belong to the depicted class respond any differently from members of other social classes? One general assumption has been that, ideally, the situation portrayed in the test should be close to the life situation of the individual taking the test.

Veroff et al. tested the effects of picture content in relation to the prediction of occupational mobility. That is, high need achievers are found to be upwardly striving, so the research question was whether the same pictures can predict this characteristic for men in different kinds of occupations. The subjects were men whose occupations could be classified as either white collar or blue collar. The TAT pictures also could be classified as representing one or the other occupational group. Mobility was defined as the prestige of the subject's occupation in relation to the prestige of his father's occupation. The subjects were interviewed and tested in their homes as part of a nationwide survey.

It was found that achievement imagery predicted upward mobility best when the picture content was different from the subject's actual occupation. That is, for men in white-collar occupations, the best predictor of mobility was the imagery aroused by the picture showing two men in work clothes, working in a shop at a machine. For men in blue-collar occupations, the best predictor was in response to a picture of men grouped around a table, possibly at a conference or a committee meeting. The results were interpreted as indicating that the most appropriate measure of motives is provided by tests that place the person in a situation with which he is not intimately familiar. When familiar situations are shown, the responses can involve habitual activities and outcomes rather than underlying motives and fantasies.

ANTECEDENTS OF NEED FOR ACHIEVEMENT

Theoretical Background

The antecedents of individual differences in the achievement motive have been of considerable interest to those working with this variable. McClelland, et al. (1953) hypothesized that motives are learned on the basis of the type of affective experiences which are associated with specific kinds of behavior. With *n* Ach, the relevant behavior should be that which occurs in situations involving standards of excellence and competition to attain these standards. If a child is raised in such a way that competition is stressed, such as when the child is expected to perform well on various tasks by himself, and positive reinforcement is provided for doing well and negative reinforcement provided for failure, the strength of the child's motive to achieve should be relatively high. On the other hand, if competition is not stressed, if little encouragement is given to compete for standards of excellence, and if parents are equally accepting of success and failure, a strong achievement motive would not be expected to develop.

We could assume on general grounds that there are marked differences among cultures in their stress on achievement and success and marked differences among families within a culture. McClelland, et al. (1953) suggested the hypothesis that individuals with high achievement motivation had been forced to master problems on their own more often and earlier than individuals with low achievement motivation.

Child-Rearing Practices Attributed to Parents

Severity. In the Wesleyan project, McClelland, et al. (1953) obtained data dealing with life history and family background. After a two-hour interview, a psychiatrist and each subject were asked to rate the subject's parents with respect to several aspects of child-rearing practices. For both the subject's own ratings and those made by the psychiatrist, the higher the *n* Ach score of the sons, the more the parents tended to be seen as autocratic, rejecting, unprotective, unsolicitous, and tending toward neglect and rigidity. Among the individual scales, the highest single correlation (.49) was between *n* Ach and perceived rejection by the father. The more the sons felt loved and accepted by their fathers, the lower their achievement need.

Duties and Responsibilities. Two samples of ten- to eleven-old boys were given the TAT and a scale asking for their description of their parents' behavior (Cox, 1962). In both samples, a significant relationship existed between achievement themes in the stories and the number of household duties and responsibilities in which the child said he participated. It was suggested that this measure reflects parental demands and expectations concerning distribution of duties and responsibilities in the home and perhaps also their more general demands and expectations.

Measures of Parental Behavior and *n* Ach of Offspring

Independence Training. Children in all cultures have various skills and accomplishments which must be mastered at some point in the developmental process. They must learn to walk, to talk, to feed themselves, to urinate and defecate in specific places under specific circumstances, and to dress themselves. There are differences among families with respect to how early the child is expected to master a given behavior. It has been hypothesized that parental insistence on early mastery leads to higher achievement need and greater independence.

Winterbottom (1958) obtained *n* Ach scores on boys in the eight-to-ten age group. In addition, the mothers of the boys were interviewed in order to obtain their attitudes concerning independence training. For example, each mother was asked to indicate the age by which she demanded her son to learn of a series of behaviors, including "to know his way around his part of the city so he can play where he wants without getting lost," "to take part in his parents' interests and conversations," "to be able to undress and go to bed by himself," and "to earn his own spending money."

The subjects were divided into high *n* Ach and low *n* Ach subgroups, and the responses of their mothers were compared. The mothers whose sons were high in *n* Ach expected the independence demands to be met at a significantly younger age than the mothers of low *n* Ach sons. For example, the mothers of high *n* Ach sons expected 60 percent of the behaviors to be learned by age seven, whereas the mothers of those with low scores expected only 33 percent of the behaviors to be learned by that age. The greatest differences in demands were with respect to the child's knowing his way around the city, trying new things for himself, doing well in competition, and making his own friends. Winterbottom also asked the mothers how they responded when the child was learning to do these behaviors. The *n* Ach scores of the sons of those mothers who reported responding with physical affection (kissing or hugging) were significantly higher than the *n* Ach scores of those whose mothers did not respond with physical affection. Thus, not only do the mothers of high need achievers expect and demand independent behavior at an early age, they provide affectional reinforcements when the achievement demands are met.

More recent research (Teevan and McGhee, 1972) has extended these findings by differentiating positive and negative attitudes toward achievement. For example, an individual who is highly concerned about achievement can be motivated primarily on a positive basis in that he is hoping for success or primarily on a negative basis in that he is afraid of failure. It was found that fear of failure develops when mothers respond in a neutral way to satisfactory behavior and with punishment when behavior is unsatisfactory. When there is reward for satisfactory behavior and a neutral response for unsatisfactory behavior, a positive achievement motive is developed.

Early Independence Training and Adolescent Achievement. Feld (1967) pointed out that when maternal independence training and the offspring's achievement need are measured at the same point in time, a relationship may not necessarily indicate that the mother's behavior has lasting effects on the son's behavior. In order to explore the long-term effects of early independence training, she was able to obtain a number of Winterbottom's original subjects; the boys were six years older and had reached adolescence.

There was a small amount of consistency (r = .38) in need for achievement over the six-year period between experiments. When the early maternal attitudes were correlated with the later *n* Ach of the sons, the relationship was much less strong than in the original study.

It is quite possible that a boy's achievement needs at any point in time are in large part a function of situational demands, including how his mother responds to him. If the environmental conditions remain the same, level of achievement need should remain the same. Feld obtained evidence that the mothers often responded quite differently to their adolescent sons than they did to the same boys when they were in grade school:

> What kinds of adolescent behavior might have resulted in apparent shifts in maternal attitudes? Boys who at age 8 had high *n* Achievement and showed more successful accomplishments might, at adolescence, be seen by their mothers as already sufficiently, or even excessively, independent or achievement oriented. On the other hand, the mothers who reported relatively late expectations for independent accomplishment in early childhood might be reacting to adolescent boys who are too dependent and who lack success orientation (Feld, 1967, p. 412).

It may be seen, then, that the determinants of achievement need probably are based on a continuing process of interaction between the individual and those who influence his behavior.

Achievement Training. Rosen and D'Andrade (1959) suggested that achievement training (doing things well) should be differentiated from independence training (doing things by himself). Their subjects were family groups each composed of a father, mother, and their son (age nine to eleven). Boys high and low in *n* Ach were matched for age, race, IQ, and social class. Half of each group were middle class and half were lower class. Two experimenters (one male and one female) visited the home. The parents and their son sat at a table, and the experimenters explained that the boy would be asked to perform certain tasks as part of a project investigating factors related to success in school and later success in a career.

The goal was to create a situation in which to observe the behavior of parents while the son engaged in achievement-related behavior. The experimenters were interested in parental behavior with respect to the demands they placed on their sons, the type of sanctions employed to enforce the demands, and the amount of independence the child revealed in interacting with his parents. The tasks were designed in such a way that the boys would be somewhat dependent on their parents for aid. The five tasks involved building block towers with one hand while blindfolded, solving anagrams, making patterns out of blocks, tossing rings at a peg, and constructing a hat rack using two sticks and a clamp.

A number of comparisons were made between parents of high and low need achievers. When asked how well their sons would do in stacking blocks, the parents of the high n Ach boys gave higher estimates than the parents of low n Ach boys. In the ring toss, parents were asked to decide how far away from the peg their son should stand; those with high n Ach sons selected a longer distance away than those with low n Ach sons.

In general, parents of the high need achievers seemed to be more competitive, more involved, and to feel more positively about the experimental tasks. They were more interested in their son's performance and more concerned about how well he did. They were also more likely to express approval for success and disapproval for failure.

The performance of the two groups of boys was also different. Those with high n Ach built higher block towers, constructed patterns faster, and made more anagram words than those with low n Ach. Boys high in achievement motive asked for less aid, were more likely to reject offers of help from their parents, and showed less negative and more positive affect than those low in the achievement motive.

It may seem rather obvious that independence training and achievement training are related to one another because each is found to influence the development of n Ach. Smith (1969) has provided evidence suggesting that the two aspects of child-rearing are relatively independent. High achievement motivation is most likely to develop if parents say "Do it on your own" and also say "Do it well." If parents stress just one of these values, need for achievement is less likely to develop.

THE DEVELOPMENT OF AUTONOMOUS AND SOCIAL
ACHIEVEMENT MOTIVATION

Veroff (1969), borrowing a distinction first articulated by Gough (1957), has emphasized the importance of differentiating autonomous achievement motivation and social achievement motivation. Autonomous motivation refers to internalized personal standards in which one sets his own standards of excellence. Social motivation involves a response to the standards set by others. Autonomous motivation depends on experiences in which the child acts and then evaluates what he has done; such behavior can begin to take place when he is one-and-a-half to two-and-a-half years old. He finds that it is pleasurable to accomplish goals, and he sets new and more rigorous goals for himself. Social motivation depends on comparison with others, and this process usually begins when the child starts going to elementary school, but it can obviously be fostered by nursery school experiences or by the presence of older siblings. A final stage of the development of need for achievement occurs when these two kinds of motivation become integrated; both can be operative, depending on the specific situation.

It also follows from this analysis that a well developed and mature achievement motive requires that a child experience an early sense of effectiveness and later that he have some degree of success in social comparisons. A successful mastery of autonomy is possible if the parents allow free exploration of a stimulating environment and if they give the child an opportunity to master appropriate challenges on his own. Even a restriction such as a playpen (McClelland, 1961) may give the child less opportunity to explore and to succeed. When the child is criticized or ridiculed for what he does at this age, autonomous achievement motivation fails to develop. He has to be allowed to strive to attain goals, to be successful in accomplishing what he set out to do, and to feel pleasure in his accomplishment. Successful mastery of social comparison is possible if the child compares favorably to others of his age and sex with respect to something valued by the group. He has to feel adequate in comparison to others, and he has to receive social approval from his peers. Veroff proposes that the appropriate time for such comparisons is around the age of eight or nine. If it happens too early, the child can feel highly incompetent. If it happens too late, he is not challenged. Again, he must strive to do well at something within his group and then be successful at it. If both of these kinds of development take place, the stage is set for the later mastery of an integrated achievement motivation, usually in adolescence when the individual can commit himself to some very personalized and autonomous skill.

Veroff (1969) has constructed tests to differentiate these two kinds of achievement motivation.[2] Findings to date have been supportive of his general propositions about the age periods at which each type of development occurs. Research based on this formulation is beginning to contribute to our understanding of such problems as sex and age differences in achievement and the effects of racially integrated schools on subsequent achievement.

---

[2] Earlier, scales to measure these motives were included in the California Psychological Inventory.

FATHER'S OCCUPATION AS A DETERMINANT OF
THE SON'S NEED FOR ACHIEVEMENT

Middle-class families are most likely to engage in the kind of child-rearing practices that produce high need for achievement in their offspring. Turner (1970) proposed that the nature of the father's occupation was the crucial factor underlying such findings. He examined types of occupational roles across different social classes. It was proposed that the more a father worked with people rather than with things and the more autonomy and less supervision he had at work, the more he and his wife would stress achievement, independence, and self-reliance in dealing with their children.

A study was conducted in a varied set of communities in a Southern state. Subjects were seventh and eighth grade males who were given a questionnaire about their father's occupation and also the TAT measure of *n* Ach. The questionnaire information was used to classify the paternal occupations as entrepreneurial or nonentrepreneurial in each of two social class levels. White collar entrepreneurs consisted of managers for bureaucracies and owners of a business while blue collar entrepreneurs were managers in an industry or a factory or the owner of a business. Nonentrepreneurs were engaged in a routine white collar or routine blue collar job; here, there was minimal authority or autonomy.

The relationship between the father's occupation and the son's achievement need is shown in Table 5-1. Sons of entrepreneurial fathers are much

**Table 5-1. Achievement Need of Sons as a Function
of Occupation of Their Fathers**

Father's Occupation	*Need for Achievement Scores*	
	Sons of Entrepreneurs	*Sons of Nonentrepreneurs*
White Collar	9.70	4.80
Blue Collar	8.83	3.77

(Data from Turner, 1970)

higher in achievement need than are sons of fathers in routine jobs. The reason that other investigators (e.g., Rosen, 1956) find a social class effect is that there is a much higher proportion of entrepreneurial occupations among white collar workers than among blue collar workers. In Turner's sample, 50 percent of those in white collar jobs could be classified as entrepreneurs whereas only 17 percent of the blue collar jobs fit that designation.

Turner proposed two kinds of child-rearing influences that could stem from occupational differences. First, when the occupation requires responsibility, decision making, competition, and aggressiveness, there develops an achievement ideology which is shared by both the husband and the wife and is influential in their child-rearing practices. Second, a father who is supervised and has little autonomy, authority, or decision-making power develops frustrations which can only be expressed at home. Thus, non-entrepreneurial fathers exercise authority and express aggression toward their sons. Only in their family life is it possible for them to behave in this independent way and to tell someone what to do. The results of these two occupational influences lead to quite different levels of achievement motivation in the male offspring.

CROSS-CULTURAL INVESTIGATIONS

Achievement Imagery in Folk Tales. McClelland, et al. (1953) studied the relation between independence training and n Ach in cross-cultural research as well as in interview studies of American mothers. As a measure of modal n Ach for an entire culture, folk tales of eight North American Indian groups were selected and scored for achievement need in much the same way as if the stories had been produced by experimental subjects responding to TAT cards in a laboratory. As an honors thesis, G. A. Friedman selected eight Indian stories involving the same character, Coyote, a trickster hero common to several tribes. Achievement need scores were highest for the Navaho, followed in descending order by the Ciricahua Apache, Hopi, Comanche, Sanpoil, Western Apache, Paiute, and Flatheads. The scoring of the folk tales was done independently of any knowledge about the child-rearing practices of the different groups.

The ratings of independence training as practiced in the eight tribes were obtained from the Human Relations Area Files of Whiting and Child (1953). Independence training was defined in terms of initial indulgence, age at which independence training starts, and severity of training for independence. Differences among the groups in all three child-rearing variables were significantly related to tribal differences in n Ach scores. Achievement need was higher the less the initial indulgence, the earlier independence training was begun, and the more severe the training was.

Father Dominance. Bradburn (1963), on the basis of previous investigations, suggested that boys with high n Ach had dominant mothers while boys with low n Ach had dominant fathers who tended to interfere with their sons' attempts to achieve. Since families in Turkey reflect the traditional Islamic emphasis on male dominance, he hypothesized that Turkish men should be lower in achievement need than American men. He notes:

> Almost universally, the Turks interviewed described their fathers as stern, forbidding, remote, domineering, and autocratic. Few of them had ever argued with their fathers, and those who had had done so at the price of an open break. . . .
> One man reported that even after he was married and had his own family,

he did not dare smoke or even sit with his legs crossed in his father's presence
or in any way contradict him (Bradburn, 1963, pp. 464–65).

To obtain comparable groups from the two cultures, junior executives from
Turkey were compared with junior executives in the United States. The
groups were alike in age and educational background. As predicted, the
American group was found to score higher in *n* Ach than the Turkish group.

SEPARATION FROM FAMILY

Working within the Turkish culture, Bradburn (1963) hypothesized that
since father dominance is associated with low *n* Ach, Turkish males who
were separated from their fathers at a relatively early age would be higher in
n Ach than those who remained under their fathers' influence.

His subjects were teachers in a pedagogy program at the Gazi Institute, a
teacher-training college in Ankara. Approximately half of them had lived
apart from their parents since the age of 14 in Village Institutes. Life in the
Institutes is free of the repressive family influence which would be expected
to stifle the development of the need for achievement.

The hypothesis was confirmed. For those who had lived away from their
parents by the age of 14, 67% were high in *n* Ach and 33% were low. For
those who had remained with their parents, 35% were high and 65% were
low in *n* Ach.

THE PLACE OF NEED FOR ACHIEVEMENT IN THE
STRUCTURE OF PERSONALITY

ACADEMIC PERFORMANCE

Grades, Amount of Schooling, and IQ. The importance of "motivation"
among the factors influencing academic performance is universally accepted
at the anecdotal level, but efforts to obtain relevant empirical evidence run
into difficulty. For one thing, a great many variables affect academic performance, including many different motive systems. Nevertheless, one of the
variables should be *n* Achievement.

Positive relationships have been reported between *n* Ach score and school
grades (Bendig, 1958) and between *n* Ach and IQs (Robinson, 1961). It
should be noted, however, that in some investigations no relationship has been
found between *n* Ach and academic performance (Cole, Jacobs, Zubok,
Fagot, and Hunter, 1962).

Relevance of Grades to Future Success. The possibility of a more complex
relationship between achievement need and grades was proposed by Raynor
(1970). First, he considered both need for achievement and test anxiety. The

former was conceptualized as a motivation to attain success (M_s) and the latter as a motivation to avoid failure (M_f). It was anticipated that when M_s is greater than M_f, an individual should be more motivated to achieve and hence should attain good grades. Second, there is the meaning of a given grade with respect to the individual's future career. Presumably, the relevance of any specific course will be a factor in determining whether or not achievement need would influence course performance. It was hypothesized that for individuals in whom the motive to achieve success is stronger than the motive to avoid failure, course grades would be higher if the course is related to his future career than if it is not. Students with the reverse pattern of motivation $(M_f > M_s)$ would not be expected to show the difference in career-relevant and career-irrelevant course grades.

The subjects were students in introductory psychology at the University of Michigan. They were given the TAT measure of n Ach and a test anxiety questionnaire. To determine the relevance of the course to their future career, a questionnaire was given. Grades at the end of the semester were recorded and scored with A = 4, B = 3, C = 2, D = 1, and F = 0.

In Table 5-2 may be seen the effects of achievement motivation and course

Table 5-2. Course Grades in Introductory Psychology
as a Function of Achievement Motivation
and Relevance of Course to Future Success

Motivation	Relevance of Course to Future Career	
	Low	High
Need for Achievement High and Test Anxiety Low: $M_s > M_f$	2.93	3.37
Test Anxiety High and Need for Achievement Low: $M_f > M_s$	3.00	2.59

(Adapted from Raynor, 1970)

relevance on grades in the course. As predicted, when $M_s > M_f$, grades were higher if the course was relevant for the individual's future career than if it was not. When $M_f > M_s$, there was no relationship between course relevance and grades and even a slight tendency for a reverse relationship.

OCCUPATION AND ACHIEVEMENT

Perhaps occupation more than any other factor is associated with our culturally defined criteria of success, prestige, and status. If n Ach is measuring the sort of motive which involves striving for such goals, occupational aims should be a function of *n* Ach.

Occupational Goals. Minor and Neel (1958, p. 39) suggest ". . . when an occupation is chosen, the person is in a position to perceive whether the job allows him to play the role he wants to play and whether the required role is in accord with his self concept." Their subjects were male veterans of the Korean War. The *n* Ach cards were administered to each subject, and a counsellor determined the primary occupational preference of the individual at the beginning of counselling. Various occupations were ranked with respect to prestige by a separate group of judges. In the upper end of the prestige rankings were mechanical engineer, retail sales manager, high school teacher, and news reporter. At the lower end were barber, order filler, longshoreman, and guard. When the subjects were divided into high and low *n* Ach groups, the prestige of their occupational choice was found to differ. For the high *n* Ach group, 88 percent preferred high-status occupations and only 12 percent preferred low-status jobs. For the low *n* Ach group, 54 percent preferred low-status and 46 percent preferred high-status occupations. The *n* Ach scores and the rank of the preferred occupation correlated .74.

CONTROL OF TIME AND SPACE

A number of different correlates of the achievement motive may be conceptualized as sharing a common element involving control of the environment. The individual high in *n* Ach is described as one who manipulates his environment, is concerned with utilizing his time efficiently, is one who plans ahead, is on the move, and so forth. Several of the investigations of the achievement motive have dealt with such factors.

Delay of Gratification. If high need achievers are planful, forward-looking, and desirous of maximizing success, they would be expected to be able to delay gratification in order to obtain greater rewards. Mischel (1961, p. 544) suggests: "Achievement fantasies may be thought of in part as reflecting as well as sustaining and mediating the individual's strivings for future rewards and attainments of excellence." For one thing, those high in *n* Ach have presumably learned to tolerate the waiting period between the expenditure of effort and later rewards.

The subjects were black eleven-to fourteen-year olds in Trinidad who were given a TAT measure of *n* Ach. One measure of delay preference involved a choice between a small ten cent candy bar available now and a much larger twenty-five cent candy bar which would be available in a week. Two verbal items were also used to determine preference.

1. I would rather get ten dollars right now than have to wait a whole month and get thirty dollars then.

2. I would rather wait to get a much larger gift much later rather than get a smaller one now.

Those children who chose delayed reward on the behavioral measure and on both verbal measures were significantly higher in *n* Ach than those who chose immediate reward on all three.

Time Imagery. Knapp and Garbutt (1958) assumed that high achievement need leads to a desire to manipulate the environment and acute awareness of time and its value, and hence the perception that time moves rapidly. Four TAT pictures were administered to male undergraduates. The subjects were asked to rate each of twenty-five metaphors in terms of its appropriateness in evoking a satisfactory image of time. Correlations were computed between *n* Ach scores and the ratings given to each metaphor. High need achievers found metaphors involving speed and directness most appropriate for describing time, while low need achievers responded to slow or static metaphors as most descriptive. Table 5-3 gives the six metaphors which cor-

**Table 5-3. Correlation of Ratings of Appropriateness
of Time Metaphors with *n* Achievement Scores**

Preferred by High Need Achievers Metaphor	*r*	*Preferred by Low Need Achievers* Metaphor	*r*
A dashing waterfall	.41	A devouring monster	−.49
A galloping horseman	.32	A quiet, motionless ocean	−.41
A bird in flight	.30	A stairway leading upward	−.37
A winding spool	.26	A string of beads	−.31
A speeding train	.23	A vast expanse of sky	−.31
A fleeing thief	.22	A large revolving wheel	−.23

relate most positively and the six which correlate most negatively with *n* Achievement scores. The metaphors thought most appropriate by those high in *n* Ach seem to represent a much greater sense of speed and action than is true for those chosen by the low *n* Ach subjects.

Other investigations have also dealt with *n* Ach and various aspects of time perception. Ricks and Epley (1960) determined the time span covered in each of several TAT stories written by a group of business executives. Those high in *n* Ach wrote stories which took place over a longer period of time than did those low in *n* Ach.

McClelland (1961) reports a simple behavioral test of attitudes about time conducted by Cortes. The experimenter first checked his watch carefully and then announced to a class of senior high school boys. "It is now *exactly* X o'clock. Please raise your hand if your watch is fast by any amount. Now please raise your hand if your watch is slow." Of those high in achievement need, 87 percent reported that their watches were fast compared with 44 percent of those low in achievement need. McClelland (1961, p. 327) remarks, "For the individual with high *n* Achievement, time is almost literally moving faster."

Graphic Expression. One other investigation in this series involved an attempt by Aronson (1958) to determine differences in graphic expression between individuals high and low in the achievement motive. Achievement scores were obtained for male undergraduates, and they were then asked to look at an abstract design projected on a screen for 1.8 seconds and to draw what they had seen. A content analysis procedure was carried out to compare the drawings of high and low scorers on the *n* Ach measure.

Those high in *n* Ach, compared to those with low scores, drew single, unattached, discrete lines rather than overlaid and fuzzy lines, left a smaller margin at the bottom of the page, drew more diagonal designs, produced more S-shaped lines, and drew fewer lines consisting of multiple curves. Examples are shown in Figure 5-1.

The graphic scoring system for *n* Ach was undertaken without preliminary hypotheses concerning what sort of differences might be found, but McClelland (1961) suggested that high need achievers seem to doodle restlessly, to seek variety in what they draw, and to fill up as much space as possible.

SELF-IDEAL DISCREPANCY AND ACHIEVEMENT NEED

Mukherjee and Sinha (1970) proposed that individuals high in achievement need perceive themselves more positively and hence closer to their ideal selves than those low in achievement need.

The subjects were a large group of graduate students at Nagpur University in India. They were given measures of *n* Ach and a test of self-concept and ideal self-concept covering six dimensions: sociability, flexibility, general competence, emotional stability, leadership, and acceptance of others.

The relationships between *n* Ach and each aspect of the self-concept measure are shown in Table 5-4. On each dimension, those high in need for achievement indicate a closer relationship between their self-concept and their ideal self than do those low in achievement need. Those low in achievement need seem to set unrealistically high goals but realize that they cannot attain them. For those with high *n* Ach, what they want to be is what they are.

THE ACHIEVING SOCIETY

One of the most unusual aspects of the *n* Ach scoring system in contrast to most other personality measures is the fact that any prose material can be scored in the same way that TAT stories are scored. Thus, unlike IQ tests or

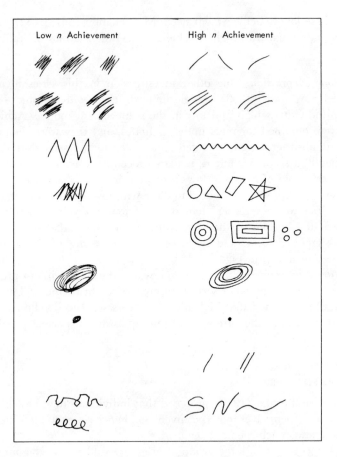

Fig. 5-1 Differences in Graphic Expression as a Function of n Achievement.

**Table 5-4. Relationship between Need for Achievement
and Self-Ideal Discrepancy**

Self-Ideal Discrepancy with Respect to	Need for Achievement		
	Low	Medium	High
Competence	26.40	16.29	13.73
Leadership	13.73	8.82	7.97
Sociability	15.64	8.85	5.67
Emotional Stability	11.33	12.18	5.67
Flexibility	11.24	8.35	5.12
Acceptance of Others	10.73	8.35	5.52

(Data from Mukherjee and Sinha, 1970)

the California F scale or almost any other widely used measure, *n* Ach scores may be obtained for any individuals who have produced written material, including those who lived centuries ago. We have seen one example of this procedure in the scoring of the Indian folk tales. The possibility of utilizing the *n* Ach scoring system in this way led to an ambitious project by McClelland and his colleagues, an unusual type of research for psychologists in that it invades the domains of history, economics, and sociology. The general background for this research is given by McClelland in *The Achieving Society*:

> From the top of the *campanile,* or Giotto's bell tower, in Florence, one can look out over the city in all directions, past the stone banking houses where the rich Medici lived, past the art galleries they patronized, past the magnificent cathedral and churches their money helped to build, and on to the Tuscan vineyards where the *contadino* works the soil as hard and efficiently as he probably ever did. The city below is busy with life. The university halls, the shops, the restaurants are crowded. The sound of *Vespas,* the "wasps" of the machine age, fills the air, but Florence is not today what it once was, the center in the 15th century of a great civilization, one of the most extraordinary the world has ever known. Why? What produced the Renaissance in Italy, of which Florence was the center? How did it happen that such a small population base could produce, in the short span of a few generations, great historical figures first in commerce and literature, then in architecture, sculpture and painting, and finally in science and music? Why subsequently did Northern Italy decline in importance both commercially and artistically until at the present time it is not particularly distinguished as compared with many other regions of the world? Certainly the people appear to be working as hard and energetically as ever. Was it just luck or a peculiar combination of circumstances? Historians have been fascinated by such questions ever since they began writing history, because the rise and fall of Florence or the whole of Northern Italy is by no means an isolated phenomenon (McClelland, 1961, p. 1).

Research was undertaken to attempt to make sense of the economic growth and decline of cultures as a function of changes in the achievement motive. The general scheme formulated by McClelland and his colleagues as connecting links between *n* Ach and the achievements of a society is outlined in Figure 5-2.

The Protestant Reformation and n *Achievement.* The German sociologist Max Weber presented a description of the new character type brought about by the Protestant Reformation—a shift toward self-reliance and the new capitalistic spirit in Western Europe. In other words, the Protestant Reformation brought about the development of high need achievers.

If this general idea has any validity, a number of specific predictions may be tested. For example, given the findings of the child-rearing studies, Protestant parents should stress earlier independence training than Catholic

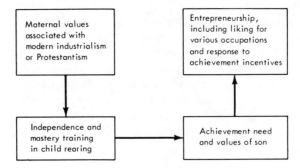

Fig. 5-2 Proposed Relationships among Mothers' Attitudes, Sons' Values, *n* Ach, and Entrepreneurial Behavior. (Adapted from McClelland, 1961, p. 58.)

parents. McClelland, Rindlisbacher, and de Charms (1955) obtained samples of Protestant, Irish-Catholic, and Italian-Catholic parents, matched for socioeconomic level, and administered Winterbottom's scale of expectancies and demands concerning independent behavior. The differences between the groups were significant and in the predicted direction, with the Protestant parents expecting independence earlier. Another prediction was that among male children, higher *n* Ach would be found for Protestants than for Catholics. With a group of German boys, the mean *n* Ach of Protestants was significantly higher than that of Catholics.

A still more general prediction would be that Protestant countries are more economically advanced than Catholic countries. As a measure of economic development, McClelland (1955) used consumption of electricity as measured by kilowatt-hours per capita as of 1950. Since advanced economies tend to be primarily in the temperate zone, and since a number of Catholic countries are in Central America and the northern part of South America, nations lying in the tropics were omitted in order to make the test more fair. The Protestant countries (Norway, Canada, Sweden, United States, Switzerland, New Zealand, Australia, United Kingdom, Finland, Union of South Africa, and Denmark) were found to have an average of 1,983 kwh/cap in 1950. A significantly lower average of 474 kwh/cap was found for the Catholic countries (Belgium, Austria, France, Czechoslovakia, Italy, Chile, Poland, Hungary, Ireland, Argentina, Spain, Uruguay, and Portugal). Even when a correction is made for differences in natural resources, the Protestant countries do better than expected and the Catholic countries do worse than expected.

n Ach and Economic Growth. To assess a nation's mean *n* Ach, the decision was made to select children's readers used in the second to fourth grades and to score the stories in these books according to the *n* Ach scoring system.

Such readers are relatively standardized within a country, are read by nearly all school children of a given age, and represent the popular culture. By going back in time one generation and obtaining n Ach scores, McClelland (1961) hoped to be able to predict the subsequent economic growth of various countries. Stories from 23 countries were collected from the time period 1920–1929 and scored for n Ach. Subsequent economic growth was measured as changes in kwh/cap between 1929 and 1950 in terms of deviation from expected growth. McClelland found that achievement need expressed in the children's stories correlated .53 with this index of economic growth. Children's stories for 1950 were also scored for n Ach, and no correlation was found between achievement scores and *previous* economic growth. It seems that this measure of a culture's n Ach level is associated with subsequent growth presumably because the n Ach was responsible for the growth.

If this proposition is correct, however, the n Ach estimates for 1950 should be related to economic growth *after* 1950. The correlation between n Ach in the 1950 children's stories and deviation from expected economic growth between 1952 and 1958 was .43. McClelland (1961) suggested that the level of n Ach present in children's readers is an index of the motivational level of the adults in the country at the time. That is, adults write the books and other adults select them for use in the school system. If these individuals express high levels of achievement motivation and if they are typical of adults in the nation, the increases in economic activity could be expected.

n *Ach and Changes within a Society.* An investigation by de Charms and Moeller (1962) sampled children's readers in the United States from 1800 to 1950. At least four books from each twenty-year period were obtained and scored for the achievement motive. As an index of achievement in the society, the investigators divided the number of patents issued by the U.S. Patent Office for each twenty-year period by the population at the middle of each period. The index was patents issued per one million population. They found that achievement imagery in the readers rose rapidly from 1800 to 1890, and then declined steadily after that period. As shown in Figure 5-3, achievement imagery and the patent index show remarkably similar patterns. The two measures correlate .79. Affiliation imagery in the stories was also scored, and this motive revealed a steady increase over the same time period. We seem to have been concerned more with affiliation than with achievement for some time now. Current novels and movies also appear to reflect an emphasis on interpersonal relationships rather than on success.

In further research, the McClelland (1961) group investigated the relationship between n Ach as estimated from various types of written material and economic growth in a variety of countries in the past. Space does not permit a full description of these studies, but a sampling of the findings provides a general picture.

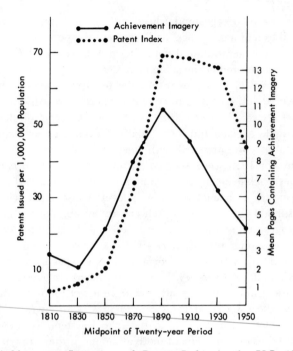

Fig. 5-3 Achievement Imagery and Patent Index in the U.S. 1800–1950. (Adapted from de Charms, R., and Moeller, G. H., "Values expressed in American children's readers: 1800–1950." *Journal of Abnormal and Social Psychology*, 1962, *64*, 139. © 1962 by the American Psychological Association and reprinted by permission.)

For ancient Greece, n Ach was highest in the early period of growth (900 B.C. to 475 B.C.), began to decline during the climax of Greek civilization (475 B.C. to 362 B.C.), and reached a low point as the nation went into economic decline (362 B.C. to 100 B.C.) (Berlew, 1956). Exactly the same pattern was found for Spain in the late Middle Ages for periods of economic growth (1200 to 1492), climax (1492 to 1610), and decline (1610 to 1730) (Cortes, 1960). For England, from the time of the Tudors to the Industrial Revolution, Bradburn and Berlew (quoted in McClelland, 1961) found a correspondence between n Ach in English literature and rates of gain in coal imports at London fifty years later.

The correspondence of n Ach and economic activity in these three cultures is shown graphically in Figure 5-4.

n *Ach and Psychogenic Death Rates.* Rudin (1968) provides a quite different kind of result of societal differences in achievement need. In contrast to the generally positive effects of high levels of achievement need stressed by others, he suggested that n Ach could also produce undesirable psychological

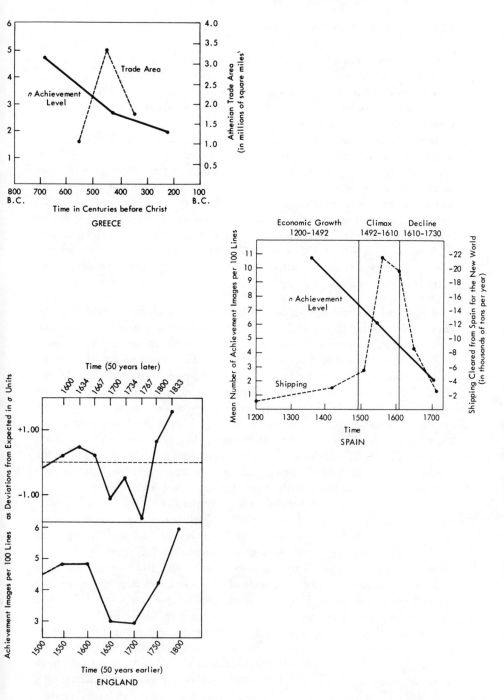

Fig. 5-4 *n* Achievement and Economic Activity in Greece, Spain, and England. (Adapted from McClelland, 1961, pp. 120, 132, and 139. Courtesy of D. Van Nostrand Company, Inc.)

effects in a society. Rudin proposed that hard-driving achievers are likely to suffer from psychogenic ailments such as ulcers and hypertension.

The need for achievement scores for sixteen countries in 1925 were obtained from McClelland (1961). Death rates in these countries for 1950 were obtained from a United Nations publication.

It was found that the need for achievement index for 1925 correlated highly with death rates in 1950 for ulcers ($r = .57$) and hypertension ($r = .52$).[3] Another proposal was that individuals in high need achieving countries would seek an escapist type of recreation and would avoid recreation that was more intellectually demanding. In support of this hypothesis, the 1925 need achievement scores were found to be positively related to per capita movie attendance in 1955–58 ($r = .55$) and negatively related to per capita book production in 1955–58 ($r = -.48$). Thus, high need achievement in a culture could be seen as associated with hard work, psychosomatic illness, and nonintellectual relaxation at the movies.

n *Ach and Interest in Business.* Still another link in the general proposal concerning the achieving society concerns individual differences in *n* Ach and individual differences in attraction to and success in the field of business.

The Strong Vocational Interest Blank (SVIB) yields scores which compare an individual's test response with the responses of individuals who are successful in various occupations. Among a group of college freshmen, the responses to the SVIB of those highest in *n* Ach were compared with the responses of those lowest in *n* Ach. The only occupational scales on which the two groups differed significantly were stockbroker, real estate salesman, advertiser, buyer of merchandise, and factory manager. In each instance, the occupation is in the field of business, and in each instance those high in *n* Ach responded more like those in the field than did those low in *n* Ach.

An entrepreneurial job involves taking responsibility for initiating decisions and for their consequences, objective feedback of the success of these decisions, and risk. Meyer, Walker, and Litwin (1961) selected managers in several manufacturing plants who held positions of this type. A group of nonentrepreneurial specialists was also chosen, and the two groups were matched for salary or status, age, years of education, and length of time with the company. The mean *n* Achievement score of the managers (6.74) was found to be significantly higher than that of the specialists (4.77).

A relationship between *n* Ach and engagement in entrepreneurial occupations does not necessarily indicate that *n* Ach is responsible for occupational choice. Among other possibilities, the demands of such jobs could well have an influence on the test scores. The latter interpretation is not supported by a

---

[3] It should be noted that a subsequent study of these same variables (Barrett and Franke, 1970) concluded that psychogenic deaths have social, economic, and medical explanations rather than a psychological one.

longitudinal study conducted by McClelland (1965a). A group of Wesleyan graduates had taken the *n* Ach measure while in college and a fourteen year follow-up was made to determine the type of occupations into which they had entered. It was found that 83 percent of those in entrepreneurial occupations had received high *n* Ach scores while in college; only 21 percent of those in nonentrepreneurial occupations had received high scores. Thus, achievement need in adolescence seems to influence later occupational choice.

n *Ach and Success in Business.* Andrews (1967) sought to trace the relationship between an individual's achievement level and his subsequent performance in the business world. Businessmen do not tend to influence the national economy by what they do as individuals but by their participation in large organizations. If business firms provide a way for high need achievers to work effectively, need achievement should lead to rapid national economic growth. If the organizations are not structured in this way, high *n* Ach may lead only to frustration.

Since high achievement motivation leads an individual to engage in hard and effective work, this would seem to insure his success in a business firm. But, what if the values and judgments of his superiors in the firm involve elements other than achievement, productivity, and success? Here, an individual's achievement need might be expected to hinder his success.

In Mexico, two firms which were quite different in value orientation were identified. One (Firm A) was highly achievement-oriented, progressive, expansive in its policies, and economically successful. The other (Firm P) was power-oriented, conservative, traditional, and less successful economically. The subjects were Mexican executives working for the two firms who had taken TAT measures as part of a testing program. In addition to *n* Ach, the stories were scored in a similar manner for need for power. Success in each firm was defined in terms of the status of the individual's job and the number of promotions received in the preceding four years.

First, a strong trend was found for the executives in Firm A to be higher in *n* Achievement and lower in *n* Power than the executives in Firm P. Second, the relationship between the motivations of individual executives and their success in each kind of firm is shown in Table 5-5. In Firm A, achievement need is positively related to success and need for power is negatively related to status in the firm. In Firm P, need for power is positively related to success; *n* Ach is negatively related to status.

Andrews concluded that the pattern of status and achievement in the two firms represented the outcome of a mutual adjustment process between men with different motivational concerns and firms with different organizational values. He also suggested that business is not always attractive to high need achievers: Only when business firms value *n* Ach would that relationship hold. Further, there should be more such firms in high *n* Achievement nations than in low *n* Achievement nations.

Table 5-5. Correlations Between Motive Scores of Executives and Two
Indices of Success in Business in Firms Oriented toward Achievement and Power

	Success in Business	
	Job Status	Promotions in Previous Four Years
Firm Oriented toward Achievement		
n Achievement of Executives	.64	.43
n Power of Executives	−.39	.11
Firm Oriented toward Power		
n Achievement of Executives	−.37	.00
n Power of Executives	.38	.34

(Data from Andrews, 1967)

DYNAMICS OF THE NEED FOR ACHIEVEMENT

RESISTANCE TO CONFORMITY PRESSURES

Those high in achievement need are described as independent, furnished
with an internal "gyroscope" of values, and oriented toward performing
tasks well rather than toward pleasing others through conformity. On these
bases, McClelland, et al. (1953) hypothesized that high n Ach should be
associated with independent, nonconforming behavior. In various conformity
tasks (e.g., Krebs, 1958), subjects high in achievement need are the least
likely to conform. McClelland, et al. (1953, p. 287) conclude: "They are
independent in action as well as thought; their independence appears almost
to be a consistant 'way of life' . . ."

TIME ESTIMATION

We all know that there is not a constant relationship between the passage of
time as measured by clocks and our subjective perception of time. For example, an hour spent in studying for an exam for a dull course can seem like
four hours while an hour spent on an enjoyable date can appear to last 15
minutes. Meade (1966) proposed that achievement need is one of the
factors that influences subjective time estimation. "Time for the high need
achiever is regarded as a commodity not to be wasted, while it is of much
less importance to the low need achiever" (Meade, 1966, p. 578). He further
hypothesized that time estimation in high need achievers would be affected
by their performance on an achievement-related activity while low need
achievers would not respond to such cues.

    The subjects were male college students who scored either extremely high
or extremely low on the TAT measure of n Ach. In the experiment, watches
were removed so that the subject had no external means of measuring time.

There was a fifteen-minute stylus maze task in which the subject was to find his way blindfolded. Each subject had twelve trials, and the experimenter gave false feedback after each trial indicating either that the subject was making slow progress at reaching the goal or fast progress. After fifteen minutes, the task was ended and the subject had to estimate how long it had taken.

In Table 5-6 are shown the time estimates. As predicted, the high need achievers overestimated the time under slow progress conditions and under-

Table 5-6. Mean Time Estimations of a Fifteen-Minute Task for High and Low Need Achievers Given Information of Fast or Slow Progress on the Task

n *Ach*	*Feedback as to Progress on Task*	
	Slow	*Fast*
High	17.9	11.6
Low	15.8	13.8

(After Meade, R. D., "Achievement motivation, achievement, and psychological time." *Journal of Personality and Social Psychology,* 1966, *4,* 579. © 1966 by the American Psychological Association and reprinted by permission.)

estimated the time under fast conditions. The low need achievers were not particularly responsive to these situational changes. Presumably, those high in achievement motivation were more involved in and challenged by the task, and information that they were making rapid progress or slow progress had a greater subjective impact than would be true for those low in *n* Ach.

PERFORMANCE IN ACHIVEMENT-RELATED TASKS

Several experimental situations have been devised which present the subject with a task to perform involving productivity, competition, or risk-taking. Such stimulus situations are hypothesized to be of greatest relevance for individuals with strong motivation to achieve.

Interaction between Motive and Performance. Atkinson (1954) has formulated a theoretical statement of the expected relationship between motivation as measured by the TAT, environmental cues as manipulated by the experimenter, and performance. Characteristic motive strength is assessed by means of fantasy productions, and the experimenter's instructions serve to indicate an association or lack of association between the outcome of the performance and the specific motivation. "When the subject is both motivated and has the expectancy that a particular performance is instrumental to attainment of the goal, then the motive is engaged and manifested in overt striving" (Atkinson, 1954, pp. 79–80). A diagram of this schema is shown in Figure 5-5. Much of the research stemming from this formulation has been compiled by Atkinson and Feather (1966).

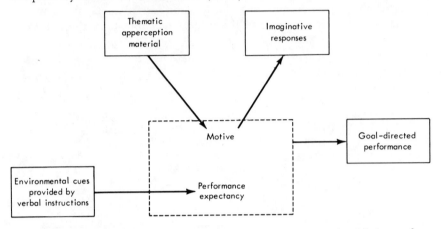

Fig. 5-5 Joint Determinants of Goal-Directed Performance by Motive and Performance Expectancy. (Adapted from Atkinson, 1954, p. 80.)

One of the early studies by Lowell (1952) investigated the relationship between *n* Achievement scores and performance on simple tasks. Groups of high *n* Ach and low *n* Ach subjects were given a series of simple addition problems to solve during a ten-minute period. Those high in *n* Ach solved more of the problems than did those low in *n* Ach.

Not only is achievement need related to performance on a task, it should also be related to an individual's expectations about how well he could perform the task, especially if the task were a somewhat difficult one. On an anagrams task described to the subjects as "moderately difficult," there was a significant positive relationship between *n* Ach and the subjects' estimates of the likelihood that they would solve all of the anagrams (Feather, 1965). This relationship did not hold when the same task was described to other subjects as a comparatively easy one. Feather hypothesized that the estimates made by the subjects were based on their past experiences of success and failure. Presumably, high need achievers have been more successful than low need achievers in performing somewhat difficult tasks.

RISK-TAKING BEHAVIOR

Theoretical Background. In extending the formulation of the interaction between motives and instructions in influencing performance, Atkinson (1957) proposed three variables as determinants of *behavior*. (1) A *motive* such as *n* Ach consists of a disposition to strive for certain kinds of satisfaction. There are avoidant as well as approach motives. Avoidant motives refer to individual differences in the painfulness of specific negative consequences of behavior. In achievement-related situations, one may assume that both the motive to achieve success and the motive to avoid failure are aroused. (2) An *expectancy* is an anticipation, usually aroused by situational cues, that a given behavior will lead to a specific consequence. (3) In addition, there is an *incentive* variable, which is the relative attractiveness of a specific goal or the relative unattractiveness of the consequences of a given goal-directed behavior. Atkinson proposed that the strength of the motivation to perform an act is a function of the strength of the motive, the expectancy or subjective probability that the act will lead to attaining an incentive, and the value of the incentive.

Without going into the details of Atkinson's theory, a few general points can be summarized. Whenever the success and failure motives are of equal strength, the resultant motivation is zero. The individual is caught between a tendency to approach the task and a tendency to avoid it; he is "frozen" halfway between, doing nothing. When the achievement motive is stronger than the fear of failure motive, the resultant motivation is positive. The individual tends to approach the task, and the motivation is strongest, when the probability of success is .50. With a 50–50 chance of success, such individuals are more highly motivated than with either very easy or very difficult tasks. When fear of failure is stronger than the achievement motive, the reverse is true. That is, the resultant motivation is negative, and it is most negative when the probability of success is .50. These individuals prefer a very easy or very difficult task. We will now see how various kinds of experimental findings fit in with these predictions. Do high *n* Ach (low fear of failure) individuals prefer an intermediate risk while low *n* Ach (high fear of failure) individuals prefer either very low or very high risk?

Preference for Different Levels of Task Difficulty. McClelland (1958) reported findings supporting these hypotheses with a group of kindergarten children engaged in a ringtoss game. Those high in *n* Ach selected an intermediate range of difficulty; that is, they chose a moderate distance from which to throw the ring at the peg. Those low in *n* Ach selected an extreme in terms of difficulty, either right on top of the peg or so far away that success was almost impossible.

Another sort of situation was utilized by Clark, Teevan, and Ricciuti (1956) who asked college students to estimate their final exam grade (the highest and lowest it could possibly be) and also to indicate what grade they would be willing to settle for if they could skip taking the final. Those who settled for an intermediate grade were significantly higher in *n* Ach than those who settled for either a grade near their maximum or minimum estimate.

In the Meyer, et al. (1961) study of managers and specialists discussed earlier, a Risk Preference Questionnaire was administered to the subjects. This instrument consisted of a list of pairs of betting choices, and the subjects were asked to choose the preferred alternative on each. Extremes of risk and nonrisk were defined as choosing 1/6 or 5/6 chance of winning. Intermediate risk was defined as choices of 2/6, 3/6, or 4/6 chance of winning. The managers (who were found to be higher in n Ach) selected the intermediate odds significantly more often than did the specialists.

Persistence at Easy versus Difficult Tasks. If an individual is presented with a task of a given difficulty level, Atkinson's theory would allow us to predict the persistence with which the task would be pursued on the basis of approach and avoidance motives. Feather (1961) used the TAT measure of n Ach as an index of M_s and the Mandler-Sarason Test Anxiety Questionnaire as an index of M_f. The subjects were male undergraduates at Michigan. For those in the upper half of the n Ach distribution and lower half of the test anxiety distribution, M_s was assumed to be higher than M_f. For those with the reverse pattern, M_f was assumed to be higher than M_s.

The subjects were presented with a "Perceptual Reasoning" test of a line diagram on a card which the subject was supposed to trace with a red pencil without lifting the pencil or retracing a line. If, within 40 seconds, the task could not be done, the subject was free to start over with the same design on a second card (again with a 40-second deadline), then with a third card, and so on. If the subject gave up, he could go on to another different design. Actually, the first design was an impossible task. Probability of success (P_s) for tracing the design correctly was manipulated by instructions to the effect that a certain percentage of college students of the subject's age level are able to solve the problem. For item one, half of the subjects were told it was easy $(P_s = .70)$, and half were told it was very difficult $(P_s = .05)$. All subjects were told that the second task was of intermediate difficulty $(P_s = .50)$.

Persistence was defined as the number of trials the subject attempted on the first design before giving up and going on to the second design. Predictions concerning differences in persistence can be made, using Atkinson's theory. For the group in which M_s is greater than M_f, subjects should persist longer on the easy task than on the hard one. For the other group $(M_f > M_s)$, subjects should persit longer on the hard task than on the easy one. Feather's data supported these predictions.

Performance on Contingent and Noncontingent Tasks. There are situations in which it is necessary to succeed in order to be able to have the opportunity to attempt future success. One must do well in undergraduate courses, for example, to be able to try his ability in graduate work. Here, success in one activity is contingent on success in other activities. Other situations are unrelated with respect to success and failure; performance in an undergraduate tennis class is irrelevant to admission to graduate school. These are noncontingent activities. Raynor and Rubin (1971) proposed that the $M_s - M_f$ relationship should be important in determining performance on contingent versus noncontingent tasks. Specifically, individuals with $M_s > M_f$ should do better on contingent than noncontingent tasks while those with $M_f > M_s$ should do better on noncontingent than on contingent tasks.

Male students at the State University of New York at Buffalo served as subjects; they were given measures of *n* Ach and of test anxiety. Subjects were led to believe that the chance of success was .5 for each of four twenty-five item arithmetic tests. Those in the contingent condition were told that the opportunity to take the second test depended on how well they do on the first test, and so on through test four. Those in the noncontingent condition were told that they would have the opportunity to take all four tests, regardless of how well they did on any one of them. Actually, only the first test was given, and then the subjects were told the purpose of the experiment and dismissed.

In Table 5-7 the results can be seen as supporting the hypothesized relationships. With respect to the number of problems attempted or the number

Table 5-7. Performance on Contingent and Noncontingent Tasks as a Function of Achievement Motivation

Performance	n *Ach* > *Test Anxiety*		*Test Anxiety* > n *Ach*	
	Contingent	*Noncontingent*	*Contingent*	*Noncontingent*
Number of Problems Attempted	18.43	15.63	8.38	14.14
Number of Problems Answered Correctly	17.43	13.00	7.00	11.86

(Data from Raynor and Rubin, 1971)

answered correctly, subjects for whom $M_s > M_f$ do better in the contingent than in the noncontingent situation. The reverse is true for those in whom $M_f > M_s$.

Another way of looking at the data is with respect to the relative performance of the high *n* Ach versus low *n* Ach groups. Achievement motive is positively related to success in the contingent condition, but it is unrelated to success in the noncontingent condition. This difference fits in well with Raynor's (1970) findings of the effect of *n* Ach on grades in courses related or not related to their future careers and with his theory of the relationship between immediate activity and its relevance to the future (Raynor, 1969).

Situational Determinants of Motivational Effects. Zander and Forward (1968) examined the effects of achievement motivation on behavior in a group situation. Motivation to achieve success or to avoid failure can presumably be aroused with respect to the activity of a group as well as with respect to an individual's personal activity. In a group, however, all participants are not equally involved in decision-making and hence in responsibility for success and failure. In that situation it would be expected that the individual's motivational pattern and his role in the group would interact to determine his response to the group's activity. Specifically, an individual in a central, decision-making role was expected to respond differently from an individual in a peripheral role; in addition, the relative strength of M_s and M_f was expected to influence this behavior.

The TAT measure of n Ach and a test anxiety questionnaire were given to a large group of eleventh-grade boys, and subgroups differing in success and failure motivation were selected. The experiment itself was described as a study of teamwork. Three-man groups were to work on a task for a series of trials to see how fast they could complete it. Their performance was to be compared with that of other groups, and they were asked to do their best. The task involved completing a design with dominoes; only the central person knew the design to be made while the two peripheral people were to slide the required dominoes under a partition when the central person asked for them. No talking was allowed, and communication was by means of written messages. Clearly, the responsibility for success fell on the central person. Each subject played different roles on different trials. The response of interest was the estimate by each group member as to how long they believed it would take to complete the next trial; examples were given to specify easy, average, and difficult goals.

It was found that intermediate group aspirations are preferred by individuals for whom $M_s > M_f$ and not for those with $M_f > M_s$ when they are in the peripheral position. The demands of the central position were so great that both motivational groups had intermediate aspirations when they were placed in that role. Another way to view the same findings is to say that the $M_s > M_f$ individuals were equally likely to chose intermediate aspirations regardless of their role whereas the $M_f > M_s$ individuals did so only when they were in the central position.

Zander and Forward noted that the $M_f > M_s$ individuals in the peripheral position chose aspirations typical of persons who tend to avoid failure, perceived themselves as less responsible for the group's outcome, and had lower evaluations of their own personal contributions. In the peripheral role these individuals could withdraw from the challenge of the group task. When they were in the central position, however, they responded just like the $M_s > M_f$ individuals. It appears that some individuals are success oriented whatever the situation. For others it takes a particular kind of situation to bring forth such behavior.

CHANGES IN NEED FOR ACHIEVEMENT

ALTERATIONS IN FAMILY STRUCTURE OR IN
CHILD-REARING PRACTICES

In considering changes in the economic growth of a society as a function of changes in *n* Achievement, McClelland (1961) in *The Achieving Society* also sought an explanation for the society-wide changes in achievement need. The two major possibilities which were suggested involved prolonged absence of the father from the home and the rearing of children by low *n* Ach servants or slaves.

Father Absence. Drawing on some of the developmental studies discussed earlier, McClelland (1961, p. 404) suggested that if dominant fathers are responsible for low *n* Ach, their absence would have the reverse effect; for example, "Wars may well have a marked and sudden effect on *n* Achievement by removing authoritarian fathers from the scene." He notes that *n* Ach showed a significant increase in both France and Germany between 1925 and 1950. Further data, obtained under more controlled conditions, are obviously needed. Nevertheless, it is intriguing to note the marked economic growth and seemingly high level of *n* Achievement since World War II in those countries most involved (for example, most of Western Europe, Russia, the U. S., Japan, China) compared to countries relatively isolated from the war (for example, Latin America, Africa, Ireland, Portugal, Turkey).

Another reason for father absence can be the occupation in which he is engaged. If a job is such that the father is away from the home for extended periods of time, the *n* Ach of the offspring should be affected in a positive direction. McClelland (1961) points out that, historically, a high incidence of sea-faring nations showed abrupt increases in economic growth. He notes as examples the Greeks, early Etruscans, British, Japanese, Scandinavians, and Genoese, and one might add the New Englanders in this country. Thus, when large numbers of dominant fathers go down to the sea in ships, the achievement need of subsequent generations seems to show an increase. As another speculation, what is the effect on future generations of the commuter culture in which the father leaves for work in early morning and returns home at the children's bed time? Functionally, these fathers are often as removed from their children's lives as if they had gone off to sea.

Child-Rearing by Slaves and Servants. Throughout history, as nations became economically and militarily powerful, slavery was instituted, and one of the tasks characteristically assigned to slaves was the rearing of the master's children. McClelland (1961) hypothesized that the slave and the slave's children should be oriented toward dependence on the master, obedience, and compliance—precisely the kind of atmosphere best suited to foster low achievement motivation. He points out that in this country, Negro slaves developed child-rearing practices emphasizing nonachievement factors. Their descendants, even though free, should still show these effects; McClelland found that lower-class blacks have the lowest average *n* Ach scores of any minority group tested. Those blacks who have moved into the middle and upper classes, on the contrary, are conspicuously high in *n* Ach.

If these general propositions about slavery are accurate, it follows that the slaveholders should also tend to develop low *n* Achievement over the generations because the slaves raise their children. The slave would be expected to respond to the master's child by indulging his every whim, thus spoiling the child. Those who founded the Southern plantations were probably high in *n* Ach, but the subsequent generations showed quite different patterns. Business enterprise in the United States has been associated with the North and even with the nonslaveholding portions of the South such as North Carolina. McClelland speculates:

> What is most fascinating about such a possibility is that it suggests a rather simple, if ironic, account of the rise and fall of many great civilizations in the past. The argument runs as follows: a people with higher level of *n* Achievement tend to pursue business enterprise more rigorously and ultimately to become more wealthy. Nearly always in the past such wealth has been used to support slaves. Certainly this was the case in Ancient Greece. Beginning around 525 B.C. when a much larger proportion of Athenian families were wealthy enough to support slaves, each child of good family was ordinarily assigned two slaves—a nurse and pedagogue to go to school with him (Glotz, 1925). Furthermore, in our sample of preliterate cultures, 45 percent of twenty cultures with high *n* Achievement versus only 19 percent of 21 low in *n* Achievement had slaves...In short, high *n* Achievement leads to increased wealth, which leads to more household slaves. But in Greece the more general use of such slaves preceded by a generation or two the marked drop in *n* Achievement....Is it unreasonable to infer that the slaves undermined the achievement training of their masters' children, although probably not consciously? So, ironically, the masters were undone by the very instrument that demonstrated, they thought, their mastery—namely, their enslavement of those they had conquered. The irony lies in the fact that what happened was certainly not *intentional* on either side. Explanations of the decline of civilizations in terms of the "decay of moral fibre," although vague and *ad hoc,* do have at least this kernel of truth in them: the institution of slavery in all probability undermined achievement training, which in turn lowered general *n* Achievement level and made civilizations less enterprising in business and more vulnerable to economic decline and ultimately attack and destruction from without (McClelland, 1961, pp. 377–78).

An analogous effect could be proposed in modern societies when low *n* Ach servants, drawn from lower socioeconomic levels, are assigned major child-rearing responsibilities by the families who can afford this luxury. As with the slave cultures, the pattern could involve enterprising activity leading to wealth and the employment of servants, leading in turn to lower *n* Ach and less business enterprise in succeeding generations.

ALTERATION IN FANTASY LIFE

Modeling Effects. If motivations are revealed in the kinds of fantasy one produces, an alteration of the content of fantasy might be expected to bring about alterations in motives. What is it that determines the content of our fantasies? Much of the content seems to have been supplied from cultural sources including myths, stories, fairy tales, songs, school readers, and so forth. At the present time, it would appear that our fantasies (and hence our motives) are at least partially determined by television, movies, and magazines.

Klinger (1967) conducted experiments with male students at the University of Minnesota. Subjects viewed models who portrayed an achievement-oriented experimenter on closed-circuit television without the audio turned on. The scene involved either achievement, affiliation, or neutral activity. The TAT was given immediately afterward.

Need for achievement as measured by the TAT was found to be influenced by these visual stimuli. Systematic long-term research is required, however, before we can state with any confidence the specific effects of our cultural fantasy factories on motivation.

A College Counselling Program. An unusual approach to bringing about a change in *n* Achievement was undertaken by Burris (1958). A group of college students enrolled in a self-improvement course wrote thematic apperception stories which were scored for achievement need. Then, in a series of eight weekly sessions lasting forty minutes each, they met to discuss the type of achievement imagery in their stories. In effect, they were directed to engage in fantasy activity centering on achievement and activity directed toward achievement goals. One matched control group of students in the same course met for counselling on how to study, while a second control group did not meet for any special sessions.

After the end of the eight weeks, the test was readministered and scored for achievement need. As predicted, the subjects in the experimental group who had discussed achievement showed a significant increase in *n* Ach. This finding alone would not be very impressive. Burris went further, however, and compared the grade-point averages the following semester of those who had shown an increase in *n* Ach versus those who were in the control groups.

He found a significantly greater increase in grade-point average for those students who had undergone the experimental treatment than for the controls.

A High School Training Program. Kolb (in press) designed a training program which was intended to increase concern for academic achievement in a group of underachieving high school boys.

The achievement motivation training program was carried out at Brown University during a six-week summer school session for high school boys. Underachievement was defined as having an IQ of 120 or higher and school grades of C or lower. The boys were divided into an experimental group which received the achievement training plus an academic summer school program and a control group receiving only the summer school program. Four major experimental ideas were incorporated in the program. It was hypothesized that need for achievement would be enhanced by the presence of effective role models, the creation of positive expectations about the effects of the program, the learning and practicing of the *n* Achievement scoring system, and participation in games that simulate various life situations relevant to achievement. In addition to extensive testing throughout the experiment, the subjects were contacted for follow-up tests at various times up to a year and a half later.

Increases in *n* Ach were, of course, shown by the experimental subjects. Improvement in school grades was the crucial variable, however. At the six-month follow-up the experimental and control groups showed no differences. By the one-and-a-half year period, however, the grade point average of the experimental group had improved significantly more than the grade point average of the control group. Kolb (in press) notes, "This would suggest that while the summer school alone gave some boost to the grades, there is a tendency for this effect to decay over time, while the addition of the [training program] to the summer program seems to promote a more permanent and perhaps increasing improvement in school grade average." When the subjects were subdivided in terms of social class, the improvement was found only for those relatively high in socioeconomic status.

The differential social class effect did not appear to be a difference in reaction to the program or ability to perform in it. Rather, it was suggested that the difference arose when the boys returned to their home environments. Boys in upper socioeconomic home environments probably received more support and encouragement for their achievement-oriented behavior.

Motivating Economic Achievement. In part influenced by the success of those various experiments, McClelland (1965b) instituted a large-scale project designed to increase *n* Achievement in business executives. Groups of individuals were brought together for one to three weeks of interaction centered on the acquisition of a high achievement motive. The general procedure includes training and practice in the production of achievement fantasy, group activities involving goal-setting and risk-taking with achievement-related tasks, role-playing activities (such as portraying a democratic father with high *n* Ach standards for his son), and an interpretation of cultural demands, values, and folklore in terms of relationship to *n* Ach. Such executive training sessions have been carried out in the United States, Mexico, and India.

McClelland and D.G. Winter (1969) reported the results of an international study attempting to alter the need for achievement. This applied research was undertaken to find out whether one could bring about a change in the spontaneous fantasies of a small segment of a nation's population and potentially bring about far-reaching economic changes.

The project began with a meeting at Harvard sponsored by the U.S. Agency for International Development (AID) attended by representatives from India, Egypt, Columbia, Tunisia, Algeria, Spain, Chili, Italy, Mexico, and Thailand. In addition to the usual complexities and lack of control typical of field research, the investigators faced extremely difficult financing problems and the inevitable red tape encountered in dealing with various government agencies and industrial concerns both in the United States and abroad. As a result of these various problems, the actual project was considerably smaller than originally planned.

Within each of two Indian cities (Kakinada and Rajahmundry), comparable groups of businessmen were chosen either to receive or not to receive achievement training. It was necessary for the subjects to leave their work to attend the special workshop in Hyderabad. The participants averaged about 36 years of age and were engaged in industry, commerce, and several professions.

The evaluation of such an ambitious endeavor is obviously difficult, and it is necessary to look at many possible kinds of changes attributable to achievement training. Table 5-8 summarizes some of the variables studied during a two-year follow-up period. The effects of achievement training may be seen when the behavior of the participants is compared with that of nonparticipants. The achievement training course appeared to influence an impressive number of indices of business and economic activities.

In addition to the statistical evidence, case studies provided a picture of the effects of the training on specific individuals (S.K. Winter, 1969, pp. 276–79):

> N is a muscular, broad-shouldered, 39-year-old businessman with curly hair and a relaxed, open smile. At the time of the course he owned a prosperous optical supply retail shop, founded by himself a number of years before on the main street...
> We were interested in interviewing N in detail because of his notable busi-

ness activity after the course. Although he had made several expansions and improvements in his business between 1950 and 1961, at the time of the achievement training there had been no changes in his firm in several years. After the course, however, N decided to become a manufacturer. Turning the routine management of his retail business over to a hired manager, he founded a small factory to manufacture a product useful in building construction. N worked persistently for over a year to overcome difficulties with licensing and procurement of raw materials, displaying a good deal of ingenuity and initiative in solving practical problems...By the time of the follow-up, the factory employed ten workers and had been in production for eight months.

Asked to recall a problem and how he surmounted it, N mentioned difficulties with licensing and financing encountered as he set up his new firm. "If it weren't for you people coming around, I would never have done it so fast." Since the achievement course, he says that he sets specific goals for himself to overcome his tendency toward procrastination. By making promises to others that he will finish a task by a given time, N says that he is more likely to get things done.

**Table 5-8. Comparison of Indian Businessmen
Receiving Achievement Training with Control Groups Receiving No Training**

	Subjects with Achievement Training		Subjects in Control Group	
	Before (1962–64)	After (1964–66)	Before (1962–64)	After (1964–66)
Entrepreneurs Classified as Active	18%	51%	22%	25%
Entrepreneurs Working Longer Hours	7%	20%	11%	7%
Entrepreneurs Starting New Businesses	4%	22%	7%	8%
Entrepreneurs in Charge of Firm Making Specific Fixed Capital Investment	32%	74%	29%	40%
Entrepreneurs in Charge of Firm Employing More People	35%	59%	31%	33%
Entrepreneurs in Charge of Firm Having Large Gross Income Increases	52%	61%	43%	38%

(Data from McClelland and D.G. Winter, 1969)

McClelland and D.G. Winter (1969) concluded that the training program worked best by strengthening the sense of efficacy among those who already wanted to feel effective and by informing them of concrete ways to reach their goals. It also worked best for those whose situations provided the opportunities to display these achievement-related characteristics.

At a more general level, the authors of the above study point out that the growing belief in social determinism has undermined man's capacity to bring about social change. They suggest an optimistic picture in which man is not necessarily seen as a hopeless victim of external forces (pp. 377–78) :

> If man's confidence in himself derived from his former conviction that he was created, looked after, and guided by an all-powerful God, where will it come from now that in popular terminology, "God is dead"? Where will he get the confidence to believe that he can act and change the course of events when he is told almost daily by the social scientists that he is not free to act, that his every reaction is predetermined by his personal and social history? Two experiences point the way to an answer to these questions. First, it is a curious paradox that the most deterministic of contemporary psychologists—namely the neo-behaviorists, followers of B. F. Skinner—are the most confident that they can create a new Utopia. The more they think they know about man, the more they think he is capable of anything. It is true that they talk in terms of creating an environment that will shape man's behavior optimally according to deterministic laws. Yet someone must act, must make the decision to create the environment and design the environment that will predetermine the best response from individuals who live in it. Where does the creator, the prime mover, get his confidence to act? From science, of course. Knowledge is the new source of power. Somehow, by thoroughly understanding how we are determined, we gain the confidence to act so as to transcend determinism.
>
> . . .Scientific knowledge is the new God, the new source of man's conviction that he has the competence to act. Yet in another sense, of course, it is a very old God, a conviction that there are certain immutable laws which exist outside of man in the universe and which, if known and obeyed, give man the power to shape his destiny.

CURRENT ISSUES IN RESEARCH ON NEED FOR ACHIEVEMENT

Objective Measurement

Given the relative difficulty involved in administering sets of TAT pictures, the subjectivity and consequent loss of reliability in the scoring system, and the amount of scoring time required per subject, it would be advantageous to be able to use a simple, objective measure of n Ach.

Among the earlier attempts to measure n Ach in an objective fashion were the California Psychological Inventory (Gough, 1952), the French Insight Test (French, 1958), and the Edwards Personal Preference Schedule (Edwards, 1959). These measuring devices do not seem to correlate with one another or with the TAT measure of achievement need (Atkinson and Litwin, 1960; Weinstein, 1969). When a series of n Ach measures were found to be uncorrelated in a study at the University of Oregon, Weinstein (1969, p. 170) concluded, "Scales with 'achievement' labels do not appear to tap the same construct, and should not be used interchangeably."

After reviewing many of the studies seeking relationships between the TAT measure and alternate objective measures, McClelland (1958, p. 38) stated: *"The conclusion seems inescapable that if the* n *Achievement score is measuring anything, that same thing is not likely to be measured by any simple set of choice-type items."* Further, he suggested that a fantasy measure of motivation is "purer" than a questionnaire measure. In a questionnaire, the subject is asked in one way or another to describe himself, and numerous extraneous factors influence such responses. In the fantasy measures, emphasis has been on what it is that individuals spontaneously think about. For example, when LeVine (1966) asked members of high (Ibo) and low (Hausa) achieving African tribes to write about how to become a successful man, they did not differ. When he asked them to write down their dreams, the Ibo produced a much higher *n* Ach content.

More recent work, however, provides evidence that objective measures may be able to do as well as the TAT. Weiner (1966) reported an attempt to validate O'Connor's (1962) objective measure, the Achievement Risk Preference Scale. It is based on Atkinson's model involving hope of success and fear of failure. Items include:

I feel:
  a) unhappy when I do something less well than I had expected.
  b) happy when I do something better than I had expected.
If I were a pinch hitter, I would like to come to bat when:
  a) my team was leading 6 to 3.
  b) the score was tied.

With results much like those reported with the TAT measure, Weiner (1966) found that the test predicted differential recall of completed and incompleted tasks for males, but not for females. Additional research with this scale has produced additional validational evidence (Weiner, 1970).

Several other investigators have also had success in developing objective measuring instruments. Mehrabian (1968c) built two objective tests to measure male and female achievement need. Items were constructed on the basis of relevant research findings with the TAT measure. On a seven-point scale of agreement-disagreement, subjects respond to such items as:

I more often attempt difficult tasks that I am not sure I can do rather than easier tasks I believe I can do.
I think more of the future than of the present and past.

Scores on these tests were found to be stable over time, to correlate moderately with the TAT measure, and to predict performance on an achievement-related task. Holmes (1971) described *n* Ach to subjects and asked them to rank themselves on this dimension with respect to their fraternity brothers or sorority sisters. For both sexes, self-rankings were correlated with grade point averages, even when the rankings were made early in their first semester of college prior to the actual report of college grades.

In an interesting approach to the problem, Sherwood (1966b) administered the TAT to naive subjects and, over the course of a semester, had them read about *n* Ach in Murray, McClelland, Atkinson, and others. Afterward, they rated themselves on achievement need. Subjects responded to three bipolar scales such as:

I frequently engage in   _ _ _ _ _ _ _ _   I seldom compete with others.
competitive activity
where winning or doing
better than someone else
is the primary concern.

The self-report measure and the projective measure correlated .35. The subjects also engaged in a scrambled words and an addition task which have been found to be related to *n* Ach. Performance on these tasks was correlated with both measures of achievement, but the best predictor was a multiple correlation using a combination of the two tests.

It would seem that there are a number of ways to measure *n* Ach objectively and that objective measures will prove to be as useful as the traditional projective approach.

CAUSE AND EFFECT INTERPRETATIONS OF
CORRELATIONAL FINDINGS

In some respects, the cross-cultural studies of *n* Achievement and the attempts to account for the achievement of nations on the basis of a personality variable are among the most exciting yet undertaken by personality psychologists. For a field still groping to develop even low-level behavioral laws, it is somewhat surprising to be in the position of predicting economic progress for nations and to be able to explain the rise and fall of empires.

The major danger in dealing with such data is the obvious one that a correlation between two variables does not necessarily mean that a causal relationship exists. McClelland is quite aware of this problem, of course, and in *The Achieving Society* he discusses a number of alternative explanations of his findings. There are two counterarguments which support McClelland's position, however.

First is the cumulative effect of a large body of consistent data. In reviewing the work on achieving societies, Mausner (1963) indicated great initial skepticism. He notes, for example, the fallacies of the correlational approach and the problems involved in measuring the modal needs of an entire nation on the basis of material such as the contents of fourth-grade readers. Nevertheless, he concludes: "This reviewer is won by the argument. The way in which the many pieces of the puzzle fit together is uncanny; the book has the feeling of a most successful detective story" (Mausner, 1963, p. 292).

The second sort of support comes from evidence aimed at making clear the connecting links between variables involved in the correlations. For example, differences between Catholic and Protestant countries in economic productivity could be explained in hundreds of ways besides that of differences in *n* Ach. When, however, parents belonging to the two religious groups are found to have different child-rearing practices and their offspring are found to differ in *n* Ach, the McClelland argument is strengthened considerably. More such links are needed. For example, James Morgan (1963), an economist, suggested that it would be convincing to see a study in which individuals whose behavior was directly contributing to a developing nation's economic growth (for example, working hard, accepting new ways of producing and consuming, taking appropriate risks) were shown to be higher in *n* Ach than individuals whose behavior was not contributing to economic growth. Positive evidence from a variety of such investigations would make the *n* Achievement thesis hard to refute.

ACHIEVEMENT NEED IN WOMEN

One of the more intriguing unresolved issues with the *n* Ach variable is the difference between males and females in achievement motivation. The general problem first became obvious in the original investigations of *n* Ach (McClelland, et al., 1953). Among other findings reported was that the achievement arousal conditions used in the construction of the test had no influence on the TAT stories of female subjects, and that some of the parent-child relationships which hold for male offspring are absent or even reversed for female offspring. One response to this state of affairs has been a tendency to direct most of the research interest to male subjects and ignore the problem of female achievement motivation. However, a few attempts have been made to explicate the reasons for the sex difference.

Men versus Women in TAT Cards. One of the first suggestions (Veroff, 1950) was that the thematic apperception pictures used to measure *n* Ach contain only male figures and hence were inappropriate for eliciting female achievement fantasy. With female high school students, responses to three male pictures and three female pictures were compared under neutral versus achievement-arousing conditions. He found that the experimental conditions had no effect on story content but that the female subjects obtained significantly higher *n* Ach scores on the *male* pictures than on the female pictures. Similar results have been reported by Lesser, Krawitz, and Packard (1963). As McClelland, et al. (1953, p. 173) noted: "...*even girls project achieve-*

ment striving primarily into the activities of men." As this statement suggests, there is apparently more to the problem than the sex of the figures in the TAT cards.

Differing Sex Roles and Achievement. One line of reasoning suggests that males and females in our culture are, in fact, basically different with respect to achievement motivation. Even with the rise of the women's liberation movement, for most members of society there are differences in the roles of the two sexes with respect to achievement. For males, achievement means success in terms of intelligence, leadership, occupational prestige, and income —all of which depend in part on the individual's own ability and hard work. For females, achievement has two meanings. First, there is personal achievement which tends to involve social acceptance or popularity with peers of both sexes, and eventually it also means the ability to run a home well as a mate, cook, housekeeper, and mother. Second, a female can achieve vicariously through the success of her husband or her sons. If these propositions have any merit, the type of conditions which would arouse n Ach and the type of behavior influenced by n Ach might well be different for females than for males.

The notion that the arousal conditions which are effective for males are inappropriate for females was tested by Field (1951). He compared the usual male-oriented arousal conditions (stressing intelligence and leadership) with conditions involving social acceptability. The subjects were told that social acceptance by others was a predictor of future social acceptance; they were then given bogus evaluations indicating either that they were socially acceptable or socially unacceptable to others. At this point the TAT cards were administered. Females receiving either type of acceptability rating had a significantly higher n Ach score than those in the control group. For male subjects, the social acceptability conditions had no effect on their n Ach scores. Thus, n Ach is aroused in males by instructions stressing leadership and intelligence and in females by instructions stressing social acceptability.

The expression of female n Ach by means of the success of their husbands is supported by the findings of Littig and Yeracaris (1965). Married females in an upstate New York community were interviewed and given a TAT measure. The interest here was in the occupational mobility of their husbands. If a woman's father and husband were both white collar workers or both blue collar workers, there was no mobility. If the father was blue collar and the husband white collar, upward mobility was indicated. If the father was white collar and the husband blue collar, there was downward occupational mobility. Mobility was found to be significantly related to n Ach. Upward mobility was more characteristic of high n Ach females and downward mobility of low n Ach females. It seems possible either that their choice of a husband was influenced by their n Ach in relation to the males' occupational potential or that their *n* Ach led them to exert influence on their husbands' occupational choice.

Achievement in School and Afterward. Still other cultural effects on female achievement need is shown in the work of Baruch (1967). She suggested that during the school years and immediately afterward women should be high in achievement motivation. Women obviously perform as well as men and often outperform them while in school or when they enter a profession. When women marry and become concerned with home and children, however, achievement motivation might be expected to decline markedly. The woman's assigned role is to be nurturant and affiliative rather than to be an achiever. Baruch also expected that in later years, there would again be a rise in *n* Ach. Her subjects were Radcliffe alumnae who constitute a highly selected and achievement-oriented group. The subjects had graduated from college 5 to 25 years prior to the study. In Table 5-9 are shown the percentage

Table 5-9. Proportion of Female Subjects Scoring High versus Medium or Low in Achievement Need as a Function of Years since Graduating from Radcliffe

	Years Since Graduation				
Achievement Need	*5*	*10*	*15*	*20*	*25*
High	57%	9%	33%	42%	33%
Medium or Low	43%	91%	67%	58%	67%

(Data from Baruch, 1967)

of high versus medium or low need achievers in each age group. It seems that shortly after graduation the high need achievers predominate; there is then a dramatic decrease in high need achievers in subsequent years. The proportion of subjects with high levels of achievement motivation rises again, but not back to the level of college and post-college days. The time period at which the decline occurs corresponds to the time that most of the subjects were having children. The later rise in *n* Ach was attributed to a growing interest in work and a return to a career. For those twenty to twenty-five years after graduation, there was a strong relationship between *n* Ach and involvement in a career. Subsequent findings with a noncollege sample indicated a more dismal picture. For poorly educated women, there is simply a steady decline of *n* Ach with age. Baruch (1967, p. 267) notes, "The opportunities are greater for the college-educated women to move from a preoccupation with achievement in fantasy to a later expression of this need through vocational behavior."

Motive to Avoid Success. An even greater barrier to female achievement has been suggested by Horner (1972). She proposes that women have learned

that successful competition and achievement actually have negative consequences. Women learn to avoid success so that they will not be rejected as
unfeminine. How many mothers have warned their daughter not to show
how intelligent she is or not to beat her date playing tennis? When a woman
sees success as likely or even possible, anxiety is aroused and achievement
strivings are thwarted. It is even found that college males indicate feelings of
high self esteem when they obtain grades of A or B while females indicate
such feelings when they are getting C's (Hollender, 1972).

A measure of individual differences in the motive to avoid success indicates
that only those females who are low on this variable perform well in competitive, mixed-sex conditions (Horner, 1968). Girls high in success avoidance
do well only in noncompetitive situations.

In her research, Horner finds that women indicate much greater fear of
success than men. An interesting sidelight is that this sex difference is reversed
for blacks. In our culture, black men are more anxious about the consequences of success than are black women. Horner suggests that the roles of
white woman and black man have much in common in contemporary American society. In both instances, it appears to be white males who have the
most to gain in maintaining such motive systems. It is a tragic waste for the
individuals themselves and for society as a whole that, for a large segment of
our population, achievement potential is systematically discouraged and hence
scarcely tapped.

SUMMARY

Achievement need is a learned motive to compete and to strive for success.
A motive or drive is a higher-order generalization and involves the concepts
of drive level, drive stimulus, instrumental responses, and goal.

Henry A. Murray is a physician, chemist, psychoanalyst, and psychologist
whose personality research at the Harvard Psychological Clinic in the 1930s
included the formulation of the *n* Achievement concept and the development
of the Thematic Apperception Test. Murray's research approach was one
involving the use of multiple investigators and multiple techniques with a
small group of subjects. The life history of a single individual was the unit
with which he chose to work. The achievement motive was defined as the
desire to do things as rapidly and/or as well as possible. The TAT is a projective test in which the subject responds to a series of pictures by making up
a story for each, presumably revealing various aspects of his personality in
his fantasies.

Current research with the *n* Ach variable was begun at Wesleyan University in the late 1940s and early 1950s by David McClelland and his associates. The approach of these investigators differed from that of Murray in
that they focused on one motive using a few subjects per experiment in a

large number of different experiments. After the effect of hunger arousal on TAT stories was determined, a similar method was utilized to manipulate and measure the achievement motive. Groups received experimental instructions designed to elicit different levels of n Achievement; four TAT slides served as the stimuli for brief stories, and the story content was compared across groups. The content categories on which the experimental and control groups differed formed the basis of the scoring system for n Ach. The assumption is made that differences in achievement fantasy in neutral situations reflect individual differences in the characteristic strength of this motive. The n Ach variable can be scored with high interjudge consistency, but its split-half and test-retest reliabilities are only of moderate magnitude. Relatively small changes in the pictures can elicit quite different responses.

The antecedents of the achievement motive are hypothesized as parental differences in stressing the importance of competition, excellence of performance, and independence plus differences in the extent to which positive reinforcement is provided for doing well and negative reinforcement provided for failure. High n Ach males have been found to perceive their parents as autocratic, rejecting, nonindulgent, and neglecting. Mothers with high n Ach sons expect independence behavior at an earlier age than do mothers with low n Ach sons, and they reward such behavior with physical affection. The response of mothers to independence behavior in children can be quite different from their response to the same individuals in adolescence. Parents who produce high n Achievement offspring expect a high level of performance, set difficult standards, display affection in response to achievement and respond negatively to failure. The general pattern is one of firm and consistent stress on independence from parents as early as possible and a continuing expectation that the son should and will do better than his competitors at any task. It appears to be useful to differentiate autonomous achievement motivation (internalized personal standards) and social achievement motivation (standards set by others). One determinant of n Ach is the father's occupation; son's with fathers in entrepreneurial occupations score higher than those whose fathers are in nonentrepreneurial jobs. Cross-cultural research lends support to the importance of early independence training as a positive factor and the presence of a dominant father as a negative factor in the development of achievement need.

Among the correlates of n Ach which have been investigated is academic performance. Achievement scores have been found to be positively related to grades and IQ. High need achievers do best in courses perceived as relevant to their future careers. N Ach has been found to be related to the prestige of the occupation which is the individual's goal and to the status of the occupation actually entered. A number of correlates of the achievement motive may be conceptualized as sharing a common element involving control of the environment. In comparison with low need achievers, high need achievers have been found to be better able to delay gratification in order to obtain greater rewards, to find metaphors involving speed and directness more appropriate for describing time than slow or static metaphors, to cover a longer time span in their stories, to have watches running fast rather than slow, and to draw different kinds of doodles. An individual high in need achievement sees himself as closer to his ideal self than does a low *n* Ach individual. One of the unusual aspects of the *n* Ach scoring system is that material may be scored for individuals no longer alive or for a cross-section of an entire group or nation. In *The Achieving Society,* McClelland attempted to make sense of the economic growth and decline of cultures on the basis of the achievement motive. If the Protestant Reformation was responsible for a shift toward self-reliance and the capitalistic spirit, a number of links between *n* Ach and religious beliefs would be hypothesized. Protestant parents have been found to stress earlier independence training than do Catholic parents, Protestant boys are higher in *n* Ach than Catholic boys, and Protestant countries are more economically advanced than Catholic countries. Using children's readers to assess a nation's *n* Ach, substantial correlations were found between *n* Achievement and subsequent economic growth for two different time periods. In the United States between 1800 and 1950 children's readers showed a steady increase in *n* Ach up to 1890 and then declined steadily; a corresponding pattern was shown by the number of patents issued per capita. For Ancient Greece, Spain in the Middle Ages, and England from the Tudors to the Industrial Revolution, a correspondence was found between *n* Ach and economic growth and decline. There is also some evidence that *n* Ach in a culture is positively associated with death rates for ulcers and hypertension. Tests show that high need achievers are more like those successfully employed in various business occupations than are low need achievers. Entrepreneurial managers are higher in *n* Ach than are nonentrepreneurial specialists; individuals involved in sales and marketing have the highest *n* Ach scores in the business community. Further, *n* Ach scores obtained in college are predictive of later entrepreneurial activity. The success of a high need achiever in business, however, only occurs in firms which are achievement-oriented.

In conformity experiments, those who yield to the incorrect majority are found to be lower in *n* Ach than are those who remain independent. When they believe they are not doing well at a task, those high in *n* Ach overestimate the time whereas they underestimate time when they believe they are doing well; low need achievers perceive time the same way in each situation. On various tasks, those high in *n* Ach perform better than those low in *n* Ach. Atkinson has formulated a theory which proposes motivation as a multiplicative function of motive strength, the subjective probability that the act will lead to the attainment of the incentive, and the value of the incentive. When both motive to achieve success and motive to avoid failure are taken into consideration, a number of behavioral predictions may be made on the basis of Atkinson's schema. For example, individuals high in n Ach prefer tasks of intermediate difficulty while those low in n Ach prefer either very easy or very difficult tasks. Similarly, those high in n Ach prefer intermediate occupational risks, while low n Ach individuals prefer occupations with very high or very low probability of success. Also, when M_s is greater than M_f there is more persistence on easy than on hard tasks; with M_f greater than M_s, there is greater persistence on difficult than on easy tasks. When success in one activity is contingent on success in another activity, individuals for whom $M_s > M_f$ perform better than on noncontingent activities; the reverse is true with individuals for whom $M_f > M_s$. Situational demands such as a position of leadership and responsibility can cause $M_f > M_s$ individuals to behave like $M_s > M_f$ individuals in preferring intermediate rather than easy or difficult goals.

McClelland has suggested that changes in n Ach might be brought about through events which remove the dominant father from the home; examples of this type of event are war or any occupation involving prolonged absence. A second hypothesized source of change is when the children of successful high n Ach parents are reared by low n Ach slaves or servants. There is some evidence that achievement need can be influenced by the behavior of models. When low achievers are directed to engage in fantasy activity centering on achievement and the attainment of achievement goals, these individuals not only show a significant increase in n Ach scores but also a significant increase in grade-point average. More elaborate studies have attempted to increase the achievement motivation of business executives. A project in India indicated that achievement training for businessmen led to dramatic changes in various economic indicators. McClelland presents an optimistic picture of the way in which science can lead to improvements for mankind.

For a number of reasons a simple, objective measure of n Ach would be advantageous, but the first such tests to be developed were unrelated to the TAT measure. More recently, a number of different investigators have constructed objective measures which appear to be extremely promising. Much of the work on n Ach can be criticized in terms of a tendency for investigators to utilize cause and effect interpretations of correlational findings. Nevertheless, the sheer volume of consistent data with respect to such concepts as the achieving society and the increasing number of "linking" studies are supportive of the present formulations.

Achievement need in women seems to be aroused by different conditions than is true for men in that acceptance and popularity are more relevant to female achievement than are leadership, intelligence, or success. Also, female n Ach can be expressed in terms of influence on a husband or on male offspring. Cultural influences can also be seen in the tremendous drop in n Ach in female college graduates when they marry and begin having children. For college-trained women who later become involved in a career, there is a tendency for n Ach to rise again; for the non-college woman, n Ach simply declines from the time she leaves school. An important motive seems to be fear of success which is relatively high for white females and black males.

6

Manifest Anxiety

Anxiety is defined as an emotional state in which there is a vague, generalized feeling of fear. Psychologists often bypass the concept of emotion and deal with anxiety simply as a motive.

Anxiety has been of considerable interest in the study of behavior, from psychoanalysis to learning theory. Therefore, one discovers with surprise that the word "anxiety" was hardly used in standard medical and psychological textbooks until the late 1930s after Freud had emphasized the importance of the concept (Sarbin, 1964a). Spielberger (1966a) reported that more than fifteen-hundred psychological studies of anxiety had been published in the literature since 1950, and this rapidly growing interest is shown graphically in Figure 6-1.

For psychologists, the focus on anxiety has been of several different kinds. First, those stimuli which evoke anxiety and the responses which define it have been studied. For example, individuals can be made fearful or anxious by means of pain or the threat of pain, by unexpected stimulus events such as a loud noise, and by that which is unusual or unknown. The effects of such stimulus events on behavior have been investigated by means of simple verbal scales and by measures of physiological responses. It has been found that fear and anxiety involve increases in heart rate, respiration rate, muscle tension, and skin moisture. There is also more adrenalin in the blood. As will be seen later in this chapter, there have been many attempts to find relationships between verbal and physiological indices of anxiety.

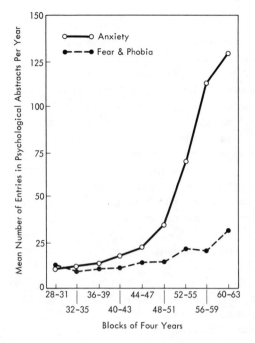

Fig. 6-1 Mean Number of Entries Per Year Indexed under the Heading "Anxiety" in *Psychological Abstracts* during the Years 1928–1963, Compared with the Combined Entries for the Headings "Fear" and "Phobia." (Adapted from Spielberger, 1966a, p. 6.)

Second, the fact that certain stimuli evoke fear or anxiety has led to research in which subjects learn to respond with fear to previously neutral stimuli through simple conditioning. One of the best known early demonstrations of learned fear was carried out by Watson and Raynor (1920). A small boy who had no fear of rats was suddenly exposed to a loud, unexpected noise while playing with a white rat. Following this experience, he was not only afraid of the rat but also of a number of things which were in some way similar to the rat in appearance. A more extensive investigation of fear as a learned motive was conducted by Miller (1948a). With rats as subjects, electric shock was used to elicit fear in a white compartment; on subsequent nonshock trials, fear (that is, tenseness, crouching, urination, defecation) was shown by the rats whenever they were placed in that compartment. Apparently any stimulus can be paired with a fear-inducing stimulus and subsequently come to evoke fear. The parallel between learned fear in the laboratory setting and the phobias, fears, and anxieties found in everyday life is a compelling one. For example, therapists are often confronted by patients for whom sexual cues evoke fear and anxiety. Why? A reasonable guess can be made on the basis of studies such as that of Hayward (1957). Baby male rats were given electric shock whenever they were placed near female rats in heat; at maturity they tended to avoid female rats in heat significantly more than did the male rats in a control group.

A third sort of interest in fear and anxiety involves drive properties. Because it is unpleasant to be fearful or anxious, any behavior which brings above drive reduction is reinforcing. The simplest drive-reducing response is physical avoidance of the stimulus. If escape is not easily accomplished, other responses which lead to the same goal may be learned. For example, in Miller's (1948a) experiment, once the rats had been taught to fear the white compartment, they were given the opportunity to escape into a black compartment if they turned a wheel which opened a door between the two compartments. Just as organisms can learn to perform instrumental responses in order to obtain food or water or sexual satisfaction, Miller's rats learned to turn the wheel to escape the white compartment and presumably to obtain fear reduction. In psychoanalytic theory, the explanation for most defense mechanisms and even more severe symptoms is that such behavior serves to reduce anxiety. Experimental evidence concerning the drive properties of anxiety suggests that Freud was probably correct in conceptualizing many behavior problems in terms of learning.

Fourth, not only is anxiety unpleasant and hence motivational in leading to anxiety-reduction, but it has another type of motivational effect which it shares with all other motives—the facilitation of whatever reaction is being made by the organism. Hull (1943) proposed that the energizing effect of drive on behavior was independent of the specific kind of drive which was aroused. Thus, any given stimulus-response sequence is facilitated equally by hunger, thirst, anxiety, or any other drive.

Finally, a fifth aspect of interest in anxiety is one which cuts across the other four: individual differences. In personality research, there has been concern with differences among individuals (1) in physiological responses to anxiety-evoking stimuli, (2) in the stimuli which have become associated with fear, (3) in the instrumental responses learned as ways to reduce anxiety, and (4) in general drive level or emotional responsiveness. A number of attempts have been made to assess individual differences in anxiety concerning classes of stimuli; for example, test anxiety is determined by responses to such items as, "When the teacher says that she is going to find out how much you have learned, do you get a funny feeling in your stomach?" (Sarason, Davidson, Lighthall, Waite, and Ruebush, 1960). Individual differences in instrumental responses which reduce anxiety have been studied with respect to many aspects of behavior, including the use of alcohol (Ullman, 1958), psychotic symptoms (Murray, 1962), and defense mechanisms (Byrne, 1961b).

In the present chapter the emphasis will be on the study of individual differences in generalized anxiety and the way in which this personality variable involves the other four aspects of anxiety.

THEORETICAL BACKGROUND OF THE CONCEPT OF ANXIETY
HULL-SPENCE LEARNING THEORY AND
EMOTIONAL RESPONSIVENESS

Background. The life and career of Clark L. Hull (1884–1952) over-lapped with that of Freud, but their background, training, and approach to a theory of behavior were markedly different. Hull was born on a farm near Akron, New York; a few years later the family moved to another farm in Michigan. His early schooling was in a one-room rural school, with atten-dance in the spring and autumn often interrupted by farmwork . At seven-teen he passed a teachers' examination and then taught for a year before entering high school. His first experience with higher education was at Alma College where he took courses in mathematics, physics, and chemistry, all of which led toward the career of mining engineer. He was working as an engineer in Minnesota when he contracted poliomyelitis, which left him a partial invalid for a year. At this point he decided that he must change his occupational plans; after considering the ministry (the Unitarian Church because it seemed to be a "free, godless religion"), he decided on psychology.

Following another two years of teaching, he and his wife had saved enough money for him to enter the University of Michigan. After receiving a bachelor's degree in psychology, Hull taught for a year at a normal school in Kentucky for $75 a month. During that time, he applied for a graduate fellowship at Cornell and at Yale but was rejected by both. Finally, he was given a teaching assistantship at the University of Wisconsin and entered graduate school there. After receiving the Ph.D. degree in 1918, he remained at Wisconsin until 1929 at which time he accepted a position at Yale. His original research interests were varied and included an investigation of the effects of tobacco on mental efficiency, work on aptitude testing which led to a book, a dissertation dealing with concept formation, and a series of experimental studies of hypnosis which resulted in another book.

At Yale, hypnotic experiments met with medical opposition, and Hull was forced to terminate this line of inquiry. For a long period, he had been inter-ested in the behaviorist approach of John B. Watson and especially in Wat-son's utilization of Pavlov's work on conditioning. In time, Hull's research interests were concentrated in the field of learning. Hull describes the theo-retical position to which he came:

> As the result of the considerations of these behavioral problems over a num-ber of years, probably influenced considerably by my early training in the physical sciences, I came to the definite conclusion around 1930 that psy-chology is a true natural science; that its primary laws are expressible quanti-tatively by means of a moderate number of ordinary equations; that all the complex behavior of single individuals will ultimately be derivable as secondary laws from (1) these primary laws together with (2) the conditions under

which behavior occurs; and that all the behavior of groups as a whole, i.e., strictly social behavior as such, may similarly be derived as quantitative laws from the same primary equations. With these and similar views as a background, the task of psychologists obviously is that of laying bare these laws as quickly and accurately as possible, particularly the primary laws. This belief was deepened by the influence of my seminar students, notably Kenneth W. Spence and Neal E. Miller. It has determined most of my scientific activities ever since, and the longer I live the more convinced I am of its general soundness (Hull, 1952, p. 155).

Hull's experimental and theoretical contributions in the 1930s and 1940s had a profound and lasting effect on the field of psychology.

At the Institute of Human Relations at Yale, behavioral scientists from various fields began working together in an attempt to produce an integrated scientific achievement. In 1936, Hull, Miller, John Dollard and O. H. Mowrer began a seminar which was concerned with seeking "...the essential identities lying in conditioned reflexes and behavior laws generally on the one hand, and, on the other, in the phenomena considered by Freud and his psychoanalytic associates" (Hull, 1952, p. 156). Among the fruits of this endeavor were work on frustration and aggression by Dollard, Doob, Miller, and Sears (1939), the experimental conceptualization of social learning and imitation by Miller and Dollard (1941), Sears's (1944) experimental approach to psychoanalytic phenomena, Miller's (1948b) exposition of the relationship between the analytic concept of displacement and the learning concept of generalization, the formulation of personality and psychotherapy by Dollard and Miller (1950), and Mowrer's (1953) application of the principles of learning theory to problems such as mental illness and psychotherapy. Hull himself had planned to include in his series of theoretical volumes one which dealt with deductions of the more elementary forms of social behavior, but his work was slowed down by poor health, and he wrote, "...as time passes I realize that I cannot possibly write this book, much as I desire to do so" (Hull, 1952, p. 162). He died in the year that statement of regret was published.

One of Hull's early associates at Yale was Kenneth W. Spence (1907–1967), who entered Yale in 1930 after receiving his undergraduate education and a master's degree at McGill University. He was awarded the Ph.D. degree in 1933 under Yerkes, became a Research Fellow at the Yale primate laboratories in Florida from 1933–1937, and then spent a year at the University of Virginia. At that point, Spence began a long, productive, and extremely influential career at the University of Iowa. Hull (1952, p. 159) notes: "He gave me detailed suggestions and criticisms regarding the text of *Principles of Behavior,* and after he became Chairman of the psychology department at the University of Iowa he directed many able empirical studies which contributed materially to the later development of the system."

From 1964 until his death in 1967, he held a professorship at the University of Texas.

One of his distinguished former students described him in the following terms (Kendler, 1967, p. 335):

> For more than three decades Spence played a major role in psychology as an experimentalist, theorist, methodologist, and teacher. These different activities were carried on in an integrated manner, cemented together by an overriding concern with experimental facts. Theory, methodology, and teaching justified themselves only in the manner they contributed to the gathering and ordering of empirical data. His concern with theory, strong and persistent, was only with postulates that had apparent experimental implications. In spite of an obvious enchantment with the philosophy of science, he avoided getting entangled with subtle issues that had no bearing on his experimental and theoretical efforts. Finally, as a teacher, he judged his success by the scientific productivity of his students.

Individual Differences in Emotional Responsiveness. In order to provide a sample of the Hull-Spence theory and to indicate the specific theoretical impetus for the development of the Manifest Anxiety Scale (MAS), one type of learning situation (classical conditioning) will be described. An *unconditioned stimulus* is one which regularly evokes an observable response (called an unconditioned response) such as the electric shock which evoked fear responses in Miller's rats. A conditioned stimulus is a stimulus which does not evoke that response until after it has been paired with or associated with the unconditioned stimulus; the white compartment was the conditioned stimulus to the overt fear responses in Miller's experiment. Once conditioning or simple learning has taken place, the conditioned stimulus comes to evoke the response which is then labeled the *conditioned response;* after being subjected to shock in the white compartment, the rats exhibited fear whenever they were placed in it again.

Even in such a seemingly simple situation, a great many variables have been found to influence the relationship between the conditioned stimulus and the conditioned response. For example, the probability of the stimulus evoking the response has been found to be influenced by the number of trials in which the conditioned stimulus and unconditioned stimulus were presented together; the more such pairings, the greater the probability that the response will follow the presentation of the stimulus. Another influence is the strength of the unconditioned stimulus; an intense stimulus (such as a strong electric shock) has a greater effect on performance than a weak one. There are individual differences in emotional responsiveness, and such responsiveness has a facilitating effect on simple conditioning. There are also a number of variables which have been found to have an adverse or inhibiting effect on performance.

Now, one could simply catalogue these variables and indicate that they have such and such an effect on performance. It would be an obvious advantage, however, to have a theoretical scheme which enabled us to conceptualize all the variables in an integrated way, which generalized to different situations, and which generated predictions about quite different kinds of behavior. Hull (1943) proposed such a system, and his approach involved the postulation of hypothetical variables which were each ultimately defined in terms of observable variables such as those just described. The relationship between the conditioned stimulus and conditioned response is conceptualized as a function of a series of different kinds of variables. Several independent variables are conceptualized as influencing the strength of whatever habits are activated in a given stimulus situation, while other independent variables are conceptualized as influencing the strength of a hypothetical emotional response, which in turn influences the strength of the total generalized drive state. In Hull's system, the strength of a response is determined by habit strength multiplied times drive minus any inhibitory factors.

This theoretical system utilizes only constructs which can be defined in terms of observable operations, and relatively precise relationships between and among variables are specified. Where does the concept of anxiety fit into such a system?

With the measurement of individual differences in emotional responsiveness, a personality variable came to be of interest to learning theorists working within this framework. Spence describes the rationale of the resulting measuring instrument:

> ...individuals differ in the magnitude of their reflex responses to a given intensity of stimulation. By analogy...we were led to assume that individuals would differ characteristically in the magnitude of this response...to the same intensity of stressful stimulation. If now there were available some means of assessing differences in this emotional responsiveness of individuals, our theoretical schema would lead to the prediction that highly emotional subjects, as assessed by the measuring device, would exhibit a higher level of performance in aversive forms of conditioning than subjects who scored low on the device.
>
> The problem thus became one of attempting to develop a test for identifying individuals in the responsiveness of this hypothetical emotional mechanism. ...It was in connection with this portion of our theory that the Manifest Anxiety or A-scale was developed. The idea of using a self-inventory test that would differentiate subjects in terms of the degree to which they admitted to prossessing overt or manifest symptoms of emotionality was suggested by Taylor (1951) in a doctoral dissertation (Spence, 1958, pp. 132–33).

The development of this test and a portion of the research utilizing it will be described. Although the original interest was in obtaining a psychometric measure which was related to drive level, work on the MAS has not been confined to the learning laboratory. In fact, much of the work is relevant to the problems which Freud discussed even though the methodology was developed in the context of Hull-Spence learning theory.

CONSTRUCTION OF THE MANIFEST ANXIETY SCALE

INITIAL ITEM SELECTION

The development of the MAS by one of Spence's doctoral students, Janet Taylor (later, Janet Taylor Spence), was first reported in an article dealing with conditioning (Taylor, 1951), but the test itself was later described in somewhat greater detail along with relevant psychometric data (Taylor, 1953).

As an item pool, approximately two-hundred items from the MMPI were given to five clinical psychologists with instructions to identify those items which indicated manifest anxiety as defined by Cameron's (1947) description of chronic anxiety reaction. On sixty-five of the items, agreement was 80 percent or better among the clinicians that manifest anxiety was being tapped. Bechtoldt (1953) attempted to improve the measuring instrument by carrying out an internal consistency item analysis. The result was a fifty-item scale made up of those items which had the highest correlations with the total score. The items and the scoring key for anxiety are given in Figure 6-2.

1. I do not tire quickly. (F)
2. I am troubled by attacks of nausea. (T)
3. I believe I am no more nervous than most others. (F)
4. I have very few headaches. (F)
5. I work under a great deal of tension. (T)
6. I cannot keep my mind on one thing. (T)
7. I worry over money and business. (T)
8. I frequently notice my hand shakes when I try to do something. (T)
9. I blush no more often than others. (F)
10. I have diarrhea once a month or more. (T)
11. I worry quite a bit over possible misfortunes. (T)
12. I practically never blush. (F)
13. I am often afraid that I am going to blush. (T)
14. I have nightmares every few nights. (T)
15. My hands and feet are usually warm enough. (F)
16. I sweat very easily even on cool days. (T)
17. Sometimes when embarrassed, I break out in a sweat which annoys me greatly. (T)
18. I hardly ever notice my heart pounding and I am seldom short of breath. (F)

19. I feel hungry almost all the time. (T)
20. I am very seldom troubled by constipation. (F)
21. I have a great deal of stomach trouble. (T)
22. I have had periods in which I lost sleep over worry. (T)
23. My sleep is fitful and disturbed. (T)
24. I dream frequently about things that are best kept to myself. (T)
25. I am easily embarrassed. (T)
26. I am more sensitive than most other people. (T)
27. I frequently find myself worrying about something. (T)
28. I wish I could be as happy as others seem to be. (T)
29. I am usually calm and not easily upset. (F)
30. I cry easily. (T)
31. I feel anxiety about something or someone almost all the time. (T)
32. I am happy most of the time. (F)
33. It makes me nervous to have to wait. (T)
34. I have periods of such great restlessness that I cannot sit long in a chair. (T)
35. Sometimes I become so excited that I find it hard to get to sleep. (T)
36. I have sometimes felt that difficulties were piling up so high that I could not overcome them. (T)
37. I must admit that I have at times been worried beyond reason over something that really did not matter. (T)
38. I have very few fears compared to my friends. (F)
39. I have been afraid of things or people that I know could not hurt me. (T)
40. I certainly feel useless at times. (T)
41. I find it hard to keep my mind on a task or job. (T)
42. I am usually self-conscious. (T)
43. I am inclined to take things hard. (T)
44. I am a high-strung person. (T)
45. Life is a strain for me much of the time. (T)
46. At times I think I am no good at all. (T)
47. I am certainly lacking in self-confidence. (T)
48. I sometimes feel that I am about to go to pieces. (T)
49. I shrink from facing a crisis or difficulty. (T)
50. I am entirely self-confident. (F)

Fig. 6-2 Manifest Anxiety Scale (MAS).

RELIABILITY AND NORMS

The internal consistency of the test was found to be relatively high; Hilgard, Jones, and Kaplan (1951) reported a split-half reliability coefficient of .92. Stability of the test scores over time is also adequate for research. The MAS has been found to have a test-retest reliability of .89 over a three-week period,

.82 over a five-month period, and .81 over nine to seventeen months (Taylor, 1953).

With almost 2,000 introductory psychology students at the University of Iowa, the mean MAS score was found to be 14.56 (Taylor, 1953). Though the female students had a slightly higher mean score than the males, the difference between the sexes in manifest anxiety was not significant. On a Greek version of this test, female subjects have been found to score significantly higher than males (Vassiliou, Georgas, and Vassiliou, 1967).

ANTECEDENTS OF MANIFEST ANXIETY

PARENTAL EXPECTANCIES

Surprisingly little research has been directed toward the problem of determining the antecedents of individual differences in characteristic anxiety level.

One variable which has been investigated is the discrepancy between parental expectancies with regard to the behavior of their offspring and the offspring's actual behavior. Presumably, a failure to live up to parental goals would be a continuing source of anxiety. Such a situation could arise because parental ideals were unreasonably high, because the offspring's behavior was actually inadequate, or from a combination of these two determinants.

A group of adolescent boys enrolled in a Summer Demonstration School at the University of California and their mothers were each given a series of items to sort (Stewart, 1958). The boys were asked to describe themselves in three separate ways—as they perceived themselves, as they would like to be, and as they thought their mothers would like them to be. In addition, they were given the MAS. The mothers sorted the cards twice—to describe their sons as they are, and as they would like them to be. The items dealt with several topics including self-control, relationships with the opposite sex, intellectual abilities, physical characteristics, and school relationships.

Stewart found that the greater the discrepancy between the son's self-description and his mother's description of her ideal for him, the more anxious the son (r = .49). Stewart (1958, p. 384) concluded that boys with low manifest anxiety ". . .were satisfied with themselves, met their perception of their mother's ideal for them, and perceived themselves as being the kind of person their mother actually wanted them to be."

MATERNAL SEPARATION

Clinical studies have provided convincing evidence that children who are separated from their mothers show a number of adverse symptoms, including anxiety. Thus, there are numerous maladjustments in children which may be instigated by a mother's death, illness, or absence. Further, children who undergo such experiences become sensitized so that any similar separations that occur later are frequently traumatic to them (Yarrow, 1964).

Experimental studies of such effects are obviously not possible with human subjects, but research with monkeys has confirmed the importance of an infant's separation from its mother. For example, when infant monkeys are taken away from their mothers even for a short time, they make cooing noises and act afraid and depressed (Kaufman and Rosenblum, 1967; Seay and Harlow, 1965). As much as a year later, subjects who are given such experiences in infancy still show the fear behavior (Mitchell, Harlow, Griffin, and Moller, 1967).

It should be possible to show that individuals who undergo early separation from their mothers have higher manifest anxiety scores than those who remain with their mothers throughout infancy and childhood, but such a study has not been reported.

THE PLACE OF MANIFEST ANXIETY IN THE STRUCTURE OF PERSONALITY

Other Verbal Measures of Anxiety

A number of investigations with the MAS have been of a semi-validational nature. That is, the MAS and one or more other verbal tests purporting to measure anxiety are administered to a sample of subjects and intercorrelated.

Separation Anxiety. A special questionnaire was built by Sarason (1958) to measure anxiety as defined by Freud: separation anxiety. An example is, "When I was a child, I often wondered how much my father loved me." If the MAS is measuring the sort of anxiety discussed by Freud, the two measures should be related. Sarason (1961) found the two tests to be positively correlated.

Test Anxiety. One rather specific type of anxiety which has been measured by means of questionnaires is that involved in test-taking situations. Mandler and Sarason (1952) developed such a test (Test Anxiety Questionnaire or TAQ) which asks subjects about their experiences in a testing situation, including uneasiness, accelerated heartbeat, perspiration, emotional interference, and worry before and during a test. Since the MAS was designed as a general measure of anxiety across various situations, a positive relationship would be expected between it and test anxiety scores. The MAS and TAQ have been found to be positively correlated in various student samples (for example, Alpert and Haber, 1960; Sarason, 1961).

Belief that the Environment is Dangerous. Lazarus (1966) has proposed that anxiety is a characteristic of individuals who believe (a) that the environment is dangerous or threatening and (b) that they have no control over it. Houston, Olson, and Botkin (1972) determined the relationship between anxiety and beliefs about the environment, using a group of undergraduates at the University of Kansas. The subjects rated various situations as to how threatening or dangerous they are. Examples include: "You are in an encounter group and on the first day you are chosen to be the first person to tell the group the three things you like least about yourself" and "Riding in a car going 95 miles an hour." It was found that the ratings of threat and danger were positively correlated with anxiety scores. In another study it was found that anxiety is associated with the belief that the individual does not have control over the environment (Watson, 1967). Thus, the individual with high anxiety appears to perceive his surroundings as potentially harmful and also as uncontrollable.

NONVERBAL MEASURES OF ANXIETY

Observations of Behavior. When a clinical psychologist or a psychiatrist makes judgments concerning a patient's anxiety level, he is probably utilizing many verbal and nonverbal cues including gestures, voice pitch, and bodily movements. If such judgments have any degree of consistency and accuracy and if the self-report approach of the MAS is measuring the same dimension as that determined by clinical observations, test scores and judges' ratings should correspond.

With a college student population, Hoyt and Magoon (1954) asked experienced counsellors to rate the degree of manifest anxiety of some of their clients over the past six months. Manifest anxiety was defined in terms of behavior indicating nervousness, tension, embarassment, and worry. The correlation between counsellor ratings and MAS scores was .47.

Buss, Wiener, Durkee, and Baer (1955) attempted to define anxiety in sufficient detail so that independent observers could agree with one another at a relatively high degree of consistency. A standard interview was conducted with patients in the presence of four psychologists. Immediately after the interview, each psychologist independently rated the patient's level of anxiety. The investigators found a correlation of .60 between the overall anxiety rating and the MAS scores.

Palmar Sweating. Changes in the moisture of the skin may be measured by placing the index finger in an anhydrous ferrous chloride solution for one minute, letting the finger dry, and then placing it on a specially treated piece of paper. An electrical device is used to measure the amount of ferrous chloride deposited on the paper, which thus indicates the amount of sweat present on the finger. Haywood and Spielberger (1966) selected a group of male undergraduates at Vanderbilt who had scored very high or very low on the MAS. When subjects reported for a verbal conditioning experiment, they were given several minutes to adapt and then the palmar sweat measure was taken. After the experimental task of constructing a series of sentences, the palmar sweat procedure was repeated. It may be seen in Table 6-1 that the palmar sweat index was larger for the high-anxious than the

Table 6-1. Palmar Sweat Index of High- and Low-Anxious Subjects
before and after an Experimental Task

	Before Task	After Task
High-Anxious Subjects	16.00	13.75
Low-Anxious Subjects	12.38	9.69

(After Haywood, H. C. and Spielberger, C. D., "Palmar sweating as a function of individual differences in manifest anxiety." *Journal of Personality and Social Psychology,* 1966, *3,* 104. © 1966 by the American Psychological Association and reprinted by permission.)

low-anxious subjects at each testing even though the anxiety level of both groups declined during the experiment. It was assumed that the subjects were initially apprehensive about the experiment and then relaxed when it turned out to be a simple task. In any event, the verbal measure and the physiological measure of anxiety were clearly related.

Multiple Physiological Measures. Based on the notion of response specificity, Lacey and Lacey (1958) have proposed that the best index of physiological activity is obtained by measuring an individual on a series of physiological variables and then using each subject's highest score, regardless of what the variable is. For one individual, the highest scored variable might be palmar sweat, for another heart rate, and so forth. As part of a larger investigation, Mandler, Mandler, Kremen, and Sholiton (1961) determined the relationship between MAS scores and this highest specific response index. Eleven measures of physiological activity were obtained, including heart rate, galvanic skin response, peripheral blood flow, and finger temperature. With a group of Harvard undergraduates as subjects, nonsignificant correlations were obtained between scores on the MAS and individual measures of physiological activity (for example, MAS and galvanic skin response correlated .06). However, when MAS scores were correlated with each subject's highest physiological scores the correlation was .60.

MALADJUSTMENT

If Freud's proposals concerning the role of anxiety in symptom-formation are correct, we would expect a high anxiety level to precede the development of psychoneurotic symptoms, a low anxiety level to follow the successful development of anxiety-reducing behavior patterns, and a high anxiety level to follow any interference with symptoms (for example, the initial stages of psychotherapy). Though research to date with the MAS has not precisely followed the pattern just outlined, there are relevant data available with respect to MAS scores and various aspects of emotional disturbance.

Population Comparisons. Taylor (1953) administered the MAS to neurotic and psychotic patients undergoing psychiatric treatment. Their median score of 34 is considerably higher than the median of 13 obtained by Iowa college students. Half of the patients had scores higher than those of 98 percent of the students. Figure 6-3 shows a comparison of the two groups.

When psychiatric patients are compared with college students, the two groups are different in many respects besides the variable of maladjustment. The students tend to be younger, brighter, and better educated, for example. An investigation comparing MAS scores of psychiatric patients and medical

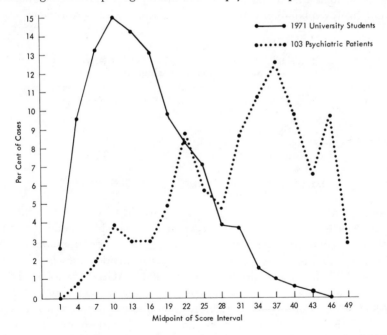

Fig. 6-3 Comparison of Normal and Psychiatric Populations on the MAS. (Data from Taylor, 1953.)

patients matched for age and intelligence was conducted by Matarazzo, Guze, and Matarazzo (1955). The neuro-psychiatric patients obtained significantly higher MAS scores (mean = 26.20) than the medical patients (mean = 13.31).

Symptoms. In an investigation of medical and psychiatric patients, the Cornell Medical Index was administered to the subjects. This index contains questions about both medical and psychiatric symptoms and serves as a standardized medical history. This test correlated .78 with the MAS (Matarazzo, Matarazzo, and Saslow, 1961). The higher the MAS score, the greater is the number of symptoms which are reported.

Intelligence and Academic Performance

There is a widely accepted belief that individuals who become anxious in situations involving intellectual skills will perform less well than individuals whose anxiety level remains relatively low. In a study conducted in Greece, there was an inverse relationship between educational level and anxiety as shown in Table 6-2 (Vassiliou, Georgas, and Vassiliou, 1967). It could be that individuals who do badly in school are especially prone to anxiety, but a more likely explanation is that anxiety interferes with performance.

**Table 6-2. Relationship between Manifest Anxiety
and Educational Attainment**

Education	Mean MAS Score
Illiterate	23.04
Grammar School	20.54
High School	18.71
University	15.36

(Data from Vassiliou, Georgas, and Vassiliou, 1967)

Since both academic ability and anxiety would be expected to influence grades, Spielberger (1966b) proposed that both variables should be considered at the same time. With a large group of male undergraduates at Duke University, high and low anxious subjects were divided into five levels on the basis of scholastic aptitude as indicated by ACE scores. Grade point averages were obtained for the semester during which each subject took the MAS. The effect of anxiety and ability on grades may be seen in Figure 6-4. For those students with the highest and lowest aptitude scores, grades were unrelated to anxiety. At the middle levels of aptitude, however, the low-anxious students consistently obtained better grades than the high-anxious students. A follow-up study of these individuals three years later provided

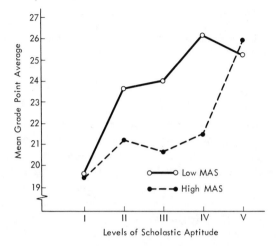

Fig. 6-4 Mean Grade Point Averages for High- and Low-Anxiety College Students at Five Levels of Scholastic Aptitude. (Adapted from Spielberger, 1966b, p. 378.)

dramatic evidence of the effect of anxiety on college performance. In each of the five levels of scholastic aptitude, the percentage of students who had dropped out of the university for academic reasons was determined. At every level except the highest, the high-anxious students were considerably more likely to have failed in college than was true for the low-anxious students. The data are shown in Table 6-3. These findings led Spielberger (1966b, pp.

Table 6-3. High- and Low-Anxious Students at Five Levels of Scholastic Aptitude Who Dropped Out of School for Academic Reasons

Scholastic Aptitude Level	High-Anxious Students % of Failures	Low-Anxious Students % of Failures
V	9.1	10.0
IV	23.8	0.0
III	22.6	4.4
II	13.6	3.8
I	27.3	13.6

(After Spielberger, 1966b, p. 380)

380–81) to suggest:

On the basis of these findings, it seemed to us that the loss to society of the full contributions of potentially able students through underachievement and/ or academic failure constituted an important mental health problem in educa- tion. But the findings also suggested that it was possible to identify members of the college population who, because of emotional problems, were not likely to function at levels commensurate with their intellectual potential. If identified early in their academic careers and offered appropriate therapeutic opportunities, could the academic mortality rate be reduced for able students whose emotional problems predisposed them to failure?

Other Relationships

Religious Conversions. Studies of sudden religious conversions suggest that they are instigated in part by guilt and that the conversion is seen as a way to solve all problems. Since the effects of conversion often do not live up to expectations, it was hypothesized by Spellman, Baskett, and Byrne (1971) that sudden converts to religion would be higher in manifest anxiety than either nonreligious individuals or regular church attenders. In a small Texas farming community, the ministers were asked to suggest about twenty names of those who would fit each of the three categories. The MAS was administered to the townspeople who had been named. Anxiety means were found to be 26.65 for the sudden converts, 18.40 for the nonattenders, and 17.81 for the regular attenders. As expected, those who had undergone a sudden religious conversion were higher in anxiety than those in the other two groups.

Birth Complications. Some evidence exists that there are differences between high- and low-anxious women in giving birth. Davids, DeVault, and Talmadge (1961, p. 76) found in two independent samples of clinic patients that: "...women who were later to experience complications in the delivery room or were to give birth to children with abnormalities obtained significantly higher manifest anxiety scores during pregnancy than did women who later had 'normal' delivery room periods."

DYNAMICS

Learning and Performance

The initial reason for constructing the Manifest Anxiety Scale was the need for a measure of individual differences in emotional responsiveness in laboratory conditioning experiments. As Taylor (1956) has pointed out, the Iowa group was not interested in the phenomenon of anxiety but in the role of drive in learning situations.

The influence of drive level (including differences in MAS scores) on behavior depends in part on the complexity of the task. As noted earlier, Hull (1943) proposed that the response strength of all habits activated in a particular stimulus situation increases as drive state increases. Using this and certain other constructs from Hull's system, Spence predicted that in a simple situation in which one habit is evoked, the higher the drive the greater the response strength. In a complex situation in which several competing responses are evoked along with the correct one, high drive interacts with each habit to increase the strength of a number of different responses. If only one response is possible, the one with the greatest habit strength will be given.

In such situations, according to Spence's predictions, if the correct response has less habit strength than one of the competing responses, a high-drive group would be expected to do less well than a low-drive group. Even in a complex situation, if the correct response were stronger than any of the competing responses, the prediction would be that a high-drive group will outperform a low-drive group.

The research testing these propositions has included a number of traditional learning tasks (for example, classical conditioning, verbal learning), other familiar laboratory problems (for example, stimulus generalization, reaction time), and miscellaneous tasks ranging from anagrams to a word-association test. Among others, Goulet (1968) has discussed some of the problems which arise in using such tasks to test drive theory. The summary presented here should demonstrate both the fruitfulness of a strong theory in stimulating research and the utility of including a personality variable in research in general experimental psychology.

Classical Conditioning. A relatively simple situation in which a single response is learned is that of classical conditioning. A typical experiment (for example, Spence, 1953) involves eyelid conditioning. Subjects are placed in a fixed position in a dental chair. The unconditioned stimulus is a puff of air which is directed at one eye, eliciting an eyeblink (the unconditioned response). The conditioned stimulus is an increase in brightness of a circular disc made of milk glass. In each conditioning trial, the puff of air is closely followed by the conditioned stimulus. The dependent variable is the number of conditioned responses (eyeblinks in response to the brightness changes) made during a given number of test trials. One would predict that high drive would lead to better performance in this situation, and hence subjects with high scores on the MAS should give more conditioned responses than subjects with low scores on the MAS.

The typical procedure has been to select subjects with extremely high or extremely low MAS scores. An illustrative finding is that of Spence and Taylor (1951). Two levels of air puff intensity (.6 lb. and 2.0 lbs. per square inch) were employed. As shown in Figure 6-5, at each puff intensity the anxious group gave significantly more conditioned responses than the non-anxious group. When subjects with scores in the middle range of the MAS are included in the sample, their conditioning performance tends to fall between the two extreme groups (Spence, 1964).

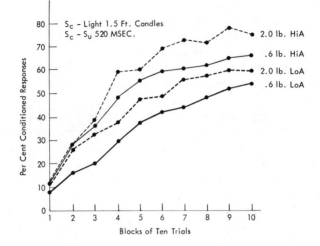

Fig. 6-5 Performance in Eyelid Conditioning Task as a Function of MAS Score and Intensity of Unconditioned Stimulus. (Adapted from Spence, 1960, p. 132.)

Stimulus Generalization. In experiments which involve stimulus generalization, the subjects learn to respond to a particular stimulus and later are presented with different stimuli. Response to the latter stimuli is a function of their similarity to the original stimulus. On the basis of drive theory, one would predict that anxious subjects would give more responses to the generalized stimuli than would nonanxious subjects. In other terminology, high-anxious subjects would be expected to have a higher generalization gradient than those low in anxiety.

Wenar (1954) trained high- and low-anxious subjects to respond to one of three stimuli, presented at twelve-second intervals, by pressing a switch. Following training, stimuli were presented at intervals longer and shorter than twelve seconds. The generalized stimuli, then, were different from the original stimulus along a temporal dimension. As hypothesized, the generalization gradient was higher for the anxious than for the nonanxious subjects.

In an investigation by Rosenbaum (1956), a rectangular training stimulus was employed, and three other rectangles differing in height served as the generalized stimuli. Subjects were male students from the extreme ends of the MAS distribution. Three levels of experimentally induced anxiety were also included (strong shock, buzzer, weak shock). The high-anxiety subjects had a higher generalization gradient than the low-anxiety subjects, but only in the strong shock condition, as shown in Figure 6-6.

Maze Learning. A maze constitutes a relatively complex situation involving a number of competing responses. Here, one would predict that the per-

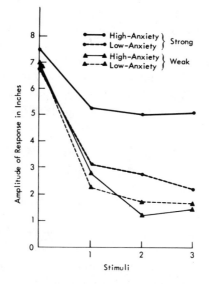

Fig. 6-6 Generalization Gradients as a Function of MAS Scores and Experimentally Induced Anxiety. The Training Stimulus is Designated as 0, and the Generalized Stimuli are Designated 1, 2, 3, in Order of Decreasing Similarity to the Training Stimulus. Weak-shock and Buzzer Conditions have been Combined in the Curves Labeled "Weak." (Adapted from Rosenbaum, G., "Stimulus generalization as a function of clinical anxiety." *Journal of Abnormal and Social Psychology,* 1956, *53,* 283. © 1956 by the American Psychological Association and reprinted by permission.)

formance of anxious subjects would be inferior to the performance of nonanxious subjects.

Taylor and Spence (1952) utilized a serial verbal maze. The learning task consisted of twenty stimulus words typed on a continuous tape. In the viewing slot of a memory drum, each word appeared in order for two seconds. After the first trial, the subject's task is to anticipate the word which will appear next. The words were "right" and "left" and appeared in the order: LLRLRRLLRLRRRLRLLRRL. Trials were continued until the subjects could go through the entire list without error for two consecutive trials. Because of interfering response tendencies such as remote associations, anxious subjects were expected to do less well than nonanxious subjects. Both in terms of number of errors and number of trials to criterion, the hypothesis was confirmed.

In an investigation at Vanderbilt University, Katahn (1966) was unable to replicate the Taylor and Spence findings but concluded that the problem lay in differences in aptitude across different samples. He found that mathematical aptitude was positively related to performance on the verbal maze task. The higher the mathematical aptitude, the better the performance.

Anxiety has a negative effect on performance for individuals with low aptitude, no effect for those with medium aptitude, and a positive effect for
those with high aptitude. He went on to show the same kind of interaction
between anxiety and aptitude in influencing grade point average. It was
noted that, "The oft quoted statement that anxiety interferes with performance on a complex task evidently needs a revision which points out that
actual or 'effective' task difficulty depends upon subjects' aptitude for that
task." (Katahn, 1966, p. 478).

Serial Learning. Spence and Spence (1966) have pointed out that when
the habit strength for the correct response is low (for example, when the task
is difficult and learning has just begun), anxiety would be expected to interfere with performance. As learning progresses, however, the habit strength
for the correct response would increase until it was stronger than that for any
competing responses. At that point (for example, late in learning) anxiety
should have a positive effect on performance. Spielberger and Smith (1966)
examined the effects of anxiety on performance at different stages of learning. Undergraduates at Duke University had to learn a list of 12 nonsense
syllables, and they were told that there is a relationship between ability on
such a task and intelligence. Under these conditions, as may be seen in Figure
6-7, the Spence and Spence hypothesis was confirmed. The high anxiety
subjects did less well than the low anxiety subjects early in learning while
the reverse was true late in learning.

In the Spielberger and Smith (1966) study, it was also possible to go one
step further and examine performance on easy (high habit strength) and
hard (low habit strength) words at various points in the learning process.
The four words at the beginning and end of the list were found to be the
easiest to learn while four in the middle were the most difficult; this common finding is known as the serial-position effect. When performance on the
two kinds of words was compared for high and low anxious subjects, the
results were as shown in Figure 6-8. For the hard words, the findings are
those predicted when initial habit strength is low. For the easy words, the
facilitative effects of high anxiety are seen very early in learning because the
correct response quickly became the one with the greatest habit strength.

Paired-Associates Learning. When subjects are presented with a stimulus
word and required to learn the response word associated with it, the experimenter can control the variables relating to response strength more precisely
than when the task is the learning of a list of words in serial order. Spence,
Farber, and McFann describe the use of this technique:

> Paired-associates learning may be conceived as consisting of a set or series
> of more or less isolated S-R associations or habit tendencies (S_1-R_A, S_2-R_B,
> S_3-R_C, etc.) that become established as a consequence of the training proce-

dure. Theoretically, if these stimulus-response items were entirely isolated from one another so that the only existent associative tendencies were between each stimulus word and its own paired response word, then *S*s with relatively high drive would be expected to perform at a higher level in learning such a series than *S*s with a lower drive strength. Essentially, the situation is similar to that of classical conditioning, except that instead of one S-R tendency being conditioned, a number of different S-R tendencies are being established simultaneously. While it may not be possible to obtain complete isolation among the S-R items, it is known how, on the basis of existing experimental knowledge, to approach this limiting condition with its minimal competition among S-Rs. Similarly, it is known how to vary the conditions so as to increase the amount of competition among them (Spence, Farber, and McFann, 1956, p. 298).

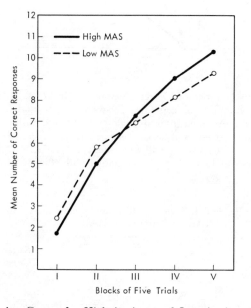

Fig. 6-7 Learning Curves for High-Anxious and Low-Anxious Subjects. The Mean Number of Correct Responses Given over Blocks of Trials. (Adapted from Spielberger, C. D., and Smith, L. H., "Anxiety (drive), stress, and serial-position effects in serial-verbal learning." *Journal of Experimental Psychology*, 1966, 72, 591. © 1966 by the American Psychological Association and reprinted by permission.)

Two experiments were reported by Spence, Farber, and McFann (1956). The word pairs are shown in Table 6-4. In one experiment the correct S-R tendencies were made strong, thus minimizing the presence of competing response tendencies; the stimulus words were very different from each other, and each was strongly associated with its response word. As hypothesized, high-anxious subjects were superior to low-anxious subjects in learning the

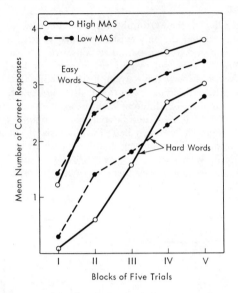

Fig. 6-8 Mean Number of Correct Responses Given by High-Anxious and Low-Anxious Subjects Over Blocks of Trials for EASY and HARD Words. (Adapted from Spielberger, C. D., and Smith, L. H., "Anxiety (drive), stress, and serial-position effects in serial-verbal learning." *Journal of Experimental Psychology*, 1966, 72, 591. © 1966 by the American Psychological Association and reprinted by permission.)

Table 6-4. Noncompetitive and Competitive Lists Used in Paired-Associates Learning*

Experiment 1 Noncompetitive		Experiment 2 Competitive and Noncompetitive	
Stimulus	*Response*	*Stimulus*	*Response*
Adept	Skillful	**Barren	Fruitless
Barren	Fruitless	Arid	Grouchy
Complete	Thorough	Desert	Leading
Distant	Remote	**Little	Minute
Empty	Vacant	Petite	Yonder
Frigid	Arctic	Undersized	Wholesome
Insane	Crazy	**Roving	Nomad
Little	Minute	Gypsy	Opaque
Mammoth	Oversized	Migrant	Agile
Pious	Devout	**Tranquil	Placid
Roving	Nomad	Quiet	Double
Stubborn	Headstrong	Serene	Headstrong
Tranquil	Quiet		
Urgent	Pressing		
Wicked	Evil		

*From Spence, Farber, and McFann, 1956, p. 300.
**Pairs with high initial association.

asociations. In the other experiment, an attempt was made to include pairs with high initial association (weak competing response tendencies) and pairs with low association but with high association across stimulus words (strong competing response tendencies). As hypothesized, high-anxious subjects made fewer errors on the four high-association pairs and more errors on the other eight pairs, when compared with low-anxious subjects.

Another method for defining relative habit strength for a response was employed by Lee (1961). The author pointed out that most verbal learning studies used normative data in assuming the relative habit strength of correct and incorrect responses. In this experiment, habit strength was manipulated experimentally by giving the subjects preliminary practice on particular sets of stimulus-response pairs that were used in the learning task. After learning a list of fifteen adjective pairs, the subjects learned a second list of 15 pairs in which there were five unchanged pairs (from the original list), five neutral pairs (new words), and five changed pairs (stimulus and response words from the initial list but paired differently). The subjects were undergraduate males at Ohio University. Analysis of variance indicated that anxious subjects did significantly better than nonanxious subjects when the dominant habit was correct (unchanged pairs) and significantly worse when the dominant habit was incorrect (changed pairs).

Performance on Other Simple and Complex Tasks. The effect of drive on response would not be expected to be confined to learning situations. Davids and Eriksen (1955) reasoned that high drive level should lead to a greater number of responses being given in any stimulus situation. Specifically, they hypothesized that anxious individuals would give more associations in response to stimulus words on a chained word association test than would nonanxious individuals. The subjects were male undergraduates. The word-association test consisted of one-hundred nouns presented by means of a tape recorder, with a twenty-second pause between words. The subjects were instructed to write down as many associations as possible to each stimulus word. Scores on the MAS were found to correlate .45 with number of associations given.

Reaction time was investigated by Wenar (1954). High-anxious subjects responded faster than low-anxious subjects. Similarly, Reynolds, Blau, and Hurlbut (1961) hypothesized that anxiety should be positively related to speed on simple tasks. One task required subjects to draw lines above the letter X and below the letter O for a group of these letters typed randomly on a sheet of paper; the score was the number completed in a two-minute period. The high-anxious subjects completed significantly more lines than the low-anxious subjects.

Katahn, Blanton, and Gipson (1967) devised a task in which subjects were supposed to press a lever when a pair of lights came on. If the wrong lever were pressed, the subject received an electric shock. The pressure exerted by each subject on the lever was measured, and the strength of this response was expected to increase as anxiety increased. As expected, the high anxiety subjects pressed the lever harder than the low anxiety subjects.

Individuals high in anxiety may respond faster and with stronger responses, but Vaught and Newman (1966) hypothesized that anxiety would interfere with performance on a simple motor steadiness test. Under competitive conditions, male subjects had to insert a stylus in a series of holes without touching the edges of the holes; the high-anxiety individuals were much less steady in performing the task.

Still another complex task was used by Taylor and Rechtschaffen (1959). Subjects had to print the alphabet upside down and backwards as rapidly as possible. Response interference should result from the incompatibility of the highly practiced patterns of normal writing versus the new patterns required by the experimental task. With undergraduates as subjects, the nonanxious subjects completed significantly more letters within the time limits than did those high in manifest anxiety.

Reducing Anxiety by Means of Humor. If anxiety inteferes with performance on difficult tasks and with performance in the relatively complex situation of the college classroom, it follows that any mechanism which would reduce anxiety should be beneficial to high-anxiety individuals. Smith, Ascough, Ettinger, and Nelson (1971) pointed out that most theories of humor include the notion of tension reduction. In various experiments (for example, Dworkin and Efran, 1967; Singer, 1968) emotional arousal has been shown to decrease when subjects are exposed to humor. Smith, et al. reasoned that the introduction of humor in a testing situation should reduce stress and hence should improve the performance of those who were anxious.

The subjects (whose anxiety had been measured early in the semester) were a large number of Purdue undergraduates who were taking a regular classroom examination in a psychology course. On a thirty-item multiple-choice examination, two forms were prepared. On the humorous form, the stem of every third item was written in a humorous way. The corresponding ten items on the nonhumorous form contained an equal number of words and had the same four alternative answers. Two examples are:

Humorous—Three years ago Prudence Sigafoos met and became enamored of Errol Raunch, who had a thin mustache. But, alas, one night Errol snatched her purse and jewelry, bound her hands and feet with baling wire, and tossed her into a passing circus wagon, where she was assaulted three times by a playful orangutan. Since that night, Prudence has claimed that men and women who have thin mustaches can't be trusted. Her reaction is an example of a(n):

Nonhumorous—Three years ago as a freshman Janet took a course from a college professor who had a beard. This professor was quite unreasonable in many respects. His lectures were disorganized and largely irrelevant to the goals of the course, his examinations contained many trick questions, and he gave over half of the class, including Janet, failing grades. Since then Janet has refused to take any courses from professors having beards. Hers is an example of a(n) :

Answers: a) stereotype
        b) archetype
        c) effectance motive
        d) projection

Humorous—Every time little Brutus pulls a typical childhood prank such as overturning and shorting out the television set by urinating on it while his mother is watching the last five minutes of "As the World Turns," Mother reacts by administering punishment with her electric cattle prod. She notes that Brutus then stomps on his playmates with his hob-nailed boots. How might this aggression be accounted for?

Nonhumorous—Every time little Tommy pulls a typical childhood prank such as passing notes to friends in his classroom, chewing gum in class, or loudly talking while the teacher is presenting the lesson, his teacher reacts by slapping his knuckles with a ruler. The teacher notes that Tommy then tends to become very aggressive toward his playmates during the following recess. How might this aggression be accounted for?

Answers: a) the teacher furnishes a model for aggression
        b) Brutus's (Tommy's) frustration level is decreased by punishment
        c) projection of aggression
        d) more than one of the above

The response measure was each student's score on the midterm examination. The results are shown in Table 6-5. It was found that students high in

Table 6-5. Performance on a Midterm Examination of High- and Low-Anxious Students with Humorous and Nonhumorous Test Items

| | Test Items | |
Anxiety Level	Humorous	Non-Humorous
High	19.27	17.67
Low	19.26	19.41

(After Smith, Ascough, Ettinger, and Nelson, 1971, p. 244)

anxiety did less well than those low in anxiety on the regular test, but this difference was eliminated when the test contained humorous material. It was concluded that the humorous items acted to reduce anxiety, and that anxiety reduction improved the performance of the high anxious subjects.

Response to Stress

Several of the investigations that were described have included a manipulation of stress as well as a differentiation of subjects on the basis of MAS scores. Saltz (1970) has concluded that individuals who score high in anxiety are those whose behavior is disrupted by failure-induced stress; those who score low in anxiety do not show behavior disruption in such situations.

Control of Autonomic Arousal. One aspect of response to stress is the individual's ability to control his autonomic reactions. When we are faced by a psychological stress such as a final examination, our bodies can respond as if we were faced with a physical danger in a primeval forest. Since we are not going to run away at top speed or to engage an enemy in combat, we are clearly better off if we can bring our physiological responses under control and moderate them. Even with physical danger, if there is a complex task to perform, as with parachutists, those with the most experience learn to control their autonomic responses so that they can function without disruption at the time when the action must occur (Fenz and Epstein, 1967). In the June, 1972, issue of *Playboy*, Grand Prix racing champion Jackie Stewart was asked by an interviewer, "Aren't you at least *nervous* before a race?" He replied:

> Of course I am, and the intensity of the nervousness is like that of a person about to go in for major surgery. But by the time the race actually starts, I see things through absolutely cold, crystal-clear eyes, without fear or apprehension of any kind. It's a strange feeling, a feeling of being totally removed from the scene and looking at it from the outside, as though I'm no longer a part of my body. But this is an acquired talent it's taken a long time to perfect, and it helps me immensely.

To determine the effect of manifest anxiety on autonomic control, Fenz and Dronsejko (1969) selected extreme scorers on the MAS and measured GSR and heart rate during conditions of real and imagined shock. On a memory drum, subjects saw the numbers 13 through 0 in that order and in the "real" condition were told that an unpleasant shock would be given when number 1 appeared. In the imagination condition, the subjects were instructed to imagine getting a shock when the number 1 appeared.

It was found that the responses of the medium-anxious group were more adaptive than those of either the high- or low-anxious individuals. In the imagination condition the medium-anxious individuals showed a gradual increase in physiological responses and peaked at the specified time; when real shock was expected, their responses rose until just before the specified time and then decreased just before the shock was to be given. Like the experienced parachutists, medium-anxious subjects controlled their autonomic responses in time to handle the real danger. Low-anxious subjects were also able to control their physiological responses at the appropriate time, but they responded no differently to the imaginary and real conditions. Subjects high in anxiety were the least adaptive in that they showed strong physiological responses at the moment of danger and responded the same to real and imaginary stress. The findings are depicted in Figure 6-9. The levels of anxiety (moderate, low, and high) can be seen as representing appropriate control, overcontrol, and undercontrol with respect to autonomic arousal.

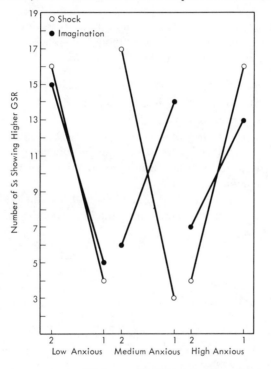

Fig. 6-9 Number of Low-, Medium-, and High-Anxious Subjects Showing Greater GSRs at Points 2 and 1 During the Time Sequence. (Adapted from Fenz and Dronsejko, 1969, p. 195.)

ANXIETY AND EXPECTANCIES

Changes in Expectancy. Rychlak and Lerner (1965) proposed that anxiety as measured by the MAS is related to expectancy. Specifically, they hypothesized that high-anxious individuals are more responsive to their recent past experience than are low-anxious individuals. Therefore, the generalized expectancy of those high in anxiety should fluctuate, while the expectancy of those low in anxiety should remain relatively stable.

The subjects were undergraduates with high or low MAS scores. They were given a series of six manual dexterity tasks. At the beginning, each subject was asked to estimate how well he would do (generalized expectancy). Next, he performed four of the tasks and received positive or negative feedback about how well he had done. Then, generalized expectancy was measured again. On the next task, they received the opposite kind of reinforcement from that they had been receiving (either positive or negative) and expectancy was measured a third time. It was found, as hypothesized, that subjects high in anxiety tended to rely on their most recent experiences in stating their expectancies. It was suggested that, "...it might be said that the anxious individual is one who is caught up in current necessities; he cannot easily transcend immediate experience, even though he might prefer to do so" (Rychlak and Lerner, 1965, p. 684).

Orientation toward Present. One way of conceptualizing such findings is to suggest that individuals high in anxiety tend to focus on the present rather than the future (Rychlak, 1972). This hypothesis was tested, using high- and low-anxious undergraduates. The subjects responded to a "time bar" in which they marked a line from a point labelled "Now" to various points in time between birth and death: one week, seven months, and nine years in each direction from now.

It may be seen in Figure 6-10 that high- and low-anxious subjects used different amounts of space is representing the time periods; the more anxious

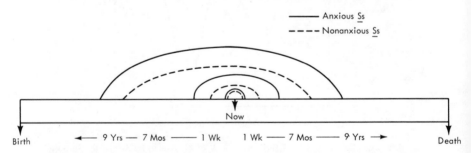

Fig. 6-10 Schematization of "Psychological Present" for Anxious and Non-anxious Subjects. The Life Span from Birth to Death is Symbolized on the Time Bar, with Successive Concentric Arcs Spanning from NOW at 1 Week, 7 Months, and 9 Years into the Past and Future. The Anxious Subjects Reveal a Constant Tendency to Extend Their Psychological Present. (Adapted from Rychlak, J. F., "Manifest anxiety as reflecting commitment to the psychological present at the expense of cognitive futurity." *Journal of Consulting and Clinical Psychology,* 1972, *38,* 74. © 1972 by American Psychological Association and reprinted by permission.

individuals appear to have literally a larger psychological present than those low in anxiety. Rychlak suggests that man is better off when he projects intentions and aspirations into the future rather than remaining tied to the present.

CHANGES IN MANIFEST ANXIETY

INCREASED ANXIETY

If scores on the MAS indicate an individual's characteristic emotional state, it would not be surprising to find that the experimental arousal of anxiety failed to bring about changes in test performance. Even though situational changes may not affect MAS performance, the use of hypnotic suggestion could conceivably have such an effect in that subjects could be led to evaluate their characteristic anxiety level differently.

Hypnotic induction of anxiety was attempted by Grosz and Levitt (1959). A group of medical and nursing students was given the MAS three times: in an ordinary waking state, in an hypnotic trance without special instructions, and in an hypnotic trance with anxiety instructions. The latter group received the following suggestions:

> I suggest to you that you will begin to feel in a certain way, that you will have certain definite feelings which I am going to suggest to you. You will begin to feel these feelings and emotions so vividly that your whole person, your whole body, every fiber of yourself, will feel that way—at first slightly, then gradually stronger and stronger. These feelings will last until I suggest to you that they are no longer there. The feelings and emotions which you will begin to experience are those of anxiety—feelings of anxiety, more and more intensely, more and more vividly. You will become more and more anxious. At first, there will just be a feeling of apprehension. Then, gradually you are beginning to feel more and more afraid but you do not know what it is that makes you feel so afraid and so anxious. You just feel that way without knowing why. You feel more and more afraid and anxious all the time, as if something dreadful is going to happen to you. Yet, you do not know what this dreadful thing is. I suggest that you will gradually begin to experience a state in which you feel really panicky, where you are so fearful that you feel an almost unbearable dread, fear, and panic. In fact, you are most likely already feeling this way and you will continue to feel this way more and more strongly (Grosz and Levitt, 1959, p. 282).

In the waking state the mean MAS score was 12.08, in the trance state 12.67, and in the anxiety trance state 25.00. Clearly the appropriate hypnotic instructions can bring about an increase in anxiety as measured by the MAS.

DECREASED ANXIETY

Psychotherapy. Effective psychotherapy should bring about a reduction in anxiety. Gallagher (1953) investigated the proposition that client-centered therapy influences MAS scores. College students were tested before and after receiving therapy. MAS scores were significantly lower after therapy (mean = 13.76) than before (mean = 17.28). Criteria of therapeutic success were a rating by the therapist, a rating by judges who read transcripts of the interviews, a rating by the client, and the ratio of negative to positive feelings expressed in the final therapy session compared to the same ratio in the first interview. Each of these criteria was found to.correlate with amount of change in MAS scores. The greater the reduction in anxiety, the greater the success of the psychotherapy.

Alcohol. The most common way in which anxiety is reduced in our culture is through the use of alcohol. At parties, on dates, after work, in restaurants, on picnics, at wakes, aboard airplanes, in bed, at wedding receptions —in short, almost everywhere and for almost all occasions, alcohol has become for many the chosen means to reduce tension and presumably to enhance pleasure. Alcohol can also be seen in a less benign light when one considers the embarassing things that are said and done by those who overdrink, those who have a crying jag, those who get into drunken arguments and fights, those who have automobile accidents, and, of course, those whose lives are destroyed by alcoholism. Interestingly enough, research provides evidence supporting both the positive and the negative effects of alcohol consumption.

Williams (1966) noted that in spite of the large number of physiological and clinical studies of drinking behavior, little research attention had been paid to the emotional effects of alcohol. He was interested in the effects of alcohol on anxiety and depression in a social situation. His investigation took place at a series of stag cocktail parties held at fraternity houses at two New York colleges. These parties began about 5 P.M. and lasted an hour or slightly longer. The subjects were told that they could do whatever they liked, and there was gin, scotch, bourbon, and mixers at the bar. Drinks could be obtained by handing in a name card to the bartender. Each drink contained two ounces of liquor. Measures of anxiety and depression were taken on the evening before the party, at the party after two drinks (4 ounces) and at the end of the party after various amounts of alcohol had been consumed (4 to 28 ounces).

The first comparison was between the preparty testing and the measures taken after two drinks. There was a significant decrease in both anxiety and depression. Such findings verify the common observation that after a couple of drinks, those at a party become more relaxed and happier. With such strong positive reinforcement, it is not surprising that the behavior would be repeated; hence there is continued drinking. Subjects in Williams's experiment varied a great deal in how many additional drinks they ordered, so the second comparison (between the 4-ounce condition and the end-of-the-party condition) was made separately for those who had consumed different amounts of alcohol. For those subjects who had only one more drink, there was a still further reduction of anxiety and depression. For those who had two additional drinks or more, there was the opposite effect; anxiety and depression *increased*. The greatest increase was for subjects who had more than 10 ounces (5 drinks) during the party.

> The decreases in anxiety and depression at low levels of alcohol consumption (from 4 to 6 ounces, generally) are consistent with clinical reports and some research on the effects of alcohol. The increases in anxiety and depression at higher levels of consumption indicated that there is a dosage effect of alcohol. At low levels of consumption it is generally agreed that the major anesthetic effect of alcohol on the brain is to remove normally prevailing inhibitions and restraints, so that emotional stimulation (feeling "high") is the most apparent feature—at least when alcohol is consumed in relaxed and natural settings. At this stage one would expect emotional changes like the decreases in anxiety and depression noted. With increasing dosage levels, however, the anesthetic effect builds, resulting in a progressive impairment of functions—These would include tiredness, dullness, nausea, a decrease in perception, inability to control one's actions, and inability to comprehand what is going on around one. Such factors are likely to create anxiety and depression in the drinker (Williams, 1966, p. 692).

Alcohol can be seen, then, as having paradoxical effects on anxiety. It is a powerful and very pleasant means to reduce anxiety, but when used to excess it can become the source of additional anxiety. A socially acceptable drug which had the former effect without the latter danger would clearly be preferable to alcohol.

STATE AND TRAIT ANXIETY

An important development in the conceptualization of anxiety has been the differentiation of two types of anxiety (Cattell and Scheier, 1961; Spielberger, 1966a). On the one hand, there is *trait anxiety* which refers to relatively stable individual differences in anxiety level; this is the construct measured by the MAS. In addition, there is *state anxiety* which refers to a temporary condition which fluctuates over time in response to situational changes. Spielberger (1966a) points out that anxiety states are characterized by subjective feelings of apprehension and tension plus the activation of the autonomic nervous system. Trait anxiety refers to a motive system or acquired tendency which predisposes the individual to respond with an anxiety state reaction to numerous situations which are perceived as threatening. The way in which these two kinds of anxiety interact is depicted in Figure 6-11.

In an effort to provide a reliable and easily administered measure of the two aspects of anxiety, Spielberger, Gorsuch, and Lushene (1970) developed

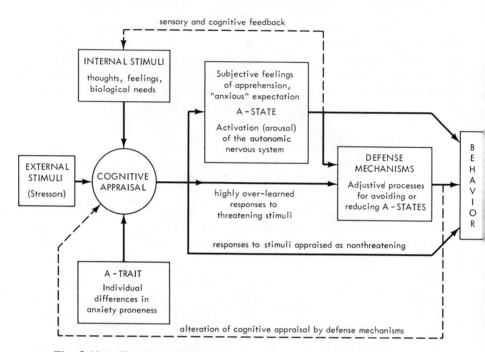

Fig. 6-11 A Trait-State Conception of Anxiety. It is Hypothesized that the Arousal of A-states Involves a Sequence of Temporally Ordered Events in which a Stimulus that is Cognitively Appraised as Dangerous Evokes an A-state Reaction. This A-state Reaction may then Initiate a Behavior Sequence Designed to Avoid the Danger Situation, or it may Evoke Defensive Maneuvers which alter the Cognitive Appraisal of the Situation. Individual Differences in A-trait Determine the Particular Stimuli that are Cognitively Appraised as Threatening. (Adapted from Spielberger, 1966a, p. 17.)

the State-Trait Anxiety Inventory. The A-Trait scale asks subjects to describe how they generally feel (almost never, sometimes, often, almost always) with respect to such statements as "I feel like crying," "I lack self-confidence," and "Some unimportant thought runs through my mind and bothers me." The A-State scale asks subjects to indicate how they feel right now, at this moment (not at all, somewhat, moderately so, very much so) with respect to such statements as "I feel calm," "I am jittery," and "I am worried." The importance of this trait-state differentiation in research on anxiety is suggested by Spielberger (1971):

> High A-Trait persons would be expected to perceive the requirement to perform on a difficult task, such as solving complex mathematical problems, as highly threatening, especially if the task were given with ego-involving instructions. Consequently, such tasks would be expected to evoke larger increments in A-State for persons who are high in A-Trait than for low A-Trait individuals. But a mathematician who is high in A-Trait is not likely to regard

this task as threatening because he has the requisite skills and experience to do well on it. On the other hand, while most persons find recreational activities such as boating and swimming to be interesting and pleasurable, a low A-Trait individual who is a poor swimmer might respond to the prospect of a boat ride with a considerable elevation in A-State. Thus, while measures of A-Trait provide useful information regarding the *probability* that high levels of A-State will be aroused, in order to assess the impact of a specific situation on a particular person, it will be necessary to take actual measures of A-State in that situation.

The way in which this conceptualization influences research is shown in the following examples.

Effects of Relaxation Training. Relaxation training involves a series of procedures in which subjects are given practice in tensing and relaxing various muscle groups (for example, arms, legs, stomach, face). Johnson and Spielberger (1968) proposed that such training would lead to a decrease in state anxiety but would not have any effect on trait anxiety.

The subjects were male psychiatric patients who were given measures of state and trait anxiety before and after two different sessions of relaxation training. As expected, this procedure had a marked effect on state anxiety in that it decreased after each session. Trait anxiety was unaffected by this experience.

Effects of Stress. The same differentiation of state and trait anxiety, but with changes in the opposite direction, was investigated by Johnson (1968). The subjects, male psychiatric patients, were all given relaxation training and then were interviewed. In the control condition, subjects were asked to talk about nonstressful topics such as their favorite hobbies or sports. In the stress condition, subjects were asked to describe their bodily reactions to fear and to describe in detail the most frightening experience of their lives. The anxiety measures were given before and after the interview.

There was a significant increase in state anxiety following the stressful interview, but there was no change in trait anxiety. Again, it appeared that the trait measure, which reflects individual differences in anxiety proneness, is not affected by changes in the situation.

Reactions to Surgery. A very real stress which would be expected to arouse anxiety is the knowledge that surgery is going to be performed. Besides the actual physical danger, there is a feeling of helplessness and uncertainty about one's fate. Spielberger, Auerbach, Wadsworth, Dunn, and Taulbee (1973) proposed that state anxiety would be aroused prior to surgery and would decline afterward; trait anxiety should remain uninfluenced by these changed situations.

The State-Trait Anxiety Inventory was given before and after surgery to a group of volunteer male patients at a Veterans Administration hospital. The first testing took place eighteen to twenty-four hours before surgery, and the second took place three to nine days after the operation was over. The second tests were given after the patient was out of pain and after his physician had informed him that he was recovering without complications.

Again, it was found that state anxiety was quite different before and after a stressful event and that trait anxiety remained constant. The investigators were also interested, however, in the effect of trait anxiety on the level of state anxiety. That is, even though state anxiety should decrease for everyone after the stress is over, its absolute level should be higher for those individuals who are chronically anxious than for those who are not. This relationship is shown in Figure 6-12.

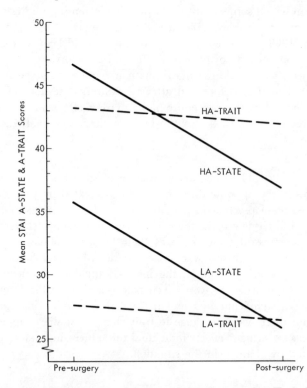

Fig. 6-12 Mean Presurgery and Postsurgery A-State and A-Trait Scores for High Anxious Trait (HA-Trait) and Low Anxious Trait (LA-Trait) Groups. (Adapted from Spielberger, C. D., Auerbach, S. M., Wadsworth, A. P., Dunn, T. M. and Taulbee, E. S., "Emotional reactions to surgery." *Journal of Consulting and Clinical Psychology*, 1973, 40. © 1973 by the American Psychological Association and reprinted by permission.)

These studies are quite consistent in indicating that state anxiety increases and decreases in response to situational changes while trait anxiety remains relatively stable over time.

CURRENT ISSUES IN RESEARCH ON MANIFEST ANXIETY

In the literature dealing with anxiety, one often finds conclusions to the effect that the very concept of anxiety is a useless one and that the Manifest Anxiety Scale only contributes to the confusion. For example, Sarbin traces the current use of the concept of anxiety to certain historical mistakes in interpreting metaphors literally. He concludes: "...the mentalistic and multireferenced term anxiety has outlived its usefulness. Unless a convention is called to decide on more precise existent referents for the term, it would be better to discontinue employing it in scientific discourse" (Sarbin, 1964a, p. 635). Whether or not Sarbin is correct in suggesting that the concept of "cognitive strain" will be more fruitful than that of anxiety, the author feels that the research cited in this chapter alone attests to the utility of anxiety as a behavioral variable.

SOCIAL DESIRABILITY

In discussing the California F Scale in Chapter 4, the measurement problem raised by acquiescent response set was indicated. With the MAS, some degree of balance exists with respect to acquiescence (39 items keyed TRUE, 11 items keyed FALSE), so one would not anticipate that the measurement of anxiety would be found to be greatly contaminated by this particular response set. To test this proposition, Chapman and Campbell (1959) reversed the wording of each MAS item in order to have a positive form (T = anxious repsonse) and a negative form (F = anxious response) of the test. The two forms were found to correlate .84. Thus acquiescent response set does not appear to influence the MAS.

Edwards (1953) published the first article in a series which raised the question of the effects of another type of response set, social desirability of the content of test items. He obtained judges' ratings of the social desirability of a series of questionnaire items. The correlation between the social-desirability value of an item as assigned by the judges and the proportion of subjects agreeing with the item content was found to be .87. This substantial relationship has been confirmed in other studies.

A related, but somewhat different, concept is Edwards's (1957) social-desirability hypothesis. He suggests that individuals differ in the tendency to give socially desirable responses to questionnaire items. He has built a Social Desirability (SD) Scale to measure this tendency. The higher an individual's score on the SD Scale, the more likely he will be to give socially desirable responses to test items. When scores on the SD Scale are found to correlate highly with scores on a given test, one interpretation is that the test is confounding social-desirability response set with whatever it is purporting to measure. SD Scale scores have been found to correlate highly with many personality tests including a correlation of −.84 with the MAS (Edwards, 1957). One caution suggested by such findings is that correlations between the MAS and other tests may simply reflect the fact that both instruments measure (at least in part) the social-desirability set.

Can something be done to eliminate this problem? With a relationship of −.84, it would be extremely difficult to measure anxiety in the way Taylor has chosen and at the same time "control for" social desirability of item content. Conceivably, items could be found which are unrelated to social desirability but which are highly related to manifest anxiety. Perhaps it is more reasonable to inquire whether the MAS and the SD Scale might best be conceptualized as measuring the same dimension and then to determine the most appropriate name for that dimension. Farber discusses this problem with respect to the MAS:

> What, then, does the test measure?
> In one sense, this is a trivial question, and requires but a trivial answer, though, unfortunately, one that constructors and users of tests sometimes fail to see, namely, that giving tests different names does not guarantee that they reflect different characteristics, and giving them the same names does not necessarily mean they reflect the same determinants. If all these highly interrelated measures are related to all other kinds of behaviors in the same way, they measure the same thing, regardless of their labels.
> Occasionally, however, this confusion among the characteristics inferred from behavior is not merely nominal. For instance, height and weight are highly correlated in the general population, yet no one supposes they are merely different names for the same thing. What if defensiveness and desire to make a favorable impression are independent, but nevertheless empirically related in a given population? How, then, could we decide whether they reflect different organismic states or processes? Or better, if the one measure is related to some other mode of behavior, which hypothetical variable is responsible for the relation?
> These are not trivial questions, and their answers are not easily come by. One kind of answer is simply the observation that there is never any guarantee in science against the inaccurate identification of determinants (Farber, 1964, p. 30).

To date, research findings suggest that the SD Scale and the MAS are measuring the same dimension of behavior. If so, the only problem is that of eventually deciding on the most appropriate name, as was discussed in Chapter 3. If, however, the two instruments are found to be measuring two different but highly related dimensions (like height and weight in Farber's example), the theoretical formulations of their respective antecedents, correlates, and consequents will eventually diverge. In either event it does not seem fruitful to consider social desirability as a "response set" which simply constitutes a methodological weakness contaminating the MAS as a measuring device. The tendency to give socially desirable responses is either another name for manifest anxiety, or it is a distinct personality variable worth studying in its own right (Block, 1965).

KINDS OF ANXIETY

As with many types of personality measures now in use, the MAS may well be superseded in the future by instruments designed to measure the variable in question more specifically. Even though there appears to be utility in the concept of a general, multi-situational anxiety level, one of the basic properties of anxiety is the ease with which it can be attached to specific cues. Tests which attempt to measure differences in anxiety evoked by classroom examinations, heterosexual stimulation, competition, or social interaction may turn out to be of greater predictive value than an omnibus measure such as the MAS which attempts to cut across many such situations.

In the typical experimental manipulation of stress, some relatively unpleasant situation is created and subjects are expected to respond with increased anxiety. There are, however, individual differences in just how threatening it is to fail an examination, to handle a snake, to appear on a stage, to receive an electric shock, or whatever. Hodges and Spielberger (1966) ran high- and low-anxious subjects in a verbal conditioning task in which they were told that they would be given several shocks. It was found that heart rate increased under these conditions, but there was no difference in the responses of individuals who scored at different extremes on the MAS. Subjects had also been given a fear of shock question two months before the experiment. This was a single item on which subjects indicated on a five-point scale how much concern or apprehension they would feel about participating in a psychology experiment in which they received an electric shock. When subjects were divided into high and low groups on the basis of their responses concerning this specific kind of threat, there was a marked difference in the heart rates of those high and low in fear of shock, as shown in Figure 6-13. Thus, the general measure of anxiety was not a predictor of physiological responses in this stressful situation, whereas the measure of anxiety which dealt specifically with this type of situation was a very good predictor.

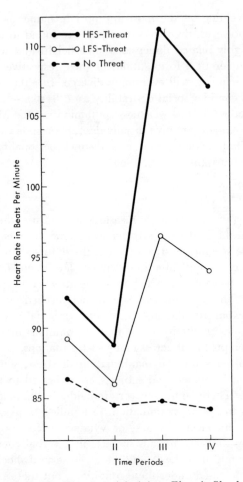

Fig. 6-13 The Effects of a Threat to Administer Electric Shock on Heart Rate for Subjects with High Fear of Shock (HFS-Threat) and Low Fear of Shock (LFS-Threat). The Heart Rate Data for Subjects in the No Threat Condition are also Shown, for Comparison Purposes. (Adapted from Hodges, W. F. and Spielberger, D. C., "The affects of threat of shock on heart rate for subjects who differ in manifest anxiety and fear of shock." *Psychophysiology*, 1966, 2, 290. © 1966 The Williams & Wilkins Co., Baltimore.)

SUMMARY

Anxiety is defined as an emotional state in which there is a vague, generalized fear. Anxiety is usually conceptualized as a motive by psychologists. Research on anxiety has been of several kinds.

1. Anxiety is studied in terms of the stimuli which evoke it and the responses which define it.
2. Through conditioning, fear or anxiety can become associated with previously neutral stimuli. This phenomenon has been of interest to experimental psychologists, clinical psychologists, and psychiatrists.
3. The motivational properties of fear and anxiety have been of research interest in that instrumental responses which lead to drive reduction can be learned.
4. In the Hull-Spence theoretical system, drive is said to have an energizing effect on behavior, and many experiments have utilized the manipulation of anxiety to test hypotheses derived from that proposition.
5. Individual differences in anxiety have been of interest with respect to each of the other four areas of research.

One approach to theory-building is represented by the work of Clark Hull and Kenneth Spence. The Hull-Spence theory is built on a base of rigorous laboratory experimentation and the testing of hypotheses deduced from the theory. Among the theoretical constructs are individual differences in emotional responsiveness. One of Spence's students, Janet Taylor, developed a personality questionnaire designed to measure this dimension.

The first step in constructing the Manifest Anxiety Scale was the presentation of two hundred MMPI items to clinical psychologists who were to judge each item as an indicator of manifest anxiety. On sixty-five of the items, 80 percent or better agreement was obtained among the clinicians. An internal consistency item-analysis reduced this number to fifty items. The reliability of the MAS, in terms of internal consistency and stability over time, is acceptably high.

The antecedents of manifest anxiety have been relatively neglected in research to date. One investigation, with adolescent boys and their mothers, found that subjects with low manifest anxiety were satisfied with themselves, met their perception of their mothers' ideal for them, and perceived themselves as being the kind of person their mothers actually wanted them to be. Clinical studies of children and experimental studies of monkeys are consistent in indicating that persistent anxiety can result when infants are separated from their mothers.

A number of correlational investigations of the MAS have been of a semivalidational nature. The MAS has been found to be significantly related to a measure of separation anxiety, test anxiety, and also the belief that the environment is threatening and uncontrollable. Scores on the MAS are found to be related to clinical judgments of anxiety level. A positive relationship is found between the MAS and physiological indicators of anxiety such as palmar sweating and the specific response index (the subject's highest score on a series of physiological variables). Psychiatric populations consistently obtain higher anxiety scores than normal groups, and the MAS is related to the number of reported medical and psychiatric symptoms. Educational level and manifest anxiety tend to be negatively related. When academic ability and anxiety are considered simultaneously, grades are found to be negatively influenced by anxiety only at middle levels of scholastic aptitude. Other findings indicate that subjects with high scores on the MAS are among those who undergo sudden religious conversions and are more likely to have difficulties with childbirth.

The initial reason for constructing the MAS was for use in learning experiments—to obtain a measure of individual differences in emotional responsiveness which in turn should be related to drive level. Hull proposed that all habits activated in a particular stimulus situation combine in a multiplicative function with total drive state to determine the strength of a response. In a simple situation in which one habit is evoked, the higher the drive, the greater the response strength. Thus, the performance of high MAS subjects should be superior to that of low MAS subjects in such situations. In a complex situation in which several competing responses are evoked along with the correct one, high drive interacts with each habit to increase the strength of a number of different responses. Thus, the performance of low MAS subjects should be superior to that of high MAS subjects in these situations. These predictions have led to a large number of investigations yielding largely confirmatory findings in situations including classical conditioning, stimulus generalization, maze learning, serial learning, and paired-associates learning. Drive level as indicated by MAS scores is also found to affect the number of word associations, reaction time, speed on a simple line-drawing task, response amplitude, motor steadiness, and speed of printing the alphabet upside down and backwards. The inclusion of humorous material in a classroom examination was found to improve the performance of high anxious students, presumably because the humor reduced their level of anxiety. In a study of autonomic arousal, it was concluded that individuals at an intermediate anxiety level showed appropriate control while those with low anxiety were overcontrolled and those with high anxiety were undercontrolled. High anxiety is also associated with changing expectancies on the basis of recent experiences and with an overemphasis on the psychological present.

Increase in anxiety has been achieved by means of hypnotic instructions suggesting anxiety, apprehension, and fear. Decrease in anxiety has been found as a function of psychotherapy. Moderate amounts of alcohol decrease anxiety; additional drinks have the opposite effect. Trait anxiety refers to stable individual differences in anxiety level while state anxiety refers to a temporary condition which fluctuates in response to situational changes. Studies of relaxation training, interview stress, and emotions surrounding surgery indicate that state anxiety increases and decreases while trait anxiety remains stable. A sufficiently large body of research has been generated to attest to the fruitfulness of the concept of anxiety and of the MAS as a measure. Though the MAS is unaffected by acquiescent response set, it is highly related to a measure of social-desirability response set. If anxiety and the tendency to give socially desirable responses are actually different variables with different antecedents, correlates, and consequents, it will be of great value if they can be measured independently. Tests which measure differences in anxiety evoked by specific stimulus situations give promise of being of greater predictive value than multisituational measures such as the MAS.

7

Intelligence

The concept of intelligence occupies a peculiar position within the field of psychology. On the one hand, intelligence tests represent perhaps the best-known and most widely influential product of psychological science. In the words of Jenkins and Paterson (1961, p. 81): "...probably no psychological innovation has had more impact on the societies of the Western world than the development of the Binet-Simon scales." At the same time, intelligence often appears to be psychology's unwanted step-child. Neither in terms of theoretical developments nor empirical research has the concept of intelligence been well integrated with other work in psychology. It is often not even considered to be an integral part of the field of personality.

In his presidential address to the American Psychological Association, McNemar said:

> The Greeks had a word for it, but the Romans had a word with better survival properties. Regardless of the word, what is now called intelligence has been talked about for at least 2,000 years. And as long as 2,000 years before the advent of attempts to measure intelligence, there seems to have been recognition of the fact that individuals differ in intellectual ability.
> The earlier attempts at measuring were based on either of two quite distinct conceptions: the Galton-Cattell idea that intellectual ability manifests itself in simple, discrimination functionng, and the Binet notion that cognitive ability reflects itself in more complex functioning. The Binet concept proved to be more fruitful, and by 1925 there was on the market, in addition to various

versions of the Binet scale, a flood of group tests of so-called general intelligence (McNemar, 1964, p. 871).

As McNemar indicates, the earliest attempts to measure individual differences in intellectual functioning consisted of the measurement of very simple responses. In the latter half of the nineteenth century, Galton worked with such characteristics as keenness of hearing and ability to form mental images. Interest in measuring intelligence in this way was furthered by James McKeen Cattell who studied psychology in Germany and returned to the United States in 1890 with a series of such tests including sensory acuity, strength of grip, and memory. This general approach to measurement was largely abandoned when Wissler (1901) correlated the scores on numerous simple tasks with college grades. The results were extremely discouraging to those who had hopes for the utility of such variables. He found, for example, that grades correlated $-.02$ with reaction time, $-.09$ with speed of cancelling letters, and .08 with color naming. Far more fruitful was the approach of Binet, and later of Terman, as will be described in the following section.

Work on intelligence has been characterized by a relative neglect of theory with the notable exception of Piaget's approach to the understanding of cognitive functioning (Phillips, 1969; Piaget, 1936, 1947). One would reasonably suppose that the items which are included in IQ tests are selected on the basis of their relevance to the test constructor's theoretical definition of intelligence. Instead, the general pattern followed has been that of Binet who "learned how to measure something without any very clear idea as to what it was he was measuring" (Hebb, 1958, p. 246). Binet's approach was to select items primarily on the basis of their ability to discriminate individuals in a consistent manner. The same sort of empiricism has prevailed in attempts to define what it is that these combined items are measuring:

> A few words about definition may be in order. First, it might be claimed that no definition is required because all intelligent people know what intelligence is—it is the thing that the other guy lacks. Second, the fact that tests of general intelligence based on differing definitions tend to intercorrelate about as highly as their respective reliabilities permit indicates that, despite the diversity of definitions, the same function or process is being measured—definitions can be more confusing than enlightening (McNemar, 1964, p. 871).

Nevertheless, those working with such instruments have proposed a variety of definitions which stress adaptation to the environment, learning ability, and/or abstract thinking. It is the latter characteristic on which Terman placed the greatest stress.

Several attempts have been made to build an integrative formulation including both genetic influences and the effects of early experience. It has been argued, for example, that the form which primate intelligence takes is the result of its development in a social context (Jolly, 1966). That is, as primate society developed, it was imperative that the young learn the rules of that society whether it involved monkeys, apes, or men. Those most adept at such learning were most likely to survive, win mates, and reproduce. Other theoretical approaches have been presented by Hayes (1962), Hebb (1949), and Hunt (1961).

BACKGROUND OF THE CONCEPT OF INTELLIGENCE

BINET AND THE IDENTIFICATION OF "FEEBLE-MINDED" CHILDREN

Alfred Binet (1857–1911) was born in Nice, France, in a family of physicians; his father and both grandfathers practiced medicine. At the age of 15, Binet was taken by his mother to Paris to attend the Lycee Louis-le-Grand from 1872 to 1875. He then entered law school, received his license in 1878, and began working on a doctorate.

In this period, an interest in "psychology" developed, and he avidly read the works of John Stuart Mill and the other British associationists. As an armchair psychologist in 1880, Binet published his first paper. In the next eleven years he published four books, had one book in press, and produced a large number of articles. Like Freud, he was interested in the work of Charcot and others who were exploring hypnosis in both medical treatment and experimental investigations. Following a period marked by stormy arguments and theoretical disputes among those interested in hypnotic phenomena, Binet in 1891 took a position at the Laboratory of Physiological Psychology at the Sorbonne, the first French psychological laboratory.

His specific interest in hypnosis shifted to a more general interest in complex mental processes. Between 1893 and 1911 he worked with and reported the use of numerous types of tests used to explore individual differences in the intellectual ability of children. In 1903, he published *The Experimental Study of Intelligence*. With only a general notion of what kinds of behavior might be appropriate indices of intelligence, Binet tried out such tests as the recall of numbers, moral judgment, mental addition, and tactile discrimination. In working with various children, including his daughters, he found that ability on simple tasks, such as reaction time and discrimination, was unrelated to ability on more complex tasks, such as those involving memory, comprehension, and mathematical manipulation.

While this work was in progress in 1904, a problem was raised within the Paris school system—the identification of "feeble-minded" children so that they could be removed from regular classes and placed in special schools. Teacher ratings could be used for this purpose, but the school administrators were afraid that teachers would make too many mistakes in classifying the children. For example, they might rate a bright troublemaker as dull to get rid of him and a dull but wealthy child as bright to avoid offending his parents. What was needed was an objective, accurate way of measuring intelligence, and the schools asked Binet if his research might be applicable to the problem.

Putting together the most successful of the various tests which he had been studying, Binet and a colleague, Th. Simon, created the Binet-Simon Scale in 1905; the test was revised in 1908 and again in 1911, the year of Binet's death.

From the very beginning, the concept of intelligence was of greatest use in solving a practical problem in an applied setting, and there was an empirical and pragmatic rather than a conceptual and theoretical basis for the selection of test items. Individual tests in the Binet-Simon instrument were arranged in order of difficulty from easiest to hardest, and the scale was made up of the same type of items in use in such tests today. This measurement technique had a great impact on psychologists and nonpsychologists alike as suggested by such statements as that by Goddard (1912, p. 326) who felt that the Binet-Simon "...scale would one day take a place in the history of science beside Darwin's theory of evolution and Mendel's law of heredity." While that evaluation seems somewhat overenthusiastic from our present perspective, it is true that the history of psychology, at least, has been closely intertwined with the history of intelligence testing.

TERMAN AND THE STANFORD-BINET

An American psychologist, Lewis M. Terman (1877–1956) became interested in Binet's work while in graduate school; later he adapted the French test for use with American children.

Terman was born on a farm in rural Indiana, the twelfth of fourteen children. He has indicated that his family was not a particularly well-educated one and that his early education in a one-room schoolhouse was decidedly inferior by modern standards. He did, however, have an early interest in individual differences:

> Whatever the cause, almost as far back as I can remember I seem to have had a little more interest than the average child in the personalities of others and to have been impressed by those who differed in some respect from the common run. Among my schoolmates or acquaintances whose behavior traits especially interested me were a feebleminded boy who was still in the first reader at the age of eighteen, a backward albino boy who was pathetically devoted to his small sister, a spoiled crippled boy given to fits of temper and to stealing, a boy who was almost a "lightning calculator," and a playmate of near my own age who was an imaginative liar and later came into national prominence as an alleged swindler and multimurderer. I am inclined to think that the associations which I had with such schoolmates were among the most valuable of my childhood experiences (Terman, 1932, pp. 300–301).

Terman did well in his classes and was promoted from the first to the third grade after being in school six months. Between the ages of eleven and eighteen, he spent half of each year working on the farm and half in school. As preparation to become a teacher he attended Central Normal College in Danville, Indiana, where he received the B.S. degree in 1896. Interspersing his college work with teaching in rural schools, he later received the "Bachelor of Pedagogy" and A.B. degrees at the Danville school. He married a fellow teacher in 1899, and after two years as a high school principal, he entered Indiana University in 1901 to study psychology. There, in two years, he received his second bachelor's and a master's degree. Obtaining a fellowship at Clark University, he moved there in 1903 for two years of graduate study.

At Clark he first learned in detail about Binet's work from students returning from Europe and from Binet's publications. His dissertation dealt with an experimental study of mental tests. He selected two groups of subjects of the same approximate age, one bright and one dull, and devised tests on which he believed they would perform differently. After receiving the Ph.D. degree at Clark, Terman accepted a job as principal of the high school in San Bernardino. He indicated that he accepted this position rather than his other offers (a Florida normal school and the University of Texas) primarily because of the climate—he had recurring difficulty with tuberculosis. After a year there, he was offered a professorship at the Los Angeles State Normal School where he remained for four years. In 1910, he accepted a position at Stanford University in the School of Education. There, he immediately began an experimental study of the Binet tests. This work culminated in the publication of *The Measurement of Intelligence* in 1916, the first of the Stanford-Binet scales.

Cronbach describes the influence of Terman's test as follows:

> The Stanford-Binet had immediate popularity and became, rightly or wrongly, the yardstick by which other tests were judged. Although there had been various previous mental tests, the outstanding popularity of the Stanford test made its conception of intelligence the standard. The acceptance of the Stanford test was due to the care with which it had been prepared, its success in testing complex mental activities, the easily understood "IQ" it provided, and the important practical results which it quickly produced. Although many criticisms have been made of the test, it was and is an exceptionally useful instrument (Cronbach, 1960, p. 161).

During World War I, Terman served under Yerkes on the committee that devised the first group intelligence tests for the armed forces. His later work at Stanford involved the development of a number of other tests, the study of gifted children, and continued work on the Stanford-Binet and its revisions. He became chairman of the Department of Psychology in 1922 and quickly developed it into an outstanding one, thanks in part to a $500,000 legacy from Thomas Welton Stanford which was earmarked for psychology.

CONSTRUCTION OF THE STANFORD-BINET INTELLIGENCE SCALE

Many different intelligence tests have been built, and these instruments tend to correlate highly with one another. Among the most widely used of these other instruments are the Wechsler Adult Intelligence Scale or WAIS (Wechsler, 1958), and the Wechsler Intelligence Scale for Children or WISC (Wechsler, 1949) and the Wechsler Preschool and Primary Scale of Intelligence (Wechsler, 1967). As an example of the construction of intelligence tests, however, only the Stanford-Binet will be described in any detail.

SELECTION OF TEST ITEMS

In selecting items for the 1916 Stanford-Binet, Terman used ninety tests of the same type that Binet had employed, primarily those involving "the more complex mental processes." Though highly useful, the 1916 test had several inadequacies and was revised in 1937 by Terman and Maud Merrill, a clinical psychologist on the Stanford faculty. The test items in the 1937 revision were similar to the earlier ones and included such subtests as analogies (Brother is a boy; sister is a —————.) ; comprehension (What makes a sailboat move?) ; vocabulary (What is an orange?) ; similarities and differences (In what way are a baseball and an orange alike, and how are they different?) ; verbal and pictorial completions (What is gone in this picture? What isn't there?) ; absurdities (One day we saw several icebergs that had been entirely melted by the warmth of the Gulf Stream. What is foolish about that?) ; drawing designs; and memory for digits and for verbal material. From a large initial sample of such items, the final test consisted of those items which (1) showed an increase in percentage of children passing it for successive age levels, and (2) were correlated with total score on the test. Subtests were arranged in age levels, and test scores obtained in terms of Mental Age (MA). The most recent revision of the Stanford-Binet (Terman and Merrill, 1960) was primarily undertaken in order to bring the test content up to date.

EVALUATION OF TEST ITEMS

Between 1950 and 1954, the 1937 test was administered to over four thousand subjects between the ages of two-and-one-half and eighteen in various communities across the country. In this way, the suitability of the old items could be determined.

As an example, we will take the vocabulary subtest. It contains a printed list of forty-five words at which the subject may look. The examiner says, "I want to find out how many words you know. Listen, and when I say a word, you tell me what it means. What is an orange?" After the subject gives his definition, the next word is asked, and so on. The words are arranged in order of difficulty as determined by the responses of the standardization group. Early in the list are words such as envelope and straw, later are words such as juggler and brunette, and still later words such as regard and disproportionate. The examiner proceeds down the list until the subject misses six consecutive words and then discontinues the vocabulary subtest and goes on to other items. A comparison of the 1937 and 1960 tests indicates that several of the vocabulary words shifted with respect to difficulty level. For example, "Mars" apparently became more familiar and hence an easier word.

When the vocabulary test was initially built, a mental age score had to be assigned for a given number of correct definitions. The assignment to a specific age level on the basis of percent passing curves is an empirical procedure. If, for example, about 50 percent of the ten-year-olds could define eleven words correctly, a vocabulary score of eleven would give the subject credit at the ten-year MA level. If older children could define a larger number of words, a subject defining more words correctly would get a higher MA score.

For the subjects in the 1960 revision, passing scores for each age level were determined, and the next step was to plot a percent passing curve as shown in Figure 7-1. From the figure we see, for example, that about 60 percent of those at age twelve receive a passing score, with 15 correct as the criterion of passing. Thus, subjects who answer 15 vocabulary items correctly receive credit at the twelve-year MA level.

The curve shown in the figure is typical of those obtained on the various Stanford-Binet items. An item passed by a set percentage of the subjects at any given age is passed by increasingly fewer subjects at younger ages and by increasingly greater numbers of subjects at older ages. The other criterion of item-acceptability is the correlation between performance on a given item and total score on the test. Terman and Merrill (1960) report that vocabulary score at age twelve (15 correct) correlates .79 with total score on the test.

INTELLIGENCE QUOTIENT

In the 1937 Stanford-Binet, the Intelligence Quotient (IQ) consisted of the Mental Age obtained on the test divided by the subject's Chronological Age (CA), with the quotient multiplied by 100. Thus, the average ten-year-old obtains an MA of 10 which is divided by his CA of 10, and the quotient times 100 equals 100 or an average IQ. Scores below 100 indicate test performance below average for an individual's age level, and scores above 100 indicate above average test performance.

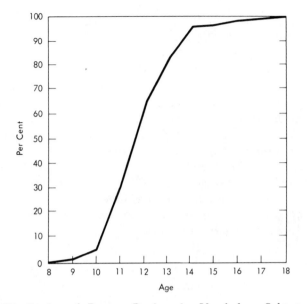

Fig. 7-1 Distribution of Percent Passing the Vocabulary Subtest at Age Twelve Level; 15 Correct = Passing. (Adapted from Terman and Merrill, 1960, p. 30.)

The MA/CA × 100 = IQ approach runs into various difficulties, especially for individuals in late adolescence and beyond. Mental age as measured by the test items does not continue showing yearly increases indefinitely. In the 1937 revision, the IQ formula could not be utilized in its pure form beyond age 13 because MA increases became smaller and smaller. By age 16, no further yearly increases occurred. For this reason, Terman and Merrill (1937) developed a "corrected CA divisor" beginning at age 13 years, 2 months. For example, at CA 16, the divisor was a CA of 15 rather than the actual CA of 16.

To get around this problem in the 1960 Stanford-Binet, IQ is defined in terms of deviations from the average performance of an individual's age group. In order to maintain continuity with the older IQ scores, the test is arbitrarily arranged so that average performance still yields an IQ of 100. The IQ score now is simply a standard score with a mean of 100 and a standard deviation of 16.

RELIABILITY

One estimate of the internal consistency of the 1960 revision is the average correlation between subtest performance and total score; the average r is .66.

For other types of reliability data, a number of findings utilizing the 1937 revision may probably be generalized to the newer test. For example, the average correlation between two forms of the 1937 test was found to be .91 (Terman and Merrill, 1937).

With respect to test-retest reliability, a number of longitudinal studies have been carried out with the Stanford-Binet. Typical of the findings of such investigations are those reported by Sontag, Baker, and Nelson (1958) dealing with stability of IQ over a ten-year period. As might be expected, the longer the interval between testings, the lower the test-retest correlation. Also, the older the child, the higher the correlation between successive testings. Tests of IQ in infancy are usually found to be unrelated to later measures of intelligence (Lewis and McGurk, 1972). IQ at age 3 correlates .83 with IQ at age 4 and only .46 with IQ at age 12. The correlation between IQ in adolescence and in adulthood has been found to be .85 (Bradway, Thompson, and Cravens, 1958). After infancy, IQ is relatively stable over time, especially from adolescence onward.

ANTECEDENTS OF INTELLIGENCE

A great deal of research interest has centered on the question of the antecedents of individual differences in intellectual ability. In addition, a good portion of this research has involved a controversy between proponents of genetic antecedents and proponents of experiential antecedents—heredity versus environment or nature versus nurture. Some of the original flavor of this sort of controversy may be ascertained from two early statements on the subject:

> By intelligence, the psychologist understands inborn, all-round, intellectual ability. It is inherited, or at least innate, not due to teaching or training; it is intellectual, not emotional or moral, and remains uninfluenced by industry or zeal; it is general, not specific, i.e., it is not limited to any particular kind of work, but enters into all we do or say or think (Burt, Jones, Miller, and Moodie, 1934, pp. 28–29).
> ...Some recent philosophers appear to have given their moral support to the deplorable verdict that the intelligence of an individual is a fixed quantity. ...We must protest and act against this brutal pessimism.... A child's mind is like a field for which an expert farmer has advised a change in the method of cultivating, with the result that in place of desert land, we now have a harvest. It is in this particular sense, the one which is significant, that we say that the intelligence of children may be increased. One increases that which constitutes the intelligence of a school child, namely, the capacity to learn, to improve with instruction (Binet, 1909, pp. 54–55).

In more recent years, there has been a shift away from such either-or questions toward an attempt to investigate all possible antecedents of personality differences, that is, an investigation of multiple determinants.

GENETIC DETERMINANTS

Family Resemblances. As was noted in Chapter 3, one of the ways to study genetic determinants of human behavior is to examine behavior similarity as a function of genetic similarity, the latter being defined in terms of closeness of family relationship.

If intelligence tests were given to a group of adults and to a group of unrelated children, the correlation between the two members of various random adult-child pairs should be .00. If, on the other hand, the adult-child pairs consist of parents and their offspring, the IQs are found to correlate about .50 (for example, Conrad and Jones, 1940). The problem with interpreting such findings, of course, is that parents and children are not only more similar than random strangers in hereditary factors, they are also more similar in environmental factors.

Another approach in family resemblance studies is to compare siblings who differ in genetic closeness. Again, random pairs of unrelated children should have IQ correlations of .00. When unrelated children are reared together, their IQ scores are found to correlate .25 (Burt, 1958). With pairs of siblings, IQs have been found to correlate about .50 (Conrad and Jones, 1940). Thus, the greater genetic similarity of siblings than of unrelated children reared together adds to similarity in IQ. Given this same sibling relationship plus *identical* genetic structure, greater IQ similarity in identical twins would further indicate the influence of heredity on intelligence. Intelligence scores of identical twins are found to correlate in the .80s (Gottesman, 1963), about as they correlate in such physical characteristics as height and weight (Newman, Freeman, and Holzinger, 1937).

Such findings seem clear, but there is a methodological weakness in comparing twin-pair similarity with other sibling-pair similarity. The twins are the same age when tested; the siblings are not. If half of the siblings are four and the other half nine, they do not correlate as highly with each other as pairs of four-year-old twins or pairs of nine-year-old twins. But we know that the four-year-olds are likely to be somewhat different in IQ by the time they are nine and conceivably more similar to their siblings in test scores. A way out of this dilemma is to compare fraternal twins with identical twins; here the pairs are the same age in each instance, but different in genetic similarity. Fraternal twins have been found to have IQ correlations ranging from .59 (Gottesman, 1963) to .70 (Richardson, 1936). Thus, fraternal twins are similar in IQ, but not as similar as identical twins. Also, apparently the only reason that fraternal twins are more similar than nontwin siblings is the fact that they are the same age. When fraternal twins are tested at different ages, their IQ scores are no more similar than other siblings (Richardson, 1936). Even during their first and second years, identical twins are more similar in mental development than are fraternal twins (Wilson, 1972).

Thus, the twin studies confirm the proposition that intellectual ability is in part a function of genetic determinants.

Experiments of Nature. With respect both to twin comparisons and to parent-child comparisons, other research has been carried out by taking advantage of "experiments of nature."

The Newman, et al. (1937) investigation included as subjects fifty pairs of identical twins reared together and nineteen pairs of identical twins who had been separated in infancy or early childhood and reared apart. The correlation between IQ scores for those reared together was .88, while for those identical twins reared apart the coefficient was .77. The homes of the separated pairs were rated in terms of several variables, including educational advantage. When the difference between the educational advantage of their homes was correlated with the difference in IQ for the nineteen separated twins, the coefficient was found to be .79. Thus, in spite of the obvious genetic influence toward similarity in IQ for identical twins, the greater the difference in their environmental opportunities, the greater the difference in their intelligence.

The study of adopted children provides the chance to investigate parent-child similarity in IQ with respect to natural parents who do not actually raise the children (genetic influence but no environmental influence) and with respect to foster parents (environmental influence but no genetic influence). Skodak and Skeels (1949) obtained a sample of children who had been placed in their adoptive homes under the age of six months. The children were given the Stanford-Binet test at various times, beginning when they were approximately two years of age and continuing until they were about thirteen. As an estimate of parental IQ, educational level was determined for the true parents and for the foster parents. In addition, the Stanford-Binet was given to the true mothers. The results were somewhat surprising. Beginning when the children were four years of age, their IQ scores correlated significantly with the educational level and with the IQ of their *true mothers.* At age 13, the children's scores correlated .32 with true mothers' educational level and .44 with true IQ. For the true fathers about whom educational level was known, this estimate of intelligence correlated .44 with child's IQ at age 13.[1] In contrast, no correlation existed between children's IQ and foster parents' educational level. At age 13, the children's scores correlated .00 with foster fathers' education and .02 with foster mothers' education. The effect of genetic factors is obvious in that the only significant parent-child correlations are with the natural parents and not with the foster parents.

Even the Skodak and Skeels data, however, offer no either-or answer for heredity and environment. The correations indicate that the *ordering* of the

[1] Computed from raw data reported by Skodak and Skeels (1949).

children along a dimension of intelligence is related to the *ordering* of their true mothers and fathers along the same dimension; it says nothing about *level* of intelligence. For the true mothers the mean IQ was 85.7, while the mean IQ of their children at age 13 was 106. The children are significantly brighter than their mothers. Since the true mothers were predominantly girls with inferior socioeconomic backgrounds and since the foster homes were relatively good in educational opportunity and socioeconomic level, this last finding could indicate that the foster home environment had a positive effect on the children's IQ. Research such as that of Skodak and Skeels has led to a conceptualization of genetic factors setting some sort of limit or maximum with respect to the development of intellectual ability with environmental factors determining the extent to which development takes place within those limits.

Selective Breeding and Intelligence. The fact that genetic determinants influence individual differences in intelligence could best be shown through research involving selective breeding. Is it possible to develop either brighter or duller offspring on the basis of deliberately matching parents on such characteristics?

Tryon in 1940 used successive generations of rats in an attempt to develop bright and dull subgroups. As a measure of "intelligence," a complicated maze learning task was employed, and each subject's learning ability was scored in terms of number of errors. There were wide individual differences in his initial group of rats with errors ranging from 7 to 214. On the basis of these error scores, Tryon selected the brightest and dullest rats and had members of each group mate only with rats similar to themselves in intelligence. This procedure was continued for eighteen generations. By the seventh generation, the experimenter had produced two distinct gruops, bright rats and dull rats. The dullest member of the bright group was brighter than the majority of the dull group and the brightest member of the dull group was duller than the majority of the bright group.

Even though selective breeding in humans is not a feasible research plan, we might note that selective breeding is actually taking place. That is, couples who marry are not randomly paired with respect to IQ. Rather, husband-wife correlations are found to be about .50. This is actually not too surprising, on several grounds. For one thing, similarity in terms of interests and abilities based on intelligence should lead to greater attraction. For another, individuals with similar IQs are more likely to come in contact with one another and hence have greater probability of meeting, dating, marrying —those who attend college, those who are assigned to technical high schools, those who live in the same neighborhood, those who have similar occupations, and so forth. Whether human beings are directing themselves toward a distant future with bright and dull subpopulations is a matter for speculation.

PRENATAL INFLUENCES

In the course of testing large numbers of mentally retarded children and obtaining case history material on them, Dr. Ruth F. Harrell noticed that bad nutrition in early life was characteristic of a large proportion of these children. Some later research with rats who were either starved or well fed during pregnancy indicated differences in the maze-learning ability of the offspring. For example, when the diets of female rats were restricted by 50 percent during pregnancy, the offspring were not only underweight at birth but as adults they made more errors on maze learning tasks than a comparison control group (Vore and Ottinger, 1970). Work with humans has indicated that the incidence of miscarriage, stillbirths, and premature births is higher among women on poor diets during pregnancy than among women on normal diets (Ebbs, Tisdall, and Scott, 1942).

Such observations and findings led to a large-scale experimental investigation of the effects of maternal diet on the intelligence of the offspring by Harrell, Woodyard, and Gates (1955). The general plan was to supplement the diet of a group of maternity patients, and then compare the IQs of their offspring with those of a control group.

In a large charity maternity clinic in Norfolk, Virginia, pregnant women served as subjects. The women were randomly assigned to one of four groups. All were given pills to be taken daily, and the pills were indistinguishable in size and color. Even the nurse who gave them the tablets at each visit did not know which subject was assigned to which group. One-fourth of the women received placebos containing inert material, one-fourth received pills containing ascorbic acid, one-fourth received pills containing thiamine, and one-fourth received pills containing thiamine, riboflavin, niacinamide, and iron (multinutrient). The pills were taken during pregnancy and while the mother was nursing the baby. The subjects visited the clinic every two weeks and were given enough pills at each visit to provide one tablet a day until the next visit. The subjects primarily were residents of slum areas in the city, and most of the women worked by the day as laundresses, cooks, or cleaning women.

The second part of the study was carried out a few years later. The offspring of the subjects were contacted on both their third and their fourth birthdays and given the Stanford-Binet. For each age group, the intelligence quotients of the four groups were compared. The mean IQs are shown in Table 7-1. We see that at each age level, the brightest children were those whose mothers had received the multinutrient pills while the least bright children were those whose mothers had not received any dietary supplement.

In explaining the effects of the vitamin supplements, several possibilities were suggested. Conceivably, the biochemical or structural characteristics of the nervous system were directly affected. Another possibility is that the

Table 7-1. Intelligence of Offspring as a Function
of Maternal Diet during Pregnancy and Breast Feeding

| Offspring | Maternal Diet Supplement | | | |
	Multinutrient	Thiamine	Ascorbic Acid	Placebo
Three-year-olds	103.3	101.8	101.0	98.3
Four-year-olds	101.6	97.6	97.9	93.7

differences were the result of more general effects on health, bodily vigor, and stamina. It has also been found that the continuation of malnutrition into early childhood can interfere with cognitive development, perhaps irreversibly (Brockman, 1966).

A cautionary note is provided by the fact that Harrell, et al. (1955) carried out a parallel study in a rural, mountain community in Kentucky and did not find that dietary supplements influenced the IQ of offspring in this setting. There were a great many differences between the samples, including a much better regular diet for the Kentucky group (home-grown vegetables for example). Also, the Kentucky children were brighter as a group than the Norfolk children. One possibility is that the Norfolk data represent a comparison of a good, balanced diet (containing vitamins) versus a deficient diet (the regular food eaten by the underprivileged members of the placebo group). If so, this would suggest that vitamin supplements during pregnancy would affect the IQ of offspring only in instances of inadequate normal diets.

SOCIOECONOMIC INFLUENCES

Intelligence is one of the major factors which determine the possibility and probability of obtaining a particular level of education and of being able to enter a particular occupation. Individuals below average in intelligence are not likely to become corporation lawyers, and individuals with very high IQs are not usually employed as unskilled laborers. Large-scale studies in both World War I (Fryer, 1922) and World War II (Stewart, 1947) found a substantial relationship between occupational level and scores on the Army intelligence examinations. Since educational and occupational levels are major criteria in defining socioeconomic status and since parent-child IQ scores are related, we would expect children from different socioeconomic levels to differ in performance on intelligence tests. A number of investigators have confirmed this expectation.

Occupational Status of Parents. The members of Terman and Merrill's standardization group for the 1937 revision of the Stanford-Binet were divided in terms of the *occupational* classification of their fathers. The IQ variations across groups for two- to five-and-one-half-year-olds are shown in Table 7-2. The higher the father's occupational level, the higher the IQ of the children.

Table 7-2. Father's Occupation and Child's IQ
(Two- to Five-and-One-Half-Year-Olds)

Father's Occupation	Child's IQ
Professional	116.2
Semiprofessional and Managerial	112.4
Clerical, Skilled Trades, and Retail Business	108.0
Semiskilled, Minor Clerical, Minor Business	104.3
Rural Owners	99.1
Slightly Skilled	95.1
Day Laborers, Urban, and Rural	93.6

Another approach is to obtain socioeconomic ratings of an entire community or subcommunity in order to compare these ratings with the IQ scores obtained by the children residing there. Maller (1933) found that the value of home rentals in a neighborhood correlated .50 with the mean IQ of the school children living in that neighborhood. Thorndike and Woodyard (1942) found that per capita income for thirty cities correlated .78 with the mean IQ scores of the sixth graders in those cities.

Social Mobility. Educational attainment is the major way in which individuals in our society are able to raise their socioeconomic status. Schmuck and Schmuck (1961) hypothesized that upwardly mobile families would exert influence on their children to succeed academically and that the children in such families would have higher IQ scores than children in non-upwardly mobile families.

Determination of upward mobility was based on the family's having moved to an area of increased socioeconomic status (for example, Europe to America, Deep South to North, farm to city, city to suburb), the father's occupation being at a higher socioeconomic level than his father's occupation, and the parents having more years of education than their parents. The subjects were fourth-grade children and their parents. The children in the upwardly mobile families were significantly brighter than those in the non-mobile families.

Interpretation of Socioeconomic Findings. The rather well-established relationship between socioeconomic status of parents and the IQ of their offspring has led to a number of different possible interpretations.

For example, it is conceivable that hereditary factors are operative in that the genetically brighter individuals do better in school, obtain better jobs, select mates similar to themselves in intelligence, are upwardly mobile, and pass on these "good" genes to offspring. Similarly, the genetically less bright individuals do worse in school, obtain lower level jobs, select less bright mates, are not upwardly mobile, and pass on these "bad" genes to their offspring.

The other major explanation involves differences across socioeconomic groups in the amount of intellectual stimulation provided for the child in his home environment. As socioeconomic status increases, the vocabulary of parents becomes larger, the amount of reading material in the home becomes greater, and the opportunity for intellectual enrichment is expanded (for example, music, art, and the theater). Given the same genetic structure, wide differences in environmental opportunities should produce different levels of intelligence.

In all probability, both explanations are partially true. We have examined some of the evidence concerning genetic influences, and we will now look more directly at the influence of different types of early experience.

EXPERIENTIAL INFLUENCES

Intellectual functioning seems to have a long period of development—stretching at least from conception to adolescence. In a relatively "standard" middle-class environment, a regular and steady increase occurs in mental age from infancy to middle or late adolescence. Given limits or boundaries set by genetic factors, intellectual functioning shows a typical growth pattern, and IQ remains more or less constant over the years. The fact that all environments are not the same leads to striking departures from this pattern. Most of the research on experiential influences on intelligence has dealt with variables which involve either environmental deprivation or enrichment over the period of development.

Environmental Deprivation. One way in which an environmental deficit can be brought about is through the isolation of a group from the cultural mainstream. For example, Gordon (1923) administered the Stanford-Binet to a group of seventy-six English canal-boat children. These youngsters seldom attended school (only when the boats were being loaded or unloaded), their parents were illiterate, and they had little contact with anyone outside of the family. The mean IQ of these children was 69.6. More important, however, is the finding that IQ and age were negatively correlated. The youngest children (4 to 6 years of age) had a mean IQ of 90 while the oldest children (12 to 22 years of age) had a mean IQ of 60. Findings consistent with these have been reported for children residing in isolated mountain areas in the United States, in rural communities, in slum areas, and in homes which are socioeconomically inferior.

Another type of environmental deprivation is represented by the institutionalization of young children. Goldfarb (1945) has emphasized the probable importance of parent-child contacts as a source of constant stimulation for young children. The child's motor and verbal responses evoke parental interest, the parent sings and talks to the child, and there is encouragement to babble, talk, sit, stand, walk, and climb. The child receives toys, is taken to see interesting things, and is encouraged to perform a variety of acts. In contrast, the institutionalized child is one of a large group, and even under the best of circumstances the amount of contact between the child and any adult figure is relatively small. Goldfarb selected a group of children who were placed in an institution in early infancy, had remained there for three years, and were then placed in foster homes. A control group consisted of children who had been placed in foster homes in early infancy rather than in institutions. The two groups were matched for age, sex, age at which they left their real parents, and background characteristics of the true mothers and foster parents. The Stanford-Binet was administered just before the institutional group left the orphanage and again after seven months in the foster homes. The control group was also tested at the same time periods. On the first testing, the control group had a mean IQ of 96 while the institutional group was significantly lower with a mean IQ of 68. Even after seven months in the foster home, there was a 26-point IQ difference between the two groups. Additional research by Goldfarb and others supports the finding that psychological deprivation in infancy produces an IQ decrement, and that subsequent placement in a home does not overcome the deficit even over an extended time period. It should be noted, however, that even with early separation from parents and placement in an institution, intelligence is not adversely affected if there is the opportunity for developing an affectionate relationship with adults or older children (Wolins, 1969).

Environmental Enrichment. Upward changes in IQ scores are likely to occur among children raised in well-educated families, presumably because these families provide greater than average intellectual stimulation (Bayley, 1954). The primary way in which "enriching" experience has been defined, however, is in terms of schooling. Intellectual stimulation in nursery school, primary and secondary schools, and even in college has generally been found to have a positive effect on IQ scores.

Though there is some controversy about the effects of nursery school on IQ, there is considerable evidence for a positive effect. Kirk (1958) studied several groups of retarded children over a period of years. One group attended a community nursery school, one group an institutional nursery school, a third group lived at home, and a fourth group lived in an institution without attending nursery school. The children in nursery school showed significantly greater increase in IQ than the children who did not have the school experience. Most of the nursery school group showed IQ gains of ten points or more. Similarly, Wellman and Pegram (1944) compared below-average orphanage children who were given a preschool experience with a matched orphanage group who were not. Those in the preschool group showed gains in IQ, and the gains were greater for those who attended regularly than for those who did not. Part of the impetus for the government's Head Start Program, in which deprived children may attend preschool classes, has been provided by studies such as these.

Quality of the school experience appears to be crucial. Worbois (1942) compared the effects on IQ of several one-room rural schools with a consolidated central rural school. All of the subjects lived in a farming area in which there was one large consolidated school and several small one-room schools. In one comparison, children in the consolidated school and in the one-room schools were tested when they entered first grade and again at the end of the school year. The two groups were not significantly different when they entered school, but those in the consolidated school had significantly higher IQ scores nine months later; there was at that time a five-point difference in mean IQ. Another comparison involved children in the two types of school who were tested as they entered school and again two years later. As before, there was no difference in IQ at the beginning, but those in the consolidated school were 13 points higher after the two-year period. Worbois found no difference between the parents of the children in the two types of schools (for example, years of education, attitude about schooling), but a number of differences between the schools were found. For example, in the consolidated school the teachers had more years of education and more teaching experience.

Finally, several studies have reported that college attendance has a positive effect on IQ. For example, Charles and Pritchard (1959) tested students at Iowa State College when they entered and again four years later. A significant increase in IQ scores occurred for both male and female students over the four-year period. In a better test of the same idea, Lorge (1945) obtained IQ scores of boys who had been tested in the eighth grade and then again thirty years later. Increase in IQ on the second test was a function of the number of years of schooling between the two testings. The more years of school, the higher the adult IQ.

Data from animal research are also consistent in showing the positive effects of environmental enrichment. When albino rats were reared in cages in which they were exposed to angular figures, as adults they out-performed control groups on a visual discrimination task (McCall and Lester, 1969). There is even evidence that brain weight increases as a function of living in an enriched environment. Henderson (1970) compared the brains of mice reared in standard cages versus those reared in larger cages provided with various small objects to climb and explore. Though total body weight was not affected, brain weight was greater for the experimental group.

BLACK-WHITE DIFFERENCES IN IQ

The search for the antecedents of individual differences in intelligence has also led to the question of racial differences. Most specifically, investigators have asked whether there are differences between blacks and whites in mean IQ and how any such differences may be explained. As controversial as those questions are, still greater concern is generated by the implications which such issues raise for educational, social, and legal policies.

It is to be hoped that such questions will seem meaningless to future generations except as historical curiosities. Up to the present time, however, much research time has been spent in seeking information about racial differences, and a great deal of emotion seems to be generated by whatever conclusions are drawn from this research.

Though the following discussion involves some common assumptions about the existence of race as a legitimate phenomenon to investigate, it should be noted that many social scientists find the concept to be a not very meaningful one. That is, race is a descriptive term which can be applied as a way of grouping people, just as we could group them by eye color or height or cephalic index or characteristics of the ear lobe. Gottesman (1968) points out that even the number of races we care to identify is a matter of one's aims and that there is no objective answer to the question of how many races there are. Thus, race tends to be a social rather than a biological concept (Baughman, 1971). The intrinsic difficulty with any such classification scheme is that the resultant groups are not homogeneously pure (mating behavior has not been limited to within-race pairs) and there are more similarities across groups than differences (Nei and Roychoudhury, 1972). The extrinsic difficulty with racial classification is that there is a strong tendency among us to evaluate groups along a superior-inferior dimension. Racial prejudice is not really different from religious prejudice, class prejudice, age prejudice, or nationality prejudice, but the identification of genetic differences as an explanation for behavioral differences and as a justification for discrimination is possible only with respect to race. Thus, efforts to find a genetic link between race and IQ can easily be interpreted or misinterpreted as racist activities. And, interestingly enough, the conclusions which are drawn from studies of black-white differences are found to be associated with various background characteristics of the investigators (Sherwood and Nataupsky, 1968). The investigators who conclude that blacks are innately inferior intellectually tend to come from higher socio-economic backgrounds than those who attribute racial differences to the environment.

We will examine some of the known facts about black-white intellectual differences, the arguments favoring genetic and environmental explanations, and the possible meaning of this research for other aspects of black-white interactions.

Mean IQ of American Blacks and Mean IQ of American Whites. Investigations stretching over half a century are consistent in reporting IQ differences between these two racial groups; white subjects obtain significantly higher mean IQ scores than black subjects (for example, Bruce, 1940; Roen, 1960; Shuey, 1966; Yerkes, 1921). Shuey (1958) estimated that the mean of blacks is 85 (compared with 100 for whites). In Figure 7-2 is shown a typical

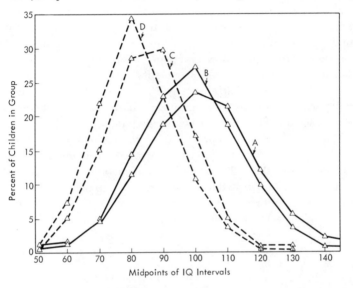

Fig. 7-2 Percentages of Children from Four Research Groups who Obtained Various IQ Scores. A = White Children in Terman and Merrill (1973) National Sample. B = White Children in Rural Area in North Carolina. C = Black Children in Rural Area in North Carolina. D = Black Children in Five Southeastern States. (Adapted from Baughman and Dahlstrom, 1968.)

distribution comparing white and black children from various sections of the country. Before we turn to the attempts to explain these racial differences, two points should be clearly understood.

First, even with group means differing by 15 points, a large overlap occurs between groups. Those who stress racial differences often speak of there being *only* 20 percent or *only* 30 percent overlap between the groups. The overlap, however, refers to the percentage of blacks falling *above the median* of the white group. Thus, 30 percent overlap indicates that about one-third of the black population is brighter than one-half of all the whites. It also indicates that 99 percent of the blacks reach or exceed the IQ scores of some whites. If the relationship between race and IQ were as strong as it is sometimes intimated, it would be possible to use these variables for prediction purposes. Obviously, however, knowledge that a given individual is black or white does not provide the kind of information which would enable you to predict his IQ. Dreger and Miller (1968) make the point even more clear by noting that knowledge of an individual's IQ does not tell you what his race is.

Second, intelligence tests ask questions drawn from a specific culture, and the testing is carried out under certain conditions. For the most part, the questions are verbal ones based on aspects of the white middle-class culture and the tests most often are administered by whites. If the individual being tested comes from a subculture in which the language patterns and the social surroundings are quite different from those represented by the test and the tester, a poor performance may represent factors other than innate intellectual deficit. Kagan (1971, p. 93) concludes that, "...the IQ test is a seriously biased instrument that almost guarantees middle-class white children higher IQ scores than any other group of children." Though the effects of the tester's race do not seem to be consistent (Gould and Klein, 1971; Sattler and Theye, 1967), the appropriateness of the test content to the subject's cultural background is clearly a crucial issue. What if intelligence tests had been developed by ghetto blacks rather than middle-class whites? A Watts social worker, Adrian Dove, developed such a test to measure the intelligence of lower-class American blacks. A few of these test items are presented in Table 7-3. The people for whom the test was developed tend to score 90

Table 7-3. Sample Items from the Dove Counterbalanced Intelligence Test*

1. A "Gas Head" is a person who has a
   a. fast moving car
   b. stable of lace
   c. "process"
   d. habit of stealing cars
   e. long jail record for arson
2. If you throw the dice and 7 is showing on the top, what faces down?
   a. Seven
   b. Snake eyes
   c. Boxcars
   d. Little Joe
   e. Eleven
3. In "C. C. Rider," what does "C. C." stand for?
   a. Civil Service
   b. Church Council
   c. Country Circuit preacher
   d. Country Club
   e. Cheatin' Charlie (The Boxcar Gunsel)

Table 7-3. (Cont.)

4. Cheap "Chitlings" (not the kind you purchase at a frozen-food counter) will taste rubbery unless they are cooked long enough. How soon can you quit cooking them to eat and enjoy?
   a. 15 minutes
   b. 2 hours
   c. 24 hours
   d. 1 week (on a low flame)
   e. 1 hour

5. "Hully Gully" came from
   a. East Oakland
   b. Fillmore
   c. Watts
   d. Harlem
   e. Motor City

6. A "handkerchief head" is
   a. a cool cat
   b. a porter
   c. an Uncle Tom
   d. a hoddi
   e. a preacher

7. "You've got to get up early in the morning if you want to ... "
   a. catch the worms
   b. be healthy, wealthy, and wise
   c. try to fool me
   d. fare well
   e. be the first one on the street

8. If a Pimp is up tight with a woman who is on the state, what does he mean when he talks about "Mother's Day"?
   a. Second Sunday in May
   b. Third Sunday in June
   c. First of every month
   d. First and fifteenth of every month
   e. None of these

9. Many people say that "Juneteenth" (June 19) should be made a legal holiday because this was the day when
   a. the slaves were freed in Texas
   b. the slaves were freed in the USA
   c. the slaves were freed in Jamaica
   d. the slaves were freed in California
   e. Martin Luther King was born
   f. Booker T. Washington died

*Correct answers are given at the end of the chapter.

percent or better. Do you think that the average white might show an "intellectual deficit" if intelligence were measured routinely on this instrument?

Black-White IQ Differences as Evidence for Genetic Superiority of Whites. An electrical engineer at Stanford, William Shockly, and an educational psychologist at Berkeley, Arthur Jensen, have in recent years been at the center of the controversy about the meaning of racial differences in IQ. Jensen (1969a, 1969b, 1969c) has presented the best documented case for interpreting the data in terms of racial genetic differences. Five major points have been made.

1. He began with a review of the studies of the effects of compensatory education on the intelligence of disadvantaged children. It was concluded that well-meaning efforts such as the Head Start Program did not result in higher IQs or in better scholastic performance.

2. He also examined the data indicating that intelligence is inherited and concluded that environmental factors play a minor role in determining individual differences. Specifically, 80 percent of the variance in IQ scores was attributed to genes.

3. The firmly established relationship between social class and intelligence was attributed in large part to genetic differences in that the innately brighter individuals tend to be successful in school and obtain better jobs. Herrnstein (1971) pushed this argument further and predicted that society will become more and more a "meritocracy" with bright people at the top of the social structure and dull people at the bottom.

4. Though Jensen regards the whole matter as a question still open to additional research, he believes that the data on racial differences in IQ strongly suggest the possibility that blacks are less well endowed genetically than whites with respect to intellectual ability. In England, Eysenck (1971) agrees with these general points but argues that they hold only for American blacks in that the slave traders specifically selected the dullest beasts of burden to work the plantations; any highly intelligent slaves would have been at a disadvantage. He adds, incidentally, that others in the United States are also "poor samples of the original populations." (p. 43).

5. Finally, Jensen feels that if society continues to ignore this difference between the races because of wishful thinking, we will actually be doing harm to the blacks in our educational system.

In the storm of criticism and debate which followed Jensen's original article, many psychologists have sought to refute the various points made by Jensen.

1. The notion that compensatory education has been unsuccessful is not consistent with achievements in other places such as in the Israeli kibbutzim (Vernon, 1970). It should also be noted that even a clearly inherited characteristic can be modified by environmental forces. For example, Japanese-Americans are considerably taller than their counterparts in Japan, presumably because of differences in what they eat (Greulich, 1957). It has been pointed out that the original Head Start projects were set up on the basis of what we know about the task-oriented middle-class child and much work is needed to discover *how* best to reach the disadvantaged (Anastasiow, 1969).

2. Many investigators have questioned Jensen's use of statistics which attribute 80 percent of the variance in IQ to inheritance (Cronbach, 1969). The percentage of the variance attributable to genetic factors depends in part on rearing conditions (Scarr-Salapatek, 1971b), and it is questionable to base variance estimates obtained in the white population and generalize

them to the black population. An example makes the problem easier to understand (Scarr-Salapatek, 1971a). Assume that you have a large box of flower seeds and randomly divide them into two subgroups. You take group W and plant the seeds in good soil and you water them regularly. You take the group B seeds and plant them in poor soil where they seldom receive any care. When they grow, you will find that the plants in groups W are superior to those in group B. The reason, obviously, is based on environmental differences. If a scientist were to study just group W, however, he would find some differences among individual plants even though they had a uniformly good environment. He would conclude, correctly, that those differences within group W were attributable to genetic factors. He then asserts, "The differences within group W are hereditary, so the differences between W and B must also be hereditary." Would he be correct?

3. There are many other variables besides that of IQ which account for success and social status. For example, success can result from hard work, from luck, from a special nonintellectual talent, from inheriting a relative's money, or from marrying the boss's daughter. Also, Vernon (1969) has noted that the majority of gifted children in recent generations have come from working-class rather than middle-class families.

4. The assertion that blacks are genetically inferior to whites in intelligence glosses over the complexity of this characteristic; for example, Jinks and Fulker (1970) conclude that at least twenty-two genes control IQ. Another weakness is that, in most studies, race is simply defined by the experimenter in terms of skin color or what the subject says his race is. Dreger and Miller (1968, p. 25) point out that, "investigations presuming to assess the effects of genetic differences on performance but failing to take obvious steps to identify genes. . . would be laughed out of court in any other field of genetic investigation."

5. A tentative and probably incorrect conclusion concerning inborn genetic differences would do a great disservice to blacks. It has been said that ". . . to assert, despite the absence of evidence, and in the present social climate, that a particular race is genetically disfavored in intelligence is to scream 'FIRE . . . I think' in a crowded theater" (Scarr-Salapatek, 1971a, p. 1228). Anastasiow (1969) points out that middle-class children come to school well prepared to function in a situation stressing verbal group instructions. The lower-class child (white or black) tends not to have been socialized in this way, and school is frequently a series of traumatic failure experiences from the very beginning. Schools are going to have to use new methods if we want to compensate for the environmental deficit of lower-class children. It has been found, for example, that intensive tutoring of black urban children leads to very large IQ gains (Eysenck, 1971). The late Sir Cyril Burt was convinced by numerous lines of evidence that there is a general factor which enters into every type of cognitive process and that this general factor depends largely

on genetic determinants. Nevertheless he pointed out that:

> A given genetic endowment is compatible with a whole range of develop-
> mental reactions and consequently of acquired attainments. All that a knowl-
> edge of a child's genetic endowment permits us to infer are the limits of that
> range, where "limit" is defined in terms of probability. The choice of a
> minimum probability will doubtless be decided in the main by financial con-
> siderations. Were more lavish funds available for the compensatory education
> of the dull and for the special education of the gifted, both would attain a
> higher level of achievement (Burt, 1972, pp. 188–89).

Black-White IQ Differences and Experiential Differences. On a great
many bases, the most likely explanation for racial differences in IQ is that of
different environmental influences for blacks and whites. The history of the
black in the United States has largely been a tragic one. From the days of
slavery to modern ghettoes, both North and South, the black has been underprivileged educationally, economically, socially, and occupationally. In other
words, all of the environmental factors known to affect intelligence have been
operating to make the average black score lower on IQ tests than the average
white. Scarr-Salapatek (1971b, p. 1287) observes that, "First, proportion-
ately more blacks than whites are socially disadvantaged, thus more black
children are reared under lower-class conditions; second, being black in the
United States may carry with it a social burden not inflicted on any white."
It has been found, for example, in both races that the absence of a father in
the home is associated with lower IQ; a higher proportion of black children
are raised in homes without fathers than is true for whites (Dreger and
Miller, 1968). As prosegregationist writers are quick to point out, the existence of negative influences does not demonstrate that the removal of such
influences would cancel black-white IQ differences. There is, however, more
convincing evidence.

First, black and white infants are found not to differ in intelligence
(Pasamanick, 1946; Gilliland, 1951). Even among preschool children, racial
differences in intelligence are absent (Anastasi and d'Angelo, 1952; Knobloch
and Pasamanick, 1953; Pasamanick and Knobloch, 1955). As children grow
older, the black and white groups begin to diverge (Osborne, 1960).

Second, given better schooling, black IQs go up. A study by Klineberg
(1935) in New York City and one by Lee (1951) in Philadelphia each
showed that the IQ scores of black children from the South increase as a
function of the number of years of schooling they have had in the North. Lee
found the highest IQs for black children born in Philadelphia, next for black
children born in the South but entering the first grade in Philadelphia, next
for black children born in the South but entering the second grade in Philadelphia, and so forth. In London, the IQs of immigrant children from the West
Indies and elsewhere is directly related to the length of time they have lived

in the city (Vernon, 1969). Consistent with such findings, after two years of school integration in Louisville, Kentucky, black IQs at every grade level increased (Stallings, 1959). Even more convincing evidence for the effects of differential schooling is the fact that blacks from New York, Ohio, and Illinois score higher than whites from Arkansas, Kentucky, and Mississippi (Benedict and Weltfish, 1943; Tyler, 1956). Presumably, the difference in ability is based on differences in the quality of education.

Third, if racial differences are genetic, interracial mating should lead to a mean IQ in the offspring which is lower than that of the "superior" race, regardless of who raises the children. In contrast, Willerman, Naylor, and Myrianthopoulos (1970) proposed that if racial IQ differences are dependent on environmental factors, the race of the mother should be a crucial factor because she is the one who has the greatest contact with the child. From a large national sample of black-white pairs, they obtained groups in which the mother was white and the father black and in which the mother was black and the father white; each pair had a four-year-old child who could be given the Stanford-Binet. As may be seen in Table 7-4, interracial matings lead to

Table 7-4. IQ Scores of 4-Year-Old Children with Interracial Parents

Race of Mother	Race of Father	Mean IQ of Child
White	Black	100.9
Black	White	93.7

(Data from Willerman, Naylor, and Myrianthopoulous, 1970)

lower IQ scores when the mother is black but not when she is white. It would again seem that environmental factors play a crucial role in bringing about black-white differences in intelligence.

Fourth, an additional relevant finding is that when black families are divided in terms of the types of socioeconomic and educational variables found to influence IQ in white samples, the same patterns are found in that better-educated, wealthier blacks with higher status occupations have brighter children than blacks without these advantages (Albee, et al., 1969; Horton and Crump, 1962; Tulkin, 1965).

Racial Differences and Racial Discrimination. "Martin Luther King had a dream—a beautiful, eloquent dream of an American society without barriers between black and white. If he had lived, he might have brought us a little closer to its realization" (Klineberg, 1971, p. 127). Even if racial differences were greater than they are and even if genetic determinants could account for all of the differences, there still would be no justification for prejudging *all* blacks as intellectually inferior and hence not capable of attending certain schools or holding certain jobs. There would be no justification for prejudging *any* individual black as unqualified to vote or eat in a particular restaurant or sit in the front of a bus. "The science of psychology can offer no support to those who see in the accident of inherited skin color or other physical characteristics any excuse for denying to individuals the right to full participation in American Democracy" (Klineberg, 1963, p. 202). It should be noted that Jensen himself cautioned that "...the full range of human talents is represented in all races of man and in all socioeconomic levels... it is unjust to allow the mere fact of an individual's racial or social background to affect the treatment accorded to him" (1969a, p. 78).

A Theory of Intellectual Development

In attempting to integrate the findings dealing with the antecedents of intelligence, Hayes (1962) has proposed a motivational-experiential theory. First, he suggests that intelligence as measured by IQ tests consists of nothing more than an accumulation of learned facts and skills. Second, genetic influence consists of motivational differences, specifically in tendencies to engage in activities conducive to learning, rather than differences in inherited intellectual capacity. He refers to these genetic tendencies as experience-producing drives. In addition to genetic determinants, experience-producing drives may be altered by a number of factors including early brain damage, the nature and variety of experiences available to the child, and presumably by such factors as adequacy of maternal nutrition during pregnancy and the occurrence of extrinsic as well as intrinsic rewards for engaging in varied activities.

Viewed in this way, no conflict exists in the data provided by genetic studies, prenatal studies, socioeconomic studies, and experiential studies. All of the findings can be conceptualized in terms of variables affecting experience-producing drives. The greater the innate drive, the more the individual will engage in the activities necessary to learn. The more rich and varied are the experiences which are available, the greater the accumulation of learned facts and skills. The greater the accumulation of such facts and skills, the higher the IQ. And, as we shall see in subsequent sections, the higher the IQ, the better the grades in school, the higher the level of possible occupational attainment, the greater the creative ability, and so on and so forth.

THE PLACE OF INTELLIGENCE IN THE
STRUCTURE OF PERSONALITY

ACADEMIC PERFORMANCE

Since IQ tests were originally constructed for the purpose of predicting academic performance and since that is the major use to which such instruments are now applied, we would expect to find that scores on intelligence tests are positively correlated with school grades. The two variables generally correlate about .50.

Frandsen (1950) found that IQ scores correlate .68 with high school grades. Some of the subtests correlated more highly with grades than others. For example, information (items such as "What does rubber come from?") correlated .56 with grades, while object assembly (similar to jigsaw puzzles) correlated .11. Using only the best subtests, Frandsen obtained a correlation of .76 between test scores and grades. The correlation between IQ and grades in college is much less than is true for lower grades because the range of ability is less broad in this group (Spielberger and Katzenmeyer, 1959). The shorter the time period between testing and grading, the better the prediction. As might be guessed from the fact that IQ is not perfectly stable over time, IQ measured in the first grade has been found to correlate only .21 with college grades (Travers, 1949).

Research reported in other sections of this book with personality variables such as *n* Achievement (Chapter 5) and manifest anxiety (Chapter 6) suggests that school performance may best be predicted with a combination of IQ tests plus quite different measures. The utility of a variety of other personality instruments has also been investigated. For example, Battle (1966) found that grades in junior high mathematics and English could be predicted by a combination of IQ scores and the student's answers to questions about his minimal standard, his certainty of reaching this standard, and the grade he expected to attain. With the same age groups, Dielman, Schuerger, and Cattell (1970) found three personality factors which improved prediction of grades over and above the prediction made by IQ. These were:

1. High speed and effectiveness at various tasks, fast judgment, and high verbal and ideational fluency.
2. Low rigidity, general competence, fast reading speed, and endurance and accuracy under stress.
3. Realistic and accurate performance on mental tasks, low imagination, reality-oriented attitudes, and low tension.

CREATIVITY

There have been various critics of both the educational emphasis on intelligence tests as selection devices and on objective examinations as the criteria for evaluating students. The picture is one of a system in which highly creative and original students are bypassed in favor of those with high IQs whose strongpoint is rote memorization of endless facts. It would be helpful to know the relationship between measures of intelligence and measures of creativity.

Much has been made of the fact that among relatively bright individuals little relationship exists between creativity and general intellectual ability (for example, Getzels and Jackson, 1962). Ripple and May (1962) rightly point out that the magnitude of the relationship is a function of the variability of the sample. With groups which do not vary much in IQ, the absence of a relationship with creativity is not very informative. They obtained various groups of seventh-grade students and administered a series of creativity tests. With groups that were homogeneous in intelligence (either all fairly high or all fairly low), IQ and creativity were found to be unrelated. In heterogenous groups (ranging from low to high intelligence), IQ and creativity were highly correlated. In the total population, then, IQ is undoubtedly related to creativity. It seems probable that a fairly high level of intelligence is necessary for creative achievement (Nicholls, 1972).

Barron (1957) found a significant correlation of .33 between IQ and creativity in a group of Air Force officers. Though the two variables are positively related, the magnitude of the relationship is such that a good many individuals must fall in the "off-quadrants"; that is, some must be bright but not creative, while others are creative but not bright.

Barron summarizes their differences:

> Subjects who are relatively original in spite of being relatively unintelligent show a lack of ego-control. They describe themselves as persons whose needs demand immediate gratification and whose aggressive impulses are out in the open. They are willful, obstreperous, and extreme individuals. One would not be inclined to select them as companions for a long trip in a submarine. By contrast, their relatively unoriginal but more intelligent fellows seem very much on the pleasant side, although perhaps a bit *too* bland and unwarlike, all things considered (Barron, 1957, p. 739).

DELAY OF GRATIFICATION

Barron (1957) argued that intelligence is a requisite for ego-control or the operation of the reality principle. This idea leads directly to another series of investigations.

Mischel and Metzner (1962) have conceptualized the capacity for postponing immediate gratification in developmental terms as involving a transition from immediate wish-fulfilling types of behavior to those requiring delay and reality testing. Since learning to delay is related to thinking, cognitive ability should be positively related to delaying capacity. As intelligence level increases, preference for delayed gratification should increase. A group of elementary school children for whom IQ scores were available served as subjects. As in other investigations by Mischel, the choice behavior was in reference to two candy bars; the children could receive a five-cent Hershey bar now or a ten-cent bar at a later time. The mean IQ of those children choosing the delayed reward (105.7) was significantly higher than the mean IQ of those choosing the immediate reward (99.0).

In other investigations, additional ego delay measures were used, including the color-word test (speed at naming colors printed in black versus speed at naming color in which the word is printed when the word and the ink color are incongruent), time estimation (estimate when thirty seconds have passed), cognitive inhibition (after learning paired-associates, subjects must respond to the stimulus words with any word other than the response words), and motor inhibition (write "New Jersey Chamber of Commerce" as slowly as possible without stopping). All of these measures were significantly related to IQ (Levine, Spivack, Fuschillo, and Tavernier, 1959; Spivack, Levine, and Sprigle, 1959).

Cognitive Functioning during Sleep

Several investigators have proposed that the brain engages in activities during sleep which are vital to its functioning. It has been found that cognitive activity can be detected in the sleeper by the presence of rapid-eye-movement (REM). Dreaming, for example, is found to be associated with periods of REM. Feinberg, Koresko, and Heller (1967) reasoned that the better the intellectual functioning as measured by IQ tests, the greater the amount of REM activity during sleep. The correlation between these variables in groups of normal and mentally deteriorated aged subjects was in the .70s.

Such results lend support to the propositions that the brain carries out necessary functions during sleep, that it is possible to measure the level at which it is functioning, and that level of brain functioning is directly associated with traditional measures of intelligence.

Adjustment

Terman's Gifted Children. In 1921, Lewis Terman obtained a research grant from the Commonwealth Fund of New York City which enabled him to begin an investigation of the characteristics of very bright individuals. His plan was to determine the "physical, mental, and personality traits" of gifted children and to follow the course of their lives into adulthood. The investigation extended over the remainder of professor Terman's life and then was continued by Melita Oden. Four books have been published describing the findings at various points in the lives of the subjects (Terman, 1925; Burks, Jensen, and Terman, 1930; Terman and Oden, 1947; Terman and Oden, 1959).

On the basis of their performance on the Stanford-Binet, over fifteen-hundred children with IQs of 140 or more were selected; the mean IQ of the group was 151. The parents and teachers of these individuals were urged not to tell the children about the study or how bright they were. The amount of data collected over the last half century has been enormous, and only a portion of it will be reported here.

Childhood. One major research interest was in the physique and health of the gifted children. In both height and weight, these children were above the established norms for unselected children in California. Even their mean birth weight was greater than the norm by 12 ounces. Compared with normative groups, they walked earlier, talked earlier, and reached puberty at a younger age. Compared with a control group of normal youngsters, they had fewer headaches, fewer hearing defects, and were rated as less nervous. The gifted children were found to have a lower incidence of physical defects and abnormal conditions of almost every kind than the normal population of school children. Terman and Oden note:

> The combined results of the medical examinations and the physical measurements provide a striking contrast to the popular stereotype of the child prodigy so commonly depicted as a pathetic creature, overserious and undersized, sickly, hollow-chested, stoop-shouldered, clumsy, nervously tense, and bespectacled. There are gifted children who bear some resemblance to this stereotype, but the truth is that almost every element in the picture, except the last, is less characteristic of the gifted child than of the mentally average (Terman and Oden, 1959, p. 8).

Ratings of twenty-five traits were made by teachers familiar with each child, and for comparison purposes a group of nongifted children was also rated by the teachers. As may be seen in Table 7-5, the gifted children re-

**Table 7-5. Percentages of Gifted Subjects Rated by
Teachers above the Mean of the Control Group***

	Percent	
1. Intellectual Traits:		
General intelligence	97	
Desire to know	90	
Originality	85	
Common sense	84	
Average of intellectual traits		89
2. Volitional Traits:		
Willpower and perseverance	84	
Desire to excell	84	
Self-confidence	81	
Prudence and forethought	81	
Average of volitional traits		82.5
3. Emotional Traits:		
Sense of humor	74	
Cheerfulness and optimism	64	
Permanence of moods	63	
Average of emotional traits		67
4. Aesthetic Traits:		
Musical appreciation	66	
Appreciation of beauty	64	
Average of aesthetic traits		65

Table 7-5. (Cont.)

5. Moral Traits:		
Conscientiousness	72	
Truthfulness	71	
Sympathy and tenderness	58	
Generosity and unselfishness	55	
Average of moral traits		64
6. Physical Traits:		
Health	60	
Physical energy	62	
Average of physical traits		61
7. Social Traits:		
Leadership	70	
Sensitivity to approval	57	
Popularity	56	
Freedom from vanity	52	
Fondness for large groups	52	
Average for social traits		57.4
8. Mechanical ingenuity	47	

*Adapted from Terman and Oden, 1959, p. 14.

ceived higher ratings on most of the traits. Except for leadership, the gifted group tend to be most like the control group on the social traits and slightly below the normals on mechanical ingenuity. Incidentally, the latter rating is probably in error because tests of mechanical ability consistently show gifted children to be better than normals.

Adolescence. The first follow-up investigation was carried out in 1927–1928 when most of the subjects were 16 or 17 and enrolled in high school. Not much change occurred in the composite portrait of the group. In school they were doing well, and they were still superior to nongifted children in such things as size, health, social interests, and leadership.

Adulthood. In 1939–1940, the group's average age was about 29. The subjects were interviewed and given a number of tests. Among the conclusions reached were the following:

That to near mid-life, such a group may be expected to show a normal or below-normal incidence of serious personality maladjustment, insanity, delinquency, alcoholism, and homosexuality. . . .

That in vocational achievement the gifted group rates well above the average of college graduates and, as compared with the general population, is represented in the higher professions by eight or nine times its proportional share. . . .

That marital adjustment of the gifted, as measured by the marital happiness test, is equal or superior to that found in groups less highly selected for intelligence, and that the divorce rate is no higher than that of the generality of comparable age.

That the sexual adjustment of these subjects in marriage is in all respects as normal as that found in a less gifted and less educated group of 792 married couples (Terman and Oden, 1959, pp. 21–22).

Mid-Life. The most recent follow-ups of these subjects were made in 1950–1952 and in 1955, again with interviews and the administration of a number of tests and questionnaires. Among the voluminous findings, a few will be cited.

The mortality rate for these gifted individuals was lower than the expectation for the general population not only for death caused by disease, but also with respect to accident-induced mortality. Compared to others of their generation, the gifted men were about one-and-half inches taller and the gifted women about one inch taller. With respect to emotional adjustment, 3.1 percent of the men and 3.4 percent of the women had been admitted to a hospital or sanitarium for the mentally ill at least once; these figures do not differ from expectancies for the general population.

Most of the gifted subjects report drinking alcohol moderately or heavily; nevertheless, there was a lower incidence of alcoholism in this group than in the general population. The incidence of crime and delinquency is very low. Three boys spent time in a reform school, and one man served a prison sentence for forgery. Only one woman served a jail sentence. All of these five individuals have since made normal adjustments. The incidence of homosexuality (2 percent of the men and 1.7 percent of the women) is considerably below the national figures.

Not surprisingly, the educational record of this gifted group is quite different from the general population. In their generation, the percentage of individuals graduating from college is less than 8 percent. Of the gifted, almost 90 percent entered college, and about 70 percent graduated. College grade-point averages of B or better were obtained by 78 percent of the men and 83 percent of the women. In addition, 56 percent of the men and 33 percent of the women obtained at least one advanced degree. Ph.D.s or M.D.s were awarded to 22.3 percent of the men and 5.4 percent of the women.

As adults, their occupational level was found to be quite high. A total of 45.6 percent of the men are in a profession, while 40.7 percent are in the managerial, official, and semiprofessional group. The most frequent profession is law, followed by university professors, engineers, and physicians. In the managerial group, most are executives or managers in business and industry, followed by banking, finance, insurance executives, accountants, statisticians, and sales managers. In income, these men are well above average, even when compared to others in the same occupation. Of the women, about half are housewives, while 42 percent hold full-time jobs with schoolteaching as the most frequent occupation.

Finally, with respect to recognition of achievement, the gifted group is again unusual. In terms of such honors as listing in *American Men of Science,* election to the National Academy of Sciences, listing in the *Directory of American Scholars,* and listing in *Who's Who in America,* the group has done exceptionally well. They have written 60 books and monographs, 2,000 technical and scientific articles, and have been granted 230 patents. Other writings include 33 novels, 375 short stories, and 265 miscellaneous articles. A great many members of the gifted group are nationally prominent in a variety of fields, while 8 or 10 are internationally known. Included are physical scientists, a biological scientist, social scientists, members of the U.S. State Department, and a motion picture director.

In summing up some of the implications of this large body of findings, Terman has said:

> The follow-up of these gifted subjects has proved beyond question that tests of "general intelligence," given as early as six, eight, or ten years, tell a great deal about the ability to achieve either presently or 30 years hence. Such tests do not, however, enable us to predict what direction the achievement will take, and least of all do they tell us what personality factors or what accidents of fortune will affect the fruition of exceptional ability. Granting that both interest patterns and special aptitudes play important roles in the making of a gifted scientist, mathematician, mechanic, artist, poet, or musical composer, I am convinced that to achieve greatly in almost any field, the special talents have to be backed up by a lot of Spearman's g, by which is meant the kind of general intelligence that requires ability to form many sharply defined concepts, to manipulate them, and to perceive subtle relationships between them; in other words, the ability to engage in abstract thinking (Terman, 1954, p. 224).

THE DYNAMICS OF INTELLIGENCE

In spite of the long history of psychological interest in intelligence and its measurement, the use of this variable in experimental studies has been relatively rare.

LEARNING

Since intelligence tests were originally developed in order to predict ability to learn in a school setting and since learning has been one of the major areas of psychological experimentation, we might expect to find a large number of learning experiments in which the IQ of subjects was a matter of research interest. Actually, there are few such investigations.

One of the early studies of this type was carried out by Kenneth Spence and a fellow student as a class project in an experimental psychology course at McGill University (Spence and Townsend, 1930). On the basis of an IQ test, ten high-scoring and ten low-scoring subjects were selected. The learning task was a finger maze made of copper wiring; the subjects were blindfolded.

Each trial was timed and the number of errors recorded. Trials continued for each subject until he had finished three perfect consecutive trials. Those subjects with the highest intelligence test scores took fewer trials, made fewer errors, and took less time in learning the maze than those subjects with low IQ scores. The authors concluded that the factors which make for a high score on the intelligence test also make for a better performance on the learning task.

Harlow (1951) has proposed that a relationship exists between the evolutionary level of a species and the rate at which members of that species are able to learn a learning set; the higher the point in the evolutionary scale, the greater the ability at "learning to learn" in a situation. A number of investigations have supported this proposition. Within a species, of course, individual differences in performance occur in learning-set formation. It has been proposed that IQ tests should permit prediction of these differences for human subjects. Koch and Meyer (1959) utilized preschool children as subjects. The learning task was very similar to that employed with monkeys in learning-set studies. Each child was individually run, and the experiment was described as a game. A "red penny" (poker chip) was hidden under one of two cards on each trial, and the child was instructed to find as many pennies as possible so that he could buy a toy from the experimenter. On each trial the subject could select only one of the cards. Each card had on it a square of colored paper of various sizes, and the color was the clue to which the subject had to learn to respond. Each day a subject was given twelve different problems, with six trials on each. On the first trial of any problem, the response had necessarily to be a guess, but on subsequent trials the correct response would be the selection of cards with the color under which the penny was located on trial one. Thus, the task was to acquire a set to learn. Each subject was continued until he made 90 percent correct responses in a day's session. The children varied in the time required to reach the criterion from one to fifteen days. This variable was found to correlate negatively with mental age on the Stanford-Binet. The higher the intellectual ability of the subject, the fewer days that were required to acquire the learning set. Figure 7-3 shows a comparison of the performance of the seven brightest children, the five least bright children, and a group of Rhesus monkeys who had been given the same problem by Blazek and Harlow (1955).

Concept formation as a function of IQ was investigated by Osler and Fivel (1961). Subjects consisted of elementary and junior high school students of different age levels. Each age level was divided into groups of average intelligence (IQ = 90 to 109) and high intelligence (IQ = 110 and above). Subjects were shown pairs of stimuli as part of a "game" and were told that one was "correct" and one "incorrect." If the subject chose the correct one, he received a marble. If enough marbles were collected, the subject would win a toy. One of the concepts used was *bird*. In this instance, the correct

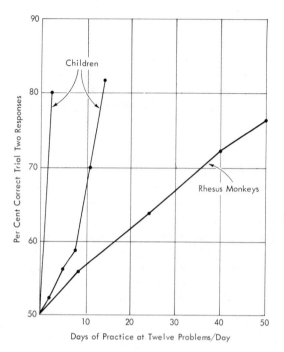

Fig. 7-3 Comparison of Learning-Set Performance of Children at Two Levels of Intelligence, and Rhesus Monkeys. (Adapted from Koch, M. B. and Meyer, D. R., A relationship of mental age to learning-set formation in the pre-school child, *Journal of Comparative and Physiological Psychology*, 1959, 52, 388. © 1959 by the American Psychological Association and reprinted by permission.)

choice on each trial would be the picture of a bird. IQ level is found to be significantly related to whether the subject can solve the problem or not (Saltz and Hamilton, 1969).

RESPONSE TO PSYCHOTHERAPY

Another type of stimulus situation in which IQ has some relevance is that of psychotherapy. The most general form which therapy takes is that of a verbal interchange between therapist and patient. Changes in the patients' behavior are often conceptualized in terms of learning. For example, Dollard and Miller (1950) and Mowrer (1953) have explained therapeutic changes in terms of concepts drawn from learning theory. Murray (1964) proposed that therapy, like learning theory, involves the acquisition, performance, and elimination of responses. It follows that response to psychotherapy should be in part a function of ability to learn, as measured by intelligence tests.

Amount of active participation in group psychotherapy was investigated by McFarland, Nelson, and Rossi (1962). The subjects were patients in group psychotherapy at the VA Hospital in Palo Alto. Their behavior in therapy was rated and their intelligence measured. Participation in group psychotherapy was found to correlate significantly with IQ and with verbal fluency. The highest coefficient (r = .56) was the correlation with an analogies test. Among the extensions of these findings suggested by the authors was the possibility of using IQ tests to select patients who would benefit from psychotherapy. In their sample, a cut-off IQ score of 100 would maximize the chances of excluding from therapy those patients who would not participate and including those who would.

A similar therapeutic problem is that of predicting those patients who will continue in psychotherapy versus those who decide to terminate it. Hiler (1958) obtained data for patients at the VA Mental Hygiene Clinic in Detroit for whom Wechsler-Bellevue scores were available. Premature termination of psychotherapy was defined as dropping out within five sessions. Those who remained in psychotherapy were significantly more intelligent (mean IQ = 112.8) than those who terminated prematurely (mean IQ = 102.8). Again, a cut-off score of 100 on the IQ test was found to maximize prediction. Most of those below 100 drop out of therapy, while most of those above 100 remain in therapy.

CHANGE IN INTELLIGENCE

Perhaps more than with most personality dimensions, the distinction between antecedent variables and change variables influencing the dimension of intelligence is a somewhat arbitrary one. As we have seen, intellectual ability shows a relatively steady process of growth from birth through adolescence. We have considered those factors influencing this process as antecedents of individual differences in IQ. We will now consider those variables which influence changes in intelligence in adulthood.

AGING

The first investigations of the effects of aging on intelligence utilized a cross-sectional design. That is, individuals of various ages were tested, and comparisons of different individuals in different age groups were made. The findings were relatively consistent and somewhat disheartening. For example, a World War I study found that Army Alpha scores decreased steadily from young (under 20) groups to older (51–60) groups of officers (Yerkes, 1921). Jones and Conrad (1933) found the same trend among individuals living in nineteen villages in New England. Wechsler (1958) plotted the standard scores on the Wechsler-Bellevue as a function of chronological age as shown in Figure 7-4. We see in the figure that intellectual growth seems to reach

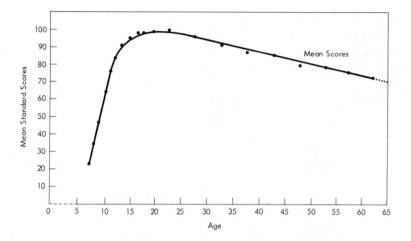

Fig. 7-4 An Age Curve of Intelligence Based on a Cross Sectional Investigation: Full Scale Scores on the Wechsler-Bellevue, Ages 7 to 65. (Adapted from Wechsler, D., *The measurement and appraisal of adult intelligence,* 4th ed. Baltimore: Williams and Wilkins, © 1958.)

a peak by late adolescence, remains relatively constant through the 20s and then begins a sharp decline. Wechsler, for one, concluded:

> Every human capacity after attaining a maximum begins an immediate decline. . . . The age at which this maximum is attained varies from ability to ability but seldom occurs beyond 30 and in most cases somewhere in the early 20s (Wechsler, 1944, p. 55).

More recently, data have become available from longitudinal studies of intelligence over the life span. In this approach, *the same individuals* are retested at various ages, and a quite different picture emerges. For example, Owens (1953) compared the test performance of a group of individuals in middle-age with their own test performance thirty years earlier as college freshmen. On every subtest of the Army Alpha their performance was better in middle age except for the arithmetic items.

One of the important variables in determining the effect of aging on IQ seems to be amount of education. Swanson (1952) retested men on a college entrance test after a twenty-year interval. Those who had graduated from college gained a mean of thirty-five points, those who attended college but did not graduate gained nine points, and those who did not attend college gained seven points.

Why does a discrepancy generally occur in the findings when different people are tested at different ages versus when the same people are retested at an older age? In the cross-sectional studies, each group is different not only in age but in the kind of life experiences they have undergone. Many things change from generation to generation—schools and technology for example. The IQ differences that are found were apparently caused by such differences in experience rather than differences in age. When the same individuals are retested, it becomes clear that intelligence dos not decline with age.

Based on the data from some of the longitudinal studies, Bayley (1955) proposed a new and more encouraging sort of curve describing the relationship between age and intellectual ability, as shown in Figure 7-5.

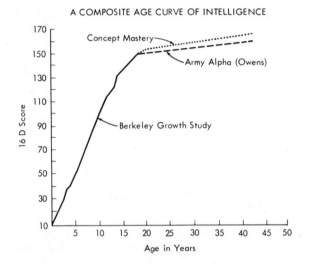

A COMPOSITE AGE CURVE OF INTELLIGENCE

Fig. 7-5 An Age Curve of Intelligence Based on Longitudinal Investigations: Data from the Berkeley Growth Study, the Terman Gifted Study, and Owen's Iowa Study. (Adapted from Bayley, N., On the growth of intelligence, *American Psychologist,* 1955, *10*, 816. © 1955 by the American Psychological Association and reprinted by permission.)

Despite the fact that longitudinal studies provide an optimistic picture of intellectual functioning during old age, it is also obvious from common observation that some individuals show a dramatic decline in mental ability as they grow older. The research goal is to identify the causes of such decline. Even though age itself may not bring about intellectual impairment, there may be some physical or psychological conditions which bring about such effects in *some* older individuals. One condition which increases with age is hypertension (high blood pressure), frequently complicated by cardiovascular disease and strokes. Wilkie and Eisdorfer (1971) hypothesized that as blood pressure increases, intelligence decreases. As part of a longitudinal study, both variables were measured over a ten-year period in a group of subjects who were aged sixty to seventy-nine when the investigation began. It was found that hypertension was related to intellectual loss over the ten years.

Subjects with normal blood pressure remained stable in their IQ scores. Such findings strongly suggest ". . . that the basis for the cognitive decline associated with aging after maturity should be considered secondary to some pathological processes and not merely as a 'normal' aging process" (Wilkie and Eisdorfer, 1971, p. 962).

CHEMICAL ENHANCEMENT OF INTELLIGENCE

From time to time, there has been an interest in the possibility of raising IQ through the use of an appropriate drug. The most notable example is that of glutamic acid. While early reports of the beneficial effects of glutamic acid on the functioning of mental defectives were encouraging, better controlled studies have been uniformly negative (Astin and Ross, 1960).

Similarly, some speculation has arisen that the use of tranquilizing drugs in treating mental illness would result in better performance on intelligence tests. Again, the findings are negative (for example, Ison, 1957).

BRAIN DAMAGE

It seems obvious that any damage to brain tissue from accidents or diseases would have a negative effect on intelligence. Strangely enough, however, it is possible to lose substantial quantities of cerebral matter without affecting test scores.

Weinstein and Teuber (1957) compared two groups of injured men for whom preinjury test scores on the Army General Classification Test (AGCT) were available. The brain-damaged group consisted of patients who had lost cerebral tissue owing to injury while the control group consisted of patients who had injuries involving peripheral nerves (for example, in the arm). Approximately ten to twelve years after the injury the AGCT was readministered. The brain-damaged group was significantly different from the control group on this postinjury testing. The difference was, however, not a function of IQ loss owing to brain damage but of *less gain* over the time span. The control group showed a mean increase of 13 AGCT points while the brain-injured group increased 1.6 points. Similarly, it has been reported that IQ scores show no change before and after a prefrontal lobotomy operation (Markwell, Wheeler, and Kitzinger, 1953).

Some investigators have reported a negative effect of brain injury on IQ (for example, Ross, 1958). A possible reason for conflicting findings involves the specification of the type of brain damage and the type of items used to measure intelligence. It has been found that left-brain lesions lead to poorer performance on verbal tests while right-brain lesions are associated with decreased performance on nonverbal scales (Satz, 1966; Satz, Richard, and Daniels, 1967).

MENTAL ILLNESS

One would not be surprised to find that an individual's ability to function intelligently declines when he becomes mentally ill.

Schwartzman and Douglas (1962) obtained intelligence test scores given by the Canadian Army during World War II and readministered the test to three groups of men. One group consisted of hospitalized schizophrenics, another was a group of schizophrenics who had been discharged from the hospital for at least a year, and the third was a group of normal veterans. The three groups were matched for IQ on the basis of the first testing, age, educational level, occupational status, and ethnic background. The study showed that on the second testing, the schizophrenic patients had lost a mean of 15.2 points on the test, the ex-patients had lost a mean of 5.1 points, and the normal group had gained 11.8 points. These differences between groups were statistically significant.

Some reports indicate no intellectual loss in schizophrenia (for example, Albee, Lane, Corcoran, and Werneke, 1963). This finding may be the result of instances of early IQ deterioration long before the schizophrenia became apparent (Lane and Albee, 1964). For example, Schaffner, Lane, and Albee (1967) examined the intelligence test scores of suburban school children who later became schizophrenics as adults. For comparison purposes, each subject was matched with a sibling who did *not* become schizophrenic in adulthood. It may be seen in Table 7-6 that the IQ scores of the preschizophrenic children were consistently lower than the IQ scores of their normal siblings.

Table 7-6. Intellectual Performance of Suburban Preschizophrenics and Their Siblings

Grade in School	IQ of Preschizophrenics	IQ of Siblings
Kindergarten to 3rd Grade	106.6	111.0
4th Grade to 6th Grade	107.6	111.1
7th Grade to 9th Grade	107.7	114.3

(After Schaffner, Lane, and Albee, 1967, p. 327)

The Schwartzman and Douglas study also suggested that as schizophrenics get better, their IQ scores go up again in that the ex-patients had higher scores than the hospitalized patients. As a more direct test of this proposition, Schwartzman, Douglas, and Muir (1962) followed up as many of the hospitalized patients as could be located eight years after the first study. Again, the Canadian Army examination was given. Of the twenty-three subjects who were tested, ten were hospitalized and thirteen had been discharged. All but three were diagnosed as chronic schizophrenics. The hospitalized patients showed a steady decline in test scores over the seventeen years. As much loss in IQ occurred between the second and third testings as did between the first and second testings. The ex-patients did not differ from the hospitalized patients in amount of loss between the first and second tests. The ex-patients did, however, show a significant gain in IQ between the second and third tests. Their mean score in 1960 was not significantly different from their original test score obtained in the army. Apparently, then, intelligence test performance is adversely affected by schizophrenia, but remission of the illness also involves a return of the lost intellectual ability.

CURRENT ISSUES IN RESEARCH ON INTELLIGENCE

Perhaps the most important developments with respect to work on intelligence involve an increasing use of the experimental method plus a variety of attempts to build a theory of intelligence. Two somewhat special types of development should also be noted: factorial approaches to intelligence and computer simulation of intelligence.

FACTORS OF INTELLIGENCE

Intelligence as measured by Binet and Terman and many others is conceptualized as a unitary variable, which Spearman (1927) designated as g or general intelligence. With the development of factor-analytic techniques, a number of investigators began to speak of a group of independent intellectual factors or of g plus a series of group factors. Thurstone, for example, found seven "primary mental abilities" which he called spatial, perceptual, number, verbal, word fluency, memory, and reasoning, and a test was built to measure each (Thurstone, 1938; Thurstone and Thurstone, 1941).

Among the many factorial studies of intelligence, the work of Guilford (1959, 1968, 1972) provides the most detailed structural framework in which intellect consists of five different abilities (cognition, memory, convergent thinking, divergent thinking, and evaluation), each of which may involve different kinds of content (figural, symbolic, semantic, and behavioral). There are also six possible kinds of products (units, classes, relations, systems, transformations, and implications). Thus, Guilford proposes a three-dimensional model with five abilities, four contents, and six products. This means that the measurement of intelligence will be best accomplished by the use of 120 independent tests. The importance of knowing about subcategories of intelligence is shown when one examines the relationship between general intelligence and one of the specific factors. For example, individuals low in general intelligence also tend to do poorly on measures of divergent thinking; those high in general intelligence may score either high or low in divergent thinking. Guilford (1968) suggests that IQ seems to set a kind of upper limit on ability to do divergent thinking but not a lower limit. The knowledge that someone is high in IQ would not give you any information about his ability to think divergently.

As convincing as the factor-analytic argument may appear, there is reason to question the notion that the future approach to intelligence will be the measurement of multiple factors (McNemar, 1964). One problem is that when tests are constructed to measure the independent intellectual factors, they are found *not* to be independent. Significant correlations between these supposedly different dimensions suggest a general factor such as Spearman's g underlying the scales. Second, the predictive ability of the factor tests with respect to such criteria as school grades is no better than that of the measures of general intelligence such as the Stanford-Binet. Unless they can be shown to yield more accurate prediction, little justification exists for conceptualizing factorially pure tests as something new, different, and better.

COMPUTER SIMULATION OF INTELLIGENCE

One of the developments in the study of intellectual functioning has been the use of digital computers to simulate intelligent behavior. Presumably, if we can design a computer to behave as human beings do, we will be able to extend our understanding of the functions involved. Computers are remarkable devices and, with suitable instructions, can perform such acts as solving equations, keeping books, and playing chess (Green, 1963). Further, computer programs can be written which are so complex that the person who wrote the program is unable to predict precisely what the computer will do with a given problem (for example, Newell, Shaw, and Simon, 1958).

With respect to the kinds of tasks that are included in intelligence tests, programs have been constructed which enable a computer to deal with such problems as verbal comprehension ("How many games did the Red Sox win by one run in 1959?") (Green, Wolf, Chomsky, and Laughery, 1961), verbal fluency (making original sentences out of words stored in the machine's memory bank) (Klein, 1964), perception and reasoning (solving problems such as geometric analogies) (Evans, 1964), numerical skills ("The distance from New York to Los Angeles is 3000 miles. If the average speed of a jet plane is 600 miles per hour, find the time it takes to travel from New York to Los Angeles by jet") (Bobrow, 1964), learning and memory (rote learning of nonsense syllables and paired-associates learning) (Feigenbaum, 1961), and reasoning (providing theorems in plane geometry and solving problems in integral calculus) (Green, 1964). Thus, a computer can be provided with the same general abilities that are involved in human intelligence.

Since computers can demonstrate these basic skills, computer specialists (for example, Green, 1964) argue that our best approach to understanding what is involved in intelligent functioning is to develop a computer model of the processes required to answer test items and then to discover what internal changes in the model lead to individual differences in performance. One potentially promising approach is that of Cunningham (1972) who has presented a theory of cognitive development in such a way that it can be tested in computer simulation research.

SUMMARY

Intelligence tests represent the best-known and most widely influential product of psychological science. At the same time, there has been little integration of the concept of intelligence with the remainder of work in psychology. The earliest attempts to measure individual differences in intellectual functioning consisted of the measurement of very simple responses, but scores on such tasks were found to be unrelated to criteria such as school grades. The use of complex tasks by investigators such as Binet and Terman proved considerably more fruitful. Perhaps the most unusual aspect of the work on intelligence is the relative neglect of theory. Definitions of intelligence tend to stress adaptation to the environment, learning ability, and/or abstract thinking.

Alfred Binet, a French psychologist, was interested in the measurement of intellectual differences among children, and in 1905 developed the first intelligence test in response to a request from the Paris school system. An American psychologist, Lewis M. Terman, became interested in Binet's work and in 1916 published the Stanford-Binet Intelligence Scale which set the pattern for all subsequent measures of intelligence.

The 1916 Stanford-Binet was revised in 1937 and again in 1960 by Terman and Merrill. The test items primarily involve the more complex mental processes and include such things as analogies, comprehension, vocabulary, similarities and differences, completions, absurdities, drawing designs, and memory for digits and verbal material. From a large pool of possible items, the final test items were selected on the basis of (1) showing an increase in percentage of children passing them at successive age levels, and (2) correlating with the total score on the test. In the 1937 Stanford-Binet, the IQ was defined as the Mental Age obtained on the test divided by the subject's Chronological Age and multiplied by 100. Because MA does not continue to show large yearly increases indefinitely, after age 13 it was necessary to substitute a corrected CA divisor in the IQ formula. In order to avoid such difficulties, on the 1960 test IQ is defined in terms of deviation from the average performance of an individual's age group. Now, IQ is simply a standard score with a mean of 100 and a standard deviation of 16. The test has high internal consistency, is stable over time, and correlates highly with other IQ tests.

A great deal of the research on the antecedents of individual differences in intelligence has involved a controversy between proponents of genetic antecedents and proponents of experiential antecedents. At the present time, there is a considerable amount of interest in determining the ways in which all factors contribute to a given behavior. Genetic determinants have been investigated by a number of means including the study of family resemblances. While the IQs of random pairs of adults and children correlate .00, parent-child correlations are .50. Similarly, random pairs of unrelated children show correlations of .00, unrelated children reared together correlate .25, sibling IQs correlate .50, fraternal twins correlate .59 to .70, and identical twins have correlations of .88. A comparison of such relationships indicates rather clearly the joint contribution of genetic and experiential variables to IQ differences. Experiments of nature include instances in which identical twins have been separated in infancy and reared apart; their IQs correlate less highly (r = .77) than do the scores of identical twins reared together but higher than the scores of ordinary siblings reared together. Another such natural experiment involves adopted children. The IQ of children is found to correlate significantly with that of their natural parents but not with their adoptive parents. In the selective breeding of rats, investigators have been able to develop subgroups of maze-bright and maze-dull subjects. Prenatal influences on IQ have been found in that the addition of vitamin supplements to the diets of pregnant women was found to have a significantly positive effect on the IQ of their offspring as measured at ages 3 and 4. Apparently, this effect is achieved only when the mother's ordinary diet is an inadequate one.

Considerable evidence also exists that the higher the occupational level of fathers, the higher the IQ of their offspring. Positive relationships are also found between IQ and upward social mobility of parents, value of home rentals in the child's neighborhood, and per capita income in the city in which he lives. When children are isolated from normal environmental stimulation in infancy and childhood, a negative influence on IQ occurs. This deprivation effect has been found for canal-boat children and others in isolated or inferior home settings. Also, IQ is lower for children raised in an institution rather than in a regular home. Environmental enrichment has the opposite effect; a positive influence on IQ is attributable to well-educated parents and to attending nursery school, high quality elementary schools, and college. Environmental enrichment has even been shown to increase the brain size of mice.

A number of investigators have dealt with the question of racial differences in IQ, especially black-white differences. Such studies tend to ignore the problem of defining race and they tend to raise the emotionally laden issues of racism and prejudice. Studies have shown that whites obtain a higher mean score on IQ tests than blacks. There are, however, large group overlaps and biases in the tests favoring middle-class whites. A few scientists have concluded that the evidence argues for the genetic superiority of whites over blacks, though most social scientists disagree with such conclusions. The most likely explanation for racial differences in IQ appears to rest on different environmental influences for blacks and whites. Black and white infants do not differ in intelligence, the IQ of blacks goes up with improved schooling, the IQ of interracial offspring is dependent on the race of the parent who raises the child, and when black parents are well educated and at a high socioeconomic level, their children are brighter than the children of less fortunate parents.

In attempting to integrate the findings dealing with the antecedents of intelligence, Hayes has proposed a motivational-experiential theory. He suggests that intelligence consists of nothing more than an accumulation of learned facts and skills. Genetic influence consists of motivational differences in the tendency to engage in activities conducive to learning. In addition to genetic determinants, experience-producing drives may be modified by a number of factors.

As would be expected, scores on intelligence tests show a positive relationship with grades in school, with an average correlation of about .50. Prediction is better as the time between testing and grading is shortened. Scores on intelligence tests are also found to correlate positively with creativity, ability to delay gratification, and cognitive functioning during sleep as measured by rapid eye movements. The most inclusive study of overall adjustment as a function of IQ has been carried out by Terman and his associates. Beginning in 1921, over fifteen hundred gifted children (IQ of 140 and above) were selected, and they have been studied at regular intervals ever since. Terman found that gifted children were taller, heavier, and healthier than normal children and were above average on a large number of characteristics. As adults, they were below average in the incidence of serious personality disturbances, insanity, delinquency, alcoholism, homosexuality, and in mortality rate. Their educational and vocational attainments are remarkable in terms of grades, degrees, income, accomplishments, and honors. Both achievement and adjustment appear to be facilitated by high intelligence.

The use of intellectual measures in experimental studies has been relatively rare. Scores on IQ tests have been found to be related to performance in learning a maze, in acquiring a learning set, and in solving concept formation tasks. Response to psychotherapy also appears to be a function of IQ in terms of amount of active participation in group psychotherapy and of positive response to individual psychotherapy.

When cross-sectional investigations of different age groups were carried out, intellectual growth was consistently found to reach a peak by late adolescence, remain relatively constant through the twenties, and then begin a sharp decline. When longitudinal investigations are conducted, however, intellectual ability is found to *increase* over the total age span, and this trend is especially true for well-educated individuals. Presumably, the descrepancy in findings is caused by differences across generations in educational opportunities and other factors. Specific disorders, such as hypertension, are associated with intellectual decline in old age. Attempts to raise intelligence by means of drugs, such as glutamic acid or tranquilizers, have not been successful. Damage to brain tissue has much less effect on IQ than might be expected; brain-damaged patients, however, tend to show *less gain* over time than nondamaged control subjects. Also, the location of the injury within the brain and the type of intelligence measured appear to be crucial factors. Finally, evidence exists that intellectual impairment is brought about by schizophrenia, and that IQ returns to normal when the patient improves.

Perhaps the most important developments with respect to work on intelligence involve an increasing use of the experimental method plus a variety of attempts to build a theory of intelligence. Intelligence is most often conceptualized as a unitary variable, designated as g or general intelligence. With the development of factor-analytic techniques a number of investigators began to conceptualize a group of independent intellectual factors. Among the difficulties with this approach is that the scales measuring the independent factors are found to be correlated with one another, and such tests yield no better predictions than the measures of general intelligence. One development has been the use of digital computers to simulate intelligent behavior. Computers have been programmed in such a way as to demonstrate the same kinds of abilities that are involved in human intelligence. Proposals have been made that the building of computer models which yield individual differences in performance will lead to an increased understanding of intellectual functioning.

* Answers to Dove Counterbalanced Intelligence Test (pp. 244–45): 1-d, 2-a, 3-c, 4-c, 5-e, 6-c, 7-e, 8-c, 9-a.

8

Self-Concept

Many psychologists who have studied personality have expressed the conviction that the most fruitful approach is to deal with man as an organized whole rather than in terms of atomistic units such as authoritarianism and achievement need. In attempting to conceptualize behavior in terms of a single, unified process, many theorists have found the notion of self-concept to be a useful one. Self-concept may be defined simply as the total collection of attitudes, judgments, and values which an individual holds with respect to his behavior, his ability, his body, his worth as a person—in short, how he perceives and evaluates himself. In the present chapter the point of view is presented that the self-concept is an important aspect of personality and that individual differences along this dimension are as meaningful as differences in attitudes, motives, and abilities, but not necessarily more so.

Self-theorists are concerned with extremely important variables, and this theoretical orientation has generated a great deal of research. Among the proponents of self-theory have been Mead (1934), Angyal (1941), Hilgard (1949), Snygg and Combs (1949), Symonds (1951), Wylie (1968), and Carl R. Rogers, whose work will serve as a base for our presentation of research dealing with the concept of self. We will see that Rogers' approach involves observation, generalization, experimental verification of hypotheses, and theory building. Therefore, the question may arise as to whether any differences exist between the theoretical approach of stimulus-response psychologists as represented by the Hull-Spence tradition and that of self-theorists such as Rogers. Rather than a basic quarrel about how to build a science of behavior, the differences lie in what is emphasized and in the language used to describe behavior. In contrasting his point of view with that of stimulus-response psychologists, Rogers says:

> ...I have been asked to cast our theoretical thinking in the terminology of the independent-intervening-dependent variable, in so far as this is feasible. I regret that I find this terminology somehow uncongenial. I cannot justify my negative reaction very adequately, and perhaps it is an irrational one, for the logic behind these terms seems unassailable. But to me the terms seem static— they seem to deny the restless, dynamic, searching, changing aspects of scientific movement. There is a tendency to suppose that a variable thus labeled, remains so, which is certainly not true. The terms also seem to me to smack too much of the laboratory, where one undertakes an experiment *de novo*, with every-thing under control, rather than of a science which is endeavoring to wrest from the phenomena of experience the inherent order which they contain. Such terms seem to be more applicable to the advanced stages of scientific endeavor than to the beginning stages. . . .
>
> It should be quite clear from the foregoing that the model of science which I find most helpful is not taken from the advanced stages of theoretical physics. In a field such as psychotherapy or personality the model which seems more congenial to me would be taken from the much earlier stages of the physical sciences (Rogers, 1959, pp. 189–90).

A few aspects of self-theory, it seems, are quite different from modern stimulus-response psychology, and these aspects will be discussed in the fol-lowing section. Included are an emphasis on the total individual rather than on bits and pieces of behavior and an emphasis on the importance of the phenomenal field. The latter term refers to the individual's total subjective perception of experience; his behavior is presumably based on this perception rather than on an externally defined environment.

THEORETICAL BACKGROUND

ROGERS AND CLIENT-CENTERED THERAPY

Carl Rogers (1967a) has described his own background in terms of the in-fluence of his early family experiences on his work. Born in Oak Park, Illinois, in 1902, he moved with his family to a farm near Chicago at the age of twelve. His was a large, hard-working, conservative, Protestant family whose religious beliefs he describes as more or less fundamentalist. As a teenager, Rogers became interested in the study of night-flying moths and in scientific agriculture which led him to an understanding of the experimental method. He describes himself in his youth as a loner without close friends outside of his family circle, living in a world of his own created by the books he read. The interest in scientific agriculture carried over to some degree in his under-graduate work at the University of Wisconsin. It was at Wisconsin that he first found friendship and companionship beyond his family through participation in a YMCA group. He became a history major and after graduation spent two years at the Union Theological Seminary where he first became acquainted with clinical psychology. His philosophical position eventually moved him away from religious work, and he transferred to Teachers College, Columbia University. After a clinical internship at the Institute for Child Guidance, he received the Ph.D. degree in educational and clinical psychology in 1931; his thesis involved the development of a test for measuring the personality adjustment of children. He then spent twelve years at the Child Study Department of a clinic in Rochester, New York. In 1938, he became the first director of the Rochester Guidance Center. His efforts to conceptualize the work of psychotherapists and to understand the behavior of their clients involved a continuing quest for a theoretical mode to account for psychotherapy and, more generally, personality.

During this period he taught courses at Columbia and Rochester, but Rogers' move into a university setting was not until 1940 (Ohio State University) when his ideas concerning client-centered psychotherapy were crystallizing. His appointment was as a Full Professor, and he notes, "I heartily recommend starting in the academic world at the top level. I have often been grateful that I have never had to live through the frequently degrading competitive process of step-by-step promotion in university faculties, where individuals so frequently learn only one lesson—not to stick their necks out" (Rogers 1967, p. 361). He moved from Ohio State in 1945 to spend an extremely productive twelve years at the University of Chicago. His therapeutic work at the Counseling Center there, his research, his development of theory, and his influence on graduate students and colleagues brought Rogers a major role in the field of psychology. He served as president of the American Psychological Association in 1946–1947. In 1957, he became Professor of Psychology and Psychiatry at the University of Wisconsin. At that point, his interest was directed toward the problem of more serious behavior disorders, and a large-scale project was undertaken to investigate the effects of psychotherapy with schizophrenics. There were a number of difficulties with the department of psychology at Wisconsin and with his own research group. In 1964 Rogers decided to leave the academic setting and accepted a position at the Western Behavioral Sciences Institute at La Jolla, California. His present interests have centered on encounter groups, working primarily with normal individuals, and with the development of a philosophy of the behavioral sciences.

The personality theory which Rogers formulated grew out of his work in psychotherapy, just as did the theory of Freud. As Rogers developed his own particular approach to psychotherapy, he concurrently proposed theoretical formulations to account for the apparent success of the nondirective or client-centered method and for the changes observed in clients. The therapeutic methods developed by Rogers and his co-workers represented a departure from traditional procedures such as psychoanalysis. The therapist is not seen in an interpretive, evaluative role, and the process of therapy is not viewed as an intellectual enterprise in which insightful interpretations help to bring unconscious material into consciousness. Rather, the therapist is one who simply facilitates the natural growth processes of the client by offering acceptance, understanding, and empathy. Rogers proposes:

> In the emotional warmth of the relationship with the therapist, the client begins to experience a feeling of safety as he finds that whatever attitude he expresses is understood in almost the same way that he perceives it, and is accepted. He then is able to explore, for example, a vague feeling of guiltiness which he has experienced. In this safe relationship he can perceive for the first time the hostile meaning and purpose of certain aspects of his behavior, and can understand why he has felt guilty about it, and why it has been necessary to deny to awareness the meaning of this behavior. But this clearer perception is in itself disrupting and anxiety-creating, not therapeutic. It is evidence to the client that there are disturbing inconsistencies in himself, that he is not what he thinks he is. But as he voices his new perceptions and their attendant anxieties, he finds that this acceptant alter ego, the therapist, this other person who is only partly another person, perceives these experiences too, but with a new quality. The therapist perceives the client's self as the client has known it, and accepts it; he perceives the contradictory aspects which have been denied to awareness and accepts those too as being a part of the client; and both of these acceptances have in them the same warmth and respect. Thus it is that the client, experiencing in another an acceptance of both these aspects of himself, can take toward himself the same attitude. He finds that he too can accept himself even with the additions and alterations that are necessitated by these new perceptions of himself as hostile. He can experience himself as a person having hostile as well as other types of feelings, and can experience himself in this way without guilt. He has been enabled to do this (if our theory is correct) because another person has been able to adopt his frame of reference, to perceive with him, yet to perceive with acceptance and respect (Rogers, 1951, p. 41).

Over the years such formulations were extended into a theory of personality and even more broadly into theoretical implications accounting for behavior in a variety of situations, including education, interpersonal relationships, and family life.

SELF-CONCEPT

Several general points of Rogers' theoretical approach should be noted. It attempts to deal with the total individual as an organized whole. Behavior is believed to be a function of the individual's perception of events, and the frame of reference of the scientist must be internal rather than external. Thus, the manipulation of external stimuli defined in the experimenter's terms would tend to overlook the fact that the subjects are responding in terms of their own individual perceptions, and that each subject's structuring of the environment may well be different from that of another and from that of the experimenter. Related to this concern is the tendency to emphasize internally directed behavior as opposed to externally directed behavior. Behavior is not seen as a response to stimuli but *"...is basically the goal-directed attempt of the organism to satisfy its needs as experienced, in the field as perceived"* (Rogers, 1951, p. 491).

The most important aspect of an individual's phenomenal field is that portion which consists of the perceptions of "I" or "me"—the self. The one basic motive of the organism is the actualizing tendency, an inherent tendency to develop all its capacities in ways which serve to maintain or enhance the ogranism.

Either on the basis of inheritance or learning, a need for positive regard develops universally. We want to be loved and respected. The satisfaction of this need is dependent on other human beings, specifically on the individual's perception of the way in which others regard him. This need is sufficiently important that the person will be more influenced by it than by his actual organic experience. A child can learn that his feces are disgusting, that he does not hate his baby sister, or that sexual thoughts are sinful even though his own original felt experiences in each instance might have provided quite different perceptions. Developing out of the need for positive regard from others is the need for positive self-regard. The child's self-concept is formed by means of interactions with others, and the child adopts for himself or internalizes this need to be thought worthwhile. He sees himself and evaluates himself as others do. And, he comes to evaluate his own experiences in terms of the values that were acquired from others.

Almost inevitably, then, some lack of congruence occurs between an individual's experiences and the acquired values. Some experiences are in accord with his self-concept and are accurately perceived and symbolized in consciousness. He goes several hours without food, notices that he feels hungry, and decides to eat some potato chips. Some experiences are contrary to his self-concept and are perceived selectively, distorted, and denied to awareness either in whole or in part. He sees his sister in the bathtub, is unable to accept his subsequent reactions as having anything to do with sexual attraction, and is aware only of feeling disgusted and angry about her appearance. "She's dumb and careless to leave the door unlocked and some prowler may happen by and try to molest her." Such defensive processes lead to rigidity of perception, inaccurate perception of reality, and the tendency to conceptualize experience in overgeneralized and abstract terms.

Whenever an incongruency exists between self and experience, psychological maladjustment occurs, and there is vulnerability to anxiety, threat, and disorganization. For example, if feelings of dependency are inconsistent with an individual's self-concept, any situation which suggests the need for someone else's help is necessarily threatening, even though the person is not able to verbalize the reason why. Similarly, the person's own behavior may be consistent with his self-concept and accurately perceived, or it may be inconsistent with the self-concept and thus subject to distorted perception and lack of awareness. In the latter instance the individual may feel that the behavior is not really his or he may distort its meaning: "I was not myself." "I pointed out your weaknesses for your own good, not to hurt you."

If a sufficient degree of incongruence exists between self and experience, the occurrence of such experiences may lead to a breakdown of the defenses, an extreme arousal of anxiety, a disorganization of the self-structure. There may be a severe attack of anxiety, the occurrence of behavior which is quite inconsistent with the person's previous behavior, or an acute psychotic breakdown. An individual can find himself overwhelmed, without direction, and unable to function adequately as anxiety mounts. A model high school boy, described by all who know him as nice and polite, one day rapes and strangles a small neighbor girl after choir practice. A meek and submissive man comes home from work one day and shoots his wife and children.

One of the major ways in which these various negative processes (inaccurate perception, defensiveness, and breakdown) may be reversed is by receiving unconditional positive regard from another person. This may occur in psychotherapy, in marriage, or through a close friendship. This experience leads to an increase in the person's own unconditional positive self-regard. With the reduction of threat, there is less need for defense and an increased possibility of accurate perception of experience. With self and experience more congruent, psychological adjustment is increased. The individual functions on the basis of his own felt experience and not on the basis of his distorted perceptions. He can thus become a fully functioning person open to experience, free of defensive distortion, and able to have a high positive regard for both self and others.

Thus, Rogers has proposed a theory of personality development, personality functioning, and personality change with the concept of self as its central focus. We will now look at the self-concept as a dimension of personality and examine some of the research which has grown out of Rogers' theoretical framework.

MEASURING THE SELF-CONCEPT

"REALITY AS PERCEIVED"

When theorists adopt the phenomenological position and insist that psychologists should approach behavior from within a subject's frame of reference rather than from without, this general idea strikes a responsive chord. Different people do perceive the same event differently, and one may logically suggest that each person responds on the basis of reality as he perceives it rather than on the basis of reality as defined by someone else. The objective facts that the "oasis" is a mirage, that the "best of all possible girls" is stupid and shallow, that the "sinister plot against his life" is only a delusion are irrelevant in terms of the perceptual field of the individual in question. And, in terms of predicting someone's behavior, quite different predictions might be made on the basis of an observer's definition of reality versus reality as perceived by the individual himself.

As reasonable as the phenomenological approach may seem, the transition from the abstract level of speculation to the concrete level of research presents an apparently insolvable dilemma. That is, how do you operationalize the "internal frame of reference"? How do you go about determining the subject's perception of reality? There is no way of avoiding the fact that the operations utilized by the experimenter must involve observable stimuli and responses. Thus, in actual research the definition of self-concept or self-regard or any other characteristic of the self has involved the presentation of verbal stimulus material to the subject in order to obtain verbal responses from him. Whether such responses accurately reflect the phenomenal field is not an answerable question. There is no way to observe anyone else's perceptual field and hence it cannot be studied by scientists.

Stephenson (1953), in developing operations for the measurement of the self-concept, proposed that the study of self-psychology must begin from the standpoint of what a person says about himself and his beliefs about what he is like. Such verbal responses are clearly observable, may easily be operationalized, and are amenable to scientific study. Stephenson (1953) further points out that he cannot logically accept a phenomenological viewpoint in the way that self-theorists have done. Nothing seems to be gained by proposing that an unobservable phenomenal field is causing behavior. Research on self-theory, then, is not really different from other types of personality research. Variables must be operationalized, measurement problems must be met, and investigations must deal with the establishment of orderly relationships between stimuli and responses and between responses and other responses. The most widely used technique for measuring the self-concept is the Q-sort, and it will serve as our example (Block, 1961).

THE Q-SORT

The Q-technique was developed by Stephenson (1953) as a way of getting at various aspects of the self. The rationale of the Q-sort has been described by Butler and Haigh (1954). First, the assumption is made that many specific self-perceptions exist for each individual. These perceptions can be ordered along a continuum from "unlike me" to "like me." For example, one might feel that the characteristic "loyal to friends" is very much a part of himself, while the characteristic "artistically gifted" is not at all descriptive of his qualities. Further, he might indicate that "high intelligence" is even more "like me" than is "loyal to friends." Such an ordering of self-descriptions does not, however, indicate the subject's value judgments about the characteristics. For example, he might be very happy about his high intelligence but feel that being loyal to his friends is a weakness that should be overcome. To get at this evaluative aspect of the self-concept, a second assumption is that self-perceptions can be ordered along another continuum —from "like my ideal" to "unlike my ideal." This second ordering yields an ideal self-concept: that organization of self-perceptions which the individual holds as desirable and undesirable for himself. When the same series of characteristics has been ordered along both dimensions, it is possible to determine the discrepancy between the two. This measure, called self-ideal discrepancy, has been frequently used in research on self-theory as an indication of self-esteem or self-value.

The Q-sort has not been standardized into an agreed-upon set of statements or a single set of instructions given to subjects or even into a specific number of categories into which the statements are sorted. In a typical procedure, Dymond (1954) asked subjects to sort one hundred statements into nine piles, putting a prescribed number of cards into each pile as shown in Table 8-1.

Table 8-1. Normal Distribution of Q-Sort Cards

	"Least Like Me"					"Most Like Me"			
Pile Number	0	1	2	3	4	5	6	7	8
Number of cards	1	4	11	21	26	21	11	4	1

One set of self-statements was developed by Butler and Haigh (1954). A group of statements was taken at random from therapy protocols and reworded to make them more clear, and then each statement was placed on a card suitable for Q-sorting. In a subsequent investigation, Dymond (1954) obtained judgments from clinical psychologists about each statement with respect to whether a well-adjusted person should indicate that it was like him or unlike him. As shown in Figure 8-1, there was very good agreement among the judges concerning what the items indicated about adjustment.

In addition to the Q-sort, a number of related instruments are used in research on the self-concept. Most often, subjects rate themselves on a series of statements, a group of descriptive adjectives, or respond to a self-oriented questionnaire. The interrelationships of such measures of self-concept were investigated by Crowne, Stephens, and Kelly (1961). The subjects were undergraduates at Ohio State. The investigators found that these measures

Positive Items: Indicates Good Adjustment if Subject Says It Is "Like Me" (Pile Nos. 5, 6, 7, or 8)

I make strong demands on myself.
I often kick myself for the things I do.
I have a warm emotional relationship with others.
I am responsible for my troubles.
I am a responsible person.
I can accept most social values and standards.
Self-control is no problem to me.
I usually like people.
I express my emotions freely.
I can usually live comfortably with the people around me.
My hardest battles are with myself.
I am optimistic.
I am liked by most people who know me.
I am sexually attractive.
I can usually make up my mind and stick to it.
I am contented.
I am poised.
I am impulsive.
I am a rational person.
I am tolerant.
I have an attractive personality.
I am ambitious.
I have initiative.
I take a positive attitude toward myself.
I am assertive.
I am satisfied with myself.
I am likable.
My personality is attractive to the opposite sex.
I am relaxed, and nothing really bothers me.
I am a hard worker.
I feel emotionally mature.
I am intelligent.
I am self-reliant.
I am different from others.
I understand myself.
I am a good mixer.
I feel adequate.

Negative Items: Indicates Good Adjustment if Subject Says It Is "Unlike Me" (Pile Nos. 0, 1, 2, or 3)

I put on a false front.
I often feel humiliated.
I doubt my sexual powers.
I have a feeling of hopelessness.
I have few values and standards of my own.
It is difficult to control my aggression.
I want to give up trying to cope with the world.
I tend to be on my guard with people who are somewhat more friendly than I had expected.

Fig. 8-1 Q-sort Statements.

I usually feel driven.
I feel helpless.
My decisions are not my own.
I am a hostile person.
I am disorganized.
I feel apathetic.
I don't trust my emotions.
It's pretty tough to be me.
I have the feeling that I am just not facing things.
I try not to think about my problems.
I am shy.
I am no one. Nothing seems to be me.
I despise myself.
I shrink from facing a crisis or difficulty.
I just don't respect myself.
I am afraid of a full-fledged disagreement with a person.
I can't seem to make up my mind one way or another.
I am confused.
I am a failure.
I am afraid of sex.
I have a horror of failing in anything I want to accomplish.
I really am disturbed.
All you have to do is just insist with me, and I give in.
I feel insecure within myself.
I have to protect myself with excuses, with rationalizing.
I feel hopeless.
I am unreliable.
I am worthless.
I dislike my own sexuality.

Fig. 8-1 Q-sort Statements (Cont.).

tend to be interrelated—the more similar the tests, the higher the correlations.

ANTECEDENTS OF THE SELF-CONCEPT

THEORETICAL BACKGROUND

Rogers proposed that an individual's self-concept and his values are acquired on the basis of early interactions with a significant other person, usually the mother. Different kinds of parent-child interactions are described by Rogers (1951) as having quite different effects on the development of the self. For all infants, the first dawning of awareness is assumed to involve likes and dislikes, pleasure and pain. Being cold is disliked, being cuddled is liked. In addition to physical stimuli, evaluations by others come to be perceived as pleasant or unpleasant. "You're a good child," is pleasurable to hear while "You're a naughty boy" is not. Since the evaluative statements by parents often come to have greater influence than the child's own perceptions, inconsistency between them can lead to the types of distortions in perception and symbolization which were discussed earlier. For example, a child may enjoy hitting his baby brother but is told by his parents that he feels only love for him. To maintain the positive regard of his parents and of himself, the child can come to believe that he really does feel only love for his brother. Thus, the visceral reaction is hate and the self-perception is love. The consequence of such imposed distortions is maladjustment, as we have seen. Rogers suggests a more beneficial kind of interaction between parent and child which can have quite different consequents with respect to the child's self-structure. It is possible for early experience to form the basis for a psychologically well-adjusted self. The beginning would be the same, with the infant experiencing various likes and dislikes. At times, he hates his baby brother and feels good when he hits him. At this point, a different type of parental behavior is possible. The parent may (1) accept the child's feeling of satisfaction in hurting his brother, (2) at the same time accept and love the child himself, and (3) nevertheless emphasize clearly that this particular behavior cannot be accepted in the family. Rogers proposes:

> The child in this relationship experiences no threat to his concept of himself as a loved person. He can experience fully and accept within himself and as a part of himself his aggressive feelings toward his baby brother. He can experience fully the perception that his hitting behavior is not liked by the person who loves him. . . . Because the budding structure of the self is not threatened by loss of love, because feelings are accepted by his parent, the child in this instance does not need to deny to awareness the satisfactions which he is experiencing, nor does he need to distort his experience of the parental reaction and regard it as his own. He retains instead a secure self which can serve to guide his behavior by freely admitting to awareness, in accurately symbolized form, all the relevant evidence of his experience in terms of his organismic satisfactions, both immediate and longer range (Rogers, 1951, p. 502).

Given this general picture of the possible child-rearing antecedents of differential development of the self-structure, what are the relevant research findings?

PERCEIVED PARENTAL ATTITUDES AND THE SELF-CONCEPT

If the child strives to maintain parental love by introjecting their values, it follows that self-regard would depend on the degree to which the child felt he was successful in maintaining the positive evaluation of his parents. Jourard and Remy (1955) obtained attitudes about self and the subject's perception of father's and mother's attitudes toward him. For both males and females, significant correlations were found between the self-concept score and the perceived attitudes of parents toward self, as shown in Table 8-2. The authors point out that the actual attitudes of the parents may or may not

Table 8-2. Correlations Between Self-Concept and
Perceived Attitudes of Parents Toward Self

	Perceived Ratings by Mother	Perceived Ratings by Father
Female Subjects	.77	.66
Male Subjects	.70	.65

correspond to the perceptions of the offspring. Nevertheless, "If it is indeed true that self-evaluations are determined by parental evaluations of one's self, then it follows that if a person believes that his parents approve of his traits, even though this belief be false, he will tend to approve of his traits as well" (Jourard and Remy, 1955, p. 366).

Parents' Perception of Their Child. If a child's self-concept depends on the way his parents respond to him, it follows that the positiveness or negativeness of their reactions is crucial. Negative reactions from parents would be expected to lead to negative self-perceptions on the part of the child. In addition, we might guess that children caught in such a bind would be likely to have adjustment problems.

Piers (1972) compared a group of children (8-14 years of age) who were receiving psychotherapy in various clinics with a "normal" group who had never been referred for psychological treatment. A measure of self-concept was given to each child; the parents were then asked to fill out the same scale as they believed their child had answered.

As would be expected, the clinic children were less positive in their self-image than were the normal children. Of greater interest is the way the parents responded. Parents of the clinic children saw them even more negatively than the children saw themselves. Parents of normal children saw them even more positively than they saw themselves. We cannot determine from this study, of course, whether the parents' positive versus negative perceptions led to differences in the child's self-concept and adjustment or vice versa. If it can be shown in future research that negative responses from the parent at one point in time are followed by the child's negative self-perception and maladjustment at a later point in time, there would be very strong support for Rogers' formulation.

Parental Differences in Perceiving Children. If a child's self-perception or self-evaluation is based on the way significant others perceive or evaluate him, parental disagreements should result in a confused self-concept. Among the consequences suggested by Wyer (1965) are an unstable self-perception and ineffectiveness in goal seeking. Since the child in this situation could never behave so as to satisfy the expectancies of both parents, he would be unable successfully to learn behavior patterns which would make others give him a positive evaluation and he would be unlikely to learn how to work hard to reach a goal such as academic success.

Wyer's subjects were several hundred male and female university freshmen and their parents. Academic effectiveness was defined as the relationship between scores on a college entrance aptitude test and actual grade performance in the first semester at college. Self-concept and parental perceptions were measured by means of responses to a series of adjectives relevant to academic concerns such as alert, ambitious, mature, hardworking, studious, and motivated. The students rated themselves as to how well the words described them and how satisfied they were with themselves in each case. The parents rated their offspring in the same way. The differences between the responses of each mother and father were summed to yield an index of parental discrepancy.

The hypothesis that parental differences in accepting their offspring would result in academic problems was confirmed in that the mean parental discrepancy for the least effective students was greater than parental discrepancy for the most effective students. It may also be seen in Table 8-3

**Table 8-3. Mean Self-Acceptance and Parental Acceptance
for Students High and Low in Academic Effectiveness**

	Academic Effectiveness	
	High	*Low*
Self-Acceptance	90.28	86.36
Mother's Acceptance	102.49	97.21
Father's Acceptance	101.64	95.51

(Data from Wyer, 1965)

that the students who were most effective academically were more self-accepting and were more accepted by both their mothers and their fathers than were the least effective students.

SITUATIONAL INFLUENCES ON THE SELF-CONCEPT

Broken Homes. In addition to parental attitudes about the child and parental agreement on such attitudes, it is reasonable to suppose that other variables contribute to one's self-concept. One example is provided by Kaplan and Pokorny (1971) who investigated the effect of broken homes on the development of self-acceptance. Their subjects consisted of a large group of married adults in Houston and the surrounding area. Self-concept was measured by a scale on which subjects indicated degree of agreement with items such as "On the whole, I am satisfied with myself" and "At times I think I am no good at all." Interview questions dealt with whether or not they had experienced a broken home (death of parent, divorce, or separation) during their childhood.

It was found that the subjects from broken homes were more likely to express a negative self-concept if the cause was the death of the father, if a parent was sent to a mental hospital, if the child was sent to live with relatives before the age of sixteen, or if a parent remarried when the child was eight or over. It is clear from these and other similar findings that a broken home does not necessarily lead to a negative self-concept. What is important are the particular circumstances surrounding the broken home situation.

Childhood Fears and Worries. In another interview study, the same investigators (Kaplan and Pokorny, 1970a) examined the relationship between the self-concept of adults and various childhood attitudes or experiences. For subjects under thirty, a negative self-concept was found to be related to childhood worries about getting a bad report card, fear of being punished by parents, having poor grades in school, and perceiving themselves as being less physically attractive than other children. It is not certain, of course, whether these memories and perceptions of childhood are accurate, but it seems quite possible that repeated negative experiences of this type contribute to a feeling that one is inadequate and not worth as much as others. The notion that one should be bright and attractive, for example, in order to be an acceptable human being seems to be consistently fostered by what children read, the movies and television shows they see, and especially by the advertising to which they are continually exposed. You are told, in effect, that you are a failure if your school grades are bad, if your teeth are not sparkling white, if you are overweight, or if your bodily odors are not thoroughly disguised. Real or imagined deficiences in these respects might well have negative psychological consequents.

As is obvious, research dealing with the antecedents of the self-concept is only in the beginning stages. Many of the more intriguing formulations proposed by Rogers have yet to be tested.

THE PLACE OF THE SELF-CONCEPT IN THE STRUCTURE OF PERSONALITY

SELF-IDEAL DISCREPANCY AS AN INDEX OF MALADJUSTMENT

In part because of its origin in observations of therapist-client interactions, Rogers' self-theory deals extensively with the problem of maladjustment. In the theory, maladjustment is defined as the magnitude of the discrepancy between self and experience. Increasing discrepancy leads to anxiety and disorganization of the self-structure. If the discrepancy reaches its maximum, psychological breakdown is the result. Since it is not possible to operationalize self-experience discrepancy, research has simply dealt with self-ideal discrepancy as an index of maladjustment.

Population Comparisons. Two groups of boys, aged nine to twelve, were compared by Davids and Lawton (1961). The normal group consisted of boys at a YMCA camp, and the maladjusted group was made up of emotionally disturbed youngsters undergoing psychiatric treatment. The normal group was found to have a significantly more positive self-concept.

In his dissertation research at the University of Colorado, Chase (1957) selected an adjusted and a maladjusted group of hospitalized veterans. The adjusted group consisted of medical and surgical patients who had given no evidence of psychiatric difficulty. The maladjusted group was made up of psychotics, neurotics, and patients with character disorders. All subjects were given a Q-sort. The mean self-ideal correlations for the adjusted subjects was significantly higher than for the maladjusted subjects.

Other Indications of Adjustment. Kaplan and Pokorny (1969) sought to determine the relationship between self-acceptance and psychosocial adjustment. In the general community in Houston, Texas, the investigators interviewed subjects and administered a measure of self-acceptance. Among the findings was a clear negative relationship between self-acceptance and psycho-physiological symptoms. The least self-accepting subjects were most likely to report problems with sleep, trembling hands, nervousness, heart beating too hard, headaches and pressures in the head, fingernail biting, shortness of breath, damp and clammy hands, and nightmares. Feelings of depression were also associated with lack of self-acceptance.

Smith and Teevan (1971) hypothesized that there is a positive relationship between maladjustment and fear of failure. In part, they reasoned that fear of failure would lead to reduced self-satisfaction and hence a greater self-ideal discrepancy. For both male and female college students, as fear of failure increased, self-ideal discrepancy increased. The authors suggest that in an achievement-oriented culture such as our own, "...perceived inadequacy in, and avoidance of, achievement situations would have effects going beyond achievement and including a general reduction in self-acceptance. It is thus suggested that failure-avoidant motivation is one significant factor contributing to the reduction of generalized self-acceptance" (p. 52).

DEFENSIVENESS AND THE CURVILINEARITY
HYPOTHESIS

The studies just discussed have each suggested a linear relationship between self-ideal discrepancy and maladjustment. As discrepancy between self and ideal increases, maladjustment increases. A number of investigators have raised questions concerning this relationship. The problem is whether to accept as accurate the subject's statements concerning his self-concept. In part, this problem brings us back to the difficulties which arise in adopting a phenomenological approach. If self-statements are taken as accurate representations of an individual's internal world, then maladjustment should be directly related to discrepancy. If, however, self-statements are viewed simply as verbal responses to be studied, one would not be surprised to find that positive self-appraisals were a function of a number of variables including deliberate lying, unconsciously motivated mechanisms of repression, the desire to give the most socially acceptable responses, or lack of contact with reality. Given such possibilities, maladjustment could conceivably be reflected in a large discrepancy between self and ideal or in an unrealistically low discrepancy between self and ideal. In other words, a curvilinear relationship between self-satisfaction and adjustment would seem to be a likely possibility.

Repression-Sensitization. The repression-sensitization dimension involves individual differences in response to threat. At one extreme are avoidance behaviors such as denial and repression while at the other extreme are approach behaviors such as intellectualization and sensitization. Presumably, those individuals at either end of this dimension are less well adjusted than individuals falling in the middle range. Using the Repression-Sensitization (R-S) Scale as a measure of defenses, a number of investigators have reported that subjects with repressive defenses tend to present themselves positively on self-concept measures while subjects with sensitizing defenses present themselves negatively (Altrocchi, Parsons, and Dickoff, 1960; Byrne, 1961b).

The MMPI as a Measure of Adjustment. One of the early investigations in which a curvilinear relationship between self-satisfaction and adjustment was hypothesized was that of Block and Thomas (1955). A group of undergraduates was given a Q-sort, and scores on MMPI scales served as the measure of adjustment. For each subject, the correlation between his self-sort and ideal sort was obtained and used as the self-satisfaction index. This coefficient was then correlated with scores on the MMPI scales. High self-ideal discrepancy was found to indicate maladjustment in that self-dissatisfied individuals tend to score higher on scales measuring such characteristics as anxiety and depression. At the same time, evidence showed that extremely low self-ideal discrepancy was also associated with maladjustment, though of a different kind. Self-satisfied individuals tended to score higher on scales measuring such characteristics as overcontrol and denial. The authors concluded that the best-adjusted individuals were those with a medium degree of self-ideal discrepancy. One general finding which seems clear on the basis of research dealing with maladjustment and self-perception is that self-ratings alone cannot be used as a straightforward index of adjustment. Self-satisfaction may result from a realistic appraisal of psychological well-being or from a defensive denial of realistic concerns.

DYNAMICS OF THE SELF-CONCEPT

RESPONSE TO STIMULI NOT CONSISTENT WITH THE SELF-CONCEPT

Perceptual Defense. One of the major propositions of Rogers's self-theory concerns the way we respond to experiences contrary to our self-concepts. It was proposed that such experiences would not be perceived or would be perceived in a distorted form. This sort of response to threat has been labeled *perceptual defense;* by defending oneself against inconsistent stimuli, the stability of the self-concept is presumably protected. The greater the discrepancy between self and experience, the greater the potential threat from the environment and hence the more perceptual defense.

Chodorkoff's (1954) doctoral dissertation at Wisconsin reported a clever method for assessing discrepancy between self and experience. Self-concept was measured by means of a Q-sort given to male undergraduates. Then, an independent assessment of each subject was made by clinical psychologists who made a Q-sort for each subject using the same group of items. The clinicians' judgments were based on the subject's responses to a biographical inventory, the Rorschach, a word-association test, and the Thematic Apperception Test. The correlation between each subject's self-sort, and the judges' sort constituted the measure of discrepancy, an index of the accuracy of the individual's self-perception.

The perceptual defense task was specially prepared for each subject. On the basis of his reaction times for word-association items, the ten words yielding the longest reaction times (that is, most threatening) and the ten words yielding the shortest reaction times (that is, least threatening) were used. Presumably, the stimuli for each subject represented personally relevant words that were either threatening or not. These twenty words were presented randomly by means of a tachistoscope, first at .10 second exposure time and then at increasingly slower speeds until the subject perceived it correctly. The more trials necessary for correct perception of a word, the greater the perceptual *defense.* For each subject, the perceptual defense score equalled his mean recognition threshold for the threatening words minus his mean recognition threshold for the neutral words.

The correlation between the accuracy of self-perception score and the perceptual defense score was −.53. In other words, the more the self-sort was like the judges' sort, the less the perceptual defense against threatening stimuli. In addition to supporting Rogers's formulations concerning defenses, these findings also suggest that the individual with inaccurate self-perception responds to threat in a maladaptive way. Chodorkoff (1954, p. 511) asks,

"...if he does not recognize threat, how can he be expected to deal with it effectively?"

Difficulty in Recall. Proceeding from the same aspect of self-theory as did Chodorkoff, Cartwright (1956) tested the proposition that it is most difficult to recall stimuli which are not consistent with the self-concept. He further suggested that differential recall of consistent and inconsistent stimuli should be greater for maladjusted than for adjusted individuals.

Subjects who had applied for psychotherapy but had not yet begun, as well as others for whom psychotherapy was judged to be unsuccessful, constituted the maladjusted group. The adjusted group was made up of individuals for whom psychotherapy had been successful plus others who did not plan to have psychotherapy. Each subject sorted statements into piles from "most like me" to "most unlike me."

For each of the statements, a separate card had been prepared containing an adjective comparable to the statement. For example, the statement "I have an attractive personality," card was prepared with the word "attractive." While the subjects performed an unrelated task, the experimenter selected the adjective cards corresponding to the Q-sort cards which the subject had placed in the two most extreme piles as like or unlike himself. Among other learning tasks, the subjects were asked to learn these self-consistent and self-inconsistent adjectives.

For the group as a whole, recall for the consistent adjectives was significantly better than recall for the inconsistent adjectives. Also, as predicted, in the maladjusted group there was a significantly greater difference between recall for the two types of adjectives than in the adjusted group. This suggested that inconsistent stimuli constituted a greater source of threat for the maladjusted subject.

A further finding was evidence supporting Rogers's proposal that experiences inconsistent with the self may be admitted into awareness in distorted form. For example, "hopeless" was misrecalled as "hopeful" by one subject and "hostile" misrecalled as "hospitable" by another.

RESPONSE TO FRUSTRATION

For the individual who is well adjusted in terms of congruence between experience and his self-concept, frustrating conditions should lead to the arousal of hostile impulses which are accurately conceptualized. Further, these impulses should be directed toward the appropriate target, the frustrating agent. In contrast, individuals whose self-concept is such that aggressive impulses are not admitted into awareness should respond quite differently in a frustrating situation. They should not be able to verbalize feelings of hostility toward the frustrating agent, but they conceivably would express aggression in some more disguised form.

Aggression Toward an Actual Frustrating Agent. A test of the proposition that the appropriate expression of aggression is dependent on self-ideal congruence was provided by Worchel (1958). A frustrating situation was created by administering an "intelligence test" to several classes of undergraduates. Worchel describes the procedure:

> The intelligence test was then administered with the instruction that each subtest was timed but that sufficient time had been allowed for most of the students to complete the tests. As the students worked, E walked around noting the students' progress, urging faster work, belittling their efforts, and unfavorably comparing their poor performance to that of other classes. He interrupted frequently by urging them to skip over the ones they could not do and to try the easier ones first (Worchel, 1958, p. 356).

Immediately after this experience, the subjects filled out a rating scale in which their attitudes about the test administration were determined. A hostility score was obtained on the basis of attitudes expressed toward the test-administrator, the one who instigated the aggression. Those subjects with high discrepancy between self and ideal expressed significantly less hostile feelings toward the test administrator than those with low discrepancy scores. The high-discrepancy subjects were assumed to be unaware of or unable to express their hostile feelings.

Aggression Toward an Imaginary Frustrating Agent. If frustration evokes greater hostility from low-discrepancy subjects, is there any evidence that high-discrepancy individuals ever express aggression outwardly?

Rothaus and Worchel (1960) presented high- and low-discrepancy subjects with imaginary situations about which they were asked to give their probable response (for example, "Your date phones at the last minute and breaks the appointment without an adequate explanation"). The hostility of the subjects' responses was determined by two judges.

In this situation, with a hypothetical response to an imaginary situation, subjects with high self-ideal discrepancy responded with significantly more hostility than did subjects with low self-ideal discrepancy. In other words, the subjects responded exactly the opposite way to a hypothetical frustration as to an actual frustration. We might suppose from this that those individuals with high self-ideal discrepancy were not threatened by the imaginary situation and thus could express hostile impulses.

RESPONSE TO SUCCESS AND FAILURE

A number of the studies of the self-concept indicate a relationship between self-esteem and various aspects of achievement—fear of failure, school performance, and concern about school grades. It would seem likely, then, that a situation involving success or failure would have differential effects on those high or low in self-esteem.

Task Performance. Shrauger and Rosenberg (1970) point out that in everyday life, quite different responses to failure may be observed. Some individuals seem to become apathetic and lose all confidence in themselves while others are stimulated by failure to work harder and to achieve. Success also brings different reactions, with some working even more diligently after a success while others take success as a sign that they can coast along on their accomplishments. Differences in self-esteem could possibly help account for these different effects. It was hypothesized that those low in self-esteem would perform less well after failure compared to those high in self-esteem. Also, success would be more beneficial to those high in self-esteem than to those with a negative self-concept.

The subjects were male students at the State University of New York at Buffalo, selected from a large group on the basis of extreme scores on a measure of self-esteem. The subjects were asked to take part in two supposedly unrelated experiments. One involved two administrations of a digit-symbol task similar to that used on intelligence tests. In between the two administrations, subjects participated in the second experiment which was described as a study of "sensitivity to other people"; it was prearranged that each subject either succeeded or failed at this task.

The effect of success and failure at the social task on changes in digit-symbol peformance may be seen in Table 8-4. First, it might be noted that

Table 8-4. Mean Changes in Digit-Symbol Scores Following Success or Failure for Subjects High or Low in Self-Esteem

Feedback	Self-Esteem	
	High	Low
Success	+8.33	+ .89
Failure	−1.44	−5.33

(Data from Shrauger and Rosenberg, 1970)

there is a general tendency for success to lead to improved performance and failure to lead to a worsened performance. Second, there were marked differences in the high and low self-esteem groups. Those high in self-esteem improved greatly following success while the performance of those low in self-esteem deteriorated greatly following failure.

Attribution of Causality. Heider (1958) has proposed that individuals who have engaged in an activity tend to attribute the outcome to either internal or external causes. Both personality and situational variables probably contribute to which kind of cause is perceived, and self-esteem has been proposed as one of the determinants. When the outcome is successful, high self-esteem individuals would be expected to attribute the cause to their own personal qualities whereas those low in self-esteem might explain the outcome in terms of external events such as luck or fate or other variables beyond their control. Failure, on the other hand, could be seen by those low in self-esteem as attributable to their own failings, while those high in self-esteem would seek the cause elsewhere. In each instance, the reason sought for what happened would be consistent with the individual's self-concept. An alternative proposition is that all individuals would simply seek to enhance their own self-esteem and attribute success to themselves and failure to external events.

Fitch (1970) devised a test of these two opposing hypotheses of self-consistency versus self-enhancement. The subjects were given a measure of self-concept and about a month later took part in an experimental task in which they had to estimate the number of dots presented briefly on a series of slides. Afterward, false feedback was given in which they were informed that they had performed poorly or very well regardless of how well they had actually done. Causal attribution was measured by means of a questionnaire which gave the subject four choices to explain his performance. The internal causes were ability and effort while the external possibilities were luck and his physical and mental condition during the experiment. Subjects were to apportion the percentage of the cause across the four possibilities.

A control group which was given no feedback distributed causality evenly over the four possibilities as about 25 percent for each. It may be seen in Table 8-5 that *both* the self-consistency and the self-enhancement hypotheses

Table 8-5. Percentage of Causality Attributed to Internal and External Variables by High and Low Self-Esteem Subjects Following Success or Failure

Self-Esteem	*Performance Feedback*	*Causal Attribution*	
		Internal	*External*
High	Success	69.5	30.5
	Failure	52.5	47.5
Low	Success	63.0	37.0
	Failure	61.5	38.5

(Data from Fitch, 1970)

were supported. In the success condition, both kinds of subjects tended to ascribe the cause to internal variables, thus enhancing their self-esteem. In the failure conditions, the low self-esteem subjects were more likely than the high self-esteem subjects to see the cause as internal, thus reacting in a way consistent with their negative self-concept.

These various experimental investigations of personality dynamics give evidence that individual differences in the self-concept substantially affect behavior in a variety of situations. We will turn next to research dealing with efforts to bring about changes in the self-concept.

CHANGES IN THE SELF-CONCEPT

EVALUATION BY OTHERS

Self-theory proposes that self-concept is developed on the basis of evaluations by others communicated during interpersonal interactions. While the earliest and presumably most general aspects of the self-concept develop in interactions between the child and parental figures, continuing changes in the self-concept should take place as a consequence of later interactions. Thus, the reactions of siblings, peers, teachers, colleagues, spouse, offspring, and/or therapist would be expected to influence changes in the self-concept. Videbeck (1960) hypothesized that one could bring about changes in self-concept through experimental manipulation of the evaluation of an individual by others. The subjects were students who had been rated by their speech instructors as superior in speaking ability. They were asked to participate in an experiment to "determine whether men or women were better in certain forms of oral communication." In the experiment, each subject read six poems. After each poem, an individual described as a visiting speech expert evaluated the subject's performance. On a random basis, the subjects were assigned to one of two conditions: approval or disapproval. Irrespective of the quality of the performance, the "expert" gave either all positive or all negative evaluations. Before and after the poem-reading sessions, the students gave self-ratings and ideal self-ratings of adequacy with reference to speaking skills and ability to communicate effectively in various social situations.

The self-ratings of the two groups prior to the experimental treatment did not differ. After the evaluation session, the self-concepts of those in the approval group became more positive while the self-concepts of subjects in the disapproval group became more negative.

Feedback about one's success and failure on many kinds of activities seems to have a direct and immediate effect on self-esteem. In the Shrauger and Rosenberg (1970) experiment mentioned earlier, the information that the subject had done a good or bad job on the "interpersonal sensitivity inventory" led, respectively, to substantial increases or decreases in self-evaluations. Flippo and Lewinson (1971) gave subjects a perceptual reasoning task on which they could succeed 75 percent, 50 percent, or 25 percent, to produce varying degrees of failure. There was a small positive effect on self-esteem in the first condition and significant decreases in self-esteem in the conditions of 50 percent and 25 percent success.

OTHER EXTERNAL EVENTS

A general, and perhaps oversimplified, proposition that could be drawn from the previous set of studies is that anything which makes an individual feel good enhances his self-concept and anything which makes him feel bad has a detrimental effect. What other kinds of evidence are relevant to that proposition?

Environmental Competence. Koocher (1971) hypothesized that increased competence in handling one's environment should have a positive effect on the self-concept. He selected a specific environmental skill: learning to swim. He noted (p. 275):

> The selection of learning to swim as a specific case of competence development was not accidental. Aside from the almost universal recognition of swimming as a valuable skill, no great proficiency is necessary in order for a person to feel that he has succeeded in this area. Even momentary self-propulsion and unsupported control in the water can represent a quite significant mastery for many children. Simply daring to challenge the water in an attempt to gain control of oneself in the medium may carry powerful implications. In this learning situation the child needs no outside approval to tell him when he has succeeded.

The subjects were a group of boys aged seven to fifteen who were participating in a YMCA summer program. When they arrived at the camp, the boys were given measures of self and ideal self. Some already knew how to swim while others did not. During a twelve-day period there was an extensive effort to teach swimming, and afterward the measures of self-concept were readministered. Some of the nonswimmers learned to swim during this period and some did not, so there were three different groups—nonswimmers who learned to swim, nonswimmers who failed to acquire swimming skills, and those who were already able to swim when they came to camp. Changes in self-ideal discrepancy were expected only for the first of these groups.

The results are shown in Table 8-6. The only group showing a significant change between pretest and posttest were those boys who had successfully

Table 8-6. Mean Self-Ideal Discrepancy Before and After Swimming Lessons at YMCA Camp

Group	Pretest	Posttest
Learned to Swim	8.26	3.37
Failed to Learn	8.88	10.75
Already Knew How to Swim	7.83	6.30

(Data from Koocher, 1971)

learned to swim at the camp. They had less self-ideal discrepancy after that experience than when they first reached the camp. It might be noted that all three groups were approximately the same on the pretest and that there is a tendency for those who failed to learn swimming to show an increase in self-ideal discrepancy. Koocher suggested that the effects on self-concept were probably not long-lasting ones.

Interpersonal Success with a Date. A special kind of interpersonal evaluation is that of being liked by a member of the opposite sex. Coombs (1969) proposed that making a favorable impression on others in a social situation enhances one's self-concept. A favorable self-concept, in turn, leads one to participate in further such social situations. Lack of success in social situations would have a negative effect on the self-concept and lead to decreased social participation. Once again, self-concept is seen as reflecting the views of others.

The research was conducted at a dance at which male and female students had been paired by a computer. Almost all of the couples were composed of individuals who did not know one another prior to the dance. Before the dance, the self-concept measures were given. Shortly after the dance and then six months later, self-concept was measured again along with various questions about the dating experience.

It was found that those who were evaluated most favorably by their dates were most likely to view themselves positively. Coombs (1969, p. 279) indicates, "The interpretation is that self-concepts are developed by viewing oneself as one imagines others are doing. By projecting himself into the mind of a dating partner and viewing himself as he thinks the partner does, a young person develops a social 'looking glass' concept of his dating desirability." It was also found that an increase in favorable self-concept led to a greater likelihood of having subsequent dates with the partner met at the dance.

Disruptive Life Experiences. Our lives are often disrupted by events to which we must adjust—moving to a new location, the draft, illness, and countless other happenings. It would be expected that such disruptions would have a negative effect on one's self-concept.

Kaplan (1970) hypothesized that self-esteem decreases as there is an increase in the number of recent life experiences which require an adjustment in the way one lives. With a large sample of adults, it was found that self-concept becomes more negative as a function of having (during the previous year) a close friend who died, any unusual experiences, or a member of the family with a serious illness. When these and other disruptive events (for example, marriage, change of residence, birth of a baby, loss of job) are combined, the more such events that occurred during the past year, the more negative the self-concept.

MOOD FLUCTUATION

Human beings are commonly observed to have periodic variations in mood, often for reasons not at all clear to the individual himself. Investigators can obtain repeated measurements of mood over a period of time by means of self-ratings and then attempt to determine the correlates and antecedents of these mood swings.

Whatever the antecedents of mood fluctuation, one would expect that changes in mood would bring about changes in the self-concept. Wessman, Ricks, and Tyl (1960) formulated a series of hypotheses concerning mood changes including several propositions dealing with concomitant changes in self-ideal discrepancy. Their subjects were female students at Radcliffe College. Over a six-week period, the girls were asked to record their feelings each night. The Mood Scale consisted of ten phrases ranging from "complete elation, rapturous joy, and soaring ecstasy" to "utter depression and gloom. Completely down. All is black and leaden. Wish it were over." The subjects were to rate themselves just before retiring each evening. In addition, a Q-sort was given twice during the six-week period—once when mood reached an extreme high and once when it was it an extreme low.

As hypothesized, self-ideal discrepancy was greater when the subject was depressed than when she was elated. The median self-ideal correlation during an elated mood was .55. During depression, the median correlation was .07. Most of the difference resulted from changes in the self-concept rather than from changes in the ideal self. One of the additional findings was that mood tended to be lower (and hence self-ideal discrepancy greater) on the two days prior to menstruation.

These findings suggest that attempts to assess more or less enduring changes in the self-concept would do well to take into account the regular and temporary fluctuations in self-esteem.

AGE

Research dealing with personality change as a function of the age of the individual suggests that the many inevitable physical and social alterations which occur over time are accompanied by changes in various personality dimensions. The fact that a curvilinear relationship has been found between age and degree of personal happiness (Kuhlen, 1956) led Bloom (1961) to hypothesize that self-acceptance or self-esteem would also be related to age in a curvilinear fashion. The subjects were male surgical patients at a VA hospital in New York. Ages ranged from the early twenties to the late sixties. The relationship between self-acceptance and age was found to be a curvilinear one as hypothesized. Self-acceptance showed a steady increase from age twenty, reached a peak during the age period fifty to fifty-nine, and then began a steady decline.

Still other investigators report that older subjects report more positive self-attitudes than younger age groups (Grant, 1969; Parker and Kleiner, 1966), that age is unrelated to self-concept (Downing and Rickels, 1965; Schwab, Clemmons, and Marder, 1966), and that self-esteem decreases with age (Ziller and Grossman, 1967). Kaplan and Pokorny (1970b) suggested that the discrepancies among various researchers are a function of differing populations with specific characteristics. They investigated a large sample varying in age from below thirty to above sixty and found no relationship between age and self-esteem for the total group. With particular subgroups, however, a different picture emerged. For example, those older subjects whose standard of living was less than they had hoped it would be were less positive in self-concept than those who were satisfied with their standard of living. Older subjects who lived as couples expressed more positive self-attitudes than those with other living arrangements (for example, living alone, living with children or other relatives). It was proposed that aging alone does not affect the self-concept but that specific events that occur in later life can have a marked effect.

CLIENT-CENTERED THERAPY VERSUS
A CONTROL GROUP

In 1954, Rogers and Dymond edited a report of a series of investigations dealing primarily with research on psychotherapy and its effect on the self-concept. The general plan (Grummon, 1954) of the study was to obtain behavioral measures before, during, and after psychotherapy for clients at the University of Chicago Counseling Center. All of the interactions between client and therapist were recorded. The clients in the *experimental group* consisted of both university students and nonstudents. Two types of control groups were established. The *own-control group* was formed by asking half of the clients in the experimental group to postpone their therapy for sixty days. This group served to control for effects such as the degree of disturbance, personality characteristics, and motivation for psychotherapy. The *equivalent-control group* was made up of individuals who volunteered to serve as subjects for a project involving "research on personality." They were matched with the experimental group on the basis of sex, student versus nonstudent status, age, and socioeconomic class. A number of different therapists participated in the project, and each handled approximately equal numbers of clients. After subjects had agreed to participate, the first testing session took place. The schedule of testing is shown in Figure 8-2.

Self-Ideal Changes. Butler and Haigh (1954) reported that the self-ideal correlations of the client groups before therapy averaged −.01. The mean self-ideal correlation after therapy was .34, and at the time of the later

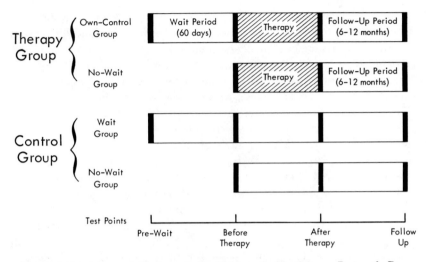

Fig. 8-2 Experimental Design of the Chicago Psychotherapy Research Project (Adapted from Rogers, C. R. and Dymond, R. F. (eds.), *Psychotherapy and personality change,* Chicago: University of Chicago Press, © 1954.)

follow-up it was .31. Thus, a change in self-ideal congruence occurred between the pretherapy period and the posttherapy period. One test of whether therapy-motivated individuals change simply with the passage of time is provided by the own-control group. When first tested, these fifteen clients had a self-ideal correlation of −.01; after the sixty-day waiting period, the correlation was still −.01. In contrast to the client groups, the equivalent control group had a mean self-ideal correlation of .58 at the beginning and .59 at the follow-up period. These subjects had less self-ideal discrepancy than the client group both before and after the clients had undergone therapy, but the crucial point is that neither group of control subjects showed any change over time. Changes in self-concept in the experimental group can be attributed to the effects of psychotherapy.

PSYCHOTHERAPY WITH PSYCHOTIC PATIENTS

Much of the early work of Rogers and his colleagues was concentrated on the relatively mild forms of emotional disturbance, and his current interests are centered on the normal person. Typically, the clients engaging in psychotherapy or participating in encounter groups have been bright, well-educated, and verbal. Rogers' self-theory was developed primarily on the basis of observations of such individuals. At Wisconsin, a large-scale six-year research project was undertaken by Rogers (1967b) in collaboration with Eugene Gendlin, Donald Kiesler, Charles Truax, and others, applying the concepts of client-centered therapy to the treatment of schizophrenics. Rogers indicates that he wanted to enlarge both his clinical and his research horizons to include the chronically hospitalized psychotic person. The project was designed to attempt to determine those aspects of therapist behavior which are most effective in bringing about behavioral changes, to identify the client behaviors which change, and to assess the outcome of the process.

The research dealt with three groups, matched with respect to sex, age, and socio-educational level. There were chronic schizophrenics, acute schizophrenics, and normals. Half of each group was given psychotherapy and half served as a control. Each therapist interacted with one client from each of the three groups. There was extensive testing of the subjects throughout the project, the therapy sessions were recorded, and the subjects were interviewed at various times by someone other than the therapist.

In a project of this scope, there is a massive amount of data and literally too many details to be able to summarize them briefly. A few of the general conclusions will be presented. There was little tendency for the schizophrenics to engage in the kind of self-exploration typical of neurotics and normals in therapy; rather, they concentrated on attempts to form a relationship with the therapist. When the most and least successful cases were examined separately, it was found that the unsuccessful therapists had very inaccurate perceptions of the relationship, perceptions which were negatively related to the perceptions of the patients and of the outside observers. It appears, then, that therapists are not reliable judges of the therapeutic relationship and thus not good predictors of the outcome of psychotherapy.

In general, it could be said that the process of psychotherapy was disappointingly noninvolving for the schizophrenic patients. They remained remote and gave little evidence of change. Both the therapy group and the control group showed a small amount of improvement on many of the measures, and there were not great differences between these two groups. One exception was that the therapy group had a slightly better rate of release from the hospital and seemed better able to maintain themselves outside of the hospital.

Perhaps the most significant findings were those of the effects of differences among therapists. The more understanding, genuine, and empathic the therapist, the more the patient engaged in self-exploration. In addition, the patients who were with the most understanding therapists showed the greatest improvement on the schizophrenia scale of the MMPI. Those with the least understanding therapists actually showed an *increase* in pathology, and were less well off after psychotherapy than the control group. Other investigators (for example, Satz and Baraff, 1962) have also found that inadequate therapy can actually be detrimental to schizophrenics. Truax and Mitchell (1971) suggest a more general problem in that the odds are two out of three that any given therapist is wasting his time and that his efforts are either ineffective or harmful. The effective therapist is one who is honest and genuine in his therapeutic encounter, who is able to provide a nonthreatening and accepting atmosphere for the client, and who is able accurately to understand the client's meaning. They conclude (p. 341) that, "Basically, the personality of the therapist is more important than his techniques." In addition, certain patient characteristics serve to influence the quality of the relationship with the therapist. The Rogers (1967b) group found that therapists were most likely to be understanding, genuine, and accepting when the patient was an expressive individual with a social-educational level similar to that of the therapist.

It may be seen that Rogers and his colleagues were able to develop a highly sophisticated research project dealing with a very difficult and complicated problem. There was an aura of disappointment about the overall results, but they were able to show that under specific circumstances there was measurable improvement in the behavior of seriously disturbed individuals.

ENCOUNTER GROUPS

Most recently, Rogers (1970) has shifted his primary focus of interest from individual psychotherapy to group experiences. He points out the proliferation of involvement with T-groups, encounter groups, and sensitivity training and the fact that much of this activity has been taking place outside of the traditional academic establishment. The movement was initially based on the conceptions of Kurt Lewin, and the first Training-group or T-group took place in 1947 in Bethel, Maine, not long after Lewin's death. These groups were designed to teach human relations skills, and the primary source of group members for the National Training Laboratories (NTL) was the executive and managerial levels of industry. Rogers traces a second impetus for the interest in groups to his own work at the University of Chicago in training counsellors for the Veterans Administration. Today, Rogers' emphasis on personal experience and growth has more or less merged with the NTL emphasis on learning human relations skills. One can see the group movement blending, in a variety of ways, the interests of clinical and social psychologists.

One feature of current encounter groups is the tendency to hold intensive marathon sessions that last for an entire weekend or even longer. The observation is that in the first hours, the participants tend to present mostly superficial aspects of themselves and only slowly do their deeper and truer feelings begin to emerge. In the course of such a process, the participant "...becomes deeply acquainted with the other members and with his own inner self, the self that otherwise tends to be hidden behind his façade. Hence, he relates better to others, both in the group and later in the everyday life situation" (Rogers, 1970, p. 9). As in his conception of individual psychotherapy, Rogers views groups as a place where the participant can experience and share feelings in an atmosphere of acceptance, thus permitting further growth. A unique feature of the encounter group is that a collection of strangers find themselves in closer contact with each other than ordinarily would happen in a lifetime of interacting with others at work, at school, with friends, or even within their own families.

One of the very real problems with encounter groups is that anyone can easily organize one, that the organizers or "facilitators" may differ greatly in motives and skills and self-awareness, and that the outcome of a badly run group can be disasterous for individual participants. The possible traumatic effects of encounter groups are minimized by many practitioners (Gibb, 1971; Rogers, 1970), but both common sense and anecdotal reports suggest that the group experience can be detrimental to some participants. With Carl Rogers as the group facilitator, one would expect only beneficial results. When the leader is a graduate student in social psychology trying to work out his own personal problems or satisfy his own unconscious needs, the outcome may well be an increase in the severity of emotional problems. The importance of the group leader is underlined by Rogers's (1970, pp. 47–48) description of himself in this role:

> I listen as carefully, accurately, and sensitively as I am able, to each individual who expresses himself. Whether the utterance is superficial or significant, I *listen*. To me the individual who speaks is worthwhile, worth understanding; consequently *he* is worthwhile for having expressed something....
>
> I...am unquestionably much less interested in the details of his quarrel with his wife, or of his difficulties on the job, or his disagreement with what has just been said, than in the meaning these experiences have for him now and the *feelings* they arouse in him. It is to these meanings and feelings that I try to respond.
>
> I wish very much to make the climate psychologically safe for the individual. I want him to feel from the first that if he risks saying something highly personal, or absurd, or hostile, or cynical, there will be at least one person in the circle who respects him enough to hear him clearly and listen to that statement as an authentic expression of himself.
>
> ...I would like the individual to feel that whatever happens *to* him or *within* him, I will be psychologically very much *with* him in moments of pain or joy, or the combination of the two which is such a frequent mark of growth.

Though it is often suggested in the psychological literature that there is little research on the effectiveness of encounter groups, Gibb (1971) has summarized 106 studies which involve an evaluation of the outcome of such group experiences and which indicate positive changes in sensitivity, the management of feelings, motivation, attitudes about self and others, and interdependence. For example, Rubin (1967) was able to show that sensitivity training not only led to an increase in self-acceptance but also to a decrease in prejudice. Campbell and Dunnette (1968) conclude that industrial managers who participate show behavioral changes, but there is little evidence that such changes lead to improvements in their work.

CURRENT ISSUES IN RESEARCH ON THE SELF-CONCEPT

ANTECEDENTS OF THE
SELF-CONCEPT

Rogers has built an elaborate and detailed picture of the antecedents of both healthy and unhealthy self-structures. The effects of conditional versus unconditional acceptance of the child and the effects of teaching accurate versus inaccurate labels for experience, for example, have been specified. Nevertheless, surprisingly little research has been directed to the task of verifying and extending such propositions.

Seemingly, research and application in this area would gain as much or more from concentration on the developmental aspects of self as from concentration on attempts to bring about alterations in the self-concepts of adults. Historically, Rogers' theory has grown out of psychotherapy, and its implications for developmental psychology have barely begun to be explored.

EFFECTS OF CLIENT-CENTERED PSYCHOTHERAPY
ON BEHAVIOR

One of the major accomplishments of Rogers and his co-workers has been that of exposing all aspects of psychotherapeutic interaction and outcome to the critical eye of research methodology. More than with any other group, the adherents of client-centered psychotherapy have welcomed the presence of recorders and cameras in therapy sessions, behavior measurement before and after therapy, detailed analysis of client-therapist interactions, and the use of control groups in the evaluation of the effectiveness of psychotherapy. Further, such research efforts have yielded the most consistent body of data now available to support the notion that psychotherapy does, in fact, bring about behavior change.

In spite of all this, there is a nagging problem concerning what it is that client-centered therapists have demonstrated. Analyses of the content of therapy sessions reveal significant changes in what clients talk about during the course of psychotherapy, such as decreased mention of symptoms and increased evidence of self-satisfaction from beginning to end of psychotherapy. Ratings are also obtained from therapists as to the client's adjustment or improvement, but in the final analysis these judgments are based primarily on the verbal behavior of the clients. The behavior measures which have been used to compare patients before and after therapy or to compare therapy groups with control groups have depended almost entirely on the verbal responses of the subjects. Whatever the measuring instrument, the focus is on what the client says about the degree to which he is anxious, depressed, self-satisfied, and so forth.

While all of this evidence may well mean that significant behavioral changes are involved, it is equally possible that the findings all represent simple alterations in verbal response patterns. Therapists reinforce certain types of verbalizations; other types are either punished or allowed to extinguish. With relatively bright, relatively verbal, not very maladjusted clients, the rapid learning of a new style of talking about themselves is not terribly surprising. Numerous experimental investigations have shown the ease with which the verbal responses of subjects can be altered by means of selective reinforcement administered by the experimenter. Reinforcement has included murmurs of "mmm-hmm" and "huh-uh" for certain classes of words (Greenspoon, 1955) and agreement or paraphrasing of the subject's statements (Verplanck, 1955). If psychotherapy is simply an extended series of verbal learning sessions, the reason for the comparative ineffectiveness of therapy with relatively dull, relatively nonverbal, severely maladjusted clients is readily apparent. Moreover, using a successful case conducted by Carl Rogers, Truax (in press) was able to show that Rogers uses empathy and acceptance in a highly selective fashion to reinforce particular kinds of verbalization, and that these reinforced verbalizations increase over time while other kinds decrease. Thus, client-centered therapy can be seen as a process of verbal conditioning. Presumably, characteristics such as empathy and acceptance serve to increase the reinforcement value of the therapist. In addition, Harmatz (1967) has shown that a conditioning experience in which positive or negative self-references were reinforced led to the expected changes in the words uttered by subjects and also changes on personality measures including the semantic differential, test anxiety scale, and a hostility scale.

What would be of considerably greater importance than the demonstration of verbal learning by clients is the determination of whether these changed verbalizations are accompanied by or result in other types of behavior change. Since the evidence to date is convincing with respect to changes in self-concept (as traditionally measured) during psychotherapy, future research on the effect of psychotherapy could go on to a somewhat different proposition. If psychotherapy brings about changes in the self-concept, all behavior related to self-structure should be different after therapy than before therapy. Based on some of the research findings reported in this chapter, for example, posttherapy grade-point average should rise, fear of failure should decrease, perceptual defense against threatening stimuli should decrease, greater hostility should be expressed toward an actual frustrating agent, and less hostility should be expressed toward an imaginary frustrating agent. A body of evidence of this sort would be relatively convincing with respect to the effects of psychotherapy on the self-concept. Negative findings, on the other hand, would suggest that the verbal changes which take place in therapy patients are severely limited in generality.

Congruency Between Self-Concept and Experience

One of the major formulations with self-theory has to do with the effects of varying degrees of congruency between an individual's self-concept and his actual experience. Thus, all forms of maladjustment are simply the result of this incongruency. Feelings of anxiety, perceptual distortions, self-deceptions, and even psychoses are all traceable to having developed a self-concept which is inconsistent with the stimuli impinging on the organism. In the research which deals with the self, however, we find that most investigators have relied on a different variable—congruency between self-concept and ideal self-concept. While self-descriptive measures such as the Q-sort have proven to be of considerable use in research, they would not seem to be an adequate operationalization of congruency between self and experience.

The reason for side-stepping this problem in most investigations is an obvious one—how do you operationalize the theoretical constructs? The most convincing solution so far has been a somewhat indirect one; self-reports are contrasted with judgments by experts. For example, Chodorkoff (1954) compared self-concept as measured by the Q-sort with descriptions of the person by clinical psychologists: Presumably the greater the discrepancy between the two measures, the greater the incongruency between self and experience. Though this approach seems closer to the theory than does a self-ideal discrepancy measure, it still appears that a more appropriate set of operations could be devised.

One possibility might be to establish a set of stimulus situations which, normatively at least, evoke certain internal experiences. Examples would be stimuli which evoke hostility, sexual excitement, or feelings of dependency. Those individuals who fail to respond in the normal way, who misperceive the stimuli, and who become anxious and disorganized, should be the ones whose self-concepts were incompatible with their experience in the situation. This sort of approach to the identification of individuals with incongruency between self and experience seems to approximate what is specified in the theory.

The more general problem involved here is the one of dealing scientifically with variables which are internal and unobservable. While we can ignore such variables and hope to build a science around them, we can also seek operations to define them. For example, we know that threatening stimuli evoke tension, but many therapists suggest that when clients are induced to think about that which threatens them, this is actually a step toward reducing the tension. How could such a proposition be investigated? Gendlin and Berlin (1961) gave subjects tape-recorded instructions to do various things followed by a period of silence in which they could carry out certain instructions. When the subjects were instructed to focus inwardly on the meanings of an unpleasant personal problem, there was a *decrease* in tension as measured by galvanic skin response, skin temperature, and heart rate. Thus, the observable consequences of internal events could be investigated.

Operationalizing the kinds of variables long stressed by self-theorists is a major challenge for future research.

SUMMARY

In attempting to conceptualize behavior in terms of a single, unified process, many theorists have utilized the notion of self-concept. Individual differences in the self-concept constitute a dimension which may be studied in the same way as any other personality dimension. The approach of self-theorists is often contrasted with the approach of stimulus-response psychologists, especially with respect to the former's emphasis on the total individual and on the importance of the phenomenal field.

Carl Rogers developed an approach to psychological treatment known as client-centered psychotherapy. The therapist is seen as one who facilitates the natural growth processes of the client by offering acceptance, understanding, and empathy. The personality theory which Rogers formulated grew out of his work in psychotherapy. Self-theory attempts to deal with the total individual as an organized whole rather than with stimulus-response units. Behavior is believed to be a function of the individual's perceptions, and thus the behavioral scientist should attempt to achieve an internal rather than an external frame of reference. Behavior is the goal-directed attempt of the organism to satisfy its needs as experienced, in the field as perceived. The most important part of the phenomenal field is the self. The satisfaction of the need for positive regard depends on other human beings, and the individual can be more influenced by this need than by his actual organic experience. Growing out of this need is the need for positive self-regard. Almost inevitably some lack of congruence occurs between the conditions of worth as defined by the self-concept and the person's experiences with respect to both internal and external events. Experiences contrary to the self-concept are perceived selectively, distorted, and denied to awareness. Such incongruency is defined as maladjustment and leaves the person vulnerable to anxiety, threat, and disorganization. A large enough degree of incongruence between self and experience can lead to a breakdown of defenses, an extreme arousal of anxiety, and a disorganization of the self-structure. Such negative processes may be reversed by receiving unconditional positive regard from another person, leading to an increase in the individual's own unconditional positive self-regard. With threat reduced, there is less need for defense and more possibility for accurate perception and symbolization of experience.

As reasonable as the phenomenological approach may seem, the experimenter cannot avoid the fact that the operations used in research must involve observable stimuli and responses. As a measure of the self-concept and ideal self-concept, Stephenson developed the Q-sort technique. The discrepancy between self and ideal is often used as a measure of self-esteem. In the Chicago Q-sort, 100 statements are sorted by the subject in a forced normal distribution: once to describe self and once to describe ideal self.

Typically, children are raised in such a way as to learn to respond on the basis of the introjected values of parents rather than on the basis of their own subjective experience. Rogers suggests that a better atmosphere is one in which parents respond to unacceptable behavior by (1) accepting the child's feelings concerning the behavior, (2) accepting and loving the child himself, but (3) showing clearly that the behavior cannot be allowed to continue. Research on the antecedents of differences in self-concept has indicated that positiveness of self-concept is related to perceiving one's parents as feeling positively toward oneself. The more different the parents are in their ideal-offspring concepts, the less academically effective is the offspring. A number of situational variables have been found to influence the development of the self-concept including the occurrence of a broken home under certain conditions and the experiencing of several kinds of childhood fears and worries.

In self-theory, maladjustment is defined as the magnitude of the discrepency between self and experience. Various groups of maladjusted individuals have been found to have more negative self-concepts and hence greater self-ideal discrepancy than normals. In addition, a negative self-concept is found to be associated with psycho-physiological symptoms and with fear of failure. Still other findings suggest that a curvilinear relationship exists between self-ideal discrepancy and adjustment. Either a very large discrepancy or an unrealistically low discrepancy may indicate maladjustment. Very low discrepancy has been found to be characteristic of individuals who utilize repressive defense mechanisms, and to be related to such variables as overcontrol and denial.

Inaccuracy in self-perception is related to perceptual defense against threatening stimuli. Similarly, recall of stimuli consistent with the self-concept is better than recall of inconsistent stimuli. For the individual whose self-concept is congruent with his experience, the hostility aroused by frustration is accurately conceptualized and directed appropriately toward the frustrating agent. When aggressive impulses are not admitted into awareness, individuals tend not to verbalize hostility toward the agent of frustration though they express greater hostility toward an imaginary frustrating agent. In responding to conditions of success and failure, those high in self-esteem improve their performance following success while those low in self-esteem show performance decrements following failure. Both groups attribute success to internal causes, while only low self-esteem individuals attribute failure to internal causes.

While the earliest and most general aspects of the self-concept develop in interaction between the child and parental figures, changes can be brought about as a consequence of later interactions. Self-concepts can be made more positive or more negative as a function of the type of evaluation received from others and success or failure. Esteem is enhanced by evidence of competence in handling the environment and by interpersonal success; disruptive life experiences have a negative effect. Fluctuations in mood also bring about changes in the self-concept. Age is another variable frequently found to be related to self-concept, but the specific events that occur at different ages seem to be crucial. Psychotherapy brings about a more positive self-concept and less discrepancy between self and ideal. When compared to individuals in various types of control groups, those receiving psychotherapy show a decrease in self-ideal discrepancy. Psychotherapy with severely disturbed psychotics has less effect on the self-concept than is true with normals and neurotics and can even make the patient worse unless the therapist is understanding, genuine, and accepting. Rogers' current interest is in encounter groups with relatively normal individuals who seem to show a number of positive changes as a function of the group experience.

Research on the antecedents of individual differences in the self-concept lags behind the many intriguing hypotheses generated by self-theorists. Historically, Rogers' theory has grown out of psychotherapy, and its implications for developmental psychology have barely begun to be explored. Research by client-centered therapists has yielded the most consistent body of data now available to support the notion that psychotherapy brings about behavior change. The evidence, however, is almost entirely based on the verbal responses of clients and may simply represent changes in verbal response patterns. What is needed now is evidence that these changed verbalizations are accompanied by other types of change in behavior. A major construct of self-theory involves the degree of congruency between an individual's self-concept and his actual experience. Research operations, however, have used only self-ideal discrepancy or discrepancy between self-ratings and ratings by an expert judge. An approach is needed which more closely approximates the theoretical description of self-experience incongruency. Operationalizing the kinds of unobservable variables stressed by self-theorists is a major challenge for future research.

III

Situational

Determinants

of

Behavior

9

Behavior as a Response

to

Stimulus Conditions

Many of our assumptions about human behavior are based on the general notion that personality characteristics are either genetically determined or learned at a very early age. Our descriptions of others not only place them at some point along dimensions of personality, the descriptions also tend to categorize other individuals with the implication that they always have been, always are, and always will be behaving in a manner appropriate to that category. If someone is said to have a sense of humor, for example, we would guess that he was the class cut-up as a youngster, that he would be equally amusing at his office and on a camping trip, and that he will be as much fun next year as he is this year. This stability, transsituational generality, and resistance to change is ordinarily what we mean by the term "personality." William James (1950, p. 121) described this stability as

> ...the enormous fly-wheel of society, its most precious conservative agent.
> ...Already at the age of twenty-five you see the professional mannerism settling down on the young commercial traveller, on the young doctor, on the young minister, on the young counsellor-at-law. You see the little lines of cleavage running through the character, the tricks of thought, the prejudices, the ways of the "shop," in a word, from which the man can by-and-by no more escape than his coat-sleeves can suddenly fall into a new set of folds. On the whole, it is best he should not escape. It is well for the world that in most of us, by the age of thirty, the character has set like plaster, and will never soften again.

When we conceptualize human behavior in terms of personality dimensions or occupational habits, we gain a simpler and more easily understandable world with which to deal. In fact, our desire for simplicity takes us a step further. Even with widely studied characteristics, the usual tendency is to translate the dimensions into simple categories so that we may speak of authoritarians and equalitarians, high and low need achievers, or those who are bright and dumb, high and low anxious, or high and low in self-ideal discrepancy. With behavior which is encountered less frequently, we not only tend to categorize but we commonly suggest that the characteristic was there even before it was manifested in observable behavior. Thus, there are homosexuals and latent homosexuals, murderers and potential murderers, suicides and those with suicidal tendencies. Though the comparison may be unfair, this identification of groups and the assignment of various characteristics to those in the group would seem to have something in common with stereotyping and prejudice. Isn't it possible that the labels "authoritarian" and "high need achiever" are somewhat analogous to the labels "criminal" and "queer" which, in turn, are somewhat analogous to the labels "kike" and "nigger"? The common factor is the idea that given behavioral characteristics are widely shared within the group and hence that identification of an individual as a member of that group is useful information in predicting his behavior. Most of us would ridicule the idea that identification of an individual as a Jew or as a black would be useful information for predicting his behavior. It is a bit more difficult to accept the idea that lawbreakers and homosexuals constitute artificial groupings of people who are not all alike. Taking this line of reasoning one step further, is it possible that knowledge of an individual's authoritarianism or achievement need is of only limited value?

CHANGING EMPHASIS IN PERSONALITY PSYCHOLOGY

There is something of a nonviolent revolution underway in personality psychology in which the emphasis is swinging away from personality variables and toward situational variables as the determinants of behavior.[1] Some of the reasons for this change of emphasis, the rationale for the stress on situational determinants, and the contrasting implications of the two viewpoints will be explored in the present chapter. The following four chapters contain descriptions of representative research which is compatible with the situational viewpoint; the specific areas are interpersonal attraction, aggression, sexual behavior, and moral behavior.

[1] As with many revolutions, this current interest can be seen as part of a cycle, a return to a much earlier psychological emphasis on the importance of the environment in determining behavior.

DISSATISFACTION WITH PERSONALITY
VARIABLES

The underlying assumption that behavioral characteristics are stable over time and generalizable across situations has led to particular kinds of measurement strategies. Heine (1969) notes that science, in its early stages, tends to involve ideas based on intuition. It is not surprising that theories of personality were first focused on those characteristics that are found "inside" the individual. From this perspective, the ideal measuring device would be one which obtained from inside the individual a limited sample of very special information which could be used to identify his basic personality characteristics. Once these were identified, a great deal would be known about the individual's past experiences, present behavior, and future activities. This type of measurement and its aims are illustrated in Figure 9-1. This general approach

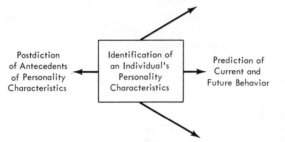

Fig. 9-1 The Identification of an Individual's Personality Characteristics as the Basis of Behavior Postdiction and Prediction.

has been utilized in astrology, palm reading, phrenology, and various other attempts to learn as much as possible about a person's behavior through a simple assessment technique.

As personality psychology developed, not only was the concept of stable personality dimensions borrowed from the culture, but the measurement strategy shown in Figure 9-1 was also followed. Even though conceptual schemes such as astrology are easily rejected on both theoretical and empirical grounds, the more respectable personality constructs were actually designed to serve the same function. That is, a sample of the individual's responses to a series of ink blots or a sample of his responses to a personality inventory was obtained in order to learn as much as possible about his past, present, and future.

In the preceding paragraphs, a series of unflattering parallels have been drawn between personality psychology and activities such as the expression of racial bigotry and reading of astrological charts. There are, of course, crucial differences. Beliefs about a given ethnic group or ideas about the influences of the stars and planets on behavior existed for centuries without the benefit or the challenge of research evidence. A primary strength of a science is in its requirement that supporting evidence be obtained and in the scientist's respect for that evidence even when it contradicts long-standing beliefs. It was on the rocky shoals of empirical studies that personality measures first began to be battered.

DISAPPOINTING RESEARCH EVIDENCE

While personality measurement was attempted in various ways in the early part of this century, the spectacular growth of personality testing occurred in the educational boom following World War II. Psychology was one of the most rapidly growing fields in this period, stimulated in part by a wide-spread interest in behavioral science, in part by the surge of servicemen returning to civilian life supported financially in college by the G.I. Bill, and in part by funds made available through federal research grants and especially through training grants and traineeships in clinical psychology. With the influx of personnel and money, clinical psychology became a booming growth industry, along with its offshoot, personality psychology.

Personality measurement was an integral part of this burgeoning activity, and projective tests constituted the most popular and promising instruments to be used. In classroom and clinic, the intricacies of the Rorschach and the TAT were taught and put into practice. Murray's imaginative dictum that the TAT provided an "x-ray of the psyche" was both encouraging and intellectually exciting. Psychologists could expose people to incomplete sentences, ask them to move cardboard figures around a miniature stage set, require them to draw a house, a tree, and a person, request them to interpret ambiguous sounds, and on the basis of such simple and yet mysterious activities, be able to peer directly into the mind, into the unconscious, and learn enough to diagnose, to describe, and to predict behavior. For a field less than half a century old, that was invigorating technology indeed.

Clinical and personality psychology were, however, academic disciplines in which research was stressed as an integral part of the educational training and as an integral part of future academic and applied activity. The emphasis on research meant that theses, dissertations, convention papers, and scholarly articles would deal in large part with correlational and experimental studies of personality tests. In the decade of research following the end of World War II, it became increasingly clear to a number of psychologists that the actual utility of the various tests was much less than had been hoped.

Julian Rotter was one of the most influential of those who perceived and were concerned about the warning signs in the research data. He was at Ohio State University as Professor of Psychology and Director of the Psychological Clinic from 1946 to 1963 and is now at the University of Connecticut. In his research, in his training of numerous clinical and personality psychologists, and most notably in the publication of *Social Learning and Clinical Psychology* in 1954, Rotter began questioning the traditional wisdom of personality measurement, and found it wanting. He examined the evaluations of the existing measuring instruments and concluded that there were serious deficiencies (Rotter, 1954, p. 334):

> We have in this field not only many hundreds of articles dealing with research investigations of reliability and validity of personality measurement, but also many published clinical studies or clinical evaluations and many years of experience that have not been formally communicated by publication. . . . The very best techniques we have are of doubtful validity for predicting the specific behavior of any person in a particular situation.

That negative reaction was soon expressed by other individuals, and it became clear to many in the field that personality measurement had serious deficiencies as a method for predicting behavior.

BUILDING MORE RELIABLE MEASURING INSTRUMENTS

As Rotter and others noted, projective tests were notoriously weak in reliability, and without reliable measurement, prediction was an impossible goal. One response to this difficulty was the effort to build better tests. This sometimes took the form of attempts to improve projective techniques by constructing reliable versions of familiar tests such as the Holtzman version of the Rorschach (Holtzman, Thorpe, Swartz, and Heron, 1961). More often, personality psychologists turned to objective tests, often in the form of carefully constructed questionnaires with highly respectable reliability coefficients such as the California Psychological Inventory (Gough, 1957). Rotter (1954, p. 334) also criticized personality tests as ". . .attempts to do too much with too little." The personality measures described in the previous five chapters represent efforts to solve the problem by measuring a specific personality dimension by means of a carefully constructed test. For example, rather than a TAT to x-ray the psyche, we have an elaborate scoring system to identify achievement-relevant content in TAT stories. The relative success of these solutions can be seen in the body of work on achievement, anxiety, and the rest.

By the late 1960s, a growing number of psychologists were once again questioning the utility of personality tests. The tenor of the criticism changed, however, and the question was not one of whether better tests should be built, but whether something was seriously wrong with the whole idea. The two types of criticism may be seen as analogous to the political choices of working within the system to effect change (building more reliable and more specific tests) and replacing the system entirely (a scientific revolution in which the very concept of personality dimensions is called into question). We will now examine the latter phenomenon in greater detail.

PERSONALITY VARIABLES VERSUS SITUATIONAL DETERMINANTS OF BEHAVIOR

It may be remembered from Chapter 2 that Harry Stack Sullivan took the position that personality was only a construct. Carson (1969), among others, has extended Sullivan's conceptualizations into current personality research. We observe behavior in social situations and generate the *idea* of personality out of those observations. In a similar vein, Rotter (1954, p. 43) pointed out, "An understanding that the constructs are instruments of the scientist, not entities, allows us to deal freely with a logical and useful set of wholly psychological and scientific constructs." One implication of this realization is that personality variables are only constructs and should be replaced by different constructs if they do not turn out to be useful. George Kelly (1958, p. 40) illustrated the way in which we tend to confuse constructs with observations:

> ...when I say that Professor Lindzey's left shoe is an "introvert," everyone looks at his shoe as if this were something his shoe was responsible for. Or if I say that Professor Cattell's head is "discursive," everyone looks at him, as if the proposition had popped out of his head instead of mine. Don't look at his head! Don't look at that shoe! Look at me; I'm the one who is responsible for the statement. After you figure out what I mean you can look over there to see if you make any sense out of shoes and heads by construing them the way I do. It will not be easy to do this, for it means abandoning one of the most ancient ways of thinking and talking to ourselves.

With respect to broad, general personality variables, it may be necessary to throw out the traditional wisdom of the culture and the traditional conceptual approach in clinical and personality psychology and start afresh from a completely different set of constructs. Peterson (1968) concluded on the basis of numerous and extensive studies in clinical psychology (e.g., Kelly and Fiske, 1951; Little and Schneidman, 1959; Meehl, 1960) that personality tests were largely unsatisfactory. His conclusion was that entirely new approaches must be developed.

THE CONSISTENCY AND SPECIFICITY OF
PERSONALITY VARIABLES

At Stanford, one of Rotter's former students, Walter Mischel, carried the criticism and reevaluation of personality dimensions and personality tests to its logical extreme. In *Personality and Assessment* Mischel (1968), questions the utility of broad personality dimensions which are supposed to reflect consistent behavior across diverse situations. His arguments and the evidence he presents are impressive. He does not, of course, deny individual differences, but he questions how consistent and general these differences may be. Such issues are profoundly important ones in personality psychology. How consistent is behavior across situations and how predictively useful is it to conceptualize behavior as determined by personality variables? With respect to each of these questions, Mischel suggests that the answer is "Not very."

Consistency of Behavior. Before considering the research evidence, it might be helpful to examine the meaning of behavioral consistency across situations and over a span of time. Partly because we know one another only imperfectly and partly because our cultural traditions assume that there is consistency, it is relatively easy to think of others as consistent. A person who is shy must be shy no matter where he is or with whom. A person who is a dishonest politician is just a grown-up version of a dishonest child. A person who is rude to us is likely to be rude to everyone. Such beliefs make for a stable and seemingly predictable world, and most people appear to agree that the world is like that.

Doubts about consistency are most likely to arise when one considers himself or anyone he knows extremely well. Are you the same wherever you are and with whomever you interact? Are you the same at school as at home? Are you the same with close friends as with your parents? Are you the same on a date as in a gym class? Are you the same when you are a customer in a store as when you are working as an employee in a store? Do you behave the same when you are alone as when you are with a group of strangers? If the answer is not "yes" to each question, what becomes of behavioral consistency, not only for you but for those with whom you interact? The surprising thing is that they, too, are different in different situations. No one really knows all the facets of his parents or his children or his friends, and certainly not of those whom he knows only casually. My children have been described as extremely attentive and eager to learn by their teachers, as extremely quiet by distant relatives, as loud-mouthed extraverts by their friends, as exasperating nuisances by their parents on occasion, and all of these descriptions are accurate and yet none really and completely fits either child for anyone who knows them well. From the narrow perspective of an outside observer, others seem consistent because we tend to be with them in a single situation or a limited array of similar situations. If you are many different people depending on where you are and with whom, you can be assured that the rest of us are also many different people.

It is also useful to consider consistency over time with respect to oneself. E. Lowell Kelly (1955, p. 659) suggests that "...because of the need to believe in consistency of one's self from moment to moment and from year to year, we tend to infer an unwarranted degree of consistency in others." But, how consistent are we from moment to moment and year to year? Personally, I can recall an extended series of different people called Donn Byrne who had, for example, different interests, different tastes, different beliefs, and quite different behavioral characteristics. I no longer believe in Santa Claus. I no longer want my mother to tuck me in before I go to sleep. I would no longer attend thirty-two consecutive Saturday matinees in order to see every episode of a Lone Ranger serial. I no longer consider the sexy scenes in movies boring or embarassing. I no longer enjoy building model airplanes or watching the Three Stooges. I no longer have uncertainties as to precisely how girls are constructed anatomically and no longer feel that large corporations would refrain from marketing a profitable product just for considerations of safety or the public welfare. I no longer wonder what I should do vocationally and no longer enjoy riding down the highway with a group of late adolescent males while sipping from a quart bottle of cheap beer. And yet, at various times in my life, I have been each of those people (and many others as well) with those interests and enjoyments and ideas and concerns. The point is not that I have had an acutely fascinating life but that each of us changes from year to year with respect to what we do and, hence, who we are.

In seeking research evidence for consistency over time and across situations, Mischel (1968) concluded that the tests which provide the best evidence for reasonable cross-situational generality and stability are the intellectual measures. Even here, the generality is greatest between similar tests or between a test and a very similar behavior such as a measure of mathematical ability and grades in a mathematical course. With other kinds of trait measures, Mischel summarized a series of investigations indicating the lack of generality of such characteristics as attitudes toward various authority figures (Burwen and Campbell, 1957), moral behavior including cheating, lying, and stealing in various settings (Burton, 1963; Hartshorne and May, 1928; Hartshorne, May and Shuttleworth, 1930), dependency (Sears, 1963), aggressive behavior (Bandura, 1960), intolerance of ambiguity (Kenny and Ginsberg, 1958), rigidity (Pervin, 1960; Wrightsman and Baumeister, 1961), anxiousness (Endler and Hunt, 1966, 1969), and perceptual defense in response to hostile words (Byrne and Holcomb, 1962). Similar results are obtained when investigators seek consistency or stability over time. These studies are more difficult to conduct and hence less frequently done. The evidence that does exist suggests that some variables such as dependency show no stability over time (Kagan and Moss, 1962), while some variables such as need for achievement show a very small degree of consistency (Moss and Kagan, 1961). E. Lowell Kelly (1955) studied a group of adults over a period of twenty years and found a relatively low degree of consistency for personality and attitude variables over that time span. Again, the greatest stability is found for intellectual traits (Bloom, 1964; Witkin, Goodenough, and Karp, 1967).

The implications of these kinds of data have only slowly begun to influence research and thinking in personality psychology. Mischel (1968, p. 37) draws the conclusion ". . . it is evident that the behaviors which are often construed as stable personality trait indicators actually are highly specific and depend on the details of the evoking situations and the response mode employed to measure them."

THE UTILITY OF PERSONALITY VARIABLES AS PREDICTORS OF BEHAVIOR

The majority of the material presented in the last five chapters has dealt with the utility of various personality variables as behavioral predictors. If our major goal is a science which leads to the prediction of behavior, it is here that the final judgments of personality variables must be made. The usefulness of the concept of broad, stable personality variables can be evaluated by asking how useful are our measuring instruments in predicting behavior?

Consider for a moment the type of findings previously discussed. Is there any pattern characterizing the following relationships?

Authoritarianism and Anti-Semitism: r = .53
Need for Achievement and Status of Preferred Occupation: r = .74
Manifest Anxiety and Cornell Medical Index: r = .78

The correlations are substantial ones, and the predictions based on those coefficients would be significantly better than chance. There is, however, something disturbing about these relationships, and it is the fact that each represents the correlation between responses in two very similar situations. That is, scores on a test are correlated with scores on another test. There is nothing wrong with seeking and finding relationships between measuring instruments, but such findings raise two questions.

1. Are two tests correlated because there is a relationship between the two constructs being measured or is the relationship artificial? At several points in the text we have touched on the problem of response sets as potential contaminators of personality tests. When the responses to two different tests are found to be correlated, there is the possibility that the underlying factor responsible for the relationship is a particular response set elicited by both tests. Thus, if a subject tends to answer "true" on a true-false test and if Test A and Test B have not been constructed so as to control for acquiescent response set, a substantial correlation coefficient probably reflects the common response set and perhaps says nothing about a relationship between Construct A and Construct B. At the very least, the relationship would very likely be a much smaller one if response set were eliminated.

From a slightly different perspective, Campbell and Fiske (1959) point out the necessity for examining simultaneously the measurement of several traits by several methods (multitrait-multimethod analysis) so that it is possible to differentiate the variance attributable to the constructs supposedly being measured and the variance determined by the testing instrument itself. For example, if inventory-taking behavior or story-writing behavior or attitude-scale behavior contributed heavily to the scores obtained on a given test, correlations between responses to two similar measures might be erroneously interpreted as a relationship between two traits when it really reflects the similarity of the methods of measurement. Campbell and Fiske (1959, p. 93) indicate that the typical finding reveals a great deal of variance attributed to method, usually more variance than is attributable to trait, which gives "...a rather sorry picture of the validity of the measures of individual differences involved."

2. Other than test-test relationships, how good are personality tests as predictors of behavior? Here we come to the crucial point in the dissatisfaction with personality tests and ultimately with the concept of general personality traits. Mischel (1968, p. 78) suggests:

> ...the phrase "personality coefficient" might be coined to describe the correlation between .20 and .30 which is found persistently when virtually any personality dimension inferred from a questionnaire is related to almost any conceivable external criterion involving responses sampled in a *different* medium—that is, not by another questionnaire.

Even if such relationships are not attributable to response set or to the method by which the constructs are measured, the magnitude of such associations is sufficiently low as to be of little practical utility in predicting behavior.

The general thrust of the argument is clear and suggests three interrelated conclusions:

> The results of research on the correlates of individual differences provide a great many overlapping networks of relations among variables. These associations tend to be of high magnitude chiefly when behaviors are measured by redundant methods, such as questionnaires whose formats and content are similar. On the other hand, when diverse behaviors are sampled by different measures, the association, although often beyond chance, generally tends at best to be of very modest strength (Mischel, 1968, p. 101).

With the possible exception of intelligence, highly generalized behavioral consistencies have not been demonstrated, and the concept of personality traits as broad response predispositions is thus untenable (Mischel, 1968, p. 146).

The real trouble is that (the trait approach) has not worked well enough, and despite the huge volume of research it has stimulated, it seems to lead to a dead end (Vernon, 1964, p. 239).

What are the implications of these conclusions for future research in the field of personality, for the measurement of personality variables, and for our conceptualizations of human behavior both in and out of the research laboratory?

IMPLICATIONS OF THE CRITICISM OF PERSONALITY VARIABLES

RESEARCH ON SITUATIONAL VARIABLES

Both Rotter (1954) and Mischel (1968) suggest social learning theory as a theoretical and empirical alternative to personality trait theory. Although the details of that specific approach will not be examined here, the general point is that behavior is in large part determined by external stimulus conditions and by the individual's past experience with those or similar stimuli. A research emphasis on stimulus determinants is not a new idea in psychology and has, in fact, been the traditional viewpoint in experimental psychology and in social psychology. It is primarily in personality and clinical psychology that the situation has been relegated to a secondary position. The pervasiveness of this orientation is suggested by Mischel (1969, p. 1015):

> When we observe a woman who seems hostile and fiercely independent some of the time but passive, dependent, and feminine on other occasions, our reducing valve usually makes us choose between the two syndromes. . . . She must be a really castrating lady with a façade of passivity—or perhaps she is a warm, passive-dependent woman with a surface defense of aggressiveness. But perhaps nature is bigger than our concepts and it is possible for the lady to be a hostile, fiercely independent, passive, dependent, feminine, aggressive, warm, castrating person all-in-one. Of course which of these she is at any particular moment would not be random and capricious—it would depend on who she is with, when, how, and much, much more. But each of these aspects of her self may be a quite genuine and real aspect of her total being.

Earlier in this chapter, in Figure 9-1, the orientation of the trait approach was depicted as one in which the behavior of the individual is sampled and that information used to predict many other responses in many other situations. A different kind of research orientation and predictive goal is depicted in Figure 9-2. Here, a given behavior is identified as important enough to be predicted and research is designed to identify the stimuli and combinations

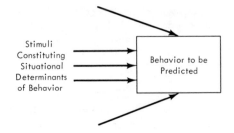

Fig. 9-2 The Prediction of Specific Behavior on the Basis of Situational Determinants.

of stimuli which affect that behavior. In other words, instead of expecting one behavior to provide predictive information about many other behaviors (trait approach), knowledge of the stimulus determinants is expected to provide predictive information about one behavior (situational approach).

The difference in research emphasis can be seen if we select a specific example. Let us say that you are interested in studying rape. As a hostile and illegal interpersonal act, there is the practical goal of preventing the occurrence of this behavior. At a theoretical level, you might be interested in rape as an expression of both sexual and aggressive impulses. If you approached the problem from the traditional viewpoint of personality psychologists, the task would be to identify the trait or traits which characterize rapists. You might begin with a clinical study in which convicted rapists were interviewed so that you could look for common patterns in their attitudes or in their childhood experiences or in various aspects of their interpersonal behavior. You might think of a number of personality variables which would logically be a part of the rapist syndrome such as hostility, psychopathy, and need for sex. You might want to identify and measure the rapist personality as a specific trait and perhaps develop a special test by determining which items on a questionnaire differentiated rapists from nonrapists. If such a personality dimension were established, its study could pursue the various directions discussed in Chapter 3. Finally, the test would be given to large numbers of males, and you could make predictions about the probability of each committing a rape. Those with high scores but no history of rape would be labeled as potential rapists or latent rapists. If this research followed the pattern of most other studies of personality variables, investigators would find moderate to high correlations between the rapist scale and various other personality questionnaires and zero to low correlations between the rapist scale and overt behavioral acts.

From the situational viewpoint, the question would be a different one. Instead of finding out the characteristics of rapists, research would begin with the determination of the conditions under which rape occurs (Menachem, 1971). For example, you might investigate the settings in which rape is most likely to be committed, the time of day, the location within the city, and so forth. It might be useful to find out if there are aspects of the victim such as physical attractiveness, style of clothing, or behavioral cues which are most likely to elicit aggressive sexual responses. You might decide to examine some of the broader societal determinants of rape. Do cross-cultural studies reveal differences in the incidence of rape which are correlated with differences in general attitudes about sexual behavior? Do repressive versus permissive pornography laws have any effect on the likelihood of rape occurring? Does the presence or absence of legalized prostitution have any effect on this behavior? It would be possible to examine the socioeconomic level, educational level, and race of rapist and victim. The latter study might disclose, for example, that the incidence of rape is greatest among less affluent and less well educated citizens. Close examination might even reveal that what is called rape among individuals at one economic level would not be so labeled at another level. The young white man who drinks too much at a fraternity party and is sexually aggressive with his date afterward is not likely to be charged with rape. The young black man who drinks too much at the corner bar and is sexually aggressive with a girl he picks up afterward may very well be charged with rape. Germaine Greer points out that a poor man may apply force to a girl by showing her a knife while a rich man may apply force by telling her she can get out of the sports car and walk home. Which act is more likely to be called "rape"? In any event, a situational orientation toward a behavioral problem tends to lead in quite different directions and to focus attention on quite different variables as compared with an individual differences orientation. Peterson (1968, p. 9) suggests:

> If one of the most effective things we can do for a disturbed or disturbing person is to alter his social environment, then we need to study the social environment systematically as an integral part of the assessment enterprise. . . .
> Designations of disease are useless. No profile of traits will do. No knowledge of dynamics is sufficient.

Most research areas in personality and social psychology tend to emphasize either the trait approach or the situational approach. In the four chapters to follow, we will examine a series of problem areas in which situational variables have been the primary concern. Whether the situational emphasis will prove more fruitful than the trait emphasis can only be answered in the future after a period of considerable research on each.

The Place of Personality Variables
in Situational Research

The way in which personality variables and stimulus variables may interact to determine behavior has been discussed in Chapter 3 as the study of personality dynamics. For those who fear that all interest in individual differences is being discouraged and that various infant traits are being tossed out with the bathwater, it will be a relief to learn that traits remain alive and well in spite of the emphasis on situational determinants. Individuals do learn different responses in a given situation and these differences tend to persist unless the situation is altered. Tests provide an efficient and useful way to get at such differences and hence to utilize them in predicting behavior. Test behavior is seen as a useful and frequently essential source of additional information on which to base predictions of the response in question. The trait model has weaknesses, but it should not be assumed that the whole idea is a useless one.

Existing tests tend to be relatively broad in scope because the aim has been to predict as much as possible from a limited sample of test responses. One possibility is that we should not look for consistency in broad, general traits but in specific behaviors in which we are interested. For example, Wallach and Leggett (1972) found that individual children were consistent over situations in drawing figures of a particular size. Thus, they argue for trans-situational consistency of behavior with respect to what might be called mini-traits. On logical grounds and on the basis of the predictive weaknesses of present tests, it could be argued that future tests need to be less ambitious in the generality of their content and more situationally specific in their inquiry. Take, for example, the following item which is typical of those found in objective personality tests: I like to go to parties. True or False. Surely anyone who has taken such a test and thought more than five seconds about his response can remember a feeling of frustration. One asks oneself, "What kind of parties? A small party with conversation or a mob scene with tightly packed bodies, formal or informal, with alcohol or with tomato juice?" "With whom? Parties with those one likes can be a great deal of fun whereas parties attended as a social duty can be something else again." "How frequently? Occasional parties may be fun; nightly parties might be seen as an inhuman torture." "What alternatives are open? One might prefer parties to a public hanging but prefer attending a Broadway play to attending a party." Turner and Fiske (1968) have shown that subjects frequently refer to a single, sometimes unusual experience, or mentally insert a qualification before selecting an answer to such questions.

It quickly becomes clear that an adequate assessment of one's general reaction to parties would require a great many questions rather than just one and a great deal of specification as to situational details. The resulting tests would be longer and more time-consuming than the present instruments, but their predictive utility should increase as a consequence. There is also the problem that some degree of mystery is lost. If I ask you whether you prefer a tub bath or a shower and then use your reply to predict your political attitudes, your racial views, your sexual habits, and your feelings about tapioca pudding, you might well be impressed with the magical powers of psychologists. If I ask you whether you tend to enjoy going to small informal nonalcoholic parties once a week with a steady date as opposed to attending a movie and then use your reply to predict your response to a party invitation, you might feel that my predictive feat was less than breathtaking. If the latter approach were effective and the former approach a waste of time, perhaps the loss of psychology's mystical aura would be tolerable.

Another aspect of testing is the probable importance of assessing the same characteristic by means of various methods. It might be, for example, that reactions to social situations could best be measured by a series of tasks such as a questionnaire plus a series of TAT stories plus a measure of physiological responses to various social stimuli plus an observation of overt behavior in a standard social setting. One implication of both the emphasis on narrow, specific traits and the use of multimethod assessment is that a lot of effort will be required to predict any given behavior. It seems likely that accurate and precise behavioral prediction will be costly in time and effort.

VIEWING HUMAN BEHAVIOR AS SITUATIONALLY DETERMINED

We have all learned to respond to behavioral differences with some kind of trait theory. What happened in Nazi Germany was a function of authoritarianism. People are on welfare because they are lazy and don't want to work. The man who commits a murder has a defective character. Women have achieved less than men in science because they think differently. Automobile accidents are caused by bad drivers. In addition to its simplicity, viewing the world in terms of inherited and learned traits has some distinct advantages. It is comforting to know that it can't happen to me, because I am not authoritarian or lazy or a potential murderer or a female or a bad driver. Problems can be solved in a straightforward manner by disarming the Germans, forcing the welfare recipients to do an honest day's work, executing the murderer, pampering the little woman with a new dishwasher so she won't have to bother her head over complicated things, and cracking down on careless drivers. The most insidious aspect of all this is that the trait explanation makes it unnecessary to examine any aspect of our political or economic or interpersonal traditions to seek either the problem or the solution. The economic and political and intellectual atmosphere of Germany in the 1930s, the exploitation and dehumanization of various classes of citizens, the lack of interest in designing safe as opposed to stylish and profitable automobiles—all such disturbing questions need not even be raised.

If we alter our focus and seek external as opposed to internal determinants of behavior, we are likely to evaluate many problems in a nontraditional manner. In Chapter 4, we examined authoritarianism from the point of view of the trait approach. The situational determinants of the same kind of behavior are suggested by Erich Maria Remarque (1929) in *All Quiet on the*

Western Front. One of the characters notes that a man who behaved one way as a postman in civilian life acts quite another way when he becomes a drill-sergeant in the army. Some stripes on a uniform and a role of authority can turn the meekest individual into a bullying tyrant.

In *The Greening of America,* Charles Reich (1970) writes of the widely held negative attitudes directed against the average man by intellectuals who ridicule his tastes and prejudices and primitive political beliefs. He suggests that the working class man and white-collar technician were not born without higher capacities and sensibilities but were systematically deprived of them by the Corporate State. Reich (1970, p. 261) views the man-in-the-street authoritarian in a way different from that traditionally expressed by liberal behavioral scientists or left-wing young people:

> The student radical of today is all too likely to call policemen "pigs," to be scornful of "straight" people and "uptight" people, to call right-wingers and George Wallace supporters "fascists," to be harshly critical of his own parents and their contemporaries. In doing this, students are reacting naturally to the anger and violence and lack of understanding directed at them, but they are nevertheless making the same mistake as those who are racial or religious bigots. Look again at a "fascist"—tight lipped, tense, crew cut, correctly dressed, church-going, an American flag on his car window, a hostile eye for communists, youth, and blacks. He has had very little of love, or poetry, or music, or nature, or joy. He has been dominated by fear. He has been condemned to narrow-minded prejudice, to a self-defeating materialism, to a lonely suspicion of his fellow men. He is angry, envious, bitter, self-hating. He ravages his own environment. He has fled all his life from consciousness and responsibility. He is turned against his own nature; in his agony he has recoiled upon himself. He is what the machine left after it had its way.

An *Esquire* reader expressed a related viewpoint in discussing an article about the My Lai massacre in Vietnam and one of the men accused of murdering civilians in that village:

> The point is simply this: There are both "hero" and "monster" in each of us. The same guy who would *save* a child's life under normal circumstances might *take* a child's life under abnormal circumstances.
> If people could take that one lesson in human behavior..., we might be able to solve some of our other problems as well.
> We're all hero-monsters in our relations with each other. With our kids. With our wives. With perfect strangers. It all depends on the circumstances. Maybe if we spent a little more time trying to control these *circumstances,* we might eventually be able to wipe most of the "monster" out of ourselves (Blumer, 1971, p. 22B).

If these general ideas are true or even partially true, the efforts of psychologists would be well spent in determining the relationship between stimulus variables and response variables. That is, we might learn more about the functioning of human beings and come closer to being able to predict and control human behavior by determining stimulus-response laws than by focusing on the individual and the ways in which individuals differ. A way of conceptualizing that kind of research will be outlined in the following section.

PARADIGM RESEARCH: GENERALIZING FROM A BASE RELATIONSHIP

The discussion of research on personality traits was organized in terms of measurement, antecedents, structure, dynamics, and change. What kind of organizational schema can be used in describing situationally oriented research? With the schema to be presented here, it may be helpful to think of it in the more general context of other sciences.

NORMAL SCIENCE

Thomas Kuhn (1970) has provided an intriguing description of the characteristics of science. He proposes that the essential step in science is the acquisition of a paradigm. By the term "paradigm" he means a body of research which is accepted by a group of scientists and which consists of specific procedures, measuring devices, and empirical laws, plus a theoretical superstructure. Without a paradigm, no field can progress. There is only random fact-gathering.

A random search for facts has been summarized by psychoanalyst Leslie Shaffer as embodying the wisdom of an ancient Patagonian proverb: He who collects enough chamberpots will one day come to possess the Holy Grail. Besides the random fact-finding, fields in the preparadigm stage of development are marked by frequent and deep debates over legitimate methods, problems, and standards of solution. As paradigms become established, time and energy are spent in developing them rather than on the question "What should we be doing?" Clearly, the field of personality is either in the preparadigm stage or is suffering from a disillusionment with the trait paradigm and hence seeking an alternative one. And, we are currently spending a considerable amount of time debating about methods, problems, and standards of solution.

Among the necessary components of scientific progress in any field is the reduction of the problem to its simplest components. Isaac Asimov (1971) points out that scientists need something simple to work with as a start.

> That is what we do in the case of the many problems in which physics and chemistry have been successful. Simplified situations are studied in the laboratory and, from these studies, general rules are evolved. With the understanding of those rules clearly in the mind, more and more details can be added, until we find ourselves working with quite complicated systems.

Newton's laws of motion were based on Galileo's experiments with balls sliding down slanting grooves; they ended up sending rockets to the moon. Dalton's atomic theory began with simple experiments involving atom-combinations ("molecules") made up of merely two or three atoms each; it ended up helping chemists to analyze the exact structure of protein molecules made up of thousands of atoms, and to put together brand new molecules that had never existed in nature before.

Put it this way—what we deal with when we look at the universe is a vast panoramic picture of enormous detail. If we try to study it directly, we are lost in complications and can make nothing of it. But suppose we find, or can construct, the artist's initial concept; the few basic lines and curves on which he built the panorama. That can give us our foundation and, if we add to it, little by little, additional items here and there, we can end up understanding large sections of the picture in detail (pp. 20, 22).

A Suggested Model for Conceptualizing Paradigmatic Research in Personality and Social Psychology

If the foregoing propositions are correct, we need to identify specific behavioral phenomena to study, narrow our initial focus to a relatively simple and understandable relationship, and study the very devil out of it in an empirically and theoretically consistent manner. What follows is a model which represents one way of thinking about such research, a way that may prove to be of some utility in the search for psychological paradigms.

Conceptualizing and Establishing a Base Relationship. One starting point in moving from the complexity of everyday experience toward a scientific interest in a phenomenon is the observation of an antecedent-consequent relationship. The relationship may involve a rare occurrence or it may take place only when very special conditions are operating. To the observer, nevertheless, it appears that X results in Y. As was pointed out in Chapter 1, it seems that human beings tend to generalize from such observations. We guess that Xs generally tend to result in Ys. When we move from generalization to attempts at verification of the observation, it is a midway step between the randomness of a preparadigm stage and the systematic concentration of research within a paradigm.

If the antecedent-consequent observation can be verified, it is possible to build on this simple beginning step by treating it as a base relationship. This base, by itself, is the first building block in the paradigm. All of the subsequent activity within the paradigm may be seen as varied approaches to extending a network of increasing generality from the base relationship.

Seeking Generality: Basic and Applied Research. In Figure 9-3 is presented an organizational schema showing the kinds of research which can grow out of a base relationship. These four categories of research will be described briefly.

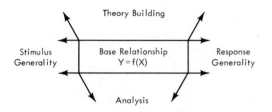

Fig. 9-3 A Schematic Model of Paradigmatic Research in Personality and Social Psychology. (After Byrne, 1971, p. 19.)

The horizontal portion of the figure describes research which is largely applied in orientation. The vertical portion of the figure describes basic research. One advantage of this conceptualization is that basic and applied research are seen as different but not antagonistic activities. That is, both are products of the same base relationship and each has implications for the other.

Analytic Research. One direction which research may take is an analysis of the elements constituting the base relationship. The goal is to isolate and to define more precisely the basic elements which are operating. In psychology, this type of research may be seen as directed toward the *identification of the stimulus* and the *isolation of the response.* Unless one has struggled directly with the problem, it is difficult to appreciate the extent to which even the simplest stimulus or response variables can turn out to be extremely complex. The identification of the basic elements, the separation of those which are relevant from those which are not, and the attaching of appropriate labels to them are each aspects of analytic research.

This concentration of nitpicking attention on the most minute and least obvious aspects of the variables under investigation tends to contribute directly to an increase in the meaningfulness, the precision, and the generality of the total conceptual structure.

Stimulus Generality. In the base relationship, the stimulus is assumed to affect the response on the basis of certain characteristics. When other stimuli are found to affect that same response, information about the essential stimulus components which influence the response is provided. For example, if varying amounts of food and water and electric shock each are able to bring about performance changes in a learning situation, we can assume that these three quite different sets of stimuli share common properties. Hence, it is necessary to postulate a more general concept such as reinforcement to account for their similar effects.

Stimulus generality also involves the establishment of boundary conditions which limit or even alter the base relationship. The investigation of stimulus generality, then, can lead to such applied problems as a specification of conditions which do and do not influence the relationship. Gravitational law may be seen as a pure base relationship. There are conditions under which apparently quite different events take place (for example, the movements of a ping pong ball near an electric fan), and prediction would require knowledge about variables beyond those included in the gravitational formula.

Response Generality. Three somewhat different kinds of research are associated with the question of the generality of the response.

First, the stimulus variable of the base relationship is manipulated and its effects on additional response variables are determined. In part because of the historical relationship with psychometric research, such investigations may be thought of as validational in that the construct validity of the original response measure is determined. As with all such research, one of the primary questions being asked is whether the label applied to the original response measure is a reasonable one in view of its relationship or lack of relationship with other response measures. That is, if one's operations are labelled "y," it is assumed that they will be found to correlate with other operations labelled "y"; if not, the label must be reconsidered.

Second, the generality of the base relationship may be sought in population samples quite different from the one originally used in establishing the relationship. A lawful function which holds only for the college sophomore suggests a quite different level of generality from a relationship which holds across groups different in age, education, and sociometric status. Similarly, cross-cultural replication of a relationship suggests a more general phenomenon than one which is limited to a single culture.

Third, a major source of the unexplained or unpredicted response variance in the base relationship is usually attributed to "individual differences." That is, individuals who differ greatly in genetic characteristics or in a lifetime of learning experiences do not respond uniformly to a given stimulus. It is here that our trait measures may be utilized to good advantage in studies of personality dynamics. When the stimulus-response relationship is found to be different at different levels of a given personality dimension, we have increased accuracy of the prediction of the responses of specific individuals.

Theory Building. Each of the other types of research provides information concerning the generality of the base relationship and about the precise nature of the phenomena under investigation. At each step, also, the experimenter is faced with the necessity of attempting to make conceptual sense out of the growing empirical network. As described in Chapter 1, attempting to answer the questions "Why?" and "How?" leads to generalizations at a higher level of abstraction which are designed to clarify the multitude of individual relationships in terms of the smallest possible set of basic principles.

The usefulness of theoretical formulations is determined by the extent to which they yield hypotheses which can be subjected to empirical test. The research which is directed at theory testing tends to lead the investigator to utilize experimental situations and operations far removed from the original base relationship. Good theories are those which unify a large number of otherwise unrelated findings under a common set of basic principles and which generate new propositions which are open to verification.

In the next four chapters, we will examine paradigms which have been developed in studying the situational determinants of several varieties of human behavior.

SUMMARY

Though it has long been assumed that personality dimensions represent broad, stable characteristics which permit us to predict a wide array of behavior, many individuals in personality psychology are changing their emphasis away from personality variables and toward situational variables as the primary determinants of behavior.

With personality variables, the ideal measuring device would be one which obtained a limited sample of information about the individual, identified his basic personality characteristics, and thus provided postdictive and predictive data about him. The interest in personality tests and testing grew tremendously with the expansion of psychology following World War II. In the years that followed, research provided results which suggested that the utility of the various tests was not as great as was originally hoped. In the mid-1950s, Julian Rotter summarized much of the research literature and concluded that both the reliability and the validity of existing tests were wanting. One reaction to such criticism was the attempt to build more reliable measuring instruments, to emphasize objective over projective tests, and to build tests to measure relatively specific constructs.

By the late 1960s, a more radical criticism of personality tests had gained numerous supporters. Among others, Walter Mischel has questioned the utility of the notion of broad personality dimensions which involve consistent behavior across diverse situations. A large body of research evidence can be interpreted as indicating that personality characteristics, except possibly for intellectual traits, are not very consistent across situations or over time. Also, our present personality tests seem to have their greatest utility in predicting responses to other personality tests; these relationships may be a function of such extraneous factors as response set or the way in which a given variable is measured. More importantly, the relationship between test scores and nontest behaviors tends to be low at best. If, as many believe, the concept of personality traits as broad response predispositions is untenable and if the trait approach leads to a dead end, what are the implications for the field of personality?

One implication is that the research on any given problem is likely to take a quite different form if the investigator is oriented toward situational determinants as opposed to trait determinants of behavior. Within the situational approach, personality variables will not be totally discarded. Rather, they will be designed to measure much more limited and much more situationally specific response tendencies. It also seems likely that our conceptions of behavior and of behavioral problems and their solutions will be greatly altered by the adoption of the situational viewpoint.

Situationally oriented research requires an organizational framework in which to conceptualize it. One approach is to consider Kuhn's concept of a paradigm as an essential step in science. That is, it is necessary to have a body of research which is accepted by a group of scientists and which consists of specific procedures, measuring devices, and empirical laws, plus a theoretical superstructure. A usual starting point in any field is the reduction of a problem to its simplest components. One way to attain such a starting point is to establish a base relationship, an antecedent-consequent relationship between a stimulus dimension and a response dimension. After this initial building-block is established, all subsequent work in a paradigm involves varied approaches to constructing an extended network of increasing generality including both basic and applied research. Analytic research refers to attempts to define more precisely the basic stimulus and response elements which comprise the base relationship. Stimulus generality refers to research in which additional stimulus determinants of the base response are sought and in which the boundary conditions of the base relationship are identified. Response generality refers to research in which the effects of the base stimulus on other response variables are determined, the generality of the base relationship is sought in quite varied population samples, and relevant individual differences are identified. Finally, theory building refers to the construction of generalizations about the components of the base relationship at the highest possible level of abstraction and the experimental testing of hypotheses derived from these generalizations.

10

Interpersonal
Attraction

Other human beings constitute the most pervasive and most important situational stimuli to which we respond. For the most part, it is not our physical surroundings but another person's behavior which makes us happy or sad, secure or insecure, contented or discontented. Others give us love and receive love from us. Others hate us and receive our hate in return. Human beings provide one another with sexual pleasure, ridicule, admiration, fear, and laughter. It is not surprising, in this context, that one area of intense psychological study has involved the determinants of how we feel about one another—interpersonal attraction.

As with any complex behavior, scientific study requires that we narrow our interests to a manageable set of problems in order to gain experimental control of the relevant variables and to permit the possibility of formulating general principles. For a starting point in the study of attraction, we will examine the effects of attitudes.

BACKGROUND: ATTITUDE SIMILARITY
AND ATTRACTION

Informal Observations and
Generalizations

It is a common observation that when two individuals express dissimilar views about the government or about moral standards or even about the quality of a television program, the subsequent interaction grows unpleasant and increasingly negative. The expression of similar views about such topics tends to lead to a pleasant and increasingly positive interaction. Not only may such responses be observed among individuals who are actually interacting, but one of the participants may be physically absent and still elicit positive and negative responses; we respond positively or negatively to a newspaper columnist or a televised political candidate on the basis of our agreement and disagreement with what they say.

Long before the field of psychology came into being, similar observations were made and communicated by a variety of individuals, including philosophers and novelists, in many different parts of the world. In the fourth century before Christ, Aristotle noted that friends tend to have similar attitudes.

Repeated historical instances of the effects of belief or attitudinal differences on behavior may easily be found. For example, the Christians of the fourth century were divided by a multitude of internal disputes about doctrine, including that between the Homoiousians and the Homoousians. The former group believed that the essence or substance of the Son is similar to, but not the same with, that of the Father. The latter group believed that the essence or substance of the Father and the Son is the same. It might seem difficult to get oneself worked up over that distinction, but this difference of opinion led to war, murder, rape, pillage, and torture. With respect to Constantius' edict to enforce the "correct" belief, Gibbon observed:

> The execution of this unjust law, in the provinces of Thrace and Asia Minor, was committed to the zeal of Macedonius; the civil and military powers were directed to obey his commands; and the cruelties exercized by this Semi-Arian tyrant in the support of the *Homoiousian,* exceeded the commission, and disgraced the reign, of Constantius. The sacraments of the church were administered to the reluctant victims, who denied the vocation, and abhorred the principles, of Macedonius. The rites of baptism were conferred on women and children, who, for that purpose, had been torn from the arms of their friends and parents; the mouths of the communicants were held open, by a wooden engine, while the consecrated bread was forced down their throat; the breasts of tender virgins were either burnt with red-hot egg-shells or inhumanly compressed between sharp and heavy boards (Gibbon, 1776, pp. 630–31).

In eighteenth century Ireland, Jonathan Swift satirized the effects of disagreements in politics and religion by discussing one of the major sources of dispute in Lilliput:

> Besides, our Histories of six Thousand Moons make no Mention of any other Regions, than the two great Empires of *Lilliput* and *Blefuscu.* Which two mighty Powers have, as I was going to tell you, been engaged in a most obstinate War for six and thirty Moons past. It began upon the following Occasion. It is allowed on all Hands, that the primitive Way of breaking Eggs before we eat them, was upon the larger End: But his present Majesty's Grandfather, while he was a Boy, going to eat an Egg, and breaking it according to

the ancient Practice, happened to cut one of his Fingers. Whereupon the
Emperor his Father, published an Edict, commanding all his Subjects, upon
great Penalties, to break the smaller End of their Eggs. The People so highly
resented this Law that our Histories tell us, there have been six Rebellions
raised on that Account; wherein one Emperor lost his Life, and another his
Crown. These civil Commotions were constantly fomented by the Monarchs
of Blefuscu; and when they were quelled, the Exiles always fled for Refuge to
that Empire. It is computed, that eleven Thousand Persons have, at several
Times, suffered Death, rather than submit to break their Eggs at the smaller
End. Many hundred large Volumes have been published upon this Controversy: But the Books of the *Big-Endians* have been long forbidden, and the
whole Party rendered incapable by Law of holding Employments (Swift, 1726,
pp. 40–41).

Thus, the idea of a relationship between attitudes and interpersonal reactions is an ancient and frequently expressed one. A very long time passed
however, before there was a formal scientific interest in such phenomena.
Just over one hundred years ago, the first step was taken to operationalize the
variables in question, to conduct systematic observations, and hence to verify
or refute the general notion of a similarity-attraction relationship.

The First Empirical Studies

In 1870 Sir Francis Galton published a report which included data on the
marriage patterns of eminent men and the members of their families. He
concluded that his findings, "establish the existence of a tendency of (like to
like) among intellectual men and women, and make it most probable, that
the marriages of illustrious men with (equivalent) women...are very common" (Galton, 1870, p. 375).

In the subsequent decades, a great many field studies were conducted
which followed Galton's general procedure. It was soon well established that
with respect to attitudes, beliefs, and values, husbands and wives were much
more similar than could be expected by chance (for example, Schuster and
Elderton, 1906; Schooley, 1936; Newcomb and Svehla, 1937). Other investigators selected pairs of friends and found that they, too, showed greater than
chance agreement about numerous topics (for example, Winslow, 1937).
These very consistent findings were extended in additional research such as
that of Terman and Buttenweiser (1935a, b) which indicated that the greater
the similarity between husband and wife, the more successful was their
marriage.

One admittedly unanswered question in all of these studies was the direction of the relationship. That is, does attitude similarity lead to attraction,
friendship, and marriage or does a close personal relationship lead people to
greater and greater agreement? Newcomb (1956, 1961) provided an answer
to this question by measuring the attitudes of a group of transfer students
before they moved to the University of Michigan to live together in co-op

housing; their developing friendship patterns were then studied during the following semester. Attitude similarity was found to be one of the determinants of friendship formation.

Whenever it is possible, scientists turn to the experimental method because there are great advantages when one can isolate, manipulate, and control the variables under investigation. During the 1950s, a number of psychologists became interested in conducting experiments in which attitude similarity was manipulated and attraction was measured (for example, Schachter, 1951; Smith, 1957). In each instance, the evidence consistently indicated that attraction is a positive function of attitude similarity.

At this point, similarity-attraction was a prime candidate for being established as a base relationship in a paradigmatic study of interpersonal attraction.

A BASE RELATIONSHIP

One of the systematic bodies of research on interpersonal attraction has been described in some detail by Byrne (1971). The initial step was to create an experimental situation in which attitude similarity could be easily manipulated, the additional determinants of attraction could be controlled, and attraction responses could be reliably measured (Byrne, 1961).

In order to have a specific set of attitudes and beliefs about which subjects could agree or disagree, a list of twenty-six topics was obtained from a pilot group and built into a twenty-six-item attitude scale which took the following form:

Belief in God (check one)

_____I strongly believe that there is a God.

_____I believe that there is a God.

_____I feel that perhaps there is a God.

_____I feel that perhaps there is no God.

_____I believe that there is no God.

_____I strongly believe that there is no God.

Political Parties (check one)

_____I am a strong supporter of the Democratic party.

_____I prefer the Democratic party.

_____I have a slight preference for the Democratic party.

_____I have a slight preference for the Republican party.

_____I prefer the Republican party.

_____I am a strong supporter of the Republican party.

The subjects who took part in the experiment were given the attitude scale and simply asked to express their opinions on each issue. A few weeks later, each of these subjects was given another copy of this attitude scale, already filled out. They were told that students in another class had responded to the same scale; they were being asked to examine each other's responses supposedly in order to determine how much they could learn about one another from this information alone. The subjects actually received a scale that had been filled in by the experimenter. For half of the subjects, the "stranger" expressed opinions just like those of each subject on all twenty-six items; for the remaining subjects, the stranger had opposite opinions on all twenty-six issues.

The response measure, the Interpersonal Judgment Scale, consisted of rating scales dealing with opinions about and evaluations of the stranger (shown in Figure 10-1). The last two items specifically deal with attraction while the first four deal with various aspects of evaluation.

Your Name:_____

INTERPERSONAL JUDGMENT SCALE

1. Intelligence (check one)
_____I believe that this person is very much above average in intelligence.
_____I believe that this person is above average in intelligence.
_____I believe that this person is slightly above average in intelligence.
_____I believe that this person is average in intelligence.
_____I believe that this person is slightly below average in intelligence.
_____I believe that this person is below average in intelligence.
_____I believe that this person is very much below average in intelligence.

2. Knowledge of Current Events (check one)
_____I believe that this person is very much below average in his (her) knowledge of current events.
_____I believe that this person is below average in his (her) knowledge of current events.
_____I believe that this person is slightly below average in his (her) knowledge of current events.
_____I believe that this person is average in his (her) knowledge of current events.
_____I believe that this person is slightly above average in his (her) knowledge of current events.
_____I believe that this person is above average in his (her) knowledge of current events.
_____I believe that this person is very much above average in his (her) knowledge of current events.

3. Morality (check one)
_____This person impresses me as being extremely moral.
_____This person impresses me as being moral.
_____This person impresses me as being moral to a slight degree.
_____This person impresses me as being neither particularly moral nor particularly immoral.
_____This person impresses me as being immoral to a slight degree.
_____This person impresses me as being immoral.
_____This person impresses me as being extremely immoral.

Fig. 10-1 Interpersonal Judgment Scale.

4. Adjustment (check one)

_____I believe that this person is extremely maladjusted.

_____I believe that this person is maladjusted.

_____I believe that this person is maladjusted to a slight degree.

_____I believe that this person is neither particularly maladjusted nor particularly well adjusted.

_____I believe that this person is well adjusted to a slight degree.

_____I believe that this person is well adjusted.

_____I believe that this person is extremely well adjusted.

5. Personal Feelings (check one)

_____I feel that I would probably like this person very much.

_____I feel that I would probably like this person.

_____I feel that I would probably like this person to a slight degree.

_____I feel that I would probably neither particularly like nor particularly dislike this person.

_____I feel that I would probably dislike this person to a slight degree.

_____I feel that I would probably dislike this person.

_____I feel that I would probably dislike this person very much.

6. Working Together in an Experiment (check one)

_____I believe that I would very much dislike working with this person in an experiment.

_____I believe that I would dislike working with this person in an experiment.

_____I believe that I would dislike working with this person in an experiment to a slight degree.

_____I believe that I would neither particularly dislike nor particularly enjoy working with this person in an experiment.

_____I believe that I would enjoy working with this person in an experiment to a slight degree.

_____I believe that I would enjoy working with this person in an experiment.

_____I believe that I would very much enjoy working with this person in an experiment.

Fig. 10-1 Interpersonal Judgment Scale (Cont.).

The mean responses of the two groups of subjects on each scale are shown in Table 10-1. Attraction could vary from 2 to 14, and the four evaluations from 1 to 7. It may be seen that the subjects responded more positively to a stranger with similar attitudes than to one who held attitudes dissimilar from their own. A similar stranger is better liked, and is evaluated as more intelligent, better informed, more moral, and better adjusted than a dissimilar one.

At this point we really did not know much more about similarity and attraction than did Aristotle or Jonathan Swift. We should note, however, that these observations were carried out in a controlled experiment which may be repeated by anyone who cares to duplicate the procedure. Further, with the variables operationalized and the behavior quantified, it is possible to move on to additional research. The next step was to move from a very limited stimulus manipulation (similarity versus dissimilarity) to a more continuous stimulus dimension.

Table 10-1. Effect of Similar versus Dissimilar Attitudes
on Attraction and Evaluation

Rating Scales	*Stranger with Attitudes Dissimilar to Those of Subject on 26 Issues*	*Stranger with Attitudes Similar to Those of Subject on 26 Issues*
Attraction	4.41	13.00
Intelligence	3.06	5.65
Knowledge of Current Events	2.65	4.65
Morality	3.47	5.76
Adjustment	2.71	6.00

(Data from Byrne, 1961)

In the experiment just described, two extreme points on a stimulus dimension were chosen: twenty-six out of twenty-six similar attitudes versus twenty-six out of twenty-six dissimilar attitudes. One might wonder whether such extreme differences in the stimulus are necessary to bring about differences in attraction; certainly it would be unusual to encounter either type of stranger in real life.

To explore this question, a new experiment was conducted (Byrne, 1962) in which only seven attitude items were used. With this small number of items, it was possible to present the subjects with all possible variations in the relative number of similar and dissimilar attitudes expressed by a stranger. Subjects filled out a seven-item attitude scale. As in the first study, the subjects later were presented with a copy of one of the scales purportedly filled out by a stranger. Subjects were randomly assigned to one of eight possible groups with respect to the relationship between the stranger's attitudes and their own. For one group, the stranger had similar attitudes on all seven topics, for a second group the stranger had similar attitudes on six topics and a dissimilar attitude on one, for a third group the stranger had similar attitudes on five topics and dissimilar attitudes on two, and so forth. In the eighth group the stranger held opinions opposite to those of the subject on all seven topics. Again, after reading through the "stranger's" scale, the subjects were asked to evaluate him on the Interpersonal Judgment Scale.

The results (shown in Table 10-2) indicated that a relationship does exist between the relative number of similar and dissimilar attitudes held by a stranger and attraction toward that stranger; complete similarity or dissimilarity is not necessary to obtain the effect. With this new information, we can say that *degree* of attitude similarity-dissimilarity significantly influences attraction—which incidentally takes us several steps beyond the original informal observations.

With this evidence of a lawful relationship between the attitude stimulus and the attraction response, it should prove useful next to be able to state the function in still more general terms. One investigation (Byrne and Nelson,

Table 10-2. Functional Relationship between Attitude
Similarity-Dissimilarity and Attraction

Experimental Condition	Mean Attraction Response
7 Similar, 0 Dissimilar	12.15
6 Similar, 1 Dissimilar	11.15
5 Similar, 2 Dissimilar	11.43
4 Similar, 3 Dissimilar	9.07
3 Similar, 4 Dissimilar	8.69
2 Similar, 5 Dissimilar	8.47
1 Similar, 6 Dissimilar	7.71
0 Similar, 7 Dissimilar	7.00

(Data from Byrne, 1962)

1965a) was conducted to determine whether the stimulus dimension consisted of *proportion* of similar attitudes, *number* of similar attitudes, or
number of dissimilar attitudes.

Using a series of attitude scales ranging in length from four items to
forty-eight items, the same general procedures were followed as described in
the two previous investigations. Proportion of similar attitudes was found to
be the only variable that exerted a significant effect on attraction. Thus, the
stimulus dimension was identified as proportion of similar attitudes.

Combining data from a series of attraction studies, the investigators then
plotted the relationship as shown in Figure 10-2. A straight-line function was
found to yield the best description of the relationship. The information shown
in Figure 10-2 can be expressed by the formula $Y = 5.44X + 6.62$. That is,
the attraction response (Y) of any subject toward a stranger can be predicted
by multiplying 5.44 times the proportion (X) of attitudes expressed by the
stranger which are similar to those of the subject and adding a constant of
6.62. We have at this point progressed to a relatively precise statement of the
relationship between a stimulus dimension and a response dimension, and
this allows us to make behavioral predictions with greater than chance
accuracy. For reasons that will be clear later in the chapter, attitude similarity
was conceptualized as a special case of the more general concept of reinforcement. Thus, the basic law of attraction states that attraction toward X is a
positive linear function of the proportion of positive reinforcements associated
with X.

One more addition to the base relationship proved necessary. What if some
attitudes have a greater effect on attraction than others? Or, what if information is available about the other person's personality, physical appearance,
race, or whatever? Some of these variables might have a much greater effect
than attitudes and some might have a much smaller effect. Such differences
could be expressed as weighting coefficients; each bit of positive or negative

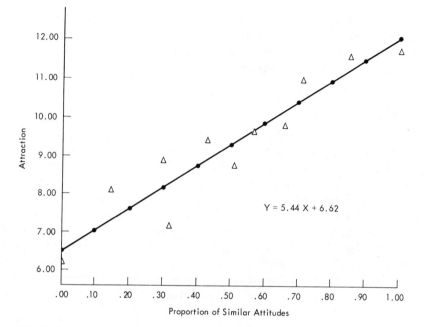

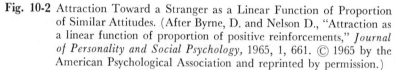

Fig. 10-2 Attraction Toward a Stranger as a Linear Function of Proportion of Similar Attitudes. (After Byrne, D. and Nelson D., "Attraction as a linear function of proportion of positive reinforcements," *Journal of Personality and Social Psychology,* 1965, 1, 661. © 1965 by the American Psychological Association and reprinted by permission.)

information from the stranger would first be multiplied by the appropriate weight and then the weighted proportion of positive reinforcements determined.

ANALYTIC RESEARCH

It was suggested in the previous chapter that analytic research involves the attempt to analyze either the stimulus or the response variable of the base relationship into still more basic elements. The experiment by Byrne and Nelson (1965a) which identified proportion of similar attitudes as the stimulus to which subjects respond is one example of analytic research. The experimental design permitted us to analyze separately the effects of number of similar attitudes, number of dissimilar attitudes, and proportion of similar attitudes; subjects were found to respond to just one of those elements.

A considerable amount of analytic research has been conducted by those interested in attraction and a number of important findings have been made.

It is generally true, however, that such research is rather tedious to explain. It tends to be of interest primarily to those deeply involved in a field and is deadly dull to everyone else. For that reason, only one further example of analytic research will be presented here.

TOPIC IMPORTANCE

It was suggested earlier that some attitudes might have more effect on attraction than others. It seems obvious that we would be more influenced by whether another person agrees with us about God than about western movies, for example. Imagine that there is 50 percent agreement between you and two different strangers. With one, you agree about important issues and disagree about unimportant ones while with the other the reverse is true. You should like the former individual better than the latter. In a similar way, at any level of similarity, a systematic difference between the importance of the agreements and of the disagreements should lead to differences in attraction.

Several experiments have tested that prediction and confirmed it. One of these findings is shown in Table 10-3. Through a procedure that it is not

Table 10-3. Mean Attraction Responses toward Strangers at Two Levels of Attitude Similarity with Different Degrees of Topic Importance for Similar and Dissimilar Items

Proportion of Similar Attitudes	Similar Items Consist of Less Important Topics than Dissimilar Items	Similar Items Consist of More Important Topics than Dissimilar Items
.75	9.30	10.00
.25	5.20	6.90
Total	7.25	8.45

(After Byrne, London, and Griffitt, 1968, p. 303)

necessary to describe here, it is possible to determine the appropriate weighting coefficients in a situation such as this. It was found that the most important topics should be given a weight of 1.5, topics of intermediate importance a weight of 1, and the least important topics a weight of .5.

From this example of analytic research on interpersonal attraction, it may be seen that the concentration of research interest on just one aspect of a seemingly simple stimulus leads to the division of that stimulus into still simpler and more basic components. The outcome of such analysis is a more complete and detailed understanding of the stimulus, a more precise prediction of the response, and more complete control of the behavior under study.

STIMULUS GENERALITY

THE STIMULUS CONTEXT

The point was made that the necessities of experimental research require that we focus our interest on a narrow and quite specific set of operations. In attraction research, for example, the stimulus can be easily manipulated by preparing an attitude scale on which the "stranger" expresses his views very precisely by means of check marks at the appropriate places on a series of items. While operational consistency is a prerequisite to cumulative scientific knowledge, one of the potential pitfalls of research limited to a given set of operations is that one's findings may be partly or even entirely a function of those operations rather than the more general construct which the operations are intended to represent. An analogous problem was discussed with respect to personality tests. Do subjects respond to the content of test questions or do they tend to agree with almost any general statement or do they give the most socially acceptable response? In attraction research, are subjects responding to the content of the stranger's attitudes or to something quite specific about the attitude scale which they have been handed by an experimenter?

Through experimentation, one way to answer that question is to vary the stimulus and determine whether the response remains the same. A series of experiments with attitudes and attraction offer convincing evidence that it is the content of the attitude statements to which subjects respond and not the form in which they are presented. It has been found that the similarity-attraction relationship holds equally well whether attitudes are expressed on a tape recording or in a sound movie (Byrne and Clore, 1966), in a face-to-face interaction with confederates expressing prearranged views (McWhirter and Jecker, 1967), or in a face-to-face interaction with two subjects expressing their genuine opinions (Brewer and Brewer, 1968). These investigations allow us to conclude with some confidence that it is the attitude content which elicits attraction responses.

OTHER KINDS OF SIMILARITY

It turns out that most individuals in a wide variety of situations tend to prefer others who express attitudes, beliefs, and values which correspond to their own. What should we expect when we turn to other characteristics? There is nothing in our formula which demands that similarity always be positively reinforcing or dissimilarity negatively reinforcing. And, in the general folklore of our culture, there is at least some support for the idea that "opposites attract." A number of researchers have proposed that with personality characteristics, there should be a law of complementarity in that dominant people should like submissive ones and vice versa, sadists and masochists should get along well with one another, and winners need to have losers around. Festinger's (1954) social comparison theory, on the other hand, suggests that we should respond most positively to similar others on most characteristics. Research, with a few scattered exceptions, tends to support Festinger and to show that even with nonattitudinal characteristics, similarity is a powerful determinant of attraction. A few examples of these studies will be given.

Personality Similarity. One of the personality variables to be studied in this way was repression-sensitization—a continuum of defense mechanisms varying from denial and avoidance on one extreme to intellectualization and approach on the other. Byrne, Griffitt, and Stefaniak (1967) administered the Repression-Sensitization Scale to a large group of subjects and some weeks later presented them with a scale supposedly filled out by an anonymous stranger. The material which they examined was not the attitudes of another person but his responses of "true" or "false" to such behavioral descriptions as "Once in a while I think of things too bad to talk about" and "At times I feel like picking a fist fight with someone."

It might be expected that attraction here would be most positive toward strangers giving the most socially acceptable responses or the least neurotic responses or toward strangers whose responses were opposite to those of the subject. Instead, there is a very strong and clear similarity effect. Subjects who give repressive responses themselves like repressers best, and sensitizing subjects like strangers who give sensitizing responses.

Ability Similarity. Intelligence, at first glance, would seem to be the kind of characteristic which would not conform to the similarity effect. That is, we all agree that intelligence is good and that the brighter someone is, the better. Or, do we in fact tend to reject the "dummies" (those less bright than ourselves) and also the "smart asses" (those who are brighter than we are)? London (1967) used the Army General Classification Test as a measure of intelligence. He divided a group of Texas undergraduates into the brightest and least bright subgroups on the basis of their scores. Later, test booklets were prepared in which a stranger supposedly answered the test items precisely as the subject had done or unlike the subject had done on two thirds of the items. Again, the task was to make judgments about the stranger.

One question was whether or not the subjects perceived the test responses as indicative of intelligence. It was found that IQ as shown on the stranger's test correlated .75 with the subjects' ratings of that person's intelligence. Even though they were reasonably accurate about the meaning of the stranger's test performance, the subjects' attraction toward the other person was determined by similarity, as may be seen in Table 10-4.

Economic Similarity. It's better to be bright than dumb, and it's also better to be rich than poor. So, those who are rich should be admired and liked. Or,

Table 10-4. Mean Attraction Responses of High- and Low-Intelligence
Subjects Responding to Strangers Who Give Similar or Dissimilar
Responses to the Army General Classification Test

Subject's Intelligence	Proportion of Similar Responses	
	.33	1.00
High	5.50	11.44
Low	6.50	11.00

(After London, 1967, p. 9)

one might guess that envy would operate and cause the economically deprived to hate those who are well off. The rich, of course, would not envy those who are poor and would certainly have no reason to dislike anyone on that basis. Byrne, Clore, and Worchel (1966) found, however, that similarity of economic status operates to determine attraction much as other characteristics do.

Economic level was determined by asking a group of Texas undergraduates to indicate their monthly spending on entertainment, miscellaneous purchases, and clothing. When they were later given similar or dissimilar economic information about strangers, it was found that the attraction of subjects who were either low or high in economic status was most positive toward an economically similar stranger and least positive toward an economically dissimilar stranger. Subjects were also asked to state their relative preference for their own economic standing versus that of the stranger. High economic status was universally preferred. Thus, subjects agreed that it is better to be rich than poor, but attraction is once again found to be greatest toward someone like oneself.

PERSONAL EVALUATIONS

The amount of research on the similarity effect should not be taken to mean that similarity is the only determinant of attraction or even that it is the most powerful determinant of attraction. Similarity is simply one of the variables to which we respond, and it is relatively convenient to manipulate experimentally.

In research conducted so far, attraction has been found to be most affected by personal evaluations. When someone tells you that he likes you or can't stand you, that you are very attractive or unbelievably ugly, that you are really sharp or hopelessly dull, your attraction toward him tends to correspond closely to the positiveness of these evaluations. We like those who like and admire us, and we dislike those who see us in a negative light. There is, of course, nothing surprising about the effect of personal evaluations on attraction. What is surprising, however, is that the effect is a precise and measurable one and that it combines with other effects in a highly predictable manner.

Byrne and Rhamey (1965) presented subjects with the attitudes of a stranger and also with a series of evaluations that the stranger was supposed to have made of the subject. Both variables influenced attraction, and it was found that each evaluation had three times the effect of each attitude item. Using these weights, the usual linear relationship with attraction is once again found. Aronson and Worchel (1966) found it difficult to believe that subjects would respond to both attitude similarity and evaluations, especially if they had actually interacted with the other person. They designed a face-to-face encounter between a subject and a confederate who exchanged attitudes about a series of issues and also wrote a message in which the confederate indicated that he enjoyed working with the subject and found him to be profound, interesting, and well-informed or that he did not enjoy working with him and found him to be shallow, uninteresting, and not well-informed. Though errors in their design and in their statistical analysis obscured the fact, their findings were just like those of Byrne and Rhamey. To demonstrate this conclusively, Byrne and Griffitt (1966b) replicated and extended the Aronson-Worchel design. During a brief interaction, the confederate agreed with the subject on seven attitudinal issues or disagreed with him on all seven issues. Then, when comments were written down and exchanged, the subject received either the positive or negative evaluative message.

The attraction means are shown in Table 10-5. Subjects were found to respond to both variables, with personal evaluations having a greater effect than attitudes.

Table 10-5. Mean Attraction Responses toward Confederate as a Function of Attitude Similarity and Confederate's Evaluation of the Subject

Proportion of Similar Attitudes	Evaluation	
	Negative	Positive
1.00	7.86	12.30
.00	5.62	10.40

(After Byrne and Griffitt, 1966b, p. 295)

PHYSICAL ATTRACTIVENESS

Still another determinant of attraction consists of various physical characteristics to which we have learned to respond in a positive or negative way. Before we even know another person or have the opportunity to learn much about him, our initial response is often a function of such variables as body build, height, weight, hair color, race, clothing style, accent, hair length, and numerous other variables which arouse particular feelings in us. In our culture, physical attractiveness seems to be a positively valued attribute and one which should influence our liking of others, however irrational this reaction may be. There is a clear stereotype that "beautiful is good" (Dion, Berscheid, and Walster, 1972).

A number of investigators (for example, Walster, Aronson, Abrahams, and Rottman, 1966) have reported a relationship between attractiveness and liking. Byrne, London, and Reeves (1968) conducted an experiment in which subjects responded to a stranger whose attitudes were given along with a photograph. The picture was actually one which had been prejudged as being attractive or unattractive by another group of students. It was initially thought that both variables would have an influence on attraction, but that physical attractiveness would have the greatest effect when the stranger was of the opposite sex. Actually, both males and females responded to both attitude similarity and physical attractiveness, regardless of the stranger. It was again possible to determine weighting coefficients and hence treat physical attractiveness as just another source of positive or negative information in the attraction formula. It turns out that an attractive stranger yields a weight of $+4$ and an unattractive one a weight of -4. That is, attractiveness is worth four agreements, and unattractiveness is worth four disagreements.

In research at Kansas State University, Moss (1969) also found a relationship between the attractiveness of females and the attraction of male subjects toward them. In addition, he found that the attractiveness of the subject exerted some influence on this relationship. The least attractive males tended to be most positive toward girls in the middle of the attractiveness dimension. Moss proposed that this response had been learned as a strategy to maximize success in obtaining dates.

RACE

With physical attractiveness, it may be seen that most individuals have learned (1) to identify those characteristics defined as physically attractive by others in the culture and (2) to respond positively to those characteristics and negatively to their opposites. For other observable characteristics, the learning is much more varied. With respect to race, for example, most white Americans have learned to identify those characteristics which categorize others as black, white, or oriental, but there are vast individual differences in learning with respect to responding to such variables as positive, negative, or as irrelevant. Thus, to predict the effect of race on attraction, it is necessary to use a personality variable—prejudice.

In a series of investigations of response by whites to blacks, the Desegregation Scale (Holtzman and Young, 1966) has constituted the measure of antiblack prejudice. It was found that high prejudiced subjects, compared with those low in prejudice, are less attracted to a stranger identified as a Negro (Wong, 1961), and assume that an unknown black college student would express more dissimilar attitudes than would an unknown white student (Byrne and Wong, 1962). When subjects are given both the attitudes and race of a stranger, however, even high prejudiced individuals are positive toward a black stranger when there are a sufficient number of similar attitudes to offset the initial negative feelings (Byrne and Wong, 1962). Low prejudiced subjects tend to ignore race; they respond to both whites and blacks on the basis of attitudes.

From the point of view of our attraction formula, race can be identified as simply another source of information which determines attraction. Specifically, for high prejudiced individuals, the identification of a stranger as black has a weight of −11. It is as if a black stranger disagreed with them on eleven topics even before any conversation could take place.

RESPONSE GENERALITY

SAMPLING OTHER POPULATIONS

Behavioral scientists who are interested in human behavior face a special problem in selecting subjects to study. Ideally, random samples are drawn from the general population, these individuals take part in our experiments, and the resulting findings are used to make inferences about the behavior of the general population. Actually, we are usually forced to utilize a very special and not at all random sample of undergraduate volunteers or students enrolled in introductory psychology courses. Despite the great difficulty in obtaining other kinds of subjects, it is necessary to do so to find out whether a given set of findings applies only to college sophomores or one which is generally applicable to a much broader range of individuals. Research on this aspect of the attraction response has proceeded in several directions.

Other Age Groups. College students constitute a relatively narrow age range, and it is possible that any given research finding (even one as stable as the similarity-attraction relationship) will not be the same for those younger or older than this. Children and adolescents in the elementary, junior high, and high schools in Austin, Texas, were studied by Byrne and Griffitt (1966a) with groups ranging from fourth graders through high school seniors. All of the subjects participated in a standard attraction experiment in which they read an attitude scale supposedly filled out by someone their own age. Attraction toward this stranger was found to be a linear function of proportion of similar attitudes, regardless of the age of the subject.

Griffitt, Nelson, and Littlepage (1972) went in the opposite direction by comparing the responses of Kansas State undergraduates with the responses of retired individuals at the local Golden Age Club. Here, the age range was sixty-two to eighty-seven. A variable of interest in addition to attitude similarity was the reported age of the stranger. Half of the strangers were described as college students and half as retired sixty-five year olds in the community. The results may be seen in Table 10-6. Both the old and young

**Table 10-6. Mean Attraction Responses as a Function
of Age of Subject, Age of Stranger, and Proportion of Similar Attitudes**

| | Proportion of Similar Attitudes | | | |
| | .18 | | .82 | |
Age of Subject	Old Stranger	Young Stranger	Old Stranger	Young Stranger
Young	7.00	8.50	11.50	10.10
Old	7.80	6.90	10.60	10.70

(After Griffitt, Nelson, and Littlepage, 1972, p. 270)

subjects responded strongly to attitude similarity, regardless of the age of the stranger. In addition, a slight effect of the generation gap is evident in responses toward the disagreeing stranger. Both old subjects and young subjects were more negative toward a dissimilar stranger who also differed from themselves in age than toward one who was their own age.

Cross-Cultural Experiments. As general as the attraction findings appear to be in our culture, the search for response generality raises still another question. Since all of the investigations were limited to one culture, "...one never can be certain the discovered relationships are valid for all mankind or whether they are an artifact of some limitation or special circumstance of the culture in which they have been discovered" (Whiting, 1968, p. 964).

The similarity-attraction relationship was examined for cultural specificity by Byrne, Gouaux, Griffitt, Lamberth, Murakawa, Prasad, Prasad, and Ramirez (1971). Subject samples were drawn from Asia and North America from two nations with highly developed economies (Japan and the United States) and from two nations with less developed economies (India and Mexico). The United States sample was further divided into a group of primarily white University of Texas students and a group of University of Hawaii students of Chinese and Japanese descent. All subjects responded to the attitudes of a stranger (translated into the appropriate language) and all of these groups yielded the usual similarity-attraction effect. Actually, the results would have been much more interesting if subjects in one or more of these groups had shown no similarity-attraction effect or even a reverse effect. It would have been possible to speculate about differences in child-rearing practices or cultural values that lead to tolerance for dissimilar views. Instead, these otherwise diverse racial and national groups are found to respond to attitudes in very much the same way.

Individual Differences in the Attraction Response

Another approach to response generality involves the exploration of the effects of personality variables. This kind of research was discussed earlier in this text as the study of personality dynamics. Though it seems obvious that personality variables should play a role in determining the effects of similarity-dissimilarity and, more generally, in influencing interpersonal behavior, there have been a great many hypothesized relationships which turned out to be nonexistent. For example, the usual similarity-attraction relationship has been found *not* to be affected by authoritarianism, dogmatism, repression-sensitization, self-ideal discrepancy, or anxiety. The only real successes in this general endeavor have been with respect to personality variables which are closely related to interpersonal behavior.

The most consistent findings are based on work with the Social Avoidance and Distress (SAD) Scale of Watson and Friend (1969). Items on this measure deal directly with feelings of discomfort and anxiety in social settings such as "I usually feel calm and comfortable at social occasions" and "I try to avoid talking to people unless I know them well." Smith (1970) and also Gouaux, Lamberth, and Friedrich (1972) hypothesized that individuals with high scores on the SAD scale would be strongly motivated to avoid social disapproval and hence they should be more responsive to the similar and dissimilar attitudes of others than would individuals scoring low on the SAD Scale. With subjects at the University of Washington and at Purdue University, this hypothesized interaction was found, as shown in Table 10-7. The

Table 10-7. Mean Attraction Responses of Individuals High and Low on Social Avoidance and Distress Scale toward Strangers Differing in Proportion of Similar Attitudes

SAD Scale Scores	Proportion of Similar Attitudes			
	.08	.17	.83	.92
High	4.37	5.70	9.87	11.39
Low	6.06	8.00	10.95	10.87

(Data from Smith, 1970; and from Gouaux, Lamberth, and Friedrich, 1972)

subjects high in anxiety about social situations are more negative toward disagreeing strangers and more positive toward agreeing strangers than the subjects low in such anxiety. Both groups show the similarity effect, but the degree to which they respond is different.

OTHER RESPONSES INDICATING ATTRACTION

In discussing stimulus generality, the point was made that it was important to distinguish between effects attributable to the specific stimuli used to operationalize attitudes and the more general characteristics theoretically ascribed to those stimuli. In the same way, attraction should not be limited to the specific paper and pencil scales which have been successfully used in much of the research. In other words, what is the construct validity of the response measure? That is, there is no single measure of any kind that constitutes the standard or ideal index of attraction. Rather, many different behaviors can be conceptualized as indicating attraction, and it is important to know the extent to which these behaviors are related to one another and the extent to which they are influenced by the same stimulus variables.

Other Paper and Pencil Measures. The IJS was used in most of this research not because it was believed to be the best of all possible measures of attraction but only because it provided very consistent data and because the use of the same dependent variable in multiple experiments is essential for science to advance. The meaning of the check marks on the two attraction items is enhanced by findings that this particular measure correlates substantially with other paper and pencil attraction measures.

Though some psychologists are critical of the use of paper and pencil response measures, it is obvious that much of human behavior is verbal and that verbal responses can be much richer and more meaningful and more indicative of our inner feelings than can simple overt physical responses. Nevertheless, response generality is extended if it can be shown that these paper and pencil responses are related to other kinds of behavior, especially behavior which is less obvious, less conscious, and less under the deliberate control of the subject. Three examples will be given.

Visual Contact. There are several lines of evidence which suggest that individuals look at objects they like more frequently and for a longer time than at objects they dislike (for example, Argyle, 1967). Efran (1969) sought to determine whether visual contact is a function of attitude similarity.

The subjects were female undergraduates, each of whom read the attitudes of a stranger who was either .00 or 1.00 similar to her. Afterward, there was a brief interaction with a confederate who was introduced as the girl whose attitudes had just been read. The subjects' visual behavior was recorded during this session, and it was found that looking time was greater when the subject believed the stranger was similar on the attitude scale than when the stranger was supposed to be dissimilar.

Proximity. There is research support for the idea that we place ourselves physically closer to those we like than to those we dislike (Duncan, 1969;

Mehrabian, 1968). The question explored by Byrne, Baskett, and Hodges (1971) was whether attitude similarity would affect voluntary proximity in the same way that it affects the making of check marks on a rating scale. In the first of two experiments, subjects were exposed to the attitudes of a similar and a dissimilar stranger followed by an opportunity to join them for a seemingly unrelated part of the procedure. The two strangers were seated apart in a semi-circular row of chairs. Female subjects were found to sit closer to the liked, similar stranger than to the disliked, dissimilar stranger; males made no distinction in their seating preferences.

Other researchers have noted sex differences in seating habits, and have suggested that males in our culture tend to avoid sitting side-by-side with other males; they prefer sitting face-to-face (Sommer, 1959). If so, the row of chairs presented a problem to our male subjects, because there was no way for them to sit across from the stranger they liked. In a second experiment, subjects were again exposed to the attitudes of a similar and a dissimilar stranger, but this time the strangers were seated at a square table, and the two empty seats were such that the subject could sit *across from* either the liked or disliked stranger. Here, males did as hypothesized and sat across from the stranger they liked whereas females showed no preference.

It appears that proximity is related to attraction but that the specific physical arrangement of the situation has quite different effects for males and females.

Compliance with Requests. Baron (1971) reasoned that verbal indicators of attraction would be much more meaningful if they could be shown to be related to an actual expenditure of effort on behalf of the other person. With sixty undergraduate females at the University of South Carolina, a situation was arranged in which each subject interacted with a female confederate who indicated either .00 or 1.00 similarity. There was also an exchange of written comments in which the confederate evaluated the subject either positively or negatively. Attraction was, of course, affected by the confederate's attitudes and evaluations.

The experiment then seemed to be over, the experimenter left the room, and at this point the confederate asked a favor of the subject. One of three requests was made, ranging from easy to difficult. The easiest request was that the subject return a notebook to a girl who lived in the subject's dormitory. The moderate request was that she return a group of books to the library, several blocks away. The most difficult request was that the subject return the books to the library, then check them out in her own name, and keep them several days until the confederate picked them up. As may be seen in Table 10-8, almost everyone was willing to comply with the easy request. With the moderate and difficult requests, though, there was a great difference between the response to the liked and to the disliked confederate. Subjects were much more likely to do a favor for someone they liked.

Table 10-8. Percentage of Subjects Complying with
Confederate's Request in Each Condition

Magnitude of Difficulty of Confederate's Request	*Proportion of Similar Attitudes*	
	.00	*1.00*
Difficult	50%	100%
Moderate	30%	90%
Easy	90%	100%

(Data from Baron, 1971)

THEORY BUILDING

In the study of interpersonal attraction, there are two major theoretical approaches. Cognitive theorists such as Leon Festinger (1957), Fritz Heider (1958), and Theodore Newcomb (1961) have tended to emphasize the homeostatic properties of elements within a closed system and the need for cognitive consistency. Reinforcement theorists such as Albert and Bernice Lott (1960), Arthur Staats (1969), and Gerald Clore and the present author (Byrne, 1971; Byrne and Clore, 1970) have tended to focus on the stimulus and response elements which constitute the attraction process, on the positive and negative properties of the relevant stimuli, and on the effectiveness of borrowing concepts from learning theory and applying them to the attraction situation.

COGNITIVE THEORY OF ATTRACTION

From the viewpoint of cognitive theorists, the most useful way to approach a problem is to focus on what individuals are thinking, on how they try to justify what they do, and on how they strive for self-consistency.

In attraction, the concern is with what is going on inside an individual's head when he communicates with another person. The other person can be regarded positively or negatively; also, the object of their conversation can be regarded positively or negatively. The important aspect of this situation is the balance or symmetry of these three elements—person, other, and object. If the two people like each other and agree about the topic of conversation, the relationship is *balanced,* and there is harmony. If the two people like each other and disagree, there is *imbalance.* Such a situation leads to attempts to restore balance. For example, one individual could persuade the other to change his attitudes, they each could misperceive the other person's attitudes, or they could decide not to like each other any more. If two people dislike one another, there is *nonbalance.* Here, there is a feeling of indifference, and it doesn't matter whether they agree or disagree about a topic.

Research on this theoretical model has included attempts to show that balanced states are more pleasant than imbalanced ones (for example, Price, Harburg, and Newcomb, 1966), that balanced relationships are easier to remember than imbalanced ones (for example, Cottrell, Ingraham, and Monfort, 1971), and various demonstrations of the ways individuals work to change an imbalanced relationship into a balanced one (Byrne and Blaylock, 1963).

REINFORCEMENT THEORY OF ATTRACTION

Byrne and Clore (1970) presented a description of the development of attraction and other evaluative responses. Positive and negative feelings become associated with a person or an object in a process analogous to classical conditioning. The evaluation of that person or object is then positive or negative to the extent that the original feelings were positive or negative. The model is shown in Figure 10-3. The origin of the feelings (or affect) is an uncon-

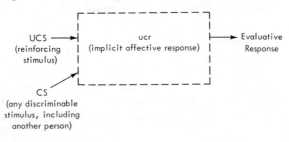

Fig. 10-3 Evaluative Responses as a Function of Association Between Any Discriminable Stimulus (CS = Conditioned Stimulus) and a reinforcing Stimulus (UCS = Unconditioned Stimulus) as Mediated by an Implicit Affective Response (UCR = Unconditioned Response). (After Byrne and Clore, 1970, p. 107.)

ditioned stimulus, one which has reinforcement properties. This stimulus may be a primary reinforcer such as pain or food or a secondary reinforcer such as praise or an attitudinal disagreement. These stimuli arouse positive or negative feelings. If asked to describe his feelings or the stimulus that aroused them, the subject's responses can be categorized on a good-bad, pleasant-unpleasant, like-dislike dimension. Whenever some other stimulus (including a human being) is present at the same time, it can (through a simple conditioning process) come to elicit implicit affective responses. The evaluation of this conditioned stimulus will therefore be a function of the positive-negative qualities of the original unconditioned stimulus.

Most of the basic components of the model have been verified in a series of experiments. Byrne and Clore (1970) were able to show that attitude statements elicit affective responses. People feel good when they agree with what they hear and bad when they disagree. In another experiment, a conditioning procedure was followed in which photographs were projected while similar or dissimilar attitude statements were simultaneously presented on a tape recording. These initially neutral pictures (conditioned stimuli) were thus paired with positive or negative attitude statements (unconditioned stimuli). Afterward, it was found that the picture that had been paired with similar attitudes now elicited positive feelings and the picture paired with dissimilar attitudes now elicited negative feelings.

It appears, then, that the general description of a conditioning process can be verified experimentally. Where else does this theory of attraction lead us? There have been four primary kinds of ideas generated by this model. The first has already been discussed in terms of the formula describing the empirical law of attraction. The linear relationship between attraction and weighted proportion of positive reinforcements was seen to be a useful concept in the study of topic importance, personal evaluations, physical attractiveness, and race. The idea that attraction responses are determined by a combination of positive and negative elements of varying weights is at once a very simple and yet a very powerful conceptual tool. The other three types of propositions generated by the theoretical model are based on the proposed relationships among reinforcing stimuli, affect, and evaluative responses. We will now examine some of the research designed to test each of them.

1. Stimuli with Reinforcing Properties Can Determine Evaluative Responses. If the general idea is correct, the association of any positive or negative reinforcement with another person will lead, respectively, to positive or negative feelings toward that person.

McDonald (1962) conducted an experiment in which subjects made up original stories in response to seven pictures, and each story was rated on a ten-point scale by another student (a confederate) who pushed a button that turned on one of ten lights to indicate how creative the story was. It was hypothesized that variations in the proportion of rewards and punishments (high and low ratings) given by the confederate would exert a significant effect on attraction toward him. Regardless of the merit of a given story, it was given a relatively high or relatively low rating according to a predetermined schedule. After the experimental session, each subject was asked to fill out the IJS with respect to the "other student." McDonald's findings were as predicted, as may be seen in Figure 10-4.

It might be noted that in the McDonald experiment the subject received reinforcement from someone else; his attraction toward that person was a function of the nature of that reinforcement. The model states that simple association is a sufficient condition and that the other person need only be present when reinforcement occurs and not necessarily the source of the reinforcement.

A test of this hypothesis was devised by Griffitt and Guay (1969) using

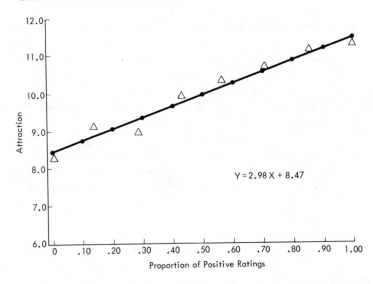

Fig. 10-4 Attraction Toward a Stranger as a Linear Function of Proportion of Positive Ratings of Creativity. (Data from McDonald, 1962.)

McDonald's story-telling procedure. In addition to the person who rated the subject's creativity, there was a second person who simply observed the procedings but provided no positive or negative reinforcement himself. It was found that attraction toward both the rater and the observer was a function of the proportion of positive reinforcements received by the subject. In a subsequent experiment, they found that the evaluation of other stimuli present during the experiment was also affected by the associated reinforcement. That is, as the proportion of positive reinforcements increased, subjects' ratings of the confederate, the experimenter, the apparatus, the pictures, and the experiment itself became more positive.

2..Stimuli That Can Determine Evaluative Responses Elicit Affective Responses and Have Reinforcing Properties. If the model is a valid description of the attraction process, any stimulus which has been shown to determine evaluative responses should be able to elicit affect and should function as a reinforcer in a learning situation.

Probably the most convincing test of the affect hypothesis was provided by Clore and Gormly (1969). When University of Illinois undergraduates were exposed to the attitudes of a confederate, their autonomic activity was recorded. Not only was a similar stranger liked better than a dissimilar one, but skin conductance was different in the two situations. It may be seen in Figure 10-5 that by the time seven attitudes had been expressed, there are clear differences in the physiological responses of the subjects.

Golightly and Byrne (1964) proposed that if the reinforcement interpretation of attitude similarity-dissimilarity is correct, attitude statements could

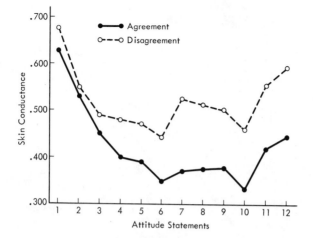

Fig. 10-5 The Effect of Attitudinal Agreement and Disagreement on Skin Conductance Level. (After Clore and Gormly, 1969.)

be used just like any other positive and negative reinforcers to alter behavior in a learning situation. The learning task consisted of a simple discrimination problem. The subjects sat in front of a wooden screen which contained a window for the presentation of stimulus cards. On each trial, a card appeared with a circle and a square on it. Each time, one was large and one small, one black and one white. Each of the eight possible combinations of shape, size, color, and position appeared in random order in each block of eight trials. A stimulus card appeared in the window, the subject chose one of the two figures and said it aloud, and immediately afterward an attitude message was presented through a slit for the subject to read. The discrimination to be learned was small-large. The choice of the correct stimulus figure was followed by the presentation of a card containing a statement agreeing with the subject's viewpoint on one of the topics from the attitude scale; the choice of an incorrect figure was followed by the presentation of a card containing a statement disagreeing with the subject's viewpoint. For example, "There is definitely a God," or "There is no God." "The Democratic Party is best," or "The Republican Party is best." For comparison, another condition involved a more traditional type of reinforcement: feedback messages read RIGHT or WRONG. A control group received no reinforcement. The findings are shown in Figure 10-6. Both the traditional reward-punishment group and the attitude similarity-dissimilarity group performed better than the control group. Thus, in a learning task, performance was significantly influenced by attitude statements. This finding lends strong support to the idea that similar and dissimilar attitudes act as rewards and punishments.

Since attraction-relevant stimuli such as attitudes are found to have reinforcement properties, it follows that various effects familiar to learning theorists should be demonstrable with these stimuli. One example is the effect

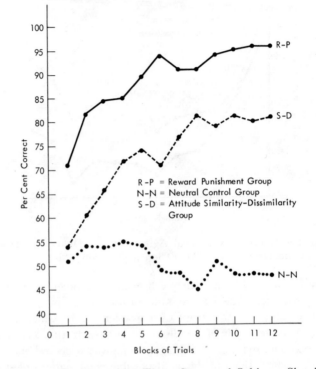

Fig. 10-6 Acquisition Curves for Three Groups of Subjects, Showing Percentage of Correct Responses over Trials as a Function of Traditional Rewards and Punishments, Attitude Statements as Rewards and Punishments, and Neutral Statements as Controls. (After Golightly, C. and Byrne, D., Attitude statements as positive and negative reinforcements, *Science*, 1964, 146, 798. © 1964 by the American Association for the Advancement of Science.)

of reinforcement magnitude. Lamberth and Craig (1970) pointed out that when animals are shifted from large to small magnitude of reward (usually food pellets of different quantities), performance declines, whereas a shift in the opposite direction facilitates performance. Conceptualizing personal evaluations as high reward magnitude and factual statements as low reward magnitude, the experimenters obtained the predicted shift effects. They concluded (Lamberth and Craig, 1970, p. 284), "The fact that they respond to changes in reward magnitude in virtually the exact way that animals respond to changes in the amount of food in a similar situation greatly strengthens the conceptualization of these stimuli as reinforcers."

3. Stimuli that Elicit Affective Responses Have Reinforcing Properties and Can Determine Evaluative Responses. In research based in part on the work of Staats (1968), Stalling (1970) was able to differentiate similarity from affect and to show that only stimuli which elicit affect have reinforcement properties. Subjects at the University of Hawaii rated a large group of adjectives with respect to pleasant-unpleasant (affect) and like me-unlike me (similarity). Even though these two characteristics are highly correlated, it is possible to select adjectives representing the four combinations of like me unpleasant, like me pleasant, unlike me unpleasant, and unlike me pleasant. In a learning task, performance was influenced only by the affect variable and not by the similarity variable.

One of the more intriguing implications of the model is that anything which influences a person's affective state will influence his evaluative responses. An experiment which is important for the theoretical model and also for potential application was conducted by Griffitt (1970). He proposed that the manipulation of negative affect would lead to changes in attraction responses. He selected increased temperature and humidity as the way to arouse negative feelings in part because of observations that the eruption of riots occurs during the "long hot summer." In a special laboratory at Kansas State University, temperature and humidity could be precisely controlled. Subjects were given the attitude scales of either a similar or dissimilar stranger under either normal or uncomfortable temperature conditions. As hypothesized, feelings were quite negative in the hot condition, and attraction was influenced by both attitude similarity and the environmental conditions. This relationship may be seen in Figure 10-7.

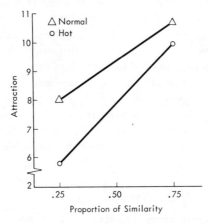

Fig. 10-7 Attraction Toward a Stranger as a Function of Effective Temperature (Normal = 67.5° and Hot = 90.6°) and Proportion of Similar Attitudes. (After Griffitt, W., Environmental effects on interpersonal affective behavior: Ambient effective temperature and attraction, *Journal of Personality and Social Psychology*, 1970, 15, 243. © 1970 by the American Psychological Association and reprinted by permission.)

APPLICATIONS

Once there had been a degree of success in identifying some of the determinants of attraction, it was inevitable that one research interest would be an attempt to manipulate these determinants in order to increase positive and decrease negative interpersonal interactions.

There are many research steps to be taken and many knowledge gaps to be filled in when moving from a highly controlled and deliberately simple experimental situation to an uncontrolled and complex "real life" situation. For example, we know that if two strangers meet in an experimental setting and are told that they agree on twelve out of twelve attitudinal issues, the best prediction is that they will like one another very much. Outside of the laboratory, if we know that two people agree on those same twelve issues and introduce them to one another, could we predict that they will become fast friends? The answer is an easy and perhaps surprising one: *of course not*. Consider some of the reasons why. (1) They may not discuss those twelve issues at all. (2) There are a countless number of possible topics besides those twelve, and we do not know how well they agree about them. (3) Attitudes are only one determinant of attraction, and we do not know about their personality characteristics, abilities, physical attractiveness, race or racial prejudice, affiliative needs, or much else that we obviously must know. (4) External influences such as temperature and recent experiences that may have influenced their current moods are not known. (5) There are undoubtedly other determinants of attraction and friendship which have not yet even been identified by experimenters but which can influence their relationship. The point is not that laws developed in a controlled situation do not apply outside of the laboratory but that we need to know all of the relevant variables operating in each situation to be able to apply our basic principles and make accurate predictions based on those laws. Application, then, must be seen not as an immediate benefit to be derived from each successful experiment but as a goal which requires the hard work of behavioral engineering. With those cautions in mind, where might a concern with application lead us in the study of attraction?

INCREASING INTERPERSONAL HARMONY

One of the more obvious areas of interest is in various two-person situations: friendship, courtship, and marriage. Research on attraction began with an interest in husband-wife similarity and current research continues to identify variables important to marital success in terms of various kinds of similarity or compatibility (for example, Cattell and Nesselroade, 1967). A somewhat intriguing finding is that spouses tend to misperceive the attitudes and values of one another in the direction of greater similarity than actually exists (Byrne and Blaylock, 1963). In addition, the happier the marriage, the greater the misperception (Levinger and Breedlove, 1966). The question must be considered as to whether interpersonal harmony would benefit from *less* open communication about various nonessential issues so that one could comfortably, though incorrectly, assume that one's spouse consistently shares his or her views. Another avenue to the study of marital happiness is to get away from broad attitudinal and personality variables and to concentrate on the specific day to day behaviors which can lead to mutual satisfaction or continuing disagreements and prolonged misery. In one example of this approach, Byrne, Cherry, Lamberth, and Mitchell (1973) determined husband-wife similarity in their responses to a series of erotic stimuli, attitudes about erotica, and the effects of this exposure on subsequent behavior. Compared to random male-female pairs, husbands and wives were similar in such reactions as negative feelings about erotic stimuli, degree of arousal, and feelings about censorship of sexual material.

Research on dating is somewhat different from studies of marriage in that it is possible to manipulate variables experimentally by placing particular couples together in various kinds of dating relationships. Studies of this kind have involved a random pairing of couples followed by assessment of their reaction to one another (Walster, Aronson, Abrahams, and Rottman, 1966) and the actual assignment of specific pairs on the basis of similarity (Byrne, Ervin, and Lamberth, 1970).

In the Byrne, et al. investigation, couples were matched on responses to personality and attitude items as either highly similar or dissimilar and were asked to spend about thirty minutes getting to know one another on a coke date at the student union. Their attraction to one another was found to be a function of both similarity and physical attractiveness, as may be seen in Table 10-9. A follow-up study at the end of the semester indicated that these

Table 10-9. Mean Attraction Responses of Males and Females with Similar or Dissimilar Dates Who Were Relatively Attractive or Unattractive

	Proportion of Similar Responses	
	Low	*High*
Male Subjects		
Attractive Date	10.55	12.00
Unattractive Date	9.89	10.43
Female Subjects		
Attractive Date	11.25	12.71
Unattractive Date	9.50	11.00

(After Byrne, D., Ervin, C. R., and Lamberth, J., Continuity between the experimental study of attraction and "real life" computer dating, *Journal of Personality and Social Psychology,* 1970, 16, 162. © 1970 by the American Psychological Association and reprinted by permission.)

same two variables influenced remembering the date's name correctly, talking to one another after the experiment was over, and desire for future dates.

Influencing Interpersonal Judgments

If evaluative responses such as attraction are a function of association with reinforcing stimuli such as attitudes, it follows that a great many decisions that people make about other people may be influenced by those same variables. If so, this fact could be used either to bring about the desired decisions or to instigate a search for ways to make decisions on more objective bases.

One type of judgment which we would expect to be related to attraction is the decision to vote for a particular candidate for public office. Byrne, Bond, and Diamond (1969) created two imaginary candidates for Congress, one consistently conservative on six issues and the other consistently liberal. Statements attributed to these candidates were read by a large group of Stanford students whose own attitudes on the issues were known. The students fell in all possible combinations of conservative and liberal views on the six issues, and their voting decisions were found to parallel their relative agreement with the two candidates as shown in Table 10-10. If one simply assumed

Table 10-10. Voting Frequencies for Liberal and Conservative Candidates by Subjects with Varying Proportions of Liberal and Conservative Attitudes

Subject Groups Based on Number of Liberal and Conservative Attitudes	Proportion of Similar Attitudes between Subject and		Voting Choice	
	Liberal Candidate	Conservative Candidate	Liberal Candidate	Conservative Candidate
6–0	1.00	.00	14	1
5–1	.83	.17	14	5
4–2	.67	.33	20	6
3–3	.50	.50	12	12
2–4	.33	.67	7	16
1–5	.17	.83	0	14
0–6	.00	1.00	0	13
Total Votes			67	67

(Data from Byrne, Bond, and Diamond, 1969, p. 256)

that an individual would vote for the candidate with whom he had the higher proportion of similar views, the votes of this group would have been predicted with 83 percent accuracy. It should be noted that the prediction in this instance is not like that of political polls in which individuals are asked for whom they will vote and then are predicted to do what they say. Here, voting response is predicted on the basis of an individual's attitudes in relation to the expressed attitudes of the candidate, and these predictions could be made even before the views of the candidate had been publicly presented.

A step farther removed from common sense is the effect of attraction relevant stimuli on judgments about the performance of others. Ideally, these judgments are made on objective bases which have nothing to do with our liking for the person being judged. In actual fact, liking seems to be a crucial variable. For example, Smith, Meadow, and Sisk (1970) had subjects observe the performance of a stranger on a learning task. Though the performance was identical in all cases, those who thought the stranger had similar attitudes judged the performance as better than did those who thought he was dissimilar. Merritt (1970) provided attitude information about prospective teachers to a large number of school principals in New York and found that response to the teachers was strongly affected by principal-teacher similarity. In a similar way applicants for a loan were found to be evaluated on the basis of irrelevant attitudes rather than relevant economic information (Golightly, Huffman, and Byrne, 1972). In all of these instances, the decisions were strongly influenced by attitudes and, as a result, constitute less accurate and less rational decisions about others.

Interpersonal judgments are serious enough when one is being rated on his performance or applying for a job or a loan, but the problem becomes even more acute when the decision takes place in a courtroom and deals with guilt versus innocence or magnitude of punishment. Griffitt and Jackson (in press) presented Kansas State students with one of two versions of a video tape description of a trial involving negligent homicide. The evidence was the same in each version, but attitudinal information was different. The supposed attitudes of the defendant involved belief in God, the American way of life, the relative ability of men and women in coping with stress and in handling the family finances, liking for sports and for dancing, and the desirability of racial integration in schools. None of these opinions, obviously, had anything to do with the facts of the case itself. Nevertheless, the more similar the defendant to the subject, the less likely he was to be found guilty, the shorter the sentence he was given, and the more positively he was rated on a series of dimensions.

An aspect of the environment which might be expected to affect our behavior is overcrowding (Griffitt and Veitch, 1971). Observations of overcrowding in ghetto living conditions plus experimental studies of the disruption caused by overcrowding in animal research led to the prediction that overcrowding results in negative affect and interpersonal dislike. The experimenters manipulated both temperature and population density (number of subjects per square foot) and found that each of these environmental variables influenced attraction toward a stranger as shown in Figure 10-8. In addition, self ratings of feelings were more negative under crowded conditions, and subjects disliked the room and the experiment more when they were overcrowded. Even in a two-person situation (sitting at a library table), when a stranger sits too close, an individual is likely to get up and leave (Felipe and Sommer, 1966) or remain seated but lean away from or otherwise block off

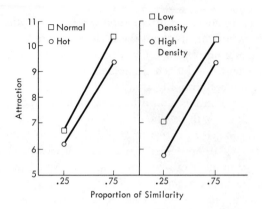

Fig. 10-8 Attraction Toward a Stranger as a Function of Effective Temperature and Proportion of Similar Attitudes (Left Panel) and of Population Density and Proportion of Similar Attitudes (Right Panel). (After Griffitt, W. and Veitch, R., Hot and crowded: Influences of population density and temperature on interpersonal affective behavior. *Journal of Personality and Social Psychology*, 1971, 17, 95. © 1971 by the American Psychological Association and reprinted by permission.)

the intruder (Patterson, Mullens, and Romano, 1971). In an unpublished follow-up study at Purdue, Capadona (1971) found that when a stranger sits too close, the result is a feeling of discomfort, dislike for the stranger, and the disruption of studying. It seems possible that much interpersonal hostility might at least be reduced if attention were focused on some of the external causes of discomfort, including temperature, population density, noise pollution, dirty air, contaminated water, traffic snarls, power failures, malfunctioning appliances, and inaccurate computer billings. If the effects of these and other annoyances combine to influence our feelings and hence our interpersonal responses, it is not surprising that happiness and friendliness are too often replaced by irritation and ill-will.

Beneficial Interpersonal Interactions

The implications of attraction research may be seen in any situation in which human beings must interact. Beyond the fact that it is more pleasant to be in a positive than in a negative interpersonal situation, other behavior is apparently affected by these feelings.

For example, there is reason to believe that learning is benefitted by a positive relationship between student and teacher (Lott, 1969). Also, attempts to persuade others or to change their opinions are enhanced by the expression of similar attitudes (Corrozi and Rosnow, 1968). Perhaps more surprising, children are found to learn better in a group in which the students like one another than in a group in which there is mutual dislike (Lott and Lott, 1966).

Still another specific interpersonal situation is that of a work setting in which one must interact with co-workers. General satisfaction and work performance are very likely a function, at least in part, of interpersonal relationships on the job. Lamberth and Padd (1972) presented students at the University of Oklahoma with an imaginary situation in which they had awakened on a Wednesday morning not feeling very well. They were told that they worked in a two-person office and were given information about their co-worker's background and education plus some attitudinal information about him. When asked to indicate whether they would go to work that day or call in sick, the decisions were found to be a function of similarity to and liking for the co-worker. With respect to actual performance, Nelson and Meadow (1971) have shown that two-person pairs who believe they hold similar attitudes actually do a better job on a simple cooperative task than pairs who believe they are dissimilar.

These kinds of studies are consistent in suggesting that a close attention to maximizing interpersonal attraction would lead to greater happiness and to more effective performance. A bit of social engineering in these areas seems reasonably easy to institute, and the potential rewards seem well worth the effort.

INCREASING TOLERANCE FOR DISSIMILARITY

Much of the research on attraction has served to emphasize the widespread tendency of people to reject and dislike others who are different from themselves. What can we do with this knowledge to make the world a better place in which to live? It has already been suggested that we can accept the basic tendency of preference for similar others and make it operate efficiently by selecting dates, marriage partners, and co-workers on the basis of similar attitudes, values, beliefs, personality characteristics, abilities, and habits. With sufficient knowledge and an efficient computer matching system, it might be possible to sort the world into increasingly homogeneous groups of similar and probably more harmonious individuals. Despite the somewhat chilling *1984* flavor of that suggestion, it actually represents only a more deliberate and effective version of what we all apparently try to do anyway. A quite different and perhaps more difficult approach would be to determine ways to increase our tolerance for dissimilarity, differentness, and disagreement. That is, if there is no realistic reason for us to be threatened by and hostile toward a dissimilar idea or person, it is clearly in our best interests to find ways to neutralize or defuse that threat.

One possibility has been explored by considering why dissimilar attitudes elicit negative affect. We seem to be threatened and are afraid of being incorrect and made to look like fools. It is easy to recall childhood experiences in which errors in our use of words or in our reasoning or in our understanding were met with ridicule by parents, older siblings, classmates, relatives, or teachers. One result of these experiences is to try to be correct, to hold tenaciously to whatever we believe, and to derogate those who differ from us. Hodges and Byrne (1972) proposed that if the dogmatic certainty could be removed from the expressions of attitudes, there would be less implied ridicule and rejection of those who disagree and hence there would be less negative feelings toward anyone expressing his views in that way. For example, one can express a belief in God dogmatically, "There's no doubt in my mind about it. There is a God." Or, the same belief can be expressed in an open minded way, "Personally I do believe there is a God, but this is a purely a matter of belief, rather than of knowledge." The belief is the same, but there is a great difference in the implied acceptance of or tolerance for the opposite belief. In two experiments, it was determined that open-minded disagreement elicited a less negative response than dogmatic disagreement. The results of both are summarized in Table 10-11.

Table 10-11. Mean Attraction Responses toward Open-Mided and Dogmatic Strangers with Similar or Dissimilar Attitudes

	Proportion of Similar Attitudes			
	.17	.25	.75	.83
Open-Minded Stranger	8.16	9.09	11.20	10.23
Dogmatic Stranger	6.85	6.64	9.71	10.88

(Data from Hodges and Byrne, 1972)

The dissimilar dogmatic stranger was disliked whereas the response to the dissimilar open-minded stranger was neutral or mildly positive. Such findings raise the possibility that people could be taught to express their views in such a way as to be less threatening to others and to elicit less negative feelings. If children, for example, could consistently be taught not to express themselves dogmatically, wouldn't their future interpersonal interactions be quite different from those now common to most of us? The different child-rearing practices of authoritarians and equalitarians described in Chapter 4 may turn out to be important determinants of later interpersonal tolerance.

In the Smith, Meadow, and Sisk (1970) study mentioned earlier in this chapter, subjects who had observed a stranger receive electric shock in a learning task were asked to indicate how painful the shock was to the stranger. Those who believed the stranger was similar to themselves rated the shock as more painful than did those who were told the stranger was dissimilar. It may be that our compassion for others decreases as they differ from us. Anecdotally, it appears that such social activities as slavery, atomic bombing, gas chambers, the dropping of napalm, or the massacre of civilian villagers is facilitated by perceiving the victims as different from oneself. What if individuals were induced to take the place of the potential victim and to see the world from his point of view? Clore and Jeffery (1972) have presented a number of examples of the way in which role playing is used to induce a perception of the world from another's perspective—a policeman spending the night in jail, a writer dying his skin black and traveling through the South, a teacher segregating students into "inferior" and "superior" brown-eyed and blue-eyed groups. The experience in each instance was an increase in empathy for others. Physical handicaps tend to elicit negative responses, perhaps in part because they identify the victim as different from the majority (Farina, Sherman, and Allen, 1968; Noonan, Barry, and Davis, 1970). Clore and Jeffery conducted an experiment with University of Illinois undergraduates in which subjects were asked to role-play the part of handicapped individuals. Some of the subjects were instructed to go across the campus in a wheelchair, have a cup of coffee at the student union, and return. This was a rather difficult task involving an uphill sidewalk, two elevator rides, several ramps and doors, and a complicated procedure to obtain coffee. Many subjects found this to be a quite emotional experience and they remarked on the way that others responded to them, glancing out of the corners of their eyes, and sneaking a look at their legs. Other subjects were in either a vicarious role-playing group (following the subjects in the wheelchair as observers) or a control group. Afterwards, all subjects were asked to respond to several questions. Attitudes about the facilities and services for the handicapped were most positive in the role-playing group and least positive in the control group. Attraction toward the experimenter (who was in a wheel chair) was also most positive for the role-playing group and least positive for the control group. A telephone survey taken four months later indicated that both the role-playing and vicarious role-playing groups were more willing to spend money on facilities for the handicapped than were members of the control group. Clore and Jeffery (1972) suggest possibilities concerning the general effects of role-playing opportunities:

> A backlog of varied role experiences would seem to be essential to the development of the ability to change perspective that typifies social maturity. If that is true, then exposing individuals to a wide range of experience (within the range of one's capacity to cope) is clearly a socially desirable end. However, if one listens to poets and novelists, many of the experiences that appear to make men wise and just involve tragedy, hardship, or loss, experiences that one would not quickly wish upon them. These considerations suggest that one is faced with being either safe-but-narrow-minded or wise-but-tortured. But an interesting possibility is that various artificial experiences (including engaging in role playing, seeing films and dramatic productions, and reading literature) enable the individual to know what it is like to be in situations which are

beyond his realm of experience. It is conceivable that the effects of emotional role playing are similar to the beneficial effects that supposedly follow from a liberal education involving exposure to art, literature, drama, and other media for vicarious emotional experience.

SUMMARY

Since other human beings constitute the most pervasive and most important situational stimuli to which we respond, the study of interpersonal attraction has long been of interest to psychologists.

A starting point for attraction research was the observation by philosophers, novelists, and others that similar attitudes are associated with liking and dissimilar attitudes with disliking. Empirical research began over one hundred years ago when Sir Francis Galton studied married couples and noted the tendency for marriage to take place between individuals who were similar in many respects. Correlational studies of spouses, fiances, and friends throughout the next several decades consistently found that such pairs tend to share similar attitudes on a variety of topics. Later, in both field and laboratory investigations, it became clear that attitude similarity is an antecedent of attraction.

In a systematic and integrated series of experiments, Byrne and his coworkers developed a methodology in which the purported attitudes of a stranger are manipulated and the resultant attraction toward that stranger is measured by means of the Interpersonal Judgment Scale. A functional relationship between attitude similarity and attraction was established, and it was found that it is the proportion of similar attitudes to which subjects respond. With attitude statements conceptualized as positive and negative reinforcements, the base relationship can be described as: attraction toward X is a positive linear function of the weighted proportion of positive reinforcements associated with X.

An example of analytic research on this base relationship is provided by the study of topic importance. It was hypothesized that attraction would be more influenced by agreement and disagreement about important than about trivial issues. It would be predicted from the formula describing the base relationship, however, that topic importance is irrelevant when there is complete similarity or complete dissimilarity of attitudes. Topic importance becomes a factor only when there is a systematic difference between the importance of the agreements and the importance of the disagreements.

Research on stimulus generality first examined the way in which attitudes are presented to the subject. It was found that the similarity-attraction effect holds constant whether the attitudes are expressed as check marks on a paper and pencil scale, on a tape recording, in a sound movie, or in a face-to-face interaction. In addition to attitudes, similarity of other characteristics also influences attraction, as shown in studies of personality characteristics, abilities, and economic status. Though similarity seems to be a consistent determinant of attraction, it is neither the sole determinant nor the most powerful one. In research to date, personal evaluations seem to have the greatest effect. One statement evaluating the individual positively or negatively is as powerful as three attitudinal agreements or disagreements, and both types of information combine to determine attraction. Another type of determinant is an observable characteristic to which positive or negative responses have been learned. Physical attractiveness and unattractiveness of both males and females is found to influence the attraction responses of both sexes. Other characteristics (such as race) elicit quite different responses in different people, and it is necessary to measure this general response (as with a measure of racial prejudice) in order to predict its effect on attraction. Compared to low prejudiced individuals, those high in prejudice are less attracted to a stranger identified as a Negro, and assume that a black stranger will disagree with them about many issues. When both racial and attitudinal information are available, it is found that high prejudiced subjects initially respond to blacks as if they had had eleven disagreements; hence, with a sufficient number of similar attitudes, the effects of racial prejudice on attraction can be overcome.

Response generality has been found in that the linear relationship between similarity and attraction established with collegiate subjects is also found outside of the college student population among children and adolescents, elderly persons, and among students in Japan, India, and Mexico. Another aspect of response generality has been the search for individual differences in the attraction response with investigations of personality dynamics. Though a surprising number of personality variables have no effect on the similarity-attraction relationship, measures which are closely related to affiliative needs have been relatively useful in predicting individual differences in attraction. For example, subjects scoring high on the Social Avoidance and Distress Scale are more responsive to attitude similarity-dissimilarity than are those with low scores. Though paper and pencil measures of attraction have been quite useful in research, the generality and/or construct validity of such measures is extended by findings linking attitude similarity and attraction with such responses as visual contact, voluntary proximity, and compliance with requests.

Both cognitive and reinforcement theories have been formulated to account for attraction. Cognitive theories stress the relationship between two individuals and any object about which they communicate. Relationships can be balanced and harmonious, imbalanced and the cause of balance-restoring behavior, or nonbalanced and a matter of indifference. Reinforcement theory has produced a classical conditioning model in which an unconditioned stimulus elicits an implicit affective response which mediates evaluative responses, including attraction. When any originally neutral stimulus is paired with an unconditioned stimulus, this conditioned stimulus comes to elicit the implicit affective response and hence evaluative responses. The basic processes of the model have been demonstrated in that similar and dissimilar attitudes evoke different affective responses; when these attitudes are paired with neutral stimuli, these conditioned stimuli come to elicit the appropriate affective responses. In addition to the linear relationship between weighted proportion of positive reinforcements and evaluative responses, three major hypotheses have been derived from the model and confirmed by subsequent research. (1) Stimuli with reinforcing properties can determine evaluative responses. It has been found that attraction is a function of direct reinforcement received from a stranger and of reinforcement simply associated with a stranger. (2) Stimuli that can determine evaluative responses elicit affective responses and have reinforcing properties. Attitudes are found to influence skin conductance levels. Attitude statements and other determinants of attraction have been shown to function as positive and negative reinforcers in various learning situations. In addition, familiar learning phenomena (for example, the effect of shifts in reward magnitude) have been shown with attraction-relevant stimuli. (3) Stimuli that elicit affective responses have reinforcing properties and can determine evaluative responses. Affect has been shown to be a necessary component of a reinforcing simulus and manipulations of temperature and humidity show how affective differences influence attraction.

The relationship between basic research findings and applications of those findings to social problems is not a simple and automatic one, but a process requiring many intermediate research steps. Attraction research has led to studies of ways to maximize interpersonal harmony with work on marital compatibility and dating. The pervasive effects of attraction on various interpersonal judgments has been shown in studies of voting, performance rating, personnel selection, loan approval, jury decisions, and the effect of overcrowding on evaluative responses. The benefits of positive interpersonal interactions have been shown in studies of the educational process, job performance, and absenteeism. An important applied goal is to discover ways to increase tolerance for dissimilarity, and it is found that tolerance is increased when views are expressed in an open-minded rather than a dogmatic fashion and when an individual is induced to play the role of the dissimilar other.

II

Aggressive Behavior

It is not difficult to demonstrate the pervasiveness of hostility, aggression, and violence in man's affairs. Our history seems all too frequently to be a chronology of war, massacre, political assassination, torture, murder, and other assorted acts of violence which we commit against one another as individuals and in organized groups. From the biblical story of Cain and Abel to last night's televised news, man can be seen as an extraordinarily aggressive animal. We have the unenviable distinction of being the only species that regularly manages to kill its own kind. H. Rap Brown suggested that "Violence is as American as cherry pie." Our nation holds no monopoly on this type of behavior, but we do lead the economically advanced Western nations in the rate at which we murder one another—once every thirty-three minutes in 1970. A notion of our level of violence is provided by observing that Philadelphia with two million citizens has the same number of homicides as England, Scotland, and Wales combined, with fifty-four million citizens. In 1971 in the United States, there was approximately one murder for every twelve thousand people and one case of aggravated assault for every six hundred people.

Even our entertainment is regularly oriented toward aggression. In our movies, novels, plays, and television, we can vicariously participate in any kind of violent act imaginable. A sampling from both real and fictional instances of aggressive behavior will provide a background for the research dealing with such problems.

Aggression can take many forms. The random violence of our cities as perpetrated by the alienated young is captured by Anthony Burgess in *A Clockwork Orange*. In one scene Alex and his friends accost an old man coming home from the library and begin to rip up his books:

> The starry prof type began to creech: 'But those are not mine, those are the property of the municipality, this is sheer wantonness and vandal work,' or some such slovos...
> Pete held his rookers and Georgie sort of hooked his rot wide open for him and Dim yanked out his fake zoobies, upper and lower. He threw these down on the pavement and then I treated them to the old boot-crush, though they were hard bastards like, being made of some new horrorshow plastic stuff. The old veck began to make sort of chumbling shooms—'wuf waf wof'—so Georgie let go of holding his goobers apart and just let him have one in the toothless rot with his ringy fist, and that made the old veck start moaning a lot then, then out comes the blood, my brothers, real beautiful (Burgess, 1962, pp. 8–9).

The opposite side of urban violence is that perpetrated by the established authorities. In a nonfictional account of one of the occurrences in the Detroit riot of 1967, John Hersey wrote in *The Algiers Motel Incident* of the interaction between the police and some innocent black male and white female suspects:

> "They started butt-stroking us on the back and shoulder blade..." Robert Green told Eggleton. "They were trying to make us say that we did know who was shooting in the building...And one of the police officers said, 'I'm gonna kill you all.' Then he turned to the two white girls, and he said, 'We have two nigger lovers here.'...So he started hitting...with a weapon; this was with a shotgun. Butt of his shotgun...He started going up and down the line hitting. One police officer pulled out his blackjack. He beat one colored guy down to the floor. Then beat him back up...
> "And there was another officer there," Michael testified on a different occasion, "he was going up and down the line beating everybody and asking where was the pistol at that was shooting at him. So everybody kept saying they didn't know nothing about no shooting and hadn't seen no shooting and hadn't seen no pistol...They was beating us, and then while our hands was on the wall, they would come by and hit us on our fingers and everything and kick us and hit us in our head..." (Hersey, 1968, pp. 264–65).

The war in Vietnam has furnished enough scenes of aggressive horror of every description to fill many volumes. North and South Vietnamese, army and guerrillas, Americans and French each contributed their own brand of aggression to the tragic story. Robin Moore in *The Country Team*, a fictionalized version of the war, describes an incident when the insurgents take a village and are challenged by an American missionary:

Two guerrillas gave the Reverend Athol sharp jabs behind the knees with pointed stakes. He collapsed with a stifled cry...

The one-eyed, one-eared guerrilla came forward. Zgret handed Mung a thin, sharpened bamboo stake. A collar of slivers had been sliced into the bamboo shaft around the base of the point. As the reverend tried to regain his feet in spite of wounded tendons and muscles behind his knees, Mung made a small circle with the thumb and forefinger of his left hand and holding both hands high slid the pointed stake through the circle. When it was all the way through, he pulled back on the stake and the slivers became barbs, catching on Mung's fingers, tearing at them as he tried to pull the stake back through the looped fingers.

The people, suspecting what was to come, groaned in horror. Zgret and two other guerrillas dragged the bloody pants and underpants off the missionary, who prayed aloud, alone. His people now were too terrified of the consequences to join in.

The Reverend Athol's buttocks were turned up, and suddenly his prayers turned to involuntary high-pitched screams as Mung forced the bamboo stake into the missionary. The villagers tried to turn away from the brutal spectacle —an ancient torture used throughout Southeast Asia—but were roughly forced back by the MFF guerrillas (Moore, 1967, p. 228).

Aggression need not be personal. The obscene technological efficiency of the Nazi program for murdering the Jews who were under their jurisdiction is presented well by Richard Condon in *An Infinity of Mirrors:*

Strass had organized the big razzias, the biggest raid of his career, to be handled entirely by the French police, under his supervision. It was a model plan and he was proud of it. Drayst had told him that it was a little master-piece. Twenty-two thousand Jews, one-fifth of the number in Paris, were to be delivered for extermination to the designated Paris transit camps. They had been divided proportionally by arrondissement so that in the future they could be transplanted geographically. Berlin wanted three trains a week, thirteen a month, each carrying one thousand Jews from Paris to Poland. It was a terrible problem to get enough rolling stock, because of the bombings and sabotage. For each shipment he needed ten boxcars or cattle trucks into which one hundred and twenty transplantees could be packed for the sixty-hour journey (the trip usually killed eighteen to twenty-one per car en route) (Condon, 1964, p. 230).

When we turn from these scenes of aggression, both real and fictional, and consider the possibility of psychological research, it is obvious that there must be some change in the focus of interest. Laboratory manipulations cannot involve beating, torture, or murder. If aggression is defined as "...*any be-havior directed toward the goal of harming or injuring another human being"* (Baron, Byrne, and Griffitt, in press), it is possible to create laboratory situa-tions in which mild forms of aggressive behavior could ethically be investi-gated. It is assumed that detailed knowledge of such aggression can be generalized to the much more extreme versions which occur outside of the laboratory.

A BASE RELATIONSHIP

Though there are a number of antecedents of aggression, as will be described in the following section, it seems that the most reliable instigator is a physical attack by another person (Buss, 1961). When you are attacked, you tend to aggress in a counterattack. This seems to be an automatic, almost involuntary response; it can even lead us to aggress against inanimate objects such as doors and hammers when they cause us pain. It is interesting to note that an isolated animal given shock will attempt to escape from the situation. When an animal is given shock in the presence of a second animal, the two will attack one another in whatever manner is usual for their species (Ulrich, 1966; Ulrich and Azrin, 1962). Thus, both anecdotal evidence and animal research would lead us to predict that the administration of pain would induce interpersonal aggression.

An experimental situation devised by Stuart Taylor and his colleagues (Gaebelein and Taylor, 1971; Taylor, 1967, 1970; Taylor and Epstein, 1967) provides a useful starting point for this research. Subjects are presented with a situation in which they believe they are competing with another subject on a reaction time task. On each trial, the slower of the two players receives an electric shock from the other, and the one giving the shock determines how strong it will be. Actually, there is no opponent and the task is rigged so that the subject will be the loser on a predetermined number of the trials. As these trials progress, the subject receives an increasingly strong shock from the opponent. There are five intensities of shock for the subject to use when it is his turn to respond. The measure of aggression is the magnitude of the shock setting the subject selects when he administers shock to the opponent.

Taylor and Pisano (1971) used this general procedure in testing the effects of two kinds of frustration on aggression. To establish the meaning of the shock to the subject, he was given several preliminary shocks of different intensities. These continued until they reached an intensity at which the subject said it was definitely unpleasant and beyond which he did not wish to feel any stronger shocks. This level was designated as #5; the other four levels were weaker than this, set at various percentages of level #5 strength. In the task itself, the subject received a series of shocks beginning at the #1 level and gradually increasing to #5.

Though frustration had no effect on the subject's aggression, there was a clear effect for the level of shock received from the opponent. As the intensity increased, the subject set higher and higher shock levels in response. The relationship between shock received and shock returned is shown in Figure 11-1.

The authors concluded that aggression research might do well to concentrate on the effects of attack and intended attack on aggressive behavior. This relationship constitutes one possible starting point for the study of aggres-

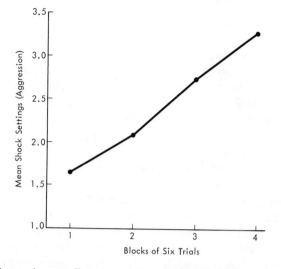

Fig. 11-1 Aggression as a Function of Physical Attack. As subjects are exposed to stronger and stronger shocks from an opponent, they respond with increasingly strong counterattacks against him. (Data from Taylor and Pisano, 1971. Figure adapted from Baron, Byrne, and Griffitt, in press.)

sion. It should be noted that in almost all of the research to be described in this chapter, the subjects are verbally or physically attacked by someone in order to instigate an aggressive response.

ANALYTIC RESEARCH

Though aggression clearly occurs in response to attack, the intent of the other person is an important determinant of our response to him. We may not like the pain caused by the dentist when he fills a tooth, but we generally do not strike him each time the drill touches a nerve ending. Actually, a much less intense pain that is administered by someone with harmful intent can result in an overtly aggressive response. Maselli and Altrocchi (1969) have suggested that one's attributions concerning another person's intent is of major importance in controlling aggression.

Using Taylor's procedure, Greenwell and Dengerink (1971) devised a clever way to separate the actual physical attack from the perceived intent of the attacker. In addition to the shock received from the opponent in the interaction task, subjects were given visual feedback on each trial which supposedly indicated the intensity of the shock. It was assumed that the information provided by the visual feedback would constitute evidence of the opponent's intention to harm the subject. If intent is a potent determinant of aggression, the subject's responses should be a function of the information rather than a function of the actual physical pain caused by the shock.

The subjects were male undergraduates at Washington State University. The visual information consisted of a series of red lights numbered one through five just like the shock intensity settings. Three experimental conditions were created. In the Information-Pain condition, both the shock intensities received from the opponent and the information conveyed by the lights were increased from trial to trial. In this condition, the information was accurate, and the subjects were expected to respond to increased attack with increased aggression as in the Taylor and Pisano experiment. In the Information condition, the lights indicated increasingly strong shock across trials, but the actual shocks remained constant at the #3 level. If subjects responded simply to pain, they should show no increase in aggression across trials. If, however, the opponent's intent is the determining factor, subject's aggression should increase as the light values increase. In the Pain condition, the actual shocks increased across trials while the light setting remained constant at #3. Again, it would be determined whether subjects responded to the physical pain or to the information provided by the lights.

The subjects' responses in each condition are shown in Figure 11-2. It may

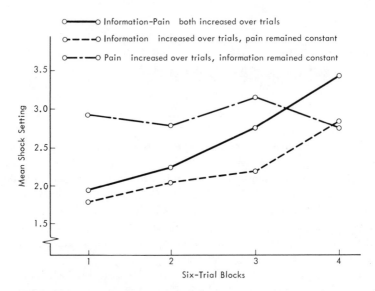

Fig. 11-2 Aggression as a Function of Physical Attack versus Information of the Opponent's Intent. If the information indicates stronger shocks, subjects respond with increasingly strong counterattacks even though the level of physical attack remains constant. If the information indicates a constant level, the subjects do not show an increase in level of counterattack even though they are exposed to stronger and stronger shocks. (Adapted from Greenwell and Dengerink, 1971.)

be seen that when information and pain were discrepant, the subjects responded to the information of intent provided by the lights rather than to the physical pain caused by the electric shock. Though it was possible that the subjects were unable to discriminate the various levels of shock and had to rely on the lights, a separate experiment indicated that subjects could distinguish the five levels of shock quite well.

It was concluded that while attack is an important determinant of aggression, the actual pain delivered in the attack is of less importance than the perceived intent of the attacker. The authors suggested that, "...when more than one source of information about attack is available and when these are discrepant, human *S*s will attend primarily to the labeled or communicated intent of an opponent rather than to the intensity of the pain they experience" (Greenwell and Dengerink, 1971). In other words, it's not what you do to me so much as what you mean to do to me. There are probably limits to this generalization, of course. If the pain were great enough, it might lead to aggression regardless of good intentions.

STIMULUS GENERALITY

Beyond the apparent effectiveness of physical attack and the perception of intent to attack, what other antecedent conditions have been found to elicit aggressive responses?

FRUSTRATION

The most widely known and most generally accepted notion for some decades has been the frustration-aggression hypothesis proposed by Dollard, Doob, Miller, Mowrer, and Sears (1939). This proposition states that when a behavior that is directed toward a goal is blocked, there is arousal of a motive to injure whatever or whoever was responsible for the frustration. Shortly after the original presentation of this idea, Miller (1941) softened the hypothesis by saying that frustration leads to various forms of behavior, including aggression. For example, frustration may lead to withdrawal or depression or to constructive efforts to overcome it. Similarly, it can be argued that some extremely aggressive acts seem to occur without any preceding frustration. An executioner may electrocute a convicted murderer without having experienced any interference with a goal-directed activity. It seems, then, that frustration does not always lead to aggression and that aggression cannot always be attributed to frustration.

A more current version of the frustration-aggression hypothesis has been proposed by Berkowitz (1969), who conceptualizes frustration as one of the multiple determinants of aggression. Specifically, it is suggested that a frustrating event will increase the probability of aggressive behavior. Much of the

relevant research has used an experimental procedure, the "aggression machine" developed by Buss (1961). Essentially, the subject is told that he and
another individual (actually a confederate) will interact in a study involving
the effect of punishment on learning. By means of a rigged drawing, the
subject is assigned the role of teacher, and other person that of the learner.
The learning task is pre-arranged so that some responses are correct and
others incorrect. The subject is supposed to respond to correct responses by
giving a simple signal and to incorrect ones by administering an electric
shock. The latter response is the measure of aggression in that the subject
chooses to push one of a series of buttons indicating different intensities of
shock. In addition, a second aggression measure is the duration of the administered shock—how long the subject presses the button. No shock is actually delivered to the confederate, of course.

In one test of the effect of frustration, Buss (1963) attempted to create
three levels of motivation to reach a goal in different experimental groups.
Subjects were then prevented from reaching the goal, and they afterward took
part in the "learning task" involving the aggression machine. The goal was to
perform well in teaching the other person. In one group, a good performance
was described as an indicator of intelligence, in a second group as a way to
win a monetary prize, and as a contributor to a course grade in a third group.
For all three, the subjects were frustrated because the learner did not master
the task in the specified number of trials. A control group was simply given
correct information as to how long it would take for the learner to master the
task. The results may be seen in Figure 11-3. Compared to the control group,
frustration was found to have only a weak effect on aggression, and the three
levels of frustration did not differ greatly from one another in their effects.

Though frustration has been found to affect aggression under specific
circumstances (for example, Geen and Berkowitz, 1967), the general conclusion is that it is not a particularly strong or consistent determinant. If frustration were great enough, however, it might be expected to lead to aggression.
For example, how might a starving man react if you prevented him from
eating?

Viewing Violent
and Aggressive Acts

One topic which is guaranteed to elicit strong opinions from social scientists,
parents, educators, and representatives of the entertainment industry is the effect of violence in movies and in television programs on the aggression of
viewers. Anyone who watches TV or attends movies can be an observer of
literally thousands and thousands of aggressive acts involving beatings, knifings,
shootings, hangings, and assorted acts of interpersonal mayhem. As technology
improves, the violence we see in movies is increasingly realistic. In addition,

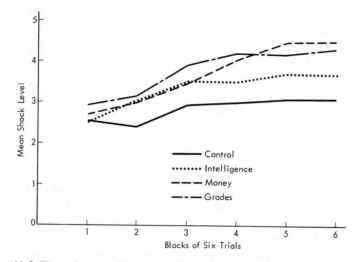

Fig. 11-3 Three Levels of Frustration Involved an Inability to Reach a Goal Described as Indicating Intelligence, Winning Money, or Obtaining a Higher Grade. Subjects in these conditions delivered slightly stronger shocks than did those in a control condition, but there were no significant differences attributable to frustration level. (Adapted from Buss, A. H., Physical aggression in relation to different frustrations, *Journal of Abnormal and Social Psychology*, 1963, 67, 6. © 1963 by the American Psychological Association and reprinted by permission.)

actual violence and real blood are an almost daily feature of television news, and we are all familiar with sights of genuine battle casualties, assassinations, and riots. What is the effect of such stimuli on our behavior? What is the effect on children? Is it possible that watching such violence tends to make us less aggressive (the catharsis effect) or does it teach us to be aggressive ourselves (the modeling effect)? These are hardly trivial questions, and the answer could have a major influence on future television programming and movie making as well as on the amount of real-life violence with which we each are threatened.

As important as the questions are, the answers are not easy to obtain. Three general approaches to the study of this problem have been undertaken. (1) Survey studies have sought the correlation between television and movie viewing habits and aggressive behavior. (2) Experimental investigations have exposed subjects to specific scenes of violence and then observed subsequent behavior. (3) Longitudinal investigations have examined viewing habits at one point in time and then examined aggressive behavior at a later point in time. We will consider examples of each kind of research to see if any general conclusions are possible.

Viewing Habits and Aggression. Eron (1963) pointed out that although television is frequently described by editorial writers and others as the cause for increased rates of crime and delinquency over the past several decades, in earlier times radios, movies, dime novels, and comic books have been singled out as responsible agents. To determine the association between television viewing and aggression, he conducted a study involving hundreds of third grade students in a semirural county in New York State. The parents of the children were interviewed with respect to the frequency of TV viewing by their children and with respect to each child's favorite programs. Aggressiveness was measured in the schools by asking each child to rate every other child in the class on a series of behaviors.

The TV programs were rated by independent judges with respect to amount of violence typically shown. For example, the *Lone Ranger* and *Perry Mason* were rated as nonviolent while *Have Gun—Will Travel* and *77 Sunset Strip* were judged to be violent. Viewing habits were classified with respect to the number of violent shows that were part of the child's favorite three.

For male third graders, a strong positive relationship was found between the level of violence in their favorite programs and their classroom aggressiveness as rated by their peers. This association between TV violence and aggression may be seen in Table 11-1. It was also found that spending many hours view-

Table 11-1. Mean Aggression Scores of Third Grade Boys as Rated by Classmates in Relation to the Violence in Their Favorite TV Programs

TV Viewing as Reported by	No Violent Programs	*Three Favorite TV Programs* One Violent Program	Two Violent Programs	Three Violent Programs
Mother	14.44	14.97	18.32	28.54
Father	12.44	14.23	18.92	20.67

(Adapted from Eron, L. D., Relationship of TV viewing habits and aggressive behavior in children, *Journal of Personality and Social Psychology,* 1970, 15, 195. © 1970 by the American Psychological Association and reprinted by permission.)

ing TV is not associated with aggression (the relationship was actually in the opposite direction); it is the *content* of the programs watched that is the important variable.

There is a built-in weakness in this and other studies like it; there is obviously no way to determine whether viewing violence on television leads to aggressive behavior, or whether aggressive habits lead to a preference for violent television programs, or whether some third factor is responsible for both behaviors.

Experimental Studies of Exposure to Aggression. One way to avoid such ambiguities inherent in correlational studies is to conduct experiments in which subjects are exposed to aggressive stimuli and then assessed as to subsequent aggression. Bandura, Ross, and Ross (1963) utilized three levels of reality (real life, film, and cartoon) in depicting an aggressive model in order to determine the effects on children's behavior. The subjects were three- to five-year-olds in nursery school. One group observed an adult acting aggressively, one group observed the same individual in a film, and a third group watched a movie depicting an aggressive cartoon character. A control group did not see an aggressive model. The aggressive behavior of the model involved hostility toward a five-foot inflated Bobo doll: sitting on it, punching it, hitting it with a mallet, tossing it in the air, and kicking it, all accompanied by appropriate verbal expressions. Subjects were tested for aggressive behavior in a different experimental room after a mild frustration. Among the available toys was a Bobo doll. Subjects in all three experimental groups were found to be more aggressive toward the Bobo doll than were subjects in the control group, and there was not much difference in the effects of the three model conditions. It was also noted that the aggressive behavior was specifically like that of the model. The authors pointed out that there was nearly twice as much aggression among the subjects in the experimental groups as in the control group.

There have been several criticisms of the Bandura et al. study and others that were patterned after it. The "aggressive" behavior was against a plastic toy rather than against another person, the stimulus was not really like actual TV programs with characters involved in a story, and it was possible for the aggression of the children to be just like that of the models when (luckily) such precise imitation is seldom possible with respect to what is seen on the screen. In an attempt to get around the criticisms of that method (and hence of the generalizability of the findings), Liebert and Baron (1972) exposed children of two different age levels (five- to six- and eight- to nine-year-olds) to a three and a half minute excerpt of violence in an actual television program, *The Untouchables.* These subjects watched a simple story involving a chase, two fist-fights, two shootings, and a knifing. Other children were shown a nonviolent program, an exciting race taken from a sports show involving athletes running around a track and jumping hurdles. Immediately after viewing one of the programs, the subjects took part in a game which was essentially a child's version of the Buss aggression machine. A subject could presumably hurt another child by pushing the appropriate button. As may be seen in Figure 11-4, children of both sexes who had seen the violent program aggressed more against their supposed victim than did those who watched the nonviolent program about a race. If three and a half minutes of televised violence can have a measureable effect on aggression, a lifetime of viewing violence could reasonably be expected to have a much greater effect.

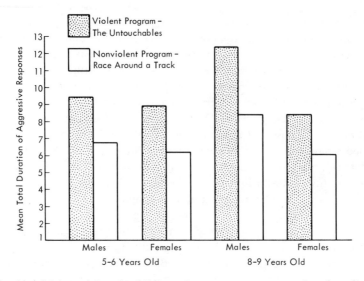

Fig. 11-4 Male and female children of two age groups were found to direct more aggression toward a nonexistent victim following exposure to three and one half minutes of television violence than following exposure to three and one half minutes of a nonviolent sports program. (Data from Liebert and Baron, 1972. Figure adapted from Baron, Byrne, and Griffitt, in press.)

These and other studies of the same general type have met with the usual criticisms directed at laboratory research; the artificial conditions of the laboratory are seen as sufficiently different from the way in which television is watched and from the way in which aggression is expressed in real life as to cast doubt on the meaning of the findings. Further, it has been argued that the effects demonstrated in such studies indicate only a momentary behavioral effect which would be of minor consequence in the nonlaboratory world. (Doob and Climie, 1972).

Longitudinal Relationship between Viewing Habits and Aggression. One type of investigation makes it possible to untangle the cause and effect relationship obscured in the survey study while bypassing the criticism of artificiality leveled at the laboratory experiment. Eron, Huesmann, Lefkowitz, and Walder (1972) carried out a follow-up investigation of the third-graders studied by Eron in the survey research described earlier. The subjects were nineteen years old when they were restudied, and again aggression was rated by their peers. The most significant finding was that the boys' preference for violent television programs while in the third grade was significantly related to aggressive behavior ten years later. A variety of statistical analyses lent strong support to the authors' conclusion that a preference for violence on television is a cause of aggressive behavior. Television habits established by the age of eight influenced aggressive behavior both at that age and a decade later.

General Conclusions Concerning Effects of Viewing Violence. As has been noted, it is possible to criticize various specific studies of the effects of violent presentations on aggressive behavior. It is difficult, however, to dismiss the very consistent findings among such different studies. Despite some contrary evidence (for example, Feshbach and Singer, 1971), it appears that exposure to violence in television and movies has both a short-range and a long-range effect on aggressive behavior, at least for males in our culture (Bryan and Schwartz, 1971).

SPECIFIC CUES TO AGGRESSION

Beyond the effects of depictions of aggression and violence on subsequent behavior, are there other cues to which we respond with increased aggression? Apparently, aggressive feelings can be aroused quite easily. For example, Wachtel and Schimek (1970) found that aggression in TAT stories increased when subjects simply overheard aggressively toned verbal interactions from the next room, even though they could not understand what was being said. Goldstein and Arms (1971) found that scores on a hostility scale increased as a function of watching the Army-Navy football game, regardless of whether the subject's preferred team won or lost. We will examine the effects of two other types of aggressive cues which are common in our environment.

Hostile Humor. Berkowitz (1970) noted that when individuals observe aggressive behavior, they tend to become more aggressive. He then raised the possibility that when the observed aggressiveness was disguised in the form of humor, it might serve to "drain off" aggressive feelings. In part, this is the sort of reasoning used to defend television programs such as *All in the Family* in which bigoted hostility is depicted humorously. His hypothesis, however, was that aggressive humor functions as a stimulus to aggressive behavior in the same way that filmed violence does.

Female students at the University of Wisconsin were placed in an experimental situation in which they were supposed to evaluate a peer who was applying for a dormitory job. By means of a tape recording, the applicant either provoked their anger (derisive, insulting message about Wisconsin coeds) or did not (bland, ordinary statements). Afterward, subjects listened to one of two four-minute tapes. Half of the subjects listened to George Carlin with a nonaggressive humorous routine, and half listened to Don Rickles whose routine involved insults to various members of his audience. The subjects then rated the job applicant on a variety of dimensions.

Expressions of hostility were significantly greater toward the insulting applicant than toward the neutral one and significantly greater following exposure to hostile humor than after non-hostile humor. It was concluded that with recognizably hostile humor, there is enhanced aggressiveness for those who are ready to act aggressively. In contrast, when angry subjects are exposed to nonhostile humor, aggressive behavior is reduced (Baron and Ball, in press; Landy and Mettee, 1969).

Cues to Aggression. Berkowitz (1964, 1965a, 1969) has stressed the importance of aggressive cues in eliciting aggressive behavior. Such cues include any aspect of the environment which is suggestive of aggression. For example, when subjects are exposed to a violent boxing film, aggression is found to be greater toward a stranger for whom there is some associative link to that film. Such links have included identifying the stranger as a college boxer (Berkowitz, 1965b), indicating that his name is the same as that of one of the actors (Berkowitz and Geen, 1966), or indicating that his name is the same as that of the film character who was the victim of aggression (Geen and Berkowitz, 1966). Thus, when someone has been associated with aggression, he seems to acquire cue value in eliciting aggressive responses.

Taking this idea one step further, Berkowitz and Le Page (1967) proposed that the presence of objects which have been associated with violence should facilitate aggressive behavior simply by their presence. Since there are approximately 115 million privately owned guns in the U.S. and since 65 percent of our killings are committed with guns, this weapon represents an obvious cue to aggression. Male students were either angered or not angered by another person and then were given a chance to aggress against him by means of electric shock. When the experimental subjects were using the aggression machine, there were a .38 caliber revolver and a 12-gauge shotgun on a nearby table. Compared to control groups who had no objects in view or who had badminton racquets on the table, the angered experimental subjects delivered more shock to the confederate. As hypothesized, the presence of weapons acted to facilitate aggression by subjects who had been provoked.

Subsequent research on this problem has been somewhat confusing in that the weapons effect seems to be difficult or impossible to replicate (Buss, Booker, and Buss, 1972; Page and Scheidt, 1971), and weapons have even been found to inhibit aggressive behavior under certain circumstances (Ellis, Weinir, and Miller, 1971). Berkowitz (1971) agrees that it is a weak effect and that other variables can interfere with it. He maintains, however, that whenever weapons are primarily associated with aggressive ideas and feelings, they would be expected to act as aggression-eliciting cues.

OTHER DETERMINANTS
OF AGGRESSIVE BEHAVIOR

Alcohol. One of the frequently observed effects of alcohol is an increase in aggressive behavior. It seems that the depressant properties of alcohol decrease feelings of anxiety and fear. Under these conditions, aggression is simply more likely to be expressed (Tucker, 1970). Considerable evidence indicates that violent crimes are most often associated with the consumption of alcohol (Shupe, 1954; Wolfgang and Strohm, 1956).

An experimental investigation of this relationship was conducted with male undergraduates at Kent State University by Shuntich and Taylor (1972). The subjects were either given two bourbon drinks, two nonalcoholic drinks which were made to appear to contain bourbon (a placebo), or nothing to drink (control group). Thirty minutes after the drinks, the subjects participated in Taylor's interaction task in which they received shocks from an imaginary opponent on some trials and administered shocks to him on others. It may be seen in Figure 11-5 that, as in previous studies, all subjects

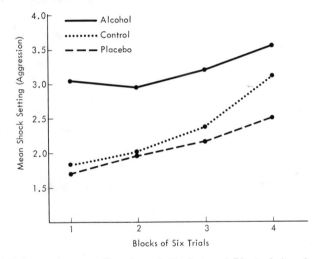

Fig. 11-5 Aggression as a Function of Alcohol and Physical Attack. As subjects are exposed to a series of increasingly stronger shocks from an opponent, their aggressive response is greatest when they have been drinking alcohol. (Data from Shuntich and Taylor, 1972.)

showed an increase in aggression over trials as the opponent gave stronger and stronger shocks, but the individuals who had first consumed alcohol responded with the greatest amount of aggression at each point during the task.

Environmental Factors. Among the possible influences on aggressive behavior are the numerous interacting variables which constitute life in a large, crowded urban environment. It has been reported that:

> ...as the population of a city increases so does the number of crimes per 100,000 citizens. In cities with less than 10,000 population, the assault rate was 28.9 per year; in cities of 100,000 to 250,000 population, the rate was 83.3; in cities over 250,000 population, the rate was 154.1...The murder rate

rose from 2.7 to 6.8 per 100,000 citizens. When a town grows from about 15,000 to over 250,000, its assault rate would likely increase 4.4 times, murder 2.8 times (Lamm, 1971, p. 18).

In Chapter 10, the effects of crowding on interpersonal attraction were reported by Griffitt and Veitch (1971). Subjects liked a stranger less under overcrowded conditions than under normal circumstances. In addition, studies of individuals confined in a limited space report the occurrence of interpersonal friction and irritability (Haythorn, Altman, and Myers, 1966; Taylor, Wheeler, and Altman, 1968). Therefore, crowdedness in a confined space would be expected to lead to a great amount of hostility and aggression. As part of a series of investigations of the effects of restricted, isolated monotony, Smith and Haythorn (1972) compared two- and three-man groups who spent twenty-one days with very little to do in a confined space. Crowded conditions consisted of seventy cubic feet of space per man while less crowded conditions involved two hundred cubic feet per man. The subjects were Navy volunteers, and the experiment was conducted in the Naval Medical Research Institute's deep isolation laboratory using soundproof, air-conditioned rooms. Hostility was measured with a scale which dealt with the subjects' feelings toward their partners. The results were surprising in that there was greater hostility in the less crowded groups than in the crowded ones, as shown in Table 11-2. Despite the occurrence of hostility and negative feelings, the

Table 11-2. Hostility Scores as a Function of Crowdedness

Condition	Days During Confinement					
	1	5	9	13	17	21
Less Crowded	65.0	58.7	61.3	61.1	56.6	57.9
More Crowded	58.5	55.9	51.8	49.9	52.0	52.3

(After Smith, S. and Haythorn, W. W., Effects of compatability, crowding, group size, and leadership seniority on stress, anxiety, hostility, and annoyance in isolated groups, *Journal of Personality and Social Psychology*, 1971, 19, 244. © 1971 by the American Psychological Association and reprinted by permission.)

subjects managed to restrain their overt expressions of hostility; angry confrontations were rare. It was proposed that increased crowdedness under these rather special conditions led the men to expend an extra effort in attempting to adapt to their partners. Quite possibly, if the conditions were continued indefinitely rather than with a known twenty-one-day limit, the effects of crowdedness might have been different.

An architect, Oscar Newman (1972), has proposed that it is not simply a matter of overcrowding leading to aggression. In studies in New York City, it was found that there is no relationship between population density and crime. Rather, crime rate depends on the way housing is designed. Crime is much more likely to occur in high-rise projects than where buildings are less than seven stories high and broken into smaller units. People in smaller and lower housing units can know one another, can see what is going on, and don't feel like anonymous ants in a hill. It appears that when there are more than six families along a corridor in a building, no one feels a sense of ownership. With relatively small units, people know each other, can recognize the presence of a stranger, and feel responsible for what goes on.

Another environmental variable which would be expected to influence aggression is temperature. Griffitt's (1970) finding of the negative effect of hot humid conditions on interpersonal attraction, as reported in Chapter 10, suggests that aggression would be greater under the same conditions. To test this proposition, Baron (1972a) investigated the responses of angered or non-angered subjects under cool or hot conditions on the aggression machine. It was hypothesized that angered subjects would respond with more aggression under uncomfortably hot conditions than under comfortably cool ones. To his surprise, the opposite effect occurred, and the heat acted to inhibit aggression under both conditions. The possibility was then raised (Baron and Lawton, 1972) that while high temperature might not have a direct effect on aggression, it would be expected to increase the likelihood of aggression if there were an aggressive model to imitate. An analogy would be the behavior of rioters during a "long hot summer"; the combination of the heat plus exposure to someone else's aggressive behavior could be the key to the expression of aggression. With the aggression machine as the response task, angered subjects were in either a cool or hot experimental room and either observed a confederate respond aggressively on the machine or did not. As may be seen in Table 11-3, the hypothesis was confirmed. When subjects had been

Table 11-3. Intensity of Shocks Delivered by Subjects under Cool or Hot Conditions after Exposure to Aggressive Model or to No Model

	Temperature	
	Cool	*Hot*
No Model	4.28	3.78
Aggressive Model	5.50	6.93

(After Baron and Lawton, 1972, p. 81)

exposed to an aggressive model, the hot conditions acted to increase the amount of aggression.

Sexual Arousal. Berkowitz (1969) has proposed that general arousal contributes to aggressive behavior. For example, it would be predicted that in any situation which evoked aggression (such as a physical attack), a high drive level (anxiety, hunger, or whatever) would lead to a more intense aggressive response. In support of this proposition, Geen and O'Neal (1969) found that subjects who were shown an aggressive boxing film and then exposed to a two-minute tape recording of white noise responded more aggressively toward a confederate than subjects who simply saw the film but were not aroused by the white noise. Even arousal in the form of physical exercise leads to increased aggression (Zillmann, Katcher, and Milovsky, 1972).

Sexual arousal presents special problems. It could be argued, for example, that sexual arousal should act like any other drive state and increase aggressive responses. In a similar vein Freud (1933) emphasized the connections between sexual and aggressive behavior, and Berne (1964) noted that aggression often precedes the sexual act and enhances its pleasure. Barclay (1969) has shown that subjects who are insulted and aggressively aroused express more sexuality in TAT stories; increase in male sexual arousal as a function of aggressiveness is even shown physiologically in the acid phosphatase found in their urine samples. Animal research, however, suggests the opposite possibility. That is, male mice tend to attack an intruding male quite viciously, but their response to an intruding female is to mount her sexually (Mackintosh, 1970). In addition, Connor (1972) has shown that such responses are controlled by smell. When male urine is placed on a female mouse, she evokes aggression; when female urine in placed on a male, he is approached sexually. Thus, rather than sexual arousal enhancing aggressive behavior, sex can function as an alternative or incompatible response and hence interfere with aggression. With respect to human subjects, this might be thought of as the "make love, not war" hypothesis. It happens that research on aggression provides support for each formulation.

Zillmann (1971) tested the general arousal hypothesis by exposing male subjects at the University of Wisconsin at Milwaukee to portions of neutral, aggressive, or erotic movies. The neutral movie was *Marco Polo's Travels* which was an educational film of a journey through China. The aggressive movie was *Body and Soul* which depicted a violent prize fight. The erotic movie, *The Couch,* depicted a young couple engaging in intimate foreplay. Following the movie, the subjects took part in the teacher-learner task on the Buss aggression machine. The results may be seen in Figure 11-6. The erotic movie strongly increased the aggressive response, even more than did the aggressive movie. Thus, it was concluded that arousal of a different emotional state such as sexuality can intensify aggression.

Support for the opposite hypothesis has been provided by Baron (1972b). Male subjects at Purdue University were either angered or not and then exposed to one of three types of pictures. Some saw erotic stimuli (nude females), others saw human stimuli that were not erotic (fully clothed females), and still others received stimuli that were neither human nor erotic (scenery, furniture, abstract paintings). Following this, the subjects took part

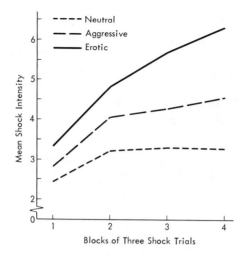

Fig. 11-6 Mean Intensity of Shocks Delivered to a Stranger Following Exposure to Neutral, Aggressive, and Erotic Movies. (After Zillmann, 1971, p. 431.)

in the aggression machine task. Though subjects rated the erotic stimuli as the most arousing and most attractive, less aggression was expressed by angry subjects who had just seen the pictures of nude or clothed females than by those exposed to impersonal stimuli. The mild sexual arousal seemed to counteract the effects of anger arousal. It was proposed that the female stimuli tended to distract the subjects from the confederate's negative response and thus reduced their degree of anger. The difference between the Zillmann and Baron findings may have been the result of different levels of sexual arousal. That is, the mild arousal of *Playboy*-type pictures served to interfere with aggression while the strong arousal of the erotic movie served to increase aggression. Additional research is obviously needed to clarify the effects of sexual arousal on aggressive behavior.

RESPONSE GENERALITY

SOCIAL AND CULTURAL DIFFERENCES IN AGGRESSIVE BEHAVIOR

Prisoners versus Undergraduates. In the study of aggressive behavior there has been little interest in extending the laboratory procedures to noncollege populations or in seeking evidence that the button-pushing response is related to nonlaboratory aggression. Wolfe and Baron (1971) have reported one of the few studies relevant to such issues.

A basic laboratory investigation involving the presence or absence of an aggressive model and subsequent responses on the Buss aggression machine was carried out in parallel studies of male undergraduates at the University of South Carolina and male prisoners in a maximum security prison who had a history of committing violent acts. All subjects were insulted by a peer who was actually a confederate and then, prior to the aggression task, some observed a highly aggressive model while others did not. The results may be seen in Table 11-4. The prisoners responded more aggressively than the stu-

Table 11-4. Mean Intensity of Shocks Delivered to Learner by Students and Prisoners with or without an Aggressive Model

Population	No Model	Aggressive Model
Students	4.92	7.37
Prisoners	6.27	8.51

(Adapted from Wolfe and Baron, 1971, p. 194)

dents, and in each group aggression was increased by exposure to an aggressive model. Thus, the generality of the laboratory findings was extended to a quite different population, and the group differences also lend support to the validity of the shock response as an indicator of aggression.

Social Class. There have not been any systematic studies of the effect of social class on aggressive responses in the laboratory setting. It may be, for example, that the Wolfe and Baron (1971) findings are at least in part attributable to social class differences between prisoners and students. Data from nonlaboratory sources suggest the strong possibility that such differences are important with respect to aggression. For example, studies in Philadelphia, Chicago, St. Louis, and Washington indicate that "Murder is almost exclusively a lower-class crime, the middle and upper classes preferring to work out their problems through suicide" (Edmiston, 1970, p. 30). One representative lower-class interaction was described:

A six-foot-two-inch Negro walks into a bar and asks for change of a dollar. The bartender, a five-foot-four-inch, 120-pound Puerto Rican, gives him some change. Halfway out of the bar, the Negro turns and comes back.
"You only gave me three quarters," he says.
"I gave you four quarters," says the bartender.
"You spic bastard, you only gave me three quarters."
"Don't call me that or I'll kill you!"
"You spic bastard..."
The bartender reaches down behind the bar, pulls out a baseball bat and brings it crashing down on the Negro's head. It kills him (Edmiston, 1970, pp. 29–30).

Additional Cultural Factors. Another relatively neglected aspect of aggression has been that of cultural variations both from nation to nation and within various geographical subgroups within a single nation. There are obviously numerous stereotypes about relatively violent and relatively passive groups and abundant anthropological evidence of vast cultural differences. Reed (1971, p. 429) turned his attention to the American South which has 30 percent of the nation's population and 45 percent of its murders:

> "Southerners," someone once remarked," will be polite until they're angry enough to kill you." He might have added that this flash-point seems to come sooner for Southerners than for other Americans. Beneath the image of a gracious, hospitable, leisurely folk has lurked that of hot-tempered, violent, even sadistic people, an image "so pervasive that it compels the attention of anyone interested in understanding the South."

Besides historical data on floggings and lynchings and current data on murder rates in the South, Reed assembled various questionnaire responses which tend to support the general notion of Southerners as more aggressive than those residing elsewhere in the United States. A portion of these findings appears in Table 11-5. Even when such factors as education, occupation, and

Table 11-5. Comparison of Responses in the South to Responses in Other Sections of the Country on Questions Relating to Aggression

Question	South	Non-South
Do you happen to have in your home any guns or revolvers?	52% say yes	27% say yes
Do you think it should be legal or illegal for private citizens to have loaded weapons in their homes?	70% say legal	44% say legal
What about the possession of pistols and revolvers—do you think there should be a law which would forbid the possession of this type of gun except by the police or other authorized persons?	63% say should not	43% say should not
Do you approve or disapprove of spanking children?	85% approve	72% approve
Do you approve of corporal punishment in schools?	81% approve	58% approve

(Data from Reed, 1971)

urban-rural differences are controlled, it was found that those residing in the South respond differently from those residing elsewhere in the nation.

INDIVIDUAL DIFFERENCES IN AGGRESSION

Sex Differences. Aggression seems to be one aspect of behavior for which there are unambiguous differences between the sexes. Animal studies, sociological data, research with children and adults, and common observation attest to the greater aggressiveness of males than females. For example, aggression is greater for boys than girls among preschool children (Pedersen and Bell, 1970) and among those in elementary school (Feshbach and Feshbach, 1969). Such findings are not surprising because aggression is a sex-typed behavior in our culture (Kagan, 1964; Maccoby, 1966). That is, boys are expected to be aggressive, and to some extent they are rewarded for aggressiveness and punished for passivity. The opposite pattern is applied to girls. It is also true, however, that even one-year-old males are more independent, engage in more gross motor activity, and play more vigorously than one-year-old females (Goldberg, Godfrey, and Lewis, 1967).

Not only are males more aggressive, but they also receive more aggression from others. For example, in the Taylor interaction task, for both college students (Taylor and Epstein, 1967) and sixth graders (Shortell and Biller, 1970), it is found that males respond with more aggression toward their opponent than do females and that opponents identified as females receive less punishment than opponents identified as males. Even females are more aggressive toward a male opponent than toward a female one. Similar results are reported when the aggression machine is used (Buss, 1963, 1966). It is interesting to find that these patterns of sex differences in aggressiveness in laboratory behavior are very much like those found in society:

> Men kill and are killed between four and five times more frequently than women. When a woman kills, a man is most likely to be her victim. She kills him with a butcher knife in the kitchen. If a woman is killed, her husband or "other close friend" is the murderer. He beats her to death in the bedroom (Edmiston, 1970, p. 31).

It has been hypothesized that cultural changes in sexual roles will eventually erase these differences between the sexes. One bit of support for such an effect has been reports of gangs of teenage girls in England who engage in violently aggressive attacks on random victims. A more desirable change would be for males to respond with decreased aggression rather than for females to show an increase.

Genetic Factors. Despite the emphasis in this chapter on aggression as a learned behavior, there is also considerable support for the idea that aggression is an inborn characteristic of man. One example is Freud's concept of the death instinct as described in Chapter 2. Current support for this position is strongest among the ethologists who describe parallels between man's aggressiveness and the very similar behaviors of our closest animal relatives. If aggression is one of man's built-in response systems, it is going to be somewhat difficult to bring about a meaningful reduction in the level of this behavior in our society. The best solution would seem to be in the development of ways to channel such behavior into harmless types of activity such as contact sports, target shooting, or fantasy activity.

A related line of research on the antecedents of extremely violent behavior has sought an explanation in genetic antecedents of aggression. It has been found that in a small percentage of the male population, there is an extra male chromosome (Owen, 1972). That is, sex is determined when the offspring receives either an X chromosome from each parent (XX = female) or an X from the mother and a Y from the father (XY = male). By accident, some males receive an additional Y chromosome (XYY). Various studies suggest that such males are taller than average, more aggressive, and are over-represented among criminal populations (Forssman and Hambert, 1963; Jacobs, Brunton, Melville, Brittain, and McClemont, 1965).

The role of this genetic accident in various behavioral problems may be seen in comparing its frequency in various populations. Among adult males, it is estimated that the XYY pattern occurs in one in eighty tall men. A much greater frequency of XYY is found among juvenile delinquents (one in four-teen), mentally defective delinquent adults (one in fifteen), adult criminals (one in twelve), and the criminally insane (one in eight) (Telfer, Baker, Clark, and Richardson, 1968).

It has been suggested that the relationship might simply be a function of height. For example, larger children would be more successful in fighting or other kinds of aggressiveness and hence would be reinforced for aggressive-ness. To test the role of height itself, Hook and Kim (1971) investigated a large group of male juvenile offenders who were genetically normal (XY) and found that the percentage of tall boys was no larger in this group than in the general population. It was concluded that the overrepresentation of XYY individuals in criminal populations cannot be explained on the basis of height. Rather, there seems to be something else about the XYY pattern which leads to aggressive behavior.

Overcontrolled and Undercontrolled Personality Types. It was noted by Megargee (1966) that a great many newspaper and magazine reports of acts of violence include a description of the individual who committed the acts as being gentle, mild, easy-going, and good natured. Relatives and friends con-sistently express their great surprise that such a quiet person could have committed violence:

> In case after case the extremely assaultive offender proves to be a rather passive person with no previous history of aggression. In Phoenix an 11-year-old boy who stabbed his brother 34 times with a steak knife was described by all who knew him as being extremely polite and soft spoken with no history of assaultive behavior. In New York an 18-year-old youth who confessed he had assaulted and strangled a 7-year-old girl in a Queens church and later tried to burn her body in the furnace was described in the press as an unemo-tional person who planned to be a minister. A 21-year-old man from Colorado who was accused of the rape and murder of two little girls had never been a discipline problem and, in fact, his stepfather reported, "When he was in

school the other kids would run all over him and he'd never fight back. There is just no violence in him." In these cases the homicide was not just one more aggressive offense in a person who had always displayed inadequate controls, but rather a completely uncharacteristic act in a person who had always displayed extraordinarily high levels of control (Megargee, 1966, p. 2).

Megargee went on the develop a theoretical description of individuals who engage in assaultive criminal acts. First, there are the Undercontrolled Aggressive individuals who fit the common stereotype of one who is chronically aggressive, antisocial, and without inhibitions with respect to expressing aggression. In contrast, the Chronically Overcontrolled individuals are extremely inhibited about the expression of aggression toward anyone in any situation. When overcontrolled individuals are instigated to aggress, they refrain from doing so. Thus, they "store up" aggression over a long period of time and, if they do aggress, they have never learned how to express an acceptable and appropriate level of aggression. The result of these two factors is that aggression from such individuals is likely to be sudden, violent, and out of all proportion to whatever event triggered it off.

The utility of this conceptualization has been demonstrated in a series of successful investigations. It has been found, for example, that groups of extremely assaultive delinquents are actually less aggressive and more controlled than groups of either moderately assaultive or nonassaultive delinquents (Megargee, 1966). An MMPI scale has been developed to identify overcontrolled hostility (Megargee, Cook, and Mendelsohn, 1967). Items include:

At times I feel like swearing. (False)
I do not mind being made fun of. (True)
It makes me nervous to have to wait. (False)

Extremely high scores on this scale are found in groups as diverse as conscientious objectors and overcontrolled delinquents imprisoned for violent crimes (Megargee, 1969). In an experimental situation, the overcontrolled individual is found to report less anger after being frustrated and to engage in less overt aggression (Vanderbeck, 1972).

This general line of research appears to have important implications for the identification of potential offenders. It also suggests that it is essential that children learn to express some degree of aggression in an appropriate manner rather than be taught to suppress all aggressive impulses. The way in which aggressive behavior is learned has been the focus of a considerable amount of research, and we will now examine a portion of this work.

Parental Determinants of Aggression. Aggression and hostility are inevitable childhood behaviors with which parents must deal. The process of socialization (training children to become members of even a simple society) necessarily involves frustration, discomfort, and imposed constraints. The child cannot eat immediately when he is hungry, cannot defecate or urinate whenever or wherever the urge arises, cannot do as he pleases with the property of others. When the child responds to such interference with aggression, that behavior also must be socialized to some extent, but the way that this is done and the limits of allowable aggression differ greatly across families.

A large-scale study by Sears, Maccoby, and Levin (1957) involved interviews with mothers of kindergarten children. When the mothers were asked about the amount of aggression shown by the child in the home, the replies ranged from none to highly aggressive. Presumably the amount of aggression shown was in part a function of the way in which the parents responded to aggressive behavior. Two variables were studied. First, mothers differed considerably in their permissiveness for aggression. Those who were not at all permissive believed that the behavior should not be allowed to occur under any circumstances and that it should be stopped the moment it began. At the other end of this dimension were mothers who were entirely permissive (child has a right to hit parents or shout angrily at them; children should fight it out if they quarrel because it is a natural part of growing up). The second parental behavior was that of the severity of punishment for aggression toward parents. At some point, even the most permissive parent stops the aggression in some way (no one allows his child to maim or kill others, for example). Again, vast differences occur among parents in what they do. Aggression toward parents was treated by some with only very mild punishment and disapproval. Parents at the other extreme responded with anger, hostility, beatings, and severe deprivation of privileges. What effects do these differences in permissiveness and punishment have on the aggressiveness of the children?

The greatest percentage of highly aggressive children had mothers who were highly permissive about aggression and who also punished it severely. The smallest percentage of highly aggressive children had mothers with the opposite pattern: nonpermissive about aggression and mild punishment. In interpreting these results, Sears, et al. point out:

> Our findings suggest that the way for parents to produce a nonaggressive child is to make it abundantly clear that aggression is frowned upon, and to stop aggression when it occurs, but to avoid punishing the child for his aggression. Punishment seems to have complex effects. While undoubtedly it often stops a particular form of aggression, at least momentarily, it appears to generate more hostility in the child and lead to further aggressive outbursts at some other time or place. Furthermore, when the parents punish—particularly when they employ physical punishment—they are providing a living example of the use of aggression at the very moment they are trying to teach the child not to be aggressive. The child, who copies his parents in many ways, is likely to learn as much from this example of successful aggression on his parents'

part as he is from the pain of punishment. Thus, the most peaceful home is one in which the mother believes aggression is not desirable and under no circumstances is ever to be expressed toward her, but who relies mainly on nonpunitive forms of control. The homes where the children show angry, aggressive outbursts frequently are likely to be homes in which the mother has a relatively tolerant (or careless!) attitude toward such behavior, or where she administers severe punishment for it, or both (Sears, et al., 1957, p. 266).

Another extensive study of parental determinants of aggression was carried out by Bandura and Walters (1959). They interviewed a large number of adolescent boys and their parents. Half of the boys had histories of aggressive antisocial behavior; the other half was made up of a matched group of nonagressive boys. The aggressive subjects each had been in repeated trouble with the law or with school authorities with antisocial, aggressive acts. Among the differences between their families was a clear pattern of hostility and the use of punitive types of discipline in the families of the aggressive subjects.

The effects of parental punishment on aggressive behavior have been verified in numerous studies, including research with animals. When rhesus monkeys are raised by punitive mothers, they are more aggressive toward peers during the first year of life (Arling and Harlow, in press), at age three (Sackett, 1965), and in adolescence (Mitchell, Arling, and Moller, 1967). The latter authors report that the aggressiveness of their subjects seemed to increase with age. Some time after the experiment was completed, the two most highly punished males "...severely aggressed against a female cage-mate and bit off several fingers. After this incident had occurred, these males were removed from the group living cage but were mistakenly returned for one weekend, during which they killed another female" (Mitchell, et al., 1967, p. 210).

In addition to the effects of parental behavior, there are data to suggest that the absence of a parent can affect aggressive behavior. It was proposed by Parsons (1947) that males in our culture have difficulties in achieving identification with a male sex role. A boy first identifies with his mother, the father frequently is not involved in child-rearing activities, and the first authority figure outside of the home is likely to be a female teacher. When a male child is finally able to reject the feminine identification, he overreacts with exaggerated masculine behavior. Thus, antisocial behavior could be seen as a desparate attempt to "act like a man." In support of this idea, Bacon, Child, and Barry (1963) found that in societies where the father does not play a large role in the household, there is a high rate of crime. Siegman (1966) took this question one step further by comparing the antisocial behavior of male adults whose fathers were absent (in the armed services) during their childhood with that of male adults whose fathers had remained at home. As expected, antisocial behavior was more characteristic of the father-absent group than of the father-present group.

Learning to Aggress. It is assumed in much of the research on aggression that this behavior is learned. Most investigators have stressed the importance of the reinforcing consequences of aggression, the reinforcement history of the individual, and the utility of aggressive responses in obtaining various kinds of satisfaction (Berkowitz, 1962; Buss, 1961; Patterson, Littman, and Bricker, 1967). The frequency of aggressive responses, the intensity of such responses, and the specific form they take are each behaviors presumably responsive to rewards and punishments. A few examples will be given in order to illustrate the way in which these general principles are reflected in empirical research.

In an experimental situation in which a subject aggresses against a stranger by administering electric shock, it would be expected that the reinforcement or nonreinforcement of such responses would determine whether or not their strength increased. Geen and Pigg (1970) ran male undergraduates on the Buss aggression machine and for half of them, the experimenter said "That's good" or "You're doing fine" whenever the subject gave the stranger a more intense shock. Half of the subjects received no verbal reinforcement for their aggressive behavior. The effect of reinforcement may be seen in Figure 11-7; the intensity of aggressive responses increased when they were reinforced.

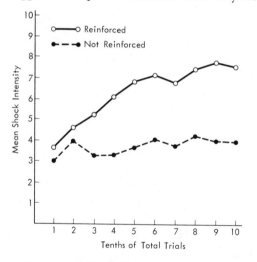

Fig. 11-7 Mean Intensity of Shocks Delivered to a Stranger as a Function of Reinforcement vs. no Reinforcement After Each Aggressive Response. (After Geen, R. G. and Pigg, R., Acquisition of an aggressive response and its generalization to verbal behavior, *Journal of Personality and Social Psychology*, 1970, 15, 167. © 1970 by the American Psychological Association and reprinted by permission.)

A second aspect of the Geen and Pigg experiment dealt with generalization. When the interaction on the aggression machine was completed, the subjects were given a word association test. After each word, the subject was to write his first five associations. The stimulus words were wash, choke, travel, walk, murder, relax, stab, sleep, torture, and listen. The experimenters were interested in the number of aggressive associations given by each subject. Those subjects who had been reinforced for aggressing against the confederate gave more aggressive associations than did the nonreinforced subjects. The effects of reinforcement on physical aggression thus increased for verbal aggression as well.

Not only does the reinforcement of physical aggression generalize to a verbal response, but the reverse is also true. Gentry (1970) gave male undergraduates at Florida State University the Picture-Frustration test (Rosenzweig, 1945) and reinforced half of the subjects whenever they gave a hostile response by saying "Very good," "That's right," or "That's an excellent response." Afterward, the subject responded on the aggression machine. It was found that those subjects whose hostile verbal responses were reinforced gave more intense shocks to the stranger than did those subjects who were not reinforced.

OTHER RESPONSES

In laboratory investigations of aggression, the responses under study have most often involved the administration of an electric shock to a stranger or else some verbal response. The validity of such responses as indicators of aggression has been questioned by the findings of Baron and Eggleston (1972). It was shown that responses on the aggression machine are apparently motivated by a desire to help the other person learn as well as by a desire to harm him. With the standard instructions indicating that it was a learning task, the amount of shock delivered to the stranger was positively correlated with questionnaire responses indicating a desire to help the other person ($r = .45$). When the instructions indicated that it was a study of the effect of shock on physiological responses, there was a negative correlation between amount of shock and desire to help the other person ($r = -.55$). It was suggested that both altruistic and aggressive motives underlie responses on the aggression machine. Thus, the "physiological" instructions may provide a better measure of aggression.

Psychophysiological Measures and the Catharsis Hypothesis: Aggressive Behavior and Tension Reduction. A somewhat different way to investigate the generality of such measures of aggression is to seek physiological indicators of aggressive feelings. Much of this work has been conducted in the context of testing the catharsis hypothesis, the idea that aggressive drives are reduced by aggressive behavior. Freud (1920) formalized the idea of catharsis with a hydrolic model in which the expression of aggression is seen as "draining the reservoir" and lowering the drive level. Hokanson (1970) has analyzed that hypothesis into two components: (1) aggressive behavior will reduce the occurrence of subsequent overt aggression and (2) aggressive behavior will serve to reduce the level of physical energy.

In pursuing these formulations experimentally, Hokanson and Shetler (1961) began by seeking the autonomic indicators of aggression. While subjects worked on an intellectual task, they were harassessed and insulted. Systolic blood pressure was found to increase under these conditions. When half the subjects were then given the opportunity to aggress against their attacker, their blood pressure quickly returned to normal; the blood pressure level of the control group remained high.

This work was expanded in another experiment (Hokanson and Burgess, 1962) in which harassed subjects were found to respond with both elevated systolic blood pressure and increased heart rate. This time, a variety of aggressive behaviors were compared—physical aggression (shock), verbal aggression (ratings of attacker), and fantasy aggression (writing a TAT story) along with a control group which did not get an opportunity to aggress in any way. Both physical and verbal aggression were found to have a cathartic effect as shown by the physiological measures, while the fantasy group and the control group each showed no decrease in physiological excitement.

Still another experiment dealt with the effects of displaced aggression or the generalization of the catharsis effect. Hokanson, Burgess, and Cohen (1963) again placed subjects in the harrassment situation and then permitted physical aggression against the attacker, against his assistant, against a "psychology major," or against another undergraduate subject. The physiological measure indicated the greatest catharsis effect when aggression was against the attacker. An intermediate level of effect was found for aggression against the assistant and the psychology major. Aggression against the other undergraduate showed no effect, much like the control group. It would seem that the catharsis phenomenon requires that aggression be directed at the instigator or at someone associated with him in some fashion.

Nonaggressive Behavior and Tension Reduction. Following the previous series of experiments, Hokanson and his associates extended their investigations by determining whether other types of behavior besides counteraggression could produce the catharsis effect. For this purpose, a new experimental situation was designed, one which is somewhat like Taylor's interaction task. Subjects believed they were interacting with a fellow subject by means of three buttons. On each interchange they could give and receive one of three messages: aggression (shock), friendliness (light), or they could ignore the other person by doing nothing.

In the investigations using this apparatus (Hokanson and Edelman, 1966; Hokanson, Willers, and Koropsak, 1968), sex differences were apparent. In interacting with same-sexed confederates, males showed the familiar physiological responses to aggression and showed the catharsis effect when they counteraggressed by shocking the opponent. Females, on the other hand, showed the catharsis effect when they made a friendly counter-response to the receipt of shock.

This difference appears to be not simply a function of sex but rather of the way in which an individual has learned to respond to interpersonal threat. Using male prisoners as subjects, Sosa (1968) divided them on the basis of case history records into those who characteristically responded to threat with violence and those who usually responded with passivity. The violent group showed the catharsis effect when they responded to aggression with aggression. The passive group showed the catharsis effect when they responded with friendliness. Hokanson (1970) proposed that the type of counterresponse which is cathartic is a learned reaction. Presumably, we can learn many alternative ways to reduce the tension aroused when others attack us. It has even been shown that subjects can be taught to respond to attack by aggressing against themselves (with shock) and that the catharsis effect can be obtained with this self-aggressive response (Stone and Hokanson, 1969). It would seem that responses to aggression as varied as counterattack, friendliness, and masochism can each be acquired and can each serve to reduce aggressive tensions.

THEORY BUILDING

Much of the research on aggression has involved tests of specific theoretical notions such as the effect of frustration, the genetic determinants of aggression, the role of overcontrol on explosive outbreaks of violence, and the catharsis effect. Many of the experiments have been based on the idea that aggression is a learned behavior. One of the most comprehensive formulations of this theoretical interpretation has been that of Bandura (1971).

ACQUIRING AGGRESSIVE RESPONSES

Bandura has proposed that aggressive responses are learned in two somewhat different ways. New behavior is acquired by means of observational learning. That is, the aggression of others is observed, and we model our behavior after theirs. The effects of violence in television and movies may be seen as examples of this kind of modeling or imitation of the aggression of others. It has even been found that the widespread publicity such as that following a spectacular murder or assassination is followed by an upsurge in similar crimes, presumably as a function of observational learning (Berkowitz, 1970). In the same way, the phenomenon of airplane hijacking is well publicized and seems to lead to imitative attempts by subsequent skyjackers. In addition, children undoubtedly learn particular modes of physical or verbal aggression as a function of seeing how adults, acquaintances, and older siblings respond to threat and attack. One of the reasons that cultures can differ greatly in the amount and type of overt aggression they express is the differential availability of particular kinds of models after which behavior can be patterned. Even in a brief interaction, the presence of a nonaggressive model can serve to inhibit the amount of aggression expressed (Baron, 1971d).

The other type of learning was discussed in the section on individual differences. Aggressive behavior can be reinforcing in that it can be successful in stopping an attack on oneself, it can lead to other types of satisfaction such as praise or the attainment of goal objects, and, as Hokanson's work indicates, aggression can be tension reducing. The frequency and intensity of an aggressive response can be increased simply through the reinforcement of that response.

Therefore, Bandura views the acquisition of aggression as based on modeling when we observe the aggression of others and on direct reinforcement when we try out the behavior ourselves.

INSTIGATION TO AGGRESSION

As we have seen, the most reliable instigator of aggression has been found to be an attack or at least the perception of an attack. Once there are well learned aggressive responses in the individual's repertoire, an attack will serve to evoke these responses. In addition, we have examined a number of stimulus conditions which increase the probability of an aggressive response. These may be seen as conditions which are part of the external situation (for example, aggressive cues, overcrowding, hot and humid surroundings) and as internal conditions of the individual (for example, the drinking of alcohol which reduces inhibition, the presence of a high level of drive). The actual expression of aggression will thus be a function of the number of such factors which are operating.

MAINTAINING AGGRESSIVE RESPONSES

The third aspect of Bandura's (1971) formulation deals with the conditions which make it likely that aggressive responses will continue to be a part of the individual's usual behavior. It is generally assumed that aggressive behavior will continue if it is associated with rewards. Thus, children can find that aggression brings them success, criminals can obtain financial gain, soldiers can become heroes, officers can win promotions, and aggressive spouses can get their own way. In addition, aggression can serve a protective function against the aggression of others and can be intrinsically rewarding as a means of reducing tension.

Presumably, aggression will cease to occur if it is not rewarded. For example, if one's environment is such that cooperation and kindness lead to social approval and to material gains whereas aggression leads to disapproval and failure, one would expect decreased aggression and increased cooperation and kindness. We have seen that individuals can even learn to reduce aggressive tension by means of nonaggressive behavior. It would seem possible that aggression could be eliminated even more effectively and quickly by means of punishment than by nonreinforcement. As will be discussed in the following section, that proposition is probably not correct. Punishment serves both as a model for aggression and as an instigator to further aggression. Thus, aggression by parents or police or military forces may be successful in controlling the immediate overt aggression of others, but such tactics are by no means successful in decreasing the likelihood of future aggression. In fact, the result is just the opposite.

APPLICATIONS

Most behavioral scientists seem to share the belief that aggression is generally undesirable and that it should be eliminated. Berkowitz (1971) has pointed out that the National Commission on the Causes and Prevention of Violence found that commercial television has an "adverse" effect on human character and attitudes in that television violence encourages violent behavior and that such behavior is "unacceptable in a civilized society." Such conclusions are, of course, based on the values of the intellectual community and not on something which could be verified by any research findings. These values are not universally shared. Feshbach (1971) points out that the reaction of the general public to the My Lai massacre of unarmed men, women, and children was not one of uniform indignation and condemnation. In fact, many people were more disturbed by the fact that the incident was made known to the public than by the incident itself. Nevertheless, most psychologists would like to see a decrease in violent behavior, and our interest in application in this area is primarily in finding ways to prevent or mitigate aggression.

It has been suggested that aggression can best be controlled physiologically by means of surgery, brain stimulation, hormones, or drugs (Moyer, 1971). Most research in this area, however, has concentrated on aspects of the social situation associated with the consequents of aggression, with cues associated with the victim, or with individual differences in responding to such cues.

Retaliation

Is aggression inhibited by punishment or threats of punishment? Many aspects of our society are based on this idea; examples include the way we frequently treat children, the way institutions such as organized religion enforce their rules of conduct, and our criminal laws. Psychologists have also endorsed this view as when Walters and Thomas (1963, p. 252) wrote, "It is only the continual expectation of retaliation by the recipient or other members of society that prevents many individuals from more freely expressing aggression." A series of experiments suggests that this seemingly obvious conclusion may be incorrect.

In two experiments with the Taylor interaction task, it was found that aggression was greater when the subject was vulnerable to counterattack on half of the trials than when he was vulnerable on only one trial out of six (Epstein and Taylor, 1967; Merrick and Taylor, 1970). Such findings suggest that there is not a direct relationship between retaliation and inhibition of aggression. In a more extensive study of inhibitors, Pisano and Taylor (1971) compared four strategies for their effectiveness in reducing physical aggression. On the interaction task, some subjects had a passive opponent who always responded with the lowest shock level, others had a matching opponent who set the same intensity as they had done, and others had a punitive opponent who always responded with the highest shock level. In a fourth condition, subjects had a punitive opponent but were told that their nonaggressive behavior would be rewarded (five cents for setting the lowest level of shock, one cent for setting the highest level, etc.). Instead of punitiveness acting to stop aggression, subjects were most aggressive toward the highly punitive opponent. The most effective strategy for inhibiting aggression, as shown in Figure 11-8, was that of a matching response. The monetary rewards and the opponent's passivity yielded intermediate effects. The authors indicated that the use of punishment by the opponent proved to be an ineffective strategy for intimidating the subject and reducing his aggression. Instead, the punishment or retaliation served to instigate greater intensities of attack. The matching behavior was an effective inhibitor and suggests that a punitive response could be successful if it were directly contingent on the level of the aggressor's response. An overpunitive response only leads to increased aggression.

On the Buss aggression machine, similar findings have been reported. Baron (1973c) had a confederate insult each subject who then had a chance to aggress against him by setting the appropriate shock level during the learning task. Half observed an aggressive model and half a nonaggressive model performing the role of teacher. Probability of retaliation was manipulated by telling some subjects that the experiment would be over after they completed the teaching task (low probability), that one of the two teachers would trade places with the learner (moderate probability), or that they would definitely trade places with the learner (high probability). It was found that after exposure to an aggressive model, threatened punishment from the victim was relatively ineffective in deterring aggression. Similarly, Baron (in press) found that high probability of retaliation was an effective deterrent for nonangered

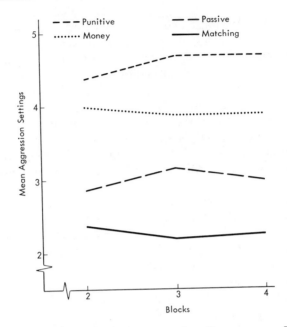

Fig. 11-8 Mean Intensity of Shocks Delivered to Opponent as a Function of Different Strategies Designed to Reduce Aggression. (After Pisano, R. and Taylor, S. P., Reduction of physical aggression: The effects of four strategies, *Journal of Personality and Social Psychology*, 1971, 19, 240. © 1971 by the American Psychological Association and reprinted by permission.)

subjects, but it was not effective when subjects had previously been insulted by the confederate.

Thus, the utility of punishment or retaliation as a way to prevent or reduce aggression may be seen to be questionable. When nations threaten to annihilate one another or to retaliate ten times over in response to any provocation, the aim is presumably to inhibit the aggressiveness of their antagonists. When societies threaten to punish wrongdoers with imprisonment, physical hardship, or death, the aim is presumably to reduce the incidence of criminal acts. The overall ineffectiveness of threats and punishments in these situations seems self-evident and is entirely consistent with the laboratory findings.

EQUITY

One aspect of aggression seems to be the informal assumption that the victim "deserves what he is getting." In wartime, every effort is made to convince the combattants of the cruelty and viciousness of the enemy. Probably, this is why Americans in World War II were horrified when the Germans killed several thousand civilians by bombing Rotterdam but were unconcerned when the Allies killed 100,000 German civilians in the fire bombing of Dresden (Blumenthal, 1972). Criminals often justify their acts in that the victim "was asking for it." Many otherwise gentle and kindly individuals respond favorably to the notion of mob violence, physical mistreatment, or the death penalty when someone acts in a way that goes beyond the bounds of "acceptable" transgressions. There is, however, another aspect of the appropriateness of aggression. That is, if a given amount of retaliatory aggression is deserved, one's aggression should not go beyond those limits. There would seem to be some idea of equitable retaliation which controls the amount of aggression directed against a victim. It may be that we feel no empathy toward someone who deserves punishment until he has received his "just deserts."

Two experiments provide evidence relevant to this proposition. Doob (1970) arranged a situation in which Stanford undergraduates were annoyed by a confederate while they were taking a personality test. The confederate finished first, and then began saying things like, "Haven't you finished yet? God, you're slow. You do go to Stanford, don't you? It's amazing they let you in." Following this, the confederate took part in a second task in which he could lose money for giving wrong answers. The confederate either lost up to $5.00, or he did not lose money in the task. The third part of the experiment involved a free association task in which the subject was supposed to shock the confederate whenever he gave a noncreative response. The response measure was the length of time the shock was administered by the subject. In Table 11-6 it may be seen that annoyed subjects tended to give shorter shocks to the annoying confederate if he had suffered a loss of money than if he had

Table 11-6. Frequencies of Long and Short Shocks
Given to Annoying Confederate Who Had Lost Money or Had Not

	Length of Shock	
	Long	Short
Confederate Lost Money	6	14
Confederate Did Not Lose Money	14	6

(After Doob, 1970, p. 295)

not. It was as though he had already paid equitably for his sins. In a control condition in which the confederate had not annoyed the subject, loss of money was unrelated to length of shock.

In a second experiment, Doob and Wood (1972) used a similar situation in which the subject interacted with an annoying confederate. Instead of loss of money, the second interaction involved a task in which the subject either administered shocks to the confederate, watched the experimenter administer shocks to the confederate, or in which the confederate received no shocks.

Finally, the free association task was presented on which the subject could shock the confederate. Once again, as shown in Table 11-7, the subject was

Table 11-7. Mean Number of Shocks Given to Annoying Confederate Who Had Been Previously Shocked by the Subject, by the Experimenter, or by No One

Confederate Shocked by Subject	Confederate Shocked by Experimenter	Confederate Had Not Been Shocked
6.80	7.60	10.67

(After Doob, A. N. and Wood, L. E., Catharsis and aggression: Effects of annoyance and retaliation on aggressive behavior, *Journal of Personality and Social Psychology*, 1972, 22, 160. © 1972 by the American Psychological Association and reprinted by permission.

less aggressive toward the annoying confederate if that person had already been punished. The authors indicate that "...the angered person who has hurt his annoyer (or seen his annoyer hurt) has 'evened the score.' Thus, the annoyed person whose annoyer has been hurt will feel less of a need to retaliate further than the annoyed person whose annoyer has not been hurt in some way" (Doob and Wood, 1972, p. 161).

Empathy

It is a truism that people can engage in literally horrifying activities designed to harm one another, and it seems equally true that most people are far from vicious when one gets to know them well. When Albert Speer writes about Adolph Hitler or Truman Capote writes about the two Kansas murderers, one can see that even the perpetrators of the most vicious acts can at times be reasonable, likeable human beings. What is the secret of this paradox? Feshbach (1971, p. 291) suggests that:

> ...except for the hardened criminal, most people find it difficult to deliberately injure another human solely for nonaggressive reasons. To reduce this inhibition, they find it necessary to dehumanize their target and invent beliefs that will enable them to hate the person they must injure. Thus, the policeman becomes a "pig," and the student, a "hippie." The Asiatic becomes a "Gook," "yellow people are treacherous," and besides, "we all know that life is cheap in the Orient."

He goes on to suggest that many influences such as television and education make it increasingly difficult to view members of other nations and races as nonhumans. If the other person is someone like ourselves, it is difficult to cause him harm. One problem, of course, is that much violence does not occur in a face-to-face situation where empathy can operate. The strategists who plan a protective retaliatory air strike do not see the terrified faces or smell the burning flesh. The bombardier who presses a button high above the clouds does not see the destruction of human bodies. The men and women who vote against an adequate welfare proposal do not have to listen to a hungry baby when he cries. It appears that we can be most vicious to one another in the abstract. What are the variables in such situations which have been found to affect interpersonal aggression?

Pain Cues. It was suggested that empathy is less likely to occur if the victim is somehow made more abstract to the aggressor. It should be more difficult, for example, to feel empathy toward an unseen victim than toward one whose pain could be directly perceived.

Baron (1971a) had angered and nonangered subjects respond on the Buss aggression machine to which a "pain meter" was added. Subjects were told that this device measured the victim's pain response physiologically and the results were supposedly shown on a meter which indicated low, moderate, or high levels of pain. As indicated in Figure 11-9, it was found that the greater

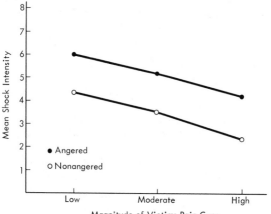

Fig. 11-9 The Effect of Pain Cues from the Victim on the Subject's Aggressive Responses. Both angered and nonangered subjects administered less intense shocks as the magnitude of the victim's pain increased. (After Baron, R. A., Magnitude of victim's pain cues and level of prior anger arousal as determinants of adult aggressive behavior, *Journal of Personality and Social Psychology*, 1971, 17, 240. © 1971 by the American Psychological Association and reprinted by permission.)

the magnitude of the victim's pain cues, the less intense the shocks subjects delivered to him. Other research (Baron, 1971b) confirmed these results; in one experiment aggression was inhibited when the subjects could hear the gasps and moans of the victim (Geen, 1970).

There are limits to the effectiveness of such cues in inhibiting aggression. At times, the pain of the victim may be reinforcing to the aggressor (Feshbach, Stiles, and Bitter, 1967). There also seem to be numerous real life instances in which the pain of the victim is enjoyed by the aggressor. There is a need to identify the specific circumstances in which pain cues increase empathy and hence inhibit aggression versus those in which the victim's pain intensifies the aggression.

Individual Differences in Empathy. With empathy defined as the capacity to view events from the standpoint of others and to experience the emotions of the other (Staub, 1971), it can be seen that individuals would be expected to differ widely in this characteristic. Feshbach and Feshbach (1969) found that among six- and seven-year-old boys, there was a negative relationship between amount of empathy and aggressiveness. For younger boys and for girls, this relationship was not found and actually tended to be in the opposite direction. Such data suggest that there is still much to be learned about the way in which empathy functions in influencing human aggression:

> Empathy, then, is a mechanism which may help terminate aggressive behavior before the object of aggression suffers serious injury. An analogy can be made between the function of empathy in humans and that of the variety of behavioral displays in many animal species which serve to inhibit intraspecies fighting (Lorenz, 1966). As Lorenz has noted, specific mechanisms for inhibiting aggression are much more highly developed in animals than in humans. An analysis of the development of empathy and the conditions which maximize its potential inhibitory effects may help foster socialization practices that, in humans, facilitate the aggressive regulating behaviors which appear to develop so naturally in animals (Feshbach and Feshbach, 1969, p. 107).

A number of observers, including psychiatrists Gilula and Daniels (1969), have pointed out that man's violence was biologically adaptive when he struggled to survive as a nomadic hunter and even when he struggled against nature or fought for food when the supply was scarce. With the advent of technology, we seem to find ourselves stuck with at least the biological capability of extreme violence but without any useful biological regulating devices. Such regulation must come from the way we structure our environmental surroundings and from the way we raise our children.

SUMMARY

Hostility, aggression, and violence are pervasive in man's affairs. In psychological research, aggression is defined as *any behavior directed toward the goal of harming or injuring another human being.*
The most reliable instigator of aggression appears to be a physical attack

by another person. On Taylor's interaction task, subjects administer increasingly strong shocks to an imaginary opponent when they receive increasingly strong shocks from him. This relationship between aggression received and aggression returned is one starting point in studying aggressive behavior.

Analytic research indicates that subjects are more responsive to the perceived intent of the attacker than to the actual physical pain he causes.

Studies of stimulus generality have sought other antecedents of aggression beyond that of attack and perceived intent. Frustration has long been conceptualized as a major determinant of aggression, but studies using such devices as the Buss aggression machine suggest that frustration is not a particularly strong or consistent instigator of aggression. Both laboratory and field studies of televised and filmed violence tend to be consistent in showing that aggressive behavior increases as a function of exposure to such stimuli. Aggression also is enhanced by the presence of aggressive cues in the situation such as hostile humor, associative links between aggressive stimuli and the victim, or the presence of weapons. Aggression is also increased by the ingestion of alcohol, crowdedness under some conditions, the design of housing units, high heat and humidity, and general drive arousal. Mild sexual arousal inhibits aggression while strong sexual arousal increases aggressiveness.

Investigations of response generality have shown population differences in that prisoners express more aggression in the laboratory than do college undergraduates, lower-class citizens commit more murders than do middle- and upper-class citizens, and residents of the American South are higher on various indices of aggression than residents of other parts of the country. Studies of individual differences report more aggression expressed by males and toward males than is true for females, an overrepresentation in criminal populations of males with an extra Y chromosome, and sudden outbreaks of extreme violence among overcontrolled individuals. A major determinant of individual differences would seem to be parental child-rearing practices, and those parents who are both permissive about aggression and severely punitive produce more aggressive children than parents who are nonpermissive but use mild punishment. In animals studies, also, punitive parents are found to produce aggressive offspring. The absence of a father in the home also appears to be an antecedent of aggressiveness. Various studies show that aggressive responses can be influenced by rewards and punishments and that these effects generalize to quite different forms of aggression. Psychophysiological responses such as systolic blood ₁ ressure and heart rate increase as a function of aggression instigation. This aggressive tension can be reduced by engaging in aggressive behavior which acts as a catharsis. It is also possible to learn to obtain catharsis through acts of friendliness and even by self-aggression.

Most approaches to aggression are based on learning formulations. Bandura's theory stresses the importance of the acquisition of aggressive

408 SITUATIONAL DETERMINANTS OF BEHAVIOR

responses (through observation and reinforcement), instigations to aggress, and the maintenance of aggressivity by means of rewards and punishments.

Psychological interest in application has primarily been in seeking to find ways to prevent or to mitigate aggression and violence. Retaliation and punishment are obvious and familiar ways to stop aggression, but they tend to have precisely the opposite effect unless there is a close matching of level of retaliation to level of aggression received. Equity studies suggest that we will not punish an instigator beyond a certain point when he has gotten what he deserves. Empathy seems to be a likely mechanism to inhibit aggression. The less abstract the victim, as when we are aware of his pain, the less we aggress toward him. Individual differences in the development of empathy are undoubtedly important, but we have only begun to study how this capacity can be developed as a way to regulate human aggression.

12

Sexual

Behavior

There are few aspects of human behavior which approach sexuality with respect to its pervasiveness in one's everyday life and in the magnitude of society's efforts to define and regulate its expression. In addition to the intertwining of sexuality with moral and legal complexities, it is obvious that sexual expression can be the source of intense pleasure and fulfillment or of crippling guilt and lifelong misery. Paradoxically, sexual abstinence can be the source of pleasure in deep spiritual commitment or the occasion of seemingly unbearable frustration. Sexual needs are cited as one of the primary reasons both for marriage and for divorce. It is also of interest that while procreation is necessary for the survival of the species, it is not necessary for the survival of the individual, so that any given person may spend a lifetime of celibacy or may engage in autosexual, homosexual, nonprocreational heterosexual behavior, or even in bestiality for a lifetime without doing himself or herself any physical harm.

A sampling of the varied scope of sexual expression is provided in the following series of quotes:

> My beloved put his hand to the hole of the door,
> And my bowels were moved for him.
> I rose up to open to my beloved;
> And my hands dropped with myrrh,
> And my fingers with sweet-smelling myrrh,
> Upon the handles of the lock.

How beautiful are thy feet with shoes,
O prince's daughter!
The joints of thy thighs are like jewels,
The work of the hands of a cunning workman.
Thy navel is like a round goblet,
Which wanteth not liquor;
Thy belly is like an heap of wheat
Set about with lilies.
    (Song of Songs which is the Song of Solomon)

It's all too swift; it's over all too soon—
The quickened pace, the gasps, the final swoon,
The sudden dying down of flame and fire,
The loosened limbs, the loss of all desire.
Let us control it; love is far more than
The itching heat of a stray dog—or man.
Let us put off the moment, let us wait
Before we lose all sense and consummate
What we might well conserve. Let lips and hands
Do all we want to answer our demands.
Let eager mouths and teasing tongues fulfill
Our deepest need until...until...until...
    (Petronius, translated 1963 by Louis Untermeyer)

Starting on your wedding night and continuing through the first year of your marriage, put one bean in a jar for every time you have intercourse. Starting with the beginning of your second year of marriage, take one bean out of the jar for every time you have intercourse. When you die there will still be some beans left in the jar. (Old folk theory quoted by Martin, 1970, p. 326)

I try to keep them from knowing too much; I approach it the same as my parents did. My parents did not tell me about it. I don't discuss it either. I think sex education corrupts the minds of 15–16 year olds! There is absolutely *no* communication between parents and kids about sex. Kids know too much already. I just tell them to behave and keep their eyes open. (Parent quoted by Libby and Nass, 1971, p. 233)

Keith (the leader of the group) went up to a car in which two people were parked and grabbed the keys from the ignition. When the man attempted to take the keys from him, he knocked the man down. Harry took the man's wallet and Keith climbed into the back seat with the girl. She asked what they were doing with her boy friend and Keith said, "They are probably beating him up." The girl agreed to do whatever Keith wanted if he would leave her boy friend alone. While Keith was in the process of having intercourse with her, some of the other boys started grabbing her breasts and pulling her blouse up so that her breasts were exposed. Don was next. (Case history reported by Blanchard, 1959, p. 260)

Police investigation revealed that the offender was driving around in his car, saw an 11-year-old white girl, and with a pellet pistol, forced her into his car and drove into a wooden area. He took her from the car, bound her hands behind her with a rope, disrobed her, attempted to rape her and performed cunnilingus on her. He beat her on the head, rolled her onto her stomach and attempted to assault her from behind...The girl's physical examination revealed bite marks on both her shoulders and privates. (Described by Berest, 1970, p. 211)

In the series of quotations which range from pre-Christian odes to the raptures and refinements of sex through wry cynicism about marital sex, negative parental attitudes about sex education, and on to incidents of gang rape and a sadistic attack on a child, it is obvious that sexual expression and sexual attitudes may take many and diverse forms.

Among the reasons for the current research interest in sexual behavior is the concern over what is often termed the sexual revolution (Cannon and Long, 1971; Christensen and Gregg, 1970). Considerable publicity has been given to such departures from conventional mores as communal marriages and mate swapping and to the sexual license now permitted in literature, movies, and the theater. Is exposure to these erotic stimuli the cause of changes in sexual behavior or is it possible that the behavior and the artistic expressions both are the result of more basic changes in our society? Before we can even begin to answer such questions, it is necessary to know a great deal about the antecedents of sexual arousal and of the determinants of the specific ways in which sexual needs are expressed. In the present chapter, we will examine several aspects of our current knowledge of heterosexual behavior.

One general point may help place this material in perspective. Of the various other physiological needs of mankind, sex holds a unique position. There is a short story which points out some of the absurdities of our sexual attitudes by presenting a society in which eating is treated in the way that we treat sexual activity. That is, sex is freely expressed and openly and publicly encouraged while eating is regarded as shameful and private and limited to a single dish which must be chosen by late adolescence. In that fictional society there were, of course, places where one could go illegally to obtain sumptuous meals cooked by women willing to sell their services. Also, cook books could be surreptitiously obtained from book dealers who specialized in such material. If we lived in such a society, the present text might well contain a chapter on eating behavior but leave sexual behavior to the physiological psychologists.

A BASE RELATIONSHIP

As yet, it is not possible to identify a body of research or a method of investigation which is central to an understanding of sexual behavior. For that reason, it will be necessary to examine a number of different ways in which investigators have approached the study of sexuality.

It is clear that in addition to the necessary physiological underpinnings of sexual excitability, man as well as other animals can be aroused through various sense modalities by what is seen, heard, smelled, or touched. Arousal can be a function of a specific cue associated with an appropriate sexual object, and a good deal of the animal research in this area has dealt with the identification of such cues. With human beings, an additional source of arousal seems to be operative in man's thoughts and fantasies about sex, and these seem to be of greater importance than any simple releasing stimulus. For this reason, in the experimental study of sexual behavior, investigators tend to utilize some relatively complex abstract stimuli such as pictorial or verbal material in which sexual activity is presented. Presumably, such material is arousing because the subject identifies with the individuals in the scene or story and hence responds to some extent as if he were actually participating in the activity rather than just remaining a spectator. Thus, it has been found repeatedly that verbal indicators of arousal are elicited by exposure to such pictorial stimuli as nude members of the opposite sex or individuals engaged in sexual acts (Brehm and Behar, 1966; Schmidt, Sigusch, and Meyberg, 1969) or verbal stimuli such as sexually descriptive passages (Byrne and Sheffield, 1965; Jakobovits, 1965). Thus, one approach to the study of sexual behavior begins with the relationship between an erotic stimulus and a verbal indication of sexual arousal.

A functional relationship can be established if there is some reasonable way to scale the stimulus along a dimension. Because of the complexity of the kinds of erotic stimuli used in these investigations, the identification of a dimension represents a more difficult conceptual task than it might appear. What is needed is a way of specifying that stimulus A is more arousing than stimulus B which is more arousing than stimulus C, and so on. How might one arrive at such a scale and on what basis?

Scaling of Heterosexual Behavior

One potentially useful approach is suggested by the work of Podell and Perkins (1957) who proposed that premarital sexual experience cumulates along a single continuum. That is, experience 1 is likely to occur first and then experience 2 and then experience 3 and so forth. Such a scale would mean, among other things, that an individual who had engaged in 3 would very likely already have experienced 2 and 1 but not necessarily 4 and 5. With a large group of unmarried male college students, the researchers administered items asking about heterosexual behavior and found that fifteen behaviors could be ordered along this Guttman scale. The behaviors, in order, were:

1. Embracing
2. Kissing on the lips
3. Manually manipulating a female's breast through clothing
4. Kissing with tongue contact
5. Manually manipulating a female's nude breast
6. Kissing a female's breast
7. Manually manipulating a female's genitals
8. Manually manipulating each other's genitals
9. Having sexual intercourse
10. Having the male's genitals manipulated to orgasm by the female
11. Sucking a female's breast
12. Touching genitals together without intromission
13. Having interfemoral relations
14. Having a female orally contact the male's genitals
15. Having oral contact with a female's genitals

The authors indicated that such data suggest, but do not prove, that premarital sexual behavior tends to follow that sequence. It also seems possible that the various acts indicate a scale of sexual excitement in that individuals tend to progress along the continuum toward increasingly exciting experiences. Experiences in the second half of the scale may be intrinsically more arousing or they may be experienced as more arousing because they are more novel or more forbidden. In any event, the fact that the behaviors could be scaled leads to the possibility of creating a stimulus dimension representing such acts. Such a stimulus scale will be designated as varying along a dimension of *eroticism*.

CREATING STIMULI WHICH ELICIT
DIFFERENTIAL AROUSAL

In a series of investigations which will be discussed in greater detail later in this chapter, Schmidt and Sigusch (1970) created motion pictures which depict a variety of sexual acts that correspond in part to the Podell and Perkins behavioral scale. If the general idea is correct that the behavioral scale corresponds to an eroticism dimension, one would expect that verbal reports of sexual arousal would be a function of the type of behavior shown on the screen.

In one experiment, male subjects at the University of Hamburg were exposed to one of four stimulus conditions in which various sexual behaviors were depicted in the form of either a movie or slides taken from the movie. In Table 12-1 is shown a description of the stimulus conditions with the corresponding self-ratings of sexual arousal on a nine-point scale. It may be seen that the arousal responses increase as the eroticism of the stimuli increases.

Table 12-1. Mean Sexual Arousal of Males
In Response to Pictorial Sexual Stimuli

Theme of Movie or Slide	*Arousal*
Male and female undress to their underclothing and engage in manual-genital petting without reaching orgasm	4.4
Male and female undress, engage in foreplay with manual-genital petting, and engage in face to face intercourse	5.3
Male and female undress and engage in manual-genital petting, cunnilingus, and fellatio, reaching orgasm	5.4
Male and female undress and engage in manual-genital petting, cunnilingus, and fellatio, followed by sexual intercourse in a variety of positions	5.6

(Data from Schmidt and Sigusch, 1970)

Extending the Eroticism Dimension

The Schmidt and Sigusch investigation involved a relatively limited range of highly erotic stimuli. It should be possible, of course, to establish a base relationship over a broader stimulus range.

Levitt and Brady (1965) utilized a series of nineteen photographs which varied in sexual content and which presumably constituted an eroticism dimension. For each of their nineteen themes, three different photographs were selected in order to minimize such extraneous characteristics as the appearance of specific individuals in the pictures.

The subjects were male graduate students who were shown each of the three sets of photographs in different orders. Their task was to rate each sex scene on a scale ranging from zero (not at all sexually stimulating) to five (very highly sexually stimulating).

It was found that the order of presentation of the stimuli did not affect the ratings, but the content of the pictures did. There was relatively high agreement among the subjects concerning the arousal value of specific themes. The content of the various photographs and the mean arousal response across the three sets are shown in Table 12-2. Once again, it is clear that subjects are responding to some sort of eroticism dimension, though the relative placement of each theme seems to vary somewhat in different investigations.

In any event, the data suggest that it is possible to identify a stimulus dimension ranging in eroticism which has a functional relationship with verbal indications of sexual arousal. The general nature of this relationship can be seen in Figure 12-1 in which the Levitt and Brady data have been graphed. It should be helpful to use such a base relationship as a starting point for our examination of research on sexual behavior.

**Table 12-2. Mean Sexual Arousal of Males
in Response to Photographs of 19 Erotic Themes**

Theme	Arousal
1. Male in undershorts	.04
2. Nude male	.13
3. Homosexual anal intercourse	.42
4. Male masturbating	.79
5. Female torturing male	.81
6. Homosexual fellatio	.84
7. Male torturing female	1.19
8. Nude females petting	1.80
9. Homosexual cunnilingus	2.08
10. Clothed female	2.63
11. Group oral sex	2.69
12. Female masturbating	2.72
13. Heterosexual cunnilingus	3.04
14. Nude female	3.17
15. Heterosexual fellatio	3.39
16. Partially clad heterosexual petting	3.43
17. Nude heterosexual petting	3.63
18. Dorsal-ventral intercourse	3.70
19. Ventral-ventral intercourse	4.13

(Data from Levitt and Brady, 1965)

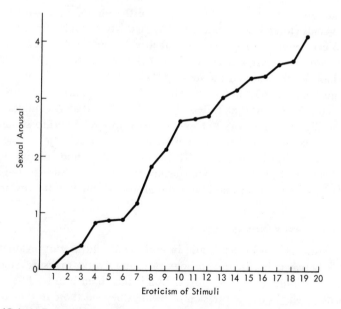

Fig. 12-1 A Base Relationship: Sexual Arousal as a Function of Stimulus
Eroticism. (Data from Levitt and Brady, 1965.)

ANALYTIC RESEARCH

It was noted earlier that the stimuli used in the study of sexual behavior tend to be both complex and varied. This is the kind of situation in which a great deal of analytic research is required in order to determine precisely which aspects of the stimulus have an effect on sexual arousal. Can we identify the various elements in an erotic stimulus which elicit sexual excitement?

Nudity versus Clothing

It seems obvious that the depiction of individuals in the nude is more arousing than is the depiction of the same individuals fully clothed. At the same time, there is a great deal of folk wisdom which suggests that nudity can be anti-erotic, that sexuality is enhanced by mystery, and that clothing and other adornments add to sexual allure.

Levitt and Hinesley (1967) sought to test these alternative propositions by comparing responses to ten photographs depicting nude individuals in various sexual acts with ten parallel photographs in which there was no bodily exposure beyond that required by the activity itself. The photographs involved such activities as intercourse, fellatio, cunnilingus, and petting. Male graduate students were shown slides of the photographs with the order of nude versus clothed pictures varied. After thirty seconds of exposure time, each subject rated his degree of sexual arousal on the five-point scale. As expected, the mean arousal response to the nude pictures (M = 2.2) was higher than for the clothed pictures (M = 1.6).

The authors (p. 66) noted, "Perhaps this is not surprising; the reader may be tempted to say that this is the kind of fact that is common knowledge. Possibly. But this does not explain why this relationship should exist, why nudity per se should be of such significance in an object which is intrinsically sexually stimulating." It seems possible that nudity has frequently been associated with sexual behavior and hence adds to the arousal value of the stimulus over and above the arousal elicited by the sex act itself.

Affection versus Nonaffection

One of the distinctions often made in both legal and literary evaluations of erotica is between hard-core pornography and erotic realism. Among the elements contributing to such a distinction is the absence in traditional hard-core pornography of any expression of feelings beyond those in the erogenous zones. In addition, it is frequently asserted that sexual arousal in females is much more dependent on the presence of elements of affection and love than on simple sexual activity.

Both male and female students at the University of Hamburg were given one of two stories to read in an investigation conducted by Schmidt, Sigusch, and Schäfer (1973). In both stories, the sexual experience of a young couple was described, and the content included flirting, petting, foreplay with oral stimulation of the genitals, and intercourse in various positions. The only difference in the stories was in the amount of affection displayed by the characters. In one, the two individuals were bound together only by their sexual experience while in the other it was clear that there was a great deal of affection between the partners. Among the response measures was a rating of sexual arousal on a nine-point scale.

The results are shown in Table 12-3. There was no difference between

Table 12-3. Mean Sex Arousal of Males and Females to Erotic Stories with and without Affectional Content

Type of Story	Males	Females	Total
Story without Affection	5.4	5.2	5.3
Story with Affection	6.0	5.4	5.7
Total	5.7	5.4	

(Data from Schmidt, Sigusch, and Schäfer, 1973)

the stories in their effect on sexual arousal, and there was no sex difference in responding to the two kinds of stories. Among the conclusions of the authors was the proposal that "Affection is not a necessary precondition for women to react sexually to sexual stimuli in the same manner as men" (Schmidt, Sigusch, and Schäfer, 1973).

ANALYZING THE ELEMENTS OF A PICTORIAL STIMULUS

If a given stimulus such as a photograph is identified as arousing, analytic research should be able to determine precisely those elements which elicit sexual excitement. This procedure has not been systematically followed with the kind of erotic stimuli discussed so far, but it was used by Wiggins and Wiggins (1969) as a way of determining the characteristics of female bodies to which males respond. The specific interest was in determining whether there is, in fact, a typology among males which corresponds to such culturally popular terms as "breast man," "ass man," and "leg man."

The investigators constructed silhouettes of females in which the size of breasts, buttocks, and legs were independently varied. A large group of male undergraduates was asked to respond to 105 pairs of nude silhouettes of the type shown in Figure 12-2. Factor analysis indicated that there are

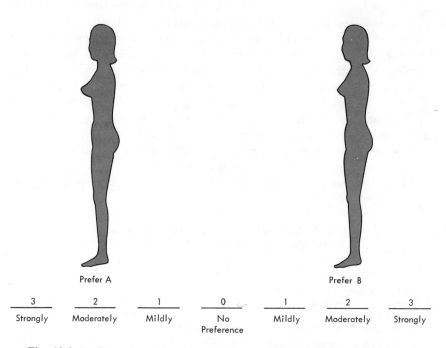

Prefer A   Prefer B

| 3 | 2 | 1 | 0 | 1 | 2 | 3 |
| Strongly | Moderately | Mildly | No Preference | Mildly | Moderately | Strongly |

Fig. 12-2 An Example of the Stimulus Pairs to Which Subjects Were Asked to Respond by Indicating Their Preference. (After Wiggins and Wiggins, 1969.)

at least five distinct groups in terms of their somatic preferences with breast men, leg men, and three somewhat more complex groups involving combinations of characteristics.

For the present discussion, the primary point is that the Wiggins' technique could be used in studying the characteristics of complex erotic stimuli in which variables such as nudity, visibility of genitalia, physical attractiveness of the participants, race, age, or whatever, could be manipulated along a continuum to determine effects on sexual arousal.

STIMULUS GENERALITY

As Mann (1971) points out, the stimuli used in experimental studies of sexual arousal have usually been selected on the basis of consensual assumptions about their erotic value. Until such time as a genuine base relationship is established, the determination of stimulus generality will in large part involve an examination of the kinds of stimuli and the kinds of situational contexts which influence self-reported arousal.

Types of Erotic Stimulus Material

In the studies discussed so far, the stimuli have involved words, pictures, movies, and drawings. One rather obvious question has to do with whether the medium in which erotic stimuli are presented has any effect on sexual arousal.

Photographs versus Drawings. Levitt and Hinesley (1967) proposed that the closer a stimulus resembles reality, the greater would be its arousal value. Thus, it follows that "...a line drawing, no matter how excellently executed and how closely it resembled actual physical objects, would not be as effective a stimulus as a photographic reproduction" (p. 63).

For comparison purposes, twelve line drawings were matched with twelve photographs with respect to the kinds of sexual activity depicted and the approximate position and appearance of the participants. Male graduate students responded to each type of picture on the arousal scale. The mean arousal response to the photographs (M = 2.1) was found to be greater than that to the matched drawings (M = 1.6). It was concluded that the greater degree of arousal elicited by the photographs was simply a function of their being a better facsimile of "real life."

Verbal versus Pictorial Stimuli. When we move from pictorial stimuli to verbal ones, it could be argued that photographs and movies are more like real life than are verbal descriptions of sexual activity. At the same time, if the major determinant of arousal is the extent to which the individual places himself in the situation, it is clear that written material very often has the power to cause the reader to identify with the portrayed characters and thus to become part of the interaction. Thus, depending on the quality of the picture and on the skill of the writer, it would seem that words or pictures could be equally arousing. When Kutschinsky (1971a) interviewed a large number of subjects in Copenhagen, Denmark, concerning their experiences with erotic materials, both men and women indicated that they were sexually aroused by books, pictures, and films. Men, however, were more likely to mention pictorial stimuli while women were more likely to mention books as arousing. Such data suggest that both types of stimuli are arousing, but that there may be a sex difference with respect to which is more arousing.

An investigation by Byrne and Lamberth (1971) dealt with response to matched pictorial and verbal stimuli by both males and females. The subjects were married couples at Purdue University. The photographic stimuli consisted of slides of the nineteen pictures used by Levitt and Brady while the verbal material consisted of nineteen short mimeographed passages from various books; the passages were selected to match the pictures. Each couple was either shown the slides or asked to read the passages; after each theme, sexual arousal was indicated. A total arousal score was determined, and this score could range from zero (no sexual arousal in response to any theme) to ninety-five (strong arousal in response to every theme).

The results may be seen in Table 12-4. For these particular stimuli there

**Table 12-4. Mean Sexual Arousal of Males and Females
in Response to Photographic or Verbal Stimuli**

	Males	*Females*
Photographic Stimuli	22.71	19.53
Verbal Stimuli	23.07	25.60

(Data from Byrne and Lamberth, 1971)

was no difference between the two types of stimulus material, nor between males and females. There was a slight trend toward greater female than male arousal to the verbal stimuli, but this difference did not reach significance. It would seem, then, that while photographs are somewhat more arousing than line drawings, there is no demonstrable difference between photographs and verbal material in arousal value.

Imagination. The effects of erotic stimuli are presumably the result of their power to elicit the fantasies of the subject and hence place him imaginatively in the erotic situation. Just how important is this imaginative component in human sexual arousal? Beach (1969) points out the differential importance of hormonal influences on sexual behavior as one moves up the evolutionary scale. For example, in lower mammals such as the rat, sexual behavior is strongly controlled by hormones from the ovaries and testes (e.g., Lisk, 1970; Young, Goy, and Phoenix, 1964), while in higher mammals there is much greater control by the central nervous system. The neocortex, which also is responsible for such functions as memory and learning, plays the major role in determining human sexual behavior. Beach reported that monkeys, chimpanzees, and human beings engage in sexual play before puberty and that humans often remain sexually responsive even though their hormonal level has dropped markedly (for example, in old age). Other studies show that castration has a great effect on the sexual behavior of lower mammals, but that apes, monkeys, and human beings are not necessarily sexually incapacitated by castration (Luttge, 1971). Beach concludes:

> The marked freedom of erotic responsiveness from hormonal control in our species is, I believe, a direct consequence of the extreme dependence of human behavior upon the complex and intricately organized neocortex. Fish and amphibians have no neocortex, and reptiles and birds have only a rudimentary

one. In rats the cortex is well defined but small. In monkeys and apes it is much larger and more specialized; in man it constitutes 90 percent of the brain's volume (p. 34).

One implication of this line of reasoning is that anything which induces subjects to thinks about erotic events should be as arousing as an external stimulus. In fact, if the function of pictures and verbal stimuli is simply to elicit fantasy behavior, it is possible that a more direct inducement to imaginative activity would actually be more arousing than exposure to specific external stimuli.

In the Byrne and Lamberth (1971) study of pictorial versus verbal stimuli, a third arousal condition was also used. Instead of being shown any erotic material, some of the married couples were told:

> Your task is somewhat difficult in that you will need to use your imagination. As you know, sexual material can appear in movies, books, still pictures, and, less frequently, in phonograph records. We are going to ask you to consider a series of themes or activities and imagine what they would be like in movies, books, etc. You will have 20 seconds to think about each and then to indicate on the rating scale the degree to which the depiction of that scene or activity is sexually arousing to you.

The descriptive phrases, one to a page, were designed to match the slides and passages. The only external stimuli, then, were the following words:

> 1. Petting, two nude females. 2. Nude female with sadistic male. 3. Female wearing blouse and short skirt, thigh partially exposed. 4. Oral-genital contact, two males. 5. Heterosexual intercourse, face-to-face, female on bottom. 6. Group activity, two females and one male, oral-genital contact. 7. Oral-genital contact, male on female. 8. Oral-genital contact, female on male. 9. Nude female masturbating. 10. Male wearing undershorts. 11. Petting, male and female in the nude. 12. Nude female. 13. Oral-genital contact, two females. 14. Anal intercourse, two males. 15. Nude male with sadistic female. 16. Nude male masturbating. 17. Heterosexual intercourse, face-to-back, female sitting on male 18. Nude male. 19. Petting, male and female partially clad.

The findings were somewhat surprising. As shown in Table 12-5, the mean arousal responses of both males and females was almost twice as high in the

Table 12-5. Mean Sexual Arousal in Response to Photographic and Verbal Stimuli as Compared to Instructions to Imagine the Same Scenes

Pictorial Stimuli	*Verbal Stimuli*	*Imagination Instructions*
21.12	24.33	43.15

(Data from Byrne and Lamberth, 1971)

imagination condition as in response to either the photographic or verbal stimuli. It was suggested that imaginative fantasies "...can be more personally involving, can involve whomever one wishes as the imagined participants, and can be completely hidden from public scrutiny" (Byrne and Lamberth, 1971, p. 62). Individual differences in "sex drive" may in fact be a function of individual differences in learning to engage in sexual fantasies.

NOVELTY

Effect of a New Sexual Partner. In studies of the mating behavior of mammals, it is found that males of various species tend to be unresponsive sexually for a period of time following ejaculation (Beach, Westbrook, and Clemens, 1966). If the male has achieved several successive ejaculations, there is a somewhat prolonged period of sexual inactivity presumably as the result of satiation. There is another sort of finding, however, which suggests that this lack of sexual interest can be overcome. When a new female partner is provided, the male will respond with renewed sexual activity (Clemens, 1967; Wilson, Kuehn, and Beach, 1963). It is as if the "satiation" were not a general physiological depletion, but rather nonresponsiveness which is specific to a given partner.

With human subjects it is obviously not feasible to conduct experiments in which satiated males are provided with a novel partner in order to investigate man's similarity to other species in this respect. It may be noted, however, that sociological and anthropological studies of mate swapping often suggest that one of the motives of the participants is the increase in sexual arousal which is offered by new partners (e.g., Bartell, 1971). Denfield and Gordon (1970) describe mate swapping as one solution to the problems of marital sexual monotony. Consistent with the proposition that the novelty afforded by new partners affects human males just as it does representatives of infra-human species is the O'Neill (1970) finding that the majority of males report having more than one orgasm per mate swapping party. The same authors also report that many of the participants "...bored and restless with long-term sex with one mate, turn to group sex as a stimulant and sexual turn-on" (p. 110). Interestingly enough, those who engage in mate swapping tend to be better educated than the general population and are mostly in professional and white-collar occupations. It has been estimated on the basis of available research data that eight million couples in this country have engaged in mate swapping activities (Breedlove and Breedlove, 1964).

The question to be answered next is whether there is any relationship between the animal studies of the effects of a novel partner, the cultural phenomenon of mate swapping, and the laboratory study of the determinants of human sexual arousal.

Satiation and Repeated Exposure to Erotic Stimuli. Survey findings such as those of Gebhard, Gagon, Pomeroy, and Christenson (1965) suggest that those who collect a large amount of erotic materials tend to lose interest in them over time. Sonenschein (1969) has hypothesized that repeated exposure to erotic stimuli leads not to continued excitement but to boredom. Such considerations lead to the suggestion that an important variable determining the effect of erotic stimuli would be the familiarity-novelty of the stimuli. Generalizing somewhat broadly from the kinds of behavior discussed previously, it would seem reasonable to hypothesize that there would be little arousal in response to familiar erotic stimuli, while any novel erotic stimuli would elicit a sexual response.

Howard, Reifler, and Liptzin (1971) tested these hypotheses by exposing male university students to erotic films and reading material for ninety minutes per day, five days per week, for three weeks. Subjects were alone in a room and were permitted to view or read whatever they wished during this period. They were free to choose either the erotic material or nonerotic items such as the *Readers' Digest.*

During the first few sessions, most of the time was spent in examining the erotic stimuli, and the subjects' reported sexual arousal was high. By the second week of the experiment, both the amount of time spent with the erotica and the reported arousal levels began a steady decline. By the eleventh session, only 30 percent of the time was spent with the erotic stimuli.

Brock (1971) has applied commodity theory to erotic materials and has proposed that erotica is valued to the extent that it is unavailable or difficult to obtain. Thus, censorship and restrictiveness tend to increase the desirability of such material. It seems equally plausible that when erotic stimuli are relatively unavailable, their increased value is a function of their unfamiliarity under such circumstances. Freely available erotic material simply loses its novelty.

OTHER STIMULI WITH AROUSAL PROPERTIES

Odor. Animal studies provide abundant evidence of the role of smell in sexual behavior. Characteristically, various odors provide the primary cue that a member of the opposite sex is responsive. With male rats, Krames, Costanzo, and Carr (1967) found that it is the odor of the new sex partner which arouses the interest of satiated males. When allowed to sniff empty containers which smelled of either their sex partner or a novel female, male rats spent signficantly more time investigating the odor from the novel female. When females were studied in the same way, they showed only a slight and nonsignificant preference for the odor of a novel male. In studies of rhesus monkeys, Michael, Keverne, and Bonsall (1971) have shown that an interference with the sense of smell in males prevents sexual responsiveness to females. The specific substances in the vaginal secretions which were responsible for male arousal were identified as aliphatic acids. When these secretions were placed on unreceptive females, males became sufficiently excited that they attempted to mount their unwilling partners; one male monkey who was repeatedly rejected simply masturbated to orgasm.

Somewhat surprisingly, the effect of odor on human sexual arousal has been largely neglected by researchers. Not only would such effects be expected on the basis of animal studies, but the advertising of many products is clearly based on their reported ability to alter one's aroma and hence enhance one's sexual appeal. The general advertising message is that the natural odors of the human skin, mouth, armpit, feet, and (more recently) genitals are unpleasant, especially to members of the opposite sex. With the proper perfume, after shave lotion, toothpaste, mouth wash, and deodorant, however, it is possible to correct such defects and become a highly desired sexual object. Whether any natural or commercially supplied odor actually has a measurable effect on human sexual arousal is a question still to be answered by research.

Music. It is obvious that music has numerous associations with sexual activities and courtship; for example, the blatant sexual content of some rock music or the possible sexual connotations of a musical beat. The use of music to accompany strippers and belly dancers is designed to enhance their erotic appeal. When religious groups ban dancing or disapprove of specific types of music, it would seem that it is the assumed sexual stimulation to which they are objecting. In an experiment by Beardslee and Fogelson (1958) male and female college students were given two pictures and four musical selections about which to write creative stories. The music consisted of three-minute excerpts from nonvocal selections judged to be arousing or non-arousing. The stories were then scored for sexual imagery. Males and females did not differ in their response to the pictures. With the music, however, there was more symbolic sex activity and sex symbolism in the stories written in response to the arousing than to the nonarousing music; in addition, musically stimulated females scored higher than males. The authors suggested that music either innately arouses sexual responses in women, more so than for men, or that such associations are conditioned more to music for females than for males.

Schiller (1971) approached the question in a different way by the use of interviews and questionnaires with adolescent females in a school for pregnant girls and also in a junior college. Almost all of the girls reported that at least some music had stimulated their erotic feelings. It was observed that irrespective of differences in age, ethnic group, socioeconomic class, or sexual experience, music was reported to serve as a catalyst for love and a stimulus for sexual arousal. Schiller (1971, p. 195) concluded that, "...the pregnant girls did not become pregnant as a result of exposure to obscene and pornographic materials. Rather, the stimuli which typically 'turned them on' and which they labeled as erotically arousing were the ordinary forms of mass media to which practically all members of our culture are frequently exposed."

In addition to the effects of specific erotic stimuli on sexual arousal, it would be expected that various aspects of the total situation would exert an influence on arousal. For example, a constant problem in psychological research in this area is the inappropriateness of sexual arousal and the impossibility of engaging in subsequent sexual behavior in the typical laboratory situation. The findings reported in these experiments are assumed to generalize to the bedroom, the automobile, or wherever else actual sexual behavior occurs. The verification of that assumption is simply not feasible for obvious reasons. Within the laboratory setting, however, it is possible to identify the kinds of variables which enhance or interfere with sexual arousal.

Characteristics of Experimenter. More than in most research, the experimenter in sexual investigations seems to have an effect on the response. One could easily imagine different results in the same study for male versus female experimenters or for someone creating a joking versus an anxious atmosphere. Mussen and Scodel (1955) exposed male undergraduates to slides of attractive nude females and obtained ratings of the sexual attractiveness of the girls. For one group of subjects, the experimenter was a formal, professorial, stern man in his sixties. A second group was met by a young, casually dressed graduate student. After the experimenter left the room, a second investigator entered and administered a series of TAT cards. Stories told in response to the cards were scored for sexual activity, and the informal group was found to express much more sexuality than the formal group. Presumably, the original sexual arousal in response to the slides was different as a function of the differences in the two experimenters.

In a quite different experimental task, Chapman, Chapman, and Brelje (1969) provided further support for the effect of the experimenter on responses to erotic stimuli. It has been shown that pupil dilation is an indicator of interest or positive evaluation (Hess, 1965; Hess and Polt, 1966) and that males show dilation in response to pictures of nude females (Hess and Polt, 1960; Nunnally, Knott, Duchnowski, and Parker, 1967). In a study of pupillary response, Chapman, et al. used two experimenters, both male graduate students in their twenties, who differed in personality and in their style of interacting with subjects. One wore a coat and tie and was serious, businesslike, formal, and aloof. The other wore khaki trousers and a sport shirt or sweater and was energetic, buoyant, casual, and friendly. The stimuli were slides of attractive nude or seminude females, attractive males, and control pictures of landscapes. The response measure was relative amount of pupil dilation, as measured in close-up photographs of the subjects. The subjects were male students at the University of Wisconsin. It was found that with the informal, casual experimenter, the subjects responded to the female slides with more pupil dilation than to the male slides. Those subjects run by the formal, aloof experimenter did not show this differentiation. It appears once again that erotic interest was fostered by a casual, permissive interaction with an experimenter and inhibited by a formal, businesslike interaction.

Alcohol. The influence of alcohol on sexual behavior is a familiar aspect of our culture as expressed by such bits of advice as "Candy is dandy, but liquor is quicker." Because alcohol is a depressant, its effect is not as a physiological aphrodisiac but rather as a reducer of anxiety about sexual responsiveness.

Clark (1952) presented undergraduate males with photographic slides of attractive nude females or with nonsexual slides and then obtained TAT stories from the subjects. It was found that there was less manifest sex content in the stories of the experimental group than in the stories of the control group. It was proposed that sexual arousal in response to the nude slides was accompanied by anxiety and that the anxiety exerted an inhibitory effect on the expression of sexual imagery in the stories. As a test of this hypothesis, the experiment was run again at a beer party. Under these conditions, the erotic slides led to more manifest sexual content in TAT stories than was true for stories not preceded by erotic slides. It was proposed that the beer reduced the anxiety associated with arousal and made it possible for sexual responses to be expressed.

Situational Influences on Real-Life Sexual Behavior. To emphasize the point that situational effects are not limited to experimental settings, two findings in studies of actual behavior will be presented. These data again suggest that sexual behavior is a function of a number of influences beyond that of immediate erotic stimuli.

In a survey, Schmidt and Sigusch (1971) compared the sexual behavior of West German workers and students. All of the subjects were twenty or twenty-one years of age and all were single. The two groups were found to be quite different in their sexual activity. By the age of twenty, 81 percent of the male workers but only 44 percent of the male students had engaged in sexual intercourse. The comparable figures for the females were 83 percent and 33 percent. The workers reported that their first intercourse experience occurred on the average of four years earlier than did the students. For those who were sexually active, there was also a student-worker difference in that both male and female students reported a higher incidence of manual-genital contact, cunnilingus, fellatio, and total nudity during intercourse than did the workers. Thus, both age at which intercourse began and the specific sexual activities which occur tend to be a function of worker versus student status. These findings are quite comparable to those reported for American samples two decades earlier (Kinsey, Pomeroy, and Martin, 1948; Kinsey, Pomeroy, Martin, and Gebhard, 1953). The two German groups were found to be similar to one another in their general attitudes about sex; in addition, physiological differences seem quite improbable. The reasons for the differences in sexual behavior would seem to lie in situational factors (Schmidt and Sigusch, 1971, p. 103):

> Since the time of sexual maturity is probably the same for the two classes, the average difference of four years shows how strong the beginning of coitus relationships is influenced by social factors. Workers, especially unskilled and semiskilled ones, reach relatively greater financial independence sooner than students. They do not remain as long as students under the pressure of parents and school.

Many extraneous situational factors undoubtedly influence both sexual arousal and the incidence of overt sexual behavior, even within a marital relationship. Examples include fatigue, illness of one's children, worries about finances, and amount of free time. Udry and Morris (1970) proposed that coitus is influenced by the day of the week. They obtained daily reports of sexual behavior from a group of white, educated females. Subjects reported their sexual behavior each day for ninety days. As shown in Figure 12-3, for

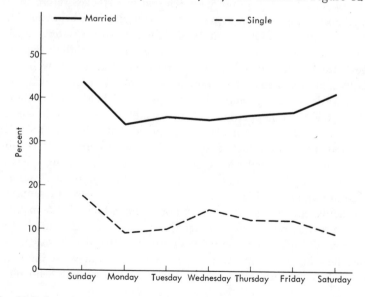

Fig. 12-3 Sexual Intercourse as a Function of Day of the Week for Educated White Females. (After Udry and Morris, 1970, p. 230.)

married women intercourse was most likely to occur on Saturday and Sunday, while for single women Sunday was the most likely day for intercourse. It was suggested that most people do not work on the weekend, and many stay in bed longer in the morning. In addition, there is the possibility of sexual interaction during the day, and there is less interference by fatigue and preoccupation. It is interesting to note that for a sample of black males and females, predominantly low in socioeconomic class and educational level, there was no tendency for the weekend pattern at all. As Udry and Morris (1970, p. 234) suggest, "It appears that the 'weekend theory' was generated from the experience of educated whites, and is perhaps limited in applicability to them."

RESPONSE GENERALITY

Sampling Biases in the Study of Sexual Behavior

While it is true that psychological research almost never approaches the ideal of a truly random sample of the population, research on sexual behavior presents more than the usual problems in this respect. Because sex is a much more taboo topic in our culture than are attraction, altruism, aggression, or any other behavioral area, a great many individuals refuse to volunteer as subjects for sexual research and many who do nevertheless refuse to answer questions about their own personal sexual attitudes and behavior. Data in this area are quite possibly based on samples which are systematically different from the total population. For example, subjects in these experiments may be more sexually liberal, more interested in sex, and may have quite different sexual preferences than those who do not take part in such research. If so, the various findings and relationships would hold true only for that portion of the total population which resembles the research volunteers. For example, Maslow and Sakoda (1952) found that volunteers for a Kinsey study scored significantly higher in self-esteem than nonvolunteers. Since it had also been found that high self-esteem is associated with unconventional sexual attitudes and nonvirginity, it was argued that the research sample for a sex study would be biased in the direction of over-representation of sexually active and sexually unconventional individuals. Even in attempts to establish a base relationship between erotic stimuli and arousal, it seems possible that the relative erotic value of stimuli depicting acts such as cunnilingus, fellatio, and unusual intercourse positions may be different for individuals who volunteer for such research and individuals who refuse to participate.

These are difficult problems for researchers to solve satisfactorily, but Kaats and Davis (1971) devised a way to explore several aspects of sample differences. They administered a sexual standards questionnaire to various large groups of male and female students. The questionnaire dealt with the acceptability of various sexual acts for an unmarried couple, the sexual experiences of the subject, and attitudes which involved sexual liberalism. For comparison purposes, the subjects were divided into a control group which simply was given the questionnaire during a regular class session, a voluntary completion group which took the questionnaire home and returned it if they wished, and a voluntary selection group composed of subjects who signed up for a study labeled "Sexual Attitudes and Behaviors." In the control group, 98 percent completed the questionnaire, in the voluntary completion group 63 percent did so, and the voluntary selection group consisted only of students who deliberately placed themselves in this kind of research situation.

The control group and the voluntary completion group were virtually the same on all of the measures. The voluntary selection group, however, tended to be more sexually liberal than either of the other two groups, especially for female subjects. Thus, it appears that there are no sexually-relevant differences between those who are willing to complete sexual questionnaires and those who are not. Kaats and Davis (1971, p. 32) note, however, that, "...quite a different picture emerges with respect to the kind of individuals who voluntarily attended the announced study of sexual behavior. The evidence is quite compelling, particularly for the women; these individuals are much more likely to hold liberal sexual attitudes and have more noncoital experience."

Sex Differences

The idea that males and females differ in their responses to erotic stimuli finds support both in everyday observations and in the existing body of survey research in which subjects have been asked to indicate what is arousing to them or to describe their experiences with erotic material. Men indicate much greater interest in erotica and report a greater degree of sexual arousal in response to such material than women (e.g., Kinsey, Pomeroy, Martin, and Gebhard, 1953). Among subjects who are asked to recall their experiences, a much higher proportion of males than females say that they feel sexually aroused when exposed to visual depictions of nudes or sexual activity and also erotic stories. It was suggested that it is "...likely that most females are indifferent to the existence of such material because it means nothing to them erotically" (Kinsey, et al., 1953, p. 662). With societal changes in books, movies, and magazines in the direction of increasing candor and explicitness, one might expect a change in female responsiveness to erotic stimuli. Nevertheless, relatively recent survey studies involving a nation-wide sample of Americans (Abelson, Cohen, Heaton, and Suder,

1971) report the same kind of sex differences found by Kinsey and his colleagues two decades earlier. It also is true that commercial productions with explicit sexual content are aimed almost exclusively at males, and that the patrons of sexploitation movies and "adult" book stores are predominantly males (Nawy, 1971).

It has very frequently been proposed that such sex differences are rooted in biological differences in that males are naturally more sexually aggressive and curious while females are oriented toward love, affection, and motherhood. As Gordon and Shankweiler (1971) found, the best-selling marriage manuals of the past two decades assume that women have less sexual interest than men and that the husband's job is to cultivate his wife's sexuality. Others suggest that the differences simply reflect the conditioning and molding of a male-dominated culture in which women are assigned and taught the passive roles of sex object and housewife. Perhaps females are simply more reluctant to express their sexual interests overtly.

Recent experimental investigations complicate the picture somewhat by presenting evidence that sex differences in response to erotica can be nonexistent and that for certain themes, females may actually be more aroused than males.

Erotic Themes Designed Specifically for Males and Females. In a study of primarily unmarried students at Hamburg University, Sigusch, Schmidt, Reinfeld, and Wiedemann-Sutor (1970) presented slides depicting twenty-four themes. Some of the pictures involved sexual activity and were shown to both sexes while some involved a single individual of the opposite sex from the subject. For example, males were shown a seminude girl with exposed breasts and genitals while females were shown a man removing his pants and revealing his genitals. Subjects participated individually, and the experimenter was out of the room. Each picture was judged with respect to sexual arousal on a seven-point scale.

It was found that there were no significant differences in arousal to eight of the themes, while males were more aroused than females in response to sixteen themes. On the three themes showing couples kissing and otherwise showing affection, the females had higher mean scores than the males. The findings are summarized in Table 12-6. The authors noted that there were large individual differences and that many of the females indicated greater arousal than the average male.

It was noted that the greatest absolute differences were in response to the pictures of a solitary member of the opposite sex. "In our society, pictures showing female seminudes and nudes are constantly offered to the public while pictures of male seminudes and nudes are comparatively rare. Men, therefore, are so to speak, 'conditioned' to these stimuli—that is, they learn much more than women to react sexually to these stimuli, and it is also expected of them" (Sigusch, et al., 1970, p. 20).

Table 12-6. Response of Unmarried Males and Females to Specific Erotic Themes

Themes More Arousing to Males and Females	Themes Equally Arousing to Males and Females
Opposite sex individual in bathing suit	Couple kissing, shoulders naked
Opposite sex individual in bikini bathing suit	Couple in bathing suit kissing and embracing
Close-up of legs of opposite sex	Couple in bed naked above waist showing affection
Opposite sex individual with clothing partially open	Close-up of genitals of opposite sex
Opposite sex individual partially clothed	Naked couple with man stimulating girl's breasts
Opposite sex individual naked	Naked couple in face-to-face coitus, man above
Close-up of breasts or nonerect penis	Naked couple engaging in cunnilingus
Opposite sex individual with genitals exposed	Close-up of genitals in coitus
Seminudity with genitals exposed	
Opposite sex individual naked in posing position	
Seminude couple, female handling penis	
Naked couple, female handling penis	
Naked couple in coitus, from rear	
Naked couple engaging in fellatio	
Close-up of fellatio	
Naked couple in coitus	

(Data from Sigusch et al., 1970)

Response to Erotic Themes by Married Males and Females. In the Byrne and Lamberth (1971) investigation of married couples at Purdue University, the nineteen sexual themes of Levitt and Brady were presented one at a time as either pictorial, verbal, or imaginative stimuli. Arousal responses were obtained from each individual following the presentation of each theme.

It was found that the total arousal response of the males (M = 28.99) did not differ from that of the females (M = 30.08). There also was no difference between the sexes in the relative arousal value of the three types of stimuli. There were, however, several themes which were significantly more arousing to one sex or the other, as shown in Table 12-7. It will be noted

Table 12-7. Sex Differences in Response to Specific Erotic Themes by Married Males and Females

Themes More Arousing to Males than to Females	Themes More Arousing to Females than to Males
Clothed female	Homosexual fellatio
Group oral sex	Male in undershorts
Nude female	Male masturbating
	Nude male

(Data from Byrne and Lamberth, 1971)

that the four themes most arousing to women involve males either alone or interacting with another male. The typical erotic magazine, book, or movie which is oriented toward heterosexual males would be unlikely to include any of these four themes. It is possible that females would find erotica aimed at male homosexuals more arousing than the usual male-oriented hetero- sexual erotica. Because Sigusch, et al. (1970) did not find such themes es- pecially arousing for their female subjects, the possibility is raised that the difference lies in the marital status of the subjects in these two investiga- tions. Perhaps frequent exposure to a nude male in marriage brings about increased sexual responsiveness to male nudity. Still another possibility is that the females in each of the two studies were equally aroused but that mar- ried females find it less threatening to admit that they are aroused by nude males.

Another aspect of sex differences to themes may be in response to mate- rial which is too blatantly erotic or "shocking." In the Schmidt and Sigusch (1970) study of response to the four sexual movies described earlier, there were no sex differences in response to the two milder movies, but females were somewhat less aroused than males by the two stronger movies. Mosher (1971) found the same kind of difference in response to those films by American college students. Again, marital status may affect such responses.

The Byrne and Lamberth data indicated that the most arousing themes for married males *and* females were the themes of cunnilingus, intercourse, fellatio, and nude petting.

Arousal and Projected Arousal of Males and Females. Another question relevant to sex differences in response to erotica concerns the beliefs held by each sex about the arousability of the other sex. Griffitt (1973) was the first to study expectations concerning the response of the opposite sex to such stimuli. He presented the nineteen Levitt and Brady slides to unmarried undergraduate males and females at Kansas State and obtained their arousal ratings plus each subject's predictions of the responses of a member of the opposite sex.

As in the Byrne and Lamberth study of married couples, there was not a significant sex difference in total sexual arousal to the nineteen themes. On specific themes, there were again sex differences very much like those re- ported for married couples with males more aroused by some themes and females by others.

With projections of arousal to the opposite sex, females expected that males would be much more aroused than males expected females to be. In addition, females thought males would be much more aroused than they actually were. Thus, males are more accurate in guessing the total level of female arousal than were females about male arousal. Males did, however, tend to believe that females would be most aroused by themes which they themselves found arousing and hence were frequently incorrect in this respect.

Griffitt (1973) observed one major difference between his findings with unmarried students and the Byrne and Lamberth findings with married couples, suggesting a possibly important point to pursue in future research.

> For the married males and females, the most arousing theme was the portrayal of "oral-genital activity, male on female" while the most arousing theme for the present unmarried females was "petting, male and female partially clad" and for males the portrayal of the "nude female" was considered most arousing. . . It might be speculated that the differing ranks across samples represent, in part, differential experiences across samples with respect to the portrayed activities. For the (presumably) less sexually experienced unmarried individuals, petting and viewing nude portrayals are more frequently encountered than are oral-genital activities. Among the married couples, the "old-hat" themes of petting and nude portrayals are relegated to lower positions concerning degree of arousal elicited than are oral-genital activities in which they are more experienced than are the unmarried subjects.

Sex Differences in Arousal at Different Points in Time. In most instances, sexual arousal is measured in experimental studies following exposure to the stimulus. The findings of Kutschinsky (1971b) raise the possibility that males and females may not differ in their arousal level after exposure to erotica but that they may reach that point in different ways.

His subjects were predominantly married graduate students in Copenhagen, Denmark, who were exposed to one hour of hard-core pornography. The erotic material consisted of a fifteen-minute color film of two girls and a boy performing various kinds of triangular foreplay and intercourse, five color magazines containing 167 erotic pictures, an audio presentation of a selection of pornographic literature, and then another fifteen-minute film showing the activities of a heterosexual couple and a lesbian couple.

Among the many findings of this study was a retrospective report of the degree of sexual arousal experienced at various points during the one-hour session. It may be seen in Figure 12-4 that a much higher percentage of males indicated feeling sexually aroused at the beginning of the session than was true for females, the two groups were slightly closer together at the middle of the session, and by the end there were no differences in arousal between males and females. As Kutschinsky (1971b) suggested, it appears that the women tended to "heat up" during the session while the men tended to "cool down." Perhaps the sexes differ in speed of arousal rather than in absolute levels of arousability to erotica.

While these various experimental studies leave us with several unanswered questions as to male-female differences in response to erotic stimuli, they

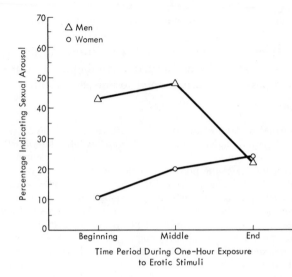

Fig. 12-4 Male and Female Arousal at Beginning, Middle, and End of a One-
Hour Exposure to Erotic Stimuli. (Data from Kutschinsky, 1971b.)

are consistent in indicating that the myth of female indifference to erotica
and immunity from the arousing effects of erotica may be laid to rest. In
future research, such variables as the content of the stimuli, familiarity with
the depicted activity, and time-relavant variables will undoubtedly be pursued in greater detail.

Individual Differences

Given the enormous range of expression of sexual impulses and of attitudes
about sex and sexuality, it is not surprising that a considerable amount of
research has been aimed at identifying relevant personality variables. Primarily, research has dealt with the identification of personality traits which
are associated with sexual arousal and personality traits which are associated
with attitudes or feelings about sex and with identifying the antecedents of
these individual differences.

Individual Differences in Sexual Arousal. In general, researchers have
had little success in establishing relationships between personality characteristics and self-reported arousal in experimental situations. There are,
however, a number of findings involving correlates of overt sexual activity.

Mosher (1961, 1966, 1968) defines sex guilt as a generalized expectancy
for self-punishing responses for violating standards of proper sexual conduct
and even for anticipating the violation of such standards. An individual high
in sex guilt would be expected to resist sexual temptation and to inhibit

sexual behavior in order to avoid the unpleasantness of feeling guilty. Mosher developed a scale to measure sex guilt, and sample items are:

As a child, sex play
   a. was a big taboo and I was deathly afraid of it
   b. was common without guilt feelings
When I have sexual desires
   a. they are quite strong
   b. I attempt to repress them

Mosher and Cross (1971) administered this scale to unmarried male and female students at the University of Connecticut along with a measure of sexual experiences (Brady and Levitt, 1965) which ranged from kissing, through manual manipulation of the female breast, to heterosexual and homosexual intercourse. The number of experiences of each subject was summed and could range from zero (never having done any of the acts) to twelve (having engaged in all of the sexual activities listed). The means were 7.60 for the males and 6.43 for the females. It was found that for both males (r = −.60) and females (r = −.61) there is a strong negative relationship between sex guilt and sexual experience. The higher the guilt, the less the experience. Specifically, low-guilt males compared to high-guilt males were likely to have manually manipuated a female's genitals, had oral contact with a female's breast, been masturbated by a female, engaged in cunnilingus, and engaged in intercourse. Low-guilt females were more likely than high-guilt females to have had their unclad breast manually manipulated, been manually masturbated by a male, masturbated a male, experienced cunnilingus, and engaged in intercourse. As in any correlational study, of course, it cannot be known whether sex guilt inhibited sexual behavior, the occurrence of sexual behavior reduced sex guilt, or whether the two variables are related for some other reason. Nevertheless, the association seems to be a substantial one.

   A different measure of sex guilt was developed by Leiman and Epstein (1961) who reported that the higher an individual's sex guilt, the lower his frequency of orgasms per week. Kutner (1971) pursued this same general line of research but argued that the sexual response should be analyzed into a number of more specific elements. He developed a rating scale on which subjects indicate the strength of their desire for sex, responsiveness during intercourse, passion during intercourse, frequency of orgasm during intercourse, ease of obtaining an orgasm, and amount of relief from sexual desire as the result of intercourse. The subjects were female patients (94 percent of whom were married) who were taking routine examinations at the Kaiser Foundation Hospital in Santa Clara. Sex guilt was found to be negatively correlated with each of the six aspects of sexual behavior. Also, sex guilt was negatively correlated with sexual adjustment, actual frequency of intercourse, preferred frequency of intercourse, and perception of their mates' passion.

Hans Eysenck utilizes factor analysis to identify basic personality variables, and the three primary dimensions are labeled introversion-extraversion, neuroticism, and psychoticism. In numerous investigations he has studied the relationship between sexual responses and the first two dimensions. He finds, for example, that those high in neuroticism are relatively inactive sexually (though high in desire) while those high in extraversion tend to be relatively active. Since both dimensions are related to sexual behavior, Eysenck (1971) proposed that the combined effects of the two dimensions would be of interest. He compared the attitudes and behaviors of hysterical personalities (high in both neuroticism and extraversion) and stable introverts (low on both dimensions). The subjects were a large group of unmarried university students who responded to sex questionnaires and the Eysenck Personality Inventory (Eysenck and Eysenck, 1965). The sexual responses of the extreme hysterics and extreme introverts were then compared. Among the numerous findings were those reported in Table 12-8 indicating those items on which

**Table 12-8. Comparison of Hysterical Personalities
and Stable Introverts on Sexual Responses**

Item	*Response More Characteristic of:*
Having engaged in sexual intercourse, face to face	Hysterical Personality
Having engaged in mutual manual fondling of genitals	Hysterical Personality
All in all I am satisfied with my sex life	Stable Introverts
My conscience bothers me too much	Hysterical Personality
The thought of a sex orgy is disgusting to me	Stable Introverts
I worry a lot about sex	Hysterical Personality
If I loved a person I would do anything with them	Hysterical Personality
At times I have been afraid of myself for what I might do sexually	Hysterical Personality
I have many friends of the opposite sex	Hysterical Personality
Sometimes sexual feelings overpower me	Hysterical Personality
I think about sex almost every day	Hysterical Personality

(Data from Eysenck, 1971)

hysterics and introverts of both sexes were found to differ. Eysenck (1971, p. 280) summarizes these and other findings as indicating that, compared to stable introverts, those with hysterical personalities

> ...are far more active sexually, have much stronger libidinal desires, are more excited by sexual stimuli, pay less regard to social taboos on sexual matters, and are more strongly affected by perverted thoughts (as well as

carrying on perverted activities more frequently). They also, however, have strong inhibitions which produce guilt feelings, worries, nervousness, and trouble with their conscience. All in all, the resulting conflict creates an overwhelming dissatisfaction with their sex lives.

Individual Differences in Attitudes about Sexuality. An especially important aspect of individual differences in the area of sexual behavior is the generally positive or negative attitude each person holds with respect to sexuality. That is, in general there seems to be a consistent response to sexual stimuli, sexual feelings, and sexual activity as pleasurable, interesting, and desirable or as disgusting, anxiety-arousing, and undesirable. It is likely that various aspects of sexual behavior are strongly influenced by these general sexual attitudes.

One personality dimension which appears to be related to these general reactions to sexuality is liberalism-conservatism. For example, in Chapter 4 it was reported that those high in authoritarianism indicated that sexual arousal was a negative experience for them, that sexual stimuli were pornographic, and that there should be legal restrictions on the production and sale of such material. Schmidt, Sigusch, and Meyberg (1969) pursued the effects of conservatism on sexual attitudes with a group of primarily unmarried male students at Hamburg University. Each subject was shown seventy-two black and white photographic slides representing twenty-four sexual themes. In addition to arousal ratings, each subject was asked to indicate how he felt about each picture on a seven-point favorable-unfavorable scale. Prior to the experimental session, subjects were given various questionnaires, including a measure of conservatism. It was found that the liberal and conservative subjects did not differ in their favorability ratings with respect to the mild sexual themes (kissing, affection) or in response to nude or partially clothed females. In fact, the conservatives were more favorable than the liberals in response to a picture of a girl in a bikini. With the more blatant and more arousing themes, however, the conservatives consistently responded with more negative responses than the liberals. This difference was apparent in response to themes of nude and seminude petting, coitus, fellatio, and cunnilingus.

These liberal-conservative differences were placed in a more general context of intellectualism and anti-intellectualism by Peckham (1969). He proposed that an intellectual tends to defend the existence of erotica, even if he finds it personally distasteful, because he wants to be the final judge of his own behavior rather than to have the judgment dictated by a higher authority. Legal restrictions are seen as threatening his own mastery. The anti-intellectuals, however:

...condemn not only the objectionable and offensive presentations of sex facts and indecent and suggestive illustrations but also anything that smacks of "disrespect for authority." Their condemnation of pornography and their mode of defining it, then, have their sources in political and social interests, in, as they always say, the stability of society (Peckham, 1969, p. 11).

Wallace and Wehmer (1972) undertook the task of measuring these differing attitudes toward sexual behavior. They assessed the sexual attitudes of a large group of male and female Detroit residents. Judges were able to classify the subjects as sexual liberals or sexual conservatives, corresponding to Peckham's intellectuals and antiintellectuals. The liberals indicated that they more frequently obtained or viewed erotic materials and that they were aroused by them. Conservatives indicated a mixture of arousal and disgust. The conservatives also were against the use of sex scenes in movies and were in favor of antipornography laws even if such materials were shown to have no harmful effects. When the subjects were exposed to sixty slides, showing various sexual themes, several differences between intellectuals and antiintellectuals were found. Compared to the sexually liberal, the conservatives found the pictures to be more offensive, more arousing, less entertaining, and less acceptable. For the conservatives, the most arousing pictures were also the most offensive; for the liberals, the most arousing pictures were the most entertaining. These very different correlates of sexual arousal would seem to suggest pervasive differences in attitudes about sexuality.

Antecedents of Differential Sexual Responses. Most of the studies of individual differences in sexuality suggest that the antecedents lie in various childhood experiences and in differing emotional climates among families. Questionnaire studies tend to support these propositions in that sexually liberal individuals report more permissive and sexually less repressive family attitudes. Studies of actual early behavior or of the effects of specific experiences are, of course, lacking because of the obvious barriers to such research. One possible avenue of investigation, however, is by means of animal research. A great deal of stress has been placed on the mother-child relationship. When an infant is deprived of this relationship by the death of its mother, hospitalization of either mother or child, placement in an institution, and so forth, a number of observational reports indicate that there are devastating effects on the infant's health and behavior. As part of the ongoing work at the primate laboratory at the University of Wisconsin, Harlow (1962) has reported a number of studies dealing with the effects of early experience on the adult behavior of monkeys. At one point, the investigators were in the process of creating unfriendly and inconsistent substitute mothers in order to study the development of neuroses in infant monkeys. Though the early efforts were not successful forty-seven infant monkeys were separated from their mothers at birth and raised in cages, some with substitute mothers and some without, where they had no physical contact with peers though they could see and hear other infants. After these subjects were five to seven years old and sexually mature, it became obvious that they were not normal.

In addition to various neurotic behaviors, the monkeys who had experienced such an unusual childhood showed no interest in normal sex behavior. When male and female pairs were placed together in the same cage, they did not mate. Next, an attempt was made to mate these animals with normal animals of the opposite sex, again without success. Harlow describes this:

> At this point we took the 17 oldest of our cage-raised animals, females showing consistent estrous cycles and males obviously mature, and engaged in an intensive re-education program, pairing the females with our most experienced, patient, and gentle males, and the males with our most eager, amiable, and successful breeding females. When the laboratory-bred females were smaller than the sophisticated males, the girls would back away and sit down facing the males, looking appealingly at these would-be consorts. Their hearts were in the right place, but nothing else was. When the females were larger than the males, we can only hope that they misunderstood the males' intentions, for after a brief period of courtship, they would attack and maul the ill-fated male. Females show no respect for a male they can dominate.
> The training program for the males was equally unsatisfactory. They approached the females with a blind enthusiasm, but it was a misdirected enthusiasm. Frequently the males would grasp the females by the side of the body and thrust laterally, leaving them working at cross purposes with reality. Even the most persistent attempts by these females to set the boys straight came to naught. Finally, these females either stared at the males with complete contempt or attacked them in utter frustration. It became obvious that they, like their human counterpart, prefer maturer men. We realized then that we had established, not a program of breeding, but a program of brooding (Harlow, 1962, p. 7).

Since other laboratory-raised monkeys show normal heterosexual behavior, the deviancy of these subjects was apparently the result of the early isolation experience. Further work was undertaken in which infant monkeys were separated from their real mothers, raised by an artificial mother (cloth-covered wire frame) but given the opportunity to play with other monkeys in infancy and childhood. In these subjects, normal sexual responses developed.

OTHER MEASURES OF SEXUAL AROUSAL

Though the research discussed so far in this chapter has relied primarily on self-rating scales, sexual arousal is one of the rare motives for which there are direct physiological indicators. That is, various changes in the genital organs are associated with sexual excitement. In addition, several less direct physiological correlates of arousal have been identified.

Verbal Reports of Physiological Reactions. An intermediate step between asking subjects to indicate their arousal on a rating scale and obtaining a physiological measure is to ask them to describe specific physiological changes that they are experiencing. Surprisingly, this relatively simple approach to measuring sexual arousal has not been used a great deal.

In the study of male students at Hamburg University described earlier, Schmidt, Sigusch, and Meyberg (1969) not only assessed arousal on a rating scale but they also administered a questionnaire asking about physiological reactions while the slides were being shown. Altogether, 80 percent of the subjects reported some kind of physiological response to the slides. Most (79 percent) indicated that they had an erection during the experiment, 27 percent indicated that there had been a pre-ejaculatory emission, and one subject had an ejaculation as the pictures were shown. Such findings constitute a convincing validation of the self-report scales and suggest that the kinds of erotic stimuli used in these experiments are effective determiners of sexual responsiveness.

This approach to measurement was extended to female subjects in the Schmidt and Sigusch (1970) study of the petting and coitus movies. Both males and females were asked about their physiological-sexual reactions during the showing of one of the films or of a series of slides taken from the films. Table 12-9 indicates that the male reactions reported in the previous

Table 12-9. Physiological-Sexual Reactions of Male
and Female Students to Erotic Films or Slides

Male Subjects		*Female Subjects*	
Any physiological reaction		Any physiological reaction	
No	13%	No	28%
Yes	87%	Yes	72%
Erection		Genital sensations of warmth,	
None	14%	pulsation, or itching	
Slight, Moderate	55%	Don't know	6%
Full	31%	No	29%
Pre-ejaculatory emission		Yes	65%
Don't know	23%	Vaginal Lubrication	
No	52%	Don't know	18%
Yes	25%	No	54%
Ejaculation		Yes	28%
No	96%	Sensations in the Breasts	
Yes	4%	Don't know	7%
		No	84%
		Yes	9%
		Orgasm	
		No	100%
		Yes	0%

(Data from Schmidt and Sigusch, 1970)

investigation were replicated and that the responses of the females closely paralleled those of the males. As with the studies of verbal response, these physiological reports once again suggest that males and females are remarkably similar in the way they are affected by erotic stimuli.

Indirect Measures of Physiological Responses to Erotic Stimuli. In Zuckerman's (1971) review of physiological measures, various response measures were described as indicative of sexual arousal. Many of these may indicate a more general response (such as anxiety) which is not specifically an indicator of the effects of erotic stimuli (Craig and Wood, 1971). Examples of such measures include the galvanic skin response (Dean, Martin, and Streiner 1968), heart rate (Corman, 1968), and dilation of the pupils (Hess, 1968).

Another measurement approach is through biochemical analysis. Clark and Treichler (1950) suggested that variations in the level of urinary acid phosphatase may indicate sexual arousal in male subjects, and they were able to demonstrate that it increased following the presentation of sexual stimuli. In a series of studies, Barclay and his colleagues (Barclay, 1970, 1971; Barclay and Little, 1972) have provided evidence that acid phosphatase is a useful index of sexual responsiveness. It has also been shown, however, that this kind of physiological measure is responsive to other situational variables. For example, when Barclay (1970) informed some subjects about the purpose of the study, there was actually more increase in acid phosphatase in the urine of the nonaroused subjects than in that of the aroused ones; unaware subjects responded in the usual manner. Even with physiological measures of sexual responsiveness, it appears that there are pervasive cognitive influences on sexual arousal.

Direct Measurement of Physiological Reactions. The most extensive research dealing directly with observed sexual behavior in human subjects has been that of Masters and Johnson (1966). Their subjects engaged in various forms of sexual activity to the point of orgasm, and descriptive data were obtained by the experimenters. The initial response to sexual stimulation is erection in the male and vaginal lubrication in the female. This is followed by a slight increase in the size and elevation of the testacles in the male and by nipple erection and a thickening of the vaginal walls and a flattening and elevation of the external female genitalia. As excitement builds to the plateau stage, there is rapid breathing, a more rapid heart rate, and an increase in muscle tension in both sexes plus emission from Cooper's gland in males and from Bartholin's gland in females. When orgasm is reached, there are involuntary muscle contractions plus contractions of the genitals and of the anus, accompanied by perspiration. Clearly, any attempts to quantify or even simply observe any of these reactions could be undertaken only in highly specialized research facilities such as those of Masters and Johnson in St. Louis.

It has, however, proven possible to study one aspect of the physiological response to excitement in other laboratories. Freund, Sedlacek, and Knob (1965) described the development of a device to measure the volume of the penis and hence to detect changes resulting from an erection. This penile plethysmograph fits around the male organ and provides a sensitive index of physical reactions to sexual cues. Several variations of this instrument have also been developed to measure either volume or circumference of the penis. It should be noted that once again, cognitive influences are of great importance. Laws and Rubin (1969) reported that subjects could inhibit erections while watching an erotic film and could produce an erection in the absence of an external stimulus; in each instance the subjects indicated that they concentrated on appropriate topics to produce the desired effect.

One of the more elaborate studies of response to erotic stimuli utilized a combination of the various types of response measure we have discussed. Howard, Reifler, and Liptzin (1971) exposed male college students to various kinds of pornography for ninety minutes per day for fifteen days. The subjects' reactions were assessed with paper and pencil scales, acid phosphatase measurement, and a direct measure of penile circumference. After a screening procedure, the experiment began with the showing of a stag movie, followed by a control week, and then two weeks during which erotic movies, pictures, magazines, and novels were available (as well as non-pornographic materials). In the third week, new erotic stimuli were provided for three days, then all nonpornography was removed during the last two days. A second stag movie was shown and eight weeks later a third stag movie was shown. A group of control subjects saw the first and second movies but were not exposed to daily erotica in the period between them. Urine samples were obtained after each session to determine acid phosphatase levels. The measure of erections was obtained during each movie showing.

Earlier in this chapter in the discussion of the effects of novelty on sexual arousal, it was reported that Howard, et al. (1971) found steadily decreasing interest after repeated exposure to the erotic stimuli. Interest increased somewhat when novel erotic stimuli were introduced to the subjects. An important parallel finding is shown in Figure 12-5. The daily mean levels of urinary acid phosphatase show the same pattern as the verbal reports of sexual interest. That is, there is a general decline over the ten days of repeated exposure followed by a sharp increase when novel stimuli are introduced and then a decline once again. The other finding of interest was in the measures of erection taken during the movie showings. In Figure 12-6 it may be seen that the typical pattern of response was for an initial rapid increase in penis size followed by a gradual decrease during the course of the movie. It should also be noted that when the second movie was shown,

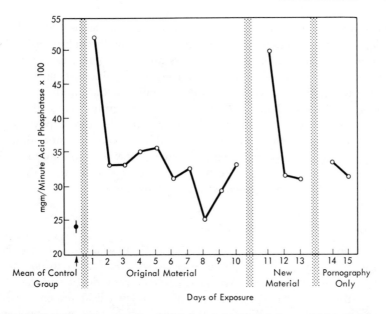

Fig. 12-5 Daily Mean Levels of Urinary Acid Phosphatase of Male Subjects Exposed to Erotic Stimuli Showing a Decline of Arousal with Repeated Exposure Followed by Increased Arousal in Response to Novel Stimuli. (After Howard, Reifler, and Liptzin, 1971, p. 117.)

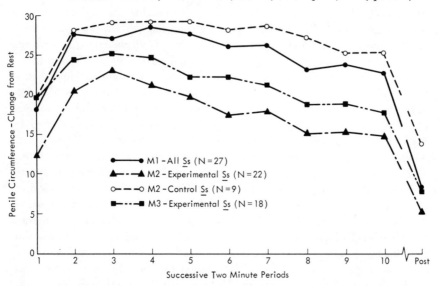

Fig. 12-6 Sexual Arousal as Measured by Changes in Penis Circumference During Showing of Erotic Movies. M1 = movie shown before experimental sessions began, M2 = movie shown after experimental sessions were completed, and M3 = movie shown eight weeks later. (After Howard, Reifler, and Liptzin, 1971, p. 118.)

the control subjects gave evidence of as much or more arousal as to the first movie, while the experimental subjects who had gone through three weeks of exposure to erotic stimuli were much less aroused. Finally, it may be seen that the experimental subjects after an eight-week interval showed more response to the third movie than to the second, but they were not back to the original response level or that of the control group. Thus, the verbal reports, the indirect physiological measure, and the direct physiological measure were consistent in indicating arousal in response to erotic stimuli, in indicating a decline in sexual arousal following repeated exposure to erotica, and in showing the renewed effectiveness of erotic stimuli when they were novel or when they were presented after a lapse of time.

EFFECTS ON SUBSEQUENT BEHAVIOR

From a number of viewpoints, one of the most important and most difficult to answer questions about response to erotic stimulation has to do with its effect on subsequent behavior. We have learned a great deal about the effects of such stimuli on verbal responses and on physiological responses within an experimental setting. What are the lingering effects of such experiences on sexual behavior? It is just such a question which elicits the most vehement opinions when pornography and censorship are discussed. Erotic stimuli have been characterized as an evil poison to body and soul (letter to the St. Louis *Globe-Democrat*), as a means of brutalizing the populace so that they are not shocked by the sight of a Vietcong flag carried down the streets of Washington (Indiana congressman quoted in Lafayette *Journal and Courier*), as a greater menace to humanity than carbon monoxide or mercury poisoning (letter to the Norman *Transcript*), as beneficial or at least harmless (three psychiatrists quoted by a UPI newspaper release), as a tool to distract Czechoslovaks' attention away from politics and hence as a capitalist plot (Soviet Young Communist League), and as an aphrodisiac used by males rendered sexless by alcohol and tobacco (George W. Crane in his syndicated column). Among college students, a 1972 poll indicated that 53.2 percent felt that pornography was harmful or very harmful to society.

One of the primary reasons for the establishment of the Commission on Obscenity and Pornography by Congress in 1967 and the appointment of its members by President Johnson in 1968 was to obtain relevant information on the effects of pornography and to make recommendations concerning relevant legislation. Essentially three kinds of data were examined. First, the effects of nonrestrictiveness could be studied by obtaining data from Denmark which had passed permissive laws concerning erotica. Second, individuals (including convicted sex criminals) could be questioned about their past experiences with pornography and about its effects on them. Third, experimental investigations could be conducted and the effects of controlled exposure could be determind by means of follow-up questionnaires. We will briefly examine each of these lines of research.

The Danish "Experiment." Legislation was passed in Denmark removing restrictions on the production, advertising, and sale of erotic material. One of the more impressive findings comes from an analysis of police records in Copenhagen over a twelve-year period extending before and after passage of the law. During this time, there was a dramatic decrease in reported sexual crimes, and the decrease began at the the time the law was changed. This decrease has been shown to be a genuine one and not attributable to changes in the legal definitions of sex crimes, to changes in attitudes about reporting sex crimes, or to changes in police record-keeping procedures. Such data cannot be taken as conclusive proof that freely available erotic stimuli act as a benefit to society and a deterrant to crime. They are, however, certainly not consistent with the belief that uncensored sexual material evokes harmful sexual activity.

Surveys of Experience and Effects. Survey studies also indicate that there is no demonstrable connection between reported experiences with erotic material and subsequent antisocial sexual behavior. In fact, sex offenders seem to have had less experience with erotica during adolescence than is true for nonoffenders (e.g., Goldstein, Kant, Judd, Rice, and Green, 1971).

Experimental Studies of Effects of Erotica on Behavior. Despite the possible importance of the question, the amount of experimental data on this question was negligible until the early 1970s (Cairns, Paul, and Wishner, 1971). Primarily in response to the explicit requests of the Commission on Obscenity and Pornography, a number of investigators conducted experiments designed to identify the behavioral effects of experimentally induced sexual arousal. In general, these studies involved the presentation of erotic stimuli and a follow-up in which the subjects were asked questions about various aspects of their sexual behavior following exposure to erotica in comparison with the same period of time prior to the experiment. The data reveal that a relatively brief exposure to explicit erotic stimuli has no really consistent effects. There is a general tendency for subjects to report an increase in feelings of tension, happiness, and sexual desire. In some of the studies, there is a reported increase in talking about sex and in masturbation. Other forms of sexual behavior, including behavior imitating that in the erotic stimuli, do not appear to be affected.

It should be noted that none of these investigators claim that their findings provide the final word on the effects of long-term exposure to erotic stimuli. For example, if subjects were bombarded over a five-year period with nightly television programs depicting explicit sexual activity, it seems quite possible that their behavior would be influenced by this experience. The data so far available suggest, however, that the probable effect would be one of an increased incidence of the kinds of sexual behavior in which they already engage. Further, the findings with respect to repeated exposure suggest that novelty would be essential to maintain any erotic effect at all.

THEORY BUILDING

Though numerous limited theories have been proposed to deal with specific aspects of sexual behavior, there is no inclusive theoretical formulation which has wide acceptance. Perhaps it would be useful to outline some of the general elements which might eventually go into the making of such a theory.

LEVEL I. SIMPLE PROCREATIVE BEHAVIOR

Human sexual behavior may be conceptualized in terms of a series of complexities added onto or fused with the rather straightforward biological sex act. As a starting point, we can consider the simplest sort of sexual behavior and then see how it can become more complicated. First, take the situation in which mature and receptive representatives of each sex are in a setting permitting or encouraging sexual activity. The Stimulation Phase is initiated by an appropriate cue. In common with other animal species, human beings could be expected to become excited or aroused by stimuli emitted by the member of the opposite sex. Examples would be the other's appearance or smell or vocalizations. Some of these cues may well be genetically determined. Once the two individuals are in close proximity, the excitement is maintained and enhanced as the participants move to the Behavioral Phase. Here, tactual stimulation of various areas of the body and direct friction of the genitals culminates in the sexual act itself. Again, survival of the species has obviously been dependent on the likelihood of genital contact being made. The end point of this activity is the Orgasm Phase with the sperm being ejaculated by the male into the female's vagina.

It seems very likely that most of the sexual behavior of our primitive ancestors and of the members of other animal species has consisted of little more than this simple progression from excitement to orgasm. One additional element is the tendency of male mammals to respond positively to a new sexual partner. Such a tendency would be of evolutionary benefit in insuring the widest possible dissemination (literally) of any given set of genes.

LEVEL II. INTELLECTUAL DEVELOPMENT:
IMAGINATION AND LEARNING

As was pointed out earlier in this chapter, one of the concomitants of progress as one moves up the evolutionary scale is the development of the cerebral cortex. There is, of course, no magic dividing line between human beings and other animals, and a number of the characteristics at Level II can be seen at times in other species, especially those closest to man.

At the Stimulation Phase, two major changes are introduced by these intellectual changes. First, any stimulus in any sensory modality can be associated with sexual arousal and hence become an effective elicitor of arousal. Common observation and clinical case histories suggest that man is infinitely plastic in his ability to attach arousal properties to diverse stimuli. Thus, human beings can learn to be sexually excited in response to particular objects of clothing or ornamentation, various parts of the human body of either sex, particular settings, particular odors, music, foods, pain—seemingly in response to anything. Rather than excitement elicited only by an appropriate sexual object, human beings may be aroused by members of their own sex or children or dead bodies, by the smell of public rest rooms or the smell of Chanel No. 5, by Beethoven or Burt Bachrach or Three Dog Night, by oysters or champagne or marijuana, by enemas or whips. It has been shown in an experimental setting, for example, that subjects can learn by association to be sexually aroused by shoes (Rachman, 1966) and to replace one set of arousing stimuli with another (Davison, 1968).

The second influence of intellective factors on the stimulation phase has been discussed in some detail previously. That is, the role of imaginative processes in human sexuality seems to be a powerful one. Presumably the effectiveness of photographs, words, or movies as stimuli for sexual arousal lies in their serving as cues for imagination. Thus, individuals vicariously participate in the imagined scenes and their bodies respond as if there was actual participation rather than simply ideation. Besides the imaginative component in response to erotic stimuli, individuals report that erotic fantasies frequently play an integral role while sexual behavior is actually occurring as in masturbation fantasies or fantasies during intercourse. Thus, the overt behavior which is taking place and the covert processes of the imagination may occur simultaneously and may not correspond with one another at all. Man's ability to learn by association and his imaginative skills thus have considerable influence on the Stimulation Phase. The stimuli for human sexual excitement can range from the simplest, genetically based cue to the most varied and creative products of man's experience and imagination.

At the Behavioral Phase, the tactual and genital responses may take on a variety of forms beyond that of a manual caress or the simple interaction of penis and vagina. The penis or clitoris or vaginal walls can be involved in frictional excitement through contact with various parts of the body of a member of the same or opposite sex. Individuals engage in sexual activities alone, with inanimate objects, and with animals. Again, the ability to learn means that the sexual act can depart dramatically from that characteristic of straightforward intercourse. From oral-genital sex to anal intercourse to battery-powered vibrators to bestiality, the Behavioral Phase can obviously involve quite different specific acts.

The effect of these variations on the Orgasm Phase is simply that the ejaculation of semen and the female climax need not necessarily involve male-female genital-genital contact.

LEVEL III. SEXUAL EXPERIENCE AND EMOTIONAL RESPONSES

At the basic affective level, all aspects of the sexual experience are a source of pleasure. The strong biological need for sexual release and the pleasure derived from it were useful attributes for the survival of the species. With intellectual development, however, various informational considerations beyond that of immediate pleasure began gradually to become factors in man's response to his sexuality. It seems likely that many positive and negative ideas about sexuality were originally based on attempts to maintain and increase the size of small, powerless groups or tribes. As was pointed out at Level II, man can easily learn infinite variations in his sexual activity. Many of these behaviors would, however, be detrimental to the maintenance of the group. For example, nonprocreative sexual acts such as masturbation, oral sex, homosexuality, or bestiality may be as pleasurable to the individual as procreative acts, but their practice would pose a genuine threat to the survival of the group. Still other acts, such as incest, seem much less obviously to be dangers, and their origins are the source of some dispute. However the idea arose, it was nevertheless beneficial to obtain genetic variety by going outside of small homogeneous groups such as the family to obtain mates.

Still a different kind of negative sanction would arise in the history of civilization with respect to ideas of property rights. Here, it can be seen that difficulty could be caused by adultery. Still later in man's development, notions of individual rights would suggest that sexual relations should not be imposed against someone's will (rape) or imposed on someone not capable of making a valid judgment (youngsters or the mentally disturbed). In response to threats to survival and evolving ideas of property and individual rights, ideas about sexuality were gradually adopted, customs were developed, and religious taboos and legal sanctions were devised to enforce them.

Two major problems arise with these various negative sanctions about sexual behavior. First, technological changes render some of the ancient wisdom and prohibitions non-functional. When human beings are currently threatened by overpopulation, the customs which encourage conception become ironically maladaptive. The development of increasingly effective and increasingly safe contraceptive devices make it truly feasible to separate the pleasurable aspects of sexual activity from the complications of conception. Our customs and laws and taboos, of course, lag behind these changes, though alterations slowly occur. In this period of transition in which social customs do not fit well with the reality of mankind's new problems and new technology, it is not surprising that there are vast differences among people in their attitudes and beliefs about sexuality, including differences across generations.

The second problem rests on the difficulty imposed in teaching the youth in a culture the fine and sometimes arbitrary distinctions between those aspects of sexual activity which are good, right, and proper and those that are bad, wrong, and improper. For example, it has customarily been taught in our culture that sex before marriage is a sin while sex after marriage is good and that desire for one's sibling is reprehensible while desire for one's spouse is to be commended. Most of us have learned these kinds of distinctions with varying degrees of success. A major pitfall has always been that with such fine distinctions the negative feelings which are deliberately associated with some sexual stimuli and some sexual responses often generalize to all or almost all sexual stimuli and sexual responses. Thus, anything having to do with sex can come to evoke negative emotional responses.

With respect to the three phases, it may be seen that positive and/or negative emotional responses may be elicited by any aspect of sexuality. Thus, any stimuli which are sexually arousing may also lead to feelings of pleasure, or feelings of disgust, or a mixture of the two. Some individuals will spend both time and money to see a movie depicting explicit sexual acts while others would find the idea shocking and nauseating. Sexual excitement itself can be viewed as a positive or negative experience or an experience which combines elements of both reactions. It is possible for sexual orgasm to be perceived as one of life's great pleasures, as a not-very-nice necessity analogous to defecation, or as a source of guilt and shame. The effects of these emotional responses on sexual behavior and on sexual attitudes are undoubtedly of great importance and will probably be the subject of much future psychological research.

The three phases of sexual activity and the three levels of development are summarized in Figure 12-7.

In research by Byrne, Fisher, Lamberth, and Mitchell (1974), several aspects of these emotional responses were investigated. Married couples who had been exposed to a series of erotic stimuli were asked to indicate their feelings immediately afterward on a series of rating scales. As might be expected in the context of the present discussion, the erotic material was found to evoke both positive and negative feelings, and these were found by factor analysis to cluster into two groups as shown in Table 12-10.

Somewhat surprisingly, response to the sexual stimuli was not simply along a single positive-negative dimension but along two separate dimensions, one positive and the other negative. Total scores on the positive group are unrelated to total scores on the negative group. When the subjects were divided into high and low subgroups on each dimension, all four combinations of emotional response were found. Thus, some subjects responded

	Stimulation Phase	Behavioral Phase	Orgasm Phase
Level I. Simple Procreative Behavior	Sexual excitement is elicited by appearance, smell, or vocalizations of sexual object	Sexual act involves tactual stimulation of partner, culminating in insertion of penis into vagina	Semen is ejaculated into vagina
Level II. Intellectual Development Fostering Imaginative Activity and the Learning of Alternative Stimuli and Responses	A. By association, any stimulus in any sensory mode can become sexually arousing B. Cognitive activity induces the individual to respond physiologically as if he were the participant in the imagined sexual encounter	The sexual act can involve an almost unlimited variety of possible responses	The male's ejaculation of semen or the female's climax can occur as the result of various types of genital friction
Level III. Any Aspect of Sexual Experience May Become a Stimulus for Positive and Negative Emotional Responses	Sexual excitement itself or any of the overt or covert stimuli eliciting arousal can evoke positive and/or negative feelings	Any sexual act can evoke positive and/or negative feelings	Orgasm can evoke positive and/or negative feelings

Fig. 12-7 The Effect of Three Levels of Development of Human Sexual Behavior on Three Phases of Sexual Activity

Table 12-10. Independent Factors of Positive and Negative
Feelings Aroused by Erotic Stimuli

Factor 1 Positive Feelings	Factor 2 Negative Feelings
Excited	Disgusted
Entertained	Nauseated
Sexually Aroused	Angry
Anxious	Depressed
Curious	
Not Bored	

(After Byrne, D., Fisher, J. D., Lamberth, J. and Mitchell,
H. E., Evaluations of erotica: Facts or feelings? *Journal of
Personality and Social Psychology*, 1974, 29, 113. © 1974 by
the American Psychological Association and reprinted by permission.)

only positively, others responded only negatively, some expressed both high
positive and high negative feelings, and still others indicated neither a positive nor a negative response. At the very least, it would seem that erotic
stimuli can arouse quite different emotions in different people.

The next question was the relationship between these emotional reactions
and other sex-related behavior. It would be expected that those individuals
for whom erotic stimuli arouse more negative than positive feelings would
hold generally anti-eroticism views. That is, the uncomfortable feelings
elicited by erotic stimuli would lead to a negative evaluation of such stimuli.
The subjects were given a dictionary definition of pornography as "obscene
or licentious; foul, disgusting, or offensive; tending to produce lewd emotions." For each of the nineteen erotic stimuli, they were asked to judge
whether it was pornographic or not. As may be seen in Table 12-11, those

Table 12-11. Number of the 19 Themes Judged to be
Pornographic as a Function of Self-Reported Affect

	Male Subjects Negative Affect		Female Subjects Negative Affect	
Positive Affect	Low	High	Low	High
High	6.60	5.70	4.28	9.00
Low	1.38	10.50	3.42	9.96

(After Byrne, D., Fisher, J. D., Lamberth, J. and Mitchell, H. E., Evaluations of
erotica: Facts or feelings? *Journal of Personality and Social Psychology*, 1974, 29,
113. © 1974 by the American Psychological Association and reprinted by permission.)

individuals who were low in positive affect and high in negative affect judged the greatest number of stimuli to be pornographic.

There is still another way in which these differential emotional responses should affect sexual behavior. Positive and negative feelings about a stimulus not only influence one's general evaluation of it, but there is a tendency to attempt to justify those feelings and evaluations in more general terms. That is, it seems to be difficult for most people to say that something makes them feel good or bad and hence they like or dislike it and let it go at that. Most of us are inclined to attribute various benefits to that which arouses our positive feelings and various evils to that which arouses our negative feelings. This same group of subjects was given a series of questions concerning their support of restrictive or non-restrictive legal measures concerning the production and sale of erotic material. Subjects were asked whether books, pictures, and movies dealing with the nineteen erotic themes should be forbidden entirely, forbidden in public display and advertising, forbidden to unmarried individuals, to teenagers, and/or to children. Total restrictiveness could range from zero (no restrictions on erotic stimuli) to five (total suppression of erotic stimuli). As may be seen in Table 12-12, it is those indi-

Table 12-12. Restrictiveness toward Erotic Stimuli as a Function of Self-Reported Affect

	Male Subjects			*Female Subjects*	
	Negative Affect			*Negative Affect*	
	Low	*High*		*Low*	*High*
Positive Affect			*Positive Affect*		
High	2.00	1.40	High	1.42	2.83
Low	.63	3.38	Low	2.14	3.16

(After Byrne, D., Fisher, J. D., Lamberth, J. and Mitchell, H. E., Evaluations of erotica: Facts or feelings? *Journal of Personality and Social Psychology*, 1974, 29, 113. © 1974 by the American Psychological Association and reprinted by permission.)

viduals with low positive and high negative affect who are most restrictive and most in favor of the censorship of erotica.

Much more research is required to determine the extent to which such positive and negative emotional responses to sexuality influence other sex-related behaviors. There is evidence as suggested in work on authoritarianism and on liberalism-conservatism that these general attitudes about sex become linked with a much broader array of attitudes about the family, about mankind, and about the structure of society. These interconnections also suggest why it is that the sexual behavior of others or changes in sexual customs can assume such importance. There is the implication, and perhaps an accurate one, that those who seek to change sexual behavior also seek to change political structure. It seems to be true that a tightly controlled, repressive political system in part functions to suppress and control potentially dangerous emotional reactions. The work of the state (whether in the People's Republic of China under Communism, or in Greece under a right-wing dictatorship) can best be carried out if sexual stimuli are avoided and sexual activity curtailed. If these observations have any validity, it follows that an efficient organization such as business, government, or the military functions best in an atmosphere of highly controlled and highly restricted sexuality in which negative emotions elicited by sexual cues act to inhibit behavior. In contrast, individual freedom and pleasure and perhaps creativity function best in an atmosphere of unrestricted sexuality in which positive emotions are elicited by sexual cues. Much of man's political activity can be seen in part as a struggle between these two extremes.

APPLICATIONS

Perhaps to a greater extent than is true for other areas of behavior, any proposed application of research knowledge concerning sex tends to bring forth immediate and spirited opposition. In part because of the strong affective components associated with all aspects of sexuality, any legislative or educational or therapeutic proposal seems almost certain to be viewed as threatening by a large portion of the population. For example, after more than two years of research and careful consideration, the Commission on Obscenity and Pornography (1970) made several relatively mild recommendations based on current knowledge about exposure to erotic stimuli and its effects. Specifically, it was recommended that a massive sex education program be launched, that open discussion of the facts be continued, that research be encouraged, that laws should not prohibit the sale or exhibition of sexual material to consenting adults, and that the public display or unsolicited mailing of explicit sexual material be prohibited. These seemingly innocuous suggestions were quickly rejected by Nixon and Agnew, who did not wish to "turn Main Street into Smut Alley," by an overwhelming majority of the United States Senate, and by numerous editorial writers and columnists around the country.

An overriding difficulty in even discussing such topics is the polarization of emotions about the part that sex should play in our lives. If sex is perceived as a somewhat inconvenient and embarassing necessity, a potential source of danger if unleashed, a somewhat dirty and shameful activity in most of its forms, and a debilitating distraction from the important and serious work of society, one's plans for applications would concentrate on the most effective way to suppress sexual stimulation and to control and discourage sexual expression. On the other hand, if sex is perceived as a source of pleasure, a vital aspect of establishing a close interpersonal relationship, and a natural and joyful expression of life, then application would stress ways to increase sexual stimulation and encourage sexual expression. From this viewpoint, sex is simply a very special activity which is inexpensive, fun, and non-fattening.

These two broad anti-sex and pro-sex aims are directly opposed to one another and seemingly cannot be resolved. There is no way to demonstrate that one orientation is superior to the other. Very successful societies and very successful individuals have functioned in accordance with each model. As examples of the ways in which these quite different orientations would affect application, consider just a few aspects of child rearing, the entertainment media, education, and adult behavior.

From the repressive viewpoint, sexual awareness and sexual activity would be postponed as long as possible. Small children would be taught to name all other parts of the body ("This is your nose. This is your tummy. These are your toes."), but the sexual organs would remain unnamed and hopefully unnoticed. Dolls would be constructed without sexual organs. Children would be discouraged from touching themselves in the genital area and nudity would be avoided. Insofar as possible, children would be protected from information in conversation, in the entertainment media, in school, or wherever, which dealt with sexual behavior. In movies and on television, they could be exposed to all aspects of their environment, including violence and murder, so long as sexuality were excluded. Formal sex education would concentrate on the facts of reproduction, preferably with stylized drawings of a sperm penetrating an ovum. An ideal accomplishment can be seen in British research with the newly developed antisex pill, Anquil, which greatly reduces or totally abolishes sexual desire. Strict censorship would prevent adults from coming in contact with imagination-stirring ideas about sex and strict laws would proscribe imaginative variations in the sex act, even between spouses.

That rather familiar orientation toward sexuality can be contrasted with the opposite orientation. Parents would be as free and open about sexuality as about eating. Penis and vagina would be as familiar as eyebrow and elbow in the child's language and in the dolls given as toys. Children could be taught that touching some parts of the body is a source of pleasure and would be encouraged to do so whenever they wished. Nudity would depend on personal comfort, and sex would be an integral part of the stories, plays, movies, and television programs. Very young children would probably be as uninterested in a television show about positions of sexual intercourse as they are in programs dealing with political conventions, but there would be no curtain of ignorance drawn over the subject. In this atmosphere, sexual education would occur in a more frank and less emotionally charged atmosphere and would not represent an alien subject matter suddenly thrust with some embarrassment into the curriculum. Education would deal with the specifics of reproduction, contraception, and venereal disease as well as with the details of sexual excitation, variations of sexual pleasure, and the intricacies of interpersonal relationships including affection and love. To push this alternative to an extreme, an ideal goal would be an increase in the frequency of sexual activity and an increase in sexual pleasure; thus, any chemical or psychological means to increase desire or intensify pleasure would be highly valued. Television, movies, billboards, and novels would be designed to stimulate imagination and to encourage more and ever better sexual encounters.

One reason for drawing these two extremes is to suggest the vast differences among us in our emotional responses to sex and to suggest the vast differences in application to which these sexual attitudes would lead us. One aspect of sex research which would be of great potential value would be an attempt to determine the consequences of these different approaches to sexuality. The very complex and very important question is whether man's total condition is better or worse in an atmosphere of sexual repression, sexual expression, or some intermediate point.

SUMMARY

Sexuality is pervasive in everyday life and in society's efforts to define and regulate its expression. Current research interest in sex in part is based on concern over apparent changes in the sexual attitudes and behaviors of much of our population and over the increasing sexual permissiveness in movies, books, magazines, and the theater.

One starting point for psychological research has been attempts to establish a base relationship between erotic stimuli and sexual arousal. Presumably, words and pictures are arousing because of their effect on an individual's imaginative processes. The identification of an appropriate stimulus dimension has involved the scaling of sexual behaviors with respect to experience and the ordering of erotic stimuli with respect to self-reported sexual arousal.

Analytic research on erotic stimuli has indicated that sexual pictures are more arousing when there is total nudity than when the depicted participants are partially clothed, that the presence of affection in stories does not influence arousal, and that males respond in different ways to specific bodily components in the pictorial representations of females.

In studying stimulus generality, it has been found that photographs are more arousing than drawings, that verbal and pictorial stimuli are equally arousing to both males and females, and that instructions to imagine sexual activity results in greater arousal than the presentation of explicit stimuli.

Animal research indicates that, for males at least, new partners elicit renewed activity even in seemingly satiated individuals. With human subjects, a possibly analogous finding is that repeated exposure to erotic stimuli leads to less and less arousal, while the introduction of novel stimuli is somewhat more exciting. Additional stimuli which have been found to be sexually arousing are odors (in animal research) and music (with female subjects). In experimental studies, the arousal effects of erotic stimuli can be inhibited by the personality characteristics of the experimenter and enhanced by alcohol. With actual behavior, both the age at which intercourse is first experienced and the specific sexual activities which occur are a function of social class. Another situational determinant of sexual behavior is the day of the week in that upper class whites tend to report greater sexual activity on Saturday and Sunday than during the week.

One problem with generalizing about the findings of sex research is the possible bias in the subject samples; subjects who volunteer for sex research are different in several respects from subjects who refuse to participate. Survey research consistently indicates that men are more interested in erotica and are more aroused by it than is true for females. Experimental studies, however, suggest that such findings reflect cultural influences rather than basic sex differences. With specific erotic stimuli, either males or females may be more highly aroused; for some stimuli, there is simply no difference in arousal. Females assume that males are more aroused than they actually are, while males are more accurate in guessing the level of female arousal. Other findings suggest that males are aroused quickly by erotic stimuli and then become less excited while females show a steady increase from beginning to end of exposure. Individual differences in sexual arousal and sexual behavior are found to be related to sex guilt and to introversion-extraversion. Relatively broad positive versus negative attitudes about sexuality are associated with more general liberal-conservative attitudes. Animal studies of early experience indicate that adult sexual behavior is detrimentally affected by isolation from peers during infancy and childhood. Though most of the psychological research on sexual behavior has relied on self-rating scales to assess sexual arousal, the validity of these scales has been shown in research dealing with verbal reports of physiological reactions, biochemical analysis of urinary acid phosphatase, and direct measures of changes in penis size. While there are many firmly held opinions about the negative effects of erotic stimuli on subsequent behavior, data suggest that exposure to such stimuli has relatively little effect. In Denmark, the passage of permissive legislation about pornography was followed by a decline in sex crimes, and there seems to be no relationship between reported early experiences with pornography and later delinquency. Experimental studies suggest that the short-term effects of exposure are minimal.

Though no inclusive theory of human sexual behavior has yet been constructed, some of the necessary elements can be outlined. Sexual behavior may be divided into three phases: stimulation, sexual activity, and orgasm. At the simplest level, these phases include stimulation by an appropriate partner of the opposite sex, sexual intercourse, and ejaculation of semen in the vagina. Because of man's intellectual skills, a second level of development can be seen as the ability to learn to be aroused by an infinite array of stimuli (including imagined ones) and the ability to seek sexual satisfaction in an infinite array of behavioral acts. Orgasm thus may have nothing to do with procreation. A third level of development has led to the association of positive and negative emotional responses to sexual stimuli, sexual acts, and to orgasm. Research has shown, for example, that erotic stimuli can elicit any combination of positive and negative feelings in an individual and that these emotional reponses are associated with evaluations of erotica and with attitudes about the value of censorship.

Any proposed application of research knowledge concerning sex tends to bring forth opposition. Two broad orientations may be seen as the perception of sex as something dangerous, to be controlled and suppressed, versus the perception of sex as something joyful to be encouraged and expressed. Such differences profoundly affect ideas about the appropriate way to apply knowledge with respect to childrearing, entertainment, education, and adult behavior. The direction that application takes depends on a society's basic position with respect to permissiveness-restrictiveness.

13

Altruistic
Behavior

Much of man's behavior can be described as a function of enlightened self-interest. We attempt to act in ways that maximize our rewards and minimize our punishments. If everyone actually behaved in whatever way gave him the most immediate personal pleasure, grabbing what he wished to grab and destroying whatever interfered with his pleasure, the world would be an even more savage place than it is at present. In Chapter 2, Freud's formulation of man's development was discussed. He depicted an initial stage of id functioning based entirely on the desire for pleasure and for the immediate gratification of all needs. The reality principle first operates as the infant begins to learn that delay of gratification is frequently necessary, that the physical world cannot always be made to conform to one's wishes. In time, the growing child also learns about the world of social reality with rules, laws, sanctions, prohibitions, incentives, and punishments designed to restrain and restrict behavior in socially acceptable ways. If ego functioning were the final developmental stage, man could be either a wild beast, caged by the restraining influences of his physical and social surroundings, or an intellectual being who rationally abides by the reasonable constraints imposed by his environment.

There are many behaviors which would be difficult to explain on either basis. There are instances in which individuals refrain from acts which would benefit them even though the behavior is physically possible and no one could possibly catch them at it. When someone finds a valuable belonging and returns it to its rightful owner, refuses to cheat on an important examination, or helps a stranger caught in a dangerous predicament, it is apparent that some additional force is operating. It is as if there are internal rules and constraints as well as external ones. Freud's concept of superego—what others have labeled the conscience—refers to an internalization of certain values and rules of conduct. These values and rules undoubtedly began with external influences but no longer depend on them. Those individuals who reach this developmental stage would feel uncomfortable (guilty) if they took possessions which did not belong to them, received a grade which was not honestly deserved, or left a threatened stranger without providing any aid. They would feel guilty, that is, if they had learned these particular cultural values with respect to stealing, cheating, and being a good Samaritan.

Kelley (1971) points out that psychologists in recent years have shown an upswing of interest in matters of morality, moral behavior, and social responsibility. A portion of this research activity is described in the present chapter.

BACKGROUND: PROVIDING AID FOR A STRANGER IN DISTRESS

Latané and Darley (1970) selected a specific type of situation which was of both theoretical and practical interest as a starting point in studying altruistic behavior. Both history and the daily newspaper provide thousands of examples of individuals who have accepted pain or even death rather than betray a cause or permit their companions to suffer. There are also many examples of those who have taken great personal risks to save the life of a total stranger. For example, a newspaper account tells of an event in Fort Wayne, Indiana, in August of 1970:

> At night fire broke out in the living room of a second-floor apartment where Melissa, aged 17 months, and Jackie, aged 2 months, were asleep in separate bedrooms while their mother was visiting neighbors. Among those attracted to the fire was Thomas Bettis, aged 25, a pharmaceutical salesman. He entered the smoke-filled apartment and, making his way past the flames, reached the first bedroom. In dense smoke he located a window, opened it, and thrust his head outside briefly for air. He then moved to the bed and picked up Melissa, who was unconscious. After handing her to a man outside the window, Bettis made his way to the other bedroom. He bumped into a crib, in which he found Jackie unconscious. Bettis carried her to the open window in the first bedroom. After handing her to the man outside, Bettis climbed through the window opening and jumped to the ground. Melissa and Jackie recovered from the effects of the smoke.

Even less dramatic instances suggest that individuals will abide by an inner code of values which is not, strictly speaking, in their own self interest:

> Annette Ronealla, a 14-year-old, found $12,300 in a brown paper shopping bag. Annette was on her way home from church in Queens Sunday when she

noticed two boys in a supermarket parking lot peeking in the bag. "Don't go there—that's gangsters' money," they warned. But Annette looked anyway, found three stacks of $20s and quickly reported her find to police. Asked why she turned the money in, Annette said: "Well, I'm honest...That's the way I was brought up at home and in church."

In contrast to these accounts, several contemporary events suggest that quite different kinds of behavior may be equally prevalent:

> Kitty Genovese is set upon by a maniac as she returns home from work at 3 A.M. Thirty-eight of her neighbors in Kew Gardens come to their windows when she cries out in terror; none come to her assistance even though her stalker takes over half an hour to murder her. No one even so much as calls the police. She dies.

> Andrew Mormille is stabbed in the stomach as he rides the A train home in Manhattan. Eleven other riders watch the 17-year-old boy as he bleeds to death; none come to his assistance even though his attackers have left the car. He dies.

In these last two instances, why didn't the bystanders do something? Explanations for these events have been offered in newspaper editorials, psychiatric pronouncements, and in themes expressed in plays, novels, and sermons. Can we explain these incidents in terms of apathy, the alienation caused by big cities, mass psychosis, or the breakdown of moral values? Anecdotal evidence, at least, suggests that the unresponsive bystanders are not necessarily indifferent or apathetic. Instead, they are fascinated by what is going on and distressed by the stranger's plight. Nevertheless, they are unwilling to provide help. Is is possible to study such behavior in an experimental setting and to learn the determinants of altruism and the absence of altruism?

A BASE RELATIONSHIP

Darley and Latané proposed that the presence of other bystanders exerted an inhibiting influence on the altruistic behavior of any given bystander. They suggest (Darley and Latané, 1968, pp. 377–378):

> In certain circumstances, the norms favoring intervention may be weakened, leading bystanders to resolve the conflict in the direction of nonintervention. One of these circumstances may be the presence of other onlookers. For example, in the [Kitty Genovese] case, each observer, by seeing lights and figures in other apartment house windows, knew that others were also watching. However, there was no way to tell how the other observers were reacting. These two facts provide several reasons why any individual may have delayed or failed to help. The responsibility for helping was diffused among the observers; there was also diffusion of any potential blame for not taking action; and finally, it was possible that somebody, unperceived, had already initiated helping action.

When only one bystander is present in an emergency, if help is to come, it must come from him. Although he may choose to ignore it (out of concern for his personal safety, or the desire "not to get involved"), any pressure to intervene focuses uniquely on him. When there are several observers present, however, the pressures to intervene do not focus on any one of the observers; instead the responsibility for intervention is shared among all the onlookers and is not unique to any one. As a result, no one helps.

They hypothesized, then, that the more bystanders to an emergency, the less likely, or more slowly, any one bystander will intervene to provide aid. In their initial experiment on this problem, the subject arrived at the laboratory supposedly to take part in a discusison (via an intercom system) of personal problems associated with college life. The experimenter gave the instructions and then left, indicating the he would return when the discussion was over. The discussion began with each participant introducing himself; suddenly, one of the other participants seemed to undergo an epileptic-like seizure. The stimulus variable of interest was the number of other people the subject believed were participating in the discussion group: just the subject and the victim, the subject and one additional participant, or the subject and four additional participants. The response variable was the time which elapsed from the beginning of the fit until the subject reported the emergency to the experimenter.

As expected, the number of bystanders had a substantial influence on the likelihood of responding and on the speed with which they sought help. These results are shown in Table 13-1. The effect of group size on both probability

Table 13-1. Likelihood and Speed of Responding to a Stranger in Distress as a Function of Number of Bystanders

Number of Bystanders	Percentage of Subjects Responding During Victim's Seizure	Number of Seconds to Respond
1 (Subject only)	85	52
2 (Subject and one other)	62	93
5 (Subject and four others)	31	166

(Data from Darley, J. M. and Latané, B., Bystander intervention in emergencies: diffusion of responsibility, *Journal of Personality and Social Psychology*, 1968, 8, 380. © 1968 by the American Psychological Association and reprinted by permission.)

of helping and speed of helping is shown in Figure 13-1. The groups were composed of various combinations of male and female subjects and male or female victims, but sex had no effect on the general findings. It seems, then, that there is something about the presence of others which can inhibit altruistic behavior. When subjects were later asked what crossed their minds

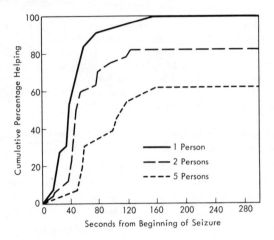

Fig. 13-1 Cumulative Distributions Showing Helping Behavior as a Function of Number of Bystanders. (After Darley, J. M. and Latané, B., Bystander intervention in emergencies: diffusion of responsibility, *Journal of Personality and Social Psychology,* 1968, 8, 380. © 1968 by the American Psychological Association and reprinted by permission.)

when the other person was calling for help, replies included, "I didn't know what to do" and "I didn't know exactly what was happening." They did not feel that the presence of others influenced their own behavior, but the results indicate that there was a very strong influence.

The authors did not observe apathy or indifference toward the victim; instead, the subjects seemed to be caught in an avoidance-avoidance conflict. They were worried and guilty about not helping, but they also did not wish to make fools of themselves by overreacting or somehow ruining the experiment.

ANALYTIC RESEARCH

If the presence of other bystanders in an emergency situation tends to inhibit and slow down altruistic behavior, the first question that arises is "why?" Attempts to answer that question lead not only to theory-building but also to a slightly different form of the question, "What are the specific stimulus cues provided by other bystanders which inhibit altruism?" The identification of those cues constitutes analytic research.

It has been observed by Latané and Darley (1970) that each individual in a group knows that others are aware of his behavior, and he will attempt to behave in such a way as to avoid being ashamed or embarrassed. The rules of public behavior tend to constrain us in a variety of ways, and these constraints tend to act against our helping a stranger in distress. For example, it is frowned upon if we stare closely at strangers or attempt to overhear their conversations, but if we are to notice that an emergency exists, we have to pay close attention to what strangers are doing. Once an emergency is perceived, the decision to intervene requires that we behave in an unusual way and do things that are out of the ordinary, such as trying to stop someone from doing harm to another or calling the police or lending a helping hand. When others are around, the decision to admit that we know what a stranger is doing and the decision to engage in some possibly undignified public behavior involve a risk. We may be mistaken about the emergency or we may attempt to help in an inappropriate way. In either event, we may be laughed at. The notion that we have unnecessarily lost our "cool" and inaccurately proclaimed an emergency is a potent inhibitor because no one wants to be the object of ridicule. When there is just one individual and what seems to be an emergency, such factors would be much less salient than if others were also present. In addition, the others provide cues which influence our decisions about what is going on and what to do about it. When several people face this indecision and conflict together, each one resists being the first to react publicly. In one of Shelly Berman's monologues, he suggests that an airplance passenger who believes that one of the engines is on fire would rather crash in flames than risk making a fool of himself by calling the stewardess. In trying to understand the effect of others on altruistic behavior, an important stimulus aspect might be what it is that these other individuals do.

REACTING TO REACTIONS OF OTHERS TO THE EMERGENCY

Latané and Darley (1968) devised an experimental situation in which a subject was presented with a possible emergency situation. The question was whether his response would vary as a function of being alone, being with others, or being with confederates who deliberately remained passive and unconcerned.

Male students at Columbia were invited to take part in an interview about life at an urban university. When they arrived for the interview and were seated in a waiting room, a stream of smoke began flowing from a vent in the wall. The subject was either alone, with two other subjects, or with two confederates who made no comment and continued filling out questionnaires as the smoke billowed in. The experimenters were interested in how much time elapsed before the subject left the room to report the emergency. If six minutes passed without the subject having responded (sufficient time for the room to fill with smoke and obscure vision), the experiment was terminated.

The results were as expected. When subjects were alone, 75 percent left the room to report the problem before the six minutes were up. When three naive subjects were waiting together, in only 38 percent of the groups did even one person report the smoke within the time limit. With two confederates who acted passive and indifferent, only 10 percent of the subjects responded to the emergency; the remaining 90 percent ". . . coughed, rubbed their eyes, and opened the window—but they did not report the smoke" (Latané and Darley, 1968, p. 218). These results are shown graphically in Figure 13-2

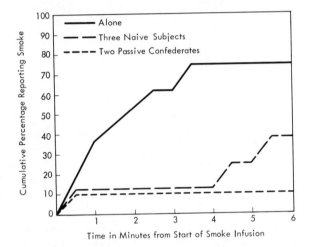

Time in Minutes from Start of Smoke Infusion

Fig. 13-2 Cumulative Distributions Showing Reporting of Emergency as a Function of Number of Bystanders and Behavior of Fellow Bystanders. (After Latané, B. and Darley, J. M., Group inhibition of bystander intervention in emergencies, *Journal of Personality and Social Psychology*, 1968, 10, 218. © 1968 by the American Psychological Association and reprinted by permission.)

with responses plotted as a function of time. At each interval of one minute, it may be seen that the subjects in the room alone behaved quite differently from subjects who were in the presence of others, and that the presence of deliberately passive strangers was a strikingly inhibitory influence. Because the subjects were observed through a one-way mirror, it was possible to note the exact moment when they first noticed the smoke. Somewhat surprisingly, when others were present, a longer time passed before the smoke was seen. It seems that individuals are much less inclined to let their eyes wander around the room when strangers are present, and it therefore takes longer even to perceive the possibility of an emergency.

Thus, the presence of strangers has been shown to have an inhibitory effect on response to two kinds of emergency, and the specific behavior of the strangers can inhibit responsiveness even more. If others are present and are passively indifferent to the emergency event, very few individuals seem willing to ignore that implied social pressure and make a response.

FRIENDS VERSUS STRANGERS
AS FELLOW-BYSTANDERS

It was suggested that groups of strangers inhibit altruistic behavior because each individual is caught in a conflict between wanting to help and wanting to avoid being ridiculed for misinterpreting the situation and overreacting. Strangers tend to avoid communicating and sharing their ideas about what is happening; therefore, they have difficulty in discerning the reactions of one another. If the bystanders in an apparent emergency situation were friends, it would seem plausible to guess that both communication and discernment would be improved; hence, a stranger in distress would be more likely to receive help and to receive it more quickly. This hypothesis was tested by Latané and Rodin (1969).

The subjects were male undergraduates at Columbia who were waiting to take part in a market research study. Subjects were either in the waiting room alone, with a confederate who remained passive and unresponsive, with a friend, or with another subject who was a stranger. A female experimenter took each subject to the waiting room which was next to her office, separated only by a curtain which divided the rooms. She left and could be heard shuffling papers and opening drawers. Four minutes after leaving the subjects, the experimenter turned on a stereo tape recorder to present the emergency event. There was the sound of climbing up on to a chair followed by a loud crash and a scream as the chair collapsed and a body was heard to fall. She then called out, "Oh, my God, my foot . . . I . . . I can't move it. Oh . . . my ankle. I . . . can't get this . . . thing . . . off me." This was followed by about one minute of cries and moans which gradually got more subdued and controlled. Finally, she pulled herself up, went to the door, and slammed it as she left. The incident took 130 seconds.

The results are depicted in Figure 13-3. Once again the inhibiting effect of strangers may be seen, and once again the effect of a deliberately nonresponsive stranger is the most inhibiting factor of all. The new finding is that of the effect of being with a friend when the emergency arises. Here, an altruistic response seems to be as likely and as rapid as when an individual is in the situation alone.[1] There is thus further support for the idea that it is not simply the presence of others which inhibits response to an emergency but the uncertainty about the situation and about how to respond. With a friend present, one can act almost as freely as when one is alone. Latané and Rodin (1969,

[1] This is not quite true because with two people present, each of whom has a 70 percent probability of responding, the chances of at least one of them responding would be 91 percent. Two friends obviously are closer to this figure than are two strangers, but there is still a degree of inhibition here compared to the alone condition. From the victim's point of view, she would be just as likely to get help from one person as from two friends and much more likely to get help in either of those situations than from two strangers.

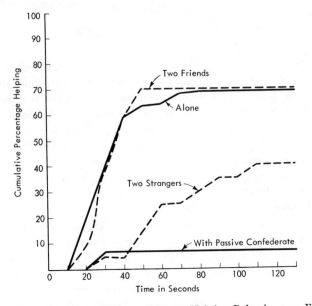

Fig. 13-3 Cumulative Distributions Showing Helping Behavior as a Function of Number of Bystanders, Behavior of Fellow Bystanders, and Relationship Between Bystanders. (After Latané and Rodin, 1969, pp. 193 and 195).

p. 200) observed:

   When strangers overheard the emergency, they seemed noticeably confused and concerned, attempting to interpret what they heard and to decide on a course of action. They often glanced furtively at one another, apparently anxious to discover the other's reaction yet unwilling to meet eyes and betray their own concern. Friends, on the other hand, seemed better able to convey their concern nonverbally, and often discussed the incident and arrived at a mutual plan of action.

This line of research has provided convincing evidence that the presence of others inhibits response to an emergency situation. The most powerful inhibitory cue is the presence of strangers who fail to show concern over the emergency and who fail to respond to it. Less inhibitory, but still with a strong effect, is the simple presence of strangers. An individual is most likely to respond appropriately to an emergency and to offer help to a person in distress if he confronts that situation all by himself.

STIMULUS GENERALITY

In the studies of altruistic behavior which have been discussed, the research strategy did not involve one specific experimental situation of unknown generality. Instead, a degree of generality was built into each new experiment in that a different setting and a different kind of emergency was employed each time. That strategy can sometimes lead to confusion because inconsistent findings across experiments may be the result of unknown stimulus differences from situation to situation. In the present instance, however, the consistent effect of number of bystanders on response to different situations, (an epileptic seizure, smoke coming through a vent, and an accidental fall) indicates a stable relationship across quite varied conditions. Additional studies of generality involve the investigation of still more situational variations, the determination of the effects of specific variables relevant to the victim or the emergency or the bystander, and an examination of the effects of increasingly complex combinations of these factors both in the laboratory and in nonlaboratory settings.

Response to Stealing

When an individual becomes aware that someone has committed a theft, the problem is in many ways quite different from the kinds of emergency created in the previous experiments. There is no physical threat to the subject or anyone else, and the only harm done is the loss of money or property. In fact, if a bystander reports the crime, he is bringing harm to the thief and facing the possibility of retribution. Nevertheless, the moral and legal issues are quite clear. Theft is wrong, and the thieves should be reported, caught, and punished. An interesting research question is whether or not the same situational determinants affect response to theft as affect response to an emergency. More specifically, does the presence of additional witnesses to such a crime inhibit the tendency of any one of them to report the crime?

Stealing Money. Latané and Darley (1970) reported an experiment in which male undergraduates at Columbia were supposedly to take part in an interview. Each subject was either the sole witness to a theft or one of two witnesses. In the waiting room was "another subject" who was a clean-cut student wearing a conservative sport coat with an open shirt. The receptionist told them that they would be interviewed individually. On a desk was a large envelope from which she took two dollars for each subject as their payment for participating. It was made clear that much more money remained in the envelope (between thirty dollars and fifty dollars). Soon afterward, a buzzer sounded, and the receptionist left the room to answer the call. At this point, the thief went to the desk, clumsily but unsuccessfully tried to conceal his actions, and placed the remaining money in his coat pocket. He said nothing throughout his performance and, if a subject said something to him he replied, "I don't know what you are talking about." A minute later the receptionist returned; half a minute later the thief was called out for his interview. The subject could report the theft as soon as the receptionist came back, after the thief was out of the room, or not at all.

When subjects were alone, 24 percent of them spontaneously reported the theft to the receptionist. If bystanders had no inhibiting effect, with two witnesses at least one of them would report it in 42 percent of the pairs. In fact, in only 19 percent of the pairs did someone tell the receptionist. There were thirty-two subjects who were in the two-witness condition, and only three of these individuals informed the girl that she had been robbed.

A great many subjects indicated in a later interview that they did not notice the theft even though it was carried out in an obvious manner in a small room. Observers through a one-way mirror felt that most subjects actually did see the theft and that they responded with a certain amount of surprise and shock, but the subjects denied it steadfastly. Whether this means they were unconsciously denying the perception or simply justifying their acquiescence to the crime is not clear.

Once again, the presence of others exerted an inhibitory effect on moral behavior. The reasons given by subjects who said they saw the theft but then failed to report it were not very convincing. Some said they believed that the thief was only making change, that he had stolen the money by accident, that he was poor and needed the money (even though he was well dressed), or that there must not have been much money in the envelope anyway.

Stealing Beer. Latané and Darley (1970) extended the study of the effect of bystanders to a different kind of theft and into a real-life setting as opposed to a laboratory. A major concern was whether or not the behavior of individuals who know they are subjects in a psychological experiment is generalizable to nonlaboratory situations in which the respondents are simply going about their everyday lives.

The setting was a discount store in Suffern, New York. For the experiment the robber was a husky Columbia undergraduate dressed in T-shirt and chinos. The store employees were, of course, participants in the experiment. The robbery was timed to take place when either one or two customers were in the store. The robber would go to the cashier and ask the name of the most expensive beer. The cashier replied, "Lowenbrau," and then went to the back of the store to see how much was in stock. The robber then picked up a case of beer near the front of the store saying, "They'll never miss this," walked out, placed the beer in his car, and drove off.

Not too surprisingly, no one tried to intervene and stop the robbery. Males and females did not differ in their tendency to tell the storekeeper about the crime. Once again, however, the number of bystanders was found to influence the response. When customers were alone in witnessing the crime, 65 percent reported it. This leads to the expectation that with two customers one or the other would report it 87 percent of the time. In fact, in only 56 percent of the two-person situations was there even one witness who informed the cashier of the theft.

RACE AND SEX

Race and Sex in the Supermarket. Wispé and Freshley (1971) were interested in whether black victims and white victims would be equally likely to receive help from black or white bystanders. The victims were young female students at the University of Oklahoma. The experiment took place at a series of supermarkets. One of the girls would stand near the front exit of the store; she held a large bag of groceries. As the designated subject left the supermarket, the girl turned slowly away, tearing the bottom of her bag. The groceries fell to the pavement, the girl made a gesture of surprise, and she slowly circled the pile for a few seconds in dismay. It was arranged so that the subject was about ten feet away and approaching the confederate when the accident occurred. Subjects were selected on the basis of being alone when they left the store and having their hands free enough to help. Both sex and race of the potential helper were of interest, so the selection of subjects involved an equal number of black women, white women, black men, and white men.

The race of the victim did not affect the likelihood of help being offered. It was found that blacks and whites were equally likely to receive help or to give help. There was a significant sex difference among black subjects in that black males were more helpful to both the black and the white victims than were black females.

Helping Dependent Males or Females. Gruder and Cook (1971) tested the proposition that females in our culture are easily cast into a dependent role and hence are more likely to elicit helping responses from others than is true for males. When males assume a dependent role, it was hypothesized that they should actually receive less help than nondependent males.

The subjects were undergraduates at the University of Illinois at Chicago Circle. Individually, a subject reported to an experimental room where there was a note left by a male or a female experimenter. The note explained that the experimenter was called away, and the subject was requested to assemble and staple questionnaires which were left in the room. In the high dependency condition, the questionnaires were supposedly needed for a project starting in two hours while in the low dependency condition they were not needed until the following week. The measure of helping was the number of questionnaires stapled by the subject.

It may be seen in Figure 13-4 that a dependent female experimenter re-

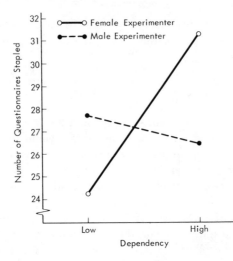

Fig. 13-4 Number of Questionnaires Assembled to Help an Experimenter as a Function of Experimenter's Sex and Degree of Dependency. (After Gruder, C. L. and Cook, T. D., Sex, dependency, and helping, *Journal of Personality and Social Psychology*, 1971, 19, 293. © 1971 by the American Psychological Association and reprinted by permission.)

ceived much more help than a nondependent one. A dependent male experimenter received slightly less help than a nondependent one. Both male and female subjects responded in the same way.

Thus, females are helped more than males when they are dependent. When females ask for help and are not immediately dependent, help isn't given very readily, perhaps because such females are seen as exploiting their role as women. Men, on the other hand, are supposed to be independent and competent. When they ask for help, they must really need it. When they are dependent and ask for help, however, there is a tendency not to respond. It is as if a man who gets himself into that kind of predicament doesn't deserve help.

Race on the Subway. Both the race of a male victim (black or white) and the type of problem (drunkenness or illness) were varied by Piliavin, Rodin, and Piliavin (1969). It was hypothesized that help would be offered most readily by members of the victim's own race and that illness would elicit more helping behavior than drunkenness. The emergency scene was staged on a branch of the New York subway system during a seven-and-a-half-minute express run between two stations. The experimenters were Columbia University students. The victim stood next to a pole in the center of one end of the subway car. About seventy seconds after the subway left one of the stations, he staggered forward and collapsed on the floor where he remained staring at the ceiling. The setting is shown in Figure 13-5. The victims were dressed identically. For the drunk condition, the victim smelled of liquor and carried a bottle wrapped in a brown paper bag. In the ill condition, the victim carried a black cane.

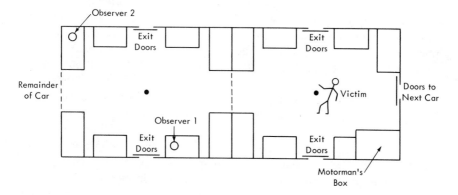

Fig. 13-5 Layout of Subway Car in Which Victim Falls. (After Piliavin, I. M., Rodin, J., and Piliavin, J. A., Good samaritanism: an underground phenomenon? *Journal of Personality and Social Psychology*, 1969, 13, 291. © 1969 by the American Psychological Association and reprinted by permission.)

In many respects, the findings were not very much like those reported in the other studies discussed so far. Spontaneous help was offered to the ill stranger in almost every trial, and even the drunk received help on half of the trials. There was no relationship between number of bystanders and speed of helping. There was a tendency for racial factors to interact with the condition of the victim in determining who offered help. For the presumably ill victim, race was not a determinant of help, but with the drunk victim, help was offered primarily by members of his own race.

Asking for Help

One of the pervading themes of these studies is the ambiguity faced by the subjects. They are presumably faced with the task of interpreting the situation, evaluating whether or not help is needed, and then deciding whether or not to act. It would follow from this analysis that anything which reduced the ambiguity of the situation would increase the likelihood of altruistic behavior. For example, it may be that help was readily given in the subway study because the victim was clearly visable and the problem was not at all ambiguous.

The Cry for Help. Yakimovich and Saltz (1971) presented subjects at Wayne State University with a situation in which the need for help was unmistakable. The experiment took place in a deserted wing of an old building in an isolated corner of the campus. Each subject participated individually and was given a questionnaire to fill out. The experimenter then left the room. A confederate who was dressed as a workman was washing windows on the floor just beneath the experimental room. When the subject was on the last page of the questionnaire, the confederate knocked over his ladder and pail, screamed, and lay down on the pavement, clutching his ankle. In one condition, the confederate continued to moan and hold his foot, but did not actually call for help. In the second condition, the situation was identical except that the injured workman occasionally cried out for assistance.

All subjects jumped up to look out the window when they heard the accident. When there was no verbalization by the victim, only 29 percent of the subjects helped him; the remaining 71 percent simply stared out the window and then went back to complete the questionnaire. When the victim cried out for help, 81 percent of the subjects provided help and only 19 percent ignored the request.

It seems that verbal cues make the situation clear enough that most subjects are willing to help the victim.

Reason for Requesting Help. In situations in which someone has been injured or otherwise incapacitated, the reason that help is needed is obvious. When help of other kinds is requested, it stands to reason that the nature of the request and the amount of justification which is provided would influence whether or not help is given.

Latané (1970) conducted a simple field study in which undergraduates at Columbia went out into various sections of New York and asked passersby for a dime. The sample of citizens to whom the request was made constituted a reasonably representative group of New Yorkers in public places. The way in which the request was made and the reasons given were varied, and these variations markedly affected the percentage of subjects who complied with the request. The results are shown in Table 13-2. It may be seen that only a third of the subjects responded positively to a simple request whereas the addition of the requester's name elicited a positive response from almost half of the subjects. The statement that the requester has spent all of his money does not meet with much success, but the statement that the dime is needed for a telephone call or that the requester's wallet has been stolen elicits help from about two thirds of the subjects.

Latané suggested that the differential effects may be the result of differential justification or of the establishment of a closer bond between the requester and the subject.

Table 13-2. Manner of Requesting Help from Strangers
and Response to the Request

Manner of Request	*Percentage of Subjects Responding Positively to Request*
"Excuse me, I wonder if you could give me a dime?"	34
"Excuse me, I wonder if you could give me a dime? I've spent all my money."	38
"Excuse me, I wonder if you could tell me what time it is? . . . and could you give me a dime?"	43
"Excuse me, my name is_____ I wonder if you could give me a dime?"	49
"Excuse me, I wonder if you could give me a dime? I need to make a telephone call."	64
"Excuse me, I wonder if you could give me a dime? My wallet has been stolen."	72

(Data from Latané, 1970)

CHARACTERISTICS OF OTHER BYSTANDERS RELEVANT TO PROVIDING HELP

Though the inhibitory effect of bystanders on the helping response was established in several experiments, it seems likely that various characteristics of an individual's fellow-bystanders could serve to weaken that effect. For example, if a subject and two policemen witnessed a theft, the subject would probably not be likely to take the responsibility for reporting the theft. If a subject and two preschool children witnessed a theft, the likelihood of the subject's responding would almost certainly increase. Variations on this theme have been explored in a few experiments.

Ability of Other Bystanders to Help. Bickman (1971) pursued the idea of diffusion of responsibility as the determinant of the bystander effect by varying the purported characteristics of the other bystanders. He proposed that if the others are perceived as being unable to help, there should be little or no diffusion of responsibility. As an example, he suggests that if someone is drowning and other bystanders cannot swim, a subject would be as likely to help as if he were alone

The actual situation used was one in which female Brooklyn College students were told they were participating in an ESP experiment. Each subject was either informed that there was one other student or two other students taking part in the study in separate cubicles connected by microphones. Actually, the "other students" were tape recordings. There was an alone condition (the subject and the victim), an able bystander condition (the subject, the victim, and another student in a nearby cubicle), and a condition in which a bystander was unable to help (the subject, the victim, and another student whose cubicle was located in a different building about 1000 feet away). The supposed study of ESP proceded until the victim was heard to say, "Wait a minute, I think something is falling off the bookcase. I'd better fix it." There was the sound of movement and rearranging objects, and then the victim cried out, "It's falling on me!" followed by a scream, a loud crash, and then silence.

The results may be seen in Figure 13-6. As predicted, subjects in the alone

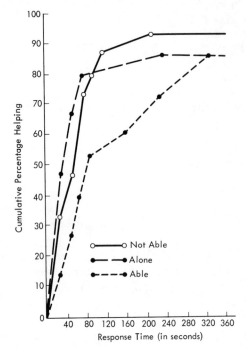

Fig. 13-6 Cumulative Distributions Showing Helping Behavior as a Function of Ability of Fellow Bystanders to Help. (After Bickman, 1971, p. 373.)

condition and in the condition where the other bystander was not able to help responded most quickly to help the victim, and these conditions did not differ from one another. Much less rapid help was provided when the subject believed that there was another bystander who was equally able to report the emergency.

It was concluded that diffusion of responsibility occurs only when bystanders are perceived as able to help.

Children as Fellow-Bystanders. Ross (1971) proposed that the presence of children as bystanders would not inhibit helping behavior and would perhaps even enhance it. The subjects were college students at the University of Toronto who were placed in an emergency situation either alone, with two adults, or with two children (ages 4 and 6). In the latter instance, the children were supposed to be waiting to take part in another experiment; they simply sat and played with coloring books. Two different emergencies were used, but the results were the same in each instance. The subjects were told that the experiment involved a problem-solving task in which instructions were given by means of a tape recorder. After about twenty minutes, one of the "emergencies" occurred. Half of the subjects were in a condition in which smoke began pouring into the experimental room while the remainder heard an accident nearby in which a workman hurt his leg.

The percentage of subjects who responded to the emergency by leaving the room in order to obtain help was once again found to be influenced by the presence of bystanders and by the characteristics of those bystanders. In Table 13-3 it may be seen that the greatest response was when the subjects

Table 13-3. Percentage of Subjects Responding to the Emergency

Emergency	Adults	Bystander Conditions Children	Alone
Smoke	16	50	100
Accident	16	50	83

(Data from Ross, 1971)

were alone and the least when other adults were present. With children in the room, there was an intermediate degree of helping. Thus, bystanders again were found to inhibit behavior, even when the bystanders were small children.

FAMILIARITY WITH THE SITUATION AND EXPLICIT RESPONSIBILITY

Altruistic behavior seems to decrease as ambiguity increases. When subjects are not sure of what has happened or not sure of the responses of others, for example, they tend to delay any helpful response or neglect to respond altogether. One reason that a group of people may be unresponsive to an emergency is that they find themselves in an unfamiliar and unusual situation and simply do not know exactly what to do. A second theme of many of these studies has been the role of diffusion of responsibility. Again, as the number of bystanders increases, it is less certain as to who should respond. If someone has the responsibility explicitly assigned to him (males versus females, policemen versus civilians, physicians versus laymen), the presence of bystanders should not be a deterrent to his providing help. Two experiments have dealt specifically with situation familiarity and explicitness of responsibility.

Familiarity with the Setting. We have all had the experience of having to function in a new and unfamiliar setting and know that it can be confusing and unsettling. Your first week at college was very probably much more hectic than was last week, for example. It follows that if altruistic behavior is restrained in part by ambiguity and confusion, individuals in an unfamiliar situation should be less likely to provide help in an emergency than individuals in a familiar situation.

Latané and Darley (1970) staged a situation in which a victim needed help in two different settings—an underground subway station and La Guardia Airport. A young man on crutches with a heavily taped left knee would, with great effort, make his way until he approached a male stranger sitting alone and somewhat isolated from others. At this point, the young man would trip and fall to the ground, clutching his knee in apparent pain.

It was found that in the subway, 83 percent of the strangers helped the fallen victim while in the airport only 41 percent did. It was possible to determine the social class of those who did and did not help and to rule this out as the explanation. Instead, the determining variable seemed to be familiarity with the particular setting. In an airport, there are simply more individuals who find themselves in a strange setting than is true for the subway. Even in the subway station, however, interviews revealed that help was more likely to be given by those most familiar with that setting.

It was proposed that (Latané and Darley, 1970, p. 119) :

> ...a person who is more familiar with the environment is more aware of the way in which the environment works. He is not overloaded with stimuli and his fears of embarrassment...have moderated. He may have a greater stake in keeping that environment safe. He is "in control." Thus he is more likely to help.

Explicit Responsibility of Bystander. In Chapter 4, the work of Stanley Milgram was described in which subjects are told to administer electric shock to another subject; many would continue even though the "victim" cried out in pain and banged on the wall to signal that they should stop. Tilker (1970) hypothesized that individuals would interfere with such a state of affairs if they were explicitly responsible for the safety and well-being of the victim and if they were clearly aware of his condition.

The subjects were freshmen at Michigan State University. All were told that the experiment involved a teacher, a learner, and an observer. A rigged drawing was held, and the subject became the observer while two confederates assumed the other two roles. The learner was strapped into an electric chair apparatus; electrode paste was applied "to provide a good contact and to avoid blisters and burns." The learner expressed fear about the strength of the shock and asked whether he could be hurt. The experimenter said, "Although the shocks can be extremely painful, no permanent damage can be done." The subject also received a sample shock to lend credibility to the situation. The experiment was described as a verbal learning task in which the teacher was to give a shock after each incorrect answer. The voltage started at 15 and was to be increased on each subsequent wrong answer until 375 volts was reached. The bogus generator with power switch, pilot lights, and amperage indicator was designed to impress subjects that it was genuine.

The subjects were assigned to one of three responsibility conditions. The well being of the learner was described as being the total responsibility of the subject, as being no responsibility of the subject (the "teacher" was made responsible), or the responsibility was ambiguous. Feedback from the victim was either absent, auditory, or auditory and visual. When protests were made by the subject, the teacher gave a set of increasingly strong responses, "I think I should go on." "Although the shocks may be painful, no damage is being done." "Shut up! This is the way it is!" The behavior of interest was whether the subject stopped the experimental procedures. Those subjects who did try to help the victim made verbal protests, reported the problem to the experimenter, and some even attacked the teacher or the apparatus.

The subjects who were given total responsibility were found to be most likely to intervene on behalf of the victim. The ambiguous responsibility condition resulted in the least amount of protest from the observers. Physical interference occurred most frequently in the condition where the victim could be seen writhing in pain and could be heard crying out; all of the totally responsible subjects in this condition interfered physically with the experiment. In addition to the importance of responsibility, it was again made clear that a cry for help is crucial. In the no feedback condition, four out of five subjects made no protest. In the feedback conditions, all but two subjects made some protest.

In general, then, it was concluded that socially responsible behavior can be greatly enhanced by the assignment of total responsibility for another's well being plus maximum feedback about his condition.

RESPONSE GENERALITY

Two aspects of response generality have been an integral part of the research strategy employed in studying altruistic behavior. While the laboratory investigations have been confined to the usual college students, a large proportion of the studies were conducted in the field and involved such subject samples as subway patrons, discount store customers, random pedestrians, and shoppers at a supermarket. There are not any systematic cross-cultural studies of this behavior, but the general U.S. population has been better sampled than is true with most psychological phenomena.

In addition, the specific response identified as altruism or helping behavior has consisted of a varied array of behaviors. Thus, subjects were called upon to report a problem, to help a fallen stranger to his feet, to pick up groceries, to go to the aid of a seizure victim, to give a dime to someone who asked for it, and to intervene when one student was administering excessive pain to another. Any general conclusions that may be drawn are obviously not restricted to a single behavioral response.

The third aspect of response generality involves individual differences in altruistic or moral behavior. Several of the investigations of helping behavior tried, without success, to identify personality variables which would differentiate those who responded and those who did not. Among these nonpredictive variables were authoritarianism, need for approval, and social responsibility (Darley and Latané, 1968), ascription of responsibility to self or others (Schwartz and Clausen, 1970), and new left ideology, trustworthiness, independence, and altruism (Yakimovich and Saltz, 1971). Despite the rather consistent lack of significant correlations between personality scales and helping behavior, there has been another more successful approach to individual differences.

The Development of Moral Behavior

A great many theorists have considered the way in which human beings develop into moral and immoral adults and the reasons for differences in this development. Three kinds of necessary processes may be identified as underlying such behavior.

First, individuals must learn to function in terms of abstract conceptualizations as opposed to concrete events and in terms of future consequents as opposed to present sensations. If we responded just to maximize our immediate pleasure and to avoid any immediate pain, our behavior would be seen as irresponsible and immature by most standards. For example, we would not attend school, get innoculated against diseases, brush our teeth, utilize contraceptives, or save money. In addition, there would be no reason to interrupt our ongoing activity and take the time and trouble to assist a stranger in distress. The study of individual differences in this ability to delay immediate gratification in order to obtain future benefits has been of interest to a number of researchers.

Second, individuals must be exposed to a specific set of values or rules of conduct which specify good and bad behavior for a given group of individuals. It is clear from anthropological and historical evidence that these values and rules can be quite different from culture to culture and in the same culture at different points in time. The cultural norms with respect to sexual behavior, courage, self-sacrifice, aggression, or whatever, can take an amazing variety of forms. Thus, one can learn that public nudity and premarital sexual experimentation are an accepted part of adolescence or one can learn to hide one's body with shame and to believe that sexual intercourse should only occur between married partners. One can learn that killing is evil or that it is admirable to decapitate members of neighboring tribes. One can learn to obey the formal laws of the nation or the informal but equally explicit laws of the Mafia. Whatever moral standards are learned, children must be exposed to them by the examples set by parents and others; by formal teaching; and by the informal teaching of the myths, songs, legends, stories, poems, and examples as presented by storytellers, minstrels, the printed page, records, radio, movies, and television. Whether our model is the "trickster" of the Central Woodland Indians, Beowulf, Robin Hood, John Wayne, or James Bond, each of us in any given cultural setting learns what it is that is acceptable and unacceptable behavior, what is good and what is bad, what wins praise and what wins censure.

Third, for the moral standards to operate effectively, there must be the kind of internalization or conscience development or superego functioning that was discussed at the beginning of this chapter. What is it that parents do or fail to do, what experiences, what kinds of child-rearing practices are responsible for the development of moral human beings? Can we identify the antecedents which differentiate the sadistic thrill killer from the compassionate samaritan? Freud's influence on research of this type is tremendous, but there are other influences as well which we will explore briefly.

DELAY OF GRATIFICATION

Civilization is built on a foundation of impulse control in which physiological drives of hunger, sex, elimination, and so forth, are satisfied in particular ways at particular times in specific contexts. One of the greatest tasks facing children and their parents is the development of behavior which involves delay and postponement of drive satisfaction. And, the teaching varies in its success; there are vast differences among individuals in willingness to delay gratification. For example, consider the student who attends college and goes through graduate school in order to obtain advanced scientific or professional training. The entire process revolves around delay and at least partial nonsatisfaction of primary and secondary needs in the expectation of greater future rewards. By way of comparison, consider the person who drops out of school, commits minor burglaries to obtain money, and participates with a gang in a sexual assault on a young woman. Is there any way to measure these dramatic differences in impulse control and to study this dimension as a personality variable?

Many investigations have utilized some variation of a technique in which subjects must choose between a small immediate reward and a larger reward which is available after a time delay. This research has been reviewed in some detail by Mischel (1966). As we saw in earlier sections (including intelligence), experimenters have measured this variable by giving children several choices, and in each instance the decision involves a small immediate reward versus a large delayed reward. For example, they must choose between a small notebook now and a larger one in a week and fifteen cents now or thirty cents in three weeks.

Relationship between Delay of Gratification and Cheating. Mischel and Gilligan (1964) hypothesized that those who are unable to postpone gratification in order to receive a larger reward would be likely to succumb to temptation and to cheat in situations in which success was of importance to them. Their subjects were sixth-grade boys in Boston who had to indicate seventeen choices between immediate and delayed reward. The situation providing the opportunity to cheat was a ray gun game in which each boy shot at a moving rocket target. Points were given for hitting the target, and brightly colored sportsman badges were given for those setting a sufficient number of points. Actually, the game was arranged so that the subject could not get enough points to win a badge unless he reported a false score. To make such cheating possible, the experimenter left the room during each game and asked the subject to write down his own scores and add them up. If they wrote down their actual score of 17, no prizes would be given. With a score of 20, they would win a badge, and with more points earned even better badges. So, the measure of cheating was the number of points over seventeen which a subject reported. Preference for immediate reward correlated .31 with amount of cheating in the game. Those who were not willing to delay gratification in order to get a larger reward were also not willing to resist the temptation to cheat.

Relationship between Delay of Gratification and Age. Since tolerance for postponement is almost certainly learned over a relatively long period of time rather than all at once, we would expect differences in this behavior across age levels. That is, with increasing age a higher and higher proportion of children should be able to delay the gratification of their impulses.

As part of a cross-cultural investigation in Trinidad, Mischel (1958) obtained data on male and female children, aged 7, 8, and 9. The subjects consisted of blacks and East Indians. In a preliminary study with other subjects, the investigator found that two reinforcements, a one-cent and a ten-cent piece of candy, were clearly perceived as different and that all of the children preferred the ten-cent candy. In the main investigation, the children filled out a research questionnaire, and then the experimenter explained that he wanted to give each child a piece of candy. Everyone could have a one-cent piece today, but if they were willing to wait until the following week, a ten-cent piece would be available. The children were divided into those who preferred the immediate reinforcement and those who preferred the delayed reinforcement. When they were further divided into separate age groups, as shown in Table 13-4, the proportion of subjects who preferred the larger delayed reinforcement to the smaller immediate reinforcement increased as age increased.

Table 13-4. Relationship Between Age and Preference for Immediate vs. Delayed Reinforcement

	Age		
	7	8	9
Proportion Choosing Delayed Reinforcement	.19	.52	.80
Proportion Choosing Immediate Reinforcement	.81	.48	.20

Delay of Gratification and Impulse Control. Reasoning from Freud's (1900) formulations of the relationship between ability to delay gratification and ability to control impulses, Roberts and Erikson (1968) studied a group of delinquent adolescent males. The subjects were chosen from a group of incoming inmates who smoked. During the first two or three weeks of imprisonment, they were not allowed to smoke. Ability to delay gratification was measured in two ways. Each subject wrote an essay about a boy who won $1,000 as a prize in a contest and what he would do with the money. The stories were scored with respect to immediate spending of the money versus saving for the future. In addition, each subject was given a coupon which could be exchanged immediately for one cigarette or a week later for a package of cigarettes. Impulse control was indicated by the ratings of supervisors who observed them during this two- to three-week period. Each subject was rated as falling into the category of "shit sticks" who fight, mouth off, manipulate, and are general nuisances or "good guys" who cause no trouble, are quiet, and obey the rules and regulations.

The relationship between delay of gratification and ratings is shown in Table 13-5. The correlations between ratings and the essay measure was .83; for the coupon choice the correlation was .75. Thus, those who are willing or able to delay gratification were found to respond with more impulse control than those who tend toward immediate gratification of impulses.

Delay of Punishment. The tendency to chose a large delayed reward rather than a small immediate one is one aspect of mature and controlled functioning. Punishment can involve a conceptually similar choice. What if you are faced with an unavoidable unpleasantness such as having a cavity filled at the dentist? Should you do it now or postpone the inevitable? On a number of grounds, it could be argued that it is advantageous to "get it over with"

Table 13-5. Number of Subjects with Each Impulse Control Rating
and Their Choices on Two Measures of Delay of Gratification

Measures	"Good Guys"	Ratings of Impulse Control Intermediate	"Shit Sticks"
Essay			
Subjects who wrote about delayed reward	23	10	1
Subjects who wrote about immediate reward	5	22	15
Cigarette Coupon			
Subjects who chose delayed reward	22	15	1
Subjects who chose immediate reward	6	17	19

(Data from Roberts and Erikson, 1968)

rather than let the threat hang over your head. It has been found that normal subjects tend to prefer an immediate punishment such as electric shock over one that is delayed (Cook and Barnes, 1964).

Hare (1966) proposed that individuals who are deficient in conscience development are likely to avoid immediate discomfort and to be relatively unconcerned about the long-term consequences of their behavior. On this basis, he hypothesized that psychopaths would not be as likely to choose immediate punishment as would normals.

The subjects were male inmates at the British Columbia Penitentiary who were classified as either psychopathic or nonpsychopathic; there was also a group of male students. Each subject was seated in front of a panel on which there was a green light and two telegraph keys about one foot apart. The subject's hand was placed midway between the keys. When the light came on, he had to press one of the keys. The subject would then receive a reasonably painful electric shock; labels indicated that one key would signal an immediate shock and the other a shock delayed by 10 seconds. After a demonstration of the way in which each key worked, there were six trials on which the subject could chose immediate or delayed shock.

The choices made by each group of subjects are shown in Table 13-6. It is clear that the psychopathic subjects were much less likely to choose the immediate shock and much more likely to choose the delayed shock than either of the other two groups of subjects.

The results can be interpreted as supporting the idea that the emotional significance of future punishment is of relatively less concern to psychopaths than to nonpsychopaths. Conscience development, then, is related both to delay of gratification and to delay of punishment.

**Table 13-6. Percentage of Subjects Choosing
Immediate versus Delayed Electric Shock**

	Psychopathic Prisoners	*Nonpsychopathic Prisoners*	*Students*
Immediate Shock	55.5	87.5	78.9
Delayed Shock	44.5	12.5	21.1

(Data from Hare, 1966)

Modifying Delay-of-Gratification Behavior. Bandura and Mischel (1965) suggested that delay of reward behavior should be influenced by the way in which others behave with respect to immediate versus delayed gratification. For example, parental behavior seems to serve as a model which determines in part the behavior of their children in this respect (Mischel, 1958). In addition, the moral of many stories ("The Grasshopper and the Ant," for example) concerns the benefits of delayed gratification, while some literature (*The Rubaiyat*) delivers the opposite message.

Bandura and Mischel (1965) compared the relative power of both live and symbolically presented models in modifying this kind of choice behavior. The subjects were elementary school children in the fourth and fifth grades. The first step was to determine whether each subject tended to choose immediate or delayed rewards. The choices included a small rubber ball today or a large rubber ball in two weeks. Those subjects who most consistently chose the immediate reward and those who most consistently chose the delayed reward were selected for a modelling experiment.

About four weeks after the initial testing, different experimenters conducted the second portion of the project. In the live model condition, an adult was given a series of appropriate small-immediate or large-delayed choices (books, records, money). The model behaved in each instance in a way opposite from that of the subject on the pretest. In addition, the idea was verbalized. For the high-delay children, the model who behaved in the opposite way said, "You probably have noticed that I am a person who likes things now. One can spend so much time in life waiting that one never gets around to really living. I find that it is better to make the most of each moment or life will pass you by." For the children who originally had chosen immediate rewards, the model chose the larger delayed rewards and also said, "You have probably noticed that I am a person who is willing to forego having fewer or less valuable things now, for the sake of more and bigger benefits later. I usually find that life is more gratifying when I take that carefully into account." The model left the room before the subject was tested again. In the symbolic model condition, the subject was told that the adult had already left but he was informed of the choices that had been made. In the control condition, the subjects were shown the kind of choices available to the adults but were informed that the adult couldn't be there to do it. Immediately afterward, each subject had a new choice test of fourteen paired items. Finally, there was a follow-up test four to five weeks later in which children again made choices between small-immediate or large-delayed rewards. This last procedure was designed to determine whether the effects of the modelling experience generalized to subsequent situations.

The results can best be seen by examining Figures 13-7 and 13-8. For both

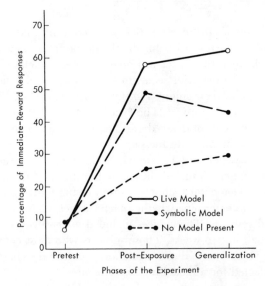

Fig. 13-7 Percentage of Immediate-Reward Responses by Delayed-Reward Children after Exposure to Immediate-Reward Model. (After Bandura, A. and Mischel, W., Modification of self-imposed delay of reward through exposure to live and symbolic models, *Journal of Personality and Social Psychology*, 1965, 2, 702. © by the American Psychological Association and reprinted by permission.)

groups of children, it is clear that their delay-of-gratification behavior was markedly altered by exposure to either a live or symbolic model and that the changes tended to persist at least over the several weeks following the experiment. Once again, the importance of situational determinants was convincingly demonstrated.

LEARNING THE APPROPRIATE
VALUES AND CONDUCT

As was suggested earlier, our moral code is culture-specific. It is not surprising that children raised in a specific culture or subculture learn the moral code of that group just as they learn the group's language, eating habits, and

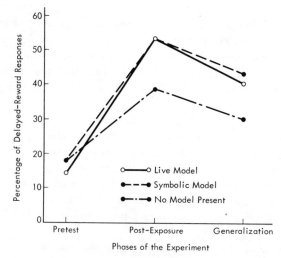

Fig. 13-8 Percentage of Delayed-Reward Responses by Immediate-Reward Children after Exposure to Delayed-Reward Model. (After Baudura, A. and Mischel, W., Modification of self-imposed delay of reward through exposure to live and symbolic models, *Journal of Personality and Social Psychology*, 1965, 2, 703. © by the American Psychological Association and reprinted by permission.)

manner of dress. Beyond these broad generalizations, however, there is still much to understand about how this learning takes place and why it sometimes does not. Studies such as that of Bandura and Mischel (1965) which was just described suggest the importance of models, both live and symbolic, in shaping behavior. Much of this research has been summarized by Bryan and London (1970) who conclude that children learn a norm which dictates, for example, whether they will come to the aid of others; the tendency to follow such a norm increases with age.

Implicit and Explicit Rules of Conduct with Children. Staub (1970) studied helping behavior in children and was surprised to find that while helping behavior increased from kindergarten through the second grade, it rapidly declined again through the fourth to sixth grades. The same pattern was found whether the children were alone or in pairs.

Staub (1971) then conducted a series of follow-up experiments in an attempt to explain those findings. In the earlier study, post-experimental interviews suggested that the older children were afraid that the experimenter would disapprove if they acted when they were not supposed to and that they did not want to engage in inappropriate behavior. During socialization children learn many rules that regulate polite, appropriate behavior, and these rules tend to be inhibitory, indicating what should not be done. "Individuals in our culture seem to learn, for example, not to interfere with another's affairs, to 'mind their own business,' to respect the privacy of others, not to embarrass others, and not to behave in idiosyncratic ways" (Staub, 1971, p. 137). In many situations, obedience to such rules would inhibit attempts to help someone in distress. Staub (1971) hypothesized that it was just such influences which prevented the older children from engaging in helping behavior.

In one experiment, seventh graders were alone in the experimental room and were instructed to make a drawing. It was indicated that a girl was working alone in the next room. Subjects were either told nothing else or the experimenter said, "If you need more drawing pencils, you may go into the other room and get some. There are some in there on the windowsill." The experimenter left and a minute and a half later, there was a crash and sounds of distress from the adjoining room (a tape recording made by a seven-year-old girl).

The behavior of the subjects was clearly affected by the explicit information that it was permissable to enter the adjoining room. As may be seen in Table 13-7, half of those who were given permission helped the stranger

**Table 13-7. Percentage of Children Helping
the Stranger in Distress**

	Provided Help	*Did Not Provide Help*
Given Permission to Enter Other Room	50%	50%
No Information about Entering Other Room	15%	85%

(Data from Staub, 1971)

in distress while only 15 percent of those without such permission provided help. An interesting observation was provided by Staub (1971, p. 139):

> The relevance to helping behavior of concern with inappropriate actions was dramatically indicated by the behavior of one in the permission group. This girl listened for a while to the distress sounds, then broke the points of both of her drawing pencils in quick, deliberate movements, apparently to provide justification for going into the other room, and then ran into the adjoining room.

Implicit and Explicit Rules of Conduct with Adults. Staub (1971) extended the findings with children by repeating some of the same procedures with a group of adult women. Again each subject was taken to the experimental room individually and given a task to do. It was made clear that someone else was working in the next room. The subjects were assigned to either a no information, a permission, or a prohibition group. In the no information group, the experimenter simply indicated that she had work to do and would be back later. In the permission group she said, "I just plugged in a pot of coffee while I was in the other room. It should be ready in a few minutes. If you would like some, go in and help yourself, when you think it is ready. Cream and sugar are beside it." She then indicated that she would return later after attending to some work. In the prohibition group, she said, "I just plugged in a pot of coffee while I was in the other room. It should be ready in a few minutes. You'd better not go in to get any, because the girl in there is working on a timed task and I don't want her to be interrupted. But if you would like some, I will get you some in a while. I have some work to do now, but I'll be back in a while." About two minutes later, there was a crash and the sounds of distress from the other room. The subject's response or lack of response was observed.

In Table 13-8 is shown the effect of explicit and implicit rules on helping

Table 13-8. Percentage of Adults Helping the Stranger in Distress

	Provided Help	*Did Not Provide Help*
Given Permission to Enter Other Room	89%	11%
No Information about Entering Other Room	89%	11%
Prohibited from Entering Other Room	61%	39%

(Data from Staub, 1971)

behavior. With these adult subjects, it may be seen that the explicit prohibition served to inhibit helping behavior but that the no information condition did not differ from the condition where explicit permission was given.

The major difference between the children and the adults was that a situation with no information seems to be interpreted in different ways. For children, no information functions as an implicit prohibition while with adults no information functions as implicit permission. It is possible that in teaching children how to behave we place more stress on what they should not do than on such positive acts as helping a stranger in distress. By the time we reach adulthood, we begin to ignore some of those implied prohibitions.

Model's Preaching versus Model's Practicing. Bryan and Walbek (1970) dealt with another aspect of a model's influence—what they tell others to do as opposed to what they actually do themselves. There is considerable anecdotal evidence and folklore suggesting that what children are told to do with respect to cheating, smoking, drinking, washing their hands, or whatever is not as important as what they observe others to be doing.

The subjects were third-, fourth-, and fifth-grade children. Subjects played a miniature bowling game and whenever they obtained a score of 20 (which they did on half of the trials) they received three one-cent gift certificates. If they wished, some of these could be donated to poor children. A donation box with a few certificates already in it was placed nearby. After the first ten games, an adult model was introduced and he also played ten games. For half of the subjects the model placed one of his three certificates in the donation box after each win, and for the other half the model donated no certificates. While the model played, he either made a number of remarks praising generosity ("I think that we should give some of our money to poor children." "People ought to share with other people.") or remarks praising selfishness ("If I win any more money, I am going to keep it all myself." "Children don't have to help other children."). Thus, the model either practiced generosity or selfishness and either preached generosity or selfishness. After the model left, the subject played 20 more games and the behavior of interest was whether or not he donated any of his certificates. Would he be influenced by the model's behavior and, if so, by the model's words or by his deeds?

The results are shown in Table 13-9. It was found that the greatest effect

**Table 13-9. Percentage of Children Donating to Charity
as a Function of Model's Practicing and Preaching**

	Practicing	
Preaching	*Model Practiced Generosity*	*Model Practiced Selfishness*
Model Preached Generosity	64%	47%
Model Preached Selfishness	62.5%	27%

(Data from Bryan and Walbek, 1970)

on the subject's behavior was what the model did rather than what he said. There was also a tendency for the greatest effect to be obtained by the consistent models. That is, the greatest percentage of donations occurred when the model both preached and practiced generosity and the smallest percentage of donations occurred when the model both preached and practiced selfishness. In a subsequent experiment, a child model was used with very similar results.

An interesting sidelight in a series of studies following this general design was an assessment of the subject's liking of the model. It was found that attraction is greater toward the model who practices generosity than toward one who practices selfishness and also is greater toward the model who preaches generosity than toward one who preaches selfishness. Strangely enough, inconsistency did not have a negative effect on attraction. It was apparently seen as good to donate to the poor or to talk about doing so; if a model was hypocritical or otherwise inconsistent, however, this did not make him disliked. One possibility is that children are exposed to hypocrisy so often in real life that they see nothing peculiar in the model's inconsistency.

Observation and Identification. When we are exposed to a powerful novel or motion picture, we often find ourselves identifying with one or more of the characters. For a brief period of time, their problems and their joys become ours. It stands to reason that such experiences serve to influence our attitudes and values. It is difficult to document the long-term general influences of those sources on our attitudes about race relations or war or premarital intercourse, but it would be difficult to believe that modelling does not occur. In the laboratory, however, it is possible to investigate many aspects of this kind of influence.

Aderman and Berkowitz (1970) cited a number of studies which show that helping behavior increases after the observation of a model who helps (Bryan and Test, 1967; Rosenhan and White, 1967) and also after the observation of someone in need of help (Aronfreed, 1970). They sought to determine more precisely what happens when an individual is exposed to such situations. They proposed that altruism is motivated by empathy which is an emotional response to the emotions of others. Further, they suggest that there are different types of empathic response which can be differentiated. For example, if one observes another person in need of help, he may feel bad especially if that person does not receive help. This empathic response of feeling bad should increase the likelihood that one will help someone else in the future. On the other hand, if one observes a helping model, the empathic response should be a pleasant one. If the model is rewarded for helping, the response is even more positive. In any event, these positive feelings should lead to subsequent helping behavior. This reasoning leads to the prediction that helping behavior can be motivated by observing and identifying with a needy person who receives no help or by observing and identifying with a helping person who is rewarded. The underlying feelings in the two situations are quite different, but the altruistic result is the same.

The subjects in the experiment were undergraduate males at the University of Wisconsin. They were asked to listen to a tape recording which was of a conversation between two students, Bruce and Tom. Each subject was instructed to identify with one of the participants by imagining his feelings and reactions during the conversation. All subjects heard a conversation in the library in which Tom indicates that he is working on a bibliographic assignment for a Shakespeare course. Bruce took an easier version of the course last year. At this point, the end of the scene is either that Bruce gives no help to Tom, Bruce helps Tom, or Bruce helps Tom and Tom expresses his appreciation. Afterward, there were scales to fill out and a postexperimental interview. During a brief waiting period, the experimenter told the subject that "if you want you can just sit here, or perhaps you could do me a favor." There was a stack of data sheets on which four circled numbers were to be added and recorded on a separate sheet. After 10 minutes the experimenter returned. The index of helping was the number of pages the subject voluntarily scored during the 10 minutes.

The results are shown in Table 13-10. When subjects identified with the

Table 13-10. Mean Number of Data Sheets Scored to Help Experimenter

| | Outcome on Tape Recording | | |
Instructional Conditions	*Bruce Doesn't Help Tom*	*Bruce Helps Tom*	*Bruce Helps Tom and Is Thanked*
Identify with Tom	72.75	65.20	66.40
Identify with Bruce	55.50	62.75	73.75

(Data from Aderman and Berkowitz, 1970)

person who needed help, their own subsequent helping behavior was greatest when that person received no help. When subjects identified with the other person in the interaction, their own subsequent helping behavior was greatest when that person gave help and was thanked for it. There were also the expected differences in feelings in these two situations with those in the former rating themselves high in sadness and aggression and those in the latter rating themselves high in elation.

Thus, it appears that observations of others can influence subsequent behavior and that the influence depends on the particular individual in an interaction with whom we identify and on the outcome of the observed interaction.

Child-Rearing Antecedents of
Moral Behavior

If it can be assumed that moral behavior is learned, the study of the way in which such learning takes place is of both theoretical and practical importance. Children are rarely, if ever, deliberately taught to be devoid of feeling for others and to be indifferent to all societal values. Yet, almost all societies, including our own, regularly turn out their full quotas of murderers, sadists, cheats, liars, and thieves. Aronfreed (1968), among others, conceptualizes conscience development in terms of internalization. That is, a given behavior is internalized to the extent that its maintenance has become independent of external outcomes; internal reinforcement keeps the behavior going rather than externally administered reward and punishment. An important research task, then, is to identify the crucial factors in parent-child interactions and other childhood learning situations which lead to the development of internalization.

Cheating and Child-Rearing. The work of Hartshorne and May (1928) was mentioned in Chapter 9 in reference to their failure to find behavioral consistency across situations with respect to traits such as honesty. A somewhat different approach to this research problem was undertaken by Mac-Kinnon (1938) a few years later. As one of the participants in Murray's personality project at the Harvard Psychological Clinic (see Chapter 5), MacKinnon was interested in creating a setting in which subjects were tempted to do something about which they would feel guilty. One by-product of that research was an intriguing hint of a relationship between child-rearing practices and subsequent moral behavior.

The subjects were asked to write down the solutions to twenty problems. On the table at which the subject worked were booklets containing the correct answers, and subjects were allowed to look up some of the solutions but not others. Each subject was led to believe that he was alone and unobserved, but the experimenter actually noted his behavior through a one-way screen. It was found that 54 percent responded to the task honestly while 46 percent cheated on one or more of the problems.

MacKinnon noted several differences between the cheaters and the non-cheaters. As they worked, the cheaters tended to verbalize anger toward the problems ("You bastard." "These are the God damnedest things I ever saw."), while none of the noncheaters did so. The cheaters also exhibited a destructive, aggressive kind of behavior in scuffling their feet, stamping on the floor, kicking the table, and pounding their fists. The noncheaters tended to behave with restlessness and fidgeting such as crossing and uncrossing their legs or hunching their shoulders. The most striking difference was in oral activity (touching the mouth, biting finger-nails) which was twice as frequent among the noncheaters as among the cheaters. Similarly, the non-cheaters were more often engaged in nose-picking and hair twisting than the cheaters. MacKinnon interpreted these differences in psychoanalytic terms, suggesting that the cheaters directed aggression externally while the non-cheaters aggressed against themselves.

The two groups were asked various questions about their parents, and again there were notable differences. The fathers of cheaters were described as using physical punishment in disciplining their children while the fathers of noncheaters used methods that made the child feel "he had fallen short of an ideal or was not worthy of the parents' love." Asked how they reacted to such punishment, subjects receiving physical punishment indicated that they were angered, they sulked, they disliked the punisher, and that they sometimes secretly repeated whatever they had been punished for. The psychological punishment led to feelings of shame, of sorrow, and to resolutions to be good and behave as expected.

The themes emerging from MacKinnon's research have tended to influence much of the subsequent research and theorizing on this problem.

Effect of Maternal Warmth and Punishment Techniques on the Development of Conscience. Sears, Maccoby, and Levin (1957) carried out a large-scale investigation of the effect of various child-rearing practices on selected aspects of the behavior of children. Interviews were conducted with a great many mothers of kindergarten-age children. The two-hour interviews were taped, and judges later used this material to rate numerous variables, including the development of conscience (aggression was described earlier).

Ratings of the children's conscience development revealed marked differences. Some gave no indication of a conscience; the child was reported to hide, deny, or show no signs of unhappiness when naughty. Others appeared to have a highly developed conscience; the child was described as feeling unhappy when naughty, confessing his wrongdoings, and wanting to be forgiven.

Two variables were found to be of importance in the development of conscience. *Maternal warmth* involves love, acceptance, enthusiasm, and outgoing affection toward the child. Ratings of the interview material were based on a variety of statements. For example, a mother rated high in warmth said:

> Well, as soon as my work is done, if she's around, I'll call her and say, "Come on, let's have some fun"; and we'll sit down and she'll sit on my lap, and sometimes I rock her back and forth, and kiss her. She likes to be kissed, she loves it, and I'll cuddle her, and she loves to be cuddled. Or I'll play a game with her (Sears, et al., 1957, p. 53).

A mother rated low in warmth said such things as:

> I, as a child, never kissed my parents, but I'll kiss him goodnight, or kiss him good-bye, something like that, hug him, that's about all. We're not over— not overdo it (Sears, et al., 1957, p. 55).

Punishment techniques used in training the child constituted the second variable. One type of punishment technique was *withdrawal of love*. The mother may look coldly at the child, turn her back, refuse to listen to him, keep him out of the family circle, threaten to go away and leave him unless he is good, or tell him that he is making her sad. The essence is that parental warmth and affection are dependent on the child's good behavior.

Children rated high on conscience development were found to be those whose mothers were high in emotional warmth and who often used withdrawal of love as a punishment technique. The authors suggest that conscience development is dependent upon identification with the parents; identification is fostered by warmth and by punishment involving withdrawal of love.

Obedience and Child-Rearing. Lester and Crowne (1970) devised an unusual experimental task which allowed them to investigate obedience and its correlates.

Their subjects were female students at the University of Connecticut. Before the experiment they indicated their feelings of aversion to a variety of things including toads, spiders, and cockroaches. The experiment in which they then participated was described as a study of animal learning and the effect of experimenter bias. The task involved the handling and maze-running of two giant South American cockroaches each of which was approximately three inches long. The insects had to be picked up, placed in the maze, and afterward returned to their original containers. If a subject refused to obey the directions, Milgram's procedure was followed in which the experimenter said such things as "Please continue." "You are required to continue." "It is absolutely essential that you continue." "You have no choice; you must continue."

Subjects were divided into the obedient ones who completed both trials with both roaches and the nonobedient ones who refused in spite of the experimenter's verbalizations. Obedience was greatest among subjects whose parents used love-oriented rewards and punishments, imposed strict regulations, and demanded obedience.

This investigation may be seen as pointing up a paradox in the study of moral behavior. When there are demands from authority figures or from society to follow the rules, obey the laws, work hard even if the job is distasteful, and otherwise do as you are told, the response of a "good" citizen with a mature conscience is seen as compliance with those demands. When the demands from authority figures or from society are considered to be immoral, the "good" citizen with a mature conscience is supposed to defy the demands. Events in the Vietnam War suggested that whether someone is labeled a war hero or a war criminal is not something on which we can all agree. Such differentiations are clearly difficult to make and even more difficult to teach our children.

THEORY BUILDING

One approach to making sense out of the experimental findings in this area of research has been the descriptive analysis of Latané and Darley (1970).

They have attempted to identify the basic elements which determine whether or not one individual will come to the aid of another. They describe an emergency as a situation which is at least potentially dangerous or threatening, a rare and unusual event requiring a possibly unique set of actions or skills. Further, the emergency is unforeseen and often requires a rapid decision and response. For any individual to decide to do something to help someone in need, he must make a series of decisions. First, he must notice that something is happening; the event must become the focus of his attention so that he becomes aware that something out of the ordinary is going on. Second, he must decide that the event is an emergency, and there are often a variety of alternative hypotheses which are equally reasonable. Third, he must decide that he should assume responsibility for helping. Fourth, he has to decide what action he should take. Fifth, he must actually engage in the helping behavior. Such an analysis is a useful pretheoretical step in that it suggests the kinds of variables to be studied and the kinds of determinants that may be of importance. Much of the research on helping behavior has been oriented around this descriptive model.

There are other more generalized kinds of theoretical formulations which are relevant to this areas of research, and they will be discussed in some detail.

The Development of Conscience

Aronfreed (1968) has traced the concept of conscience through various historical periods. In the writings of Plato and Aristotle concerning morality, the emphasis was on rational judgments rather than on what we have conceptualized as conscience. Much later in time, the emphasis of many philosophers such as Bentham and John Stuart Mill was still on the intellectual as opposed to the affective components of morality. The idea that moral behavior is determined by feelings and internal compulsion can be traced from St. Augustine and St. Thomas Acquinas through Locke and Hume and Kant. In more modern times, the traces of these two emphases may still be seen in the cognitive theory of Piaget and the affective theory of Freud.

Piaget (1948) proposed a theoretical model in which children are seen as developing conscience or morality in terms of a set of rules. This cognitive formulation describes different stages in which children first evaluate behavior with respect to the wishes of authority figures and the consequences of the acts regardless of intent. They take rules in a literal sense and are concerned with the letter of the law and not with the spirit. As the child matures, moral evaluations become more relative to situations and circumstances and intentions. Kohlberg (1963a, b) developed a method for assessing the developmental level of moral judgment as it proceeds from the avoidance of punishment, to social conformity, to an autonomous and internalized set of values.

The developmental sequences of Piaget and Kohlberg are rejected in favor of a five-factor theory of moral conduct recently formulated by Hogan (1973). The model rests on the general assumptions that our behavior is governed in large part by a system of man-made rules and that morality is a natural phenomenon which makes evolutionary sense. An individual's moral development is based on two cognitive and three affective dimensions. Cognitively, he has to learn the rules of conduct, and he has to learn moral reasoning. Affectively, certain interactions are necessary for him to become socialized by internalizing the rules, to feel empathy for others, and to develop a sense of autonomy. One interesting feature of the model deals with the consequences of differential development of these dimensions. Consider socialization and empathy as an example. An individual low on both will tend to become a delinquent. A highly socialized person low in empathy will rigidly follow the rules but without warm interpersonal concerns. An individual low in socialization but high in empathy will be unconcerned about conventional rules and will feel free to break the rules (for example, smoking marijuana or engaging in unusual sexual behavior) so long as it causes no harm to others. An individual high on both dimensions will be "morally mature," in that his compliance with social rules is tempered by his feeling for other people. Hogan has developed measures for each of the five dimensions, and their usefulness in research has been shown in a number of investigations.

To date, Freud's concept of guilt has had the greatest influence on psychological research and theorizing. The general outlines of the psychoanalytic conception of conscience development have been discussed earlier in the present chapter and also in Chapter 2. When various instinctual needs such as sex and aggression are renounced, any impulse toward satisfying them triggers guilt, and it is the guilt feelings which induce the individual to behave in ways which satisfy the internalized moral code.

Two examples will be presented to show the way in which the concept of guilt has been utilized in research on moral behavior.

Guilt and Compliance. Carlsmith and Gross (1969) pointed out that most of the research on obedience and compliance has focused on the strong external pressures which elicit such behavior. They were interested, however, in the way in which compliance can be obtained with minimal external pressure. Other research (for example, Brock and Becker, 1966; Wallace and Sadalla, 1966) strongly suggested that compliance can be obtained under circumstances in which the subject feels guilty and acts in order to reduce that guilt.

In one experiment, subjects were assigned the role of teacher in a learning situation in which the learner (a confederate) either received an electric shock after each mistake or simply heard the sound of a buzzer. The subject's task was to pull a switch to activate the shock or the buzzer each time the learner made a mistake. When the experiment was apparently over, the confederate told the subject that he was a member of a committee attempting to prevent a freeway being built through a grove of redwood trees in Northern California. He said that he needed volunteers to telephone people who would be asked to sign a petition to save the trees. The people to be called and their telephone numbers were written on index cards, of which the confederate had several stacks. He said that each call would take two or three minutes, and he asked the subject if he would help by making some of the calls. If the subject agreed to help, he was asked how many cards he was willing to take. In the nonshock condition, about 25 percent of the subjects agreed to help while in the shock condition 75 percent of the subjects agreed to help. Of the subjects who complied with the request, the mean number of phone calls to be made was sixteen in the nonshock condition and thirty-two in the shock condition. Thus, compliance with a request is much greater after the subject had delivered shock to the requester than in the control condition. One interpretation of this finding is that the subjects felt guilty about hurting the confederate and agreed to help him because of these feelings. It was also possible that the subject just felt sorry for the victim or just wanted to make restitution to him; by doing him a favor, the subject could try to make up for the harm that was done. A second experiment was undertaken in order to differentiate these possible determinants of compliance.

The general task was the same except that there were, in addition to the teacher and the learner, an observer whose task was just to record the responses and the feedback. The subject was assigned the role of either teacher or observer. After the experiment, the request to help "save the redwoods" was either made by the learner or by the observer. There were four experimental conditions. In a condition like the previous experiment, the subject was the teacher, and help was requested by the learner; here, the response could be motivated by guilt, sympathy, or the desire to make restitution. In the sympathy condition, the subject was simply an observer, and help was requested by the learner; here there is no guilt and no reason to make restitution. In the guilt condition, the subject was the teacher, and help was requested by the observer; neither sympathy nor restitution could be operating. In the control condition, the subject was the teacher, help was requested by the learner, but no shock was given.

The effect of these various conditions on the number of phone calls accepted by the subject is shown in Table 13-11. The greatest compliance was obtained for subjects who were presumably responding to their guilt feelings and the least for subjects whose response could be attributed simply to sympathy. Other research (Freedman, Wallington, and Bless, 1967) indicated similar effects even where the person making the request had not observed the situation and hence could not know what the subject had done; thus, the feelings of guilt would seem to be an internal matter and not a reaction to the supposed judgments of the observer. The authors conclude that,

Table 13-11. Number of Telephone Calls Subject
Agrees to Make when Requested to Help

Experimental Condition	*Help Requested by*	*Subject's Role*	*Mean Number of Telephone Calls*
Sympathy	Learner	Observer	6.5
Control (no shock)	Learner	Teacher	13.0
Restitution, Sympathy, or Guilt	Learner	Teacher	23.5
Guilt	Observer	Teacher	39.0

(Data from Carlsmith and Gross, 1969)

"... guilt arising from personal implication is a necessary precondition for obtaining compliance in this situation" (Carlsmith and Gross, 1969, p. 238).

Labeling One's Arousal as Guilt. One very interesting line of research has focused on the question of the level of internal arousal to which subjects respond and the label which they apply to their internal state (Nisbett and Schachter, 1966; Schachter and Latané, 1964). For example, the concept of guilt arousal implies various internal events, both physiological and psychological. When the individual perceives these internal events, he must label his feelings as guilt in order for his subsequent behavior to be affected. If anything interferes with either the arousal or the labeling process, the effects of guilt would be less powerful.

Following this reasoning, Dienstbier and Munter (in press) hypothesized that it is not simply emotional arousal which influences one to avoid an immoral act such as cheating but rather one's interpretation of the meaning of that arousal. When there is temptation to commit such an act, there should be emotional arousal. The individual can interpret this arousal as a sample of how bad he will feel if he commits an immoral act (guilt) or if he is caught (fear). Either label should inhibit his behavior. If, however, he believed that his emotional state had some other, quite different, cause, there should be no inhibition.

The subjects were undergraduates at the University of Nebraska. The experiment supposedly involved the effect of a vitamin supplement on vision. In the experimental room, the pill (actually, it was gelatin) was administered and the subjects were asked to read about the kind of side effects they might experience. Each subject either learned that he had taken Suproxin with side effects of "a pounding heart, hand tremor, sweaty palms, a warm or flushed face, and a tight or sinking feeling in the stomach" or Supraxin with side effects of "an increased tendency to yawn, a lessening of eye blink rate, and tired eyes." It was assumed that any sympathetic nervous system arousal caused by the temptation to cheat would resemble the effects attributed to "Suproxin." The temptation was in the form of a vocabularly test which was supposed to be highly predictive of success in college. The subjects were also told that if they scored lower than 20, the score of the average college freshman, a board of psychologists would like to examine them to determine the reasons for the subnormal performance. The thirty-word test was very hard, and the highest score by a noncheating subject was nineteen. Following the vocabulary test, there was a vision test. Then they were given the opportunity of going over the correct answers for the vocabulary test and cautioned not to change any answers. The experimenter was called out of the room for a long distance phone call. Through the use of a special booklet, it was possible to detect any changed answers.

It had been hypothesized that subjects would cheat more in the Suproxin condition because any arousal would be interpreted as drug effects and hence would not inhibit their actions. The percentage of cheaters in each condition is shown in Table 13-12. When the arousal could be attributed to the effects

**Table 13-12. Percentage of Cheaters as a Function
of Supposed Reason for Emotional Arousal**

Reason for Emotional Arousal	*Cheaters*	*Noncheaters*
Drug Side Effects	49%	51%
Guilt or Fear	27%	73%

(Data from Dienstbier and Munter, in press)

of the drug, almost twice as many subjects cheated as when the arousal could be attributed to guilt or fear. It appears that a person's interpretation of his internal state can have a substantial effect on his moral behavior.

MORAL BEHAVIOR AS A FUNCTION OF POSITIVE AND NEGATIVE REINFORCEMENT

Latané and Darley (1970) point out a number of ways in which altruism could be rewarding to the individual. For example, another's distress may make us feel uncomfortable until the distress is relieved. Also we want to look good in the eyes of others. It is also possible to conceptualize our internal moral values in terms of reward and punishment. Farber (1964, p. 22) recalled an insight he once had

> ...while listening to Frank A. Logan describe some of his animal experiments at Yale, in which delay of reward was balanced against amount of reward in simple choice situations. The experimental results showed that, within limits, rats will choose a longer delay, if the reward is large enough, in preference to shorter delays with lesser rewards. Probably because of obtuseness, it had never before occurred to me quite the same way that the morality

of human beings in giving up the pleasures of this world for the sake of eternal salvation may have something in common with the morality of rats in giving up an immediate reinforcement for the sake of a bigger piece of Purina dog chow.

Much of the research already discussed could be interpreted in reinforcement terms, but there are investigations directly relevant to this theoretical interpretation.

Consequences of Helping. In ascertaining the likelihood of a given individual taking action to help another, it seems useful to identify the positive and negative elements which might influence his behavior. For example, what are the positive effects of living up to one's moral code versus the negative effects of making a fool of oneself? Presumably, the relative number and relative importance of these positive and negative determinants are the crucial variables affecting the final course of action. In many instances, we can only guess at what some of these positive and negative factors might be. Latané and Darley (1970) report the research of Harvey Allen who manipulated the probable consequences of helping in order to study effects of these anticipated outcomes on altruistic behavior.

In a preliminary study, one confederate boarded a subway and asked whether the car was going uptown or downtown. A second confederate always gave the wrong answer, saying "uptown" if it was going downtown and vice versa. This interaction took place beside an unwitting subject. The question was whether the subject would correct the second confederate by giving the right information. About half of the subjects were found to intervene and give the correct answer.

This situation was then used to test the effects of different probable consequences. The confederate who would be giving the misinformation first created a role for himself. He sat in the subway car with his legs outstretched; another confederate walked past and stumbled over his feet. The seated confederate then responded either by doing nothing, by looking up from his muscle-building magazine and shouting physical threats, or by making embarrassing comments about the person's clumsiness. Afterward, a third confederate asked the role-playing confederate about the direction the car was going and was misinformed. At this point, a subject who witnessed the scene had either perceived the misinformer in a neutral role, as a person who would resort to physical violence, or one who would make a loud and unpleasant scene. The latter possibilities represent negative consequences for helping, so there should be less helping behavior in those conditions.

The results are shown in Table 13-13. As expected, there was considerably less helping behavior when the consequences of helping were purposefully made negative.

Table 13-13. Percentage of Subjects Correcting Confederate
Who Provided Misinformation

Consequences	Percentage Helping
Neutral	50%
Unpleasant: embarrassment	28%
Dangerous: physical harm	16%

(Data from Latané and Darley, 1970)

Rewarding and Punishing Altruistic Behavior. When an act of helping is rewarded, such behavior should be more likely to occur the next time that kind of situation arises. If helping is punished, such behavior should be less likely to occur in the future. Moss and Page (1972) tested this hypothesis in a field experiment.

On the main street of Dayton, Ohio, a female confederate would approach a subject and ask for directions to a local department store. When the subject provided this information, he received either a reward (a thank you and indication that the help was appreciated) or a punishment ("I can't understand what you're saying. Never mind, I'll ask someone else.").

Farther down the street, a second female confederate waited for the subject to approach. She then dropped a small bag and walked on as if the accident had not been noticed. Would the subject try to help her or not? If the subject had just been rewarded by the first confederate, 92.5 percent helped the girl who dropped the bag. If the subject had just been punished, only 42.5 percent provided help. Thus, the consequences of altruistic behavior were found to influence subsequent altruism.

Feelings about the Person in Need of Help. The general feelings of an individual toward the person needing help would seem to be another deciding factor. For example, one would undoubtedly risk more negative consequences to aid a loved one than to aid a stranger or an enemy. Baron's (1971) experiment, described in Chapter 10, in which subjects agreed to do a difficult favor for a liked confederate more frequently than for a disliked confederate, will be remembered. On this basis, one might hypothesize a number of variables in the attraction literature that could be expected to operate in influencing helping.

Lerner (1970) has approached this general problem from a somewhat different perspective. He asks how it is possible for any of us to allow our fellow human beings to live in poverty, to be without adequate education or medical care, or to be confined in inadequate and underfinanced institutions of various kinds. Obviously, we do find it possible to sit in a comfortable home attended by well-fed pets and sip expensive liquor while watching a documentary about some of these appalling conditions on our color television set.

Lerner suggests that we are able to react with either compassionate concern or with cruel indifference to the suffering of others. We conceptualize these various events and defend our own reactions in terms of a "just world."

> We want to believe we live in a world where people get what they deserve or, rather, deserve what they get. We want to believe that good things happen to good people and serious suffering comes only to bad people...
>
> Unfortunately, we are regularly confronted with incidents which seem to contradict this belief. We learn of an innocent child killed or brutalized, or of a man whose security derived from a lifetime of hard work is wiped out by an illness, a flood, the closing down of a mine, the act of a criminal. Each such incident may be frightening or sickening. We do not want to believe that these things can happen, but they do. At least we do not want to believe they can happen to people like ourselves—good decent people. If these things can happen, what is the use of struggling, planning, and working to build a secure future for one's self and family? No matter how strongly our belief in an essentially just world is threatened by such incidents, most of us must try to maintain it in order to continue facing the irritations and struggles of daily life. This is a belief we cannot afford to give up if we are to continue to function.
>
> ...Any evidence of underserved suffering threatens this belief. The observer then will attempt to reestablish justice. One way of accomplishing this is by acting to compensate the victim; another is by persuading himself that the victim deserved to suffer, after all. In our culture, and probably many others, suffering is seen as deserved if the person behaved poorly or if he is inherently "bad," or undesirable. (Lerner, 1970, pp. 207–208).

We are motivated to help those in distress because we feel compassion, and helping is the right thing to do. When we fail to do so, it can be because we have redefined the situation such that the innocent victim does, in fact, deserve his fate. We don't have to help him because we do not like him and he is getting what is coming to him. Lerner and his associates have conducted a number of experiments which tend to confirm this general proposition. One response to an innocent victim is to derogate him; otherwise, one's belief in a just world might be threatened.

Altruism as Reinforcement. A direct test of the reinforcement value of altruism has been provided by Weiss, Buchanan, Altstatt, and Lombardo (1971). They utilized an experimental situation in which a subject learns to terminate a noxious stimulus—instrumental escape conditioning. The behavior that serves to terminate the noxious stimulus is an instrumental response. In many studies of such behavior the noxious stimulus has been electric shock or an uncomfortably loud noise. In this experiment, the stimulus was the supposed suffering of another human being. The response was the pushing of a button which relieved the other person's discomfort. If this act of helping another person is, in fact, rewarding, the acquisition of this response should conform to known learning principles.

Each subject participated along with a confederate who was introduced as a fellow subject. The confederate pretended to experience intense pain as he tried to hold a metal stylus steady in a tunnel while receiving continuous electric shock. When the stylus touched the edge, the subject was supposed to set three dials to evaluate the performance. Afterward, a signal light came on and the subject pushed the button to reactivate the apparatus. The button pushing supposedly turned off the electricity, and the confederate breathed a sigh of relief as he got a ten-second break before the shock was resumed. What was actually of interest to the experimenter was the speed with which the button was pushed after the signal light went on. If it was rewarding to end the other person's suffering, the subject should learn to push the button faster and faster. In escape conditioning, this learning is faster when the reward is given on every trial (continuous reinforcement) than when it is given on only a portion of the trials (partial reinforcement). To determine whether an altruistic reward conforms to this law, some of the subjects received continuous reinforcement on the twenty-four trials (button pressing relieved the confederate's suffering each time) and some received partial reinforcement (button pressing relieved confederate's suffering on only half of the trials). Subjects in control groups went through the same procedures except that the confederate was not receiving electric shock.

In Figure 13-9 it may be seen that the control group showed a small but regular practice effect as speed improved over the course of the trials. The groups in which the response involved an altruistic act performed at a much higher level, and, as hypothesized, the continuous reinforcement group was superior to the partial reinforcement group.

The authors (Weiss, et al., 1971, p.1263) note:

> Classical political philosophers, such as Hobbes, Locke, Rousseau, and Comte, as well as their modern descendants, have found it essential to address themselves to the problems of selfishness and altruism in human nature. Ample psychological evidence is available to indicate that man is neither wholly selfish nor wholly altruistic in his behavior. It has not previously been demonstrated, however, that the roots of altruistic behavior are so deep that people not only help others, but find it rewarding as well. Much interest has been shown in the question of how socially constructive or altruistic instrumental behavior can be learned and maintained through extrinsic rewards. However, our research demonstrates that instrumental behavior can be learned and maintained solely through the rewarding function of altruism. The results further indicate that there is a profound similarity between the action of altruistic and conventional, nonaltruistic rewards.

APPLICATIONS

The origin of research interest in moral behavior has been in real-life situations, and much of the research in this area has been conducted in relatively

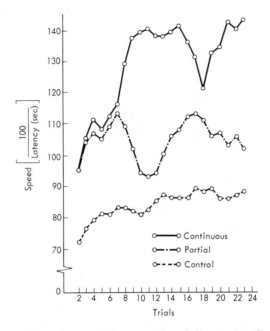

Fig. 13-9 Acquisition Curves of Response Speed Comparing Groups Receiving Continuous or Partial Altruistic Reinforcement with Control Group. (After Weiss, Buchanan, Altstatt, and Lombardo, 1971, p. 1263.)

realistic laboratory settings or has consisted of nonlaboratory field studies. For those reasons, the applied implications of most of the research is immediately obvious. It might be helpful, however, to stress two of the underlying themes of the findings in order to emphasize their relevance.

First, these investigations are quite consistent in showing that those who fail to act in an emergency or who fail to help a stranger in distress are not really indifferent, cruel, apathetic, or alienated. Rather, they seem to be confused and apprehensive about what is going on and what should be done about it. There is a pervasive fear of appearing ridiculous in the eyes of our fellow men, and the best protection is to do nothing and play it cool. One remedy for this situation is for society to make a purposeful and continuing effort to clarify such situations by making them familiar and to suggest the appropriate role for bystanders to play in helping others. In school, on television, in books, and in various youth organizations, our children learn a great deal about how to recognize poison ivy, how to find one's way out of the woods when lost, and what to do when bitten by a snake. For a great many city dwellers whose wildlife adventures are limited to the Jungle Cruise at Disneyland, these nature problems are in the realm of fantasy. It could be argued that as much or more time should be spent in learning what to do if a prowler enters a neighbor's apartment or what to do if a drunk passes out on the sidewalk. To some degree, we all need to learn to pay attention to and to recognize the dangers of such situations; in addition, we need to learn the appropriate response to make. We need examples and models and the chance to practice (at least vicariously) the appropriate behaviors. Also, a victim should be aware that an explicit cry for help increases the chances of obtaining aid.

Second, early childhood experiences seem to influence the development of an internal value system. When children experience an atmosphere of warmth and love which is at least partially contingent upon appropriate behavior, they seem to be most likely to develop internal values which guide their subsequent behavior. When children experience a cold and unaccepting environment and when discipline is enforced primarily through physical punishment and threats of physical punishment, they seem to be least likely to develop the internal guides of conscience. Those are rather sweeping conclusions, and we obviously need to know much more about details of child-rearing, but the available data seem consistently to lead to just these generalizations. In addition, it is obvious that the models who influence behavior (parents, teachers, television performers) must behave in the manner that we consider most desirable and appropriate. For example, children need to see these models choose to delay gratification, help others in distress, and refrain from cheating, if they are to become adults who behave in these ways. Commercials which tell us to "Enjoy now and pay later" and fictional heroes like James Bond provide precisely the opposite message.

SUMMARY

When individuals refrain from acts which would benefit them or risk personal harm in order to help a stranger, they seem to be responding to internalized values that go beyond simple self-interest. Latané and Darley approached the study of this behavior by attempting to identify the variables that determine whether or not an individual will go to the aid of a stranger in distress. It was found that the more bystanders there are to an emergency, the less likely it is that any given bystander will provide aid.

Analytic research on this base relationship between number of bystanders and the probability of helping a stranger in distress has indicated that individuals are strongly influenced by the reactions of their fellow bystanders and that friends inhibit altruistic behavior less than strangers do.

The generality of this relationship has been tested across a variety of stimulus conditions both in the laboratory and in field settings. For example, the presence of bystanders decreases the likelihood of reporting a monetary theft in an office or a shoplifting episode in a discount store. The race of a girl in need of help in a supermarket accident does not influence the amount of help received from either black or white strangers; dependent females receive more help than nondependent ones while the reverse tends to be true for males; and though race has no effect on whether a sick individual is helped, a drunk victim is most likely to be helped by members of his own race. Help is more likely when a victim specifically requests it, and the explicit justification for needing help is an important determinant of whether help will be given. The inhibitory effects of fellow bystanders is less if they are unable to help or if they consist of children rather than of other adults. Altruistic behavior is more likely in a familiar than in an unfamiliar setting and is more likely for someone who is formally assigned responsibility than for someone without that responsibility.

Response generality for these various findings has been demonstrated across diverse subject populations and with a variety of different behavioral acts. While the search for personality scales which predict altruistic or moral behavior has been notably unsuccessful, a great many studies have concentrated on the developmental aspects of such behavior. Three underlying processes of interest are delay of gratification, the learning of specific values or rules of conduct, and the internalization of these values. Delay of gratification is operationally defined in research as the choice of a large reward in the future in preference to a small immediate reward. The tendency to postpone gratification has been found to be negatively related to cheating behavior and positively related to age and to impulse control. Psychopaths are found to differ from nonpsychopaths in indicating a relative preference for delayed rather than immediate punishment. Both live and symbolic models can alter preference for delayed versus immediate gratification. One's particular moral code is culture-specific, and the necessary learning involves numerous elements including the implicit and explicit rules of conduct, the verbalizations and the behavioral practices of models, and empathic identification with others. A number of developmental studies suggest that child-rearing practices involving physical punishment are not as effective as those involving withdrawal of love in determining subsequent characteristics such as cheating, conscience development, guilt, and obedience.

Theory building has centered on two broad concerns: conscience development and reinforcement theory. The motivating force underlying the construct of "conscience" is guilt, and it has been shown in various experiments that guilt can facilitate compliance with the requests of others and can inhibit transgressions such as cheating. The importance of reinforcement variables has been shown in investigations which manipulate the consequences of helping a stranger, which manipulate feelings toward the stranger, and in an investigation in which altruism was shown to act as a reinforcer in an instrumental escape conditioning task.

The applied implications of this type of research are readily apparent. As overall conclusions, it might be seen that society would benefit from making a purposeful and continuing effort to clarify potential emergency situations by making them familiar and by providing models for behavior in such situations. Further, research has emphasized the crucial importance of child-rearing practices and of the behavior of available models on the development of internal guides to behavior.

IV

The Individual:
Integrating
Personality Research

14

Describing and Predicting Human Behavior

Throughout much of this text, the term "personality" has been used to denote specific kinds of behavioral variables: dimensions of individual differences. In studies of the situational determinants of behavior, the term was broadened to include the responses of persons to specific stimulus conditions. A more familiar usage has to do with the overall combination of an individual's various characteristics. Most definitions of personality, in fact, include some aspect of a unified description of a "whole person." For example, McClelland (1951, p. 69) defined personality as ". . . the most adequate conceptualization of a person's behavior in all its detail that the scientist can give at a moment in time."

What becomes of this holistic conception when personality research is pursued in the atomistic, variable-by-variable manner described in the preceding thirteen chapters? One possibility has been raised by Allport (1961, p. 27) who rejects the operational approach of "extreme positivistic behaviorism." He suggests that with such an approach, "only outer, visible, manipulable operations are tolerated. Personality as such evaporates in a mist of method." More recently, Carlson (1971) has explored Allport's complaint further. All of the 1968 articles appearing in the *Journal of Personality* and the *Journal of Personality and Social Psychology* were reviewed. This survey indicated that personality research concentrates on undergraduates, uses experimental methods, obtains only a limited number of responses from each subject, and involves primarily a highly impersonal relationship between an experimenter and a conscripted subject. It was noted that "...*not a single published study attempted even minimal inquiry into the organization of personality variables within the individual*" (Carlson, 1971, p. 209). It was concluded that the person is not really studied in current personality research.

Without disagreeing with their objective descriptions, is there any way to refute the kind of conclusions drawn by Allport and by Carlson? Can one take such bits and pieces of behavior as authoritarianism, achievement need, anxiety, intelligence, self-concept, attraction, aggression, sex, and altruism and reassemble them in order to present a coherent picture of a specific and perhaps unique individual? Two answers are relevant to that question. On the one hand, the viewpoint represented by the present text is that the *only* way we are likely to be able to obtain a coherent picture of any single individual is by knowing as much as possible about the dimensions of individual differences and about the laws governing behavior in various situations. On the basis of such knowledge we will eventually be able to "reconstruct the individual" by combining the separate bits of information about him and his situational context. We can then understand his behavior in that we can predict and, at times, control it. On the other hand, it is true that not many occasions arise when we will even want to know enough about any particular single individual to be able to predict the totality of his behavior.

Before discussing these two considerations in any detail, a somewhat better perspective may be gained by turning to the more general problem of what is meant by describing an individual. Descriptions written by novelists, psychiatrists, and clinical psychologists will be sampled.

PERSONALITY DESCRIPTION

NOVELISTS

We live in a culture grown accustomed to the presentation of fictional characters whose behavior, motives, abilities, and needs are displayed in varying depths of detail. By means of plays, movies, and television programs, we are familiar with legions of imaginary individuals, some more real and better known to us through the artistry of their creators than are our real acquaintances. Like the multi-wall television of Ray Bradbury's (1953) future world in which the imaginary TV "family" makes the viewer one of them, existing media allow us to know countless different personalities.

To create such beings with words alone as the writer of novels or short stories must do is more difficult. The attempt to present word pictures of either real or imaginary personalities has a relatively short history considering the length of time man has been on this planet. And, once the attempt was first made, a long period was required for individual artists to progress from two-dimensional characters with stylized attributes to complex, highly differentiated personalities.

What is the technique by which words bring life and individuality to a fictional character? Briefly, we will take a look at one of Dickens' familiar creations, our annual Christmas visitor, Ebanezer Scrooge:

> Oh! but he was a tight-fisted hand at the grindstone. Scrooge! a squeezing, wrenching, grasping, scraping, clutching, covetous, old sinner! Hard and sharp as flint, from which no steel had ever struck-out generous fire; secret, and self-contained, and solitary as an oyster. The cold within him froze his old features, nipped his pointed nose, shrivelled his cheek, stiffened his gait; made his eyes red, his thin lips blue; and spoke out shrewdly in his grating voice. A frosty rime was on his head, and on his eyebrows, and his wiry chin. He carried his own low temperature always about with him; he iced his office in the dog-days, and didn't thaw it one degree at Christmas.
>
> External heat and cold had little influence on Scrooge. No warmth could warm, no wintry weather chill him. No wind that blew was bitterer than he, no falling snow was more intent upon its purpose, no pelting rain less open to entreaty (Dickens, 1943, p. 18).

What, then, do authors do? In order to describe individuals to us, authors present a description of the physical attributes of the individual and a great deal about the character's personality traits. That is, by presenting something of the specific behavior and general traits of the person, the author can assemble a unique individual. Most often, by the way, this process has involved the tendency to overplay the consistency of individuals and the stability of traits as Andre Gide (1946, p. xxxi) and Michel de Montaigne have noted:

> ...it was necessary to establish for the time being a somewhat rudimentary psychology, on general and sharply defined lines, as a preliminary to the construction of a classical art. Lovers had to be nothing but lovers, misers wholly misers, and jealous men a hundred per cent jealous, while good care had to be taken that no one should have a share of all these qualities at once. Montaigne speaks of those "good authors" (and what he says is even truer of those who followed him than of those he was acquainted with) "who select a prevailing characteristic of a man, and adapt and interpret all his actions in accordance with that image; and if they can not sufficiently bend them, they attribute them to dissimulation."

PSYCHIATRISTS

The traditional medical history bears little relation to the novel. It provides instead relevant background information (for example, age and sex of patient), previous illnesses and accidents and operations, and those symptoms and signs which indicate a particular diagnosis. Ideally, the latter information conveys a great deal in that a given disease entity is known to be brought about by a specific cause, that disease runs a typical course, and it can be cured by a specific treatment procedure.

As psychiatry and psychoanalysis developed, a different approach was needed. Behavioral problems required that various bits and pieces be described and brought together in the report. Observations were not reducible to labels or summary background data. Even after diagnostic categories were developed, they conveyed little information about cause, course, or treatment. What came to be accepted as more important was a detailed, insightful description of personality. In a curious way, the attempts by physicians interested in behavioral disorders to describe their patients involve the use of techniques similar to those of novelists. In 1884, Freud wrote to his fiancé that "...I am becoming aware of literary stirrings when previously I could not have imagined anything further from my mind." Somewhat later, in *Studies on Hysteria,* he wrote, "It still strikes me as strange that the case histories I write should read like short stories and that, as one might say, they lack the serious stamp of science." In the decades since, psychoanalytic reports have frequently maintained this literary flavor.

With psychoanalytic descriptions of personality, there are behavioral sketches plus an attempt to interpret behavior in Freudian terms. An example is Savitt's description of a heroin addict who was in analysis:

> A precocious young musician had had his promising career disrupted by his morbid cravings. From birth the mother left his care to others, and not until the age of four was he somewhat integrated into the family group. When he entered treatment he was in one of his periodic states of exile from his family, living occasionally with his grandparents. Usually, however, he wandered around in the demoralizing atmosphere of the various "pads" occupied by fellow addicts.
>
> One of his earliest statements was, "Once I get something into my body I feel safe." He spoke of himself as a milk addict and lover of sweets. An injection of heroin proved to be unconsciously equated with the incorporation of mother-breast-food. He had previously gone through the gamut of oral substitutive gratifications: alcohol, marijuana, and opiates by mouth; also several periods of abnormal craving for food during which he became moderately obese. From sixteen to eighteen he passed through a stage of sexual promiscuity and hypersexuality from which he had regressed into occasional homosexuality.
>
> For this patient the incorporation of heroin also meant being swallowed and engulfed by mother. Thus, in one intravenous injection a mutual incorporation of mother and child was achieved (Savitt, 1963, pp. 45–46).

CLINICAL PSYCHOLOGISTS

In many respects, clinical psychologists have had an unenviable goal in their approach to personality description. Like psychiatrists, they have attempted to combine the descriptive power of novelists with the physician's emphasis on symptoms and diagnosis. In addition, the psychologist brings to the task a background of research training and a scientific concern with evidence and prediction.

Thus, the typical descriptive productions of clinicians include specific data such as test responses, test scores, and comparison with normative groups, plus a tendency to predict future behavioral probabilities and to make recommendations to bring about personality change. An example will serve to illustrate these points.

A college student at a large Midwestern university applied to the university counselling center for assistance. Holtzman, Thorpe, Swartz, and Herron present the following background material:

> A slightly effeminate, physically unattractive white male, Jack first came to the counsellor in the middle of his freshman year for help in deciding upon his major field of study. Although he had originally planned to major in geology, he was now considering a change to psychology and wanted to learn more about himself in relation to an occupational choice. During the initial interview it soon became apparent that Jack was worried about much more than choosing a field of study. He expressed little self-confidence, remarked that he had few friends, and vaguely mentioned difficulties in getting along with his parents. He said that he had been forced to argue for a long time to get their approval for majoring in geology, and he thought he would have even more difficulty in getting them to agree to his proposed change to psychology. Moreover, he was not certain that he possessed the right personality characteristics for success as a psychologist.
>
> Jack expressed considerable concern about the security of highly personal information revealed to the counsellor. Toward the end of the first interview he hesitantly confided that he thought he had strong homosexual tendencies, hastening to add that he had never really had an overt homosexual experience. However, he mentioned that he did spend a good deal of time reading magazines dealing with male physical culture or sex and hanging around with several boys who were actively homosexual. He stated that he lacked the nerve to plunge into active homosexual relations and wondered whether homosexuality would prevent him from becoming a successful psychologist.
>
> Jack's scholastic aptitude, though not outstanding, was above average for freshmen. He had ranked in the second quarter of his graduating class in a large high school and scored at the seventy-sixth percentile on the university's admission test. His grades during the first semester of college work were mediocre but not quite low enough to place him on probation. Jack agreed to take a battery of psychological tests, and arrangements were made for a series of interviews with an experienced counselling psychologist (Holtzman, Thorpe, Swartz, and Herron, 1961, pp. 222–23).

Psychological testing in this instance included the Holtzman Ink-blot Technique. The summary of what was learned from the ink-blot responses was as follows:

> In summary, it can be said with some confidence that Jack has a severe personality disorder bordering on overt schizophrenia and characterized by excessive preoccupation with homosexual fantasies. Although he may be able to maintain sufficient control of his autistic thought processes to cope with a daily routine and appear superficially normal, the sexual confusion, hostility, bizarre associations, and complete lack of conventionality characteristic of his ink-blot responses suggest that he is a seriously disturbed individual. In spite of this generally disturbed picture, some hopeful signs are present. In side remarks

and subtle verbal qualifications, Jack indicates some awareness of the bizarre, confused nature of his fantasies. On a number of ink-blot variables related to developmental level, and, possibly, degree of ego differentiation, he scores rather well, indicating that he may have sufficient inner resources to improve in an intensive course of psychotherapy (Holtzman, et al., 1961, pp. 226–47).

Having briefly examined three different, though related, general approaches to personality description, what is the possible contribution of the field of personality to this task? What could the methods and the goals of science contribute?

PREDICTION AS THE GOAL OF DESCRIPTION

PREDICTION VERSUS UNDERSTANDING

As in Chapter 1 when the goals of science were discussed, we must consider the purpose of the activity being undertaken. For the novelist, it is sufficient to entertain and to provide something of interest to the reader. If he succeeds further in creating an emotional bond of recognition and empathy and identification between reader and fictional creation, the artistic goal is achieved. For the psychiatrist, as an applied medical scientist, presumably the diagnostic goal is paramount. With a sufficient body of knowledge and well-developed techniques for accurate diagnosis, the assignment of the proper "disease" label would provide a considerable amount of useful information about an individual. Unfortunately, the actual situation is quite different from that. Quite possibly the basic idea of a medical model for behavioral problems is an inadequate and inaccurate approach because maladjusted behavior is not a disease caused by some biological agent. At best, however, the present state of knowledge renders the diagnostic goal less useful in psychiatry than in other fields of medicine. Diagnostic labels serve primarily a descriptive function rather than a predictive one.

In the role of applied behavioral scientists, the clinical psychologist brings to the problem the potential of a quite different framework. The goal of personality description need not be entertainment, interest, emotional involvement of the reader, or the assignment of a diagnostic label. Most important, there is no necessary reason to help anyone "get the feel" of the person being described. Rather, the task is to say something meaningful, to provide predictive accuracy.

The importance of prediction versus understanding is more than just a scientific bias. In the pragmatic world of the clinic, the industrial concern, or the courtroom, a great need exists for accurate predictions about specific behaviors. Word pictures which provide a vague feeling of emotional understanding are of questionable utility.

The Contribution of Case History Material to Prediction

What is the role of background data or the subject's case history if our only goal is that of prediction? Consider for a moment the following individual.

Charles is a 28-year-old unmarried clerk whose education was terminated after he graduated from high school. He was the third of five children, and his family regularly attended the Lutheran church in their small rural community.

He describes both his father and mother as affectionate. His father has been a semi-invalid for some years, and his early home conditions were perceived as constituting near-poverty. Charles expressed some feelings of dislike toward school, had a relatively poor record of deportment, but earned fairly good grades.

After leaving high school, he obtained a position as a clerk in a small store. He expresses his enjoyment of his occupation and feels he has done well at it. His approach to religion is on a shallow and intellectualized level, and his participation is little more than a formal ritual acquired from his parents.

Charles has had an average number of dates, but his heterosexual adjustment is described as relatively poor. He does not have an adequate sexual outlet. Otherwise, his social adjustment is relatively good, and he seems to be adept in social skills and poise. His recreational interests include a mixture of solitary and social pursuits. His interests are broad, his level of aspiration high, and he has a clear life plan. With respect to stability, Charles is described as moderately variable.

Now, what do we know about Charles that we did not know before—with respect to being able to make predictive statements about him? Very little. In fact, all that we can assert with greater than chance accuracy is that Charles is more likely to be characterized as normal than as schizophrenic. This statement is based on the fact that Charles is a hypothetical individual drawn from an excellent, but rare, investigation of the meaning of case history data.

Schofield and Balian (1959) obtained comprehensive personal history statistics of a sample of schizophrenics at the University of Minnesota Hospitals. For comparison purposes, a group of normals was investigated. These subjects consisted of hospital patients, hospital employees, students, employees of a large industrial firm, and office workers. By "normal" is meant that each of the subjects was free of psychiatric disturbance and had no history of a previous mental disorder. Further, the normals were matched with the schizophrenics with respect to age, sex, and marital status. Each subject was given a comprehensive clinical interview lasting forty-five to ninety minutes. In our "case history" of Charles, the first paragraph simply describes the average normal subject. All of the other "facts" are simply items which were significantly more true of the normal sample than of the schizophrenic sample. Schofield and Balian say:

The single most impressive feature of the data...is the sizable overlap of the normal Ss and schizophrenic patients in the distributions of the various personal history variables. Of the 35 separate tests which were run, 13 (or 37%) failed to reveal a reliable difference between the two samples. Further, on 5 of the remaining 22 variables, the distributions showed a reliably greater presence in the normals of negative or undesirable conditions. In those instances where the statistical tests did indicate a reliable characterization of the schizophrenics by prevalence of a pathogenic variable, the normals generally also showed a closely approximating degree of the same factor (Schofield and Balian, 1959, p. 222).

They go on to suggest:

It seems necessary that we turn some of our research energies toward a discovery of those circumstances or experiences of life which either contribute directly to mental health and emotional stability or which serve to delimit or erase the effects of pathogenic events. For this purpose, we will need to make extensive psychological study of the biographies of normal persons as well as of patients, with such biographies recorded so that their coverage and uniformity facilitate analysis (Schofield and Balian, 1959, p. 224).

Though a few such investigations have been undertaken (for example, Dohrenwend and Dohrenwend, 1967; Livson and Peskin, 1967; Vestre and Lorei, 1967), without a vast body of such data, little or nothing will be gained by including case history material in our descriptions of personality. Other than a dubious literary exercise or the possible titillation of being able to peek into keyholes, case history material would seem to belong on data sheets in research projects; for predictive purposes, they tend only to provide facts which serve no actual function.

CONTRIBUTION OF GENERAL TRUTHS

Another class of material appears in personality description. Before discussing it, let us examine another brief personality sketch. A female undergraduate was given a personality test which was then analyzed by a psychologist. She was told:

Some of your aspirations tend to be pretty unrealistic. At times you are extroverted, affable, sociable, while at other times you are introverted, wary, and reserved. You have found it unwise to be too frank in revealing yourself to others. You pride yourself as being an independent thinker and do not accept others' opinions without satisfactory proof. You prefer a certain amount of change and variety and become dissatisfied when hemmed in by restrictions and limitations. At times you have serious doubts as to whether you have made the right decision or done the right thing. Disciplined and controlled on the outside, you tend to be worrisome and insecure on the inside. Your sexual adjustment has presented some problems for you. While you have some personality weaknesses, you are generally able to compensate for them. You have a great deal of unused capacity which you have not turned to your advantage. You have a tendency to be critical of yourself. You have a strong need for other people to like you and for them to admire you.

What has been said about the young lady? Actually, she found out nothing beyond what she could learn from reading random pages of an astrology book, but people tend to feel that such descriptions are actually providing them with useful information. Snyder and Larson (1972) gave that same set of statements to each of a large group of undergraduates after they had supposedly been measured on a "Personality Profile Test." Each was asked to rate how accurate the interpretation was. The mean response was between "good" and "excellent." The authors point out that people place great faith in the results of psychological tests and accept the results as being true for themselves. The difficulty is that many such descriptions consist of general propositions that can apply to anyone and everyone. They are glittering generalizations which apply to most people and hence are distinctive for no one. How useful is it for me to tell you that you breathe through your nose? In terms of prediction, such statements obviously supply no differential information.

The general truths of the type described here say no more about a given individual than would a simple sentence indicating that he is a human being raised in the contemporary American culture. Of course, general truths which involve established behavioral laws applicable to all individuals would be *extremely* useful for predictive purposes. Nevertheless, no reason would exist to include them in the personality description of a *specific individual*. To do so would be like describing the qualities of an Oldsmobile by stating Newton's laws of motion.

CONTRIBUTION OF KNOWLEDGE CONCERNING
PERSONALITY DIMENSIONS

Though they do not produce an exciting flow of descriptive prose, an individual's scores on a series of personality dimensions do provide a considerable amount of information relevant for behavior prediction. Given a body of data concerning a particular dimension, the fact that an individual obtains a specific score on an instrument designed to measure that dimension permits a large number of predictions to be made about him.

As an example, let us take authoritarianism as measured by the California F Scale. On the basis of the research findings presented in Chapter 4, what could you say about a person who obtains a high score? Normative data permits you to state where he stands in relation to other people on this particular dimension and with respect to the ideology represented by the individual items. More importantly, perhaps, quite specific predictions could be made about his attitudes concerning family structure along an autocratic-democratic continuum, the type of disciplinary techniques he prefers to use with children, his relative restrictiveness or permissiveness in child-rearing attitudes, the authoritarianism of his parents, and the authoritarianism of his

spouse. Still other predictions could be made concerning his attitudes toward Jews, his degree of ethnocentrism, his attitudes toward blacks, the type
of hostility expressed in his dreams, his tendency to establish blame and
advocate punishment, and his attitudes about the Vietnam War, sex education, and pornography. You could predict his political and economic conservatism, his response to the idea of socialized medicine, his voting behavior
in any given election, his reaction when faced by a requirement to sign a
noncommunist loyalty oath, his intelligence and scores on several aptitude
tests, his grade-point average, his religious preferences, and the regularity
of his church attendance. In specified situations, one could predict his
ability to perceive ambiguous sexual and aggressive stimuli, his response to
fictional characters portraying sexual roles, his evaluation of the artistic
depiction of nudes as pornographic, his feelings about censorship, his aggressiveness toward low-status victims, his ideas about how best to motivate
others, and the degree to which liking for a defendant would influence his
response as a juror. Estimates could be made of his tendency to conform to
group pressure and his resistance to changing his opinion on the basis of new
data. Finally, you could specify certain conditions under which his authoritarianism would be expected to increase or decrease. Those statements may
seem grandiose, but they are based on empirical evidence and actually are
fairly conservative when compared with statements made in many personality descriptions. Some of the behavior predicted above could be ascertained much more easily and accurately with a direct approach (for example,
religious preference). If anything of importance depended on the decision
made, more research data would be highly useful in that many of the obtained relationships account for only a small proportion of the variance of
the behavior to be predicted. For example, while choice of a particular
political candidate is related to authoritarianism, voting behavior is a function of many other variables in addition to that measured by the F Scale.
Such limitations obviously are not unique to predictions based on personality dimensions.

Ideally, one would know more about an individual than simply his score
on one personality measure. What could be predicted on the basis of knowing an individual's score on several dimensions? As an exercise, the student
might list the predictions that could be made about an individual's behavior
if he had taken the California F Scale, a series of *n* Ach pictures, the Manifest Anxiety Scale, an intelligence test, and a self-ideal Q-sort.

We can envision a time at which a large number of well-designed and
highly reliable personality tests are available along with a large body of
research findings dealing with the antecedents, correlates, and consequents
of each. With such a battery of measuring devices (ten tests?, twenty tests?,
one hundred tests?), the scores made by an individual would yield a profile
describing his standing on each dimension. A further step (probably carried

out by a computer in which all relevant data were stored) would be the determination of *all* other behaviors which would be predicted on the basis of the person's scores on the various tests and combinations of tests. The end result might be a profile sheet plus a long list of predictive statements.

The way of arriving at such a set of dimensions is a matter of controversy. One major approach is the piecemeal, one-variable-at-a-time research described throughout this text. The other major approach involves the use of many variables at a time and the identification of the underlying dimensions by means of factor analysis. Tests emerging from this multivariate, factor-analytic methodology should constitute internally homogeneous dimensions relatively independent of one another. Proponents of the multivariate approach include H. J. Eysenck at the University of London, J. P. Guilford at the University of Southern California, and Raymond B. Cattell at the University of Illinois. Psychologists agree on the general goal, but they differ in their estimate of the best strategy. One could argue, for example, that the clarification of personality dimensions by way of factor analysis would be more meaningful after a period of time spent in isolating, operationalizing, and conducting research with individual variables. Cattell (1959) argued that the dimensions should be determined as a preliminary step in personality research and that the time has arrived for using this methodology in experimental investigations (Cattell, 1966).

However the dimensions are determined, agreement exists that a finite set will ultimately be specified. If personality description were defined in terms of an individual's profile of scores on the dimensions, the product would be quite different from that of the novelist, the psychiatrist, or the present clinical psychologist. Personality description as an art form would have given way to personality description as a series of predictions about the probable behavior of a given person. A number of psychologists, including Cattell, believe that this is precisely what the field of personality is all about:

> *Personality is that which permits a prediction of what a person will do in a given situation.* The goal of psychological research in personality is thus to establish laws about what different people will do in all kinds of social and general environmental situations (Cattell, 1950, pp. 2–3).

Cattell's emphasis on prediction *in a given situation* brings us back to the point made in Chapter 1. When psychologists conceptualize a predictive science of behavior, this is done in terms of predicting responses made to particular stimuli. Thus, general laws of behavior take the form: $R = f(S)$. The contribution of knowledge about personality dimensions is the refinement or further specification of those laws in order to permit the differential prediction of the behavior of individuals.

HAS PERSONALITY "EVAPORATED IN A MIST OF METHOD"?

Returning to criticisms made by Allport and by Carlson, can we say that they have been answered? When we assemble a personality profile based on scores obtained from a large battery of measures and make a series of predictions with greater-than-chance accuracy, have we reconstructed in scientific form the sort of personality which Allport and others are talking about?

In one sense, the answer must be no. The artist's view of the unique individual is being replaced by the scientist's view of the predictable organism. Allport (1961, pp. xi-xii) says: "My own view is that, taken in the large, the evidence before us does not depict man as a reactive robot." Frankly, the present author would like to be able to agree. It is pleasant to think of man (oneself) as having a special destiny and as somehow rising above his physical surroundings. As the knowledge of biological functioning, cellular chemistry, the molecular secrets of heredity, and even of stimulus-response relationships grows more complete each day, our conception of man inevitably changes. Those who conceive of man as something uniquely different in the universe, operating with a degree of independence from natural laws, and having special qualities placing him forever beyond the realm of science are increasingly hard-pressed by contrary evidence. The special qualities of man are suggested by Allport: "He is more than a bundle of habits, more than a point of intersection of abstract dimensions. He is more than a respresentative of his species, more than a citizen of the state, more than an incident in the movements of mankind. He transcends them all" (Allport, 1961, p. 573). It is a bit sad to contrast the poetic figure of man as historically pictured with the mechanistic picture which has been emerging over the past century or two. But, man has had to adjust to a universe in which his planet is not the hub and to a classification of himself as simply one of the primate species in an evolutionary chain; surely the idea of man's behavior being lawfully determined by antecedents poses no greater threat than these previous revolutions in the history of ideas. The response to Skinner's (1971) depiction of man is frequently negative, but probably not as much so as was the initial response to the ideational changes instigated by Galileo and Darwin.

In another sense, the emerging conception of human personality in quantified, predictable terms does encompass the sort of phenomena described by the nonbehavioristic theorists. It is not as if knowledge about man's behavior and the ability to predict and control it will destroy the human qualities which we value. When we know the relationship between pressure applied to the keys of a piano and the nature of the subsequent vibrations of air molecules, the music is no less beautiful. Knowledge of antecedent-consequent relationships in behavior will not somehow prevent the occurrence of a Brahms or a Shakespeare or a Lincoln or an Einstein. On the contrary, future developments may enable us to increase the incidence of such personalities and to decrease the incidence of less desirable representatives of our species. Humanistic values need not be dashed aside simply because we are gaining the ability to predict and control human behavior. Precisely the opposite result seems to be a more likely possibility.

THE GENERAL UTILITY OF PERSONALITY DESCRIPTION

NEED FOR PERSONALITY DESCRIPTION

At that distant date when all basic personality dimensions have been identified and an enormous body of data has been assembled, the task of producing a complete personality description of just one subject will be a formidable one. Testing time alone might well consume days or even weeks. The task of scoring the test instruments and assembling the data could presumably be adapted to mechanical and electronic procedures. The outcome which describes one individual could quite conceivably constitute a good-sized book of predictive statements. Is it sufficiently worthwhile to obtain a complete personality description to warrant the required lavish expenditure of time, effort, and money?

Though we may only guess about the future, the author's opinion is that the need for complete personality descriptions will be relatively limited. Only one type of situation would seem to be clearly appropriate to warrant all the necessary work. When a key individual is being selected for a position in which his behavior in a variety of situations has widespread consequences for others, it would seem well worth the investment to be able to predict that behavior as accurately and as completely as possible. Examples are candidates for the presidency or astronauts to be sent on a long and expensive interplanetary mission. Knowledge of every strength and weakness of such individuals in responding to many different stimulus situations could be of crucial importance.

If these possibilities arouse fears of a regimented future world, the points made in Chapter 1 concerning the application of scientific knowledge should be noted again. Decisions must be and are being made about presidential candidates and astronauts. The only question is on what basis they are made and the relationship between the decision and the ensuing consequences.

PREDICTING AND CONTROLLING LIMITED ASPECTS OF HUMAN BEHAVIOR

There are numerous inappropriate questions which people ask psychologists in good faith, but which behavioral science cannot be expected to answer. "How can I find happiness?" "What is the meaning of man's existence?"

Appropriate questions are those that have to do with the prediction of behavior.

When examined closely, most predictions which psychologists would reasonably be asked to make in practical situations are in relation to specific questions about limited aspects of behavior. Two kinds of circumstances arise in which behavioral predictions are of great value. First, there are questions about the behavior of individuals. An example would be, "How well will John Jones do in college?" As indicated by the research presented in this text, it may be seen that if we ascertained his performance on an intelligence test, his need for achievement, and his standing on the Manifest Anxiety Scale, it would be possible to provide a meaningful response to that question. We do not need to know everything about John Jones, and we are not asked to describe everything he will do everywhere. Second, there are questions about the responses of people in general. An example would be, "What kinds of books or movies would be the most sexually arousing?" On the basis of the research summarized in Chapter 12, it is clear what kinds of erotic content elicit the greatest excitement. Again, the question has to do with a relatively limited concern and the answer can be quite specific and reasonably accurate. The more we learn in research, the more accurate the answers will be to both types of question.

There is a further, and potentially more dramatic, use for the knowledge of behavioral science. Neither individuals nor their stimulus world need be conceptualized in static terms. Change is possible in both. When our science is sufficiently advanced, it should be possible to alter the personality structure of an individual to insure maximally rewarding behavior in a given situation. For example, driving could be made more safe either by refusing licenses to unsafe drivers *or* by changing drivers into models of safety and skill. In a similar way, it should be possible to alter situations to insure maximal benefits. For example, if violence on TV and movie screens is clearly shown to increase the incidence of aggression, aggression could be decreased by making recommendations that such entertainment be avoided *or* by altering the content of all productions so that prosocial rather than antisocial behavior is elicited. Instead of just predicting how well John Jones will do in college, we will eventually be able to bring about an optimal level of functioning with respect to intelligence, achievement, and anxiety. Instead of just predicting which erotic stimuli are most arousing, we can manipulate stimuli to bring about the desired degree of arousal.

Whether such manipulations bring about utopia or hell depends on the values of the manipulators in relation to one's own values. Laser beams can be used in performing delicate eye surgery and in guiding "smart bombs" to their targets of destruction. Some individuals place greater value on healing the sick while others become more enthusiastic about being able to kill enemy troops. It appears that one man's utopia is, in fact, another man's hell. The best that any of us, scientists and nonscientists alike, can do is to attempt to persuade others to share our own, obviously correct, views.

Beyond the problem of agreement concerning values is another criticism which is sometimes raised against the idea of changing individuals and stimulus situations in the manner suggested here. It is argued that we would be moving toward a colorless, bland society. The specter arises of mindless masses marching in lock-step. Certainly such an outcome is not a necessary result of instituting beneficial influences on behavior. An analogy is provided by the application of medical science. Compared to the previous century, we now have greater "blandness" in that, for example, people need no longer be disfigured by smallpox, be crippled by poliomyelitis, or be labeled as lepers to roam the countryside with a warning bell hanging from their necks. Even in the social sphere, sufficient changes have been brought about to remove some of the color and interest of previous times. We can no longer see galley slaves rowing great ships, attend public executions as a family outing, or visit the auction block to buy our servants and laborers. Equally great changes in personality would deprive us of the human variety represented by schizophrenics, muggers, sadists, political assassins, or those who are unloved and lonely. For many of us, blandness seems preferable to this kind of human variability. Those are not the only alternatives, however. Rather than bland human robots, the individuals of the future can be creative, bright, happy, democratic, kind, loving, and so on, within the limits of our applied skills and the shared values of our society.

Man has refused to accept the limitations imposed by his physical and biological world. Transportation, communication, comfort, physical health, and conception, for example, are increasingly under man's control. We have no reason to believe that behavior should be or will be left out of man's technological progress.

SUMMARY

Most definitions of personality include the idea of a unified description of an individual. If personality is defined in terms of a series of dimensions plus the situational determinants of behavior, the problem of combining separate bits of information to describe a person is sometimes seen as a difficult or impossible one.

Personality description began with novelists who over the centuries developed techniques which infused life and individuality into fictional characters. Authors tend to present a description of the physical attributes of the individual and a great deal about the character's specific behavior and general traits. Psychiatrists have the traditional medical interest in symptoms and diagnoses which (at least eventually) should convey information about the cause, course, and treatment for specific behavioral problems. In addition, an attempt is made to describe personality in much the way that novelists do. Clinical psychologists have tended to follow the pattern of psychiatrists with respect to such descriptions except that they add a scientist's concern with evidence and with prediction.

The goals of those engaged in personality description are varied. The novelist hopes to entertain and engage the emotions of the reader. The psychiatrist strives for diagnostic accuracy. The primary goals of the clinical psychologist include accurate prediction. The reason for describing the personality of an individual is to make possible the prediction of behavior rather than to elicit a feeling of understanding in those who read the description. From this viewpoint, items of case history information serve no purpose in personality description unless evidence shows that particular background data lead to specific predictions. General truths which hold for almost everyone serve no purpose in descriptions of personality. In contrast, knowledge of an individual's score on a personality dimension provides a considerable amount of predictive information to the extent that research has been done with that dimension. If an individual's standing on each of several personality dimensions were known, a very large number of behavior predictions could be made. A battery of measuring devices would yield an individual's personality profile. This in turn could yield a long list of research-based predictive statements concerning that individual. The most appropriate strategy for arriving at the best possible set of dimensions is a matter of some controversy. Approaches vary from univariate research in which one variable at a time is isolated and investigated to multivariate research in which many variables are investigated simultaneously in order to clarify the underlying dimensions by means of factor analysis. The conception of personality in antecedent-consequent terms does not satisfy some theorists, but the lawfulness of man's behavior becomes more and more difficult to refute.

In the future, when all basic personality dimensions have been identified and an enormous body of data has been assembled, the task of producing a complete personality description of just one subject will be a formidable one. Very likely the need for such a description will be limited. Possibly the only justifiable use will be when a key individual is being selected for a position in which his behavior has widespread consequences for others. Much more frequently, the problem of behavior prediction arises in relation to specific questions about limited aspects of behavior. Such questions have to do both with the behavior of an individual and with the responses of people in general. A future goal is the development of psychological technology which will enable man to alter the personality structure of an individual and/or the appropriate aspects of the situation in order to bring about the best possible human behavior.

Appendix

Understanding Correlational Statistics

An undergraduate student in a research-oriented psychology course is confronted with one of three alternative approaches concerning his required knowledge and utilization of statistics. (1) It can be assumed that the student has in the past or will possibly in the future become familiar with statistics, but that it is preferable to omit statistical details when the major purpose of a course is to communicate what is known about a problem area. Those who conducted the original research and those who attempt to communicate such research findings to a broader audience are assumed to be knowledgeable and trustworthy with respect to statistical procedures. Hence, the student can relax and deal with the content of the research rather than having to contend with the way statistics were used to bridge the gap between raw data and conclusions about what was discovered. (2) It can be assumed that students should know at least the basic logic and meaning of the more familiar statistical procedures. Without some familiarity of this sort, it is difficult to interpret statements about correlations or significance levels for example. Even a little knowledge of statistical concepts helps to clarify research descriptions and to make them more meaningful. (3) It can be assumed that the research process will remain unnecessarily mysterious unless students can personally and actively engage in the process of analysis. It has been said that one learns by doing and not by hearing that others have done it.

Each of these three approaches makes sense, and each can be defended.

The present text is organized in such a way as to make possible any of the three ways of dealing with the study of personality research. (1) The main body of the text omits all but the most essential references to statistics. Thus, a student well versed in statistical concepts or a student totally unfamiliar with statistics should be able to read the text with equal ease and understanding; each may omit reading this Appendix. (2) With the optional material in the present section, however, it is also possible for the student to become acquainted with some of the logic and reasoning underlying a few of the commonly used statistical tools. In order to understand this section, the student need only be familiar with concepts such as arithmetic mean and standard deviation, which are commonly taught in introductory psychology. It is the author's bias, incidentally, that familarity with the concept of correlation is a necessity for all students while familiarity with more advanced concepts such as analysis of variance is useful only for those planning a professional research career. (3) Finally, the examples and exercises make it possible for the student to become directly involved in actual statistical calculations if he wishes to do so.

THE CORRELATION COEFFICIENT

Relationships between Variables

If a relationship between two variables is a linear one, its direction and its magnitude can be expressed by a single statistic: the correlation coefficient or r. "Direction" refers to whether high scores on one variable are associated with high or with low scores on a second variable. A positive correlation indicates that those who obtain high scores on variable X tend to obtain high scores on variable Y, and that low scores on X tend to go with low scores on Y. For example, a positive correlation is found between IQ scores and grades in school; students with high IQs tend to get higher grades than students with low IQs. A negative correlation indicates that those who obtain high scores on variable X tend to obtain low scores on variable Y, and vice versa. For example, a negative correlation has been found between test anxiety and grades in school; students high in test anxiety tend to get lower grades than students low in test anxiety.

The "magnitude" of a relationship indicates the *degree* to which two variables are related. A perfect positive correlation is indicated by a coefficient of 1.00 while a perfect negative correlation is -1.00. When there is absolutely no relationship between two variables, the correlation is 0.00. In order to be able to interpret the meaning of correlation coefficients which fall at other points between plus and minus 1.00, we must know several additional facts about this statistic.

A correlation describes the relationship between two sets of variables. The most usual situation is one in which each individual has been measured on two different variables (or on the same variable on two different occasions) or in which each member of a pair of individuals (parent-child, husband-wife, twins, pairs of friends) has been measured on the same variable. In any event, the data sheet is made up of a list of pairs of numbers. In Table A-1, six subjects and their scores on two variables are shown. As will be seen later in this section, the correlation between X and Y is found to be .89. Since 1.00 is a perfect relationship, it is obvious that .89 indicates a very high relationship. Two questions need to be answered, however. How likely is the relationship to be found in another sample? What does an r of .89 tell us?

Table A-1. Scores Obtained by Six Subjects on Two Variables

	Variable X	*Variable Y*
Subject 1	10	12
Subject 2	30	28
Subject 3	41	38
Subject 4	6	22
Subject 5	19	20
Subject 6	8	15

STATISTICAL SIGNIFICANCE

The inferences that psychologists make about their experimental findings are expressed as *levels of significance*. If an investigator reports that he performed an experiment to test problem-solving ability and found that in his sample of 80 subjects the mean score of boys was higher than the mean score of girls at the 5 percent level of significance, he is indicating that the chances are only 5 out of 100 (probability of .05) that this same difference would fail to hold true in the total population; the chances are 95 out of 100 (probability of .95) that they *would* hold true. Such a statement requires the application of probability theory to samples of data. We will not go into the details of the mathematical theory or the statistical manipulations by which one arrives at such statements. Suffice it to say that with a sample of a given size, a difference of a given magnitude between groups, and variations of a given amount within each group, one can apply formulas and utilize tables and arrive at a significance level. In the example, there is no way to know with absolute certainty whether boys and girls in the general population *really* differ in problem-solving ability or whether this particular research sample yielded a chance finding which is not generalizable to the total population. If boys and girls really do not differ in this ability and if 100 experimenters with 100 different samples of subjects had conducted the same experiment, five of them would be expected to find sex differences significant at the .05 level. When an experiment is repeated and yields the same findings, we can be more certain of its validity. Whatever the probability figure, the best a scientist can ever do is make an estimate or bet. At the 5 percent (.05) level of significance, the odds are 95 to 5 (or 19 to 1) that the finding is a real one. If the finding reaches the 1 percent (.01) level of significance, the odds reach 99 to 1. At the .1 percent (.001) level, the odds are 999 to 1 that the finding is a true one, one that would be found again if the study were repeated on a new sample, one that holds true for the entire population. Obviously, the higher the significance level, the more confident we can feel about the results. Scientific facts are never a *complete* certainty unless the total population is available for study, which is highly unlikely. As experiments are repeated, however, and findings replicated, the probability of their being attributable to chance shrinks to a negligible quantity.

With correlation coefficients, inferences must be made concerning the likelihood of finding the same relationship in the general population as in your research sample. The significance level of a particular correlation coefficient depends entirely on its magnitude and on the number of subjects who make up the sample. The larger the correlation and the bigger the sample, the greater the probability of the relationship holding true for the total population.

In order to obtain an idea of the way size of sample and magnitude of correlation coefficient influence the level of significance, a series of values is presented in Table A-2.

Table A-2. Magnitude of Correlation, Size of Sample, and Significance Level

Size of Sample	r at .05 Level	r at .01 Level
3	.997	.999
4	.95	.99
5	.88	.96
6	.81	.92
7	.75	.87
8	.71	.83
9	.67	.80
10	.63	.77
20	.44	.56
30	.36	.46
40	.31	.40
50	.28	.36
60	.25	.33
70	.24	.31
80	.22	.29
90	.21	.27
100	.20	.26
500	.09	.12
1,000	.06	.08

As the table indicates, a correlation may be of a very small magnitude and yet indicate a valid relationship. With 1,000 subjects, for example, a correlation of only 0.8 is still significant at the .01 level. A correlation coefficient that small is not very useful for predictive purposes, but the best bet is that there is a real relationship between the variables. This brings us to the second question about correlations: What does a correlation of a given magnitude tell us?

INTERPRETATION OF A CORRELATION COEFFICIENT:
PREDICTIVE ACCURACY

When the correlation between two variables is a real one, we can predict a score on one variable from knowledge of the score on the other with greater than chance accuracy. The higher the correlation (the closer to plus or minus 1.00), the more accurate the prediction. The prediction of one variable from another involves the use of a regression equation. The accuracy or precision of this prediction is determined by the standard error of estimate. We will take an example of a significant relationship which was discussed in Chapter 7 and follow through in some detail the way in which one variable can be predicted from another when the two are correlated.

A number of investigators have found (Anastasi, 1958) that the IQ score of either parent (variable X) correlates approximately .50 with the IQ score of their offspring of either sex (variable Y). Since this is a relatively stable finding across a number of samples, we can use this information to predict a child's IQ on the basis of the IQ of either of his parents. To make such a prediction, we must know the correlation between the two variables, the mean of the population on each variable, and the standard deviation of the population on each variable. If we use the Wechsler Adult Intelligence Scale or WAIS (Wechsler, 1958) for the parents and the Wechsler Intelligence Scale for Children or WISC (Wechsler, 1949) for the offspring, the population means are approximately 100 and the standard deviations approximately 15 on each variable. So: $r = .50$, $M_x = 100$, $M_y = 100$, $SD_x = 15$, and $SD_y = 15$. The general formula for predicting Y (the IQ of a child) from X (the IQ of a parent) is:

$$Y' = r\frac{SD_y}{SD_x}X + \left(M_y - r\frac{SD_y}{SD_x}M_x\right)$$

In the formula, X is the IQ score of any specific parent, and Y' is the predicted IQ score of that parent's offspring.

As an example, let us assume that a father has an IQ of 150, and you wish to predict the eventual IQ of his new born son. To gain some understanding of the meaning of a correlation, we will take three different levels of possible relationships of parent-child IQs. First, we will look at the prediction which would be made if the correlation between X and Y were zero.

Then, we will examine the differences in prediction when there is some relationship, in this case the actual one of .50. Finally, we will look at the perfect prediction situation, a correlation between X and Y of 1.00.

$r = 0.00$. A correlation of zero between the two variables would mean that the IQ of parents gave you absolutely no information which would help in predicting the IQ of their offspring. Using the regression equation with a correlation of zero, you would predict that the father with an IQ of 150 would have a son with the following IQ

$$Y' = 0 \frac{15}{15} 150 - \left(100 - 0 \frac{15}{15} 100\right)$$

$$Y' = 100$$

In other words, with no relationship between X and Y, the best prediction of Y' is the population mean on the Y variable no matter what score is obtained on the X variable. Whether the father has an IQ of 150 or 82, the best prediction would be that the child would have an IQ of 100.

The accuracy with which you can predict one variable from another is shown by a statistic which utilizes the correlation coefficient, the standard error of estimate. $SD_{y \cdot x}$ is the standard error of the Y' scores as predicted from the X scores and the formula is:

$$SD_{y \cdot x} = SD_y \sqrt{1 - r^2}$$

The larger the correlation coefficient, the smaller the standard error of estimate and hence the greater the accuracy of prediction. In our example, had the correlation been zero, $SD_{y \cdot x}$ would equal $15 - \sqrt{1 - 0.00^2}$ which equals 15. Thus, where there is no relationship between variables, the standard error of estimate of the predicted Y scores is simply the standard deviation of Y in the population.

The standard error of estimate allows you to state the precision of your prediction in terms of probability within certain limits. In this instance, the prediction is that all sons will have an IQ of 100 with $SD_{y \cdot x}$ equal to 15. This means that with a father whose IQ is 150 (or a father with any IQ), about two-thirds of the time such a prediction is made, the son's actual IQ will fall between 100 ± 15 or between 85 and 115. About 95 percent of the time the actual IQ will be between 100 and $\pm (2 \times 15)$ or between 70 and 130. Almost always, the actual IQ will be between $100 \pm (3 \times 15)$ or between 55 and 145. Here, predictions are simply being made in terms of multiples of the standard error utilizing a normal curve table which may be found in any introductory text on statistics.

Another way to conceptualize such predictions is with respect to the percentage of the variance in the predicted variable which can be accounted for on the basis of knowledge of the predictor variable. The square of the correlation coefficient indicates how much of the variance of Y can be accounted for by X in making predictions with the regression equation. With a correlation of 0.00, you can account for 0 percent of the variance in Y by a knowledge of X. As has been indicated, with a zero correlation it does not help to know anything about X because the prediction is the same no matter what. With respect to predictive accuracy, none exists, except that errors can be minimized by utilizing population statistics and betting that everyone will have a mean score. Betting on the mean is the best guess that can be made in such situations since the prediction is the least wrong the greatest number of times. If the mean is predicted each time, the standard error of estimate indicates how often the prediction is wrong by how much. With a zero correlation the standard error of estimate is the same as the standard deviation of Y, and the variance accounted for by a knowledge of X is zero.

$r = .50$. The actual correlation between parental IQ and that of their offspring is .50. What does this knowledge do for us? What does a correlation of this magnitude mean? How does it affect our predictive accuracy?

Looking at the regression equation, if a father had an IQ of 150, what could you predict about the eventual IQ of his newborn son? Substituting in the formula:

$$Y' = .50 \frac{15}{15} 150 + \left(100 - .50 \frac{15}{15} 100\right)$$

$$Y' = 125$$

Now we have a prediction which is specific for this son and this father, one which actually utilizes the known relationship between the variables. The IQ of any father (or mother) could be put into the formula and the specific IQ of a son (or daughter) could be predicted. With fathers of varying IQs, the prediction of the sons' IQs would also vary.

How accurate is this prediction? The standard error of estimate is $SD_{y.x} = 15 - \sqrt{1 - .50^2}$ or 13. In terms of accuracy, this means that about two-thirds of the time we make such a prediction about the sons of fathers with 150 IQ, the son's actual IQ will fall between 125 ± 13 or between 112 and 138. About 95 percent of the time the actual IQ of the son will be between $125 \pm (2)(13)$ or between 99 and 151. Almost always, the actual IQ will be between $125 \pm (3)(13)$ or between 86 and 164.

With these data, our prediction is a more specific one and also a more accurate one. We have narrowed the range of predictive accuracy. We have gone from predicting that everyone will fall on the population mean to predicting a very specific number, and the range of inaccuracy around this prediction is more narrow. The narrowness or precision of this range is a function of the magnitude of the relationship between X and Y. We have gone from a situation in which our predictive powers account for zero percent of the variance (0.00^2) to one in which our prediction accounts for 25 percent of the variance $(.50^2)$.[1] This also informs us that 75 percent of the variance is as yet not accounted for and is as yet unpredicted.

$r = 1.00$. If the correlation had been 1.00, prediction would be perfect. The IQ of a parent would tell you exactly the IQ of his offspring. For the 150 IQ father, the regression equation would be

$$Y' = 1.00 \frac{15}{15} 150 + \left(100 - 1.00 \frac{15}{15} 150\right)$$

$$Y' = 150$$

How accurate is this prediction? The standard error of estimate is $SD_{y \cdot x} = 15 - \sqrt{1 - 1.00^2}$ which equals zero. This means that every time we make a prediction about the IQ of an offspring of fathers with an IQ of 150, the offspring's actual IQ will be 150. When the correlation coefficient is squared, it tells us that 100 percent of the variance is accounted for. All variations in Y are predicted.

The three examples which have been discussed are shown in Table A-3. As the magnitude of the relationship increases, the prediction of Y' changes, the standard error of estimate becomes smaller, the percentage of variance in the predicted variable which can be accounted for becomes greater, and the range of error becomes narrower. With this discussion as a background, the student should be better able to evaluate correlation coefficients of various sizes.

COMPUTATIONAL EXAMPLE

Computation of the Pearson product-moment correlation coefficient (named in honor of Professor Karl Pearson who developed this statistic) may be undertaken in any one of several ways. The defining formula is:

$$r = \frac{\Sigma xy}{NSD_x SD_y}$$

The x represents the difference between each X score and the mean of the X scores, and y is the difference between each Y score and the mean of the

---

[1] The variance of a distribution of scores is the mean of squared deviations of each individual score from the mean of the distribution. The variance may be determined by squaring the standard deviation. Thus, the variance of the WISC scores is 15^2 or 225. If we knew everything there was to know about the antecedents of intelligence, our predictor variables would account for all of that 225; each individual's IQ would be predicted without error. With a parent-child correlation of .50, we would say that 25 percent of the variance can now be accounted for (or predicted) on the basis of parental intelligence and 75 percent cannot be accounted for or predicted. These figures can be obtained by squaring the standard error of estimate: $13^2 = 169$. This figure is the variance which is not predicted from X. And, 169 is 75 percent of 225; the amount of the variance which *is* predicted is the difference between 169 and 225 or 56, which is 25 percent of 225.

Table A-3. Predicting Y from X on the Basis of Correlations of Different Magnitudes between X and Y

Magnitude of r	*0.00*	*.50*	*1.00*
Prediction of Son's IQ when Father's IQ is 150	100	125	150
Standard Error of Estimate	15	13	0
Percentage of Variance in Y Accounted for by X	0%	25%	100%

Actual IQ of Offspring Will Fall Within the Following Ranges:

68.27% of the time	85–115	112–138	150–150
95.45% of the time	70–130	99–151	150–150
99.73% of the time	55–145	86–164	150–150

Y scores. The sum of the products of these difference scores is divided by the product of the number of pairs of scores times the standard deviation of the X scores times the standard deviation of the Y scores. An easier method of calculation is through the use of a scatter diagram as described in most beginning statistics texts. Still easier, if a desk calculator is available, is the use of the gross score formula:

$$r = \frac{N\Sigma XY - \Sigma X\Sigma Y}{\sqrt{N\Sigma X^2 - (\Sigma X)^2}\sqrt{N\Sigma Y^2 - (\Sigma Y)^2}}$$

As an illustration of the latter method, we will return to the imaginary data for the six subjects in Table A-1. The necessary quantities are shown in Table A-4. When these figures are substituted in the formula:

$$r = \frac{(6)(3150) - (114)(135)}{\sqrt{(6)(3142) - (114)^2}\sqrt{(6)(3481) - (135)^2}} = .89$$

Table A-4. Quantities for Computing a Correlation Coefficient Using the Gross Score Formula

Subjects	*X*	*Y*	*X²*	*Y²*	*XY*
1	10	12	100	144	120
2	30	28	900	784	840
3	41	38	1681	1444	1558
4	6	22	36	484	132
5	19	20	361	400	380
6	8	15	64	225	120
N = 6	ΣX = 114	ΣY = 135	ΣX² = 3142	ΣY² = 3481	ΣXY = 3150

MULTIPLE CORRELATION COEFFICIENT

In the preceding discussion, the impression may have been given that the correlation coefficient as an indicator of predictive accuracy only applies to the two-variable situation. Not only can we have a relationship between X and Y and hence predict Y from X, but Y can also be related to any number of other variables which may be combined to predict Y. The statistic which describes such a situation is the *multiple correlation coefficient*. The interpretation of a multiple *r* through utilization of a regression equation, standard error of estimate, and percentage of the variance accounted for is like that of the ordinary correlation coefficient. Returning briefly to the IQ example, would prediction of a child's IQ be any better if we knew the IQ of each of his parents? The only additional bit of information needed for the formula is the fact that the IQ's husbands and wives correlate .50. If r_{12} is the correlation between offspring and father, r_{13} the correlation between offspring and mother, and r_{23} the correlation between mother and father, the multiple correlation is:

$$r_{1.23} = \sqrt{r_{12}\left(\frac{r_{12} - r_{13}\,r_{23}}{1 - r_{23}^2}\right) + r_{13}\left(\frac{r_{13} - r_{12}\,r_{23}}{1 - r_{23}^2}\right)}$$

$$r_{1.23} = .57$$

Thus, knowledge about that IQs of both parents provides slightly greater power in predicting the IQ of their offspring; 32 percent of the variance can be accounted for. The standard error of estimate is computed as before: $SD_{1.23} = SD_y \sqrt{1 - r_{1.23}^2}$ which equals 12.33. A regression equation can be written in which information about both parents contributes to the prediction of the child's IQ.

The use of the correlation coefficient is appropriate for any situation in which the variables represent continuous measures and in which the relationship is a linear one. Other types of situations frequently arise, however, and the student should refer to an introductory statistics text for further information about the use of other types of correlation coefficients, their computation, and their interpretation.

STATISTICAL TEXTS

For the student who wishes to pursue the kind of statistical problems touched on here and to go beyond this brief introduction, a number of excellent texts are available. Among the possibilities are:

Edwards, A. *Statistical methods.* New York: Holt, Rinehart, and Winston, 1967.

McNemar, Q. *Psychological statistics.* New York: John Wiley, 1969.

Winer, B. J. *Statistical principles in experimental design.* New York: McGraw-Hill, 1971.

References

ABELSON, H., COHEN, R., HEATON, E., & SUDER, C. National survey of public attitudes toward and experience with erotic materials. In *Technical Report of the Commission on Obscenity and Pornography*. Vol. VI. Washington, D.C.: U.S. Government Printing Office, 1971. Pp. 1–37.

ADERMAN, D., & BERKOWITZ, L. Observational set, empathy, and helping. *Journal of Personality and Social Psychology*, 1970, **14**, 141–48.

ADORNO, T. W., FRENKEL-BRUNSWICK, E., LEVINSON, D. J., & SANFORD, R. N. *The authoritarian personality*. New York: Harper, 1950.

ALBEE, G. W., et al. Statement by SPSSI on current IQ controversy: Heredity versus environment. *American Psychologist*, 1969, **24**, 1039–40.

ALBEE, G. W., LANE, E. A., CORCORAN, C., & WERNEDKE, A. Childhood and intercurrent intellectual performance of adult schizophrenics. *Journal of Consulting Psychology*, 1963, **27**, 364–66.

ALLPORT, G. W. *Pattern and growth in personality*. New York: Holt, Rinehart, & Winston, 1961.

ALPER, T. G., & GREENBERGER, E. Relationship of picture structure to achievement motivation in college women. *Journal of Personality and Social Psychology*, 1967, **7**, 362–71.

ALPERT, R., & HABER, R. N. Anxiety in academic achievement situations. *Journal of Abnormal Psychology*, 1960, **61**, 207–15.

ALTROCCHI, J., PARSONS, O. A., & DICKOFF, H. Changes in self-ideal discrepancy in repressors and sensitizers. *Journal of Abnormal and Social Psychology*, 1960, **51**, 67–72.

ANASTASI, A., & D'ANGELO, R. Y. A comparison of Negro and white preschool children in language development and Goodenough Draw-a-Man IQ. *Journal of Genetic Psychology*, 1952, **81**, 147–65.

535

ANASTASIOW, N. Educational relevance and Jensen's conclusions. *Phi Delta Kappan,* 1969, **51,** 32–35.

ANDREWS, J. D. W. The achievement motive and advancement in two types of organizations. *Journal of Personality and Social Psychology,* 1967, **6,** 163–68.

ANGYAL, A. *Foundations for a science of personality.* New York: Commonwealth Fund, 1941.

ARGYLE, M. *The psychology of interpersonal behavior.* Middlesex, England: Penguin, 1967

ARISTOTLE. *The rhetoric.* New York: Appleton-Century-Crofts, 1932.

ARLING, G. L., & HARLOW, H. F. Effects of social deprivation on maternal behavior of rhesus monkeys. *Journal of Comparative and Physiological Psychology,* in press.

ARONFREED, J. *Conduct and conscience.* New York: Academic Press, 1968.

ARONFREED, J. The socialization of altruistic and sympathetic behavior: Some theoretical and experimental analyses. In J. Macaulay and L. Berkowitz (eds.), *Altruism and helping behavior.* New York: Academic Press, 1970. Pp. 103–26.

ARONSON, E. The need for achievement as measured by graphic expression. In J. W. Atkinson (ed.), *Motives in fantasy, action, and society.* Princeton: Van Nostrand, 1958. Pp. 249–65.

ARONSON, E., & WORCHEL, P. Similarity versus liking as determinants of interpersonal attractiveness. *Psychonomic Science,* 1966, **5,** 157–58.

ASCH, S. E. Studies of independence and submission to group pressure: 1. A minority of one against a unanimous majority. *Psychological Monographs,* 1956, **70,** (Whole no. 416).

ASIMOV, I. Is cancer's cure in outer space? *Indianapolis Star Magazine,* March 21, 1971, 20–25.

ASTIN, A. W., & ROSS, S. Glutamic acid and human intelligence. *Psychological Bulletin,* 1960, **57,** 429–34.

ATKINSON, J. W. Explorations using imaginative thought to assess the strength of human motives. In M. R. Jones (ed.), *Nebraska symposium on motivation 1954.* Lincoln: University of Nebraska Press, 1954. Pp. 56–112.

ATKINSON, J. W. Motivational determinants of risk-taking behavior. *Psychological Review,* 1957, **64,** 359–72.

ATKINSON, J. W., & FEATHER, N. T. (eds.) *A theory of achievement motivation.* New York: Wiley, 1966.

ATKINSON, J. W., & LITWIN, G. H. Achievement motive and test anxiety conceived as motive to approach success and motive to avoid failure. *Journal of Abnormal and Social Psychology,* 1960, **60,** 52–63.

ATKINSON, J. W., & McCLELLAND, D. C. The projective expression of needs. II. The effect of different intensities of the hunger drive on thematic apperception. *Journal of Experimental Psychology,* 1948, **38,** 643–58.

AUMACK, L. Effects of imprisonment upon authoritarian attitudes. *Psychological Reports,* 1956, **2,** 39–42.

BACON, H. K., CHILD, I. L., & BARRY, H. A. A cross-cultural study of correlates of crime. *Journal of Abnormal and Social Psychology,* 1963, **66,** 291–300.

BANDURA, A. Relationship of family patterns to child behavior disorders. Progress Report, U.S.P.H.S. Research Grant M-1734, Stanford University, 1960.

BANDURA, A. Social learning theory of aggression. In J. F. Knutsen (ed.), *Control of aggression: Implications from basic research.* Chicago: Aldine, 1971.

BANDURA, A., & MISCHEL, W. Modification of self-imposed delay of reward through exposure to live and symbolic models. *Journal of Personality and Social Psychology,* 1965, **2,** 698–705.

BANDURA, A., ROSS, D., & ROSS, S. A. Imitation of film-mediated aggressive models. *Journal of Abnormal and Social Psychology,* 1963, **66,** 3–11.

BANDURA, A., & WALTERS, R. H. *Adolescent aggression.* New York: Ronald Press, 1959.

BARCLAY, A. M. The effect of hostility on physiological and fantasy responses. *Journal of Personality,* 1969, **37,** 651–67.

BARCLAY, A. M. Urinary acid phosphatase secretion in sexually aroused males. *Journal of Experimental Research in Personality,* 1970, **4,** 233–38.

BARCLAY, A. M. Information as a defensive control of sexual arousal. *Journal of Personality and Social Psychology,* 1971, **17,** 244–49.

BARCLAY, A. M., & LITTLE, D. M. Urinary acid phosphatase secretion resulting from different arousals. *Psychophysiology,* 1972, **9,** 69–77.

BARON, R. A. Magnitude of victim's pain cues and level of prior anger arousal as determinants of adult aggressive behavior. *Journal of Personality and Social Psychology,* 1971, **17,** 236–43. (a)

BARON, R. A. Aggression as a function of magnitude of victim's pain cues, level of prior anger arousal, and aggressor-victim similarity. *Journal of Personality and Social Psychology,* 1971, **18,** 48–54. (b)

BARON, R. A. Exposure to an aggressive model and apparent probability of retaliation from the victim as determinants of adult aggressive behavior. *Journal of Experimental Social Psychology,* 1971, **7,** 343–55. (c)

BARON, R. A. Reducing the influence of an aggressive model: The restraining effects of discrepant modeling cues. *Journal of Personality and Social Psychology,* 1971, **20,** 240–45. (d)

BARON, R. A. Behavioral effects of interpersonal attraction: Compliance with requests from liked and disliked others. *Psychonomic Science,* 1971, **25,** 325–26. (e)

BARON, R. A. Aggression as a function of ambient temperature and prior anger arousal. *Journal of Personality and Social Psychology,* 1972, **21,** 183–89. (a)

BARON, R. A. Effects of exposure to erotic and nonerotic stimuli on subsequent aggression. Paper presented at the meeting of the Midwestern Psychological Association, Cleveland, May, 1972. (b)

BARON, R. A. Threatened retaliation as an inhibitor of human aggression: Mediating effects of the instrumental value of aggression. Paper presented at the meeting of the Midwestern Psychological Association, Chicago, May, 1973.

BARON, R. A., & BALL, R. L. The aggression-inhibiting influence of nonhostile humor. *Journal of Experimental Social Psychology,* in press.

BARON, R. A., BYRNE, D., & GRIFFITT, W. *Social psychology: Understanding human interaction.* Boston: Allyn and Bacon, in press.

BARON, R. A., & EGGLESTON, R. J. Performance on the "aggression machine": Motivation to help or harm? *Psychonomic Science,* 1972, **26,** 321–22.

BARON, R. A., & LAWTON, S. F. Environmental influences on aggression: The facilitation of modeling effects by high ambient temperatures. *Psychonomic Science,* 1972, **26,** 80–82.

BARRETT, G. V., & FRANKE, R. H. "Psychogenic" death: A reappraisal. *Science,* 1970, **167,** 304–6.

BARRON, F. Some personality correlates of independence of judgment. *Journal of Personality,* 1953, **21,** 287–97.

BARRON, F. Originality in relation to personality and intellect. *Journal of Personality,* 1957, **25,** 730–42.

BARTELL, G. D. *Group sex: A scientist's eyewitness report on the American way of swinging.* New York: Peter H. Wyden, 1971.

BARUCH, R. The achievement motive in women: Implications for career development. *Journal of Personality and Social Psychology,* 1967, **5,** 260–67.

BATTLE, E. S. Motivational determinants of academic competence. *Journal of Personality and Social Psychology,* 1966, **4,** 634–42.

BAUGHMAN, E. E. *Black Americans.* New York: Academic Press, 1971.

BAUGHMAN, E. E., & DAHLSTROM, W. G. *Negro and white children: A psychological study in the rural South.* New York: Academic Press, 1968.

BAYLEY, N. Some increasing parent-child similarities during the growth of children. *Journal of Educational Psychology,* 1954, **45,** 1–21.

BAYLEY, N. On the growth of intelligence. *American Psychologist,* 1955, **10,** 805–18.

BEACH, F. A. It's all in your mind. *Psychology Today,* 1969, **3,** (2), 33–35, 60.

BEACH, F. A., WESTBROOK, W., & CLEMENS, L. G. Comparisons of the ejaculatory response in men and animals. *Psychosomatic Medicine,* 1966, **28,** 749–63.

BEARDSLEE, D. C., & FOGELSON, R. Sex differences in sexual imagery aroused by musical stimulation. In J. W. Atkinson (ed.), *Motives in fantasy, action, and society.* Princeton, N. J.: Van Nostrand, 1958. Pp. 132–42.

BECHTOLDT, H. P. Response defined anxiety and MMPI variables. *Iowa Academy of Science,* 1953, **60,** 495–99.

BECHTOLDT, H. P. Construct validity: A critique. *American Psychologist,* 1959, **14,** 619–29.

BENDIG, A. W. Predictive and postdictive validity of need achievement measures. *Journal of Educational Research,* 1958, **52,** 119–20.

BENEDICT, R., & WELTFISH, G. *Races of mankind.* New York: Public Affairs Commission, 1943.

BEREST, J. J. Report on a case of sadism. *Journal of Sex Research,* 1970, **6,** 210–19.

BERGMANN, G. The contribution of John B. Watson. *Psychological Review,* 1956, **63,** 265–76.

BERKOWITZ, L. *Aggression: A social psychological analysis.* New York: McGraw-Hill, 1962.

BERKOWITZ, L. Aggressive cues in aggressive behavior and hostility catharsis. *Psychological Review,* 1964, **71,** 104–22.

BERKOWITZ, L. The concept of aggressive drive: Some additional considerations. In L. Berkowitz (ed.), *Advances in experimental social psychology.* Vol. 2. New York: Academic Press, 1965. (a)

BERKOWITZ, L. Some aspects of observed aggression. *Journal of Personality and Social Psychology,* 1965, **2,** 359–69. (b)

BERKOWITZ, L. The frustration-aggression hypothesis revisited. In L. Berkowitz (ed.), *Roots of aggression.* New York: Atherton, 1969.

BERKOWITZ, L. Aggressive humor as a stimulus to aggressive responses. *Journal of Personality and Social Psychology,* 1970, **16,** 710–17. (a)

BERKOWITZ, L. The contagion of violence. In W. J. Arnold and M. M. Page (eds.), *Nebraska symposium on motivation.* Lincoln: University of Nebraska Press, 1970. (b)

BERKOWITZ, L. The "weapons effect," demand characteristics, and the myth of the compliant subject. *Journal of Personality and Social Psychology,* 1971, **20,** 332–38. (a)

BERKOWITZ, L. Bad aggression and good (or bad) sex: Some observations on the reports of the violence and pornography commissions. Paper presented at the meeting of the American Psychological Association, Washington, D.C., September, 1971. (b)

BERKOWITZ, L., & GEEN, R. G. Film violence and the cue properties of available targets. *Journal of Personality and Social Psychology,* 1966, **3,** 525–30.

BERKOWITZ, L., & LePAGE, A. Weapons as aggression-eliciting stimuli. *Journal of Personality and Social Psychology,* 1967, **7,** 202–7.

BERLEW, D. The achievement motive and the growth of Greek civilization. Unpublished bachelor's thesis, Wesleyan University, 1956.

BERNE, E. *Games people play.* New York: Grove, 1964.

BICKMAN, L. The effect of another bystander's ability to help on bystander intervention in an emergency. *Journal of Experimental Social Psychology,* 1971, **7,** 367–79.

BINET, A. *L'etude experimentale de l'intelligence* (1903). Paris: Alfred Costes, 1922.

BINET, A. *Les idees modernes sur les enfants.* Paris: Ernest Famarion, 1909.

BIRNEY, R. C. The reliability of the achievement motive. *Journal of Abnormal and Social Psychology,* 1959, **58,** 266–67.

BISCHOF, L. J. *Interpreting personality theories.* New York: Harper & Row, 1970.

BLANCHARD, W. H. The group process in gang rape. *Journal of Social Psychology,* 1959, **49,** 259–66.

BLAZEK, N. C., & HARLOW, H. F. Persistence of performance differences on discriminations of varying difficulty. *Journal of Comparative and Physiological Psychology,* 1955, **48,** 86–89.

BLOCK, J. Personality characteristics associated with fathers' attitudes toward childrearing. *Child Development,* 1955, **26,** 41–48.

BLOCK, J. *The Q-sort method in personality assessment and psychiatric research.* Springfield, Ill.: Charles C. Thomas, 1961.

BLOCK, J. *The challenge of response sets: Unconfounding meaning, acquiescence and social desirability in the MMPI.* New York: Appleton-Century-Crofts, 1965.

BLOCK, J., & THOMAS, H. Is satisfaction with self a measure of adjustment? *Journal of Abnormal and Social Psychology,* 1955, **51,** 254–59.

BLOOM, B. S. *Stability and change in human characteristics.* New York: Wiley, 1964.

BLOOM, K. L. Age and the self concept. *American Journal of Psychiatry,* 1961, **118,** 534–38.

BLUMENTHAL, M. D. Predicting attitudes toward violence. *Science,* 1972, **176,** 1296–1303.

BLUMER, B. Calley continued. *Esquire,* 1971, **75** (4), 22B.

BOBROW, D. G. *Natural language input for a computer problem solving system.* Cambridge Mass.: MAC-TR-1, Project MAC, M.I.T., 1964.

BRADBURN, N. M. *N* Achievement and father dominance in Turkey. *Journal of Abnormal and Social Psychology,* 1963, **67,** 464–68.

BRADBURY, R. *Fahrenheit 451.* New York: Ballantine Books, 1953.

BRADWAY, K. P., THOMPSON, C. W., & CRAVENS, R. B. Preschool IQs after twenty-five years. *Journal of Educational Psychology,* 1958, **49,** 278–81.

BRADY, J. P., & LEVITT, E. E. The scalability of sexual experiences. *Psychological Record,* 1965, **15,** 275–79.

BREEDLOVE, W., & BREEDLOVE, J. *Swap clubs.* Los Angeles: Sherbourne, 1964.

BREHM, J. W., & BEHAR, L. B. Sexual arousal, defensiveness, and sex preference in affiliation. *Journal of Experimental Research in Personality,* 1966, **1,** 195–200.

BREWER, R. E., & BREWER, M. B. Attraction and accuracy of perception in dyads. *Journal of Personality and Social Psychology,* 1968, **8,** 188–93.

BROCK, T. C. Erotic materials: A commodity theory analysis of availability and desirability. In *Technical Report of the Commission on Obscenity and Pornography.* Vol. I. Washington, D.C.: U.S. Government Printing Office, 1971. Pp. 131–37.

BROCK, T. C., & BECKER, L. A. "Debriefing" and susceptibility to subsequent experimental manipulations. *Journal of Experimental Social Psychology,* 1966, **2,** 314–23.

BROCKMAN, L. The effects of severe malnutrition on cognitive development in infants. Unpublished doctoral dissertation, Cornell University, 1966.

BROWN, J. S. *The motivation of behavior.* New York: McGraw-Hill, 1961.

BRUCE, M. Factors affecting intelligence test performance of whites and Negroes in the rural South. *Archives of Psychology,* 1940, no. 252.

BRYAN, J. H., & LONDON, P. Altruistic behavior by children. *Psychological Bulletin,* 1970, **73,** 200–211.

BRYAN, J. H., & SCHWARTZ, T. Effects of film material upon children's behavior. *Psychological Bulletin,* 1971, **75,** 50–59.

BRYAN, J. H., & TEST, M. A. Models and helping: Naturalistic studies in aiding behavior. *Journal of Personality and Social Psychology,* 1967, **6,** 400–407.

BRYAN, J. H., & WALBEK, N. H. Preaching and practicing generosity: Children's actions and reactions. *Child Development,* 1970, **41,** 329–53.

BUDNER, S. Intolerance of ambiguity as a personality variable. *Journal of Personality,* 1962, **30,** 29–50.

BURGESS, A. *A clockwork orange.* New York: W. W. Norton, 1962.

BURKS, B. C., JENSEN, D. W., & TERMAN, L. M. *The promise of youth: Follow-up studies of a thousand gifted children.* Vol. III of *Genetic studies of genius,* by Terman, L. M. (ed.), Stanford University Press, 1930.

BURRIS, R. W. The effect of counseling on achievement motivation. Unpublished doctoral dissertation, Indiana University, 1958.

BURT, C. The inheritance of mental ability. *American Psychologist,* 1958, **13,** 1–15.

BURT, C. Inheritance of general intelligence. *American Psychologist,* 1972, **27,** 175–90.

BURT, C., JONES, E., MILLER, E., & MOODIE, W. *How the mind works.* New York: Appleton-Century-Crofts, 1934.

BURTON, R. V. Generality of honesty reconsidered. *Psychological Review,* 1963, **70,** 481–99.

BURWEN, L. S., & CAMPBELL, D. T. The generality of attitudes toward authority and nonauthority figures. *Journal of Abnormal and Social Psychology,* 1957, **54,** 24–31.

BUSS, A. H. *The psychology of aggression.* New York: Wiley, 1961.

BUSS, A. H. Physical aggression in relation to different frustrations. *Journal of Abnormal and Social Psychology,* 1963, **67,** 1–7.

BUSS, A. H. Instrumentality of aggression, feedback, and frustration as determinants of physical aggression. *Journal of Personality and Social Psychology,* 1966, **3,** 153–62.

BUSS, A. H., BOOKER, A., & BUSS, E. Firing a weapon and aggression. *Journal of Personality and Social Psychology,* 1972, **22,** 296–302.

BUSS, A. H., WIENER, M., DURKEE, A., & BAER, M. The measurement of anxiety in clinical situations. *Journal of Consulting Psychology,* 1955, **19,** 125–29.

BUTLER, J. M., & HAIGH, G. V. Changes in the relation between self-concepts and ideal concepts consequent upon client-centered counseling. In C. R. Rogers and R. F. Dymond (eds.), *Psychotherapy and personality change.* Chicago: University of Chicago Press, 1954. Pp. 55–75.

BYRNE, D. Interpersonal attraction and attitude similarity. *Journal of Abnormal and Social Psychology,* 1961, **62,** 713–15. (a)

BYRNE, D. The repression-sensitization scale: Rationale, reliability, and validity. *Journal of Personality,* 1961, **29,** 334–49. (b)

BYRNE, D. Response to attitude similarity-dissimilarity as a function of affiliation need. *Journal of Personality,* 1962, **30,** 164–77.

BYRNE, D. Repression-sensitization as a dimension of personality. In B. A. Maher (ed.), *Progress in experimental personality research.* New York: Academic Press, 1964. Pp. 169–220.

BYRNE, D. Parental antecedents of authoritarianism. *Journal of Personality and Social Psychology,* 1965, **1,** 369–73.

BYRNE, D. *The attraction paradigm.* New York: Academic Press, 1971.

BYRNE, D., BASKETT, G. D., & HODGES, L. Behavioral indicators of interpersonal attraction. *Journal of Applied Social Psychology,* 1971, **1,** 137–49.

BYRNE, D., & BLAYLOCK, B. Similarity and assumed similarity of attitudes between husbands and wives. *Journal of Abnormal and Social Psychology,* 1963, **67,** 636–40.

BYRNE, D., BOND, M. H., & DIAMOND, M. J. Response to political candidates as a function of attitude similarity-dissimilarity. *Human Relations,* 1969, **22,** 251–62.

BYRNE, D., CHERRY, F., LAMBERTH, J., & MITCHELL, H. E. Husband-wife similarity in response to erotic stimuli. *Journal of Personality,* 1973, **41,** 385–394.

BYRNE, D., & CLORE, G. L. Predicting interpersonal attraction toward strangers presented in three different stimulus modes. *Psychonomic Science,* 1966, **4,** 239–40.

BYRNE, D., & CLORE, G. L. A reinforcement model of evaluative responses. *Personality: An International Journal,* 1970, **1,** 103–28.

BYRNE, D., CLORE, G. L., & WORCHEL, P. The effect of economic similarity-dissimilarity on interpersonal attraction. *Journal of Personality and Social Psychology,* 1966, **4,** 220–24.

BYRNE, D., ERVIN, C. R., & LAMBERTH, J. Continuity between the experimental study of attraction and "real life" computer dating. *Journal of Personality and Social Psychology,* 1970, **16,** 157–65.

BYRNE, D., FISHER, J. D., LAMBERTH, J., & MITCHELL, H. E. Evaluations of erotica: Facts or feelings? *Journal of Personality and Social Psychology,* 1974, **29,** 111-16.

BYRNE, D., GOUAUX, C., GRIFFITT, W., LAMBERTH, J., MURAKAWA, N., PRASAD, M. B., PRASAD, A., & RAMIREZ, M., III. The ubiquitous relationship: Attitude similarity and attraction. A cross-cultural study. *Human Relations,* 1971, **24,** 201–7.

BYRNE, D., & GRIFFITT, W. A developmental investigation of the law of attraction. *Journal of Personality and Social Psychology,* 1966, **4,** 699–702. (a)

BYRNE, D., & GRIFFITT, W. Similarity versus liking: A clarification. *Psychonomic Science,* 1966, **6,** 295–96. (b)

BYRNE, D., GRIFFITT, W., & STEFANIAK, D. Attraction and similarity of personality characteristics. *Journal of Personality and Social Psychology,* 1967, **5,** 82–90.

BYRNE, D., & HOLCOMB, J. The reliability of a response measure: Differential recognition-threshold scores. *Psychological Bulletin,* 1962, **59,** 70–73.

BYRNE, D., & LAMBERTH, J. The effect of erotic stimuli on sex arousal, evaluative responses, and subsequent behavior. In *Technical report of the Commission on Obscenity and Pornography.* Vol. VIII. Washington, D.C.: U.S. Government Printing Office, 1971. Pp. 41–67.

BYRNE, D., LONDON, O., & GRIFFITT, W. The effect of topic importance and attitude similarity-dissimilarity on attraction in an intrastranger design. *Psychonomic Science,* 1968, **11,** 303–4.

BYRNE, D., LONDON, O., & REEVES, K. The effects of physical attractiveness, sex, and attitude similarity on interpersonal attraction. *Journal of Personality,* 1968, **36,** 259–71.

BYRNE, D., & NELSON, D. Attraction as a linear function of proportion of positive reinforcements. *Journal of Personality and Social Psychology,* 1965, **1,** 659–63.

BYRNE, D., & RHAMEY, R. Magnitude of positive and negative reinforcements as a determinant of attraction. *Journal of Personality and Social Psychology,* 1965, **2,** 884–89.

BYRNE, D., & SHEFFIELD, J. Responses to sexually arousing stimuli as a function of repressing and sensitizing defenses. *Journal of Abnormal Psychology,* 1965, **70,** 114–18.

BYRNE, D., & WONG, T. J. Racial prejudice, interpersonal attraction, and assumed dissimilarity of attitudes. *Journal of Abnormal and Social Psychology,* 1962, **65,** 246–53.

CAIRNS, R. B., PAUL, J. C. N., & WISHNER, J. Psychological assumptions in sex censorship: An evaluative review of recent research (1961–1968). In *Technical Report of the Commission on Obscenity and Pornography.* Vol. I. Washington, D.C.: U.S. Government Printing Office, 1971. Pp. 5–21.

CAMERON, N. *The psychology of behavior disorders: A bio-social interpretation.* Boston: Houghton Mifflin, 1947.

CAMPBELL, D., & FISKE, D. Convergent and discriminant validation by the multitrait-multimethod matrix. *Psychological Bulletin,* 1959, **56,** 81–105.

CAMPBELL, J. P., & DUNNETTE, M. D. Effectiveness of T-group experiences in managerial training and development. *Psychological Bulletin,* 1968, **70,** 73–104.

CANNON, K. L., & LONG, R. Premarital sexual behavior in the sixties. *Journal of Marriage and the Family,* 1971, **33,** 36–49.

CAPADONA, J. Library seating: The relationship of distance and sex to disruption of studies, comfort, and attraction. Unpublished manuscript, Purdue University, 1971.

CARLSMITH, J. M., & GROSS, A. E. Some effects of guilt on compliance. *Journal of Personality and Social Psychology*, 1969, **11**, 232–39.

CARLSON, R. Where is the person in personality research? *Psychological Bulletin*, 1971, **75**, 203–19.

CARSON, R. C. *Interaction concepts of personality*. Chicago: Aldine, 1969.

CARTWRIGHT, D. S. Self-consistency as a factor affecting immediate recall. *Journal of Abnormal and Social Psychology*, 1956, **52**, 212–18.

CATES, J. Psychology's manpower: Report on the 1968 national register of scientific and technical personnel. *American Psychologist*, 1970, **25**, 254–63.

CATTELL, R. B. *Personality: A systematic, theoretical, and factual study*. New York: McGraw-Hill, 1950.

CATTELL, R. B. Personality theory growing from multivariate quantitative research. In S. Koch (ed.), *Psychology: A study of a science*. New York: McGraw-Hill, 1959. Pp. 257–327.

CATTELL, R. B. Multivariate behavioral research and the integrative challenge. *Multivariate Behavioral Research*, 1966, **1**, 4–23.

CATTELL, R. B., & NESSELROADE, J. R. Likeness and completeness theories examined by Sixteen Personality Factor measures on stably and unstably married couples. *Journal of Personality and Social Psychology*, 1967, **7**, 351–61.

CATTELL, R. B., & SCHEIER, I. H. *The meaning and measurement of neuroticism and anxiety*. New York: Ronald Press, 1961.

CAWS, P. Psychology without a psyche. *The New Republic*, 1971, **165** (16), 32–34.

CHAPMAN, L. J., & CAMPBELL, D. T. Response set in the F Scale. *Journal of Abnormal and Social Psychology*, 1957, **54**, 129–32.

CHAPMAN, L. J., & CAMPBELL, D. T. Absence of acquiescence response set in the Taylor Manifest Anxiety Scale. *Journal of Consulting Psychology*, 1959, **23**, 465–66.

CHAPMAN, L. J., CHAPMAN, J. P., & BRELJE, T. Influence of the experimenter on pupillary dilation to sexually provocative pictures. *Journal of Abnormal Psychology*, 1969, **74**, 396–400.

CHARLES, D. C., & PRITCHARD, S. A. Differential development of intelligence in the college years. *Journal of Genetic Psychology*, 1959, **95**, 41–44.

CHASE, P. H. Self concepts in adjusted and maladjusted hospital patients. *Journal of Consulting Psychology*, 1957, **21**, 495–97.

CHODORKOFF, B. Self-perception, perceptual defense, and adjustment. *Journal of Abnormal and Social Psychology*, 1954, **49**, 508–12.

CHRISTENSEN, H. T., & GREGG, C. F. Changing sex norms in America and Scandinavia. *Journal of Marriage and the Family*, 1970, **32**, 616–27.

CHRISTIE, R. Changes in authoritarianism as related to situational factors. *American Psychologist*, 1952, **7**, 307–8. (abstract)

CLARK, L., & TREICHLER, M. Psychic stimulation of prostatic secretion. *Psychosomatic Medicine*, 1950, **12**, 261–63.

CLARK, R. A. The projective measurement of experimentally induced levels of sexual motivation. *Journal of Experimental Psychology*, 1952, **44**, 391–99.

CLARK, R. A., TEEVAN, R., & RICCIUTI, H. N. Hope of success and fear of failure as aspects of need for achievement. *Journal of Abnormal and Social Psychology*, 1956, **53**, 182–86.

CLEMENS, L. G. Effect of stimulus female variation on sexual performance of the male deermouse, *peromyscus maniculatus. Proceedings, 75th Annual Convention, APA,* 1967, 119–20.

CLORE, G. L., & GORMLY, J. B. Attraction and physiological arousal in response to agreements and disagreements. Paper presented at the meeting of the Psychonomic Society, St. Louis, November, 1969.

CLORE, G. L., & JEFFERY, K. McM. Emotional role playing, attitude change, and attraction toward a disabled person. *Journal of Personality and Social Psychology,* 1972, **23,** 105–11.

COLE, D., JACOBS, S., ZUBOK, B., FAGOT, B., & HUNTER, I. The relation of achievement imagery scores to academic performance. *Journal of Abnormal and Social Psychology,* 1962, **65,** 208–11.

Commission on Obscenity and Pornography. *The Report of the Commission on Obscenity and Pornography.* Washington, D.C.: U.S. Government Printing Office, 1970.

CONANT, J. B. *On understanding science.* New York: New American Library, 1947.

CONDON, R. *An infinity of mirrors.* New York: Random House, 1964.

CONNOR, J. Olfactory control of aggressive and sexual behavior in the mouse (*Mus musclus L.*). *Psychonomic Science,* 1972, **27,** 1–3.

CONRAD, H. S., & JONES, H. E. A second study of familial resemblance in intelligence: Environmental and genetic implications of parent-child and sibling correlations in the total sample. *39th Yearbook, National Society for the Study of Education,* 1940, Part II, 97–141.

COOK, J. O., & BARNES, L. W. Choice of delay of inevitable shock. *Journal of Abnormal and Social Psychology,* 1964, **68,** 669–72.

COOMBS, R. H. Social participation, self-concept and interpersonal valuation. *Sociometry,* 1969, **32,** 273–86.

CORMAN, C. Physiological response to a sexual stimulus. Unpublished bachelor's thesis, University of Manitoba, 1968.

CORROZI, J. F., & ROSNOW, R. L. Consonant and dissonant communications as positive and negative reinforcements in opinion change. *Journal of Personality and Social Psychology,* 1968, **8,** 27–30.

CORTES, J. B. The achievement motive in the Spanish economy between the 13th and 18th centuries. *Economic Development and Cultural Change,* 1960, **9,** 144–63.

COTTRELL, N. B., INGRAHAM, L. H., & MONFORT, F. W. The retention of balanced and unbalanced cognitive structures. *Journal of Personality,* 1971, **39,** 112–31.

COX, C. C. *The early mental traits of three hundred geniuses.* Vol. II of *Genetic studies of genius,* by Terman, L. M. (ed.). Stanford: Stanford University Press, 1926.

CRAIG, K. D., & WOOD, K. Autonomic components of observers' responses to pictures of homicide victims and nude females. *Journal of Experimental Research in Personality,* 1971, **5,** 304–9.

CRONBACH, L. J. *Essentials of psychological testing* (2nd ed.). New York: Harper, 1960.

CRONBACH, L. J. Heredity, environment, and educational policy. *Harvard Educational Review,* 1969, 338–47.

CROWNE, D. P., STEPHENS, M. W., & KELLY, R. The validity and equivalence of tests of self-acceptance. *Journal of Psychology,* 1961, **51,** 101–12.

CRUTCHFIELD, R. S. Conformity and character. *American Psychologist,* 1955, **10,** 191–98.

CUNNINGHAM, M. *Intelligence: Its organization and development.* New York: Academic Press, 1972.

DARLEY, J. M., & LATANÉ, B. Bystander intervention in emergencies: Diffusion of responsibility. *Journal of Personality and Social Psychology,* 1968, **8,** 377–83.

DARWIN, C. *On the origin of species by means of natural selection* (1859). New York: Heritage Press, 1963.

DAVIDS, A. The influence of ego-involvement on relations between authoritarianism and intolerance of ambiguity. *Journal of Consulting Psychology,* 1956, **20,** 179–84.

DAVIDS, A., DEVAULT, S., & TALMADGE, M. Anxiety, pregnancy, and childbirth abnormalities. *Journal of Consulting Psychology,* 1961, **25,** 74–77.

DAVIDS, A., & ERIKSEN, C. W. The relation of manifest anxiety to association productivity and intellectual attainment. *Journal of Consulting Psychology,* 1955, **19,** 219–22.

DAVIDS, A., & ERICKSEN, C. W. Some social and cultural factors determining relations between authoritarianism and measures of neuroticism. *Journal of Consulting Psychology,* 1957, **21,** 155–59.

DAVIDS, A., & LAWTON, M. J. Self-concept, mother concept, and food aversions in emotionally disturbed and normal children. *Journal of Abnormal and Social Psychology,* 1961, **62,** 309–14.

DAVISON, G. C. Elimination of a sadistic fantasy by a client-controlled counter conditioning technique: A case study. *Journal of Abnormal Psychology,* 1968, **73,** 84–90.

DEAN, S. J., MARTIN, R. B., & STREINER, D. L. The use of sexually arousing slides as unconditioned stimuli for the GSR in a discrimination paradigm. *Psychonomic Science,* 1968, **13,** 99–100.

DE CHARMS, R., & MOELLER, G. H. Values expressed in American children's readers: 1800–1950. *Journal of Abnormal and Social Psychology,* 1962, **64,** 135–42.

DENFELD, D., & GORDON, M. The sociology of mate swapping: Or the family that swings together clings together. *Journal of Sex Research,* 1970, **6,** 85–100.

DICKENS, C. A Christmas carol (1843). In C. Dickens, *Five Christmas novels.* New York: Heritage Press, 1939. Pp. 17–88.

DIELMAN, T. E., SCHUERGER, J. M., & CATTELL, R. B. Prediction of junior high school achievement from IQ and the objective-analytic personality factors U.I. 21, U.I. 23, U.I. 24, and U.I. 25. *Personality: An International Journal,* 1970, **1,** 145–52.

DIENSTBIER, R. A., & MUNTER, P. O. Cheating as a function of the labeling of natural arousal. *Journal of Personality and Social Psychology,* in press.

DION, K., BERSCHEID, E., & WALSTER, E. What is beautiful is good. *Journal of Personality and Social Psychology,* 1972, **24,** 285–90.

DOHRENWEND, B. S., & DOHRENWEND, B. P. Field studies of social factors in relation to three types of psychological disorder. *Journal of Abnormal Psychology,* 1967, **72,** 369–78.

DOLLARD, J., DOOB, L. W., MILLER, N. E., & SEARS, R. R. *Frustration and aggression.* New Haven: Yale University Press, 1939.

DOLLARD, J., & MILLER, N. E. *Personality and psychotherapy.* New York: McGraw-Hill, 1950.

Doob, A. N. Catharsis and aggression: The effect of hurting one's enemy. *Journal of Experimental Research in Personality*, 1970, **4**, 291–96.

Doob, A. N., & Climie, R. J. Delay of measurement and the effects of film violence. *Journal of Experimental Social Psychology*, 1972, **8**, 136–42.

Doob, A. N., & Wood, L. E. Catharsis and aggression: Effects of annoyance and retaliation on aggressive behavior. *Journal of Personality and Social Psychology*, 1972, **22**, 156–62.

Downing, R. W., & Rickels, K. Q-sort patterns of self-evaluation in three neurotic clinic populations. *Journal of Clinical Psychology*, 1965, **21**, 89–96.

Dreger, R. M., & Miller, K. S. Comparative psychological studies of Negroes and whites in the United States: 1959–1965. *Psychological Bulletin Monograph Supplement*, 1968, **70**, Part 2, 1–58.

Duncan, S., Jr. Nonverbal communication. *Psychological Bulletin*, 1969, **72**, 118–37.

Dustin, D. S., & Davis, H. P. Authoritarianism and sanctioning behavior. *Journal of Personality and Social Psychology*, 1967, **6**, 222–24.

Dworkin, E. S., & Efran, J. S. The angered: Their susceptibility to varieties of humor. *Journal of Personality and Social Psychology*, 1967, **6**, 233–36.

Dymond, R. F. Adjustment changes over therapy from self-sorts. In C. R. Rogers and R. F. Dymond (eds.), *Psychotherapy and personality change*. Chicago: University of Chicago Press, 1954. Pp. 76–84.

Ebbs, J. H., Tisdall, F. F., & Scott, W. A. The influence of prenatal diet on the mother and child. *Milbank Memorial Fund Quarterly*, 1942, **20**, 35–45.

Edmiston, S. Murder, New York style: A crime of class. New York, 1970, **3** (33), 29–35.

Edwards, A. L. The relationship between the judged desirability of a trait and the probability that the trait will be endorsed. *Journal of Applied Psychology*, 1953, **37**, 90–93.

Edwards, A. L. *The social desirability variable in personality assessment and research.* New York: Dryden, 1957.

Edwards, A. L. *Edwards Personal Preference Schedule manual.* New York: Psychological Corporation, 1959.

Edwards, A. L. *Statistical methods.* New York: Holt, Rinehart, and Winston, 1967.

Efran, M. G. Visual interaction and interpersonal attraction. Unpublished doctoral dissertation, University of Texas, 1969.

Eliasberg, W. G., & Stuart, I. R. Authoritarian personality and the obscenity threshold. *Journal of Social Psychology*, 1961, **55**, 143–51.

Ellis, D. P., Weinir, P., & Miller, L., III. Does the trigger pull the finger? An experimental test of weapons as aggression-eliciting stimuli. *Sociometry*, 1971, **34**, 453–65.

Elms, A. C., & Milgram, S. Personality characteristics associated with obedience and defiance toward authoritative command. *Journal of Experimental Research in Personality*, 1966, **1**, 282–89.

Endler, N. S., & Hunt, J. McV. Sources of behavioral variance as measured by the S-R inventory of anxiousness. *Psychological Bulletin*, 1966, **65**, 336–46.

Endler, N. S., & Hunt, J. McV. Generalizability of contributions from sources of variance in the S-R inventory of anxiousness. *Journal of Personality*, 1969, **37**, 1–24.

ENTWISLE, D. R. To dispel fantasies about fantasy-based measures of achievement motivation. *Psychological Bulletin,* 1972, **77,** 377–91.

EPSTEIN, R. Authoritarianism, displaced aggression, and social status of the target. *Journal of Personality and Social Psychology,* 1965, **2,** 585–89.

EPSTEIN, S., & TAYLOR, S. P. Instigation to aggression as a function of degree of defeat and perceived aggressive intent of the opponent. *Journal of Personality,* 1967, **35,** 265–89.

ERON, L. D. Relationship of TV viewing habits and aggressive behavior in children. *Journal of Abnormal and Social Psychology,* 1963, **67,** 193–96.

ERON, L. D., LEFKOWITZ, M. M., HUESMANN, L. R., & WALDER, L. O. Does television violence cause aggression? *American Psychologist,* 1972, **27,** 253–63.

EVANS, T. G. A heuristic program to solve geometric analogies problems. *AFIPS Conference Proceedings,* 1964, **25,** 327–38.

EYSENCK, H. J. Hysterical personality and sexual adjustment, attitudes and behavior. *Journal of Sex Research,* 1971, **7,** 274–81. (a)

EYSENCK, H. J. *The IQ argument: Race, intelligence, and education.* New York: Library Press, 1971. (b)

EYSENCK, H. J., & EYSENCK, S. B. G. *The Eysenck Personality Inventory.* London: University of London Press, 1965.

FARBER, I. E. A framework for the study of personality as a behavioral science. In P. Worchel and D. Byrne (eds.), *Personality change.* New York: Wiley, 1964. Pp. 3–37.

FARINA, A., SHERMAN, M., & ALLEN, J. G. Role of physical abnormalities in interpersonal perception and behavior. *Journal of Abnormal Psychology,* 1968, **73,** 590–93.

FEATHER, N. T. The relationship of persistence at a task to expectation of success and achievement-related motives. *Journal of Abnormal and Social Psychology,* 1961, **63,** 552–61.

FEATHER, N. T. The relationship of expectation of success to need achievement and test anxiety. *Journal of Personality and Social Psychology,* 1965, **1,** 118–26.

FEIGENBAUM, E. A. The simulation of verbal learning behavior. *AFIPS Conference Proceedings,* 1961, **19,** 121–32.

FEINBERG, I., KORESKO, R. L., & HELLER, N. EEG sleep patterns as a function of normal and pathological aging in man. *Journal of Psychiatric Research,* 1967, **5,** 107–144.

FELD, S. C. Longitudinal study of the origins of achievement strivings. *Journal of Personality and Social Psychology,* 1967, **7,** 408–14.

FELIPE, N. J., & SOMMER, R. Invasions of personal space. *Social Problems,* 1966, **14,** 206–14.

FENZ, W. D., & DRONSEJKO, K. Effects of real and imagined threat of shock on GSR and heart rate as a function of trait anxiety. *Journal of Experimental Research in Personality,* 1969, **3,** 187–96.

FENZ, W. D., & EPSTEIN, S. Gradients of physiological arousal of experienced and novice parachutists as a function of an approaching jump. *Psychosomatic Medicine,* 1967, **29,** 33–51.

FESHBACH, N. D., & FESHBACH, S. The relationship between empathy and aggression in two age groups. *Developmental Psychology,* 1969, **1,** 102–7.

FESHBACH, S. Dynamics and morality of violence and aggression: Some psychological considerations. *American Psychologist,* 1971, **26,** 281–92.

FESHBACH, S., & SINGER, R. D. *Television and aggression*. San Francisco: Jossey-Bass, 1971.

FESHBACH, S., STILES, W. B., & BITTER, E. The reinforcing effect of witnessing aggression. *Journal of Experimental Research in Personality*, 1967, **2**, 133–39.

FESTINGER, L. A theory of social comparison processes. *Human Relations*, 1954, **7**, 117–40.

FESTINGER, L. *A theory of cognitive dissonance*. Stanford, Calif.: Stanford University Press, 1957.

FIELD, W. F. The effects on thematic apperception of certain experimentally aroused needs. Unpublished doctoral dissertation, University of Maryland, 1951.

FITCH, G. Effects of self-esteem, perceived performance, and choice on causal attributions. *Journal of Personality and Social Psychology*, 1970, **16**, 311–15.

FLIPPO, J. R., & LEWINSOHN, P. M. Effects of failure on the self-esteem of depressed and nondepressed subjects. *Journal of Consulting and Clinical Psychology*, 1971, **36**, 151.

FORSSMAN, H., & HAMBERT, G. Incidence of Klinefelter's syndrome among mental patients. *Lancet*, 1963, **1**, 1327.

FRANDSEN, A. N. The Wechsler-Bellevue intelligence scale and high school achievement. *Journal of Applied Psychology*, 1950, **34**, 406–11.

FREEDMAN, J. L., WALLINGTON, S. A., & BLESS, E. Compliance without pressure: The effect of guilt. *Journal of Personality and Social Psychology*, 1967, **7**, 117–24.

FRENCH, E. Development of a measure of complex motivation. In J. W. Atkinson (ed.), *Motives in fantasy, action, and society*. Princeton: Van Nostrand, 1958. Pp. 242–48.

FRENCH, J. W. & MICHAEL, W. B. *Standards for educational and psychological tests and manuals*. Washington, D.C.: American Psychological Association, 1966.

FRENKEL-BRUNSWIK, E. Intolerance of ambiguity as an emotional and perceptual personality variable. *Journal of Personality*, 1949, **18**, 108–43.

FRENKEL-BRUNSWIK, E. Dynamic and cognitive personality organization as seen through the interviews. In T. W. Adorno, E. Frenkel-Brunswik, D. J. Levinson, and R. N. Sanford (eds.), *The authoritarian personality*. New York: Harper & Row, 1950. Pp. 442–67.

FREUD, S. Jenseits des Lustprinzips. In *Gesammelte Werke*, 1920, Vol. XIII. London: Imago Publishing Co., 1940.

FREUD, S. On the grounds for detaching a particular syndrome from neurasthenia under the description "anxiety neurosis." (1895) In J. Strachey (ed.), *The standard edition of the complete psychological works*. Vol. 3. London: Hogarth and Institute of Psychoanalysis, 1959.

FREUD, S. *The interpretation of dreams* (1900). London: Hogarth, 1953.

FREUD, S. Inhibitions, symptoms and anxiety (1926). In J. Strachey (ed.), *The standard edition of the complete psychological works*. Vol. 20. London: Hogarth and Institute of Psychoanalysis, 1959, Pp. 77–175.

FREUD, S. *New introductory lectures on psycho-analysis*. New York: W. W. Norton, 1933.

FREUD, S. *An autobiographical study* (1935). London: Hogarth, 1946.

FREUD, S. Formulations regarding the two principles in mental function. In *Collected papers*. Vol. 4. London: Hogarth, 1946. Pp. 13–21.

FREUND, K., SEDLACEK, F., & KNOB, K. A simple transducer for mechanical plethysmography of the male genital. *Journal of the Experimental Analysis of Behavior*, 1965, **8**, 169–70.

FROMM, E. *Escape from freedom.* New York: Holt, Rinehart & Winston, 1941.

FRYER, D. Occupational intelligence standards. *School and Society,* 1922, **16**, 273–77.

GAEBELEIN, J., & TAYLOR, S. P. The effects of competition and attack on physical aggression. *Psychonomic Science,* 1971, **24**, 65–67.

GALLAGHER, J. J. Manifest anxiety changes concomitant with client-centered therapy. *Journal of Consulting Psychology,* 1953, **17**, 443–46.

GALTON, F. *Hereditary genius: An inquiry into its laws and consequences* (1870). New York: Horizon, 1952.

GARDNER, R. A., & GARDNER, B. T. Teaching sign language to a chimpanzee. *Science,* 1969, **165**, 664–72.

GEBHARD, P. H., GAGON, J. H., POMEROY, W. B., & CHRISTENSEN, C. U. *Sex offenders.* New York: Harper & Row, 1965.

GEEN, R. G. Perceived suffering of the victim as an inhibitor of attack-induced aggression. *Journal of Social Psychology,* 1970, **81**, 209–15.

GEEN, R. G., & BERKOWITZ, L. Name-mediated aggressive cue properties. *Journal of Personality,* 1966, **34**, 456–65.

GEEN, R. G., & BERKOWITZ, L. Some conditions facilitating the occurrence of aggression after the observation of violence. *Journal of Personality,* 1967, **35**, 666–76.

GEEN, R. G., & O'NEAL, E. C. Activation of cue-elicited aggression by general arousal. *Journal of Personality and Social Psychology,* 1969, **11**, 289–92.

GEEN, R. G., & PIGG, R. Acquisition of an aggressive response and its generalization to verbal behavior. *Journal of Personality and Social Psychology,* 1970, **15**, 165–70.

GENDLIN, E. T., & BERLIN, J. I. Galvanic skin response correlates of different modes of experiencing. *Journal of Clinical Psychology,* 1961, **17**, 73–77.

GENTRY, W. D. Effects of frustration, attack, and prior aggressive training on overt aggression and vascular processes. *Journal of Personality and Social Psychology,* 1970, **16**, 718–25.

GETZELS, J. W., & JACKSON, P. W. *Creativity and intelligence: Explorations with gifted students.* New York: Wiley, 1962.

GIBB, J. R. The effects of human relations training. In A. E. Bergin and S. L. Garfield (eds.), *Handbook of psychotherapy and behavior change.* New York: Wiley, 1971. Pp. 839–62.

GIBBON, E. *The decline and fall of the Roman Empire* (1776). Vol. 1. New York: Heritage Press, 1946.

GIDE, A. Introduction. In *The essays of Michel de Montaigne.* New York: Heritage Press, 1946.

GILLILAND, A. R. Socioeconomic status and race as factors in infant intelligence test scores. *Child Development,* 1951, **22**, 271–73.

GILULA, M. F., & DANIELS, D. N. Violence and man's struggle to adapt. *Science,* 1969, **164**, 396–405.

GODDARD, H. H. *The Kallikak family.* New York: Macmillan, 1912.

GOLDBERG, S., GODFREY, L., & LEWIS, M. Play behavior in the year-old infant: Early sex differences. Paper presented at the meeting of the Society for Research in Child Development, New York, March, 1967.

GOLDFARB, W. Effects of psychological deprivation in infancy and subsequent stimulation. *American Journal of Psychiatry,* 1945, **102**, 18–33.

GOLDSTEIN, J. H., & ARMS, R. L. Effects of observing athletic contests on hostility. *Sociometry,* 1971, **34,** 83–90.

GOLDSTEIN, M., KANT, H., JUDD, L., RICE, C., & GREEN, R. Experience with pornography: Rapists, pedophiles, homosexuals, transsexuals, and controls. *Archives of Sexual Behavior,* 1971, **1,** 1–15.

GOLIGHTLY, C., & BYRNE, D. Attitude statements as positive and negative reinforcements. *Science,* 1964, **146,** 798–99.

GOLIGHTLY, C., HUFFMAN, D. M., & BYRNE, D. Liking and loaning. *Journal of Applied Psychology,* 1972, **56,** 521–23.

GORDON, H. *Mental and scholastic tests among retarded children.* Education Pamphlet No. 44. London: Board of Education, 1923.

GORDON, M., & SHANKWEILER, P. J. Different equals less: Female sexuality in recent marriage manuals. *Journal of Marriage and the Family,* 1971, **33,** 459–66.

GORFEIN, D. Conformity behavior and the "authoritarian personality." *Journal of Social Psychology,* 1961, **53,** 121–25.

GOTTESMAN, I. I. Heritability of personality: A demonstration. *Psychological Monographs,* 1963, **77,** No. 9 (Whole no. 572).

GOTTESMAN, I. I. Biogenetics of race and class. In M. Deutsch, I. Katz, and A. R. Jensen (eds.), *Social class, race, and psychological development.* New York: Holt, Rinehart, and Winston, 1968.

GOUAUX, C., LAMBERTH, J., & FRIEDRICH, G. Affect and interpersonal attraction: A comparison of trait and state measures. *Journal of Personality and Social Psychology,* 1972, **24,** 53–58.

GOUGH, H. G. *Manual for the California Psychological Inventory.* Palo Alto, Calif.: Consulting Psychologists Press, 1957.

GOULD, L. J., & KLEIN, E. B. Performance of black and white adolescents on intellectual and attitudinal measures as a function of race of tester. *Journal of Consulting and Clinical Psychology,* 1971, **37,** 195–200.

GOULET, L. R. Anxiety (drive) and verbal learning: Implications for research and some methodological considerations. *Psychological Bulletin,* 1968, **69,** 235–47.

GRANBERG, D., & CORRIGAN, G. Authoritarianism, dogmatism and orientations toward the Vietnam war. *Sociometry,* 1972, **35,** 468–76.

GRANT, C. H. Age differences in self-concept from early adulthood through old age. *Proceedings, 77th Annual Convention, American Psychological Association,* 1969, 717–18.

GREEN, B. F. *Digital computers in research.* New York: McGraw-Hill, 1963.

GREEN, B. F. Intelligence and computer simulation. *Transactions of the New York Academy of Science,* 1964, **27** (1), 55–63.

GREEN, B. F., WOLF, A. K., CHOMSKY, C., & LAUGHERY, K. Baseball: An automatic question answerer. *AFIPS Conference Proceedings,* 1961, **19,** 219–24.

GREENBERG, D. S. Biomedical policy: LBJ's query leads to an illuminating conference. *Science,* 1966, **154,** 618–20.

GREENSPOON, J. The reinforcing effect of two spoken sounds on the frequency of two responses. *American Journal of Psychology,* 1955, **68,** 409–16.

GREENWELL, J., & DENGERINK, H. A. The role of perceived vs. actual attack in human physical aggression. Paper presented at the meeting of the Midwestern Psychological Association, Detroit, May, 1971.

GREULICH, W. W. A comparison of the physical growth and development of American-born and native Japanese children. *American Journal of Physical Anthropology,* 1957, December, 489–516.

GRIFFITT, W. Environmental effects on interpersonal affective behavior: Ambient effective temperature and attraction. *Journal of Personality and Social Psychology,* 1970, **15,** 240–44.

GRIFFITT, W. Response to erotica and the projection of response to erotica in the opposite sex. *Journal of Experimental Research in Personality,* 1973, **6,** 330–338.

GRIFFITT, W., & GUAY, P. "Object" evaluation and conditioned affect. *Journal of Experimental Research in Personality,* 1969, **4,** 1–8.

GRIFFITT, W., & JACKSON, T. The influence of ability and nonability information on personnel selection decisions. *Psychological Reports,* 1970, **27,** 959–62.

GRIFFITT, W., NELSON, J., & LITTLEPAGE, G. Old age and response to agreement-disagreement. *Journal of Gerontology,* 1972, **27,** 269–74.

GRIFFITT, W., & VEITCH, R. Hot and crowded: Influences of population density and temperature on interpersonal affective behavior. *Journal of Personality and Social Psychology,* 1971, **17,** 92–98.

GROSSMAN, J. C., & EISENMAN, R. Experimental manipulation of authoritarianism and its effect on creativity. *Journal of Consulting and Clinical Psychology,* 1971, **36,** 238–44.

GROSZ, H. J., & LEVITT, E. E. The effects of hypnotically induced anxiety on the Manifest Anxiety Scale and the Barron Ego-Strength Scale. *Journal of Abnormal and Social Psychology,* 1959, **59,** 281–83.

GRUDER, C. L., & COOK, T. D. Sex, dependency, and helping. *Journal of Personality and Social Psychology,* 1971, **19,** 290–94.

GRUMMON, D. L. Design, procedures, and subjects for the first block. In C. R. Rogers and R. F. Dymond (eds.), *Psychotherapy and personality change.* Chicago: University of Chicago Press, 1954. Pp. 35–52.

GUILFORD, J. P. *Personality.* New York: McGraw-Hill, 1959.

GUILFORD, J. P. Intelligence has three facets. *Science,* 1968, **160,** 615–20.

GUILFORD, J. P. Thurstone's primary mental abilities and structure-of-intellect abilities. *Psychological Bulletin,* 1972, **77,** 129–43.

HABER, R. N., & ALPERT, R. The role of situation and picture cues in projective measurement of the achievement motive. In J. W. Aktinson (ed.), *Motives in fantasy, action, and society.* Princeton: Van Nostrand, 1958. Pp. 644–63.

HALL, C. S., & LINDZEY, G. *Theories of personality.* New York: Wiley, 1970.

HANDLON, B. J., & SQUIER, L. H. Attitudes toward special loyalty oaths at the University of California. *American Psychologist,* 1955, **10,** 121–27.

HARE, R. D. Psychopathy and choice of immediate versus delayed punishment. *Journal of Abnormal Psychology,* 1966, **71,** 25–29.

HARLOW, H. F. Primate learning. In C. P. Stone (ed.), *Comparative psychology.* Englewood Cliffs, N.J.: Prentice-Hall, 1951. Pp. 183–238.

HARLOW, H. F. The heterosexual affectional system in monkeys. *American Psychologist,* 1962, **17,** 1–9.

HARMATZ, M. G. Verbal conditioning and change on personality measures. *Journal of Personality and Social Psychology,* 1967, **5,** 175–85.

HARRELL, R. F., WOODYARD, E., & GATES, A. I. *The effect of mothers' diets on the intelligence of offspring.* New York: Bureau of Publications, Teachers College, Columbia University, 1955.

HART, I. Maternal child-rearing practices and authoritarian ideology. *Journal of Abnormal and Social Psychology,* 1957, **55,** 232–37.

HARTSHORNE, H., & MAY, M. A. *Studies in the nature of character.* Vol. I. *Studies in deceit.* New York: Macmillan, 1928.

HARTSHORNE, H., MAY, M. A., & SHUTTLEWORTH, F. K. *Studies in the nature of character.* Vol. 3. *Studies in the organization of character.* New York: Macmillan, 1930.

HAYES, K. J. Genes, drives, and intellect. *Psychological Reports,* 1962, **10,** 299–342.

HAYTHORN, W. W., ALTMAN, I., & MYERS, T. I. Emotional symptomatology and stress in isolated pairs of men. *Journal of Experimental Research in Personality,* 1966, **4,** 290–306.

HAYWARD, S. C. Modification of sexual behavior of the male albino rat. *Journal of Comparative and Physiological Psychology,* 1957, **50,** 70–73.

HAYWOOD, H. C., & SPIELBERGER, C. D. Palmar sweating as a function of individual differences in manifest anxiety. *Journal of Personality and Social Psychology,* 1966, **3,** 103–5.

HEBB, D. O. *The organization of behavior.* New York: Wiley, 1949.

HEBB, D. O. *A textbook of psychology.* Philadelphia: Saunders, 1958.

HEIDER, F. *The psychology of interpersonal relations.* New York: Wiley, 1958.

HEINE, R. W. Foreword. In R. C. Carson, *Interaction concepts of personality.* Chicago: Aldine, 1969. Pp. v-viii.

HENDERSON, N. D. Brain weight increases reulting from environmental enrichment: A directional dominance in mice. *Science,* 1970, **169,** 776–78.

HERRNSTEIN, R. I.Q. *Atlantic,* 1971, **228** (3), 44–64.

HERSEY, J. *The Algiers Motel incident.* New York: Alfred A. Knopf, 1968.

HESS, E. H. Attitude and pupil size. *Scientific American,* 1965, **212,** 46–54.

HESS, E. H. Pupillometric assessment. *Research in Psychotherapy,* 1968, **3,** 573–83.

HESS, E. H., & POLT, J. M. Pupil size as related to interest value of visual stimuli. *Science,* 1960, **132,** 349–50.

HESS, E. H., & POLT, J. M. Changes in pupil size as a measure of taste difference. *Perceptual and Motor Skills,* 1966, **23,** 451–55.

HILER, E. W. Wechsler-Bellevue intelligence as a predictor of continuation in psychotherapy. *Journal of Clinical Psychology,* 1958, **14,** 192–94.

HILGARD, E. R. Human motives and the concept of the self. *American Psychologist,* 1949, **4,** 374–82.

HILGARD, E. R., JONES, L. V., & KAPLAN, S. J. Conditioned discrimination as related to anxiety. *Journal of Experimental Psychology,* 1951, **42,** 94–99.

HODGES, L. A., & BYRNE, D. Verbal dogmatism as a potentiator of intolerance. *Journal of Personality and Social Psychology,* 1972, **21,** 312–17.

HODGES, W. F., & SPIELBERGER, C. D. The effects of threat of shock on heart rate for subjects who differ in manifest anxiety and fear of shock. *Psychophysiology,* 1966, **2,** 287–94.

HOGAN, R. Moral conduct and moral character: A psychological perspective. *Psychological Bulletin,* 1973, **79,** 217–32.

HOKANSON, J .E. Psychophysiological evaluation of the catharsis hypothesis. In E. I. Megargee and J. E. Hokanson (eds.), *The dynamics of aggression.* New York: Harper & Row, 1970. Pp. 74–86.

HOKANSON, J. E., & BURGESS, M. The effects of three types of aggression on vascular processes. *Journal of Abnormal and Social Psychology,* 1962, **64,** 446–49.

HOKANSON, J. E., BURGESS, M., & COHEN, M. F. Effects of displaced aggression on systolic blood pressure. *Journal of Abnormal and Social Psychology,* 1963, **67,** 214–18.

HOKANSON, J. E., & EDELMAN, R. Effects of three social responses on vascular processes. *Journal of Personality and Social Psychology,* 1966, **3,** 442–47.

HOKANSON, J. E., & SHETLER, S. The effect of overt aggression on physiological arousal. *Journal of Abnormal and Social Psychology,* 1961, **63,** 446–48.

HOKANSON, J. E., WILLERS, K. R., & KOROPSAK, E. The modification of autonomic responses during aggressive interchange. *Journal of Personality,* 1968, **36,** 386–404.

HOLLENDER, J. Sex differences in sources of social self-esteem. *Journal of Consulting and Clinical Psychology,* 1972, **38,** 343–47.

HOLMES, D. S. Conscious self-appraisal of achievement motivation: The self-peer rank method revisited. *Journal of Consulting and Clinical Psychology,* 1971, **36,** 23–26.

HOLT, R. R. Individuality and generalization in the psychology of personality. *Journal of Personality,* 1962, **30,** 377–404.

HOLTZMAN, W. H., THORPE, J. S., SWARTZ, J. D., & HERON, E. W. *Inkblot perception and personality.* Austin: University of Texas Press, 1961.

HOLTZMAN, W. H., & YOUNG, R. K. Scales for measuring attitudes toward the Negro and toward organized religion. *Psychological Reports,* 1966, **18,** 31–34.

HOOK, E. B., & KIM, D. S. Height and antisocial behavior in XY and XYY boys. *Science,* 1971, **172,** 284–86.

HORNER, M. Sex differences in achievement motivation and performance in competitive and noncompetitive situations. Unpublished doctoral dissertation, University of Michigan, 1968.

HORNER, M. The motive to avoid success and changing aspirations of college women. In J. M. Bardwick (ed.), *Readings on the psychology of women.* New York: Harper & Row, 1972. Pp. 62–67.

HORTON, C. P., & CRUMP, E. P. Growth and development: XI. Descriptive analysis of the backgrounds of 76 Negro children whose scores are above or below average in the Merrill-Palmer scale of mental tests at three years of age. *Journal of Genetic Psychology,* 1962, **100,** 255–65.

HOUSTON, B. K., OLSON, M., & BOTKIN, A. Trait anxiety and beliefs regarding danger and threat to self esteem. *Journal of Consulting and Clinical Psychology,* 1972, **38,** 152.

HOWARD, J. L., REIFLER, C. B., & LIPTZIN, M. B. Effects of exposure to pornography. In *Technical Report of the Commission on Obscenity and Pornography.* Vol. VIII. Washington, D.C.: U.S. Government Printing Office, 1971. Pp. 97–132.

HOYT, D. P., & MAGOON, T. M. A validation study of the Taylor Manifest Anxiety Scale. *Journal of Clinical Psychology,* 1954, **10,** 357–61.

HULL, C. L. *Principles of behavior.* New York: Appleton-Century-Crofts, 1943.

HULL, C. L. *A behavior system.* New Haven, Conn.: Yale University Press, 1952.

HUNT, J. McV. *Intelligence and experience.* New York: Ronald, 1961.

IMMERGLUCK, L. Determinism-freedom in contemporary psychology: An ancient problem revisited. *American Psychologist*, 1964, **19**, 270–81.

ISON, M. G. The effect of "thorazine" on Wechsler scores. *American Journal of Mental Deficiency*, 1957, **62**, 543–47.

IZZETT, R. R. Authoritarianism and attitudes toward the Vietnam war as reflected in behavioral and self-report measures. *Journal of Personality and Social Psychology*, 1971, **17**, 145–48.

JACKSON, D. N., & MESSICK, S. J. Content and style in personality assessment. *Psychological Bulletin*, 1958, **55**, 243–52.

JACOBS, P. A., BRUNTON, M., MELVILLE, M. M., BRITTAIN, R. P., & McCLEMONT, W. F. Aggressive behavior, mental subnormality, and the XYY male. *Nature*, 1965, **208**, 1351–52.

JACOBSON, F. N., & RETTIG, S. Authoritarianism and intelligence. *Journal of Social Psychology*, 1959, **50**, 213–19.

JAKOBOVITS, L. A. Evaluational reactions to erotic literature. *Psychological Reports*, 1965, **16**, 985–94.

JAMES, W. *The principles of psychology.* New York: Dover, 1950.

JENKINS, J. J., & PATERSON, D. G. (eds.), *Studies in individual differences.* New York: Appleton-Century-Crofts, 1961.

JENSEN, A. R. How much can we boost IQ and scholastic achievement? *Harvard Educational Review*, 1969, **39**, 1–123. (a)

JENSEN, A. R. Heredity and environment: A controversy over IQ and scholastic achievement. *Berkeley Centennial Fund, University of California*, 1969, **2** (4), 4–6. (b)

JENSEN, A. R. *Environment, heredity, and intelligence.* Cambridge, Mass.: *Harvard Educational Review*, 1969. (c)

JINKS, J. L., & FULKER, D. W. Comparison of the biometrical genetical, MAVA, and classical approaches to the analysis of human behavior. *Psychological Bulletin*, 1970, **73**, 311–49.

JOHNSON, D. T. Effects of interview stress on measures of state and trait anxiety. *Journal of Abnormal Psychology*, 1968, **73**, 245–51.

JOHNSON, D. T., & SPIELBERGER, C. D. The effects of relaxation training and the passage of time on measures of state- and trait-anxiety. *Journal of Clinical Psychology*, 1968, **24**, 20–23.

JOLLY, A. Lemur social behavior and primate intelligence. *Science*, 1966, **153**, 501–6.

JONES, M. B. Religious values and authoritarian tendency. *Journal of Social Psychology*, 1958, **48**, 83–89.

JONES, H. E., & CONRAD, H. S. The growth and decline of intelligence. *Genetic Psychology Monographs*, 1933, **13**, 223–98.

JOURARD, S. M., & REMY, R. M. Perceived parental attitudes, the self, and security. *Journal of Consulting Psychology*, 1955, **19**, 364–66.

JUNG, C. G. *Psychological types.* London: Routledge & Kegan Paul, 1923.

JUNG, C. G. *Two essays on analytical psychology,* London: Bailliere, Tindall, and Cox, 1928.

JUNG, C. G. *Modern man in search of a soul.* New York: Harcourt, Brace & World, 1933.

JUNG, C. G. *The integration of the personality.* New York: Farrar & Rinehart, 1939.

JUNG, C. G. *Freud and psychoanalysis.* Vol. 4 of H. Read, M. Fordham, and G. Adler (eds.), *The collected works of C. G. Jung.* New York: Pantheon, 1961.

JUNG, C. G. *Memories, dreams, reflections.* New York: Pantheon, 1963.

KAATS, G. R., & DAVIS, K. E. Effects of volunteer biases in studies of sexual behavior and attitudes. *Journal of Sex Research,* 1971, **7,** 26–34.

KAGAN, J. Acquisition and significance of sex typing and sex role identity. In M. L. Hoffman and L. W. Hoffman (eds.), *Review of child development research.* Vol. 1. New York: Russell Sage Foundation, 1964.

KAGAN, J. The magical aura of the IQ. *Saturday Review,* 1971, **54** (49), 92–93.

KAGAN, J., & MOSS, H. A. *Birth to maturity: A study in psychological development.* New York: Wiley, 1962.

KAGITCIBASI, C. Social norms and authoritarianism: A Turkish-American comparison. *Journal of Personality and Social Psychology,* 1970, **16,** 444–51.

KAHN, R. L., POLLACK, M., & FINK, M. Social attitude (California F Scale) and convulsive therapy. *Journal of Nervous and Mental Diseases,* 1960, **130,** 187–92.

KAPLAN, H. B. Self-derogation and adjustment to recent life experience. *Achives of General Psychiatry,* 1970, **22,** 324–31.

KAPLAN, H. B., & POKORNY, A. D. Self-derogation and psychosocial adjustment. *Journal of Nervous and Mental Disease,* 1969, **149,** 421–34.

KAPLAN, H. B., & POKORNY, A. D. Age-related correlates of self-derogation: Report of childhood experiences. *British Journal of Psychiatry,* 1970, **117,** 533–34. (a)

KAPLAN, H. B., & POKORNY, A. D. Aging and self-attitude: A conditional relationship. *Aging and Human Development,* 1970, **1,** 241–50. (b)

KAPLAN, H. B., & POKORNY, A. D. Self-derogation and childhood broken home. *Journal of Marriage and the Family,* 1971, **33,** 328–37.

KATAHN, M. Interaction of anxiety and ability in complex learning situations. *Journal of Personality and Social Psychology,* 1966, **3,** 475–79.

KATAHN, M., BLANTON, R. L., & GIPSON, M. T. Speed and amplitude of response as a function of anxiety and degree of conflict. *Journal of Experimental Research in Personality,* 1967, **2,** 169–72.

KAUFMAN, I. C., & ROSENBLUM, L. A. Depression in infant monkeys separated from their mothers. *Science,* 1967, **155,** 1030–31.

KELLEY, H. H. Moral evaluation. *American Psychologist,* 1971, **26,** 293–300.

KELLY, E. L. Consistency of the adult personality. *American Psychologist,* 1955, **10,** 659–81.

KELLY, E. L., & FISKE, D. W. *The prediction of performance in clinical psychology.* Ann Arbor: University of Michigan Press, 1951.

KELLY, G. A. Man's construction of his alternatives. In G. Lindzey (ed.), *Assessment of human motives.* New York: Rinehart, 1958. Pp. 33–64.

KELLY, J. G., FERSON, J. E., & HOLTZMAN, W. H. The measurement of attitudes toward the Negro in the South. *Journal of Social Psychology,* 1958, **48,** 305–17.

KELMAN, H. C., & BARCLAY, J. The F Scale as a measure of breadth of perspective. *Journal of Abnormal and Social Psychology,* 1963, **67,** 608–15.

KENDLER, H. H. Kenneth W. Spence: 1907–1967. *Psychological Review,* 1967, **74,** 335–41.

KENNY, D. T., & GINSBERG, R. The specificity of intolerance of ambiguity measures. *Journal of Abnormal and Social Psychology,* 1958, **56,** 300–304.

KERLINGER, F. Social attitudes and their criterial referents. *Psychological Review,* 1967, **74,** 110–22.

KINSEY, A. C., POMEROY, W. B., & MARTIN, C. E. *Sexual behavior in the human male.* Philadelphia: Saunders, 1948.

KINSEY, A. C., POMEROY, W. B., MARTIN, C. E., & GEBHARD, P. H. *Sexual behavior in the human female.* Philadelphia: Saunders, 1953.

KIRK, S. A. *Early education of the mentally retarded.* Urbana: University of Illinois Press, 1958.

KLEIN, E. B. Stylistic components of response as related to attitude change. *Journal of Personality,* 1963, **31,** 38–51.

KLEIN, S. *Control of style with a generative grammar.* Santa Monica, Calif.: SP 1633 System Development Corporation, 1964.

KLINEBERG, O. *Negro intelligence and selective migration.* New York: Columbia University Press, 1935.

KLINEBERG, O. Negro-white differences in intelligence test performance: A new look at an old problem. *American Psychologist,* 1963, **18,** 198–203.

KLINEBERG, O. Black and white in international perspective. *American Psychologist,* 1971, **26,** 119–28.

KLINGER, E. Modeling effects on achievement imagery. *Journal of Personality and Social Psychology,* 1967, **7,** 49–62.

KNAPP, R. H., & GARBUTT, J. T. Time imagery and the achievement motive. *Journal of Personality,* 1958, **26,** 426–34.

KNOBLOCH, H., & PASAMANICK, B. Further observations on the behavioral development of Negro children. *Journal of Genetic Psychology,* 1953, **83,** 137–57.

KOCH, M. B., & MEYER, D. R. A relationship of mental age to learning-set formation in the pre-school child. *Journal of Comparative and Physiological Psychology,* 1959, **52,** 387–89.

KOGAN, N. Authoritarianism and repression. *Journal of Abnormal and Social Psychology,* 1956, **53,** 34–37.

KOHLBERG, L. The development of children's orientations toward a moral order: 1. Sequence in the development of moral thought. *Human Development,* 1963, **6,** 11–33. (a)

KOHLBERG, L. Moral development and identification. In H. Stevenson (ed.), *Child psychology.* Chicago: University of Chicago Press, 1963. Pp. 383–431. (b)

KOLB, D. A. Achievement motivation training for underachieving high school boys. *Journal of Personality and Social Psychology,* in press.

KOOCHER, G. P. Swimming, competence, and personality change. *Journal of Personality and Social Psychology,* 1971, **18,** 275–78.

KRAMES, L., COSTANZO, D. J., & CARR, W. J. Responses of rats to odors from novel versus original sex partners. *Proceedings, 75th Annual Convention, APA,* 1967, 117–18.

KREBS, A. M. Two determinants of conformity: Age of independence training and *n* Achievement. *Journal of Abnormal and Social Psychology,* 1958, **56,** 130–31.

KUHLEN, R. G. Personality change with age. In P. Worchel and D. Byrne (eds.), *Personality change.* New York: Wiley, 1964. Pp. 524–55.

KUHN, T. S. *The structure of scientific revolutions.* Chicago: University of Chicago Press, 1970.

KUTNER, S. J. Sex guilt and the sexual behavior sequence. *Journal of Sex Research,* 1971, **7,** 107–15.

KUTSCHINSKY, B. Pornography in Denmark: Pieces of a jigsaw puzzle collected around New Year 1970. In *Technical Report of the Commission on Obscenity and Pornography.* Vol. IV. Washington, D.C.: U.S. Government Printing Office, 1971. Pp. 263–88. (a)

KUTSCHINSKY, B. The effect of pornography: A pilot experiment on perception, behavior, and attitudes. In *Technical Report of the Commission on Obscenity and Pornography*. Vol. VIII. Washington, D.C.: U.S. Government Printing Office, 1971. Pp. 133–69. (b)

LACEY, J. I., & LACEY, B. C. Verification and extension of the principle of autonomic response-stereotype. *American Journal of Psychology*, 1958, **71**, 50–73.

LAMBERTH, J., & CRAIG, L. Differential magnitude of reward and magnitude shifts using attitudinal stimuli. *Journal of Experimental Research in Personality*, 1970, **4**, 281–85.

LAMBERTH, J. & PADD, W. Student's attitudes and absenteeism: A possible link. *Psychological Reports*, 1972, **31**, 35–40.

LAMM, R. D. Urban growing pains. Is bigger also better? *The New Republic*, 1971, **164** (23), 17–19.

LANDY, D., & METTEE, D. Evaluation of an aggressor as a function of exposure to cartoon humor. *Journal of Personality and Social Psychology*, 1969, **12**, 66–71.

LANE, E. A., & ALBEE, G. W. Early childhood intellectual differences between schizophrenic adults and their sibling. *Journal of Abnormal and Social Psychology*, 1964, **68**, 193–95.

LATENÉ, B. Field studies of altruistic compliance. *Representative Research in Social Psychology*, 1970, **1**, 49–61.

LATANÉ, B., & DARLEY, J. M. Group inhibition of bystander intervention in emergencies. *Journal of Personality and Social Psychology*, 1968, **10**, 215–21.

LATANÉ, B., & DARLEY, J. M. *The unresponsive bystander: Why doesn't he help?* New York: Appleton-Century-Crofts, 1970.

LATANÉ, B., & RODIN, J. A lady in distress: Inhibiting effects of friends and strangers on bystander intervention. *Journal of Experimental Social Psychology*, 1969, **5**, 189–202.

LAWS, D. R., & RUBIN, H. B. Instructional control of an autonomic sexual response. *Journal of Applied Behavior Analysis*, 1969, **2**, 93–99.

LAZARUS, R. S. *Psychological stress and the coping process*. New York: McGraw-Hill, 1966.

LEE, E. S. Negro intelligence and selective migration: A Philadelphia test of Klineberg's hypothesis. *American Sociological Review*, 1951, **61**, 227–33.

LEE, L. C. The effects of anxiety level and shock on a paired-associate verbal task. *Journal of Experimental Psychology*, 1961, **61**, 213–17.

LEIMAN, A. H., & EPSTEIN, S. Thematic sexual responses as related to sexual drive and guilt. *Journal of Abnormal and Social Psychology*, 1961, **63**, 169–75.

LERNER, M. J. The desire for justice and reactions to victims. In J. Macaulay and L. Berkowitz (eds.), *Altruism and helping behavior*. New York: Academic Press, 1970. Pp. 205–29.

LESSER, G. S., KRAWITZ, R. N., & PACKARD, R. Experimental arousal of achievement motivation in adolescent girls. *Journal of Abnormal and Social Psychology*, 1963, **66**, 59–66.

LESTER, L. F., & CROWNE, D. P. A strict behavioral test of obedience and some childrearing correlates. *Personality: An International Journal*, 1970, **1**, 85–93.

LEVENTHAL, H., JACOBS, R. L. & KUDIRKA, N. Z. Authoritarianism, ideology and political candidate choice. *Journal of Abnormal and Social Psychology*, 1964, **69**, 539–49.

LEVINE, M., SPIVACK, G., FUSCHILLO, J., & TAVERNIER, A. Intelligence and measures of inhibition and time sense. *Journal of Clinical Psychology*, 1959, **15**, 224–26.

LEVINE, R. *Dreams and deeds: Achievement motivation in Nigeria*. Chicago: University of Chicago Press, 1966.

LEVINGER, G., & BREEDLOVE, J. Interpersonal attraction and agreement: A study of marriage partners. *Journal of Personality and Social Psychology*, 1966, **3**, 367–72.

LEVINSON, D. J., & HUFFMAN, P. E. Traditional family ideology and its relation to personality. *Journal of Personality*, 1955, **23**, 251–73.

LEVITT, E. E. The effect of a "causal" teacher training program on authoritarianism and responsibility in grade school children. *Psychological Reports*, 1955, **1**, 449–58.

LEVITT, E. E., & BRADY, J. P. Sexual preferences in young adult males and some correlates. *Journal of Clinical Psychology*, 1965, **21**, 347–54.

LEVITT, E. E., & HINESLEY, R. K. Some factors in the valences of erotic visual stimuli. *Journal of Sex Research*, 1967, **3**, 63–68.

LEWIS, M., & MCGURK, H. Evaluation of infant intelligence. *Science*, 1972, **178**, 1174–77.

LIBBY, R. W., & NASS, G. D. Parental views on teenage sexual behavior. *Journal of Sex Research*, 1971, **7**, 226–36.

LIEBERT, R. M., & BARON, R. A. Some immediate effects of televised violence on children's behavior. *Developmental Psychology*, 1972, **6**, 469–75.

LINDGREN, H. C. Authoritarianism, independence, and child-centered practices in education: A study of attitudes. *Psychological Reports*, 1962, **10**, 747–50.

LIPPMANN, W. The university. *New Republic*, 1966, **154** (22), 17–20.

LISK, R. D. Mechanisms regulating sexual activity in mammals. *Journal of Sex Research*, 1970, **6**, 220–28.

LITTIG, L. W., & YERACARIS, C. A. Academic achievement correlates of achievement and affiliation motivations. *Journal of Psychology*, 1963, **55**, 115–19.

LITTIG, L. W., & YERACARIS, C. A. Achievement motivation and intergenerational occupational mobility. *Journal of Personality and Social Psychology*, 1965, **1**, 386–89.

LITTLE, K. B., & SCHNEIDMAN, E. S. Congruencies among interpretations of psychological test and anamnestic data. *Psychological Monographs*, 1959, **73** (6, Whole no. 476).

LIVSON, N., & PESKIN, H. Prediction of adult psychological health in a longitudinal study. *Journal of Abnormal Psychology*, 1967, **72**, 509–18.

LOFTON, J. A perspective from the public at large. *American Psychologist*, 1972, **27**, 364–66.

LONDON, O. H. Interpersonal attraction and abilities: Social desirability or similarity to self? Unpublished master's thesis, University of Texas, 1967.

LORENZ, K. *On aggression*. New York: Harcourt, Brace, and World, 1966.

LORGE, I. Schooling makes a difference. *Teachers College Record*, 1945, **46**, 483–92.

LOTT, A. J. The potential power of liking as a factor in social change. Paper presented at the meeting of the Southwestern Psychological Association, Austin, Texas, May, 1969.

LOTT, A. J., & LOTT, B. E. Group cohesiveness and individual learning. *Journal of Educational Psychology*, 1966, **57**, 61–73.

LOTT, B. E., & LOTT, A. J. The formation of positive attitudes toward group members. *Journal of Abnormal and Social Psychology,* 1960, **61,** 297–300.

LOWELL, E. L. The effect of need for achievement on learning and performance. *Journal of Psychology,* 1952, **33,** 31–40.

LUTTGE, W. G. The role of gonadal hormones in the sexual behavior of the Rhesus monkey and human: A literature survey. *Archives of Sexual Behavior,* 1971, **1,** 61–88.

LYNES, R. After hours. Ouch! *Harper's,* 1968, **237** (1420), 23–26.

MACCOBY, E. (ed.). *The development of sex differences.* Stanford: Stanford University Press, 1966.

MACKINNON, D. W. Violation of prohibitions. In H. A. Murray, *Explorations in personality.* Oxford: Oxford University Press, 1938. Pp. 491–501.

MACKINTOSH, J. H. Territory formation by laboratory mice. *Animal Behavior,* 1970, **18,** 177–83.

MAHLER, I. Attitudes toward socialized medicine. *Journal of Social Psychology,* 1953, **38,** 273–82.

MALLER, J. B. Mental ability and its relation to physical health and social economic status. *Psychological Clinic,* 1933, **22,** 101–7.

MANDLER, G., MANDLER, J. M., KREMEN, I., & SHOLITAN, R. D. The response to threat: Relations among verbal and physiological indices. *Psychological Monographs,* 1961, **75** (Whole no. 513).

MANDLER, G., & SARASON, S. B. A study of anxiety and learning. *Journal of Abnormal and Social Psychology,* 1952, **47,** 166–73.

MANN, J. Experimental induction of human sexual arousal. In *Technical Report of the Commission on Obscenity and Pornography.* Vol. I. Washington, D.C.: U.S. Government Printing Office, 1971. Pp. 23–60.

MARKWELL, E. D., JR., WHEELER, W. M., & KITZINGER, H. Changes in Wechsler-Bellevue test performance following prefrontal lobotomy. *Journal of Consulting Psychology,* 1953, **17,** 229–31.

MARTIN, J. D. Note on a mathematical "theory" of coital frequency in marriage. *Journal of Sex Research,* 1970, **6,** 326–31.

MARX, M. H. The general nature of theory construction. In M. H. Marx (ed.), *Psychological theory.* New York: Macmillan, 1951. Pp. 4–19.

MASELLI, M. D., & ALTROCCHI, J. Attribution of intent. *Psychological Bulletin,* 1969, **71,** 445–54.

MASLING, J. M. How neurotic is the authoritarian? *Journal of Abnormal and Social Psychology,* 1954, **33,** 21–42.

MASLOW, A. H., & SAKODA, J. M. Volunteer-error in the Kinsey study. *Journal of Abnormal and Social Psychology,* 1952, **47,** 259–67.

MASTERS, W. H., & JOHNSON, V. *Human sexual response.* Boston: Little, Brown, 1966.

MATARAZZO, J. D., GUZE, S. B., & MATARAZZO, R. G. An approach to the validity of the Taylor Anxiety Scale: Scores of medical and psychiatric patients. *Journal of Abnormal and Social Psychology,* 1955, **51,** 276–80.

MATARAZZO, R. G., MATARAZZO, J. D., & SASLOW, G. The relationship between medical and psychiatric symptoms. *Journal of Abnormal and Social Psychology,* 1961, **62,** 55–61.

Mausner, B. Entrepreneurial behavior. *Contemporary Psychology,* 1963, **8,** 291–92.

McCall, R. B., & Lester, M. L. Differential enrichment potential of visual experience with angles versus curves. *Journal of Comparative and Physiological Psychology,* 1969, **69,** 644–48.

McClelland, D. C. *Personality.* New York: Holt, Rinehart & Winston, 1951.

McClelland, D. C. Some social consequences of achievement motivation. In M. R. Jones (ed.), *Nebraska symposium on motivation 1955.* Lincoln: University of Nebraska Press, 1955.

McClelland, D. C. Methods of measuring human motivation. In J. W. Atkinson (ed.), *Motives in fantasy, action, and society.* Princeton: Van Nostrand, 1958. Pp. 7–42.

McClelland, D. C. *The achieving society.* Princeton: Van Nostrand, 1961.

McClelland, D. C. *n* Achievement and entrepreneurship: A longitudinal study. *Journal of Personality and Social Psychology,* 1965, **1,** 389–92. (a)

McClelland, D. C. Toward a theory of motive acquisition. *American Psychologist,* 1965, **20,** 321–33. (b)

McClelland, D. C., Atkinson, J. W., Clark, R. A., & Lowell, E. L. *The achievement motive.* New York: Appleton-Century-Crofts, 1953.

McClelland, D. C., Clark, R. A., Roby, T. B., & Atkinson, J. W. The effect of the need for achievement on thematic apperception. *Journal of Experimental Psychology,* 1949, **37,** 242–55.

McClelland, D. C., Rindlisbacher, A., & de Charms, R. C. Religious and other sources of parental attitudes toward independence training. In D. C. McClelland (ed.), *Studies in motivation.* New York: Appleton-Century-Crofts, 1955.

McClelland, D. C., & Winter, D. G. *Motivating economic achievement.* New York: Free Press, 1969.

McDonald, R. D. The effect of reward-punishment and affiliation need on interpersonal attraction. Unpublished doctoral dissertation, University of Texas, 1962.

McFarland, R. L., Nelson, C. L., & Rossi, A. M. Prediction of participation in group psychotherapy from measures of intelligence and verbal behavior. *Psychological Reports,* 1962, **11,** 291–98.

McGuire, W. J. Vital statistics. *Personality-Social Newsletter,* May 1968, 1–2.

McNemar, Q. Lost: Our intelligence? Why? *American Psychologist,* 1964, **19,** 871–82.

McNemar, Q. *Psychological statistics,* New York: Wiley, 1969.

McWhirter, R. M., & Jecker, J. D. Attitude similarity and inferred attraction. *Psychonomic Science,* 1967, **7,** 225–26.

Mead, G. H. *Mind, self and society.* Chicago: University of Chicago Press, 1934.

Meade, R. D. Achievement motivation, achievement, and psychological time. *Journal of Personality and Social Psychology,* 1966, **4,** 577–80.

Meehl, P. E. The cognitive activity of the clinician. *American Psychologist,* 1960, **15,** 19–27.

Meer, S. J. Authoritarian attitudes and dreams. *Journal of Abnormal and Social Psychology,* 1955, **5,** 74–78.

Megargee, E. I. Undercontrolled and overcontrolled personality types in extreme antisocial aggression. *Psychological Monographs,* 1966, **80** (Whole no. 611).

Megargee, E. I. Conscientious objectors' scores on the MMPI *O-H* (Overcontrolled Hostility) Scale. *Proceedings, 77th Annual Convention, APA,* 1969, 507–8.

MEGARGEE, E. I., COOK, P. E., & MENDELSOHN, G. A. The development and validation of an MMPI scale of assaultiveness in overcontrolled individuals. *Journal of Abnormal Psychology,* 1967, **72,** 519–28.

MEHRABIAN, A. *An analysis of personality theories.* Englewood Cliffs, N.J.: Prentice-Hall, 1968. (a)

MEHRABIAN, A. Relationship of attitude to seated posture, orientation, and distance. *Journal of Personality and Social Psychology,* 1968, **10,** 26–30. (b)

MEHRABIAN, A. Male and female scales of the tendency to achieve. *Educational and Psychological Measurement,* 1968, **28,** 493–502. (c)

MENACHEM, A. *Patterns in forcible rape.* Chicago: University of Chicago Press, 1971.

MERRICK, R., & TAYLOR, S. P. Aggression as a function of vulnerability to attack. *Psychonomic Science,* 1970, **20,** 203–4.

MERRITT, D. L. The relationships between qualifications and attitudes in a teacher selection situation. Unpublished doctoral dissertation, Syracuse University, 1970.

MEYER, H. H., WALKER, W. B., & LITWIN, G. H. Motive patterns and risk preferences associated with entrepreneurship. *Journal of Abnormal and Social Psychology,* 1961, **63,** 570–74.

MICHAEL, R. P., KEVERNE, E. B., & BONSALL, R. W. Pheromones: Isolation of male sex attractants from a female primate. *Science,* 1971, **172,** 964–66.

MILGRAM, S. Behavioral study of obedience. *Journal of Abnormal and Social Psychology,* 1963, **67,** 371–78.

MILGRAM, S. Some conditions of obedience and disobedience to authority. *Human Relations,* 1965, **18,** 57–76.

MILLER, N. E. The frustration-aggression hypothesis. *Psychological Review,* 1941, **48,** 337–42.

MILLER, N. E. Studies of fear as an acquirable drive: I. Fear as motivation and fear-reduction as reinforcement in the learning of new responses. *Journal of Experimental Psychology,* 1948, **38,** 89–101. (a)

MILLER, N. E. Theory and experiment relating psychoanalytic displacement to stimulus-response generalization. *Journal of Abnormal and Social Psychology,* 1948, **43,** 155–78. (b)

MILLER, N. E., & DOLLARD, J. *Social learning and imitation.* New Haven: Yale University Press, 1941.

MILTON, W., & WAITE, B. Presidential preference and traditional family values. *American Psychologist,* 1964, **19,** 844–45.

MINOR, C. A., & NEEL, R. G. The relationship between achievement motive and occupational preference. *Journal of Counseling Psychology,* 1958, **5,** 39–43.

MISCHEL, W. Preference for delayed reinforcement: An experimental study of a cultural observation. *Journal of Abnormal and Social Psychology,* 1958, **56,** 57–61.

MISCHEL, W. Delay of gratification, need for achievement, and acquiescence in another culture. *Journal of Abnormal and Social Psychology,* 1961, **62,** 543–52.

MISCHEL, W. Theory and research on the antecedents of self-imposed delay of reward. In B. A. Maher (ed.), *Progress in experimental personality research.* Vol. 3. New York: Academic Press, 1966. Pp. 85–132.

MISCHEL, W. *Personality and assessment.* New York: Wiley, 1968.

MISCHEL, W. Continuity and change in personality. *American Psychologist,* 1969, **24,** 1012–18.

MISCHEL, W., & GILLIGAN, C. Delay of gratification, motivation for the prohibited gratification, and responses to temptation. *Journal of Abnormal and Social Psychology*, 1964, **69,** 411–17.

MISCHEL, W., & METZNER, R. Preference for delayed reward as a function of age, intelligence, and length of delay interval. *Journal of Abnormal and Social Psychology*, 1962, **64,** 425–31.

MISCHEL, W., & SCHOPLER, J. Authoritarianism and reactions to "sputniks." *Journal of Abnormal and Social Psychology*, 1959, **59,** 142–45.

MITCHELL, G. D., ARLING, G. L., & MØLLER, G. W. Long-term effects of maternal punishment on the behavior of monkeys. *Psychonomic Science*, 1967, **8,** 209–10.

MITCHELL, G. D., HARLOW, H. F., GRIFFIN, G. A., & MØLLER, G. W. Repeated maternal separation in the monkey. *Psychonomic Science*, 1967, **8,** 197–98.

MITCHELL, H. E., & BYRNE, D. The defendant's dilemma: Effects of jurors' attitudes and authoritarianism on judicial decisions. *Journal of Personality and Social Psychology*, 1973, **25,** 123–29.

MONTAGU, A. *Human heredity.* New York: New American Library, 1959.

MOORE, J. C., JR., & KRUPAT, E. Relationships between source status, authoritarianism, and conformity in a social influence setting. *Sociometry*, 1971, **34,** 122–34.

MOORE, R. *The country team.* New York: Crown, 1967.

MORGAN, H. H. Measuring achievement motivation with "picture interpretations." *Journal of Consulting Psychology*, 1953, **17,** 289–92.

MORGAN, J. N. Entrepreneurial behavior. *Contemporary Psychology*, 1963, **8,** 289–91.

MOSHER, D L. The development and validation of a sentence completion measure of guilt. Unpublished doctoral dissertation, Ohio State University, 1961.

MOSHER, D. L. The development and multitrait-multimethod matrix analysis of three measures of three aspects of guilt. *Journal of Consulting Psychology*, 1966, **30,** 25–29.

MOSHER, D. L. Measurement of guilt in females by self-report inventories. *Journal of Consulting and Clinical Psychology*, 1968, **32,** 690–95.

MOSHER, D. L. Psychological reactions to pornographic films. In *Technical Report of the Commission on Obscenity and Pornography.* Vol. VIII. Washington, D.C.: U.S. Government Printing Office, 1971. Pp. 255–312.

MOSHER, D. L., & CROSS, H. J. Sex guilt and premarital sexual experiences of college students. *Journal of Consulting and Clinical Psychology*, 1971, **36,** 27–32.

MOSS, H. A., & KAGAN, J. Stability of achievement and recognition seeking behaviors from early childhood through adulthood. *Journal of Abnormal and Social Psychology*, 1961, **62,** 504–18.

MOSS, M. K. Social desirability, physical attractiveness, and social choice. Unpublished doctoral dissertation, Kansas State University, 1969.

MOSS, M. K., & PAGE, R. A. Reinforcement and helping behavior. *Journal of Applied Social Psychology*, 1972, **2,** 360–71.

MOWRER, O. H. Neurosis, psychotherapy, and two-factor learning theory. In O. H. Mowrer (ed.), *Psychotherapy: Theory and research.* New York: Ronald Press, 1953.

MOYER, K. E. The physiology of aggression and the implications for aggression control. In J. L. Singer (ed.), *The control of aggression and violence: Cognitive and physiological factors.* New York: Academic Press, 1971. Pp. 61–92.

MUKHERJEE, B. N., & SINHA, R. Achievement values and self-ideal discrepancies in college students. *Personality: An International Journal*, 1970, **1**, 275–301.

MURRAY, E. J. Direct analysis from the viewpoint of learning theory. *Journal of Consulting Psychology*, 1962, **26**, 226–31.

MURRAY, E. J. Sociotropic-learning approach to psychotherapy. In P. Worchel and D. Byrne (eds.), *Personality change*. New York: Wiley, 1964. Pp. 249–88.

MURRAY, H. A. *Explorations in personality* (1938). New York: Science Editions, 1962.

MURRAY, H. A. What should psychologists do about psychoanalysis? *Journal of Abnormal and Social Psychology*, 1940, **34**, 150–75.

MURRAY, H. A. Preparations for the scaffold of a comprehensive system. In S. Koch (ed.), *Psychology: A study of a science*. Vol. 3. New York: McGraw-Hill, 1959. Pp. 7–54.

MURSTEIN, B. I. *Theory and research in projective techniques*. New York: Wiley, 1963.

MUSSEN, P. H., & SCODEL, A. The effects of sexual stimulation under varying conditions on TAT sexual responsiveness. *Journal of Consulting Psychology*, 1955, **19**, 90.

NADLER, E. B. Yielding, authoritarianism, and authoritarian ideology regarding groups. *Journal of Abnormal and Social Psychology*, 1959, **58**, 408–10.

NAWY, H. The San Francisco erotic marketplace. In *Technical Report of the Commission on Obscenity and Pornography*. Vol. IV. Washington, D.C.: U.S. Government Printing Office, 1971. Pp. 155–224.

NEI, M., & ROYCHOUDHURY, A. K. Gene differences between caucasion, Negro, and Japanese populations. *Science*, 1972, **177**, 434–36.

NELSON, D., & MEADOW, B. L. Attitude similarity, interpersonal attraction, actual success, and the evaluative perception of that success. Paper presented at the meeting of the APA, Washington, D.C., September, 1971.

NEWCOMB, T. M. The prediction of interpersonal attraction. *American Psychologist*, 1956, **11**, 575–86.

NEWCOMB, T. M. *The acquaintance process*. New York: Holt, Rinehart, & Winston, 1961.

NEWCOMB, T., & SVEHLA, G. Intra-family relationships in attitudes. *Sociometry*, 1937, **1**, 180–205.

NEWELL, A., SHAW, J. C., & SIMON, H. A. Chess-playing programs and the problem of complexity. *IBM Journal of Research and Development*, 1958, **2**, 320–35.

NEWMAN, H. H., FREEMAN, F. N., HOLZINGER, K. J. *Twins: A study of heredity and environment*. Chicago: University of Chicago Press, 1937.

NEWMAN, O. *Defensible space*. New York: Macmillan, 1972.

NICHOLLS, J. G. Creativity in the person who will never produce anything original and useful: The concept of creativity as a normally distributed trait. *American Psychologist*, 1972, **27**, 717–27.

NISBETT, R. E., SCHACHTER, S. Cognitive manipulation of pain. *Journal of Experimental Social Psychology*, 1966, **2**, 227–36.

NOONAN, J. R., BARRY, J. R., & DAVIS, H. C. Personality determinants in attitudes toward visible disability. *Journal of Personality*, 1970, **38**, 1–15.

NUNNALLY, J. C., KNOTT, P. D., DUCHNOWSKI, A., & PARKER, R. Pupillary response as a general measure of activation. *Perception and Psychophysics*, 1967, **2**, 149–55.

O'CONNOR, P. An achievement risk preference scale: A preliminary report. *American Psychologist,* 1962, **17,** 317. (Abstract)

O'NEILL, G. C., & O'NEILL, N. Patterns in group sexual activity. *Journal of Sex Research,* 1970, **6,** 101–12.

OSBORNE, R. T. Racial differences in mental growth and school achievement: A longitudinal study. *Psychological Reports,* 1960, **7,** 233–39.

OSLER, S. F., & FIVEL, M. W. Concept attainment: I. The role of age and intelligence in concept attainment by induction. *Journal of Experimental Psychology,* 1961, **62,** 1–8.

OWEN, D. R. The 47, XYY male: A review. *Psychological Bulletin,* 1972, **78,** 209–33.

OWENS, W. A., JR. Age and mental abilities: A longitudinal study. *Genetic Psychology Monographs,* 1953, **48,** 3–54.

PAGE, M. P., & SCHEIDT, R. J. The elusive weapons effect: Demand awareness, evaluation apprehension, and slightly sophisticated subjects. *Journal of Personality and Social Psychology,* 1971, **20,** 304–18.

PARKER, S., & KLEINER, R. J. *Mental illness in the urban Negro community.* New York: Free Press, 1966.

PARSONS, T. Certain sources and patterns of aggression in the social structure of the western world. *Psychiatry,* 1947, **10,** 172.

PASAMANICK, B. A comparative study of the educational development of Negro infants. *Journal of Genetic Psychology,* 1946, **69,** 3–44.

PASAMANICK, B., & KNOBLOCH, H. Early language behavior in Negro children and the testing of intelligence. *Journal of Abnormal and Social Psychology,* 1955, **50,** 401–2.

PATTERSON, G. R., LITTMAN, R. A., & BRICKER, W. Assertive behavior in children: A step toward a theory of aggression. *Monographs of the Society for Research in Child Development,* 1967, **32,** No. 5, 1–43.

PATTERSON, M. L., MULLENS, S., & ROMANO, J. Compensatory reactions to spatial intrusion. *Sociometry,* 1971, **34,** 114–21.

PECKHAM, M. *Art and pornography: An experiment in explanation.* New York: Basic Books, 1969.

PEDERSEN, F. A., & BELL, R. Q. Sex differences in preschool children without histories of complications of pregnancy and delivery. *Developmental Psychology,* 1970, **3,** 10–15.

PERVIN, L. A. Rigidity in neurosis and general personality functioning. *Journal of Abnormal and Social Psychology,* 1960, **61,** 389–95.

PETERSON, D. R. *The clinical study of social behavior.* New York: Appleton-Century-Crofts, 1968.

PHILLIPS, J. L., JR. *The origins of intellect: Piaget's theory.* San Francisco: W. H. Freeman, 1969.

PIAGET, J. (1936) *The origins of intelligence in children.* New York: International Universities Press, 1952.

PIAGET, J. *The moral judgment of the child.* Glencoe, Ill.: Free Press, 1948.

PIERS, E. V. Parent prediction of children's self-concepts. *Journal of Consulting and Clinical Psychology,* 1972, **38,** 428–33.

PILIAVIN, I. M., RODIN, J., & PILIAVIN, J. A. Good samaritanism: An underground phenomenon? *Journal of Personality and Social Psychology,* 1969, **13,** 289–99.

PISANO, R., & TAYLOR, S. P. Reduction of physical aggression: The effects of four strategies. *Journal of Personality and Social Psychology,* 1971, **19**, 237–42.

PODELL, L., & PERKINS, J. C. A Guttman scale for sexual experience—a methodological note. *Journal of Abnormal and Social Psychology,* 1957, **54**, 420–22.

PRICE, K. O., HARBURG, E., & NEWCOMB, T. M. Psychological balance in situations of negative interpersonal attitudes. *Journal of Personality and Social Psychology,* 1966, **3**, 265–70.

RACHMAN, S. Sexual fetishism: An experimental analogue. *Psychological Record,* 1966, **16**, 293–96.

RAMIREZ, M., III. Identification with Mexican family values and authoritarianism in Mexican-Americans. *Journal of Social Psychology,* 1967, **73**, 3–11.

RAYNOR, J. O. Future orientation and motivation of immediate activity: An elaboration of the theory of achievement motivation. *Psychological Review,* 1969, **76**, 606–10.

RAYNOR, J. O. Relationships between achievement-related motives, future orientation, and academic performance. *Journal of Personality and Social Psychology,* 1970, **15**, 28–33.

RAYNOR, J. O., & RUBIN, I. S. Effects of achievement motivation and future orientation on level of performance. *Journal of Personality and Social Psychology,* 1971, **17**, 36–41.

REED, J. S. To live- and die-in Dixie: A contribution to the study of southern violence. *Political Science Quarterly,* 1971, **86**, 429–43.

REICH, C. A. *The greening of America.* New York: Random House, 1970.

REMARQUE, E. M. *All quiet on the Western Front* (1929). New York: Heritage Press, 1969.

REYNOLDS, W. F., BLAU, B. I., & HURLBUT, B. Speed in simple tasks as a function of MAS score. *Psychological Reports,* 1961, **8**, 341–44.

RICHARDSON, S. K. The correlation of intelligence quotients of siblings of the same chronological age levels. *Journal of Juvenile Research,* 1936, **20**, 186–98.

RICKS, D., & EPLEY, D. Foresight and hindsight in the TAT. Paper read at Eastern Psychological Association, New York, April, 1960.

RIM, Y. Values and attitudes. *Personality: An International Journal,* 1970, **1**, 243–50.

RIPPLE, R. E., & MAY, F. B. Caution in comparing creativity and I.Q. *Psychological Reports,* 1962, **10**, 229–30.

ROBERTS, A. H., & ERIKSON, R. V. Delay of gratification, Porteus Maze Test performance, and behavioral adjustment in a delinquent group. *Journal of Abnormal Psychology,* 1968, **73**, 449–53.

ROBINSON, P. The measurement of achievement motivation. Unpublished doctoral dissertation, Oxford University, 1961.

RODGERS, D. A. In favor of separation of academic and professional training. *American Psychologist,* 1964, **19**, 675–80.

ROEN, S. R. Personality and Negro-white intelligence. *Journal of Abnormal and Social Psychology,* 1960, **61**, 148–50.

ROGERS, C. R. *Client-centered therapy.* Boston: Houghton Mifflin, 1951.

ROGERS, C. R. A theory of therapy, personality, and interpersonal relationships, as developed in the client-centered framework. In S. Koch (ed.), *Psychology: A study of a science.* Vol. 3. *Formulations of the person and the social context.* New York: McGraw-Hill, 1959. Pp. 184–256.

ROGERS, C. R. Carl R. Rogers. In E. G. Boring and G. Lindzey (eds.), *A history of psychology in autobiography*. Vol. 5. New York: Appleton-Century-Crofts, 1967. Pp. 341–84. (a)

ROGERS, C. R. *The therapeutic relationship and its impact: A study of psychotherapy with schizophrenics*. Madison: University of Wisconsin Press, 1967. (b)

ROGERS, C. R. *Carl Rogers on encounter groups*. New York: Harper & Row, 1970.

ROGERS, C. R., & DYMOND, R. F. (eds.), *Psychotherapy and personality change*. Chicago: University of Chicago Press, 1954.

ROKEACH, M. *The open and closed mind*. New York: Basic Books, 1960.

ROKEACH, M. Authoritarianism scales and response bias: Comment on Peabody's paper. *Psychological Bulletin*, 1967, **67**, 349–55.

RORER, L. G. The great response-style myth. *Psychological Bulletin*, 1965, **63**, 129–56.

ROSEN, B. C. The achievement syndrome: A psychocultural dimension of social stratification. *American Sociological Review*, 1956, **21**, 203–11.

ROSEN, B. C., D'ANDRADE, R. The psychosocial origins of achievement motivation. *Sociometry*, 1959, **22**, 185–218.

ROSENBAUM, G. Stimulus generalization as a function of clinical anxiety. *Journal of Abnormal and Social Psychology*, 1956, **53**, 281–85.

ROSENHAN, D., & WHITE, G. M. Observation and rehearsal as determinants of prosocial behavior. *Journal of Personality and Social Psychology*, 1967, **5**, 424–31.

ROSENZWEIG, S. The picture-association method and its application in a study of reactions to frustration. *Journal of Personality*, 1945, **14**, 3–23.

ROSS, A. O. Brain injury and intellectual performance. *Journal of Consulting Psychology*, 1958, **22**, 151–52.

ROSS, A. S. Effect of increased responsibility on bystander intervention: The presence of children. *Journal of Personality and Social Psychology*, 1971, **19**, 306–10.

ROTHAUS, P., & WORCHEL, P. The inhibition of aggression under nonarbitrary frustration. *Journal of Personality*, 1960, **28**, 108–17.

ROTTER, J. B. *Social learning and clinical psychology*. Englewood Cliffs, N.J.: Prentice-Hall, 1954.

RUBIN, I. M. Increased self-acceptance: A means of reducing prejudice. *Journal of Personality and Social Psychology*, 1967, **5**, 233–38.

RUDIN, S. A. National motives predict psychogenic death rates 25 years later. *Science*, 1968, **160**, 901–3.

RYCHLAK, J. F. *A philosophy of science for personality theory*. New York: Houghton Mifflin, 1968.

RYCHLAK, J. F. Manifest anxiety as reflecting commitment to the psychological present at the expense of cognitive futurity. *Journal of Consulting and Clinical Psychology*, 1972, **38**, 70–79.

RYCHLAK, J. F., & LERNER, J. J. An expectancy interpretation of manifest anxiety. *Journal of Personality and Social Psychology*, 1965, **2**, 677–84.

SACKETT, G. P. Effects of rearing conditions upon the behavior of rhesus monkeys (*Macaca mulatta*). *Child Development*, 1965, **36**, 855–68.

SALES, S. M. Economic threat as a determinant of conversion rates in authoritarian and nonauthoritarian churches. *Journal of Personality and Social Psychology*, 1972, **23**, 420–28.

SALTZ, E. Manifest anxiety: Have we misread the data? *Psychological Review*, 1970, **77**, 568–73.

SALTZ, E., & HAMILTON, H. Do lower IQ children attain concepts more slowly than children of higher IQ? *Psychonomic Science,* 1969, **17,** 210–11.

SAMUELSON, F., & YATES, J. F. Acquiescence and the F Scale: Old assumptions and new data. *Psychological Bulletin,* 1967, **68,** 91–103.

SANFORD, N. The approach of the authoritarian personality. In J. L. McCary (ed.), *Psychology of personality: Six modern approaches.* New York: Logos, 1956. Pp. 253–319.

SARASON, I. G. Interrelationships among individual difference variables, behavior in psychotherapy, and verbal conditioning. *Journal of Abnormal and Social Psychology,* 1958, **56,** 339–44.

SARASON, I. G. Characteristics of three measures of anxiety. *Journal of Clinical Psychology,* 1961, **17,** 196–97.

SARASON, S. B., DAVIDSON, K. S., LIGHTHALL, F. F., WAITE, R. R., & RUEBUSH, B. K. *Anxiety in elementary school children.* New York: Wiley, 1960.

SARBIN, T. R. Anxiety: Reification of a metaphor. *Archives of General Psychiatry,* 1964, **10,** 630–38.

SATTLER, J. M., & THEYE, F. Procedural, situational, and interpersonal variables in individual intelligence testing. *Psychological Bulletin,* 1967, **68,** 347–60.

SATZ, P. Specific and nonspecific effects of brain lesions in man. *Journal of Abnormal Psychology,* 1966, **71,** 65–70.

SATZ, P., & BARAFF, A. S. Changes in the relation between self-concepts and ideal concepts of psychotics consequent upon therapy. *Journal of General Psychology,* 1962, **67,** 291–98.

SATZ, P., RICHARD, W., & DANIELS, A. The alteration of intellectual performance after lateralized brain-injury in man. *Psychonomic Science,* 1967, **7,** 369–70.

SAVITT, R. A. Psychoanalytic studies on addiction: Ego structure in narcotic addiction. *Psychoanalytic Quarterly,* 1963, **32,** 43–57.

SCARR-SALAPATEK, S. Unknowns in the IQ equation. *Science,* 1971, **174,** 1223–28. (a)

SCARR-SALAPATEK, S. Race, social class, and IQ. *Science,* 1971, **174,** 1285–95. (b)

SCHACHTER, S. Deviation, rejection, and communication. *Journal of Abnormal and Social Psychology,* 1951, **46,** 190–207.

SCHACHTER, S., & LATANÉ, B. Crime, cognition, and the autonomic nervous system. In D. Levine (ed.), *Nebraska symposium on motivation.* Lincoln: University of Nebraska Press, 1964. Pp. 221–73.

SCHAFFNER, A., LANE, E. A., & ALBEE, G. W. Intellectual differences between suburban preschizophrenic children and their siblings. *Journal of Consulting Psychology,* 1967, **31,** 326–27.

SCHILLER, P. Effects of mass media on the sexual behavior of adolescent females. In *Technical Report of the Commission on Obscenity and Pornography.* Vol. I. Washington, D.C.: U.S. Government Printing Office, 1971. Pp. 191–95.

SCHMIDT, G., & SIGUSCH, V. Sex differences in responses to psychosexual stimulation by films and slides. *Journal of Sex Research,* 1970, **6,** 268–83.

SCHMIDT, G., & SIGUSCH, V. Patterns of sexual behavior in West German workers and students. *Journal of Sex Research,* 1971, **7,** 89–106.

SCHMIDT, G., SIGUSCH, V., & MEYBERG, U. Psychosexual stimulation in men: Emotional reactions, changes of sex behavior, and measures of conservative attitudes. *Journal of Sex Research,* 1969, **5,** 199–217.

SCHMIDT, G., SIGUSCH, V., & SCHAFER, S. Responses to reading erotic stories: Male-female differences. *Archives of Sexual Behavior*, 1973, **2**, 181–99.

SCHMUCK, R. A., & SCHMUCK, R. W. Upward mobility and I.Q. performance. *Journal of Educational Research*, 1961, **55**, 123–27.

SCHOFIELD, W., & BALIAN, L. A comparative study of the personal histories of schizophrenic and nonpsychiatric patients. *Journal of Abnormal and Social Psychology*, 1959, **59**, 216–25.

SCHOOLEY, M. Personality resemblances among married couples. *Journal of Abnormal and Social Psychology*, 1936, **31**, 340–47.

SCHUSTER, E., & ELDERTON, E. M. The inheritance of psychical characters. *Biometrika*, 1906, **5**, 460–69.

SCHWAB, J. J., CLEMMONS, R. S., & MARDER, L. The self concept—psychosomatic applications. *Psychosomatics*, 1966, **7**, 1–5.

SCHWARTZ, S. H., & CLAUSEN, G. T. Responsibility, norms, and helping in an emergency. *Journal of Personality and Social Psychology*, 1970, **16**, 299–310.

SCHWARTZMAN, A. E., & DOUGLAS, V. I. Intellectual loss in schizophrenia: Part I. *Canadian Journal of Psychology*, 1962, **16**, 1–10.

SCHWARTZMAN, A. E., DOUGLAS,V. I., & MUIR, W. R. Intellectual loss in schizophrenia: Part II. *Canadian Journal of Psychology*, 1962, **16**, 161–68.

SEARS, R. R. Experimental analysis of psychoanalytic phenomena. In J. McV. Hunt (ed.), *Personality and the behavior disorders*. New York: Ronald Press, 1944. Pp. 306–32.

SEARS, R. R. Dependency motivation. In M. R. Jones (ed.), *Nebraska symposium on motivation*. Lincoln: University of Nebraska Press, 1963. Pp. 25–64.

SEARS, R. R., MACCOBY, E. E., & LEVIN, H. *Patterns of child rearing*. Evanston, Ill.: Row, Peterson, 1957.

SEAY, B. M., & HARLOW, H. F. Maternal separation in the rhesus monkey. *Journal of Nervous and Mental Disease*, 1965, **140**, 434–41.

SHERWOOD, J. J. Authoritarianism, moral realism, and President Kennedy's death. *British Journal of Social and Clinical Psychology*, 1966, **5**, 264–69. (a)

SHERWOOD, J. J. Self-report and projective measures of achievement and affiliation. *Journal of Consulting Psychology*, 1966, **30**, 329–37. (b)

SHERWOOD, J. J., & NATAUPSKY, M. Predicting the conclusion of Negro-white intelligence research from biographical characteristics of the investigator. *Journal of Personality and Social Psychology*, 1968, **8**, 53–58.

SHONTZ, F. C. *Research methods in personality*. New York: Appleton-Century-Crofts, 1965.

SHORTELL, J. R., & BILLER, H. B. Aggression in children as a function of sex of subject and sex of opponent. *Developmental Psychology*, 1970, **3**, 143–44.

SHRAUGER, J. S., & ROSENBERG, S. E. Self-esteem and the effect of success and failure feedback on performance. *Journal of Personality*, 1970, **38**, 404–17.

SHUEY, A. M. *The testing of Negro intelligence*. Lynchburg, Va.: J. P. Bell, 1958.

SHUEY, A. M. *The testing of Negro intelligence* (2nd ed.). New York: Social Science Press, 1966.

SHUNTICH, R. J., & TAYLOR, S. P. The effects of alcohol on human physical aggression. *Journal of Experimental Research in Personality*, 1972, **6**, 34–38.

SHUPE, L. M. Alcohol and crime: A study of the urine alcohol concentration found in 882 persons arrested during or immediately after the commission of a felony. *Journal of Criminal Law, Criminology and Police Science*, 1954, **44**, 661–64.

SIEGMAN, A. W. Father absence during early childhood and antisocial behavior. *Journal of Abnormal Psychology,* 1966, **71,** 71–74.

SIGUSCH, V., SCHMIDT, G., REINFELD, A., & WIEDEMANN-SUTOR, I. Psychosexual stimulation: Sex differences. *Journal of Sex Research,* 1970, **6,** 10–24.

SIMPSON, G. G. *This view of life.* New York: Harcourt, Brace and World, 1964.

SIMPSON, M. Authoritarianism and education: A comparative approach. *Sociometry,* 1972, **35,** 223–34.

SINGER, D. L. Aggression arousal, hostile humor, and catharsis. *Journal of Personality and Social Psychology Monograph Supplement,* 1968, **8,** 1–14.

SINGER, R. D. The effects of verbal reinforcement of prodemocratic responses upon subsequent expression of authoritarian opinions and social prejudice. Unpublished doctoral dissertation, University of Pennsylvania, 1960.

SKINNER, B. F. *Science and human behavior.* New York: Macmillan, 1953.

SKINNER, B. F. *Beyond freedom and dignity.* New York: Alfred A. Knopf, 1971.

SKODAK, M., & SKEELS, H. M. A final follow-up of one hundred adopted children. *Journal of Genetic Psychology,* 1949, **75,** 85–125.

SMITH, A. J. Similarity of values and its relation to acceptance and the projection of similarity. *Journal of Psychology,* 1957, **43,** 251–60.

SMITH, B. D., & TEEVAN, R. C. Relationships among self-ideal congruence, adjustment, and fear-of-failure motivation. *Journal of Personality,* 1971, **39,** 44–56.

SMITH, C. P. (ed.). *Achievement-related motives in children.* New York: Russell Sage Foundation, 1969.

SMITH, R. E. Social anxiety as a moderator variable in the attitude similarity-attraction relationship. Paper presented at the meeting of the Western Psychological Association, Los Angeles, April, 1970.

SMITH, R. E., ASCOUGH, J. C., ETTINGER, R. F., & NELSON, D. A. Humor, anxiety, and task performance. *Journal of Personality and Social Psychology,* 1971, **19,** 243–46.

SMITH, R. E., MEADOW, B. L., & SISK, T. K. Attitude similarity, interpersonal attraction, and evaluative social perception. *Psychonomic Science,* 1970, **18,** 226–27.

SMITH, S., & HAYTHORN, W. W. Effects of compatibility, crowding, group size, and leadership seniority on stress, anxiety, hostility, and annoyance in isolated groups. *Journal of Personality and Social Psychology,* 1972, **22,** 67–79.

SNYDER, C. R., & LARSON, G. R. A further look at student acceptance of general personality interpretations. *Journal of Consulting and Clinical Psychology,* 1972, **38,** 384–88.

SNYGG, D., & COMBS, A. W. *Individual behavior.* New York: Harper, 1949.

SOMMER, R. Studies in personal space. *Sociometry,* 1959, **22,** 247–60.

SONENSCHEIN, D. Pornography: A false issue. *Psychiatric Opinion,* 1969, **6,** 11–18.

SONTAG, L. W., BAKER, C. T., & NELSON, V. L. Mental growth and personality development: A longitudinal study. *Monographs of Social Research in Child Development,* 1958, **23,** No. 2.

SOSA, J. N. Vascular effects of frustration on passive and aggressive members of a clinical population. Unpublished masters thesis, Florida State University, 1968.

SPEARMAN, C. *The abilities of man.* New York: Macmillan, 1927.

SPELLMAN, C. M., BASKETT, G. D., & BYRNE, D. Manifest anxiety as a contributing factor in religious conversion. *Journal of Consulting and Clinical Psychology,* 1971, **36,** 245–47.

SPENCE, J. A., & SPENCE, K. W. The motivational components of manifest anxiety: Drive and drive stimuli. In C. D. Spielberger (ed.), *Anxiety and behavior*. New York: Academic Press, 1966.

SPENCE, K. W. Learning and performance in eyelid conditioning as a function of the intensity of the UCS. *Journal of Experimental Psychology*, 1953, **45**, 57–63.

SPENCE, K. W. A theory of emotionally based drive (D) and its relation to performance in simple learning situations. *American Psychologist*, 1958, **13**, 131–41.

SPENCE, K. W. The empirical basis and theoretical structure of psychology. In K. W. Spence, *Behavior theory and learning*. Englewood Cliffs, N.J.: Prentice-Hall, 1960. Pp. 71–88.

SPENCE, K. W. Anxiety (drive) level and performance in eyelid conditioning. *Psychological Bulletin*, 1964, **61**, 129–39.

SPENCE, K. W., FARBER, I. E., & McFANN, H. H. The relation of anxiety (drive) level to performance in competitional and noncompetitional paired-associates learning. *Journal of Experimental Psychology*, 1956, **52**, 296–305.

SPENCE, K. W., & TAYLOR, J. A. Anxiety and strength of the UCS as determiners of the amount of eyelid conditioning. *Journal of Experimental Psychology*, 1951, **42**, 183–88.

SPENCE, K. W., & TOWNSEND, S. A comparative study of groups of high and low intelligence in learning a maze. *Journal of General Psychology*, 1930, **3**, 113–30.

SPIELBERGER, C. D. Theory and research on anxiety. In C. D. Spielberger (ed.), *Anxiety and behavior*. New York: Academic Press, 1966. Pp. 3–20. (a)

SPIELBERGER, C. D. The effects of anxiey on complex learning and academic achievement. In C. D. Spielberger (ed.), *Anxiety and behavior*. New York: Academic Press, 1966. Pp. 361–98. (b)

SPIELBERGER, C. D. Anxiety as an emotional state. In C. D. Spielberger (ed.), *Anxiety: Current trends in theory and research*. New York: Academic Press, 1971.

SPIELBERGER, C. D., AUERBACH, S. M., WADSWORTH, A. P., DUNN, T. M., & TAULBEE, E. S. Emotional reactions to surgery. *Journal of Consulting and Clinical Psychology*, 1973, **40**, 33–38.

SPIELBERGER, C. D., GORSUCH, R. L., & LUSHENE, R. E. *Manual for the State-Trait Anxiety Inventory*. Palo Alto, Calif.: Consulting Psychologists Press, 1970.

SPIELBERGER, C. D., & KATZENMEYER, W. G. Manifest anxiety, intelligence, and college grades. *Journal of Consulting Psychology*, 1959, **23**, 278.

SPIELBERGER, C. D., & SMITH, L. H. Anxiety (drive), stress, and serial-position effects in serial-verbal learning. *Journal of Experimental Psychology*, 1966, **72**, 589–95.

SPIVACK, G., LEVINE, M., & SPRIGLE, H. Intelligence test performance and the delay function of the ego. *Journal of Consulting Psychology*, 1959, **23**, 428–31.

STAATS, A. W. Social behaviorism and human motivation: Principles of the attitude-reinforcer-discriminative system. In A. G. Greenwald, T. C. Brock, & T. M. Ostrom (eds.), *Psychological foundations of attitudes*. New York: Academic Press, 1968. Pp. 33–66.

STAATS, A. W. An outline of an integrated learning theory of attitude formation and function. In M. Fishbein (ed.), *Readings in attitude theory and measurement*. New York: Wiley, 1969. Pp. 373–81.

STALLING, R. B. Personality similarity and evaluative meaning as conditioners of attraction. *Journal of Personality and Social Psychology*, 1970, **14**, 77–82.

STALLINGS, F. H. A study of the immediate effects of integration on scholastic achievement in the Louisville public schools. *Journal of Negro Education*, 1959, **28**, 439–44.

STAUB, E. A child in distress: The influence of age and number of witnesses on children's attempts to help. *Journal of Personality and Social Psychology*, 1970, **14**, 130–40.

STAUB, E. Helping a person in distress: The influence of implicit and explicit "rules" of conduct on children and adults. *Journal of Personality and Social Psychology*, 1971, **17**, 137–44. (a)

STAUB, E. The learning and unlearning of aggression: The role of anxiety, empathy, efficiency, and prosocial values. In J. L. Singer (ed.), *The control of aggression and violence: Cognitive and physiological factors*. New York: Academic Press, 1971. Pp. 93–124. (b)

STEINER, I. D., & JOHNSON, H. H. Authoritarianism and "tolerance of trait inconsistency." *Journal of Abnormal and Social Psychology*, 1963, **67**, 388–91.

STEPHENSON, W. *The study of behavior. Q-technique and its methodology*. Chicago: University of Chicago Press, 1953.

STEVENS, S. S. Psychology and the science of science. *Psychological Bulletin*, 1939, **36**, 221–63.

STEWART, L. H. Manifest anxiety and mother-son identification. *Journal of Clinical Psychology*, 1958, **14**, 382–84.

STEWART, N. A.G.C.T. scores of army personnel grouped by occupation. *Occupations*, 1947, **26**, 5–41.

STONE, L., & HOKANSON, J. E. Arousal reduction via self-punitive behavior. *Journal of Personality and Social Psychology*, 1969, **12**, 72–79.

SULLIVAN, H. S. *Conceptions of modern psychiatry*. Washington, D.C.: William Alanson White Psychiatric Foundation, 1947.

SULLIVAN, H. S. Tensions interpersonal and international: A psychiatrist's view. In H. Cantril (ed.), *Tensions that cause war*. Urbana, Ill.: University of Illinois Press, 1950. Pp. 79–138.

SWANSON, E. O. The relation of vocabulary test-retest gains to amount of college attendance after a 24-year period. *American Psychologist*, 1952, **7**, 368. (abstract)

SWIFT, J. *Gulliver's travels* (1726). New York: Heritage Press, 1940.

SYMONDS, P. M. *The ego and the self*. New York: Appleton-Century-Crofts, 1951.

TAYLOR, D. A., WHEELER, L., & ALTMAN, I. Stress relations in socially isolated groups. *Journal of Personality and Social Psychology*, 1968, **9**, 369–76.

TAYLOR, J. A. The relationship of anxiety to the conditioned eyelid response. *Journal of Experimental Psychology*, 1951, **41**, 81–92.

TAYLOR, J. A. A personality scale of manifest anxiety. *Journal of Abnormal and Social Psychology*, 1953, **48**, 285–90.

TAYLOR, J. A. Drive theory and manifest anxiety. *Psychological Bulletin*, 1956, **53**, 303–20.

TAYLOR, J. A., & RECHTSCHAFFEN, A. Manifest anxiety and reversed alphabet printing. *Journal of Abnormal and Social Psychology*, 1959, **58**, 221–24.

TAYLOR, J. A., & SPENCE, K. W. The relationship of anxiety level to performance in serial learning. *Journal of Experimental Psychology*, 1952, **44**, 61–64.

TAYLOR, S. P. Aggressive behavior and physiological arousal as a function of provocation and the tendency to inhibit aggression. *Journal of Personality*, 1967, **35**, 297–310.

TAYLOR, S. P. Aggressive behavior as a function of approval motivation and physical attack. *Psychonomic Science*, 1970, **18**, 195–96.

TAYLOR, S. P., & EPSTEIN, S. Aggression as a function of the interaction of the sex of the aggressor and the sex of the victim. *Journal of Personality*, 1967, **35**, 474–86.

TAYLOR, S. P., & PISANO, R. Physical aggression as a function of frustration and physical attack. *Journal of Social Psychology*, 1971, **84**, 261–67.

TEEVAN, R. C., & McGHEE, P. E. Childhood development of fear of failure motivation. *Journal of Personality and Social Psychology*, 1972, **21**, 345–48.

TELFER, M. A., BAKER, D., CLARK, G. R., & RICHARDSON, C. E. Incidence of gross chromosomal errors among tall criminal American males. *Science*, 1968, **159**, 1249–50.

TERMAN, L. M. *The measurement of intelligence*. Boston: Houghton Mifflin, 1916.

TERMAN, L. M. (ed.), et al. *Mental and physical traits of a thousand gifted children*. Vol. I. Stanford: Stanford University Press, 1925.

TERMAN, L. M, Trials to psychology. In C. Murchison (ed.), *A history of psychology in autobiography*. Vol. II. Worcester, Mass.: Clark University Press, 1932. Pp. 297–331.

TERMAN, L. M. The discovery and encouragement of exceptional talent. *American Psychologist*, 1954, **9**, 221–30.

TERMAN, L. M., & BUTTENWIESER, P. Personality factors in marital compatibility: I. *Journal of Social Psychology*, 1935, **6**, 143–71. (a)

TERMAN, L. M., & BUTTENWIESER, P. Personality factors in marital compatibility: II. *Journal of Social Psychology*, 1935, **6**, 267–89. (b)

TERMAN, L. M., & MERRILL, M. A. *Measuring intelligence*. Boston: Houghton Mifflin, 1937.

TERMAN, L. M., & MERRILL, M. A. *Stanford-Binet intelligence scale*. Boston: Houghton Mifflin, 1960.

TERMAN, L. M., & ODEN, M. H. *The gifted child grows up*. In. L. M. Terman (ed.), *Genetic studies of genius*. Vol. IV. Stanford: Stanford University Press, 1947.

TERMAN, L. M., & ODEN, M. H. *The gifted group at mid-life: Thirty-five years' follow-up of the superior child*. In L. M. Terman (ed.), *Genetic studies of genius*. Vol. V. Stanford: Stanford University Press, 1959.

THOMPSON, R. C., & MICHEL, J. B. Measuring authoritarianism: A comparison of the F and D Scales. *Journal of Personality*, 1972, **40**, 180–90.

THORNDIKE, E. L., & WOODYARD, E. Differences within and between communities in the intelligence of children. *Journal of Educational Psychology*, 1942, **33**, 641–56.

THURSTONE, L. L. *Primary mental abilities*. Chicago: University of Chicago Press, 1938.

THURSTONE, L. L., & THURSTONE, T. G. *Factorial studies of intelligence*. Chicago: University of Chicago Press, 1941.

TILKER, H. A. Socially responsible behavior as a function of observer responsibility and victim feedback. *Journal of Personality and Social Psychology*, 1970, **14**, 95–100.

TOWNES, C. H. Quantum electronics, and surprise in development of technology: The problem of research planning. *Science*, 1968, **159**, 699–703.

TRAVERS, R. M. W. Significant research on the prediction of academic success. In W. T. Donahue, C. H. Coombs, & R. M. W. Travers, *The measurement of student adjustment and achievement*. Ann Arbor: University of Michigan Press, 1949. Pp. 147–90.

TRUAX, C. B., & MITCHELL, K. M. Research on certain therapist interpersonal skills in relation to process and outcome. In A. E. Bergin and S. L. Garfield (eds.), *Handbook of psychotherapy and behavior change.* New York: Wiley, 1971. Pp. 299–344.

TRYON, R. C. Genetic differences in maze-learning ability in rats. *Thirty-ninth Yearbook of the Society for the Study of Education,* 1940, Part I. Pp. 111–19.

TRYON, R. C. Psychology in flux: The academic-professional bipolarity. *American Psychologist,* 1963, **18,** 134–43.

TUCKER, I. F. *Adjustment, models and mechanisms.* New York: Academic Press, 1970.

TULKIN, S. R. Race, class, and family as related to school achievement. Unpublished honors thesis, University of Maryland, 1965.

TURNER, C. B., & FISKE, D. W. Item quality and appropriateness of response processes. *Educational and Psychological Measurement,* 1968, **28,** 297–315.

TURNER, J. H. Entrepreneurial environments and the emergence of achievement motivation in adolescent males. *Sociometry,* 1970, **33,** 147–65.

TYLER, L. E. *The psychology of human differences.* New York: Appleton-Century-Crofts, 1956.

UDRY, J. R., & MORRIS, N. M. Frequency of intercourse by day of the week. *Journal of Sex Research,* 1970, **6,** 229–34.

ULLMAN, A. D. Sociocultural backgrounds of alcoholism. *Annual American Academy of Political and Social Science,* 1958, **315,** 48–54.

ULRICH, R. E. Pain as a cause of aggression. *American Zoologist,* 1966, **6,** 643–62.

ULRICH, R. E., & AZRIN, N. H. Reflexive fighting in response to aversive stimulation. *Journal of the Experimental Analysis of Behavior,* 1962, **5,** 511–20.

VACCHIANO, R. B., STRAUSS, P. S., & HOCHMAN, L. The open and closed mind: A review of dogmatism. *Psychological Bulletin,* 1969, **71,** 261–73.

VANCE, F. L., & MACPHAIL, S. L. APA membership trends and fields of specialization of psychologists earning doctoral degrees between 1959 and 1962. *American Psychologist,* 1964, **19,** 654–58.

VANDERBECK, D. J. A construct validity study of the *O-H* (Overcontrolled Hostility) Scale of the MMPI, utilizing a social learning approach to the catharsis effect. Unpublished doctoral dissertation, Florida State University, 1972.

VASSILIOU, V., GEORGAS, J. G., & VASSILIOU, G. Variations in manifest anxiety due to sex, age, and education. *Journal of Personality and Social Psychology,* 1967, **6,** 194–97.

VAUGHT, G. M., & NEWMAN, S. E. The effects of anxiety on motor-steadiness in competitive and noncompetitive conditions. *Psychonomic Science,* 1966, **6,** 519–20.

VERNON, P. E. *Personality assessment: A critical survey.* New York: Wiley, 1964.

VERNON, P. E. *Intelligence and cultural environment.* London: Methuen, 1969.

VERNON, P. E. Genes, 'G' and Jensen. *Contemporary Psychology,* 1970, **15,** 161–63.

VEROFF, J. A projective measure of the achievement motivation of adolescent males and females. Unpublished honors thesis, Wesleyan University, 1950.

VEROFF, J. Social comparison and the development of achievement motivation. In C. P. Smith (ed.), *Achievement—related motives in children.* New York: Russell Sage Foundation, 1969. Pp. 46–101.

VEROFF, J., FELD, S., & CROCKETT, H. Explorations into the effects of picture cues on thematic apperceptive expression of achievement motivation. *Journal of Personality and Social Psychology*, 1966, **3,** 171–81.

VERPLANCK, W. The control of the content of conversation: Reinforcement of statements of opinion. *Journal of Abnormal and Social Psychology*, 1955, **51,** 668–76.

VESTRE, N. D., & LOREI, T. W. Relationships between social history factors and psychiatric symptoms. *Journal of Abnormal Psychology*, 1967, **72,** 247–50.

VIDEBECK, R. Self-conception and the reactions of others. *Sociometry*, 1960, **23,** 351–59.

VORE, D. A., & OTTINGER, D. R. Maternal food restriction: Effects on offspring development, learning, and a program of therapy. *Developmental Psychology*, 1970, **3,** 337–42.

WACHTEL, P. L., & SCHIMEK, J. G. An exploratory study of the effects of emotionally toned incidental stimuli. *Journal of Personality*, 1970, **38,** 467–81.

WALLACE, D. H., & WEHMER, G. Evaluation of visual erotica by sexual liberals and conservatives. *Journal of Sex Research*, 1972, **8,** 147–53.

WALLACE, J., & SADALLA, E. Behavioral consequences of transgression: I. The effects of social recognition. *Journal of Experimental Research in Personality*, 1966, **1,** 187–94.

WALLACH, M. A., & LEGGETT, M. I. Testing the hypothesis that a person will be consistent: Stylistic consistency versus situational specificity in size of children's drawings. *Journal of Personality*, 1972, **40,** 309–30.

WALSTER, E., ARONSON, V., ABRAHAMS, D., & ROTTMAN, L. Importance of physical attractiveness in dating behavior. *Journal of Personality and Social Psychology*, 1966, **4,** 508–16.

WALTERS, R. H., & THOMAS, E. L. Enhancement of punitiveness by visual and audiovisual displays. *Canadian Journal of Psychology*, 1963, **17,** 244–55.

WATSON, D. Relationship between locus of control and anxiety. *Journal of Personality and Social Psychology*, 1967, **6,** 91–92.

WATSON, D., & FRIEND, R. Measurement of social-evaluative anxiety. *Journal of Consulting and Clinical Psychology*, 1969, **33,** 448–57.

WATSON, J. B., & RAYNOR, R. Conditioned emotional responses. *Journal of Experimental Psychology*, 1920, **3,** 1–14.

WECHSLER, D. *The measurement of adult intelligence.* 3rd. ed. Baltimore: Williams and Wilkins, 1944.

WECHSLER, D. *Wechsler intelligence scale for children.* New York: Psychological Corporation, 1949.

WECHSLER, D. *The measurement and appraisal of adult intelligence.* 4th ed. Baltimore: Williams and Wilkins, 1958.

WECHSLER, D. *Manual for the Wechsler Preschool and Primary Scale of Intelligence.* New York: Psychological Corporation, 1967.

WEINER, B. Achievement motivation and task recall in competitive situations. *Journal of Personality and Social Psychology*, 1966, **3,** 693–96.

WEINER, B. New conceptions in the study of achievement motivation. In B. A. Maher (ed.), *Progress in experimental personality research.* Vol. 5. New York: Academic Press, 1970.

WEINSTEIN, M. S. Achievement motivation and risk preference. *Journal of Personality and Social Psychology*, 1969, **13,** 153–72.

WEINSTEIN, S., & TEUBER, H. L. The role of preinjury education and intelligence level in intellectual loss after brain injury. *Journal of Comparative and Physiological Psychology*, 1957, **50**, 535–39.

WEISS, R. F., BUCHANAN, W., ALTSTATT, L., & LOMBARDO, J. P. Altruism is rewarding. *Science*, 1971, **171**, 1262–63.

WELLMAN, B. L., & PEGRAM, E. L. Binet IQ changes of orphanage pre-school children. *Journal of Genetic Psychology*, 1944, **65**, 239–63.

WELLS, W. D., WEINERT, G., & RUBEL, M. Conformity pressure and authoritarian personality. *Journal of Psychology*, 1956, **42**, 133–36.

WENAR, C. Reaction time as a function of manifest anxiety and stimulus intensity. *Journal of Abnormal and Social Psychology*, 1954, **49**, 335–40.

WESSMAN, A. E., RICKS, D. F., & TYL, M. McI. Characteristics and concomitants of mood fluctuation in college women. *Journal of Abnormal and Social Psychology*, 1960, **60**, 117–26.

WHITING, J. W. M. Methods and problems in cross-cultural research. In G. Lindzey and E. Aronson (eds.), *The handbook of social psychology* (2nd ed.). Vol. 2. Reading, Mass.: Addison-Wesley, 1968. Pp. 693–728.

WHITING, J. W. M., & CHILD, I. L. *Child training and personality: A cross-cultural study.* New Haven: Yale University Press, 1953.

WIGGINS, N., & WIGGINS, J. S. A typological analysis of male preferences for female body types. *Multivariate Behavioral Research*, 1969, **4**, 89–102.

WILKIE, F., & EISDORFER, C. Intelligence and blood pressure in the aged. *Science*, 1971, **172**, 959–62.

WILLERMAN, L., NAYLOR, A. F., & MYRIANTHOPOULOS, N. C. Intellectual development of children from interracial matings. *Science*, 1970, **170**, 1329–31.

WILLIAMS, A. F. Social drinking, anxiety, and depression. *Journal of Personality and Social Psychology*, 1966, **3**, 689–93.

WILSON, J. R., KUEHN, R. E., & BEACH, F. A. Modification in the sexual behavior of male rats produced by changing the stimulus female. *Journal of Comparative and Physiological Psychology*, 1963, **56**, 636–44.

WILSON, R. S. Twins: Early mental development. *Science*, 1972, **175**, 914–17.

WINER, B. J. *Statistical principles in experimental design.* New York: McGraw-Hill, 1971.

WINSLOW, C. N. A study of the extent of agreement between friends' opinions and their ability to estimate the opinions of each other. *Journal of Social Psychology*, 1937, **8**, 433–42.

WINTER, S. K. Case studies. In D. C. McClelland & D. G. Winter, *Motivating economic achievement.* New York: The Free Press, 1969. Pp. 275–308.

WINTERBOTTOM, M. R. The relation of need for achievement to learning experiences in independence and mastery. In J. W. Atkinson (ed.), *Motives in fantasy, action, and society.* Princeton: Van Nostrand, 1958. Pp. 453–78.

WISPÉ, L. G., & FRESHLEY, H. B. Race, sex, and sympathetic helping behavior: The broken bag caper. *Journal of Personality and Social Psychology*, 1971, **17**, 59–65.

WISSLER, C. *The correlation of mental and physical tests.* New York: Columbia University Press, 1901.

WITKIN, H. A., GOODENOUGH, D. R., & KARP, S. A. Stability of cognitive style from childhood to young adulthood. *Journal of Personality and Social Psychology*, 1967, **7**, 291–300.

Wolfe, B. M., & Baron, R. A. Laboratory aggression related to aggression in naturalistic social situations: Effects of an aggressive model on the behavior of college student and prisoner observers. *Psychonomic Science*, 1971, **24**, 193–94.

Wolfgang, M. E., & Strohm, R. B. The relationship between alcohol and criminal homicide. *Quarterly Journal of Studies on Alcohol*, 1956, **17**, 411–25.

Wolins, M. Young children in institutions: Some additional evidence. *Developmental Psychology*, 1969, **2**, 99–109.

Wong, T. J. The effect of attitude similarity and prejudice on interpersonal evaluation and attraction. Unpublished master's thesis, University of Texas, 1961.

Worbois, G. M. Changes in Stanford-Binet IQ for rural consolidated and rural one-room school children. *Journal of Experimental Education*, 1942, **11**, 210–14.

Worchel, P. Personality factors in the readiness to express aggression. *Journal of Clinical Psychology*, 1958, **14**, 355–59.

Wrightsman, L. S., Jr., & Baumeister, A. A. A comparison of actual and paper-and-pencil versions of the water jar test of rigidity. *Journal of Abnormal and Social Psychology*, 1961, **63**, 191–93.

Wrightsman, L. S., Jr., Radloff, R. W., Horton, D. L., & Mecherikoff, M. Authoritarian attitudes and presidential voting preferences. *Psychological Reports*, 1961, **8**, 43–46.

Wyer, R. S., Jr. Self-acceptance, discrepancy between parents' perceptions of their children, and goal-seeking effectiveness. *Journal of Personality and Social Psychology*, 1965, **2**, 311–16.

Wylie, R. C. The present status of self theory. In E. F. Borgatta & W. W. Lambert (eds.), *Handbook of personality theory and research*. Chicago: Rand McNally, 1968. Pp. 728–87.

Yakimovich, D., & Saltz, E. Helping behavior: The cry for help. *Psychonomic Science*, 1971, **23**, 427–28.

Yarrow, L. J. Separation from parents during early childhood. In M. L. Hoffman & L. W. Hoffman (eds.), *Review of child development research*. Vol. I. New York: Russell Sage Foundation, 1964. Pp. 89–136.

Yerkes, R. M. Psychological examining in the U. S. Army. *Memoirs: National Academy of Science*, 1921, **15**, 1–890.

Young, W. C., Goy, R. W., & Phoenix, C. H. Hormones and sexual behavior. *Science*, 1964, **143**, 212–18.

Zander, A., & Forward, J. Position in group, achievement motivation, and group aspirations. *Journal of Personality and Social Psychology*, 1968, **8**, 282–88.

Ziller, R. C., & Grossman, S. A. A developmental study of the self-social constructs of normals and the neurotic personality. *Journal of Clinical Psychology*, 1967, **23**, 15–21.

Zillmann, D. Excitation transfer in communication-mediated aggressive behavior. *Journal of Experimental Social Psychology*, 1971, **7**, 419–34.

Zillmann, D., Katcher, A. H., & Milarsky, B. Excitation transfer from physical exercise to subsequent aggressive behavior. *Journal of Experimental Social Psychology*, 1972, **8**, 247–59.

Zubin, J. Psychopathology and the social sciences. In O. Klineberg and R. Christie (eds.), *Perspectives in social psychology*. New York: Holt, Rinehart, & Winston, 1965.

Zuckerman, M. Physiological measures of sexual arousal in the human. *Psychological Bulletin*, 1971, **75**, 347–56.

Author Index

Subject Index

Achievement need, 128
Achievement training, 140
Achieving society, 149, 154
Acquiescent response set, 122
Affect, 352, 356, 448
Affection, 416
Aggression, 89, 113, 288, 369
Aging, 260, 295, 346
Alcohol, 212, 382, 426
Altruism, 458
Anal stage, 39
Analytic research, 327, 339, 373, 416, 462
Analytical theory, 44
Anima, 48
Animus, 48
Anti-intraception, 90
Anti-Semitism, 101
Anxiety, 40, 182
Anxiety reduction, 206, 211
Application, 11, 13, 58, 167, 168, 169, 170, 326, 358, 400, 453, 502, 521
Archetypes, 47
Assumptions of personality research, 15, 17
Attack, 372
Attitude, 86
  similarity, 331
Attraction, 331
Attribution, 290
Authoritarianism, 86, 323, 517

Autonomic arousal, 208
Autonomous achievement motivation, 141

Balance theory, 351
Balanced F scale, 123
Base relationship, 326, 334, 372, 411, 460
Basic research, 11, 326
Behavioral science, 3, 4
Binet, Alfred, 226
Birth complications, 198
Birth trauma, 41
Black-white differences, 242
Brain damage, 263
Business, 156, 157
Bystander effect, 460

California F scale, 92
Case history, 515
Catharsis, 396
Cheating, 480, 491
Child-rearing practices, 79, 98, 138, 139, 144, 151, 165, 191
Classical conditioning, 199, 352
Client-centered therapy, 272, 296, 301
Clinical psychology, 26, 312
Cognitive theory, 351
Collective unconscious, 46
Competence, 293

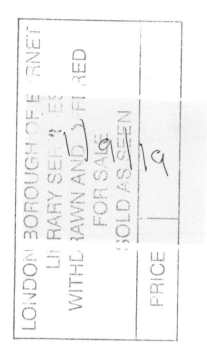

THE
BOURNE
ENIGMA

ROBERT LUDLUM was the author of twenty-seven novels, each one a *New York Times* bestseller. There are more than 225 million of his books in print, and they have been translated into thirty-two languages. He is the author of *The Scarlatti Inheritance*, *The Chancellor Manuscript*, and the Jason Bourne series – *The Bourne Identity*, *The Bourne Supremacy*, and *The Bourne Ultimatum* – among others. Mr Ludlum passed away in March 2001. To learn more, you can visit Robert-Ludlum.com.

ERIC VAN LUSTBADER is the author of numerous bestselling novels including *First Daughter*, *Beloved Enemy*, *The Ninja*, and the international bestsellers featuring Jason Bourne: *The Bourne Legacy*, *The Bourne Betrayal*, *The Bourne Sanction*, *The Bourne Deception*, *The Bourne Objective*, *The Bourne Dominion*, *The Bourne Imperative*, *The Bourne Retribution*, and *The Bourne Ascendancy*. For more information, you can visit EricVanLustbader.com. You can also follow him on Facebook and Twitter.